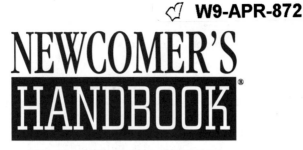

NEWCOMER'S HANDBOOK®

FOR MOVING TO AND LIVING IN

Minneapolis– St. Paul

3rd Edition

FIRST BOOKS®

6750 SW Franklin
Portland, OR 97223
503-968-6777
www.firstbooks.com

Author: Elizabeth Caperton-Halvorson
Series Editor: Linda Weinerman
Publisher: Jeremy Solomon
Cover and Interior Design: Erin Johnson Design
Maps: Jim Miller/fennana design
Transit maps courtesy of Metro Transit

ISBN-13: 978-0-912301-67-9
ISBN-10: 0-912301-67-8
ISSN: 1930-6296

Printed in the USA on recycled paper.

Published by Firstbooks.com, Inc., 6750 SW Franklin Street, Suite A, Portland, OR 97223-2542, 503-968-6777

What readers are saying about Newcomer's Handbooks:

I recently got a copy of your Newcomer's Handbook for Chicago, and wanted to let you know how invaluable it was for my move. I must have consulted it a dozen times a day preparing for my move. It helped me find my way around town, find a place to live, and so many other things. Thanks.
—Mike L.
Chicago, Illinois

Excellent reading (Newcomer's Handbook for San Francisco and the Bay Area) ... balanced and trustworthy. One of the very best guides if you are considering moving/relocation. Way above the usual tourist crap.
—Gunnar E.
Stockholm, Sweden

I was very impressed with the latest edition of the Newcomer's Handbook for Los Angeles. It is well organized, concise and up-to-date. I would recommend this book to anyone considering a move to Los Angeles.
—Jannette L.
Attorney Recruiting Administrator for a large Los Angeles law firm

I recently moved to Atlanta from San Francisco, and LOVE the Newcomer's Handbook for Atlanta. It has been an invaluable resource — it's helped me find everything from a neighborhood in which to live to the local hardware store. I look something up in it everyday, and know I will continue to use it to find things long after I'm no longer a newcomer. And if I ever decide to move again, your book will be the first thing I buy for my next destination.
—Courtney R.
Atlanta, Georgia

In looking to move to the Boston area, a potential employer in that area gave me a copy of the Newcomer's Handbook for Boston. It's a great book that's very comprehensive, outlining good and bad points about each neighborhood in the Boston area. Very helpful in helping me decide where to move.
—no name given (online submit form)

TABLE OF CONTENTS

CONTENTS

CONTENTS

THE U.S. CENSUS BUREAU DEFINES THE MINNEAPOLIS–ST. PAUL Metropolitan Statistical Area as a region of thirteen counties located in both Minnesota and neighboring Wisconsin. The seven core counties of "The Metro" are Anoka, Carver, Dakota, Hennepin (includes Minneapolis), Ramsey (includes St. Paul), Scott, and Washington, all within Minnesota. The larger 13-county area extends out to Chisago, Isanti, Sherburne, and Wright counties, also in Minnesota, and Pierce and St. Croix counties in Wisconsin. That's an area of 144 by 114 miles. In terms of population, three out of five Minnesota residents live in the Twin Cities area, with over 70% concentrated in the Western Metro counties. More than 70% of the region's jobs and traffic are concentrated on the west side as well, and projections show that the "western tilt" will continue to grow.

There's no place like the Twin Cities. The trees, the lakes, the snow . . . the orchestras, restaurants, music, and theaters! And where else can you teach your kids to drive on roads plowed across frozen lakes? Really, we've got it all.

But if all you've ever heard about Minnesota is our "bracing and invigorating" climate, the prospect of living here might be daunting. Rest assured, national surveys consistently pick Minnesota as one of the best places in the nation to raise a family. So what's so great about Minnesota? It's the quality of life!

It's 136,900 acres of parks, lakes, ski areas, and golf courses all within the metro area. It's more shopping than you could ever do, two internationally acclaimed orchestras, and nearly as many theater seats as New York City. It's Fortune 500 companies, a vibrant local music scene, vital downtowns where people like to live and want to play, and a robust economy. It's a small enough population for breathing room, but more than enough to support major league sports—plus, we have relatively safe neighborhoods, clean streets, and well-maintained houses. Most important, if you decide to move here, you'll be living in a place where art, culture, sports and recreation are not only easily accessible, but also more affordable than in the major cities on the east and west coasts.

But, what about the weather you ask? The sub-zero temperatures? The blizzards? The wind-chill factor? Well, that's what pulls Minnesotans together, giving us something to talk about and an opportunity to brag about our survival skills.

And it doesn't seem to be keeping anyone away. The Twin Cities are the 15th largest metropolitan area in the U.S., according to the 2000 census, with 3 million people (over half the state's population) living in the region. Updated figures show that we're on track to add another million by the year 2030.

Unfortunately, most of the people moving here head for the suburbs, a pattern of growth that contributes to our biggest problem, urban sprawl. Third-ring suburbs Woodbury, Eagan, and Eden Prairie all doubled their populations during the 1980s and '90s, and current growth is occurring even farther out. While urbanization on such a vast scale can have a tendency to blur or erase the unique qualities that give communities their own sense of character, here—at least for now—our communities have managed to remain distinct.

Take Minneapolis and St. Paul, for example. Although they're called the Twin Cities, they are definitely not twins. Sitting on the Mississippi's west bank, Minneapolis (population 382,618) is the power suit—it has demolished layer upon layer of its architectural history in order to create a skyline profile of sleek office towers. In contrast, St. Paul (population 287,260), across the river, even though it's the state capital, has a slower, more settled and provincial feel. Having paid attention to architectural preservation, it boasts the low-slung silhouette of some of the Midwest's last remaining Victorian Romanesque blocks. In fact, it's so low-rise that at one time a 14-story ice palace was actually the city's tallest building!

The suburbs, too, have their own look and feel, ranging from post-war practical inner-ring municipalities like Richfield, Roseville, and St. Louis Park to the resort-style villages of Lake Minnetonka and White Bear Lake. Newer suburbs, such as Hudson, Wisconsin, and Blaine, are all about soccer and golf, while upscale Edina is all about shopping; and Excelsior, Wayzata, Mound, Chaska, Elk River, Anoka, Stillwater, and Waconia, though definitely suburbs, are also traditional small towns.

Despite recent setbacks with local companies such as Northwest Airlines, the Twin Cities' economy appears to be strong and unemployment relatively low. Local corporations Target, Best Buy, 3M, Cargill, General Mills, and Medtronic are household names; and with over 200 medical research centers and a large employment concentration in surgical and medical instrument manufacturing, *Business Week* magazine has dubbed the Twin Cities "Medical Alley."

The engine that drives Minnesota's economy is our schools. The state's workforce is among the most highly educated in the country. For years, our public and private elementary and secondary schools have ranked among the best, as have our numerous colleges. The metro is home to the University of Minnesota main campus, a dozen private four-year colleges, six community colleges, nine technical institutes, and several trade schools. In 2000, Minnesota ranked seventh in the percentage of residents holding a bachelor's degree.

Affordable housing, however, is increasingly hard to come by. In 2004, the average two-bedroom apartment in the metro rented for $930 per month, and a modest home sold for around $200,000. On the plus side, this is forcing residents to rediscover "old gems," structurally sound, often beautifully crafted early 20th-century houses that are being updated to meet the needs of modern families. In another step back to the "good old days," many of the new developments are embracing "new urbanism" goals of higher-density neighborhoods, pedestrian-friendly shopping, and public spaces that facilitate community interaction.

The faces of Minnesota are changing as well. Though Minnesotans traditionally consider themselves "Scandinavian," the state is becoming more ethnically and racially diverse. In 2000, nearly 12% of Minnesotans identified themselves as African-American, Asian, American Indian, Latino, or members of two or more races. Though African-Americans make up the largest minority group in the state, the Latino population is the fastest growing, having nearly tripled, from 54,000 to 143,382, between the 1990 census and 2000. (Political rhetoric about "illegal aliens" not withstanding, according to the 2000 census, almost 60% of Hispanic/Latino people living in Minnesota were U.S.-born citizens; another 8% were naturalized citizens.) Nowhere is Minnesota's new diversity more apparent than in Minneapolis and St. Paul. St. Paul (long known for its Irish roots) is now home to the second largest urban Hmong population in the world. The Twin Cities are also host to the largest Somali and Liberian refugee communities in the U.S., as well as one of the largest Native American urban populations. But growth in the nonwhite population hasn't been confined to the cities: about 10% of the suburban population is now nonwhite and Latino, too. So while we are definitely growing in diversity, the state has a long way to go before it will mirror the 31% nonwhite and Latino population found in the U.S. as a whole.

HISTORY

A play about Minnesota history opens with the untamed rhythms of a Native American chant in raw counterpoint to the genteel strains of a Victorian waltz— a clear metaphor for the cultural conflict that accompanied the settling of Minnesota and continues today.

The first Europeans arrived in the 1680s in the person of Father Louis Hennepin, a Franciscan adventurer who traveled with a party of Dakota guides up the river to a wide falls, which he named St. Anthony. Where Hennepin was standing is now the center of downtown Minneapolis.

A hundred twenty years later, Minnesota was acquired through the Louisiana Purchase (1803), and Congress sent a military expedition to explore the new territory and find out what treasures the country had gained. Expedition leader Lieutenant Zebulon Pike found two different groups of Native American tribes living here, the Ojibwe and the Dakota. Pike signed an agreement with the Dakotas in 1805 that ceded to the U.S. nine square miles of land at the confluence of the Mississippi and Minnesota Rivers—that's the land Ft. Snelling and the airport are built on today, and includes much of the cities of Minneapolis and St. Paul. Settlement began during the 1820s, and soon fur traders and farmers were comfortably established downriver from the fort. In 1841, an earnest missionary named Lucien Galtier built a log church on the east bank of the Mississippi and named it after St. Paul, the Apostle of Nations. The name stuck for the settlement, which soon became the capital of the new state of Minnesota.

Entrepreneurs also moved upriver to St. Anthony Falls, where they used the hydraulic power of the Mississippi to mill flour and saw lumber, giving Minneapolis the nickname "Mill City." This east bank settlement was originally known as St. Anthony, but Charles Hoag, a teacher, proposed a different name for it, combining *Minne,* the Dakota word for "water," and *polis,* the Greek word for "city," into Minneapolis. Today the cobblestone street of old St. Anthony has been preserved as Saint Anthony Main, a shopping and entertainment district across from downtown on the east bank of the river, in what is known as the Mississippi Mile.

Relations between white settlers and Native Americans in the area were not always harmonious. Despite an agreement by the U.S. to send food and supplies to displaced Indians, during the recession of 1862 federal food rations were not sent, and a group of hungry and desperate Indians raided a homestead and killed the people living there. More violence followed, leading to the Dakota War of 1862. When the fighting ended, thirty-eight Dakotas were executed by hanging, and the Indians were pushed west into what are now called the "Dakotas.

It was the Mississippi River that opened Minnesota to the world, and the newborn cities on its banks became boomtowns in the late 19th century as waves of immigrants, particularly Scandinavians, Germans, and Poles, moved to the frontier. In 1867 Minneapolis was incorporated as a city. At first the transportation hub of St. Paul was the larger of the two competing hamlets. During the 1880s, however, Minneapolis began to overtake its neighbor both in population and commerce. Rivalry between the cities was fierce, leading to the Great Census War of 1890. The first census results showed that Minneapolis was population champ, but St. Paul officials charged fraud, and a scandal ensued. A deputy U.S. marshal arrested census workers in downtown Minneapolis and, when results were recounted, investigators found that counters in both cities had inflated numbers with "residents" who lived in cemeteries and office buildings! The recount, however, did confirm that Minneapolis had more residents, and it has remained the larger city ever since.

Although St. Paul has gradually garnered the reputation as the sleepier town, it hasn't always been that way. During the Prohibition years from 1920 to 1933, mobsters running liquor from Canada brought their ill-gotten gains and wild ways to the city. Ma Barker and her sons hid out here, and the infamous John Dillinger was involved in shoot-outs around town. Finally, arrests and indictments in the late 1930s led to the end of St. Paul's "gangster city" era.

With a large rural population, Minnesota was fertile ground for labor and agricultural reform movements. When the state's Farmer-Labor Party merged with the Democratic Party in 1944 (forming the Minnesota DFL), it began producing national leaders with a strong progressive bent. One of the most visible on the national stage was Hubert H. Humphrey, who served first as mayor of Minneapolis, then as Minnesota's U.S. senator. A strong advocate for civil rights, he gave up his congressional seat to serve as vice president under Lyndon B. Johnson, and was the Democratic presidential candidate in 1968, losing to Richard Nixon. Humphrey's protégé, Walter Mondale, succeeded him as U.S. senator, then served as vice president under Jimmy Carter. In 1984, he, too, ran for president. Consistent with Minnesota's progressive tradition, he chose a woman, U.S. Representative Geraldine A. Ferraro, as his running mate, making her the first woman nominated for that position by a major party. Together they campaigned in support of the Equal Rights Amendment and the need to reduce the federal budget deficit, but were defeated by Ronald Reagan and George H.W. Bush.

While the state's political reputation was growing on the national front, the Twin Cities were becoming the industrial, commercial, and cultural center of the vast fertile Upper Midwest region. Unchecked by geography, area growth erupted outward into the surrounding farmlands after World War II, and the rings of suburbs that were created lured population away from both Minneapolis and St. Paul. Extensive redevelopment, begun in the 1960s, continues to this day, bringing people back to the metropolitan core. The early 1970s construction in Minneapolis of the Investors Diversified Services (IDS) building, the area's first skyscraper, signaled the emergence of Minneapolis as a financial center for the upper Midwest. Soon many downtown offices, apartments, stores, and theaters in Minneapolis and St. Paul were connected with indoor, above-ground skyways, making it possible to live and work in the city centers during the bitter months of winter without ever having to step outside.

Also during the 1970s, investors and government officials finally became concerned with building preservation. Numerous revitalization projects were undertaken, including restoring the Landmark Center in St. Paul and renovating the Warehouse District in Minneapolis. These initiatives have kept alive some of the early history of the two boomtowns, and now the presence of these historic buildings is helping to attract affluent professionals, young families, and senior citizens back from the suburbs to live in the cities' central cores.

WHAT TO BRING

- **A car and a coat**—both in good shape to take on winter. The Twin Cities' bus system, MetroTransit, offers express connections to the suburbs, but getting around totally by bus is difficult and time-consuming. After years of legislative reluctance, light rail transit has become a reality, connecting the Minneapolis downtown to the airport and Mall of America, but light rail for the rest of the area is still a dream (see the **Transportation** chapter).
- **A map**—there are places where Twin Cities' streets and highways follow a perfect grid, and places where streets are laid out at crazy angles to the grid. This guide will help you get to know the neighborhoods, but for the full picture, you'll need to accompany it with a map. Hudson's Street Atlas (www.hudsonmap.com), which is published locally and sold online and at bookstores, is a comprehensive spiral-bound book that shows every street in St. Paul and Minneapolis and the surrounding communities. Once you get used to using it, you will never get lost.

"MINNESOTA NICE"

Everyone has concerns about moving to a new place and dealing with an entirely new culture, so rest assured the term "Minnesota Nice" is not just an expression—people here really are nice. In contrast to some other parts of the country, Minnesotans feel the need not to offend and to "make the other person feel comfortable." Consequently, they invariably display a positive demeanor when encountering strangers. You can expect them to jump start your car in the grocery store parking lot, tow your boat when it runs out of gas, lend you their favorite chainsaw, let you go first at a four-way stop. What they won't do, however, is open up to you in any meaningful way. Try to get personal, and "Minnesota Nice" quickly turns into "Minnesota Ice," making it hard to tell what a Minnesotan is really thinking or feeling about you, and making it very, very hard to make friends when you first move here. In fact, that's the main complaint of nearly everyone who's ever moved here, so don't think it's you. It's merely a cultural (and possibly weather-augmented) lack of willingness to engage at any level beyond the superficial. On the other hand, if you have to hold up the checkout line while you dump the entire contents of your purse out on the counter to find your credit card, it's nice to know that the people behind you, no matter how angry, frustrated, irritated or bent out of shape they may be, will stoically fume in silence and steadfastly refuse to show any displeasure with you!

That said, how do you develop relationships with people who are so reserved? Do the same things you'd do anywhere. Get involved. Volunteer in your child's school or sports. Join a church, club, or civic organization. The League of Women Voters (www.lwvmn.org) talks about important issues at every meeting—and it's a great way to learn about your new state; ditto the library book clubs. Organizations such as Twin Cities Transplants (www.imnotfromhere.com) sponsor events for singles and couples that range from happy hours to museum tours and New Year's Eve parties. They also maintain message boards to help people with similar interests find each other and arrange to get together. The local Newcomers Clubs (www.newcomersclub.com/mn.html) provide a similar service, sponsoring golf and tennis leagues, bridge, and many social events, though their events are only open to women.

Finally, if you've moved here in winter, just hang on. In summer your neighbors will come out of their houses—and while they may not be willing to talk about much more than the weather, at least you'll be talking!

LOCAL LINGO

Sisu. Fish house. Hotdish. What are these people talking about? Here's your Minnesota-to-English Translation Guide. For an in-depth understanding of Minnesotan, rent the movie *Fargo* (yes, we do talk like that!) or read Howard Mohr's book, *How to Speak Minnesotan.*

Bars: Cookie squares, such as brownies or lemon bars.
Borrow: Lend, as in, "Will you borrow me your chainsaw?"
Brat (rhymes with trot): Something you eat; officially named bratwurst.

Croppie: How Minnesotans pronounce the name of the panfish the rest of the country calls a "crappie."

Din't: How Minnesotans pronounce the contraction, "didn't."

Duck, duck grey duck: The circle tag game the rest of the world calls "Duck, duck, goose."

Fish house, also ice house: A structure you haul out on the ice so you can be warm and cozy sitting inside a heated shelter while you fish through a hole in the floor. For a sneak peek at what it looks like inside one of these homes-away-from-home look online at the website of Distinct Builders, http://ice-shack.com.

Hotdish: Casserole. The standard formula is some kind of meat plus some kind of soup plus some kind of cooked vegetable. In other parts of the country, if you're invited to a potluck, you typically take enough for eight to ten servings. Minnesotans, however, take enough food for the whole crowd. Not only that, but if asked to bring an appetizer, they will, without fail, arrive with two—and probably some bars for dessert (see above), as well.

Ice dam: A ridge of ice that forms at the edge of a roof and prevents melting snow (water runoff) from draining off the roof. The water that backs up behind the dam eventually gets under the shingles and leaks into the home, causing damage to walls, ceilings, insulation, and other areas. The only permanent fix for ice dams is to properly insulate, seal, and ventilate the attic so that the home's roof remains cold.

Lutefisk: Fish soaked in lye. This Scandinavian delicacy is usually served at Christmas with melted butter and mashed potatoes. Don't worry—no one will expect you to actually eat this, but they may demonstrate their own superiority to you by going back for seconds. That said, Minnesotans are nothing if not practical, and this stuff stinks, which is why those who choose to indulge normally eat it at a restaurant, church supper, or down at St. Olaf College, where they serve it in the dining hall prior to the St. Olaf Choirs' annual Christmas concerts.

Norski: Norwegian

Not too bad: Very good.

Ole and Lena: Norwegian characters in Minnesotans' favorite Scandinavian jokes. They are often joined by their Swedish friend Sven, as they are in this joke that goes around year after year: Ole died, so Lena went to the local paper to put a notice in the obituaries. Sven, the editor, after offering his condolences, asked Lena what she would like to say about Ole. Lena replied, "You yust put 'Ole died.'" Sven, somewhat perplexed, said, "That's it? Just 'Ole died'? Surely, there must be something more you'd like to say. You were married 55 years. If it's money you're concerned about, don't worry, the first five words are free." So Lena thought about it for a few minutes and finally said, "O.K. You put 'Ole died. Boat for sale.'"

Out East: East Coast

Parking Ramp: A multi-story building where you can park your car (as opposed to a surface lot), called a parking garage or parking structure in some other areas of the country.

Pop: Soda or cola

Rambler: One-level house

Sisu: Finnish word for an almost magical combination of stamina, toughness, and perseverance in the face of adversity. While the term is more commonly seen on bumper stickers than heard in everyday speech, every now and then you can expect to hear somebody say that someone has "sisu." It's most often a reference to a patient fighting a life-threatening illness, or someone who has just suffered a devastating loss—often it's as much as you'll ever hear about someone else's troubles.

Sack: Bag

So . . . then: The basic construction of a Minnesota sentence, as in: "So, are you through with the chainsaw then?"

SPAM: That iconic canned pork-shoulder-and-ham product with an indefinite shelf life that was invented and is still produced in Austin, Minnesota (www.ci.austin.mn.us) by Hormel Food Corporation (www.spam.com).

Spendy: Pricey; expensive

That's different: Expression of extreme disapproval. In ancient Viking days, those who were different were killed. Consequently, a Scandinavian's foremost wish is to fit in, and anything that is "different" is very bad, indeed.

The Range: Iron Range (www.rangecities.com); Northern Minnesota, around Virginia, Chisholm, Ely, Eveleth, Biwabik, Hibbing, etc., where iron ore and taconite have been mined since the late 1800s. This part of the state was made famous by the 2005 movie *North Country.*

Uff-da: Norwegian expletive that passes for an extreme emotional outburst in Minnesota. It signifies strong disgruntlement on the order of something a carpenter might say when he hammers his finger instead of the nail.

Up North: Northern Minnesota, above Grand Rapids.

Warming house: Temporary, seasonal shelters beside outdoor ice rinks where you put on your skates and go to warm up after skating.

Whatever: This is the ultimate expression of Minnesota's institutional passive-aggressiveness. Do not make the mistake of thinking that the person who has responded to your query by answering "Whatever" has no opinion or preference and is leaving the decision up to you. They are merely keeping you guessing.

Wild rice: Minnesota's State Grain is not actually rice, but a very high protein annual water-grass seed, "zizania aquatica." Naturally abundant in the cold rivers and lakes of Minnesota and Canada, wild rice is still harvested in the traditional Indian way, from a canoe using beater sticks to knock the seeds into the bottom of the boat. Wild rice soup, in particular, is a favorite of people who live here.

Ya: Phrase of agreement, as in "Ya sure, you betcha." You'll hear this phrase ten times a day if you go Up North, but around the metro, you're more likely to hear people say, "You bet." The Howard Mohr book, *How to Speak Minnesotan,* says that this phrase is popular because "it is pleasantly agreeable, but doesn't obligate the speaker to a strong position."

Yet: still. You will hear Minnesotans say things like, "Is it raining yet?" (meaning, "Is it still raining?") and it will grate on your nerves, but there is nothing you can do about it.

ADDRESS LOCATOR

There are places where Twin Cities' streets follow a perfect grid, and places where streets are laid out at crazy angles with no sense to east, west, north, or south. The convolutions are due primarily to the Mississippi River winding through both downtowns, oblivious to the needs of city planners. City boundaries, where streets occasionally change names, add additional confusion. Suburban communities often follow Twin Cities' street patterns, but not always. For the full picture, you'll need to accompany this guide with a map. Even better is a hefty street atlas, which offers page-by-page micro-views of every metropolitan block accompanied by an index of all streets, such as Hudson's Street Atlas of the Greater Twin Cities (www.hudsonmap.com). With one in hand, keep the following things in mind:

MINNEAPOLIS

- Street addresses are uniformly divided in hundreds, block by block. Numbers increase moving outward from the Mississippi River on the north side and from Nicollet Avenue on the south side.
- Downtown streets are laid out diagonally to the compass (the pesky Mississippi!) so try not to let compass directions throw you off. Because of their orientation to the river, numbered streets and those running parallel to them are labeled north or south, dividing at Hennepin Avenue.
- South Minneapolis (south of Grant Street) is straightforward and easy to understand. Numbered streets run east-west, with ascending numbers going southward. Avenues for the most part run north-south, and have numbers east of Nicollet Avenue and proper names west of Nicollet, which means, in South Minneapolis, the higher the numbered street, the farther south it is; the higher the numbered avenue, the farther east it is.
- In the University of Minnesota neighborhood, numbered streets generally run east-west, while numbered avenues run north-south. Streets and avenues here are labeled Southeast.
- In Northeast Minneapolis numbered avenues run east-west, with numbers ascending northward. North-south streets are numbered heading east from the river until 6th Street. East of 6th the streets are named chronologically after U.S. presidents, from Washington to Coolidge.
- In North Minneapolis numbered avenues run east-west, with numbers ascending northward. North-south streets have ascending numbers as you go west from the Mississippi, until 7th Street. West of 7th, streets have proper names.

ST. PAUL

Governor Jesse Ventura got into trouble for suggesting that St. Paul was laid out by tipsy Irishmen, but there are many who live here who would agree.

- Along with St. Paul's old-world charm comes a somewhat confusing street system. St. Paul's street numbers don't always follow tidy increments of one hundred for every block; they may change from 100 to 200 in the middle of the block so . . . get out that atlas.
- West of Downtown, the north-south dividing line is Summit Avenue. Street numbers increase going westward from Downtown.
- Downtown, Wabasha Street is the division between east and west. The Mississippi River is the north-south marker.
- East of Downtown the north-south dividing line is Upper Afton Road. Street numbers increase going eastward from Downtown.

FROM CITY TO CITY

- University and Franklin avenues keep their names going from St. Paul to Minneapolis, but Marshall Avenue in St. Paul becomes Lake Street in Minneapolis, and St. Paul's Ford Parkway becomes 46th Street in Minneapolis. Don't worry too much; there are only a handful of these streets to remember. The river breaks up most of them.
- Some suburbs, especially inner ones, number their streets according to the grid of the Twin Cities. Other older or far-flung suburbs, such as Wayzata, are laid out on their own grids. The simple advice: don't expect address numbers in the 'burbs and cities to match up.

All in all, the Twin Cities are no more difficult to navigate than any other middle-aged American city with local geographical quirks. Take a few trips to different parts of town and it won't be long before you're tooling around like a native.

MINNEAPOLIS AND ST. PAUL, THE CORE CITIES

I N 2004, FOR THE FIRST TIME IN MANY YEARS, THE TWO CENTRAL CITIES led the regional building permit race for new residential units, as inner-city developers began on a condo/loft/townhome building spree the likes of which have, until now, been reserved for the suburbs.

As a result, the Minneapolis and St. Paul downtown warehouse blocks, which began morphing into residential districts in the 1980s, have blossomed into tony glass and concrete playgrounds for the childless, with access to both cities' riverfronts and cultural attractions that is unmatched elsewhere in the metro. The Midtown Greenway through South Minneapolis and the Hiawatha LRT in Southeast have spawned a transit-oriented renaissance that has put more than 1000 multi-housing units into the construction pipeline along the light rail line alone. Not to be outdone, Northeast's bachelor-on-the-skids scruffiness has given way to a dapper elegance that has turned it into one of the Cities' most sought-after addresses. Even staid Kenwood and Lowry Hill, where you could easily look down some streets and assume that nothing much has changed in the last 100 years, now boast expensive new townhouses you can barely tell from the turn-of-the-century originals. Over in St. Paul, not only has the floodplain been given over to loft-living, but mixed-use construction between West 7th and the Mississippi River bluffs constitutes the largest housing development in the city's history.

After decades of losing population to the suburbs, both these cities are high-flying. As a result, homes in the urban core, in general, have racked up 60% price gains in the last five years, according to the Federal Reserve banking system's FedGazette. In such a market, renovation becomes economically feasible. Consequently, some of the neighborhoods that were undesirable five or ten years ago are being rediscovered, stabilized, and gentrified.

That said, there are still sections of both cities that you should check out extra-carefully: North Minneapolis, extending into Robbinsdale and Brooklyn Center, has some great, affordable houses—and a high crime rate; South Minneapolis, south of I-94 and east of Lyndale to the Mississippi River, can be dicey as far down as 46th Street; St. Paul, along University Avenue east of Snelling and north of I-94, as well as the northeastern quadrant of St. Paul, north of I-94 and east of I-35E, has seen a fair amount of drug- and gang-related violence. While these regions do, in fact, include some great older homes and fabulous amenities, there may be safer Twin Cities locales.

A few suggestions to get you started with your hunt: Many young single professionals choose to go straight to Uptown or the southwest districts of St. Paul; Bryn Mawr, in Minneapolis north of 394, has been voted one of our most livable neighborhoods more than once; young families love south Minneapolis and western St. Paul as much for the niches in the houses' plaster walls as for their easy access to bike paths and shopping; and lofts in St. Paul and Northeast Minneapolis tend to be more affordable than those in Minneapolis Downtown. As is true wherever you go in this state, the closer you are to water, the more you'll have to pay. Equally true: Parking is difficult to find in the downtowns and winter exacerbates the situation. You will save yourself a lot of headaches if you limit your search to housing that includes off-street parking.

When asked where they live, residents in Minneapolis and St. Paul are more likely to give the names of their neighborhoods than their street addresses. This can be confusing, but don't worry, it's actually quite orderly—at least in Minneapolis, which has six geographic areas (Central, South, Southwest, North, Northeast and Southeast) divided into 11 communities, and further subdivided into 81 neighborhoods organized around parks and schools. The Central community, for example, includes the following neighborhoods: Downtown East, Downtown West, Elliot Park, Loring Park, North Loop and Stevens Square/Loring Heights. Thanks to the clear-cut boundaries, in Minneapolis, people tend to be quite specific about their neighborhoods. In St. Paul, on the other hand, even though it is officially subdivided into a much more manageable 17 districts, there are nearly 130 informal "proxy" neighborhoods, many of which coincide with shopping districts, historic designations, or earlier, independent villages that are no longer there. Don't worry, though. If you move to St. Paul, just say you live in Highland or on Cathedral Hill or Frogtown, and anybody you're talking to will get the idea.

The Minneapolis Area Association of Realtors has commissioned a map that shows all the neighborhoods (and neighborhoods-within-neighborhoods) in Minneapolis and St. Paul. The map may be purchased from a member of the association, or at shops in the Minnesota History Center and at the Science Museum of Minnesota. Contact the association at 952-933-9020, www.mpls realtor.com.

Virtually every neighborhood is represented by a neighborhood organization. In Minneapolis, these associations function under the umbrella of the Neighborhood Revitalization Program (NRP), which was created in 1990 in response to a determination that neighborhood revitalization is the most urgent long-term challenge facing the city. Since that time, thousands of Minneapolis residents have used the NRP planning process to identify and meet their neighborhoods' housing, safety, economic development, recreation, health, social service, environmental, and transportation needs. They have built community centers, created jobs, and they can help you feel at home in your new community once you've moved in. Call the NRP (311, www.nrp.org), and they will put you in touch with the current president of the association of the neighborhood you are considering. Access the Minneapolis neighborhoods that have web pages through the city's web site, www.ci.minneapolis.mn.us.

In St. Paul, the 17 district councils operate as private nonprofits to engage residents, business owners, and property owners in issues and projects throughout the city. They can provide you with a neighborhood contact list as well as neighborhood profiles and the latest news. To reach them, click on a link from the city's web site, www.stpaul.gov, or call 651-266-8989.

NEIGHBORHOOD SAFETY

911 is the emergency number throughout the metro area, but for safety information, you will need to contact other sources. For Minneapolis, you can find out how one neighborhood compares with another by reading neighborhood crime reports online at CODEFOR, www.ci.minneapolis.mn.us/citywork/police/stats/codefor. Looking at these reports, you often see that the largest numbers of crimes are reported in Downtown West, Jordan, Longfellow, Lowry Hill East, Cedar Riverside, Central, Folwell, Hawthorne, Marcy-Holmes, Near North, the U of M, Whittier, Seward, Ventura Village, Phillips, and Elliot Park. Be sure, though, to look at the types of crimes and not just the numbers.

A further resource is the SAFE Crime Prevention team of specialists who work in each precinct. You can contact them by calling 311. You can also e-mail them online through clickable links on the Minneapolis police department web page, www.ci.minneapolis.mn.us/police/outreach/safe-teams.asp.

To investigate neighborhood safety in St. Paul, check with the St. Paul Police Department, 651-291-1111, www.stpaul.gov/depts/police. Free information is easily attainable from the department's web page,through the clickable link to the Community Resources (F.O.R.C.E. Unit). Here the F.O.R.C.E. Unit lists its most recent search warrant addresses—and posts pictures of the houses, as well! There is also a link to the city's crime maps where crime rates can be viewed on density grids, allowing you to compare all parts of the city by crime: murder, rape, assault, quality of life calls, etc.

Wherever you choose to live, you should also do a zip code search of the Department of Corrections web site (www.corr.state.mn.us/level3/search.asp) to see if any Level 3 sex offenders are living nearby.

A word on safety for renters: Question the landlord closely about tenant screening procedures, what they do about problem tenants, and if they participate in the **Minnesota Crime Free Multi-housing Program**. If they do, and have completed the required training, they should display a large metal sign that shows they are certified, and the building's literature and advertising should include the program logo.

Finally, once you've narrowed down your choices, give the zip codes for the addresses you're interested in to your insurance agent, who can provide you with additional statistical information, including crime rates and how much insurance coverage will cost you if you decide to move into that area.

STORMWATER UTILITY FEE

Into each life a little rain must fall, but in Minneapolis you pay for it according to how much impervious surface you have in your yard. (Impervious areas are hard surfaces, such as roofs, sidewalks, and driveways, which stop rain or melting snow from being absorbed into the ground.) Called a "stormwater utility fee," the city now separates this charge out from the rest of your bill so that you can appeal it or apply for up to a 100% credit if you install stormwater management practices, such as "rain gardens" on your property. Placed in a strategically located shallow depression in the ground, a rain garden will not only act like a sponge and prevent excessive runoff from leaving your property, but will also help to replenish our groundwater supply, all the while taking some of the pressure off the city's already overburdened storm sewer system. For more information, contact the City Utility Billing Office, 311, or check out the city's web site, www.ci.minneapolis.mn.us, and click on "Stormwater Utility Fee Information."

MINNEAPOLIS

Water has played an important role in the city's development. Known as both the "City of Lakes" and the "Mill City," Minneapolis has 18 lakes and more than 6300 acres of parks within its city limits. It's the Mississippi River, however, that made it the "Mill City." With several flour mills located alongside St. Anthony Falls, in the area we call Historic St. Anthony or St. Anthony Main, Minneapolis was the world's largest flour producer from 1882 to 1930. This era in the region's history is preserved in the Mill City Museum, 704 South Second Street, www.mnhs.org. A National Historic Landmark, this riverfront museum chronicles the ups and downs of the flour milling industry, including the story of Betty Crocker, of cooking fame, who, in 1945, was voted the second most popular woman in America behind Eleanor Roosevelt. Not bad for a gal who never existed! Better yet, she still represents the most successful branding campaign in advertising history.

Fast-forward to 2006, and though the mills are long gone, Minneapolis, in Hennepin County, is still the state's largest city. While 382,618 residents sleep in the city every night, during the day the city's population swells to more than half a million as 167,000 go downtown to work and another 100,000 travel into the city to attend the University of Minnesota and other colleges and trade schools.

At first glance, the faces of these Minneapolitans may appear to be overwhelmingly white, but according to the 2000 census, Minneapolis is now our most ethnically diverse city, with 18% Black/African Americans, 12.3% Asians, 7.8% Hispanics or Latinos, and 2.2% American Indians.

These new residents tend to settle in the same places the earlier immigrants did, making our historic districts far more diverse than the historic districts in many other cities. If you're interested in old houses, the Historic Preservation Commission leads walking tours from May through August. Check them out online at www.ci.minneapolis.mn.us/hpc/walking-tours.asp, or call the Minneapolis Heritage Preservation Commission Information Line at 311.

Web Site: www.ci.Minneapolis.mn.us

Phone Number: To reach any Minneapolis city department, if you are calling from within the city limits, even on a cell phone, call 311. If you are calling from outside the city, call 612-673-3000.

Area Code: 612

Public Schools: Minneapolis, District Office: 612-668-0000, TTY 612-668-0001, www.mpls.k12.mn.us

Parks: www.minneapolisparks.org; no matter where you choose to live, you will be within 6 blocks of a park and/or recreation facility, though only the most significant parks are mentioned below. Off-leash recreation areas are located at Franklin Terrace, Lake of the Isles, Minnehaha Park, and St. Anthony Parkway.

Community Publications: Minneapolis Star Tribune,www.startribune.com

Public Transportation: Information about all public transportation can be accessed at 612-373-3333, www.MetroTransit.org. *Buses:* Buses generally run along main thoroughfares, but routes and schedules do change, so be sure to check the web site or call. *Trains:* The Hiawatha Light Rail Transit line follows Hiawatha Avenue from the Minneapolis Warehouse District to the Mall of America. Trains run every 7–8 minutes during rush hours and every 10–15 minutes during off-hours and weekends. Fares range from 50 cents to $2.75. Trains run between 5 a.m. and 1 a.m. *Trolleys:* River City Trolley, www.rivercitytrolley.org, runs May through October between downtown attractions. Purchase tickets at the Mill City Museum, Minneapolis Convention Center, or from the driver. An all-day pass costs under $20 for adults, less for children and seniors.

CENTRAL COMMUNITY

WAREHOUSE DISTRICT AND RIVERFRONT
DOWNTOWN WEST
NORTH LOOP
DOWNTOWN EAST
STEVENS SQUARE–LORING HEIGHTS
ELLIOT PARK
LORING PARK

Boundaries: North: Plymouth Ave, Mississippi River; **West:** I-94; **South:** Franklin Ave, Hwy 12; **East:** Interstate-35W

Though this area is officially divided into East and West, people don't talk that way. They just say **"Downtown"** or **"Warehouse District"** or **"Riverfront,"** or **"North Loop."** Whatever you call it, though, if you live here you can sleep an extra hour and still get to work on time!

Downtown West centers around Nicollet Mall, an eight-block commercial strip closed to cars, and includes the restored Warehouse District that surrounds Target Center. The North Loop runs from 2nd Avenue north to Duluth

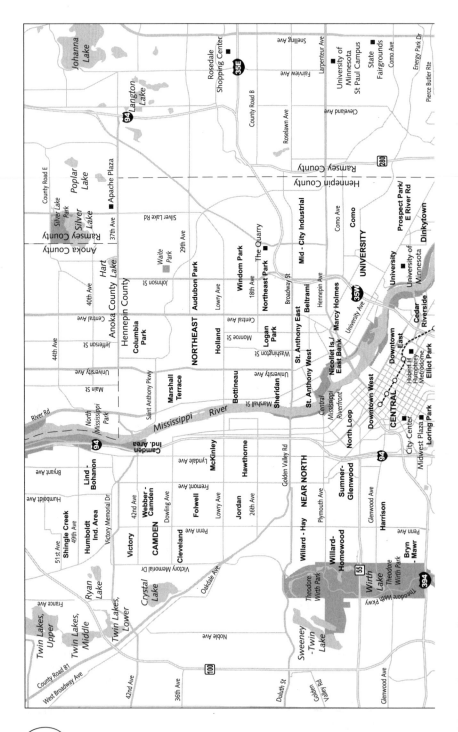

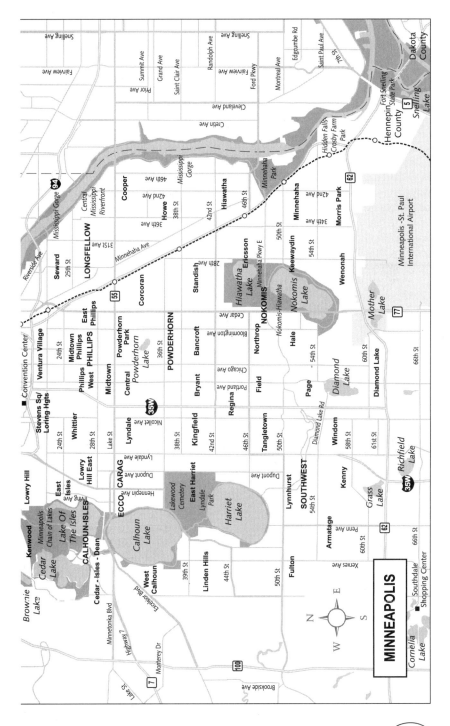

MINNEAPOLIS

Avenue, between I-94 and the river. Downtown East is the area between Park Avenue and 35W.

For years the city turned its back on this area. The warehouse blocks were an entertainment district at night, but by day they were skid row. Likewise, the riverfront was allowed to become an industrial wasteland, and the river was pretty hard to find, even if you knew it was there. Not any more. Over the past decade fashionable condo complexes have emerged in revamped warehouses, and streets of row houses have blossomed on land that used to be home to hobo camps and parking lots. Here you will find small (one- and two-bedroom) units in high-rise buildings that are sometimes connected to the sky-ways, though mostly near the ends. (Skyways are enclosed breezeways that connect building to building on the level of the second or third floors.) Larger units are rare and command premium prices. Controlled access and 24-hour security are standard, plus amenities such as fitness centers and secure parking. Many complexes also set aside space for corporate housing, providing new-comers with an easy way to get to know the area before having to commit.

New attractions have moved in as well, including the Guthrie Theater. Recreation amenities are spectacular, with trails on both sides of the river and a major park out in the middle of the Mississippi on Boom Island. With the recent construction of the Nicollet Mall Target, now Downtown has everything—even a grocery store.

The downside is transportation. With the network of bus routes that pass through downtown, as well as the LRT, you'd think if you lived here you'd be set in terms of public transportation, but in fact most downtown residents still feel they need to keep a car.

Only a short hop away, **Stevens Square–Loring Heights** is bracketed between the busy streets of Lyndale Avenue, I-35, I-94 and Franklin Avenue. The original buildings here were constructed roughly between 1890 and 1930. If you're interested in seeing where Minneapolis has come from—and where it is going—just take a walk around these simple-to-sumptuous streets. **Loring Heights**, west of Nicollet, is a neighborhood of grand houses, developed in one of the upper classes' first moves toward the south and west of the central city. Its layout of curved streets on a ridge is the classic mark of the Victorian romantic suburb. The small apartments of **Stevens Square** (www.stevens square.org), on the other hand, were built as a mill town for small families and single tradesmen. Today these apartments are home to many singles, as well as people taking the cure at nearby treatment centers. Though most properties are rental, condo conversions are increasingly popular. Nearby **Elliot Park** (www.elliotpark.org), surrounding the Hennepin County Medical Center and Metrodome, has suffered from a dicey reputation, but is starting to trend upward with projects such as the mixed-income/mixed-use East Village row house development on 11th Avenue South, which was recently named Most Innovative Housing Project (large scale) by the Minneapolis NRP.

Lovely turn-of-the-century, brick walk-up apartments and large stone houses surrounding Loring Park give the **Loring Park** neighborhood (Lyndale to 12th and Hawthorne Avenue to I-94, www.loringdowntown.com), an air of grandeur that is further enhanced by the presence of a number of beautiful public buildings—the Basilica of St. Mary, the Minneapolis Woman's Club, the Cathedral Church of St. Mark, and the Hennepin Avenue United Methodist Church. Connected to the Nicollet Mall by a picturesque pathway known as the Loring Greenway, it is easy to live here and walk to work downtown. Its days as a rental neighborhood, however, may be numbered as more and of the apartments are converted into expensive condominiums.

Long the center of gay life in the Twin Cities, these hills and hollows are well-supplied with hangouts for gay and straight alike. Visiting film crews and out-of-town celebrities are often spotted in the Café and Bar Lurcat (1624 Harmon Place, Minneapolis, 612-486-5500, www.cafelurcat.com), which overlooks the park and is arguably the Twin Cities' most cosmopolitan bistro. A slew of interesting coffee shops and cafés line the north side. On the south, the 510 Groveland Building is one of the best addresses in town, and home to what may well be the metro's best restaurant, La Belle Vie (612-874-6440, www.labellevie.us). Numerous independent theaters, such as the Red Eye Collaboration (www.theredeye.org) and Loring Playhouse (www.loringdowntown.com), are all within walking distance, and the Walker Art Center and sculpture garden (www.walkerart.org) are just across the street over the Irene Hixon Whitney pedestrian bridge.

Zip Codes: 55402, 55403, 55404, 55405, 55411, 55415

Post Offices: Main Office, 110 S 1st St; Loop Station, 110 S 8th St; Loring Station, 18 N 12th St; Butler Quarter Station, 100 N 6th St; Commerce Station, 307 4th Ave S

Police Precinct: 4th, 1925 Plymouth Ave N, 311 (non-emergency)

Emergency Hospital: Hennepin County Medical Center, 701 Park Ave, 612-873-3000, www.hcmc.org

Library: Central Library, 250 Marquette Ave, 612-630-6000, www.mpls.lib.mn.us

Community Resources: Guthrie Theater, 818 Second St S, 612-377-2224, www.guthrietheater.org; Hennepin Theatre District, includes the State, Orpheum, Pantages, Hennepin Stages, Music Box, and Illusion Theatres, all located along Hennepin Ave, www.hennepintheatredistrict.org; Hubert H. Humphrey Metrodome, 900 S 5th St, 612-335-3370, www.msfc.com; Mill City Museum, 704 S Second St, 612-341-7555. www.mnhs.org; Orchestra Hall, 1111 Nicollet Mall, 612-371-5656 or 800-292-4141, www.minnesotaorchestra.org; Target Center, 600 1st Ave N, 612-673-0900, www.targetcenter.com

Parks: www.minneapolisparks.org; Loring Park, Mississippi Riverfront

Community Publications: *Downtown Journal,* www.dtjournal.com; *Minneapolis Observer,* www.mplsobserver.com; *Southside Pride,* http://southsidepride.com

Public Transportation: 612-373-3333, www.MetroTransit.org; you can get around downtown by bus on any major street, and downtown fares are reduced. Minneapolis/St. Paul Inter-city Express buses provide connecting service between downtown Minneapolis, I-94, Snelling Ave, the Capitol Complex, and downtown St. Paul. The LRT travels along 5th St S, with stations at Hennepin Ave, Nicollet Mall, Government Plaza, and the Humphrey Metrodome.

CALHOUN–ISLES COMMUNITY

UPTOWN-EAST CALHOUN (ECCO), CARAG (CALHOUN AREA RESIDENTS ACTION GROUP), LOWRY HILL EAST (THE WEDGE) BRYN MAWR, CEDAR-ISLES-DEAN, WEST CALHOUN KENWOOD, EAST ISLES, LOWRY HILL

Boundaries: North: Bassett Creek; **West:** France Ave; **South:** 38th St; **East:** Lyndale Ave

Visitors and residents alike fall in love with Minneapolis because of the Calhoun-Isles community with its linked "Chain of Lakes" and the myriad activities possible here: shopping, running, roller-blading, biking, swimming, sailing, people-watching, etc. Calhoun is one of the top lakes for windsurfing in the Twin Cities, and the running/biking paths around all these lakes are part of the Grand Rounds Scenic Byways (see **Lakes and Parkways**).

The Calhoun-Isles community was the first Minneapolis suburb, and it's still one of the most popular places for newcomers to settle. For those who work in downtown Minneapolis, the office is only a short walk, bike ride, or brief bus ride away.

Calhoun-Isles can be divided into three distinct districts: the trendy, populous rental neighborhoods commonly known as Uptown; the meandering streets along the southwest border of the city that make up Bryn Mawr, Cedar-Isles-Dean, and West Calhoun; and the city's most expensive neighborhoods, Kenwood, Lowry Hill, and East Isles, which wrap around Lake of the Isles.

UPTOWN

EAST CALHOUN (ECCO) CARAG LOWRY HILL EAST (THE WEDGE)

The rental area of **Uptown** spreads outward from the Calhoun Square Shopping Mall, which is on the corner of Lake Street and Hennepin Avenue in East Calhoun. It includes **East Calhoun** (**ECCO**, www.eastcalhoun.org) and **CARAG** (www.carag.org), which together extend south from Lake Street to 36th Street, and east from Lake Calhoun to Lyndale Avenue. The northernmost section of Uptown, called **Lowry Hill East** or **the Wedge** (www.thewedge.org), is a large, roughly triangular shaped, rental area that stretches between Hennepin and Lyndale Avenues, north of Lake Street, to the point where the two streets meet near Loring Park. It includes the up-and-coming Lyn-Lake business district and entertainment center, at the corner of Lyndale and Lake streets. Bistros, arthouse cinemas, ethnic eateries, and beer-and-burger bars all thrive in this area, along with small performance spaces and trendy shopping.

As a general rule, housing closest to the lakes is the most expensive. Large homes, many of which have been divided into duplexes, predominate, and stately brick apartment buildings built as far back as the 1890s still survive. The major building period, however, occurred during the 1920s as part of a plan to convert East Calhoun into an "apartment district." Mediterranean-style structures from this period can be identified by their red tile roofs. Low-rise one- and two-bedroom apartment complexes built in the 1960s and '70s are still to be found, but there are also newly constructed condos, particularly near the lakes and along the Midtown Greenway. While these neighborhoods offer rental living quarters and recreation possibilities in abundance, the downside is traffic. The intersection at Hennepin and Lake is said to be one of the busiest in the Twin Cities, and the Hiawatha LRT train crossing Lake Street every few minutes has possibly made the gridlock even worse. In an effort to make commuting by bike easier, area residents have been among the most active promoters of the Midtown Greenway, the below-grade bike path that parallels Lake Street and will eventually run from France Avenue all the way across town to the Mississippi River, www.midtowngreenway.org.

BRYN MAWR, CEDAR-ISLES-DEAN, WEST CALHOUN

Close to the parks, but out of the traffic, the hilly wooded neighborhoods on the west side of the city lakes offer comfortable living in a park-like setting of architecturally varied, well-kept bungalows, ramblers, colonials, and architects' signature houses. High-rise apartment buildings in **Cedar-Isles-Dean** (www.cidna.org) and **West Calhoun**, along Highway 7 and Excelsior Boulevard, boast picture-perfect views of sailing boats beating through the deep green waters of Lake Calhoun. **Bryn Mawr**, which is sliced in two by east-west running I-394, is not overrun with recreation traffic, even though it is adjacent to both Cedar Lake and Wirth Park. Much of the shoreline on Cedar Lake is occupied by private homes, unusual in this city where most lakes are completely surrounded by public parks, Public access is provided, however, at beaches, boat launches, and fishing piers. Residents in these neighborhoods tend to be professionals or executives, many of whom work out of their homes, so there are people about throughout the day.

KENWOOD, EAST ISLES, LOWRY HILL

While Calhoun seems like a summer kind of place, **Kenwood** and the other neighborhoods that surround Lake of the Isles are at their best in winter when the crowds have gone home. Winter evenings bring groups of sledders screaming down "Suicide Hill," skaters, and scents of hot chocolate and cinnamon wafting through the frost-bitten air. On nights like these, the most important building on the block becomes the east shore warming house, even though in winter this affluent neighborhood seems twice as impressive as usual, with its large Mediterranean, Colonial, and Arts-and-Crafts homes dressed up for the holidays. So muffle-up and take the three-mile walk around the lake, and don't miss the Purcell-Cutts house at 2328 Lake Place, which is considered one of the best examples of Prairie School architecture in the country, or the "Mary Tyler Moore house" on the corner of Kenwood and 21st, where Ms. Moore hung her hat after she sailed it in the air in the opening clip of the TV show. While you are walking keep your eyes open. Some of the "old" houses here are actually new and include elegant twin homes you'd swear were built at the turn of the century. Check out the eight new "old" houses in Kenwood Crest, located next to the historic Kenwood water tower—they even have two- and three-car garages (a rarity for the city!), while fitting comfortably into the ambiance of the nineteenth-century neighborhood. You'll find that people tend to refer to this whole area as Kenwood, even though Kenwood is mostly on the western side of the lake.

Not all residents live lakeside, of course. Many of the skaters, bikers, and joggers you'll pass live between the lake and Hennepin Avenue, where the hills of **East Isles** sport blocks of architecturally significant houses and a vast number of well-maintained apartments. You will find many young professional families here, as well as young professional singles, but the area is in such high demand that to find an apartment, you should look for signs posted in yards or windows, because only rarely do the best apartments make the classifieds.

At the north end of the lake, the steep streets of **Lowry Hill**, from 22nd Street to I-394, west of Hennepin, span the arts and the ages, from turn-of-the-century mill-owners' mansions to the Walker Art Center's collection of contemporary art. Some of the houses here have been pulled down or turned into offices, but many of them still exist as private homes with craftsman details intact, creating a wonderful air of elegance and grace. Despite the heavy traffic, residents of Lowry Hill enjoy their neighborhood, happy to be so convenient to downtown.

Zip Codes: 55403, 55405, 55408, 55409, 55416
Post Offices: Loring Station, 18 N 12th St; Lake Street Station, 10 E 31st St; Elmwood Branch, 3532 Beltline Blvd, St. Louis Park
Police Precinct: 5th, 2429 Nicollet Ave, 311 (non-emergency)
Emergency Hospitals: Hennepin County Medical Center, 701 Park Ave, 612-873-3000, www.hcmc.org; Methodist Hospital, 6500 Excelsior Blvd, St. Louis Park, 952-993-5000, www.parknicollet.com/methodist
Library: Walker, 2880 Hennepin Ave, 612-630-6650, www.mpls.lib.mn.us
Community Resources: Purcell-Cutts House, 2328 Lake Place; Walker Art Center, 1750 Hennepin Ave, 612-375-7600, www.walkerart.org
Parks: www.minneapolisparks.org; Minneapolis Chain of Lakes; Parade Athletic Fields and Ice Garden; Walker Art Center Sculpture Garden, 1750 Hennepin Ave, www.walkerart.org
Community Publication: *Downtown Journal*, www.dtjournal.com
Public Transportation: 612-373-3333, www.MetroTransit.org; bus service is frequent along Lake St, Hennepin Ave, and other major thoroughfares

SOUTHWEST COMMUNITY

ARMATAGE, KENNY, WINDOM
LYNNHURST, TANGLETOWN
LINDEN HILLS, FULTON
EAST HARRIET, KINGFIELD

Boundaries: North: 38th St; **West:** France Ave, Xerxes Ave; **South:** Crosstown Hwy 62; **East:** I-35W

While young singles head straight for Uptown, hip young families usually prefer the post-Depression bungalows and mini-Tudors of the other southwest communities. Life here, while still close to the city lakes and parkways, is far enough away to make tree-lined streets and well-kept yards feel like small town living. No more than ten minutes' drive from the high-rises of downtown, this is the most heavily residential area of Minneapolis.

Single-family homes and duplexes predominate, although apartments are available, especially in the **Windom** neighborhood. Most homes date to the early 1900s through the 1940s. Homes surrounding Lake Harriet and the Lake Harriet Rock Garden are expensive and some of the most beautiful in Minneapolis. Moderately priced ideal starter homes abound away from the lakeside.

Numerous parks add to the tranquility of this community and provide entertainment, too. You can catch a concert at the Lake Harriet bandshell most summer evenings, or stroll through the park's rose garden or bird sanctuary. Lake Harriet also boasts some of the city's favorite swimming beaches. A bike path connects the rose garden to Lyndale Farmstead Park, the original home of Theodore Wirth, the turn-of-the-century "father" of Minneapolis parks. This park, too, has a garden, but it also has ballfields, ice skating rink, nontraditional "imaginative" play space, and a water fountain with a place where dogs can get a drink, too. The Minnehaha Creek Parkway and trail corridor runs through the community to the south. For pictures of Minnehaha Creek and Lake Harriet, look online at Minneapolis Phototour, www.phototour.minneapolis.mn.us.

It is important to be aware that the southern end of Minneapolis is strongly impacted by airport noise. Citing broken promises to deal with noise, Minneapolis, Richfield, and Eagan have joined in a suit against the Metropolitan Airports Commission (MAC) seeking noise-proofing for houses and a 5-decibel reduction in noise levels. Unfortunately, this is simply the latest round in a long-standing and heated battle, with very little change ever actually accomplished.

ARMATAGE, KENNY, WINDOM

Lined up on the southern border of the city, north of the 62 Crosstown Highway and south of Diamond Lake Road, **Armatage** (www.armatage.org), **Kenny** (www.kennyneighborhood.org), and **Windom** neighborhoods boast well-built two- and three-bedroom starter houses, most of which pre-date the 1940s. Houses in Kenny tend to be newer, and sometimes larger. There is a stable mix of old and new families and, according to the Kenny Neighborhood Association, the homes are about 95% owner-occupied. Apartments can be found in **Windom**, along 35W, where housing runs the gamut, dating from pre-WWII through the 1970s. Retail space in these neighborhoods consists of locally owned stores, located primarily along Penn Avenue and Lyndale. Neighborhood concerns include airport noise and freeway issues.

LYNNHURST, TANGLETOWN

The community milk-cow (you read it right) once grazed in a pasture on 46th Street, and the neighborhood of **Lynnhurst** (www.lynnhurst.org) somehow retains that idyllic sense. Extending from Lyndale west to Penn Avenue, between 46th and 54th streets, this neighborhood boasts very fine period homes as well as parks along Minnehaha Creek and the shores of Lake Harriet, and is one of the most beautiful in the Twin Cities. There has been steady upward movement in assessed values of these properties, and quick market turnover.

Step out of the hustle and bustle of the city in **"Tangletown"** (www.tangle town.org), between I-35W and Lyndale, a hilly tangle of curved, wooded streets that are unusual in the mostly grid-like South Minneapolis layout. Also unique—the neighborhood is capped by the Washburn Water Tower on Prospect Avenue. This majestic water tank is ringed by 16-foot-tall sword-wielding soldiers who have stood sentry since 1932 underneath huge concrete eagles. They're there to protect the city's water supply from typhoid, and apparently they've been effective. The water tower was built by Tangletown resident Harry Wild Jones, who also designed Lakewood Cemetery Chapel; check it out on the Minneapolis Phototours web site, www.phototour. minneapolis.mn.us/3005. About a third of the houses here are pre-1920, with most of the rest built prior to 1960. Because development happened over the course of so many years, architectural styles are highly variable, giving these tree-lined streets a real small town feel. Major issues in this vicinity are typical of South Minneapolis—airport noise and the volume and speed of traffic, as well as traffic spillover onto the residential streets. Shopping is conveniently located in five commercial districts along Penn Avenue, 50th, Bryant, and Lyndale, with many new shops and small restaurants being added every year.

LINDEN HILLS, FULTON

Linden Hills (www.lindenhills.org), on the far southwest edge of the city, was built as a "cottage city" in the 1880s to entice homebuyers away from down-town and out to the waters of Calhoun and Harriet. Only a few cottages remain. Most have been torn down and replaced by bigger houses with two-car garages. The remaining ivy-covered cottages with details like oval windows are considered desirable remodeling gems. Property values are moderate to high, even for houses in deteriorated condition.

Many families choose Linden Hills to be in Southwest High School's atten-dance district. The sense of community—wine and cheese welcomes and sum-mertime block parties—is another draw. Best of all, it's quiet—a tranquil haven in the middle of the city, with pleasant shopping centered on 43rd and Upton, near which you will find Linden Hills co-op (www.lindenhills.coop), Turtle Bread Company (www.turtlebread.com), and Wild Rumpus books (www.wild rumpusbooks.com).

Fulton (www.fultonneighborhood.org) is a bit less placid. Located between Lake Harriet and 47th streets on the north and 54th street on the south, between Penn and France avenues, it is bisected by the main artery of 50th Street, with its extended commercial district offering boutique shopping at both 50th and Penn and 50th and France. Housing here consists of 108 square blocks of well-cared-for 1920s-built bungalows. The 2000 census counted a total population of 5566, in 2590 mostly owner-occupied households. With a significant number of residents over age 65, the neighborhood association has partnered with a service agency to provide home maintenance support so that these seniors can stay in their homes. Actions such as this make Fulton feel like a friendly small town. And the location is convenient, too—residents can walk to Lake Harriet, Lund's, Walgreens, Blockbuster, the Edina Grill, and The Malt Shop at 50th and Bryant, as well as have easy access to Highway 100 and the 62 Crosstown and 35W freeways.

EAST HARRIET, KINGFIELD

Talk about quiet neighborhoods—most of **East Harriet** is occupied by Lakewood Cemetery. That's supposed to be a joke; you'll hear it a lot if you move into this neighborhood. You'll also be treated to a list of all your celebrity "neighbors," including Hubert Horatio Humphrey, Minnesota's senator for many years and vice-president of the United States. Joking aside, this neighborhood does include some of the city's finest amenities: Lake Harriet and its Rose Garden, and the T. S. Roberts Bird Sanctuary, with its boardwalk through the marsh and an osprey nesting platform. Houses in East Harriet (between 36th Street on the north and 46th on the south, west of Lyndale) tend to be large two-story Tudors, Colonials, and Mediterraneans with charming amenities such as sun-porches. The homes are set back from the streets under leafy, old growth canopies. For photos of this neighborhood's wide boulevard and handsome homes, look online at Minneapolis Phototour, www.phototour. minneapolis.mn.us.

Kingfield (www.kingfield.org), between 36th and 46th, is bordered by I-35W on the east and Lyndale on the west. It takes its name from Martin Luther King Park. Its houses are similar to those closer to Lake Harriet, but a little less expensive. Many have been updated with additional bathrooms and new kitchens. Contemporary housing options are few, but do include new multi-family residences and live/work condos on Nicollet. Kingfield, which prides itself on being a forward-looking neighborhood, is the impetus behind the 40th Street Greenway project, which, if built, will create an attractive and safe cross-town route for pedestrians and bicyclists from Kings Highway to West River Road, and provide connections to parks and additional bicycle routes located at either end.

Zip Codes: 55409, 55410, 55419

Post Offices: Lake Street Station, 110 E 31st St; Edina Branch, 3948 W 49 1/2 St, Edina; Diamond Lake Station, 5500 Nicollet Ave

Police Precinct: 5th, 2429 Nicollet Ave, 311 (non-emergency)

Emergency Hospitals: Fairview Southdale Hospital, 6401 France Ave S, 952-924-5000, www.fairview.org; Abbott Northwestern Hospital, 800 E 28th St, 612-863-4000, www.abbottnorthwestern.com

Libraries: www.mpls.lib.mn.us; Linden Hills, 2900 W 43rd St, 612-630-6750; Washburn, 5244 Lyndale Ave S, 612-630-6500

Community Resources: Bakken Library and Museum of Electricity in Life, 3537 Zenith Ave S, 612-926-3878, www.thebakken.org

Parks: www.minneapolisparks.org; Minneapolis Chain of Lakes; Lake Harriet Rose Garden; Minnehaha Creek Park

Community Publications: *Downtown Journal,* www.dtjournal.com; *Southwest Journal,* www.swjournal.com

Public Transportation: 612-373-3333, www.MetroTransit.org; buses run along the main thoroughfares and provide good transportation from this area

NOKOMIS COMMUNITY

HALE, PAGE, DIAMOND LAKE
STANDISH-ERICSSON
FIELD, REGINA, NORTHROP
KEEWAYDIN, MINNEHAHA, MORRIS PARK, WENONAH

Boundaries: North: 42nd St, Hiawatha Golf Course; **West:** I-35W; **South:** Cross-town Hwy 62; **East:** Hiawatha Ave, 47th Ave

"Say, if you'd begin to live, To Oleana you must go/The poorest wretch in Norway, becomes a Duke in a year or so." Those were the words of a song meant to lure Scandinavians to America. Oleana turned out to be a land fraud in Pennsylvania and many of the immigrants wound up here, in Minnesota. The first generation settled on "Snoose Boulevard" (Cedar-Riverside); the second generation built their sturdy post-Depression bungalows here, in Nokomis, and lived in them for a lifetime.

Nokomis, with tree-lined blocks of pleasant yards and tidy houses, is moderately priced, making it attractive to young singles and couples. Some luxurious Colonials line the curved parkways around Lake Nokomis; otherwise, what you'll find here are bungalows, mini-Tudors, and occasional one-story ranch houses. Brick apartment buildings dating to the 1920s can be found along larger streets such as Chicago Avenue and Cedar Avenue, and small commercial districts dot the area. Housing in this community is largely owner-occupied, by a local population with a range of ages and pocketbooks. However, noise from Minneapolis/St. Paul International Airport, to the south, is definitely a factor to consider if you're looking at Nokomis. Keep this in mind and ask pointed questions if you're house hunting in this area.

On the other hand, the ground transportation and recreation amenities are excellent and close at hand. The LRT on the east side of these neighborhoods makes getting downtown, to the airport, or to the Mall of America a quick and easy trip, and the heart of the community, Lake Nokomis, is an expansive body of water with more greenspace around it than any of the other lakes of South Minneapolis. Minneapolis' lake-parkway system winds through this community along Minnehaha Creek and around Lake Nokomis, leading to the public Hiawatha Golf Course and Lake Hiawatha. The Hiawatha Golf Learning Center (www.minneapolisparks.org) features a 50-station, natural grass driving range, putting greens, and a variety of sand traps to use for short iron, chipping, and bunker practice. Minnehaha Park (www.minneapolisparks.org), located at the intersection of Hiawatha Avenue and Minnehaha Parkway, is one of Minneapolis' oldest and most popular parks. In keeping with the Scandinavian roots of the community, it is the venue for the Svenskarnas Dag Scandinavian festival held every year near the end of June. The off-leash dog park is at the south end of the park, accessible from the park's 54th and Hiawatha entrance. For a description of Minnehaha Park and Minnehaha Falls, which are on the eastern edge of Nokomis, check **Lakes and Parkways**.

The **Hale, Page,** and **Diamond Lake** neighborhoods (www.hpdl.org) are located between Minnehaha Creek on the north, Highway 62 on the south, Cedar Avenue on the east and I-35W on the west. Most of the houses here have three bedrooms and were built as late as the 1960s. Some of the residents are original owners.

Standish and **Ericsson** (www.Standish-ericsson.org), north and east of Lake Hiawatha from Cedar Avenue to Hiawatha Avenue, and from 36th Street down to Minnehaha Parkway, are traditional "bungalow communities," with small well-kept stucco bungalows and 1.5-story expansions that boast details like natural woodwork, hardwood floors, and built-in buffets. New housing can be found in the redevelopment area that abuts Hiawatha Avenue and the LRT line. Rich with strong civic groups, active block clubs, and recreational facilities, Standish-Ericsson is home to Hiawatha Park and public golf course, www.minneapolisparks.org, where you can swim, walk, and bike and golf in summer and ski groomed cross-country trails in winter. The 40th Street Greenway, if constructed, will create an attractive and safe cross-town route for pedestrians and bicyclists along 40th and 42nd streets. The greenway is envisioned to extend from Kings Highway to West River Road, and to provide connections to parks and bicycle routes at either end. In between, the greenway will connect several parks and other Southside landmarks like Roosevelt High School and Sibley Field, which has a children's playground, sledding hill, and hockey and skating rinks. If you work in St. Paul, these neighborhoods have easy access to that side of the river over the Ford Parkway Bridge. In the center of Nokomis, between I-35W and Cedar Avenue, **Field, Regina**, and **Northrop** consist primarily of small, two-bedroom pre-1940s stucco, brick, and stone houses. Northrop in particular has some pretty, hilly streets (check out 12th, 13th, and 14th) and a mix of well-kept, updated housing stock. This area is popular with young couples who are looking for an affordable alternative to Lake Harriet. Shopping is nearby along Chicago Avenue.

Finally, **Keewaydin, Minnehaha, Morris Park,** and **Wenonah** are spread out from the east shore of Lake Nokomis to Minnehaha Park. Known for NRP purposes as Nokomis East (www.nokomiseast.org), these neighborhoods that abut the airport have slightly newer housing, but a higher proportion of renters. Prior to 1900, this neighborhood was a major American Indian center, and until 1880 there was actually an American Indian village here, on the site now occupied by the Nokomis Community Center. The main transportation corridors are the neighborhood boundaries: 34th and 28th avenues, 50th and 54th streets, Highway 55 (Hiawatha Avenue), and the 62 Crosstown. The area's primary shopping district is at 34h Avenue between 50th and 54th streets. There you will find the library, post office, grocery store, and a variety of other businesses. The success of the Hiawatha LRT is bringing new housing to this area, and some units are already under construction at the VA Medical Center LRT stop.

Zip Codes: 55406, 55407, 55409, 55417, 55419
Post Offices: Nokomis Station, 5139 34th Ave S; Diamond Lake Station, 5500 Nicollet Ave
Police Precinct: 3rd, 3000 Minnehaha Ave, 311 (non-emergency)
Emergency Hospital: Abbott Northwestern Hospital, 800 E 28th St, 612-863-4000, www.abbottnorthwestern.com; Fairview-University Medical Center, 2450 Riverside Ave, 612-672-6000, www.fairview.org
Library: www.mpls.lib.mn.us; Nokomis, 5100 34th Ave S, 612-630-6700
Community Resources: The Rabbithood, www.rabbithood.com: The Hale, Page, Diamond Lake Business Association has dubbed itself the "rabbit-hood" in honor of the seven-foot bronze rabbit that graces the Portland Ave at Minnehaha Pkwy gateway to the neighborhood.
Parks: www.minneapolisparks.org; Hiawatha Park and public golf course; Lake Nokomis Park; Minnehaha Creek
Community Publication: *Southside Pride,* http://southsidepride.com
Public Transportation: 612-373-3333, www.MetroTransit.org; buses travel along Chicago Ave, Minnehaha Ave, Bloomington Ave/Ford Pkwy (to St. Paul), 28th Ave S, 34th Ave, 42nd St, and Cedar Ave; the Hiawatha LRT stops at 38th, 46th, and 50th sts, VA Medical Center, and Fort Snelling

POWDERHORN COMMUNITY

POWDERHORN PARK
MIDTOWN
WHITTIER
LYNDALE
CENTRAL
CORCORAN

Boundaries: North: Franklin Ave, Lake St; **West:** Lyndale Ave, I-35W; **South:** 38th St, 42nd St; **East:** Minnehaha Ave

When the snow begins to fall, the rolling hills of Powderhorn Park (www.ppna.org) become a well-used tobogganing area, and skaters take to the only outdoor speed-skating track in Minneapolis. At the heart of Powderhorn's diverse community is this lovely park, a one-square-mile reserve of woods and wildflower-covered hills with a small powderhorn-shaped lake that is home to egrets and great blue herons. It's a welcome expanse amid these urban surroundings, and the ideal setting for Powderhorn's artistically minded neighborhood events, which include May Day (www.heartofthe beasttheatre.org), Powderhorn Festival of the Arts, Shakespeare in the Park, July 4th fireworks, and Friday night concerts.

Yet, **Powderhorn Park**, where property values increased 20% between 2003 and 2005, sits in marked contrast to some of the neighborhoods around it (**Central, Corcoran, Bryant,** and **Bancroft**), which tend to be economically depressed rental areas with high levels of unemployment, crime, poverty, and substandard housing. What is unusual is that the Powderhorn Park Neighborhood Association is working to do something about that. Most recently, their efforts have focused on transforming Lake Street. The project began with a new YWCA (www.ywcampls.org) at 22nd and Lake, and has continued with the Midtown Exchange offices/condos/global market and hotel at Chicago and Lake. The plan is to eventually revamp Lake Street all the way from the Mississippi River to Uptown, accommodating pedestrians as well as vehicles and enhancing the ethnic character of the surrounding neighborhoods. If you're interested in living in this area, contact the Powderhorn Residents Group (www.prginc.org), a nonprofit organization that helps people find quality, affordable housing in the area. With easy access to downtown via the Midtown Greenway bike trail and the Hiawatha Light Rail Transit line, as well as many houses that have had a face-lift in recent years, this neighborhood is worth more than a passing thought.

Midtown? Most Twin Citians never heard of it, with reason, because it's still being built. Spread out along East Lake Street from the Hiawatha LRT Lake Street/Midtown stop west to the Midtown Exchange (http://midtowncommunity works.org/exchange) at Chicago and Lake, it's still more of a construction nightmare than a distinct district, but it's getting there. Named with an obvious nod to the success of Uptown to its west, it is being developed in a public-private partnership that includes Wells Fargo and Allina Hospitals and Clinics, which has recently moved its corporate headquarters into the Midtown Exchange building (formerly the Sears mail-order warehouse building). At one million square feet, the Midtown Exchange project is the second largest commercial development in Minnesota, surpassed only by the Mall of America. When the conversion is complete, it will include Allina's offices, condos, senior housing, a Global Marketplace, a conference center, and a Sheraton hotel. The old Sears Tower will even feature a penthouse with 34-foot ceilings. Even though Lake Street is torn up and expected to stay that way for quite awhile, the Latino and Somali business people who own the global markets and restaurants along this strip are determined to hang on. Visit the Mercado Central at Lake Street and Bloomington Avenue, and help them stay in business. For more information, visit http://midtowncommunityworks.org/exchange/.

Closer to downtown, **Whittier** (www.whittieralliance.org), from Franklin south to Lake Street, between Garfield and I-35W, is one of the city's oldest neighborhoods. Named for the poet John Greenleaf Whittier, it is sometimes referred to as the "Arts Quarter" because of the presence of the Minneapolis Institute of Arts (www.artsmia.org), Children's Theatre Company (www.childrens theatre.org), and Minneapolis College of Art and Design (www.mcad.edu)—as well as the bohemian collection of artists and actors who live nearby. This is a largely rental area of mansions sitting next door to Section 8 housing in a patchwork of sometimes posh/sometimes sketchy blocks. With 43% of the city's supportive housing and social services concentrated in this neighborhood and nearby Phillips, Stevens Square–Loring Heights, and Central, an ongoing issue is the impact of the group homes on the community's livability and safety, as well as the potential for adverse effects on neighborhood development and revitalization efforts. On the other hand, that very abundance of iffy property is what makes this a neighborhood where you can buy something cheap, fix it up, make a profit, and move to a much better place and still stay within the neighborhood. And the neighborhood is rich with "better places." The Washburn–Fair Oaks Mansion District along 22nd Street between 1st and 2nd Avenues, near the Minneapolis Institute of Arts/Children's Theater, is listed on the National Historic Register (www.hhmuseum.org). More grand houses, some of the oldest in Minneapolis, are found along Blaisdell and Third Avenue. Stevens Avenue is home to a number of beautifully restored houses, including an in-town bed and breakfast (see **Temporary Lodgings**). Running through the middle of the neighborhood, "Eat Street," or Nicollet Avenue, offers an around-the-world tour of restaurants and groceries, as well as brand new loft housing. Four blocks east, Third Avenue South, which runs between Downtown and the Minneapolis Institute of Arts/Children's Theatre Company/MCAD, has been designated the "Avenue of the Arts," and given streetscaping improvements that include corporate-sponsored and -planted medians and a Frank Lloyd Wright–inspired freeway bridge. When checking out this area, be sure to visit the Hennepin History Museum (www.hhmuseum.org), half a block north of the Minneapolis Institute of Arts/Children's Theatre on Third Avenue. They lead walking tours around the neighborhood every summer.

Farther south, across Lake Street, the duplexes and apartments in **Lyndale** (www.lyndale.org), Lake Street to 36th and Lyndale Avenue to I-35W, are much like nearby neighborhoods in Uptown, although housing here is generally more affordable and incomes more modest. Less than a fourth of the units are owner-occupied. Back in the 1990s, the Lyndale Neighborhood Association (LNA) received national attention for its work in making the transition from a crime-infested, transient community to a diverse and vibrant neighborhood. Now the group is focusing its efforts on affordable housing and partnering with developers to build condos. A quirky collection of restaurants, galleries, and theaters makes the corner of Lyndale and Lake Street, known as Lyn-Lake, a great alternative to the busier parts of town.

In **Central**, just east of I-35 and south of Lake Street, the old-style commercial East Lake Street business district is being redeveloped for the first time in fifty years (see Midtown above). By the time of its completion in 2008, it will stretch four miles from Lake Calhoun to the Mississippi River and give space to pedestrians as well as to cars. At the west end of this stretch of Lake Street, by 35W, is the national headquarters of Wells Fargo Home Mortgage, which brings hundreds of employees a day into the neighborhood. At the east end is the new light rail station. In between, there are three key community landmarks: the Mercado Central, a thriving member-owned cooperative of Latino businesses at 15th and Lake; the Midtown Exchange (old Sears building) at Chicago and Lake, which is bringing offices, new housing, a hotel, and a global market modeled on Seattle's Pike Place Market into the community; and the YWCA fieldhouse and aquatic center at 22nd and Lake, which provides a safe place to run, play basketball, and swim. Housing in the Central neighborhood includes the grand Queen Anne Healy Block Residential Historic District of c. 1875–1899 homes located between Lake Street and East 31st Street at 3101–3145 Second Avenue South and 3116–3124 Third Avenue South. Once known as "crack alley," these historic houses have been rehabilitated, signaling a profound change in the neighborhood. In addition, new housing—both market rate and subsidized—is sprouting up just north of Lake Street along the Midtown Greenway.

At the far east end of Lake Street, the **Corcoran** neighborhood (www. corcoranneighborhood.org), East Lake Street to East 36th between Hiawatha and Cedar Avenues, is not the prettiest neighborhood in Minneapolis, but it is conveniently positioned just west of the LRT line. Home to a diverse and active Hispanic community, this neighborhood hosts the city's annual Cinco de Mayo celebration and the Midtown Public Market, a vibrant farmers' market organized around interesting theme days such as Clay Day, and Hmong Community Day.

Zip Codes: 55405, 55406, 55407, 55408, 55409

Post Offices: Powderhorn Station, 3045 Bloomington Ave; Minnehaha Station, 3033 27th Ave S; Lake Street Station, 110 E 31st St

Police Precincts: west of I-35W: 5th Precinct, 2429 Nicollet Ave, 311 (non-emergency); rest of Powderhorn: 3rd Precinct, 3000 Minnehaha Ave, 311 (non-emergency)

Emergency Hospital: Abbott Northwestern Hospital, 800 E 28th St, 612-863-4000, www.abbottnorthwestern.org

Library: www.mpls.lib.mn.us; Hosmer, 347 E 36th St, 612-630-6950

Community Resources: Children's Theatre Company, 2400 3rd Ave S, 612-874-0400, www.childrenstheatre.org; Minneapolis Institute of Arts, 2400 S 3rd Ave, 612-870-3131, www.artsmia.org; Minneapolis College of Art and Design, 2501 Stevens Ave, www.mcad.edu; Midtown YWCA fieldhouse, childcare, and athletic center, YWCA (www.ywcampls.org) at 22nd and Lake; Washburn–Fair Oaks Mansion District and Healy Block Historic District, www.hhmuseum.org

Parks: www.minneapolisparks.org; Midtown Greenway Bikeway (one block north of Lake Street from the Chain of Lakes to the Mississippi River); Powderhorn Park and Recreation Center

Community Publications: *Downtown Journal,* www.dtjournal.com

Public Transportation: 612-373-3333, www.MetroTransit.org; buses travel on all the major thoroughfares and are timed to connect with the LRT

PHILLIPS COMMUNITY

VENTURA VILLAGE

Boundaries: North: I-94; **West:** I-35W; **South:** Lake St; **East:** Hiawatha Ave

The Phillips community (www.pnn.org) in south-central Minneapolis has, for years, been the densest, poorest, most diverse community in the city. Plagued by crime and disinvestment despite years of hard work by neighborhood block clubs, corporations, and social agencies, today some parts of this community are rising out of a decades-long slump and becoming leaders in property value increases and transit-oriented infrastructure development. Though Phillips still faces problems caused by poverty and crime, at least some parts of it are experiencing a significant turnaround.

You can look at the variety of housing along these streets and see that Phillips has a complex history. Elegant Victorian mansions along Park and Portland avenues, some of the largest in the city, are signs of this neighborhood's past grandeur. So are smaller turn-of-the century houses with Queen Anne turrets and gingerbread trim. Unfortunately, urban decay, due in part to construction of interstate highways 35W and 94, laid waste to much of this area. By the 1990s, neighborhood unemployment was 14% and the streets were blighted with boarded-up drug houses and vacant lots. But then several things happened more or less at the same time. Abbott Northwestern Hospital figured out that the neighborhood murder rate was affecting its bottom line and started training and hiring locals, as well as helping employees buy houses nearby; and residents started turning the vacant lots into gardens. By 1997, 30 community gardens had sprouted here. Everyone agrees that these gardens played a key role in stabilizing the area. However, as in many cities, the "pacification" of the neighborhood resulted in pressures for redevelopment, and now many of the vacant lots are sprouting townhouses instead of flowers. The principal location for new housing here, however, is along the Midtown Greenway (one block north of Lake Street from the Chain of Lakes to the Mississippi River), particularly in the Midtown Exchange area (see **Midtown** above). Here you will find new multi-unit housing that caters to singles and small families. It's a development trend that began in Uptown, to the west, and has now moved eastward into Phillips.

Not to be outdone, homeowners at the north end of the community in **Ventura Village**, between 24th Street and I-94, are trying to create more affordable housing—without having to resort to high-rises—by building carriage houses and "granny flats" over their garages. This neighborhood's organization has also been active in working to obtain the "air rights" to build over the freeways, thus reconnecting it with Whittier, Elliot Park, Stevens Square, and downtown.

While Phillips has long been the center of Minneapolis' Native American community, according to a recent census its Hispanic population has increased five-fold since 1990, and Latinos now make up more than a quarter of the community's 20,000 residents. Somalis are making their mark here as well, as you can see by the growing numbers of small African restaurants and food stores that line Cedar Avenue. (For more information on this area see the Shopping Districts section of **Shopping for the Home**.)

Zip Codes: 55403, 55404, 55405, 55407, 55408
Post Offices: Powderhorn Station, 3045 Bloomington Ave; Minnehaha Station, 3033 27th Ave S; Lake Street Station, 110 E 31st St
Police Precinct: 3rd, 3000 Minnehaha Ave, 612-673-5703
Emergency Hospital: Abbott Northwestern Hospital, 800 E 28th St, 612-863-4000, www.abbottnorthwestern.com
Library: www.mpls.lib.mn.us; Franklin, 1314 E Franklin Ave, 612-630-6800
Community Resources: American Swedish Institute, 2600 Park Ave, 612-871-4907, www.americanswedishinst.org; Green Institute/Re-Use Center/Phillips Eco-Enterprise Center and Deconstruction Services, 2801 21st Ave S, 612-278-7100, greeninstitute.org; Minneapolis American Indian Center, 1530 Franklin Ave E, www.maicnet.org
Parks: www.minneapolisparks.org; Midtown Greenway
Community Publication: *Southside Pride,* http://southsidepride.com
Public Transportation: 612-373-3333, www.MetroTransit.org; buses travel along Franklin Ave, Chicago Ave, Bloomington Ave/Cedar Ave, Lake St, and Park Ave; I-35W express routes board where the highway crosses Lake St. LRT stations are located at Franklin and Lake St.

GREATER LONGFELLOW COMMUNITY

LONGFELLOW
SEWARD
COOPER, HOWE, HIAWATHA

Boundaries: North: I-94; **West:** Minnehaha Ave; **South/East:** Mississippi River

Greater Longfellow is the sliver-shaped bungalow community that flanks the gorge of the Mississippi River between I-94 and Minnehaha Falls Park. It is bisected by Lake Street and bordered by Hiawatha Avenue. Popular since the 1920s with working-class people, it is well-served by public transportation, including the Hiawatha LRT, with stations at Lake, 38th, and 46th streets. Early predictions estimated 7150 new housing units and millions of feet of new retail space would be built along the LRT corridor, and while current construction doesn't approach that level of building boom, a number of new condo/apartment/small-scale retail developments are going up, particularly near the 38th Street and 46th Street stations.

Ideally located, with a variety of housing, this is another neighborhood in which first-time homebuyers can buy small and (relatively) cheap and move up without having to leave the neighborhood.

Residents here also have easy access to nature. Bike trails through the Mississippi River Gorge, Minnehaha Falls Park, and the east-west Midtown

Greenway, which crosses both Longfellow and Cooper neighborhoods, combine to make the outdoor amenities in this district every bit as nice as those you will find around the Chain of Lakes—better, really, because here there is more Nature and less Traffic. Though most of the houses are fairly undistinguished, there are a few homes that have tree-top views of the city skyscrapers, and ground-level views that are all river and nature.

SEWARD

It's actually hard to find a home in **Seward** (www.sng.org), which at the end of the 1990s developed a hip reputation. Housing here ranges from deteriorated student digs to two blocks of gentrified railroad workers' houses (circa 1880) located on Milwaukee Road, and now listed on the Historic Register. In between there are new townhouses and industrial-style lofts, small apartment buildings built in the late 1800s and early 1900s, a slew of early 20th-century 1.5-story bungalows that feature built-ins and front porches, and even some fairly new family-sized in-fill houses.

COOPER, HOWE, HIAWATHA

A little farther south, a patchwork of homes in various stages of improvement characterizes the **Cooper, Howe**, and **Hiawatha** neighborhoods. Houses in the blocks closest to the river have been upgraded substantially, and more modest homes farther back are also being renovated on a block-by-block basis. At the south end of Hiawatha, Minnehaha Parkway boasts larger homes with charming decorative details, but for architecturally unique dream-houses or condos, look to the river and shop along Edmund Boulevard.

Much of Longfellow's housing is deemed worthy of rehabilitation, but may fall short of meeting the needs of modern families. Over half the houses in these neighborhoods are bungalows—two-bedroom, one-bath, single-story houses with built-in cabinets and expansion attics. Two-story, four-square houses built in the 1920s are the second-most predominant style. So popular is renovation of these existing houses that the Longfellow community commissioned a book, *The Longfellow Planbook: Remodeling Plans for Bungalows and Other Small Urban Homes,* which contains ideas for updating the area's predominant housing types. Plans have been reviewed and approved by the Minneapolis Inspections Division. The book can be purchased from the Longfellow Community Council (www.longfellow.org), for $20, or $10 for Longfellow residents.

Zip Codes: 55404, 55406, 55407, 55417
Post Offices: Minnehaha Station, 3033 27th Ave S; Nokomis Station, 5139 34th Ave S
Police Precinct: 3rd, 3000 Minnehaha Ave, 311 (non-emergency)
Emergency Hospitals: Abbott Northwestern Hospital, 800 E 28th St, 612-863-4000, www.abbottnorthwestern.com.; Fairview-University Medical Center, 2450 Riverside Ave, 612-672-6000, www.fairview.org

Library: www.mpls.lib.mn.us; East Lake, 2727 E Lake St, 612-630-6550

Community Resources: Longfellow House, located in Minnehaha Park at 4800 Minnehaha Ave S; 1849 John H. Stevens House (first frame house built west of the Mississippi) is also located in Minnehaha Park; Matthews Park, 2318 28th Ave S

Parks: www.minneapolisparks.org; Mississippi River Parks and Trails; Minnehaha Park

Community Publications: *Southeast Angle,* www.southeastangle.info; *Southside Pride,* http://southsidepride.com; *Downtown Journal,* www.dtjournal.com

Public Transportation: 612-373-3333, www.MetroTransit.org; buses travel Franklin, Minnehaha, and Lake St and connect with the Hiawatha LRT at Lake St, 38th and 46th

UNIVERSITY COMMUNITY

MARCY-HOLMES
COMO
UNIVERSITY OF MINNESOTA
CEDAR-RIVERSIDE (WEST BANK)
DINKYTOWN
PROSPECT PARK
NICOLLET ISLAND

Boundaries: North: E Hennepin Ave, I-35W; **West:** Nicollet Island, I-35W; **South:** I-94, East Bank of Mississippi; **East:** city limits

WEST BANK/CEDAR-RIVERSIDE/MARCY-HOLMES/COMO

Gold and maroon (the **University of Minnesota** colors) rule—but so do black, white, yellow, and brown, in these neighborhoods tucked in along the banks of the Mississippi close to the U, whose East Bank and West Bank campuses straddle the river. Here Somalis, Russians, Indians, Ethiopians, Kenyans, Asians, Latinos, and Minnesota farm kids of Scandinavian and German descent all crowd the streets, walking as one, talking and laughing in the melting pot of colors and cultures that has been the theme of this neighborhood since its founding.

A haven for new immigrants ever since the 1800s, when it was known as "Snoose Boulevard," **Cedar-Riverside** (www.cedarriverside.com) was slated for demolition in the mid-1960s when I-94 was built. It saved itself through a grass-roots, counter-culture movement that created the first federally funded, New-Town-In-Town urban redevelopment project in the country. Backers of the project idealistically believed that people of all incomes, ages, races, and cultures could live together in harmony in high-density, high-rise apartments close to shops and cultural activities. While this vision was never fully realized, anyone traveling I-94 between the two cities cannot help noticing the project's distinctive apartment towers with their bright-colored panels. Locally famous architect Ralph Rapson, who designed the towers, said of this complex: "We had the dream that modern or contemporary design was going to really revolutionize and change the way we lived and thought about society. I think we thought we were part of a revolution that was going to change things considerably. We always had the notion that we could do something that would make the environment better for mankind." A little radical? Maybe. Or maybe just an appropriate educational mission for a neighborhood that is home to two Twin Cities icons of higher education, the U and Augsburg College.

Though many still call the project towers "home," there is less avant-garde housing here as well. Multitudes of student duplexes and apartments are located just off-campus in **Marcy-Holmes** (www.marcy-holmes.org), west of I-35W, and in **Dinkytown** (www.dinkytownusa.com), which abuts the campus. There are also the raucous blocks of University Avenue's fraternity row. Quieter neighborhoods can be found in **Prospect Park** and **Como** (www.secomo.org). Unfortunately, due to their near-campus location, rents are not a bargain, although house prices are moderate.

Often recommended for off-campus housing, the **Como** neighborhood is a swath of modest (sometimes dilapidated) bungalows and tall, skinny two-stories. This neighborhood is home to Joe's Market and Deli at 1828 Como, one of the Twin Cities' last family-owned neighborhood groceries. Make your first visit on a Monday, otherwise known as Lebanese Omelet Day, and you'll be sure to return often. The perks of an academic community—lectures, concerts, the University Film Society—are easily accessible to people living nearby, and the University's Weisman Art Museum, on the East Bank, is the riverfront's most significant architectural landmark.

Dinkytown, between 8th Street and University Avenue on the East Bank, is the main campus commercial/entertainment district. It has plenty of cheap places to eat and many businesses named "Gopher" (for the University of Minnesota mascot). Bob Dylan (known locally as Robert Zimmerman from Hibbing, Minnesota) played at the Twelve O'clock Scholar here in the early sixties. The **West Bank** area, near the LRT station, is equally lively and packed with unique restaurants and numerous venues offering live performances, music and dance. For full information about where to go and what to do, look online at www.cedarriverside.com. Wherever you go, think about safety and take your cue from the University of Minnesota, which provides escorts to people who are out on campus at night.

PROSPECT PARK/EAST RIVER ROAD

Across the river on the East Bank, between the University and St. Paul, **Prospect Park/East River Road** (www.pperr.org) is a place where you can walk out of your modern condo door into a 100-year-old neighborhood. Security is not such a huge concern here, where quiet streets and tree-covered slopes give the neighborhood a tranquil character. People who live in "the Park" say they live in a small town with an urban beat, a place where they can walk to work, to recreation, shopping, and community events, and probably recognize everybody along the way. Residents here are 10 minutes by car from each downtown, and centrally located for travel to any place in the Twin Cities.

Their strong sense of place probably has to do with the area's clear geographic boundaries, steep hills, and its pointy green witch's hat water tower, which is visible from I-94. Once a year the whole neighborhood climbs to the top and is treated to a panoramic view of the cities all the way to the airport.

The area's civic history dates back to the late 1800s when it was a commuter suburb on the Minneapolis streetcar line. Today, imposing historic residences rub elbows with new condos and public housing on Prospect Park's meandering streets. Though there is a laissez-faire attitude toward landscaping, and the used auto parts business displays "found-art" sculptures, beautiful restoration is appreciated. Many of the homes date from the early 1900s up to the 1930s and feature art glass windows and other elegant details. Popular updates include turning butler's pantries into second bathrooms and putting in modern kitchens. Recently, the Central Corridor Partnership, which includes several groups dedicated to creating a better central corridor transit system, has begun to transform the industrial zone along University into mixed-use housing. One of the first of these projects is 212-unit Emerald Gardens, which is located on the exact border of Minneapolis and St. Paul. Shopping for this area is nearby along University and Washington Avenues.

NICOLLET ISLAND/EAST BANK

Another antique refuge with a view of the city skyline is just northwest of the university, out in the river. Forty-seven-acre **Nicollet Island** (http://nicollet island.com, www.niebna.org) is a 19th-century Victorian landmark settlement and park within the St. Anthony Falls Heritage Zone. Most of Nicollet Island's 400 graceful stone houses were built between 1880 and 1910, and have been faithfully restored. Today they are being joined by new luxury condominiums across the water on historic Southeast Main. Even if you decide not to move to this neighborhood, be sure to take the River City Trolley's narrated tour of the area, 612-673-5123, www.rivercitytrolley.org, or Mobile Entertainment's Segway guided tours of the Mississippi Riverfront, 952-888-9200, www.humanonastick.com (see **Transportation**). The Nicollet Island Inn (www.nicolletislandinn.com) is the perfect place to stay while you check out the city. To view some of the best pictures of the island's houses, click on www.umcycling.com/msp2.htm.

Zip Codes: 55455 (University of Minnesota), 55413, 55414, 55454, 55404
Post Offices: University Station, 2811 University Ave SE; Dinkytown Station, 1311 SE 4th St
Police Precinct: 2nd, 1911 Central Ave NE, 311 (non-emergency)
Emergency Hospitals: Fairview-University Medical Center, 2450 Riverside Ave, 612-672-6000, www.fairview.org
Libraries: www.mpls.lib.mn.us; Southeast, 1222 SE 4th St, 612-630-6850; University libraries, www.umn.edu
Community Resources: University of Minnesota, www.umn.edu; Cedar Cultural Center, 416 Cedar Ave S, Minneapolis, 612-338-2674, www.the cedar.org; First Bridge Park, Hennepin Ave and W River Pkwy, www.mrd

bridges.com; Frederick R. Weisman Art Museum, 333 E River Rd, University of Minnesota, Minneapolis, 612-625-9494, www.weisman. umn.edu; Minneapolis Riverfront District: Boom Island, Nicollet Island, Historic Main, Hennepin Bluff, Mill Ruins Park, and Stone Arch Bridge, www.mrdbridges.com

Parks: www.minneapolisparks.org; Minneapolis Riverfront District, www.mrdbridges.com

Community Publications: *Southeast Angle,* www.southeastangle.info; *Southside Pride,* http://southsidepride.com/; *Minnesota Daily,* www.daily.umn.edu; *Downtown Journal,* www.dtjournal.com

Public Transportation: 612-373-3333, www.MetroTransit.org; *Buses:* There are more than 30 U of M bus routes that run from many parts of the Twin Cities to campus, though most of them operate on weekdays only. Supersavers are on sale at the following campus locations: Coffman Union, the West Bank Skyway Store, the Williamson Hall Bookstore, the St. Paul Student Center, and the Fairview-University Medical Center Ticket Office. Supersavers are also sold at all MetroTransit stores and at over 130 outlets around town, and can be purchased online at www.metro council.org/transit. *Trains:* The Cedar-Riverside LRT station does not have any connecting bus routes, though buses do run north and south on Cedar Ave. To find them, follow the "To Cedar Avenue Buses" signs.

NORTHEAST COMMUNITY

ST. ANTHONY EAST (HISTORIC ST. ANTHONY)
ST. ANTHONY WEST
BELTRAMI, NORTHEAST PARK
BOTTINEAU, SHERIDAN, MARSHALL TERRACE
COLUMBIA PARK
WAITE PARK, AUDUBON PARK
HOLLAND, LOGAN PARK
WINDOM PARK

Boundaries: North: 37th Ave NE; **West:** Mississippi River; **South:** Nicollet Island, Central Ave, I-35W; **East:** city limits

In Minneapolis, the action has definitely moved to this side of the river! Once an industrial area filled with seedy bars that catered to the local workingman and University of Minnesota students, "Nord'east" (www.northeast minneapolis.com) has taken a dramatic upscale turn. Streets filled for over 100 years with Polish, Ukrainian, Scandinavian, German, and Italian laborers who came over to work in the grain and lumber mills are now teeming with empty-nest suburbanites, artists chased out the Downtown Warehouse District by escalating rents, and young executives equally attracted to the neighborhood's trendy shopping/entertainment scene and to its easy access to their offices in downtown Minneapolis, just across the river over the Hennepin Avenue/First Avenue bridge.

Though, as someone recently said on the radio, they're not giving gay walking tours of Northeast—yet—East Hennepin is also starting to develop a large concentration of gay-owned businesses and residents.

Housing in the neighborhoods is changing dramatically as well. Not that swank lofts are replacing *all* the old warehouses and cottages, but they are replacing a lot of them. The trend is being called "Edina-fication" after the Twin Cities' most fashionable suburb. Yet, the industrial and immigrant heritage of this area is still evident along the neighborhoods' stick-straight streets that were named for presidents in order to help immigrants prepare for their citizenship exams. Buildings here are a few stories, not 50, and brick, rather than glass and steel. And though fancy restaurants and stylish bars are pulling in an upscale clientele, good old Nye's Polonaise Room, Totino's, Marino's, Elsie's, and Stasiu's are still packing in the crowds, too.

While music, bars, and polka lounges have always been an important part of this community, the visual arts have recently come to prominence as well. In February 2003, the city of Minneapolis designated the area of Northeast Minneapolis bordered by Broadway, Lowry, Central Avenue, and the Mississippi River as the Northeast Minneapolis Arts District. It includes the neighborhoods of Bottineau, Sheridan, Holland, and Logan Park, but St. Anthony East, West, and Beltrami are home to many artists' studios as well.

Though the rest of Northeast is not so glam, there is still more to this community than new lofts in old buildings around East Hennepin.

While Midwestern squares and small turn-of-the-century wood frame houses built before 1940 predominate in the blue-collar blocks of most of the neighborhoods, the "Parks" (**Waite, Audubon, Windom, and Columbia**) have newer houses, as well as more white-collar workers, and are actually quite a lot like the suburbs they adjoin. They even have a South Minneapolis–style amenity, a stretch of parkway that runs along St. Anthony Boulevard from the Mississippi River on the west through Columbia Park, Waite Park, and Audubon Park, to Hillside Cemetery on the east. This parkway is part of the Minneapolis Grand Rounds, and, besides being a great place to run or bike, also connects several parks and Columbia Golf Course.

HISTORIC ST. ANTHONY/ST. ANTHONY WEST

After you have crossed the river on Hennepin Avenue, Kramarczuk's East European Deli, which has done business at 215 East Hennepin since 1954, ushers you into the city's old working-class neighborhood of **Historic St. Anthony** (www.stawno.org), the birthplace of Minneapolis—not to be confused with the nearby suburb of St. Anthony or the St. Anthony Park section of St. Paul. This wedge-shaped neighborhood, bordered by Northeast Central, Broadway, and the Mississippi River, is home to many historical places of interest including St. Anthony Falls, "discovered" by Father Louis Hennepin in 1680; the Pillsbury "A" mill, the beginning of "Mill City's" flour, lumber, and textile industry; and the Stone Arch Bridge. Architectural landmarks, the Russian Orthodox and Ukrainian Orthodox churches, Surdyk's Liquors and Nye's Polonaise Room, serve as reminders of St. Anthony's booming business district of days gone by. At the same time, new upscale restaurants and businesses are also thriving, and it is thought that someday east Hennepin could become an eight-block-long strolling and shopping boulevard. (See the Shopping Districts section of the **Shopping for the Home** chapter.)

Successive waves of redevelopment in the 1960s, '70s, and '80s demolished many of the old houses, and they have been replaced with multi-unit housing, including luxury high-rises where residents are treated to spectacular views of the river and the soaring music from National Historic Landmark Our Lady of Lourdes Catholic Church (www.ourladyoflourdes.com), the oldest continuously used church in the city. Consistent with the Northeast tradition of homeownership, nearly all the housing is owner-occupied, both new and old.

The western half of this neighborhood, **St. Anthony West** (www.stawno.org) experienced three waves of redevelopment, but came through them with some of its Victorians intact. Now designated an Historic Garden District, the demand for its vintage homes far exceeds the supply, resulting in most of St. Anthony West's residents living in some form of multi-housing such as duplexes or townhomes. For those who love the river, this is an ideal place to live. Not only is it a 20-minute walk to offices downtown, it is within biking distance of the university and has Boom Island Park for river access. This 14-acre riverside park features a day-use marina, playground, and picnic area.

BELTRAMI/NORTHEAST PARK

Heading north along Central Avenue, you'll find delis, polka lounges, and supper clubs, as well as rows and rows of small, Midwestern squares and bungalows. Here the **Beltrami** and **Northeast Park** neighborhoods, east of Central and south of Broadway, are also picking up their pace. Though two-story plain frame houses built during the early 1900s make up the bulk of the homes, more recently constructed housing can be found near the railroad tracks and along East Hennepin. While Northeast is notably lacking in good parks, Beltrami Park, off East Broadway, has a playground, pool, tennis and basketball courts, and a baseball diamond. As other warehouse districts have gentrified, some artists are choosing Beltrami for its less expensive studio space. It is also conveniently located to the university, Interstate 35W, and to shopping at the Quarry Retail Center, with its grocery store, Target, Home Depot, PetSmart, and other national retailers. The rest of the neighborhood of Northeast Park, just north of I-35W, is made up of quiet, dead-end streets. Really quiet and genuinely dead: the Hillside Cemetery occupies a full third of it. Older homes in the area (c. 1920s and '30s) are being bought by young families looking for starter homes with character, and some of its sturdy ramblers changed ownership for the first time as late as the 1990s.

SHERIDAN/BOTTINEAU/MARSHALL TERRACE

The rental working-class communities of **Sheridan** (www.sheridan neighborhood.org), **Bottineau**, and **Marshall Terrace** may lack fancier recreation amenities like field houses and health clubs, but residents can still get their workouts biking the Grand Rounds or dancing the polka at Gasthof Zur Gemutlichkeit at 2300 University. Located within the designated Northeast Minneapolis Arts District. **Bottineau** actually has some houses on the riverfront, and has become very popular with artists. The California Building, at 20th and California, a 90,000-square-foot grain mill built in 1920, now houses 75 artists' studios. The **Sheridan** neighborhood, also part of the Arts District, is a good example of Northeast's unpretentious, working-class style. Plain, often large, and in good condition, these houses are being fixed, not gentrified. A number of small apartment buildings can also be found in Sheridan. Once considered an iffy place to live, Sheridan is now thought of as desirable, in part due to its growing art scene, which includes small galleries along its 13th Avenue business corridor. The Sheridan Neighborhood Organization (SNO) emphasizes community-building by sponsoring events like the SNO Ball and the SNO Big Deal. Once the only neighborhood in the city that didn't have a park, the community has recently acquired a small, undeveloped green area on the bank of the Mississippi River where a foundry formerly stood.

Marshall Terrace (www.neighborhoodlink.com/minneapolis/mtn), between 37th Street on the north and Lowry on the south, looks like it would be 100% industrial, until you get into it. Then you see plain turn-of-the-century houses on quiet streets. The houses are affordable, and many have been purchased either by parents of University students, or young professionals. About one-quarter of the houses here are duplexes. For those concerned about living near an industrial zone, current residents say that Northern States Power Co. (NSP) and the other industries that occupy the riverfront are generally good neighbors, and the bulk of their complaints are related to noise. These neighborhoods have access to the river bike paths through West River Road.

COLUMBIA PARK/WAITE PARK/AUDUBON PARK/HOLLAND/ LOGAN PARK/WINDOM PARK

Another well-kept Northeast secret is the upscale **Columbia Park** neighborhood (www.neighborhoodlink.com/minneapolis/colpark), just a chip shot away from Columbia Park and Francis A. Gross Golf Course. Columbia Boulevard, which runs north of the golf course, looks very much like the south Minneapolis parkways, with the same type of housing—stucco and brick Tudors and two-story colonials. Curvy Architect Avenue, off Columbia Boulevard, west of Van Buren, is truly picturesque, with houses designed by prominent Twin Cities architects over the course of the 1930s, '40s, and '50s. Homes here are elaborate and well kept, with meticulous landscaping and mature trees that contribute to the park-like atmosphere.

Waite Park and **Audubon Park**, across Central from Columbia Golf Course, down to Lowry, are known as friendly, fairly safe neighborhoods with well-kept houses. The streets are quiet, the topography is hilly, with easy access to I-35W and 280. Houses with 1940s charm and contemporary renovations, located in the vicinity of Johnson Street and St. Anthony Boulevard, are popular with young professionals and their families.

South, down Central and across Lowry, the **Holland** neighborhood is often overlooked. Covering 66 blocks, this neighborhood is primarily residential, but is diagonally bisected by a busy rail line and a corridor of light industry. Over 75% of the homes were built in the early 1900s by railroad workers employed at the rail yards on the northern edge of the neighborhood. They consist mostly of modest two-story wood frame or 1.5-story stucco bungalows that lack embellishment. They were sturdy, however, and offer today's buyers an affordable housing option that is difficult to find elsewhere. Nevertheless, this neighborhood still has a lot of rental property, and homes here are only 60% owner-occupied. Though high-rise apartments can be found on Holland's borders, most of the neighborhood's rental units are duplexes or four-plexes. The neighborhood's main commercial/retail areas along Central, Lowry, and University are bustling and evolving, as old Italian and Eastern European shops and restaurants are being replaced by Hispanic and Indian-owned restaurants, a food co-op, pubs, bakeries, and art galleries.

Logan Park, just south of Holland, is defined by Broadway to the south, Central to the east, 19th Avenue to the north, and Washington Street to the west. Slightly less than half residential, it's a small neighborhood that boasts large houses, including Victorians with dining rooms, built-in buffets, and intact woodwork. Homes in this area appeal to young families. Commuters find the neighborhood nice as well, with on and off ramps to I-35W only a few blocks away. The heart of the neighborhood is Logan Park; originally a decorative city square in the late 1800s, with formal flowerbeds and a Victorian fountain in the center, it is now a recreation area. In an attempt to attract more artists, Logan Park has set aside neighborhood redevelopment money to support the arts. Other neighborhood priorities include holding on to small local businesses, controlling heavy industry, and creating a special service district to bring a mix of useful businesses and housing to Central Avenue, the main north-south thoroughfare.

Windom Park (www.windompark.org) is made up of a long strip of land running from Central Avenue, east to New Brighton Boulevard, between 18th Avenue and Lowry. Central Avenue is the main commercial corridor, but there are big box retailers (Target, Home Depot, etc.) at the Quarry Shopping Center on 18th Avenue. Johnson Street also has a mix of commercial and large residential rental units. The other major thoroughfare, Stinson, on the east side of the neighborhood, is a parkway that is included in the Grand Rounds. Craftsman and Tudor-style homes built in the 1920s and '30s are found along this parkway and to the east. Windom, the park, at the intersection of Johnson Street and Lowry Avenue, features a long, sloping hill that serves as a site for summer concerts and the annual Ice Cream Social, a carnival that attracts families from throughout Northeast. Adjacent to the park are the Pillsbury Math, Science, and Technology magnet school, for grades K–6, and the Bottineau Early Education Center for grades K–2.

Zip Codes: 55413, 55418
Post Office: East Side Station, 1600 18th Ave NE
Police Precinct: 2nd, 1911 Central Ave NE, 311 (non-emergency)

Emergency Hospital: Fairview-University Medical Center, 2450 Riverside Ave, 612-672-6000, www.fairview.org

Libraries: www.mpls.lib.mn.us Northeast, 2200 Central Avenue NE, 612-630-6900; Pierre Bottineau, 1224 Second Street NE, 612-630-6890

Community Resources: Chute Square and the Ard Godfrey House, 50 University Avenue NE, www.ardgodfreyhouse.org; Northeast Minneapolis Arts Association, www.nemaa.org; St. Anthony Main, www.saintanthonymain.com/mplsriverfrontdistrict.html

Parks: www.minneapolisparks.org; Boom Island Park; Columbia Parkand golf course

Community Publication: *Northeaster*, 2304 Central Ave NE, 612-788-9003

Public Transportation, 612-373-3333, www.MetroTransit.org; buses travel along E Hennepin, Johnson St, Stinson Blvd, Central Ave, 2nd St NE, University Ave, Marshall St, and Lowry Ave

NORTH MINNEAPOLIS

Driving through some parts of North Minneapolis now and seeing the deteriorated housing, graffiti, and groups of people hanging out in the streets, it's hard to imagine the bustling multicultural, yet peaceful, community that thrived here prior to the mid-1960s. Back then West Broadway was one of the largest retailing centers in the metro area, and Plymouth Avenue is said to have looked a lot like Grand Avenue in St. Paul looks now—a street lined with a useful mix of small owner-operated shops.

So what happened? Different things, which happened to converge at a particularly vulnerable time. The construction of I-94 fractured the neighborhoods and the more economically secure residents moved away, choosing—as many other city-dwellers did—to move to the suburbs, where newer, bigger houses were being built on larger lots. Finally, there were the race riots of 1966, when Plymouth Avenue went up in flames. At that point, much of the remaining white population put their homes on the market at fire sale prices and fled, leaving these neighborhoods to the poorest of the poor, most of whom were African American.

Today North Minneapolis exists as a paradox—still largely African American with a high concentration of poverty and crime, but with some of the city's most interesting housing stock and finest public greenspaces. Whimsical artist-designed benches installed in public places around North Minneapolis aim to pull smokers out of their houses and make them aware of the dangers of secondhand smoke. The houses on the backs of the benches are meant to represent homes that could be smoke-free. The mosaic seats symbolize the diversity of the North Side's neighborhoods.

By 2030, this community and the northwest suburbs along County Road 81 (also known as West Broadway and Bottineau) are expected to increase in population by 25%. In preparation, a number of projects are in various stages of development, including the Humboldt Greenway housing development, redevelopment of Lowry Avenue, a bus rapid transit corridor along County

Road 81 (www.northwestcorridor.info), and a mixed-use development on the corner of Penn Avenue and Lowry that may include new apartments and an Aldi's grocery store.

WEBBER–CAMDEN COMMUNITY

MCKINLEY, FOLWELL, CLEVELAND
LIND-BOHANON
SHINGLE CREEK
VICTORY

Boundaries: North: 53rd Ave N; **West:** Xerxes Ave N; **South:** Lowry Ave N; **East:** Mississippi River

Webber-Camden is "like a great big flea market," says one resident, "a place where people can find real treasures at affordable prices." With no industrial zones within its borders, about a third of Webber-Camden is taken up by a cemetery. The rest is housing. Although there are some post–World War II apartment buildings, approximately 80% of the houses are single-family two-story wood-frames and Craftsman-style bungalows or 1.5-story stucco Tudors built between 1910 and 1932. Many are considered on the small side for today's families, though just right for first-time home-buying singles or childless couples. Organizations such as Habitat for Humanity, A Brush with Kindness, and Christmas in April have worked hard to improve the housing stock here, and many of the most derelict buildings have been torn down and replaced. In the late 1990s, the neighborhood took off, drawing buyers who might traditionally be looking to buy in Uptown or Highland Park in St. Paul, including young families attracted to Patrick Henry High's International Baccalaureate program, artists, and gays. Webber-Camden's business area is located along 44th Street North and includes a homey coffeehouse, Camden Coffee Company, on the corner of 44th and Humboldt.

In the Shingle Creek (www.neighborhoodlink.com/minneapolis/shingle) and Victory areas, homes are slightly more expensive and incomes slightly higher when compared with the rest of Camden, although all of the neighborhoods are modest in comparison to the rest of Minneapolis. **Shingle Creek**, west of Humboldt and north of 49th Avenue, is made up of bungalows and ramblers (one-level homes) built primarily in the 1950s after the lowlands were drained. The creek cuts diagonally through the neighborhood and creates a natural greenspace, which connects with a mixed-use trail on the north side of 49th Avenue near the main entrance to the North Mississippi Regional Park and Interpretive Center, www.minneapolisparks.org. This area is home to one of the metro's "New Urban Neighborhoods," the Humboldt Greenway community of two-story, single-family homes and townhouses that went on the market in 2005.

Victory, west of Penn, between Dowling Avenue and the Humboldt Industrial Area, contains vintage homes from the 1920s and '30s through the 1960s, as well as some of the city's nicest public greenspaces, among them Victory Memorial Drive, which has been designated a State Historic District.

While most of the housing here is single-family, there are several small apartment buildings along Thomas Avenue North, which is also a major bus route. Most home sales here, as in the rest of North Minneapolis, are to first-time buyers. But, in contrast to other nearby neighborhoods, the median value of houses in Victory rose more than 30% between the censuses of 1990 and 2000. If you're interested in this area, be sure to check out the pictures of Victory Memorial Drive posted on the Minneapolis Park Board web site, www.minneapolisparks.org/grandrounds.

North of Webber-Camden, **Lind-Bohanon** (www.neighborhoodlink. com/minneapolis/l-bna), which stretches from 43rd Avenue to the north city limits, between the Mississippi River and Humboldt Avenue, has a reputation for being a relatively quiet neighborhood with a low resident turnover rate. Some families have lived in their houses here for two or three generations. One of the first public housing projects in the nation—Mississippi Courts—was built in Lind-Bohanon in the 1940s to house soldiers returning from World War II. Recently, long-time and former residents have started gathering at the Carl Kroening Interpretive Center (CKIC) to share photos, stories, and memories of this historic housing project. Other ongoing activities at CKIC, which is located in North Mississippi Regional Park (www.minneapolisparks.org), include hiking or cross-country skiing along the Mississippi River, or taking a 1973 Barracuda "for a spin" and discovering the impact that I-94 had on the community. You can look around and see for yourself that it wasn't good.

On the southernmost edge of the community, between Dowling and Lowry, the neighborhoods of **McKinley** (which includes the North River Industrial Area), **Folwell** (www.folwell.org), and **Cleveland** are areas of deteriorated housing and significant poverty, although there are a number of community improvement efforts underway.

The Minneapolis public schools in this area run several innovative programs including a Hmong bilingual magnet at Loring School (K–5), off Victory Memorial Drive in the Victory neighborhood; and the Afro-Centric Academy at 1601 Aldrich. The Elizabeth Hall School, also at 1601 Aldrich, operates an International Baccalaureate Primary Years magnet program with Chinese language instruction and an all-day kindergarten.

Zip Codes: 55412, 55430
Post Offices: Lowry Avenue Station, 2306 Lowry Ave N
Police Precinct: 4th, 1925 Plymouth Ave N, 311 (non-emergency); the 4th Ward CARE Task force web site, http://4thwardcaretaskforce.org, is designed to inform residents about public safety issues in these neighborhoods
Emergency Hospital: North Memorial Medical Center, 3300 Oakdale Ave N, Robbinsdale, 763-520-5200, www.northmemorial.com
Library, www.mpls.lib.mn.us: Webber Park, 4310 Webber Pkwy, 612-630-6640
Community Resources: Folwell Center for Urban Initiatives and City Kids Co-op, 1206 37th Ave N, 612-521-2100; Pillsbury United Communities and Clothing Closet, 612-529-9231; A Brush with Kindness volunteer neighborhood assistance, 612-788-8169

Parks: www.minneapolisparks.org; North Mississippi Regional Park

Community Publications: *Camden Community News*, P.O. Box 11492, 612-521-3060, www.camdenews.org; *North News*, 2304 Central Ave NE, 612-788-9003; *Insight News*, 1815 Bryant Ave N, 612-588-1313, www.insight news.com

Public Transportation: 612-373-3333, www.MetroTransit.org; buses travel along 26th Ave, Lowry, Thomas, West Broadway, Oakdale, Fremont, Lyndale, and Penn. Bus Route 5, which travels through this community, has a history of having more problems than most. Extra transit officers are sometimes assigned to ride this route, but for your own safety, you may not want to ride this or other routes alone.

NEAR NORTH COMMUNITY

HAWTHORNE
JORDAN, WILLARD-HAY, WILLARD HOMEWOOD
SUMNER-GLENWOOD
NEAR NORTH
HARRISON

Boundaries: North: Lowry Ave; **West:** Xerxes Ave; **South:** Bassett Creek; **East:** I-94, Mississippi River

The North Side of Minneapolis is one of the city's oldest neighborhoods and has been home to many different ethnic populations through the years. Today it is home to the city's biggest redevelopment project ever, Heritage Park.

   Hawthorne (www.hawthornecommunity.org), located north of Broadway to Lowry, and east of Emerson Avenue to the Mississippi River, is a 77-square-block area bisected by I-94. About two-thirds of this neighborhood consists of rental property. Creating rainwater gardens is a priority of the Hawthorne Area Community Council, as is trying to change the perception of Hawthorne as a crime-ridden area by honoring members of the community who are helping to make it a better place. Well over a hundred "Hawthorne Neighborhood Champions" have been recognized so far.

   In **Jordan**, north of Broadway and west of Emerson, where there is a higher rate of home ownership, there is a trend toward rehabilitating houses, rather than tearing them down. The same is true in **Willard-Hay**, south of Broadway, from approximately Penn Avenue to Xerxes. Willard-Hay, which has many dilapidated houses, is also the unlikely location of "the poor-man's Kenwood," otherwise known as **Willard-Homewood**, located south of Plymouth Avenue, abutting Theodore Wirth Parkway. This area of large, architecturally interesting Tudor, Spanish, and Arts-and-Crafts style houses was one of the city's first planned developments. Most of the houses were built between 1905 and 1930. Residents fled this neighborhood in the 1960s when north Minneapolis was the scene of racial rioting, and houses here have been selling at fire-sale prices ever since. You can get a lot of house for the money—sun porches, high ceilings, fireplaces, built-in bookcases and buffets, beamed ceilings, hardwood floors, front and back staircases and libraries. This is, however, a neighborhood for those who have a high tolerance for urban interactions.

The easternmost neighborhoods in this community, **Sumner-Glenwood** and **Near North**, are part of a broad redevelopment plan being undertaken by the City of Minneapolis, the result of the settlement of a 1990s lawsuit that required Minneapolis to demolish ghettos of public housing and replace them with mixed-income development. In 2005, the 145-acre mixed-income, mixed-density, culturally diverse redevelopment project, now named Heritage Park, was dedicated and people started moving back in. When completed in approximately 2009, it will stretch roughly from I-94 on the east to Humboldt Avenue on the west, and from 12th Avenue on the north to Glenwood Avenue on the south. The eastern edge of this project is conveniently located about six blocks west of the downtown business district. The most extensive from-the-ground-up development the city has ever undertaken, it includes two new parks, a greenway named for Van White, the city's first black councilmember, and 900 rental, for-sale, market-rate, and subsidized houses and townhomes, www.ci.minneapolis.mn.us/cped/heritage_park.asp.

Nearby, the historic 1915 Sumner Library, on the corner of Olson Highway (55) and Van White Memorial Boulevard, houses the largest black history collection in Minneapolis. Further reminders of Minneapolis' proud past, a strip of Queen Anne "painted ladies" can be found in the 1500 block of Dupont Avenue, just north of Plymouth Road. Dating from 1875–1899, at least one of these houses is listed on the National Historic Register. Located in the 30-square-block Old Highland (www.oldhighland.org) district of Near North, between Plymouth Avenue and West Broadway, and Aldrich Avenue and Girard, the "Painted Ladies" and their Arts-and-Crafts neighbors are some of the biggest houses in North Minneapolis. Many have already been renovated. Be sure to check the Old Highland web site for pictures.

The **Harrison** neighborhood, which is south of Highway 55, abuts Theodore Wirth Park on the west, and is adjacent to the more prosperous Bryn Mawr neighborhood on its south border. It is bisected by Glenwood Avenue. While there is some rehabilitated housing here, there is also considerable dispute about whether the southern part of Harrison should remain residential or be zoned for light industrial use. As in the other North Side communities, arts and the involvement of artists are a big factor in the efforts to revitalize this district. Unfortunately, most of their projects have been short-lived. There has also been much discussion about "daylighting" Bassett Creek, a small, shallow stream that begins at Medicine Lake in Plymouth and winds through Golden Valley and this neighborhood before draining into the Mississippi River in downtown Minneapolis. It is thought that if Bassett Creek could be cleaned up and uncovered where it's been diverted through tunnels, it would provide the North Side with an amenity on the order of Minnehaha Creek in South Minneapolis. While projects upstream in Plymouth and Golden Valley have focused on improving the creek's water quality, not much has been done to reclaim it at the Minneapolis end, except by volunteers who call themselves the Friends of Bassett Creek, www.mninter.net/%7Estack/bassett/index.htm.

Zip Codes: 55405, 55411

Post Offices: Loring Station, 18 N 12th St; Lowry Avenue Station, 2306 Lowry Ave N

Police Precinct: 4th, 1925 Plymouth Ave N, 311 (non-emergency)

Emergency Hospitals: North Memorial Medical Center, 3300 Oakdale Ave N, Robbinsdale, 763-520-5200, www.northmemorial.com; Hennepin County Medical Center, 701 Park Ave, 612-873-3000, www.hcmc.org

Libraries: www.mpls.lib.mn.us: North Regional, 1315 Lowry Ave N, 612-630-6600; Sumner, corner of Olson Hwy and Van White Memorial Blvd, 612-630-6390

Community Resources: North Community YMCA, 1711 W Broadway, 612-588-9484, www.ymcatwincities.org

Parks: www.minneapolisparks.org; North Mississippi Park; Theodore Wirth Park and Golf Course

Community Publications: *North News*, 2304 Central Ave NE, 612-788-9003; *Insight News*, 1815 Bryant Ave N, 612-588-1313, www.insightnews.com

Public Transportation: 612-373-3333, www.MetroTransit.org; buses travel along Fremont, Emerson, Broadway, Penn, Plymouth Ave, Lyndale Ave, Glenwood, Cedar Lake Rd, and Hwy 55 (Olson Memorial Blvd)

ST. PAUL

Situated in Ramsey County, St. Paul, the state capital, is often called "The Last City of the East" because early developers laid it out in an East Coast style, with city squares and broad boulevards, and filled it with buildings that featured elaborate ornamentation. Look for examples of the city's superb early architecture in its five designated historic districts: Dayton's Bluff, Historic Hill District, Irvine Park, Lowertown, and Summit Avenue West, and in University-Raymond Commercial Historic District. Maps of the districts are posted on the city's web site at www.stpaul.gov/depts/liep/hp.

From the horse-drawn golden chariot on the state capitol's marble dome to Summit Avenue, the longest and best-preserved boulevard of Victorian mansions in the nation, a stately, 19th-century elegance pervades much of this city. Though St. Paul was settled only slightly earlier than Minneapolis, it seems older because so much of the early city survives: blocks of Victorian Romanesque brick buildings, divided boulevards, established neighborhoods—even the trees are old.

Now modern loft conversions are breathing new life into the old buildings. A commitment by the city to build 5000 new units of housing by the end of 2005 fast-tracked a lot of construction, but rather than triggering the demolition of existing buildings, it has served to encourage historic renovation and the reclamation of former industrial sites. The 1917 Union Depot, for example, which is listed on the National Register of Historic Places, has had its upper floors converted into two-level loft condominiums. As one of the few loft buildings in Downtown that is skyway connected, there is also a big push to return its lower floors to their glory days as the center of St. Paul rail travel, and thus connect the skyways with commuter and high-speed rail. Several of the bigger, neighborhood-scale projects are being developed around the riverfront. One of them, the Upper Landing condos (www.upperlanding.net/home.html), sits on a swath of land considered flood plain before developers elevated it above the 100-year-flood level. Another, the 65-acre reclamation of an oil tank storage site between West 7th and the Mississippi River bluff on the city's southwestern edge, is St. Paul's largest housing project ever.

St. Paul's population (287,260) and economy have always trailed Minneapolis, which actually is one of the reasons people like to live there—it feels more like a small town than a big city. The downtown is compact and the streets are more wholly residential than the streets of Minneapolis. At the same time, grocery stores, restaurants, bookstores, and the city's many historical and cultural sites are easily accessible by foot or bus from most neighborhoods. Housing on the east side of the metro also tends to be cheaper than on the west side. Expect rents to be about $100 less per month than in Minneapolis, and for houses to cost proportionately less, as well.

A true sense of community is fostered within St. Paul's 17 neighborhoods (here called districts), assisted by district councils that work together with city government, giving neighborhoods a voice in city decisions. District councils are also active in civic beautification, community gardening, home improvement, and recycling, and work closely with the St. Paul Police Department on crime prevention. Call the district councils listed at the end of each neighborhood profile for more information about a specific neighborhood.

St. Paul's police force is organized into three districts, western (north and south), central, and eastern. Each district has several neighborhood substations. For information about crime in a particular neighborhood, call the St. Paul Crime Prevention Coordinator at 651-266-5625. The police department's annual crime reports and maps of crime locations (STATMap) are posted on the internet at www.st.paul.gov/police. According to the STATMap, St. Paul's "hot spots" for crime tend to be located in the parts of town north of I-94, particularly in the Frogtown, Summit-University, and Dayton's Bluff neighborhoods. But don't read this and automatically mark these neighborhoods off your list; Dayton's Bluff, in particular, has a very involved community council that is working hard to deal with its relatively small proportion of troublesome blocks—and the police have targeted all these areas for additional patrols.

Web Site: City of St. Paul, 651-266-8989, www.stpaul.gov
Area Code: 651
Public Schools: St. Paul, District Office: 651-767-8100, www.stpaul.k12.mn.us
Parks: www.stpaul.gov/depts/parks; St. Paul has 160 parks and open spaces, 41 recreation centers, three 18-hole golf courses, over 100 miles of trails, indoor and outdoor pools, and a public beach. Its principal parks are Como and Phalen in the northern part of the city, and Highland and the Mississippi riverfront in the south. Book tee times online at http://www.usegolf.net/golferstpaul. Only the most significant parks are listed below.

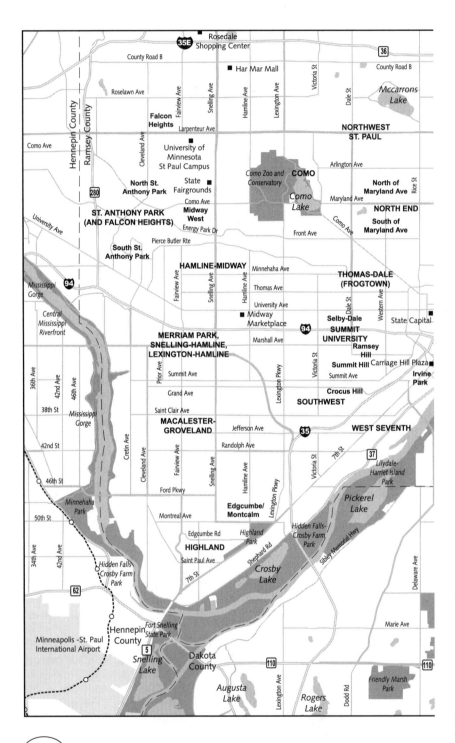

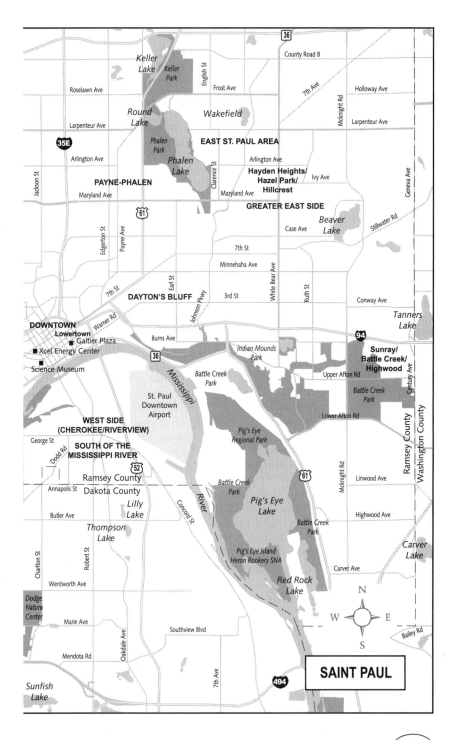

Community Publications: *St. Paul Pioneer Press,* 651-222-5011, www.twincities.com; *St. Paul Villager and Avenues,* 757 Snelling Ave S, 651-699-1462, www.villagercomm.com; *Sun Newspapers,* www.mn sun.com; *The Bugle,* P.O Box 8126, 651-646-5369; *Minnesota Women's Press,* 771 Raymond Ave, 651-646-3968

Public Transportation: Information about all public transportation can be accessed at 612-373-3333, www.MetroTransit.org. Buses generally run along main thoroughfares, but routes and schedules do change, so be sure to check the web site or call.

DOWNTOWN DISTRICT

DOWNTOWN/LOWERTOWN

Boundaries: North: University Ave; **West:** Marion St, Irvine Ave; **South:** Kellogg Blvd, Mississippi River; **East:** I-94, Lafayette Rd

The beauty of living downtown is that most everything is within walking distance—although, since St. Paul is built on hills, people sometimes opt to take the bus up and then walk down. Bus service is convenient; you can take the bus anywhere within downtown for fifty cents, or, use it to get to downtown Minneapolis, the Mall of America, or the Rosedale Shopping Mall. In fact, immediate amenities are so accessible by public transportation that many residents don't even own a car. However, since downtown shopping is limited, residents who otherwise live blissfully car-free recommend joining "HourCar" (www.hourcar.org), a nonprofit pay-as-you-go car sharing service managed by the St. Paul Neighborhood Energy Consortium (www.spnec.org). HourCars are conveniently stashed in a couple of Downtown and Lowertown parking ramps and near the University of Minnesota. (See the **Transportation** chapter in this book.)

The other beauty of living in **Downtown** is all the new housing. While Downtown has long been dotted with high-rise apartment buildings containing both moderate-rent and luxury apartments, at the time of the writing of this book, many of the old corniced and dentiled office buildings are being converted into condos. They include the 1908 Shubert Theater building adjacent to the Fitzgerald Theater, home stage of the Prairie Home Companion radio show. All in all, there are over 2500 condos either in the works or planned for this district, where units are generally described as "cozy" (as small as 370 square feet) and often equipped with space-saving Murphy beds. Though the units are decked out with the same high-end appliances and trendy finishes, prices tend to be lower than in similar units in Minneapolis, the smallest starting at $85,000 in 2006. Most of these units are being targeted at first-time homebuyers or those who work downtown. The State Capitol building and state offices are here, as are headquarters for a few large companies. Many of these offices are connected by skyways (enclosed breezeways that connect building to building on the level of the second or third floors). On weekdays these skyways bustle with restaurants and food-courts, coffee shops, grocery stores, a fresh fruit and vegetable stand, video rentals, a branch library, and branch post office, Most of the shops are closed in the evenings, however, and stay shuttered on weekends and holidays. Three hotels, the Central Library, Children's Museum, RiverCentre, and Xcel Energy Center can also be reached through the skyways, and the Science Museum is just a short jog across Kellogg Boulevard from the system. Download a map of the skyway system from the City of St. Paul's web site at www.stpaul.gov/maps.

Despite the weekday buzz in the skyways, Downtown is not a world-class shopping destination, though with more people living in the district, that may change. Already, Downtown has a full-service small grocery, drug store, fruit market, discount bookstore, and Macy's. (For more specialized shopping, see the Shopping Districts section of the **Shopping for the Home** chapter.)

What the district does have is nightlife. The Ordway Theater (www. ordway.org), with its concerts and Broadway musicals, is in the center of downtown on Rice Park, and there's a wellspring of nearby restaurants, clubs, and coffee shops to go to before and after performances. In Lowertown, Fourth Street, between Sibley and Wall streets, is turning into a Midwest "Tin Pan Alley," with venues that showcase live music, from touring bands to local artists' jam sessions. The Minnesota Museum of American Art at Kellogg and Market Street (www.mmaa.org) draws a crowd all year for its "ArtHere First Fridays" that feature local artists and live bands. (For more information, see the **Cultural Life** chapter.) To stay on top of the St. Paul scene, be sure to check out www.stpaulafterhours.com or sign up for their e-mailed newsletters.

In the 1970s, developers completed several high-rise apartments and renovations, including an overhaul of **Lowertown**, the city's unique warehouse district and artists' colony, located near the river, between Robert Street and Broadway, on the east side of downtown. Lowertown takes its name from a nearby steamboat stop called Lower Landing. With over 500 sculptors, potters, painters, and performance artists living in the district, it's one of the largest concentrations of working artists in any city in the Midwest. Each April and October, the members of the Art Collective open their studio doors for the St. Paul Art Crawl. Check www.lowertown.org or www.stpaulartcrawl.org for more information. Site of one of St. Paul's two early river landings, this neighborhood contains large, old brick buildings that have been converted into offices, artists' lofts, and apartments. New construction is going up here as well, including 44 condo units being built above the new year-round indoor farmers' market at 5th and Wall Streets.

Open space, while not as plentiful as elsewhere in the Twin Cities, is available in five small city parks tucked in amid the tall buildings, and in a regional park on Harriet Island. Rice Park is a formal square bordered by the Ordway Music Theatre, Landmark Center, the Central Library/James J. Hill Library, and the grand old St. Paul Hotel. More of a plaza than a park, the ice sculpture contest is held here during the St. Paul Winter Carnival. Kellogg Park is a narrow strip of greenspace that runs between the edge of the river bluff and Kellogg Boulevard, from the Robert Street Bridge to the Wabasha Street Bridge. A popular setting for weddings, it includes sculptures depicting St. Paul's history. Mears Park is a beautifully landscaped square at 5th and Sibley that features a bandshell, and is home to popular summer concerts. Visit in the spring for a stunning display of thousands of tulips. The newest downtown parks are Landmark Plaza located along Market Street, where there is an ice rink in winter, and Wacouta Commons, a neighborhood greenspace in the new North Quadrant development. Harriet Island Regional Park is just a short walk from downtown across the Wabasha Bridge. The region's leading venue for outdoor festivals, the St. Paul Yacht Club, is located here, as is the University of Minnesota Showboat and the Padelford tourist boats.

Historic and cultural sites and annual events abound in downtown, making it easy to entertain out-of-town visitors. People flock to events at the RiverCentre auditorium and convention center (www.xcelenergycenter.com), the Ordway (www.Ordway.org) and Fitzgerald theaters (www.fitzgeraldtheaterpublicradio.org), the Science Museum of Minnesota (www.smm.org), the Children's Museum (www.MCM.org), and the Minnesota History Museum (www.mnhs.org), and to numerous festivals throughout the year. During the summer, on Friday and Saturday evenings, Kellogg Boulevard is closed off between Robert Street and Wabasha for antique car shows, complete with food vendors and live music. The car shows are an intimate tête-à-tête compared to the serious food-fest, the Taste of Minnesota, which is held over the Fourth of July weekend. Then restaurants from all over the Twin Cities set up booths in front of the Capitol, live bands play throughout the park, and each evening ends in fireworks. There are more fireworks in January during the 120-year-old St. Paul Winter Carnival, a major event that includes an ice castle, sled dog races, parades, and a treasure hunt. The ice castles have always been the highlights of the Winter Carnivals, and throughout the event's history, palaces of all sizes and designs have been constructed. The 1888 ice castle, at 14 stories, was the tallest building in the city at the time; the 1992 ice palace, at 15 stories, was the tallest ice palace on record in the world at the time. (For pictures of some of the more notable ice castles, check out the Winter Carnival web page, www.winter-carnival.com/history/icepalaces.html.) Those who enjoy a wee bit of rowdiness will love St. Paul's raucous St. Patrick's Day street party. Rooted in the city's Irish heritage, the festivities kick off at noon with a parade down Fourth Street to Rice Park (www.stpatsassoc.org), and continue into the night with (it seems) nearly everyone in town wearing a "Kiss Me I'm Irish" button and partaking of green beer.

Web Site: Capitol River District Council (District 17), 445 Minnesota St, Suite 524, 651-221-0488, www.capitolrivercouncil.org

Zip Codes: 55101, 55102, 55107

Post Offices: Main Office, 180 E Kellogg Blvd; Pioneer Station, 141 E 4th St; Uptown-Skyway, 415 W Wabasha St; Riverview Station, 292 Eva St

Police: Central District Patrol Team, 651-291-1111 (non-emergency), www.stpaul.gov/depts/police

Emergency Hospitals: Regions Hospital, 640 Jackson St, 651-254-2191, www.RegionsHospital.com; HealthEast St. Joseph's Hospital, 69 W Exchange St, 651-232-3000, www.healtheast.org

Library: www.stpaul.lib.mn.us; Central, 90 W 4th St, 651-266-7000

Community Resources: Ordway Center for the Performing Arts, 345 Washington St, 651-224-4222, www.ordway.org; Landmark Center, 75 W 5th St, 651-292-3233, www.landmarkcenter.org; Minnesota Children's Museum, 10 W 7th St, 651-225-6000, www.MCM.org; Minnesota History Center and Minnesota Historical Society, 345 W Kellogg Blvd, St. Paul, 651-296-6126, 651-282-6073 (TTY) or 800-657-3773 (toll free), www.mnhs.org; Minnesota Museum of American Art, 50 W Kellogg Blvd, 651-266-1030, www.mmaa.org; Science Museum of Minnesota, 120 W Kellogg Blvd, 651-221-9444, www.smm.org

Parks: www.stpaul.gov/depts/parks; Harriet Island Regional Park

Public Transportation: 612-373-3333, www.MetroTransit.org; numerous city bus lines run through downtown, and you can get around downtown by bus on most major streets. Pick up a free transit map at the MCTO store in the American National Bank building at 5th and Minnesota sts.

SOUTHWEST DISTRICTS

SUMMIT HILL DISTRICT

CROCUS HILL
SUMMIT AVENUE
SUMMIT HILL

Boundaries: North: Summit Ave; **West:** Ayd Mill Rd; **East:** Ramsey St; **South/East:** I-35E; **South:** Summit Hill is separated from W 7th by the bluffs

St. Paul's counterpart to Kenwood in Minneapolis, the neighborhoods of the Southwest district have the ambiance of a library filled with leather-bound books: old, hefty, and rich with historical detail. Variations include the more trendy east end of Summit, and the more academic west end, but all the people who live here have access to the restaurants and shops of Grand Avenue, one of St. Paul's great pleasures. The one surprise is the number of rental units contained within the huge old houses.

The mansions and historic buildings poised high on **Summit Hill** epitomize the grandeur and wealth of boom-era St. Paul. The traditional home of the city's aristocracy, this broad boulevard is lined with superior examples of many styles of turn-of-the century architecture and ornamentation, including a possible decorative coffin on the roof of Number 456 (on the north side of the street, just west of the University Club). Summit's first mansion, erected in 1862 at 432, also created quite a stir when it was built because it incorporated those new-fangled features—steam heating, hot and cold water, and gas lighting.

In the 1880s and 1890s the Crocus Hill and Grand Hill neighborhoods also became fashionable locations for wealthy families. **Crocus Hill** (south of Summit) is still one of the Twin Cities' most desirable and eccentric neighborhoods. If you buy a house in this maze of cobblestone streets, it may come with a ghost, but your garage could be four blocks away. Crocus Hill, the street, is only half a block long, which is long enough for most deliverymen, because house numbering is not consecutive. One is the first house built on the street, but the second house, built at the opposite end of the street, is Four. In between are Twelve, Two, Eleven, and Sixteen—and Five is around the corner. Only two of the early 1880s houses remain; the rest were built between the 1920s and '40s. Crocus Hill, the neighborhood, extends to St. Clair, and, mercifully, its streets do employ sequential numbering.

All five miles of **Summit Avenue**, in the Summit Hill District, are protected, either as a national or local Historic District. Out of 440 original homes built along this avenue in the late 1800s, an amazing 373 have survived. Summit Avenue has also survived as St. Paul's power address. The Minnesota governor's official residence is at 1006, although recent governors have chosen not to live there. Railroad baron James J. Hill's 45-room red sandstone mansion, a few blocks away at 240 Summit, was the largest house in the Midwest when it was built in 1891. Across the street is the Renaissance-style Catholic Cathedral of the Archdiocese of Saint Paul and Minneapolis, which looks across at the other domed building in town, the Minnesota State Capitol. The cathedral is host to many concerts, the most popular of which is the annual Christmas performance of Handel's *Messiah*. F. Scott Fitzgerald was born in the neighborhood, and returned to write *This Side of Paradise* in a shabby-genteel red stone row house on the corner of Summit and Dale. You can learn about these and many of the other historic buildings and gardens by joining one of the Minnesota Historical Society's guided walking tours, held every Saturday from May through September. Another tour called "These Old Houses" is held every other year on the first Sunday after Mother's Day, and is popular with locals and tourists alike. Contact the Minnesota Historical Society for information, 651-296-6126, www.mhs.org.

Step away from Summit Avenue and you'll find more than a museum that pays homage to the lavish excesses of the late 19th century. Residential opportunities abound in Summit Hill, and not everyone living here is a millionaire. The neighborhood's last housing boomlet, in the 1920s, included the building of many apartments, particularly along the streetcar lines on major thoroughfares like Grand Avenue. In addition, during the Depression of the 1930s a lot of families found they could no longer afford to live in their expensive homes, and subsequently many single-family houses were converted into duplexes or rooming houses, which remain today, making up much of the housing that's available in Summit Hill. While vacancy rates are low, it is possible to find an apartment with refinished hardwood floors, tall windows, and fireplaces. The least expensive apartments generally are found on Cathedral Hill. Also try the area south of Grand Avenue for more modest housing. People from all walks of life live here, including faculty, staff, and students from nearby colleges.

Proximity to Grand Avenue, one of the Twin Cities' most attractive commercial districts, is another perk to living in Summit Hill. Grand Avenue is loaded with interesting restaurants, specialty stores, taverns and bookstores. The southwest districts' principal summer festival, Grand Old Days, attracts crowds from all over the Twin Cities. Then the street is closed off and its entire length becomes one long party, with live bands, food, beer, games, a parade, and great people watching.

However, the area's popular shopping, coupled with the presence of so many apartments, has created three problems: burglaries, traffic, and parking. Be assured the St. Paul police department is working on these issues. A word to the wise, don't park your car even for a minute in a space that requires a resident's sticker. For more information about shopping in this district, see the **Shopping for the Home** chapter.

Web Sites: Summit Hill Association (District 16), 860 St. Clair Ave, 651-222-1222, www.summithillassociation.org

Zip Codes: 55102, 55105

Post Offices: Main Office, 180 E Kellogg Blvd; Elway Station, 1715 W 7th

Police Non-Emergency: Western District Patrol Team, North: 651-266-5512, South: 651-266-5549; General Information, 651-291-1111; www.stpaul.gov/depts/police

Emergency Hospitals: Regions Hospital, 640 Jackson St, 651-254-2191, www.RegionsHospital.com; HealthEast St. Joseph's Hospital, 69 W Exchange St, 651-232-3000, www.healtheast.org

Libraries: www.stpaul.lib.mn.us; Central, 90 W 4th St, 651-266-7000; Rondo Outreach Community Library, University and Dale

Community Resources: James J. Hill House and Library (www.mnhs.org/places/sites/jjhh); F. Scott Fitzgerald sites at 481 Laurel, 240 Summit, 260 Summit, University Club at 420 Summit, 475 Summit, 501 Grand Hill, 626 Goodrich (www.stpaulcvb.org); Cathedral of St. Paul (www.cathedralsaintpaul.org); St. Paul Curling Club, 470 Selby Ave, 651-224-7408

Parks: www.stpaul.gov/depts/parks: Linwood Park and Recreation Center

Public Transportation: 612-373-3333, www.MetroTransit.org; buses travel along Selby, Grand, St. Clair, Dale and Snelling

SUMMIT–UNIVERSITY DISTRICT

SELBY–DALE
CATHEDRAL HILL/RAMSEY HILL (SOUTH OF SUMMIT)

Boundaries: North: University Ave; **West:** Lexington Pkwy; **South:** Summit Ave; **East:** Irvine Ave, Marion St (also includes buildings on the north side of Irvine St located immediately below Summit Ave, east of Ramsey St)

Much like Summit Hill to the south, the streets of Summit-University contain many of the city's oldest buildings, including stone row houses, fortress-like Victorian wood frames, and elegant 19th-century brick storefronts and row houses.

"Before there was Interstate 94 . . . there was Rondo," said Mary Sanders in a 1992 book that details the destruction of this district's legendary Rondo neighborhood by the construction of I-94. The book, *In Voices: A Collection of Writings and Stories for a Diverse Community,* compiled by Mark Clark and available from the Minnesota Historical Society, tells the story of Rondo Avenue, which was the heart of St. Paul's largest black neighborhood. When the freeway went through, the Cedar-Riverside community, to the west, was able to rally and find a way to remain more or less intact—Rondo was not. The construction erased it, displacing thousands of African Americans and leaving a legacy of poverty and crime that continues today, especially in the half of this district that is north of I-94.

More like two distinct neighborhoods than one, "Summit-U" straddles the freeway. The north side is heavily commercial and crime-ridden, though currently the subject of much transit-oriented development, including one of the nation's most unusual mixed-use projects, the Rondo Community Outreach Library and Apartments at University and Dale. With three floors of apartments above the library, it will be a home for almost 100 renters and a home base for many small businesses as well as reading literacy and education programs. It is one of a handful of such projects in the nation in which a library shares a facility with a housing development.

The south of I-94 side of the district, at least once you get a few blocks away from the freeway, is the part we think of as trendy. Stretching out from the St. Paul Cathedral to Lexington, it, too, was a hotbed of porno shops and crime as recently as the early 1990s. At one point, someone even bombed the Selby-Dale police station and blew out all the windows in the neighborhood. Today, those times are past, and the corner of Selby and Dale has become the center of one of St. Paul's most charming residential and entertainment quarters. Houses and brownstone apartments have been restored to the glory of their golden days, and pricey restaurants like The Vintage are always full.

Selby and Dale streets create a clear-cut crossroad through this neighborhood. Selby, a main thoroughfare, has been lined with businesses and apartments since the 1880s. Dale acts as the dividing line between modest homes on the west, many of which were built in the 1960s or '70s, and grand houses on the east in the area known as **Ramsey Hill** or **Cathedral Hill**.

The Ramsey Hill neighborhood (www.ramseyhill.org), east of Dale to the Cathedral, between Summit and I-94, is one of the largest, best preserved contiguous Victorian districts in North America and the largest and oldest Registered National Historic District in Minnesota. Every other year the Ramsey Hill Association sponsors the Gables Gardens and Ghosts House & Garden Tour to showcase this neighborhood's beauty and rich history. While most of these properties are single-family homes, in some of them you can find huge apartments with "character" (sometimes even fireplaces) at rents that are lower than in Uptown in Minneapolis.

If you're in the market to buy, **Selby-Dale** used to be a great place to find a fixer-upper, especially for those looking for two-story frame houses with front porches and picture windows. That isn't so much the case anymore, though with some homes as small as 700 square feet, this can still be a good neighborhood for first-time homebuyers. In the blocks adjacent to Summit, truly large Italianate and Queen Anne houses can also be found. Thanks to urban renewal, some houses now sit on a lot-and-a-half, with owners having purchased land when next-door derelict houses were torn down. Still, lots are small in proportion to the houses, and it's hard to garden because there's so much shade. Pocket gardens and boulevard gardens are popular, and they have the additional advantage of bringing people out onto the streets where they can keep an eye on what's going on.

Like the other neighborhoods surrounding Summit, shopping on Grand Avenue is within easy walking range, but some of the best local dining is to be found right on Cathedral Hill. Sweeney's (www.sweeneyssaloon.com) at Dale and Ashland has an old Irish pub atmosphere, and The Vintage serves excellent food accompanied by even better wine. Mississippi Market natural food co-op, at the corner of Selby and Dale, offers a fine selection of food in its deli and is known for its coffee.

The lack of a large open space in the area may be problematic for some. While people walk, run, and bike the city streets—and the Twin Cities Marathon comes right down Summit—there is no place to play ball; in fact, the closest open area is along the Mississippi River. However, there are playgrounds every few blocks and an unofficial off-leash dog area at Marshall-Webster Park.

Prospective residents will want to be aware of the concentration of lower income housing in a section of Summit-University, north of Selby, though numerous community initiatives and revitalization projects have been accomplished or are in the works there. The area is now home to the Hallie Q. Brown/Dr. Martin Luther King Community Center, which provides daycare services and other activities, and to the well-known Penumbra Theater, 270 Kent Street, 651-224-3180, which features plays with African-American themes.

Web Sites: Summit-University Planning Council (District 8), 627 Selby Ave, 651-228-1855, www.district8stpaul.org; Ramsey Hill Association, www.ramseyhill.org

Zip Codes: 55102, 55103, 55104

Post Office: Industrial Station, 1430 Concordia Ave

Police Non-Emergency: Western District Patrol Team, North: 651-266-5512, South: 651-266-5549; General Information, 651-291-1111; www.stpaul.gov/depts/police

Emergency Hospitals: Regions Hospital, 640 Jackson St, 651-254-2191, www.RegionsHospital.com; HealthEast St. Joseph's Hospital, 69 W Exchange St, 651-232-3000, www.healtheast.org

Library: www.stpaul.lib.mn.us: Rondo Community Outreach Library at University and Dale, 651-266-7000

Community Resources: Ramsey Hill Historic District, www.ramseyhill.org; Cass Gilbert Society (historical architecture), www.cassgilbert society.org/; Saint Paul's Cathedral, 239 Selby Ave, 651-228-1766, www.cathedralsaintpaul.org; Hallie Q. Brown/Dr. Martin Luther King Community Center, 270 Kent St, 651-224-4601; Farm in the City operates a summer produce market in the Great Harvest Bread Company parking lot, 534 Selby Ave, www.farminthecity.org; Mississippi Market (www.msmarket.coop) and St. Paul Neighborhood Energy Consortium (www.spnec.org), 622 Selby Ave, 651-310-9499; Penumbra Theatre Company, 270 N Kent St, 651-224-3180, www.penumbratheatre.org; Rondo Avenue Inc. (sponsors of Rondo days), www.rondodays.org

Parks: www.stpaul.gov/depts/parks; Marshall/Webster Park at Laurel and
St. Albans
Public Transportation: 612-373-3333, www.MetroTransit.org; buses
travel along University, Selby, and Dale

MACALESTER–GROVELAND DISTRICT

Boundaries: North: Summit Ave; **West:** Mississippi River; **South:** Randolph
Ave; **East:** Ayd Mill Rd

Universities and colleges located in or near the Mac-Groveland district
(Macalester College, the University of St. Thomas, St. Paul Seminary, The
College of St. Catherine, and William Mitchell College of Law) give this district
a friendly, college-town feel.

Created in the 1880s when a group of Macalester College trustees bought
a farm west of St. Paul and divided it into a campus and lots for houses, Mac-
Groveland has become one of St. Paul's epicenters, bustling with academic and
commercial energy. Grand Avenue, the main east-west thoroughfare, includes
specialty retail shops, restaurants, and scores of places to eat, drink, and argue
politics and religion—but there is very little parking.

Once a farm, then a commuter suburb, the history of Mac-Groveland has
resulted in an interesting mixture of housing sizes, prices, and designs, with
rents and house prices among the highest in St. Paul. Because of high student
demand, the best time to look for an apartment is in late spring to early summer when students move out and sublets and leases become available.

More than three-fourths of Mac-Groveland's homes were built before
1940, and range from two- and three-bedroom homes on the east end to luxurious Mississippi River–front residences. On and near Grand Avenue, two- to
four-story brick apartments from the 1920s are interspersed with the cafés and
retail businesses that make Grand Avenue St. Paul's most lively commercial district. Architectural styles range from 19th-century Tudor-style cottages and
meticulous Arts-and-Crafts bungalows to contemporary designs from the
1960s. Roomy homes with front porches line the curvy streets skirting
Macalester College. Bordering the neighborhood to the north are the impressive houses of Summit Avenue (read more about this elegant boulevard in the
description of Summit Hill). Residential streets in Mac-Groveland are attractive
and tranquil, lined with mature oaks and maples.

The bluffs and the Mississippi River gorge lie at the western end of the
neighborhood. Land adjacent to the St. Paul Seminary is relatively wild and picturesque, and miles of river walking or bike riding are accessible from Mac-
Groveland via the river parkway.

Web Sites: Macalester-Groveland Community Council (District 14), 320
Griggs St S, 651-695-4000, www.macgrove.org
Zip Code: 55105
Post Office: Elway Station, 1715 W 7th St
Police Non-Emergency: Western District Patrol Team, North: 651-266-5512,

South: 651-266-5549; General Information, 651-291-1111; www.
stpaul.gov/depts/police

Emergency Hospitals: Regions Hospital, 640 Jackson St, 651-254-2191,
www.RegionsHospital.com; HealthEast St. Joseph's Hospital, 69 W
Exchange St, 651-232-3000, www.healtheast.org

Library: www.stpaul.lib.mn.us; Merriam Park, 1831 Marshall Ave, 651-642-
0385

Community Resources: Macalester College, the University of St. Thomas,
St. Paul Seminary, The College of St. Catherine, and William Mitchell
College of Law

Parks: www.stpaul.gov/depts/parks; Mississippi Riverfront

Public Transportation: 612-373-3333, www.MetroTransit.org; buses
travel along Grand Ave, Snelling, Smith Ave, and Randolph

MERRIAM PARK, SNELLING-HAMLINE, LEXINGTON-HAMLINE

Boundaries: North: I-94, Cleveland Ave, University Ave; **West:** City limits at
33rd Ave, Mississippi River; **South:** Summit Ave; **East:** Lexington Pkwy

Merriam Park's identity derives not only from the atmosphere of its scenic
riverfront and well-kept homes, but also from the interesting people who live
here. From the long-distance racer who trains by running a marathon every day
to the president of the University of Minnesota, Merriam Parkers treasure their
neighbors as well as their neighborhood's aura of urbane wilderness.

Bordered by the magnificent gorge of the Mississippi to the west and by
the mansions of Summit Avenue to the south, Merriam Park is conveniently
located midway between downtown Minneapolis and St. Paul, with
Minneapolis and the Hiawatha LRT just a short hop away, across the Lake
Street/Marshall Avenue bridge. It includes the residential areas of Desnoyer
Park, Iris Park, Merriam Park, and Shadow Falls located on or near the
Mississippi River, and the business areas of Snelling Crossing (Snelling at
Marshall Avenue and Selby), Cleveland and Marshall, Cretin and Marshall,
Grand Avenue west of Snelling, and University Avenue.

Although it is in the center of urban activity today, Merriam Park was actually one of the Twin Cities' first suburbs, located a couple of trolley stops outside of early St. Paul. Colonel John Merriam, who in the 1880s owned much of
the neighborhood's bluff land, envisioned the creation of a rural village built on
large estates separated by abundant parkland. He built himself a luxurious
house and sold lots to those who would agree to his requirement that homes
built on this land cost at least $1,500—a sizable amount at the time.

Traces of Merriam Park's exclusive beginnings are still apparent along the
Mississippi, where turn-of-the-century Tudor and Arts-and-Crafts style houses
line streets shaded by mature, graceful trees. The green and fittingly groomed
land surrounding the Town and Country Club, located along the river north of
Marshall Avenue, adds to the neighborhood's air of grandeur. During winter,
the country club's gates are left open for cross-country skiers.

It seems every size and style of architecture is represented here, from the opulent Queen Annes, Gothic, and Italianate styles reflective of Victorian taste, to the colonial revivals, Dutch colonials, Tudors, American foursquares, and prairie style houses of today. Built to last, these homes exhibit solid construction and craftsmanship and loving attention to detail. Generally you'll find housing to be less expensive than in Highland, with houses near the University of St. Thomas campus occupied by students and university-related folk. Merriam Park did, however, see a 20% increase in median home value between 2004 and 2005.

The northernmost part of **Snelling-Hamline**, located to the east of Merriam Park between Snelling and Hamline, was decimated by the construction of I-94. However, the southern streets near Summit are now being rehabilitated. Here you can find old brownstone apartments, a few new duplexes, and some single-family houses. The neighborhood pub, O'Gara's at Snelling and Selby (www.ogaras.com), has a micro-brewery and offers music that ranges from an Irish jam session on Sunday nights to rock. They also offer free shuttle service to all Vikings and Wild home games.

Further east, **Lexington-Hamline** also straddles I-94 between Lexington and Hamline Avenues from University to Summit. South of I-94, most people live in single-family houses, while those north of I-94 live in high-rise apartments. With 504 units, Skyline Tower is the largest residential community in Lex-Ham and the gateway to St. Paul for hundreds of families new to the state. This neighborhood is also noted for its 19th- and early 20th-century houses and community enthusiasm, as well as for being home to St. Paul Central High School and Concordia University. Farm in the City uses the facilities of Concordia University and the community schools and parks to provide garden-based summer programs for children and community garden plots for deaf Hmong farmers.

The major cross streets, Cretin, Selby, Marshall, Snelling, and Lexington, are busy and commercial, and add to the general convenience of the district. Events at the University of Minnesota and University of St. Thomas and other campuses in the area are only a walk, bike, or bus ride away, and residents can easily stroll to many of the restaurants, shops, and conveniences of Grand Avenue to the south. (For more about Grand Avenue, see **Shopping for the Home**.) Coffeehouses, bakeries, and specialty shops are found on Marshall and Cleveland and other Merriam Park street corners, and the Midway Shopping Center, also nearby at University and Snelling avenues, offers staples at discount stores and supermarkets.

Merriam Park Community Center, 2000 St. Anthony Avenue, is a symbol of the neighborhood to many area residents. The center offers a variety of services to area families, including a preschool, adult community education programs, recreation, a community food shelf, seniors' programs, and "The Wordsmiths" toastmasters club.

Though not over-endowed with neighborhood parks and playgrounds, life here does offer the open splendor of the Mississippi bluffs. A pleasant hike along the river begins at Merriam Park, goes south to the Ford Parkway Bridge, then across the river and back up to the Marshall Avenue Bridge. Don't miss the color extravaganza in October.

Web Sites: Merriam Park Community Council (District 13), 1684 Selby Ave, 651-645-6887, www.merriam-park.org/mpcc.htm; Snelling-Hamline Community Council (also District 13), 1684 Selby Ave, 651-644-1085, www.snellham.org; Lexington-Hamline Community Council (also District 13), Dunning Recreation Center, 1221 Marshall Ave, 651-645-3207, www.lexham.org

Zip Code: 55104

Post Office: Industrial Station, 1430 Concordia Ave

Police Non-Emergency: Western District Patrol Team, North: 651-266-5512, South: 651-266-5549; General Information, 651-291-1111; www.stpaul.gov/depts/police

Emergency Hospitals: Regions Hospital, 640 Jackson St, 651-254-2191, www.RegionsHospital.com; HealthEast St. Joseph's Hospital, 69 W Exchange St, 651-232-3000, www.healtheast.org; Fairview-University Medical Center, 2450 Riverside Avenue, Minneapolis, 612-672-6000, www.fairview.org

Library: www.stpaul.lib.mn.us; Merriam Park, 1831 Marshall Ave, 651-642-0385

Community Resources: Lex-Ham Community Band, www.lexham arts.org/band/index.html; Town and Country Club, 2279 Marshall Ave, 651-646-7121; Farm in the City, www.farminthecity.org; Merriam Park Community Center, 2000 St. Anthony Ave, 651-645-0349; University of St. Thomas

Parks: www.stpaul.gov/depts/parks; Mississippi Riverfront

Public Transportation: 612-373-3333, www.MetroTransit.org; buses travel along Grand Ave, Snelling, University, St. Clair, Cleveland, Cretin, Randolph, and Marshall/Lake Street

HIGHLAND DISTRICT

Boundaries: North: Randolph Ave; **West/South:** Mississippi River; **East:** I-35W, Homer St from W 7th St to Shepard Rd

Highland Park is a neighborhood where moving up doesn't necessarily mean moving out. From homes with character to ultra-luxe penthouses, there is housing here to fit most tastes and pocketbooks, although demand is such that it is much easier to sell a home here than it is to find one to buy or rent.

The south and west sides of the district are embraced by the river, which runs in a gorge far below these hills. The houses here, along Mississippi River Boulevard, are not actually on the water, but have views across the parks and parkways. Near the Ford Plant off Ford Parkway, which crosses the river into the Hiawatha neighborhood of Minneapolis, you will find small 1950s and '60s ramblers in good condition, laid out on grid streets. More substantial brick and stucco homes on correspondingly larger lots line Mt. Curve Boulevard and Highland Park Golf Course. The architect-designed houses in the **Edgcumbe/Montcalm** neighborhood near the golf course have their own river views, and near the College of St. Catherine, well-kept rental duplexes and apartment buildings are in high demand.

Highland is home to two of the Twin Cities' only "Streamlined Moderne" buildings, the 1939 Highland Theater on Cleveland, and a house at 1775 Hillcrest Avenue, that was also built in '39. Of less architectural but more historical interest, the elegant house at 1590 South Mississippi River Boulevard served as a prohibition era speakeasy known as the Hollyhocks Inn.

Historically the city's primary Jewish neighborhood, this is where you will find kosher Cecil's Deli (651 Cleveland) and most of the city's synagogues.

Highland's main commercial area is clustered around the intersection of Cleveland Avenue and Ford Parkway. This shopping destination has it all—bookstores, groceries, department stores, bank, an historic movie theater, and some of the metro's favorite restaurants. Other assets in this district include O'Shaughnessy Auditorium at the College of St. Catherine, which is the St. Paul home of the Minnesota Orchestra and also provides an intimate venue for a wide variety of dance groups and other performances. Well-regarded private schools Cretin-Derham Hall and St. Paul Academy/Summit School are located here as well.

In fact, Highland residents often say that everything they want is right here and within walking distance—and yet no place is more convenient when they need to leave. Handily located between the State Capitol and Minneapolis, Highland is only about ten minutes from the airport or the capitol, and only a bus ride across the Ford Bridge from connecting with Minneapolis' light rail.

The other major perk of living in this district is its proximity to greenspace and recreation areas. Highland Park (the park) is a hilly expanse with a municipal golf course, outdoor swimming pools, and cross-country ski trails. On the wild side, Hidden Falls and Crosby Farm Regional Park, adjacent to the southern end of Highland, offer walking and biking trails through the woods. The confluence of the Mississippi and Minnesota Rivers, which includes Minnehaha Falls, the Fort Snelling State Park, and the Minnesota River National Wildlife Refuge are just across the Ford Bridge.

Web Sites: Highland Park District Council (District 15), 1978 Ford Pkwy, 651-695-4005, www.highlanddistrictcouncil.org

Zip Code: 55116

Post Office: Elway Station, 1715 W 7th St

Police Non-Emergency: Western District Patrol Team, North: 651-266-5512, South: 651-266-5549; General Information, 651-291-1111; www.stpaul.gov/depts/police

Emergency Hospitals: Regions Hospital, 640 Jackson St, 651-254-2191, www.RegionsHospital.com; HealthEast St. Joseph's Hospital, 69 W Exchange St, 651-232-3000, www.healtheast.org; United Hospital, 333 N Smith Ave, 651-241-8000, www.allina.com; Fairview-University Medical Center, 2450 Riverside Ave, Minneapolis, 612-672-6000, www.fairview.org

Library: www.stpaul.lib.mn.us; Highland Park, 1974 Ford Pkwy, 651-292-6622

Community Resources: Highland Fest Art Fair, www.highlandfest.com; College of St. Catherine and O'Shaughnessy Auditorium, 2004 Randolph Ave, 651-690-6700, www.stkate.edu/oshaughnessy

Parks: www.stpaul.gov/depts/parks; Highland Park Golf Course
Public Transportation: 612-373-3333, www.MetroTransit.org; buses
travel along Snelling Ave, Randolph, Cleveland, Cretin, and Ford Pkwy,
connecting with the Hiawatha LRT at the 50th Street Station

WEST SEVENTH DISTRICT

Boundaries: North: Bluffs of Summit Hill and I-35E; **West:** I-35E, Homer St;
South: Mississippi River; **East:** W Kellogg Blvd

Just to the west of downtown is St. Paul's old Uppertown, named for being the
location of the "upper" of St. Paul's two boat landings on the Mississippi River.
Known also as West Seventh, Fort Road (because the main drag, West Seventh
Street/Shepard Road, leads to Fort Snelling) or the West End, this traditional
immigrant neighborhood is St. Paul's historic heart and soul. It is where notori-
ous bootlegger "Pig's Eye" Parrant set up his still and founded the city of "Pig's
Eye," which we know as St. Paul. It is also the flood-prone docklands where
many of St. Paul's earliest residents stepped off riverboats to begin making their
homes on the frontier. Don't get this district confused with "The West Side,"
which is across the river.

While the houses of West Seventh were not built on as grand a scale as the
homes along Summit Avenue, many of them are older and at least as historic.
Amid streets laid out around elegant **Irvine Park** at Walnut Street and Ryan,
you'll find such treasures as stone houses built before the Civil War, pioneer-era
Greek Revivals, restored red brick row houses, and lap-sided Victorian Queen
Annes. This National Historic District is also the setting for Governor Alexander
Ramsey's stone, two-story Second Empire house at 265 Exchange Street,
which, together with its surrounding English garden, is open for tours and hol-
iday dances. To see pictures of this neighborhood, look online at St. Paul
Phototour, www.geomyidae.com/index.php?TopicID=pxirvinepark.

As St. Paul expanded, earlier residents moved "up the hill" to Summit in
the first of many flights away from the docklands, and West Seventh became
the destination of workers arriving from Europe in search of jobs on railroads
and in grain mills. Irish, German, Italian, and Czech—all the immigrant groups
that built St. Paul passed through here, not unlike Ellis Island. By the late 1800s,
there were so many Czechs living in the neighborhood that Czech composer
Antonin Dvorak stopped in at the now refurbished Czecho-Slovak Protection
Society Hall on South Michigan Street while on his concert tour across America.
Poles, too, began moving to the neighborhood in the late 19th century, and
their Saint Stanislaus Catholic Church still stands on Western Avenue.
Eventually, these immigrants moved on as well and, as is often the case with
urban areas, the large old houses became too big to manage for the working
classes who were left and were divided up for flophouses and even more dis-
reputable purposes. Many of them, including a house designed by state capitol
architect Cass Gilbert, became so derelict they had to be torn down.

Another part of the history of West Seventh has literally been washed away.
As early as the 1850s, Italian families built houses along the levee below 7th

Street (the site of today's Shepard Road). Their community, known as Little Italy, with its flocks of chickens and community ovens, was condemned in 1959 after being inundated by a series of floods. Cossetta's Restaurant on West 7th (www.cossettaeventi.com), a block from the Xcel Energy Center, was moved up from the flood plain and has an awning reminding us all that it is "just a piece of the levee." In the meantime, the land along Shepard Road was left to become an industrial mess, with breweries, power plants and a petroleum "tank-farm."

Finally, in the 1970s, when all of West Seventh was close to being bull-dozed for an industrial park, a group of residents stepped in, rolled up their sleeves and formed the West 7th/Fort Road Federation. Their efforts resulted in the area's designation as an Historic District, and the subsequent renovation of a number of the old houses. The federation has also undertaken several rede-velopment projects. In 2003, 1000 Friends of Minnesota (www.1000fom.org) gave the Federation a Smart Growth award for its Brewery Breakthrough Project. Developed by the Federation with funding assistance from the City of Saint Paul, Metropolitan Livable Communities, and other agencies, the Brewery Project is a three-block, 44-unit development located near the Minnesota Landmark Brewing Company on West Seventh. It includes new and rehabili-tated single-family housing, new townhouse units, restoration of an historic mansion, and the creation of a park overlooking the river bluff. Several other projects are already completed or in the works for this organization, including the conversion of the old St. Paul Gas and Light Company power plant at Shepard Road and Randolph into condos. Take a look at that project online at www.islandstation.com.

Today's West Seventh district is a convenient location that offers blocks of modest Midwestern squares mixed with brick workers' cottages and a few Victorians, as well as condos, duplexes, and the two newest, biggest housing developments in the city's history: 600-unit Upper Landing, off Shepard Road at Washington and Spring Streets, and 850-unit Victoria Park, along Otto Avenue, between Shepard Road and West Seventh. Victoria Park will eventually include townhomes, a Sholom Home senior housing complex, single-family homes, moderately priced condos, retail shops, and a new city park. You can check out its web site at www.lovethyneighborhood.com.

The bedrock that creates the river channel and underlies this neighbor-hood sometimes makes renovation of houses and upgrading of utilities diffi-cult, but the river itself is a source for neighborhood recreation. The bike trail along Shepard Road offers a bird's eye view of the Mississippi, and Crosby Farm Park, off Shepard Road, is a bluff and floodplain forest complete with a board-walk running through its marsh and a network of hiking and biking trails.

Visitors come to West Seventh for the antique shops at the east end of the street and the fine dining at Forepaugh's, located in a mansion on Exchange Street in Irvine Park, 651-224-5606. At the opposite end of the spectrum, the region's classic diner, Mickey's Diner at 1950 West 7th, serves pancakes, burg-ers, and fries 24 hours a day.

Web Site: West 7th/Fort Road Federation, 974 W 7th St, 651-298-5599, www.fortroadfederation.org

Zip Codes: 55102, 55116
Post Offices: Main Office, 180 E Kellogg Blvd; Elway Station, 1715 W 7th
Street
Police Non-Emergency: Central District Patrol Team, 651-266-5563;
General Information, 651-291-1111; www.stpaul.gov/depts/police
Emergency Hospitals: Regions Hospital, 640 Jackson St, 651-254-2191,
www.RegionsHospital.com; HealthEast St. Joseph's Hospital, 69 W
Exchange St, 651-232-3000, www.healtheast.org; United Hospital, 333 N
Smith Ave, 651-241-8000, www.allina.com
Library: www.stpaul.lib.mn.us: Central Library, 90 W 4th St, 651-266-7000;
West Seventh Library, 265 Oneida St, 651-298-5516
Community Resources: Governor Alexander Ramsey House, 265 Exchange St
Parks: www.stpaul.gov/depts/parks; Irvine Park, 281 Walnut St (Ryan Ave
& Walnut St) is a popular setting for wedding photographs; Linwood
Park and Recreation Center; Mississippi Riverfront and Crosby Farm
Regional Park
Public Transportation: 612-373-3333, www.MetroTransit.org; buses
travel along Grand Avenue, W 7th Street, St. Clair, Randolph

NORTHWEST ST. PAUL

(West of I-35E and North of University)

ST. ANTHONY PARK DISTRICT (AND FALCON HEIGHTS)

Boundaries: *St Anthony Park:* **North:** city limits (Larpenteur); **West:** city
limits (Hwy 280); **South:** I-94, B.N. Railroad; **East:** Cleveland Ave, Snelling Ave,
St. Paul Campus of the University of Minnesota, and the Minnesota State Fair
Grounds; *Falcon Heights:* **North:** Roselawn Ave; **West:** Fulham St; **South:**
Hoyt Ave and Como; **East:** Hamline Ave

Tame hills and mature trees provide a park-like setting for a variety of stolid
brick apartments and stately older houses in these neighborhoods. Falcon
Heights is technically a St. Paul suburb, but hard to differentiate from the rest of
this community.
     The lovely curved streets of **St. Anthony Park** were laid out in the 1870s
by landscape architect Horace Cleveland. His idea was to build a community of
large rural estates adapted to the natural contours of the land, thus creating
the meandering streets and oddly shaped parks and greenways that make up
this district.
     Although "The Park" still offers the original tranquility its designer sought,
the city has long since grown up around it, and now the Burlington Northern
industrial/commercial rail corridor divides it into northern and southern halves.
North St. Anthony Park is an affluent twist of wooded residential streets containing larger Colonials and variations of Midwestern squares, the majority of
which were built between 1900 and 1929. Many of the newer buildings are

apartments, where university faculty and students make up a good number of the residents. South St. Anthony Park is a more modest area made up mostly of single-family bungalows and Midwestern-square style houses. In 2003, the warehouse district that sits in between these neighborhoods was designated the **University-Raymond Historic District**. Groups dedicated to creating a better central corridor transit system have recently begun transforming this area from industrial to mixed-use, transit-oriented residential. One of the first of these projects was 212-unit Emerald Gardens, which is located on the exact border of Minneapolis and St. Paul. Emerald Gardens has received awards for its creative, pedestrian-friendly architecture, which incorporates elements of the site's industrial roots into its present multi-use environment.

Two small commercial districts containing numerous locally owned businesses are within walking distance of most homes in the St. Anthony Park District. At the west end of Como, and often credited with putting St. Anthony on the map, are the Luther Northwestern Theological Seminary and the surrounding shopping area that includes Micawbers Bookstore (www.micawbers.com), Muffuleta Cafe, and The Bibelot Shop. The Raymond-University shopping area is the site of several small cafes and restaurants, as well as a grocery co-op.

Following the eastern "arm" of the neighborhood, **Midway West (Energy Park Drive)** is a mixed-use strip of development that went up in the 1980s and includes apartment complexes, office space, and the Municipal Stadium, home of the St. Paul Saints Northern League baseball team. Although the Saints are a minor league team, their games are quite popular, due in part to their wacky promotions, such as free back rubs during games and the famed pig that carries out new balls.

As befits a neighborhood of professional and academic households, a Carnegie library, endowed in 1917 by "the patron saint of libraries," Andrew Carnegie, is the neighborhood centerpiece. St. Anthony also has its own band, and is home to the Music in the Park Sunday Concert Series. The highlight of the year is a 4th of July celebration that starts with a morning run, features a neighborhood bike/trike/lawnmower brigade parade and a patriotic speech contest, and ends with an evening concert and dance.

Several small parks provide children's playgrounds, tennis courts, winter skating rinks, and picnic tables. Access to the trails and parks along the Mississippi River is gained from city streets.

While St. Anthony Park is distinctly residential, major employers located near or within the district include the University of Minnesota, Luther Seminary, H.B. Fuller Company, and the Waldorf Corporation.

The vast open spaces that take up two-thirds of **Falcon Heights**—the University of Minnesota St. Paul Campus, the Minnesota State Fairgrounds, U of M Golf Course, and Gibbs Farm Museum—create the impression of an almost rural area, and don't leave much room for housing. In fact, most of this 2-square-mile city's streets are east of Snelling, between Hoyt and Roselawn Avenue. Laid out in a standard grid pattern, they are in marked contrast to the west side of the city, where the curvy blocks of the University Grove development take their cue from neighboring St. Anthony Park. Situated on University-owned land, University Grove consists of 103 architect-designed homes built for professors and administrators over a 60-year period from the 1920s into the 1990s. They were described as an "architectural time capsule" of modern America in a 1989 article about the neighborhood in *The New York Times*. While homeownership there is basically limited to University faculty and staff, there are occasional rentals available, usually when professors go on sabbatical. Check the University Grove web page for pictures and information, www1.umn.edu/ugrove/index.html. Nature is as important here as the houses, with common areas of woods and gardens connecting the backyards of most homes, and a former trolley line transformed into a rustic trail that leads from Folwell Avenue to the U's St. Paul campus.

In 2005 Falcon Heights got its first new development in years, Town Square, on the southeast corner of Snelling and Larpenteur. This award-winning development combines apartments and townhouses with service-oriented businesses like restaurants, an optician, and a beauty salon. More new construction may be in Falcon Heights' future, as the University is also proposing to build a new home for its Bell Museum of Natural History on land it owns at Larpenteur and Cleveland. Nearly three-fourths of the residents of Falcon Heights have a bachelor's degree or higher.

While sleepy most of the time, this neighborhood wakes with a start during the state fair. Then most Falcon Heights streets have parking restrictions to ensure that they remain accessible to emergency vehicles, but the city does provide residents with special parking permits. While the fair can be a nuisance, the increasing willingness of fair visitors to use the bus has made a big difference to traffic in this area over the last few years.

Web Sites: St. Anthony Park Community Council (District 12), 890 Cromwell Ave, 651-649-5992, www.sapcc.org; City of Falcon Heights, 2077 W Larpenteur Ave, 651-792-7600, www.ci.falcon-heights.mn.us
Zip Codes: 55104, 55108, 55114, 55108, 55113
Post Office: Industrial Station, 1430 Concordia Ave
Police Non-Emergency: Western District Patrol Team, North: 651-266-5512, South: 651-266-5549; General Information, 651-291-1111; www.stpaul.gov/depts/police; Falcon Heights contracts police service from the City of St. Anthony.
Emergency Hospitals: Regions Hospital, 640 Jackson St, 651-254-2191, www.RegionsHospital.com; HealthEast St. Joseph's Hospital, 69 W Exchange St, 651-232-3000, www.healtheast.org; United Hospital, 333 N Smith Ave, 651-241-8000, www.allina.com; Fairview-University Medical Center, 2450 Riverside Ave, Minneapolis, 612-672-6000, www.fairview.org
Library: www.stpaul.lib.mn.us: St. Anthony Park, 2245 Como Ave, 651-642-0411
Public Schools: Falcon Heights is part of the Roseville School District, 651-635-1600, www.isd623.org
Community Resources: Municipal Stadium and the Saint Paul Saints baseball team, 1771 Energy Park Dr, 651-644-6659, http://saintsbaseball.com; Arts Festival, www.stanthonyparkartsfestival.org; St. Anthony Park Community Band, www.stanthonyparkband.org; Gibbs Farm Museum of Pioneer and Dakotah Life, 2097 W Larpenteur Ave, www.rchs.com/

gbbsfm2.htm; University of Minnesota St. Paul Campus; Minnesota State Fairgrounds; University-Raymond Historic Area; Minnesota State Horticultural Society headquarters; Bell Museum of Natural History

Public Transportation: 612-373-3333, www.MetroTransit.org; buses travel along Snelling Ave, Como Ave, Cleveland, Buford, Gortner, Fairview, University Avenue, Larpenteur, and Raymond. U of M #52 routes run from many parts of the Twin Cities to the St. Paul campus on weekdays; the University Circulator is free and provides service every 15 minutes during the regular University school calendar to bus connections on the St. Paul and Minneapolis campuses. A Park & Ride lot is located at Eustis and Como aves.

HAMLINE–MIDWAY DISTRICT

Boundaries: North: Burlington-Northern Railroad; **West:** Cleveland Ave; **South:** University Ave; **East:** Lexington Pkwy

Just east of St. Anthony Park, midway between the downtowns of Minneapolis and St. Paul, the Hamline-Midway neighborhood is one of the busiest parts of the Twin Cities. In fact, University and Snelling is *the* busiest intersection in the entire state of Minnesota.

University was an early route between the two Twin Cities—first by horse-drawn carriage, then electric streetcar, then by car. As the cities grew toward each other, the Hamline-Midway neighborhood emerged haphazardly as a checkerboard of mixed residential and commercial uses, including processing plants. Much of the low- to moderately priced housing stock went up before 1940, although pleasantly landscaped residences lining the narrow streets immediately surrounding Hamline University, off Snelling, were built as late as the 1960s. While the Midway area has traditionally had some of the best transit service in the metro, with frequent buses and the Amtrak passenger train station, local groups are working to make the transit corridor even better. The Central Corridor Partnership has begun transforming industrial property along University Avenue into mixed-use, transit-oriented development. They are also supporting a proposal to connect downtown St. Paul with Downtown Minneapolis via light rail down University Avenue.

Despite the fact that the Midway area appears to be engaged in a period of significant transition, derelict housing is still a concern, and so is crime. Prostitution and drug-related crime are a given, and in recent years, bank robberies, restaurant hold-ups, and murder have all taken place here, too.

Web Site: Hamline-Midway Coalition (District 11), 1564 Lafond Ave, 651-646-1986, www.hamlinemidwaycoalition.org

Zip Code: 55104

Post Office: Industrial Station, 1430 Concordia Ave

Police Non-Emergency: Western District Patrol Team, North: 651-266-5512, South: 651-266-5549; General Information, 651-291-1111; www.stpaul.gov/depts/police

Emergency Hospitals: Regions Hospital, 640 Jackson St, 651-254-2191, www.RegionsHospital.com; HealthEast St. Joseph's Hospital, 69 W Exchange St, 651-232-3000, www.healtheast.org; United Hospital, 333 N Smith Ave, 651-241-8000, www.allina.com

Library: www.stpaul.lib.mn.us; Hamline-Midway Branch Library, 1558 Minnehaha Ave W, 651-642-0293

Community Resources: Hamline University; University United coalition of Midway citizens and businesses working to revitalize the University Ave corridor, www.universityunited.com; St. Paul Area Revitalization Corporation, 843 Rice St, 651-488-1039, www.sparcweb.org, offers low-interest home improvement loans to south Como homeowners and landlords, and provides housing resource information to homeowners, including information on loan programs, city permit procedures, and contractors.

Parks: www.stpaul.gov/depts/parksNewell Park

Public Transportation: 612-373-3333, www.MetroTransit.org; buses travel along Snelling Ave, Como Ave, Cleveland, Buford, Gortner, Fairview, University Avenue, Larpenteur, and Raymond

THOMAS-DALE (FROGTOWN) DISTRICT

Boundaries: North: B.N. Railroad; **West:** Lexington Pkwy; **South:** University Ave; **East:** I-35E

In the 1880s, when Germans first settled here to be near rail yard jobs, they called their marshy new home, Froschburg, or Frog City, probably for their croaking companions outside. Today, the marshes, with their frog choruses, are long gone.

In their place are modest worker cottages built by the state's earliest residents, as well as newer two-story Midwestern squares and ramblers. Some of the lots are narrow, apparently the result of subdivisions by enterprising residents, and in some places two houses are built on a single lot, one house behind the other. Over half of the housing is pre-1940, and many of the cottages are over 100 years old. The Ramsey County Historical Society (www.rchs.com) did a survey and found houses dating from the 1860s and 1870s along Sherburne, Charles, and Como avenues east of Rice Street. They also discovered a concentration of 1880s houses along the streets extending westward between Rice and Dale. The historical society says you can recognize these oldest houses by their arched window and door openings, brick window hoods, and frilly open porches. Though much of this area has been obliterated by urban renewal, it is still the city's most intact working class neighborhood.

It is also one of the city's most diverse. According to the 2000 census, nearly 40% of Frogtown's residents are of Asian background, 27% are white, and 23% are black. The neighborhood also boasts a large Vietnamese business district with scores of restaurants and markets along University Avenue.

Many of the churches here have ethnic origins, including a striking monument to the area's early European immigrants, the baroque masterpiece Church of St. Agnes at 550 Lafond Avenue, which has a 200-foot-high onion dome roof. The Twin Cities Catholic Chorale and members of the Minnesota Orchestra present orchestral Masses of the Viennese tradition at the solemn Mass, which is celebrated in Latin, on Sundays at ten o'clock. Check the church web site for pictures and more information, www.stagnes.net.

Though the neighborhood is still beset by poverty and crime, many good things are happening here, including the new Rondo Community Outreach Library and Apartment complex at University and Dale, which includes three floors of housing above the library (see Summit-University section in this chapter for more information). The library will offer small business assistance, reading literacy, and education programs, and is one of a handful of such projects in the nation in which a library shares a facility with a housing development.

Web Sites: Thomas-Dale (District 7), 689 Dale St N, 651-298-5068 (no web site)
Zip Codes: 55103, 55104
Post Offices: Rice Street Station, 40 Arlington Ave; Industrial Station, 1430 Concordia Ave
Police Non-Emergency: Western District Patrol Team, North: 651-266-5512, South: 651-266-5549; East of Rice St: Central District Patrol Team, 651-266-5563; General Information, 651-291-1111; www.stpaul.gov/depts/police
Emergency Hospitals: Regions Hospital, 640 Jackson St, 651-254-2191, www.RegionsHospital.com; HealthEast St. Joseph's Hospital, 69 W Exchange St, 651-232-3000, www.healtheast.org; United Hospital, 333 N Smith Ave, 651-241-8000, www.allina.com
Library: www.stpaul.lib.mn.us; Rondo Community Outreach Library at University and Dale, 651-266-7000
Community Resource: Church of St. Agnes, 550 W Lafond Ave, on the National Historic Register, www.stagnes.net
Public Transportation: 612-373-3333, www.MetroTransit.org; buses travel along Como, Thomas, Rice St, University Ave, Dale St

COMO DISTRICT

Boundaries: North: Hoyt Ave, Larpenteur Ave, and the City of Roseville; **West:** Snelling Ave and the City of Falcon Heights; **South:** B.N. Railroad, Como Park, W Maryland Ave; **East:** Dale St

When it's minus 25 degrees, and the rest of the folks in the Twin Cities are fantasizing about someplace warm, all Como residents have to do is step next door to the tropical park inside the glimmering glass Victorian Conservatory in Como Park. With one million visitors each year at the zoo alone, Como (www.comozooconservatory.org) is the most-used park in the seven-county metro area. St. Paul's equivalent of Central Park, 450-acre Como Park comprises over 40% of this district. The centerpiece of what is known as St. Paul's "Garden District," the park features the city's main recreation lake, a zoo, amusement park, 18-hole golf course, miles of trails, a Japanese garden, bandshell, and extensive picnic grounds where throngs of picnickers enjoy summer evenings much as they did at the turn of the century when they rode out to the lake in horse-drawn omnibuses.

While this cozy upper-middle-class neighborhood surrounds the park and Lake Como, none of the homes are lakeside, although many of them enjoy lake and park views. The oldest houses were built on the lake's south and west sides, some of them as summer villas for visitors from the South. Later waves of building in the 1940s, '70s, and '80s added Craftsman homes with sun porches and moderately priced bungalows to the streets close to Snelling Avenue. Today, about one-third of the houses are less than thirty years old. Two-thirds of the homes in the district are owner-occupied.

On the western edge of this neighborhood lies the Minnesota State Fairgrounds, which is viewed alternately as an asset and a liability. A perennial controversy at State Fair time has to do with those residents who allow fairgoers to park in their yards. While this brings in extra cash for some, it also clogs traffic and turns the usually tranquil neighborhoods into noisy parking lots for almost two weeks each August.

Shopping is close by at the Midway shopping area, to the south, where there are banks, groceries, discount stores, and big-box retail, and at Rosedale Shopping Center, as well as at the strip malls along Highway 36 to the north in Roseville.

Web Sites: Como Park Community Council (District 10), 1556 Como Ave, www.comopark.org

Zip Codes: 55103, 55108, 55117

Post Offices: Como Station, 2286 Como Ave; Rice Street Station, 40 Arlington Ave E

Police Non-Emergency: Western District Patrol Team, North: 651-266-5512, South: 651-266-5549; General Information, 651-291-1111; www.stpaul.gov/depts/police

Emergency Hospitals: Regions Hospital, 640 Jackson St, 651-254-2191, www.RegionsHospital.com; HealthEast St. Joseph's Hospital, 69 W Exchange St, 651-232-3000, www.healtheast.org; United Hospital, 333 N Smith Ave, 651-241-8000, www.allina.com

Library: www.stpaul.lib.mn.us: Hamline-Midway Branch Library, 1558 Minnehaha Ave W, 651-642-0293

Community Resources: Bandana Square and Twin Cities Model Railroad Museum, 1021 Bandana Boulevard E (east of Lexington off Energy Park Dr, 651-647-9628; St. Paul Area Revitalization Corporation, 843 Rice St, 651-488-1039, www.sparcweb.org, offers low-interest home improvement loans to south Como homeowners and landlords, and provides housing resource information to homeowners, including information on loan programs, city permit procedures, and contractors

Parks: www.stpaul.gov/depts/parks: Como Park, Conservatory, Golf Course, and Zoo; Comotown Amusement Park (www.comotown.com)

Public Transportation: 612-373-3333, www.MetroTransit.org; buses travel along Front St/Energy Park Dr, Horton, Larpenteur, Victoria, and Dale

NORTH END DISTRICT

Boundaries: North: Larpenteur Ave; **West:** Dale St, Lexington Pkwy; **South:** B.N. Railroad; **East:** I-35E

Heading north from the State Capitol on Rice Street, you cross the railroad tracks and enter the city's North End District, a mix of residential and light industrial properties. The North End District is bisected by Maryland Avenue, and the streets **south of Maryland** include an intact working-class enclave of small Victorian wood frames built by rail yard and mill workers at the end of the 19th century. **North of Maryland** there is a more suburban feel with curving streets, larger lots, and houses built in the 1930s, '40s, and '50s. Housing here is fairly evenly divided between single- and multi-family dwellings, including many large apartment complexes. Consider the North End if you want easy access to Interstate 35E or Highway 36.

The neighborhood's older, blue-collar section centers around two large cemeteries. Pre–Civil War Oakland Cemetery, east of Rice Street, is a designated historic site where many of St. Paul's early statesmen, including founding father Henry Sibley, are buried. Calvary Cemetery, which dates from 1866, is west of Como Avenue. Besides the Victorian houses, many sturdy Midwestern squares and small worker cottages line the streets. Newer North End housing includes a Lewis Park development that offers townhomes and barrier-free apartments.

Wheelock Parkway, which begins in Como, also winds through the North End, following the edge of a sheer bluff, and overlooking a third cemetery, Elmhurst, which was established in 1865. The tracts here of more recently built houses and apartment complexes have more in common with the surrounding suburb of Maplewood than with St. Paul. Convenient shopping is available on thoroughfares, including Rice Street, and Maplewood Mall is a short drive north on White Bear Avenue.

Pictures of some of the old houses and other buildings in this neighborhood are posted on the St. Paul Phototour web site, www.geomyidae.com/index.shtml. Plans to bring new "higher density" housing to this community, particularly in the areas of Loeb Lake and Marydale Park (intersection of Maryland Avenue and Dale Street), are still in the discussion stage, with discussions centering, in part, on whether the city should exercise its right under recent Supreme Court rulings to condemn property in this area for the benefit of private developers.

Web Site: District 6 Planning Council, 213 Front St, 651-488-4485, www.neighborhoodlink.com/stpaul/dist6
Zip Codes: 55101, 55103, 55117
Post Office: Rice Street Station, 40 Arlington Ave E
Police Non-Emergency: Western District Patrol Team, North: 651-266-5512, South: 651-266-5549; Central District Patrol Team, 651-266-5563; General Information, 651-291-1111; www.stpaul.gov/depts/police

Emergency Hospitals: Regions Hospital, 640 Jackson St, 651-254-2191, www.RegionsHospital.com; HealthEast St. Joseph's Hospital, 69 W Exchange St, 651-232-3000, www.healtheast.org; United Hospital, 333 N Smith Ave, 651-241-8000, www.allina.com

Library: www.stpaul.lib.mn.us; Rice Street Branch, 995 Rice St, 651-558-2223

Community Resources: Jackson Street Roundhouse train museum, off I-35E and Pennsylvania, 651-228-0263; St. Paul Area Revitalization Corporation, 843 Rice St, 651-488-1039, www.sparcweb.org, offers low-interest home improvement loans to homeowners and landlords, and provides housing resource information to homeowners, including information on loan programs, city permit procedures, and contractors

Parks: www.stpaul.gov/depts/parks: Gateway Trail, www.dnr.state.mn.us/state_trails/gateway

Public Transportation: 612-373-3333, www.MetroTransit.org; buses travel Jackson St, Rice St, Dale, Arlington, Maryland, Front St, Larpenteur

EAST ST. PAUL AREA

(East of I-35 and North of I-94)

East St. Paul covers nearly a third of the city of St. Paul, a huge area that has always been working-class and industrial, but became severely blighted over the last 25 years, as the factories that used to be here closed and the workers who lived near them lost their jobs. The area began suffering from deteriorating property, increasing poverty, and rising crime. Then, in the late 1990s, in an attempt to turn this district around, the St. Paul Port Authority and a number of nonprofits, as well as corporations such as Wells Fargo and 3M, came together to create the Phalen Corridor (www.phalencorridor.org). This 10-year, hundreds of millions of dollars project has won numerous awards, including the EPA's 2005 Phoenix Award, and the "Most Heart Warming Revival of the Metro Area in 2004" from *Twin Cities Business Monthly Magazine.* It includes the construction of a new street, 2.5-mile-long Phalen Boulevard, which runs from 35-E east to Johnson Parkway, a new YMCA (www.ymcatwincities.org) and connected public school, new single-family homes and townhomes, and the conversion of rundown Phalen Shopping Center into senior housing. It also created Ames Lake, the nation's first wetland reclaimed from a shopping center parking lot. New recreation amenities in the area now include linkage of the Willard Munger and Gateway bike trails, Vertical Endeavors indoor rock-climbing facility (www.verticalendeavors.com, 651-776-1430), and an extreme skate park. New housing includes several mixed-income projects such as The Brownstones on Swede Hollow Park, just steps from downtown, and Phalen Crossings, near the lake.

PAYNE–PHALEN DISTRICT

Boundaries: North: Larpenteur Ave; **West:** I-35E; **South:** Grove St, B.N. Railroad; **East:** Johnson Pkwy, McAfee St

A September 1999 report from the Community Revitalization Center for Urban and Regional Affairs at the University of Minnesota states that "the greatest concentration of crime along St. Paul's East Side is located south of Maryland and east of Edgerton along Arcade Street and Payne Avenue"—the very center of the Payne-Phalen neighborhood. Seven years later, despite hard work by the St. Paul police, this is still a tough neighborhood, particularly south of Maryland.

If you choose to live here, however, you will not only have easy access to I-35 and I-94, you will also be close to excellent recreation amenities. Lake Phalen is surrounded by a substantial expanse of rolling hills, a golf course, and a paved running path. In the summer you can rent sailboats and in the winter, the park offers cross-country ski lessons.

While modest two-story frame houses, bungalows, and Midwestern squares (as well as a smattering of unique turn-of-the-century Victorian houses) are found on the southern end of this neighborhood, attractive, well-built, larger Colonials and bungalows line the streets near the lake. As part of the Payne/Phalen Boulevard redevelopment, new senior lofts have been built on the corner of Payne and Phalen Boulevard, and there is more mixed-income, mixed-use housing either planned or under construction, including row houses and condominiums on Whitall and Edgerton. There are also plans for commercial redevelopment along Payne Avenue.

Web Site: District 5 Planning Council, 1014 Payne Ave, 651-774-5234 (no web site)

Zip Codes: 55101, 55106

Post Offices: Dayton Bluff Station, 1425 Minnehaha Ave; Seeger Square Station, 886 Arcade St

Police Non-Emergency: Eastern District Patrol Team, 651-266-5565; General Information, 651-291-1111; www.stpaul.gov/depts/police

Emergency Hospitals: Regions Hospital, 640 Jackson St, 651-254-2191, www.RegionsHospital.com; HealthEast St. Joseph's Hospital, 69 W Exchange St, 651-232-3000, www.healtheast.org; United Hospital, 333 N Smith Ave, 651-241-8000, www.allina.com

Library: www.stpaul.lib.mn.us; Arlington Hills, 1105 Greenbrier St, 651-793-3930

Community Resources: East Side Neighborhood Development Company, 900 Payne Ave, 651-771-1152, www.esndc.org, builds and sells housing in this district; Minnesota Humanities Commission, 987 E Ivy, www.thinkmhc.org

Parks: www.stpaul.gov/depts/parks: Gateway Trail, www.dnr.state.mn.us/state_trails/gateway; Phalen Park and Golf Course; Arlington/Arkwright Off-Leash Dog Area

Public Transportation: 612-373-3333, www.MetroTransit.org; buses travel along Westminster, Edgerton, Arcade, Prosperity, Larpenteur, English, County Road B, Maryland, Skilman, Desoto, and White Bear Ave. A Park & Ride lot is located at Larpenteur Ave and Arcade St.

DAYTON'S BLUFF DISTRICT

Boundaries: North: Grove St and B.N. Railroad; **West:** Lafayette Rd and State Hwy 3; **South:** Warner Rd; **East:** US Hwy 61, Birmingham St, Hazelwood St, Johnson Pkwy

Dayton's Bluff consists of two distinct parts: the upper neighborhood, or bluff; and the lower neighborhood, known as "Swede Hollow." Since the mid-1800s, this area has been home to waves of Scandinavians, Italians, Eastern Europeans, African-Americans, Asians, Hispanics, and, most recently, Somali and Eritrean refugees.

Sitting high atop Dayton's Bluff, just east of downtown, the charming restored houses have a spectacular "front-porch" view of the Mississippi River valley and the St. Paul cityscape below. Developed in the 1850s by land speculator Lyman Dayton, who built a house on this land (hence the name, Dayton's Bluff), this was St. Paul's first upscale neighborhood. Now it is one of St. Paul's five historic districts, and though many of its Victorian "painted ladies" have been rehabilitated, there are some still waiting. Fans of old houses will appreciate the cupolas, dormers, gables, turrets, parapets, and pediments that are common architectural elements in the historic area.

Like Payne-Phalen to the north, this is another neighborhood in transition. In fact, it's always been in transition. While the lower part of the district, "Swede Hollow," was basically a "stepping-stone" where immigrants squatted until they saved enough money to move to better digs, the upper part of the neighborhood—the Bluff—was once called "the most picturesque and beautiful district of the city" (*St. Paul Pioneer Press,* January 1, 1887). In the two decades between 1970 and 1990, however, the Bluff suffered job losses, deteriorated housing, and soaring crime, becoming much more like its lower sector for awhile. Then in 1992, the community got organized. An historic district was established, and young professionals started moving in and rehabing the old houses. The Upper Swede Hollow Neighborhood Association also started buying troublesome properties and turning them around. As a result of the community's efforts, East 7th Street has been largely cleaned up and turned into an ethnic business corridor that is home, now, to the Mexican consulate (797 East 7th Street, 651-771-5494) as well as to a new HealthEast clinic. The neighborhood association has also been instrumental in creating the Phalen Corridor, a public-private model for addressing problems by creating mixed-income, mixed-use development (see East St. Paul introduction above).

And though Dayton's Bluff still has the second-highest rate of police calls in the city, crime did decline 20% between 1997 and 2002, as residents and police worked together to clear out the pockets of trouble.

At the southern end of Dayton's Bluff there is a steep hilltop with a breath-taking view of the Mississippi River Valley and both downtowns. As early as 1000 B.C. the Hopewell Indians chose this area as a burial site, leaving behind a series of oval-shaped burial mounds along the edge of the bluff. The overlook, with the six gravesites that remain, is now Indian Mounds Park, complete with walking paths, picnic areas, and playgrounds.

For those who are curious about what Dayton's Bluff used to look like, old postcard views of the neighborhood are posted on the Web at www.tc.umn.edu/~cosim001/Postcards.html. Minnesota Historical Society photographs of "Dayton's Bluff and the Saint Paul Winter Carnival" can be viewed at www.tc.umn.edu/~cosim001/WinterCarnival.html.

Web Site: Dayton's Bluff Community Council (District 4), 798 E 7th St, 651-772-2075, www.daytonsbluff.org

Zip Codes: 55101, 55106

Post Offices: Dayton's Bluff Station, 1425 Minnehaha Ave; Main Office, 180 E Kellogg Blvd

Police Non-Emergency: Eastern District Patrol Team, 651-292-3565; Dayton's Bluff Community Police Office, 651-774-3437; General Information, 651-291-1111; www.stpaul.gov/depts/police

Emergency Hospitals: Regions Hospital, 640 Jackson St, 651-254-2191, www.RegionsHospital.com; HealthEast St. Joseph's Hospital, 69 W Exchange St, 651-232-3000, www.healtheast.org; United Hospital, 333 N Smith Ave, 651-241-8000, www.allina.com

Libraries: www.stpaul.lib.mn.us Arlington Hills, 1105 Greenbrier St, 651-793-3930; Sun Ray Branch, 2105 Wilson Ave, 651-501-6300

Community Resources: Mexican Consulate; Dayton's Bluff Historical Area (roughly the four blocks east of Mounds Blvd), www.ci.stpaul.mn.us/depts/liep/HPC; Metropolitan State University, www.metrostate.edu; Twin Cities Neighborhood Housing Services, www.tcnhs.org; Hmong American partnership, www.hmong.org

Parks: www.stpaul.gov/depts/parks; Indian Mounds Park

Community Publications: *Dayton's Bluff District Forum* newspaper is pub-lished monthly, March through December, and is downloadable from the internet (www.daytonsbluff.org/news.html) or delivered to residents free of charge; Dayton's Bluff Community Blog, http://daytons-bluff.journalspace.com

Public Transportation: 612-373-3333, www.MetroTransit.org; buses travel along Burns Ave, Pacific, Mounds Blvd, 3rd St, Minnehaha, Payne, Arcade, White Bear Ave

GREATER EAST SIDE
HAYDEN HEIGHTS/HAZEL PARK/HILLCREST

Boundaries: North: Larpenteur Ave; **West:** Hazelwood St, Johnson Pkwy, McAfee St; **South:** East Minnehaha Ave; **East:** McKnight Rd

Driving up the gradual slope of Minnehaha Avenue and crossing White Bear Avenue, one comes upon a plateau of small- to mid-sized post-1940s Cape Cods and ramblers, some of them on curving, suburban-style streets. This is **Hayden Heights/Hazel Park/Hillcrest,** which, together with several other small subdivisions, comprises the northeastern corner of the city. It is a residential area with a mix of young families, especially Southeast Asians, and retirees. Hillcrest Country Club, in the neighborhood's northeastern corner, occupies almost a quarter of the acreage in Hayden Heights. Some houses face the golf course's meticulously groomed grounds, and many others benefit from the quiet roads that parallel the course. When compared to many of St. Paul's other neighborhoods, there is a dramatic difference between this area's post–World War II suburban-style ramblers and the older housing that predominates in much of the rest of the city. While home values are about the same as in Payne-Phalen and Dayton's Bluff, the small, well-tended yards appear to have more in common with the suburb of Maplewood next door than with most of St. Paul.

Maplewood, surrounding this district to the north and east, is the relatively affluent suburban home to 3M Company's international headquarters. Hayden Heights/Hazel Park/Hillcrest residents enjoy some of the commercial amenities of living next to this well-off suburb, including Maplewood Mall, a large indoor shopping center on White Bear Avenue. Hayden Heights and Hazel Park have several small parks, and Lake Phalen is close enough to the neighborhood for easy visits. (See Ramsey County for more about Maplewood.)

Web Site: Greater East Side Council (District 2), 1961 Sherwood Ave E, 651-774-2220 (no web site)
Zip Codes: 55106, 55119
Post Office: Eastern Heights Station, 1910 Suburban Ave
Police Non-Emergency: Eastern District Patrol Team, 651-266-5565; General Information, 651-291-1111; www.stpaul.gov/depts/police
Emergency Hospitals: Regions Hospital, 640 Jackson St, St. Paul, 651-254-2191, www.RegionsHospital.com; HealthEast St. Joseph's Hospital, 69 W Exchange St, 651-232-3000, www.healtheast.org; United Hospital, 333 N Smith Ave, 651-241-8000, www.allina.com
Library: www.stpaul.lib.mn.us; Hayden Heights Branch, 1456 White Bear Ave N, 651-793-3934
Community Resource: Hillcrest Country Club
Parks: www.stpaul.gov/depts/parks; Furness Parkway, while not a park, has a wide, park-like median and bike trails

Public Transportation: 612-373-3333, www.MetroTransit.org; buses travel along Maryland Ave, Larpenteur, Stillwater Ave, White Bear Ave

SUNRAY/BATTLE CREEK/HIGHWOOD

Boundaries: North: Minnehaha Ave; **West:** Hazelwood St, Birmingham St, Warner Rd; **South:** Mississippi River, city limits; **East:** McKnight Rd

If you're looking for open space, the wide expanse of Sunray/Battle Creek/Highwood has it. Making up St. Paul's southeastern corner, much of this area consists of the wetlands of Pig's Eye Lake Park and Battle Creek Park, as well as a railroad and industrial zone that occupies a slice of land along State Highway 61.

Because of the steep, wooded bluffs in the Battle Creek area east of Highway 61, and immense stretches of marshy land surrounding Pig's Eye Lake along the Mississippi River, this area remained undeveloped until after World War II, except for Highwood, where there was an unsuccessful attempt in the late 1880s to develop a commuter suburb. A handful of architect-designed Queen Anne and shingle style homes dating from this era can be found along Point Douglas Road and East Howard Avenue.

Most of the rest of the houses have been built since the 1970s. Tract housing runs along grid streets and culs-de-sac in the north. Split-levels and ramblers (ranch houses) sit on large lots in the south. Large apartment and condominium complexes were built on the northern and central streets in the 1970s. As a result of its more recent construction and relatively low density, the neighborhood has the newer look of nearby Maplewood and Woodbury. The exception to this suburban appearance is the northwestern corner of Sunray, which is made up of simple, turn-of-the-century bungalows and Midwestern squares, much like those in adjacent Dayton's Bluff.

Rents and prices for the tidy houses, condos, and townhouses are above average for St. Paul, comparable to prices in Como, but well below the most expensive Twin Cities neighborhoods. Houses also tend to be less expensive than in the nearby suburban communities of Maplewood and Woodbury.

The most recent census shows that this community is developing an increasingly diverse population, with big gains in Black and Asian populations. There has also been a large increase in the number of school-age children. Just over half the people in this neighborhood own their own homes.

Sunray/Battle Creek/Highwood is close to shopping centers along I-94, including the Sun Ray Shopping Center and a highly developed area across I-94 from Sunray that is home to the St. Paul Byerly's grocery store and a wide selection of big box retail. Ample hiking and biking areas can be found along the rocky ravines of Battle Creek Park and at other green spaces in the neighborhood. Across State Highway 61 from Battle Creek, Pig's Eye Lake Park, which is home to nesting great blue herons, egrets and cormorants, is a favorite of birdwatchers.

Web Sites: None
Zip Codes: 55106, 55119

Post Office: Eastern Heights Station, 1910 Suburban Ave
Police Non-Emergency: Eastern District Patrol Team, 651-266-5565;
Sunray Shopping Center Storefront, 651-702-6770; General Information,
651-291-1111; www.stpaul.gov/depts/police
Emergency Hospitals: Regions Hospital, 640 Jackson St, 651-254-2191,
www.RegionsHospital.com; HealthEast St. Joseph's Hospital, 69 W
Exchange St, 651-232-3000, www.healtheast.org; United Hospital, 333 N
Smith Ave, 651-241-8000, www.allina.com
Library: www.stpaul.lib.mn.us; Sunray Branch, 2105 Wilson Ave, 651-501-
6300
Community Resources: Battle Creek-Highwood (District 1) District
Council, 2090 Conway St, 651-501-6345
Parks: www.stpaul.gov/depts/parks; Battle Creek Regional Park
Public Transportation: 612-373-3333, www.MetroTransit.org; buses
travel along White Bear Ave, Burns, Ruth, McKnight Rd, Upper Afton Rd,
Lower Afton Rd, Londin Rd, and Century (Hwy 120), Hwys 10 and 61;
transit center at SunRay Shopping Center

SOUTH OF THE MISSISSIPPI RIVER

WEST SIDE (CHEROKEE/RIVERVIEW)

Boundaries: North/West/East: Mississippi River; **South:** Annapolis St

Cross the arching Smith Avenue High Bridge, and you're in another world—St.
Paul's West Side, a world filled with the strains of mariachi bands and the seduc-
tive rhythms of salsa music. If you can't tell by the murals and Spanish-
language signs along Cesar Chavez Boulevard, you can tell by the lively mix of
cantinas and ethnic markets that you are in the oldest Hispanic neighborhood
in the Twin Cities. Though Chicanos have been settling here in large numbers
since the 1920s, this community is also richly diverse. For over one hundred
years, Neighborhood House (www.neighb.org), the local settlement house,
has opened its arms to waves of immigrants, first from Russia and Lebanon,
then from Latin and Central America, Africa, Mexico, Cambodia, and, most
recently, from Thailand. At Neighborhood House the newly arrived learn to
speak English and are assisted with their transition to American life. The vibrant
flux of these new immigrants has turned this drab industrial area into a techni-
color melting pot guaranteed to overcome any case of winter blues.

Known for years as "the West Side," the name is confusing to newcomers
and oldtimers alike, since the neighborhood, which sits on the west bank of the
Mississippi River, is actually south of Downtown. To clear up the confusion, the
papers have started listing properties here as being in "Cherokee/Riverview," a
reference to the neighborhood's Cherokee Heights bluff area that overlooks the
river and downtown St. Paul.

The earliest buildings here are farmhouses and workers' cottages dating
from the mid-19th century. Many of the other houses are Midwestern squares

and variations on bungalows, intermingled with newer split-levels and new apartments and townhouses. More than half the housing was built before 1940, and includes a smattering of renovated Victorians. Much to the dismay of many of the current residents, developers now have their eyes on the neighborhood's riverfront. One developer has proposed a twelve-story condo project on the area's West Side Flats, at the foot of the Wabasha Street bridge. Another is already taking reservations for units in a 74-acre, 30-story residential, retail, hotel, and entertainment complex between Robert Street and Highway 52. Both projects, according to the West Side council, will fly in the face of the surrounding neighborhood's character and existing streetscape, violate a host of neighborhood and river corridor plans, and chase poor working families out of the district. Consequently, residents have geared up to fight. One can only imagine that developers looked around at the rather handmade texture of this neighborhood and thought it would be a pushover. They must never have shopped here.

The busy commercial streets teem with civic engagement and entrepreneurial spirit. Robert Street, which runs north-south, is a commercial district where you can find everything from cowboy boots to used cars. Cesar Chavez Boulevard (formerly Concord Street) from the Lafayette Bridge to Plato Boulevard is the axis for the Latino strip, newly revitalized and now known as District del Sol (www.districtdelsol.com). Check out the margaritas at Boca Chica, 11 Cesar Chavez Boulevard, and the cherry empanadas at El Burrito Mercado, at 215 Wabasha. La Placita Marketplace's peaceful courtyard is the setting for lively music, plays, and lectures (www.laplacitamarket.org). On the far eastern side of the neighborhood, on the flats across the river from downtown, Holman Field, a small airplane landing strip used mostly by private aviation and the Minnesota Air National Guard, is only slightly less quiet than this commercial area.

Even if you don't move here, be sure to visit during Cinco de Mayo, when the whole neighborhood turns into one big street carnival. Or go over for one of the productions of Teatro del Pueblo (www.teatrodelpueblo.org). While you're there, stop in at the Riverview Branch Library. On the National Historic Register, this Carnegie library has a special section for Spanish-speaking patrons.

Go over to commune with Nature, too. Set atop a steep sandstone bluff, Cherokee Park offers an awesome panorama of river barges and downtown St. Paul. This is a place for solitude, and an occasional glimpse of the river's wildlife. Bird watchers can spot herons and egrets riding updrafts over the bluff's edge and, once in a great while, a bald eagle soaring overhead. Below the bluffs are the sandstone walls and marshy river flats of Lilydale Park, which contain small caves created by eons of percolation and erosion. At the turn of the century, some of the caves were used by Yoerg's Brewery for cold storage of their product, which was subsequently marketed as "Yoerg's Cave-Aged Picnic Beer." Nearly all of the cave openings are now barred because of cave-ins and other accidents, but the foundations of the brewery, the ruins of an old brick foundry, and the massive cottonwoods standing along the Mississippi flats still make for interesting exploring.

For a preview of this neighborhood, tune in to Radio Rey, 630 AM, and La Nueva Ley, 740 AM (www.radiorey630am.com). Their programming in Spanish and Hmong audibly reflects the diversity of the district.

Web Site: West Side Citizens' Organization (District 3), 127 W Winifred St, 651-293-1708, www.wsco.org
Zip Code: 55107
Post Office: Riverview Station, 292 Eva St
Police Non-Emergency: Central District Patrol Team, 651-266-5565; General Information, 651-291-1111; www.stpaul.gov/depts/police
Emergency Hospitals: Regions Hospital, 640 Jackson St, 651-254-2191, www.RegionsHospital.com; HealthEast St. Joseph's Hospital, 69 W Exchange St, 651-232-3000, www.healtheast.org; United Hospital, 333 N Smith Ave, 651-241-8000, www.allina.com
Library: www.stpaul.lib.mn.us; Riverview Branch, 1 E George St, 651-292-6626
Community Resources: Cinco de Mayo Celebration, www.district delsol.com/cinco.html; Neighborhood House, 179 E Robie St (in the Paul and Sheila Wellstone Center for Community Building), www.neighb.org, offers food shelf, recreation, English lessons, social services of all kinds, computer labs, and partners with East Metro Music Academy to offer music and performing arts programming.
Parks: www.stpaul.gov/depts/parks: Cherokee Park; Lilydale Park, has fossil hunting (by permit only).
Community Publications: *The West Side FYI*, www.westsidefyi.org; *La Prensa De Minnesota*, www.laprensa-mn.com; *La Voz Latina*, 1643 S Robert Street, 651-457-1177, www.stpaulpublishing.com
Public Transportation: 612-373-3333, www.MetroTransit.org; buses travel along Stryker Ave, Smith Ave, S Robert St, Concord St, Plato, Filmore, and George

WEST METRO SUBURBS

HENNEPIN COUNTY

Boundaries: Northeast: Anoka County (Mississippi River); **Northwest:** Wright County (Crow River); **West:** Wright County; **South:** Scott County (Minnesota River); **Southeast:** Carver County, Dakota County; **East:** Ramsey County (Mississippi River); **Area:** 606 square miles; **Population:** 1,120,897

Seventy percent of the population, jobs, and traffic in the Twin Cities are concentrated in the metro's west side, and this percentage is expected to increase to 75% in the near future. Hennepin County also tends to have the most expensive homes in the state, with three of the metro's A-list addresses: "Kenwood" (in Minneapolis), and Edina and Lake Minnetonka in the western suburbs.

But there's more to this county than posh addresses; there are good values here as well. The northern suburbs (Robbinsdale, Crystal, New Hope, and Brooklyn Park) are chock full of smaller, generally well-maintained economical homes and rentals, as are Richfield and Bloomington in the south. Surprisingly, posh Edina offers good values in apartments, condos, and older homes; and St.

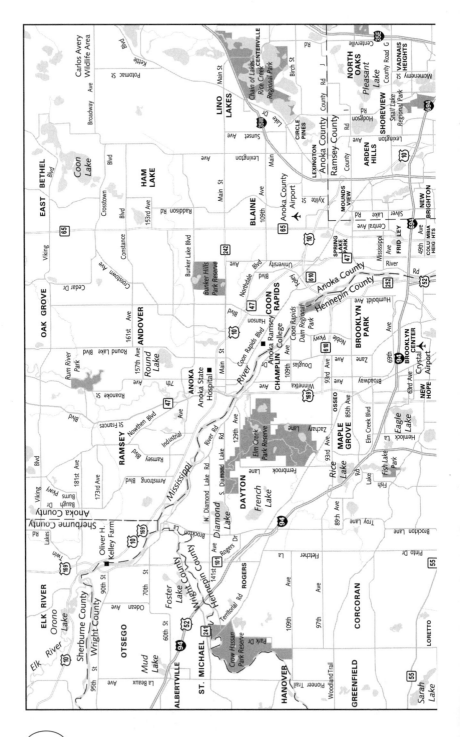

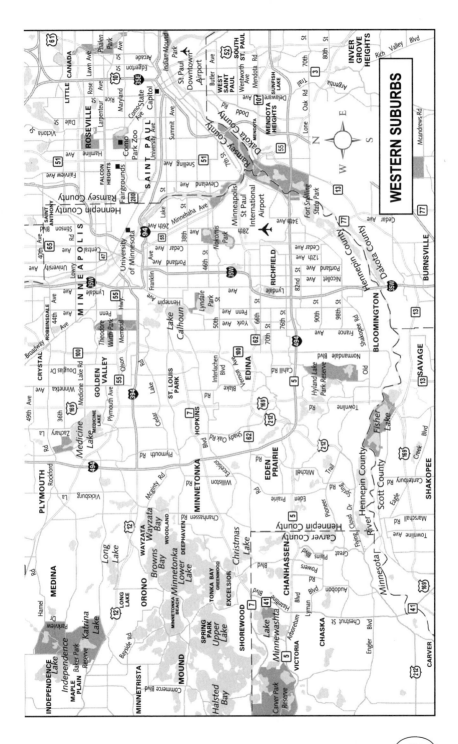

WESTERN SUBURBS

Louis Park, a first-ring suburb, is filled with cute blocks of starter homes, as is the City of Minnetonka. Even Wayzata has a couple of neighborhoods of starter homes, although they're priced considerably higher. And you can get on "The Lake" at a reasonable price—if you're willing to live at the far western end and can handle the killer commute. But probably the county's best kept secret is Golden Valley, north of I-394, which has easy access to the core cities, while featuring mature neighborhoods of older, more affordable, custom-built houses on winding, pretty streets.

Regardless of where you choose to live, shopping will be handy, with grocery and specialty stores scattered throughout. But be forewarned: this is car country, and there are very few places in these suburbs where you can live and be within walking distance of anything.

Another car issue—while the county's web site is great for renewals, you'll need to go in person to register your vehicle and get a driver's license the first time. Save yourself hours of standing in line and get your driver's license in one of the surrounding counties. Chaska, in Carver County, is popular. If you must take a road test, most people find the course at the Plymouth Motor Vehicles Service Center (2455 Fernbrook Lane, 952-476-3042) extremely confusing, and, again, prefer Chaska, where road tests are conducted on city streets. For other Department of Public Safety locations, check the department's web site at www.dps.state.mn.us/dvs/index.html.

Area Codes: 952 (south of I-394) and 763 (north of I-394)

Hennepin County Web Site: www.hennepin.us; Service centers are located throughout the county: Hennepin County Government Center (Downtown), 300 South 6th Street—Public Service Level, Minneapolis, 612-348-8240 (Information), 612-348-9677 TDD; Brookdale, Brooklyn Center; Ridgedale, Minnetonka; Southdale, Edina; Maple Grove Service Center, 9325 Upland Ln N; Eden Prairie Service Center, 479 Prairie Center Dr. Drive-up windows and drop boxes are available at most service centers for license tab renewals.

Police: Hennepin County Sheriff's Office, Minneapolis City Hall, 350 S Fifth St, Minneapolis; Emergency: 911; Non-emergency, 612-348-3744, TDD 612-348-6480

Library: Hennepin County Library System, www.hclib.org

Emergency Hospitals: Abbott Northwestern Hospital, 800 E 28th St, Minneapolis, 612-863-4000, www.abbottnorthwestern.com; Fairview Southdale Hospital, 6401 France Ave S, Edina, 952-924-5000, www.fairview.org; Fairview-University Medical Center, 2450 Riverside Ave, Minneapolis, 612-672-6000, www.fairview.org; Hennepin County Medical Center, 701 Park Ave, Minneapolis, 612-873-3000, www.hcmc.org; Methodist Hospital Park Nicollet Health Services, 6500 Excelsior Blvd, St. Louis Park, 952-993-5000, www.parknicollet.com; North Memorial Health Care, 3300 Oakdale Ave N, Robbinsdale, 763-520-5200, www.north memorial.com; Waconia Ridgeview Medical Center, 500 S Maple St, Waconia, 952-442-2191, 800-967-4620, www.ridgeviewmedical.org (this is the preferred hospital of many who live in the western suburbs).

Parks: Three Rivers Park District (www.threeriversparks.org) operates nearly 27,000 acres of park reserves, regional parks, and special use areas, including three nature centers, four golf courses, two downhill ski and snowboard areas, snow-tubing hill, extensive trails for hiking, biking, horseback riding and cross-country skiing, as well as areas for camping, swimming, fishing/boating, picnicking, and snowshoeing

Community Publication: Sun Newspapers, 612-829-0797, www.mn sun.com

Public Transportation: MetroTransit, 612-373-3333, www.metro transit.org

SOUTH/SOUTHWESTERN SUBURBS

BLOOMINGTON (EAST AND WEST)
RICHFIELD
EDINA

BLOOMINGTON

Boundaries: North: I-494; **West**: Town Line Rd; **South**: Minnesota River; **East**: Minnesota River; **Area**: 35.5 square miles; **Population**: 85,172

Like yin and yang, the disparate halves of Bloomington fit together to form the state's third-largest city. The eastern half, known locally and in the classifieds as East Bloomington, has flat streets laid out in grids, and a large proportion of property that is zoned for business and commercial/industrial uses. When you go shopping at Mall of America, you are in East Bloomington. The western side of the city, which is largely residential, more affluent, and hilly, is known locally as West Bloomington. When you're driving on I-494 and see the ski jump just south of the freeway, you are in West Bloomington. The two halves of Bloomington are treated separately below.

RICHFIELD AND EAST (HALF OF THE CITY OF) BLOOMINGTON

Boundaries: *Richfield:* **North**: 62 Crosstown; **West**: Xerxes Ave; **South**: I-494; **East**: Minneapolis–St. Paul International Airport; **Area**: 7 square miles; **Population**: 34,440; *East Bloomington* (the eastern half of the City of Bloomington): **North**: I-494; **West**: approximately Penn Ave; **South**: Minnesota River; **East**: Minnesota River

At the end of WW II, returning veterans and their growing families needed homes, and so residential development of the area commenced. The result: street after street of modest ramblers on small, flat lots.

The grid-style streets, Cape Cods, and small ramblers are with us still, along with some 1970s split-levels. While the bulk of homes in this area are "maturing," many have been replaced with contemporary housing or "transformed" into more valuable commercial real estate. Look for executive-level homes and condos around Wood Lake in Richfield and along the river bluffs in East Bloomington. That said, most houses still run around 1500 square feet, have detached single-car garages, and sell in the $200,000 range. Because of their size and affordability, these houses go quickly (particularly in Richfield), often to young, single professionals.

Surprisingly, for cities that have so many little commercial and retail areas, neither Richfield nor Bloomington has a real downtown. Bloomington is rectifying that, however, by building a walkable, mixed-use downtown around its Hiawatha Light Rail Transit stop. Condos here are pricey, but feature fabulous views across the river bottoms.

Both Bloomington and Richfield have a number of programs in place to assist homeowners. Richfield will help finance new buyers, and supply a free "remodeling advisor" for those looking to remodel. Each January the city also holds a very useful "Street of Possibilities Remodeling Fair" at the Richfield High School. A great reference book, *Cape Cods & Ramblers: A Remodeling Planbook for Post-WWII Houses,* provides ideas and vision for homeowners who want to remodel their homes, and features plans for this area's three most common house designs: a rambler with a detached garage, a rambler with an attached garage, and a 1.5-story Cape Cod. The planbook is available at the city halls for $10 (resident) or $15 (non-resident). Call the Richfield City Hall, 612-861-9760, for more information or to order one.

When looking here, keep in mind that these cities abut Minneapolis–St. Paul International Airport and are affected by airplane noise, even at night. Despite this, they are desirable areas, particularly for renters, due in part to their central location along freeways 494 and 35W. About one-third of all housing units are rentals, and include apartments, double bungalows, and single-family.

Both cities have many recreation facilities including Richfield's **Wood Lake Nature Center** (www.woodlakenaturecenter.org) and the **Minnesota Valley National Wildlife Refuge**, www.fws.gov/midwest/minnesotavalley, in Bloomington.

Richfield is served by Independent School District #280, www.richfield.k12.mn.us. It is also home to Academy of the Holy Angels (6600 Nicollet Avenue, 612-798-2600, www.ahastars.org), a Catholic, coeducational high school. Bloomington is served by Independent School District #271, www.bloomington.k12.mn.us.

City of Richfield, 6700 Portland Ave, 55423; 612-861-9700, www.ci.Richfield. mn.us

City of Bloomington, 2215 W Old Shakopee Rd, 55420; 952-948-8700, www. ci.bloomington.mn.us

EDINA AND WEST (HALF OF THE CITY OF) BLOOMINGTON

Boundaries: *Edina:* **North**: St. Louis Park and Hopkins; **West**: Washington Ave and Hwy 169; **South**: I-494; **East**: France Ave north of 54th St, Xerxes south of 54th St; **Area**: 16 square miles; **Population**: 54,901; *West Bloomington:* **North**: I-494; **West**: Town Line Rd; **South**: Minnesota River; **East**: Penn Ave

The upscale ambiance of Edina and West Bloomington contrast markedly with the more working-class atmosphere of easterly neighbors Richfield and East Bloomington, though they, too, exhibit an enormous diversity of housing.

Although there is no official boundary line, somewhere between Penn Avenue and France Avenue the apartment buildings, hotels, and 1940s tract housing of East Bloomington give way to curved streets, modern housing with multi-car garages, and residents who tell you that they live in West Bloomington. Custom-built homes grace many of these hilly streets, particularly around Hyland Hills Ski Area and along the Minnesota River Bluffs. In fact, this end of Bloomington is indistinguishable from Edina to the north.

Much is made of Edina and its affluent residents' supposed high-flying lifestyle. But, in many ways, Edina (pronounced Ee-die-nah) is more mystique than fact. Though a number of its residents are corporate kings and prominent professionals, at least one fourth of Edina's population is retired and over age 65. And while Edina certainly does have plenty of houses that sell for over a million, it also has a nice selection of plain ramblers dating from the 1950s and '60s, subsidized apartment units, condominiums, and townhouses, as well. Look for less costly real estate near the freeways and major arteries, and in the vicinity of Pamela Park. More typical of what's considered Edina are the city's multi-million-dollar, brick-and-ivy neighborhoods, among them the 1920s to 1940s houses surrounding the Edina Country Club, which are listed on the National Register of Historic Places. These houses are large in proportion to their lots, a pattern has served as the template for much of the rest of Edina's development. The classic styles of these homes offer formal rooms such as first-floor libraries and dining rooms, and many of them boast home theaters and computer-controlled wine cellars, as well. Look for similar amenities in newer homes in the Braemar and Indian Hills neighborhoods, and around Interlachen Country Club, where newer homes nestle beneath canopies of mature trees. With very little open land available for development, Edina's current building boomlet is taking place as older homes are torn down and replaced with new construction that is particularly luxurious! A 2005-built $4.95 million dream home at 6429 Indian Hills Road has so far been the most expensive home ever shown on the fall Parade of Homes tour, www.paradeofhomes.org. The one-acre lot alone cost $1.2 million, which should give you an idea of what to expect with respect to prices if you're interested in living in one of the swankier sections of the city.

While both Edina and West Bloomington have significant percentages of rental housing, the units tend to be clustered in park-like settings and offer amenities such as tennis courts. One Edina high-rise complex, Edina Park Plaza (www.emporis.com/en/wm/bu/?id=127895), off France Avenue and I-494, has an indoor park with real trees and huge indoor playground (www.ci.edina.mn.us/content/facilities/edinborough_park). The **Residence Inn**, which is part of this complex (3400 Edinborough Way, 952-893-9300, 800-410-9649, www.marriott.com), is a great place to stay while you're looking over the city.

In the City of Bloomington, 25% of the land is set aside for parks and nature areas, mostly located in the western half of the city. The parkland also includes Hyland Hills Ski Area (see **Sports and Recreation**) and the Minnesota Valley National Wildlife Refuge (see **Lakes and Parkways**). In Edina, you'll find groomed parks and carefully tended golf courses in each of its four corners.

Most children in Edina attend Edina District 273 schools (www.edina.k12.mn.us), although some students in the northern part of the city are in the Hopkins District 270 attendance area (www.hopkins.k12.mn.us). West Bloomington is served by Independent School District #271, www.bloomington.k12.mn.us.

While Bloomington and Edina are both known for their shopping, Edina's reputation is more up-market, with a cluster of boutiques, and restaurants centered on Fiftieth and France (www.50thandfrance.com), and Southdale and the Galleria malls, farther down France between the 62 Crosstown and I-494. Both these cities are also rich with public transportation. Buses travel along the major roads, and there are transit hubs at 76th Street and Southdale Center.

Finally, for those who do crossword puzzles, Edina is the answer to the clues, "Five-letter suburb of Minneapolis" and "Minnesota cake-eaters."

City of Edina, 4801 W 50th St, 55424; 952-927-8861, www.ci.edina.mn.us
City of Bloomington, 2215 W Old Shakopee Rd, 55420; 952-948-8700, www.ci.bloomington.mn.us

WESTERN SUBURBS

MINNETONKA
HOPKINS
EDEN PRAIRIE
GOLDEN VALLEY
ST. LOUIS PARK

MINNETONKA

Boundaries: North: Ridgemont Ave; **West**: Woodland, Deephaven, Shorewood; **South**: 62 Crosstown; **East**: St. Louis Park, Hopkins, and Edina; **Area**: 8 square miles; **Population**: 51,100

The city of Minnetonka barely touches Lake Minnetonka at Gray's Bay, so it isn't the lake that has fueled the city's growth—it's jobs. Major international employers such as Cargill, Carlson Companies, and General Mills, as well as numerous smaller businesses, provide an abundance of white-collar jobs and have placed Minnetonka among the top three cities in the state with respect to job creation.

Another city with a gilded reputation, Minnetonka's neighborhoods are constructed on wooded lots with rolling terrain. Many neighborhoods are built around wetlands, and land ownership often involves following wetlands policies, which can affect the way you may use your yard.

While the city boasts numerous upper-bracket homes throughout, for the most affordable housing, check in the neighborhoods that were built circa 1970, off Minnetonka and Excelsior boulevards. Those looking for larger apartments or reasonably priced condominiums will find them around Ridgedale Shopping Center and Cedar Lake Road in the north, or highways 101 and 7 in the southern portion of the city. Settle anywhere in Minnetonka and you won't be far from a playground or park. Among the city's many sport and recreation amenities are city-owned **Williston Fitness Center**, which offers low-cost memberships to residents, and an extensive network of paved paths. The paths through **Purgatory Park**, off Excelsior Boulevard east of Highway 101, are particularly good for walking your dog.

Minnetonka School District #276 (www.minnetonka.k12.mn.us), covers most of the city, but children in the northernmost sections attend Wayzata District #284 (www.wayzata.k12.mn.us). Neighborhoods east of I-494 (more or less) are in the Hopkins #270 school district (www.hopkins.k12.mn.us). Hopkins is the district believed by many to be the best in the state. (For more information, see **Childcare and Education**.) Bus service is organized around commuter service and routes that connect at Ridgedale Shopping Center or the Plymouth Road Transit Center.

City of Minnetonka, 14600 Minnetonka Blvd 55345; 952-939-8200, www.ci. minnetonka.mn.us

HOPKINS

Boundaries: North: St. Louis Park and Minnetonka; **West**: Minnetonka; **South**: Edina and Minnetonka; **East**: St. Louis Park and Edina; **Area**: 4 square miles; **Population**: 17,000

An affordable place to rent or buy a home and a convenient 15-minute commute to Minneapolis, Hopkins is one of the few suburbs that offers a bona fide downtown where you can catch a movie, grab a bite to eat, go to the dentist, or get your car repaired. Other major attractions: the **Hopkins Center for the Arts**, 1111 Main Street (www.hopkinsmn.com/_hca), which is home to **Stages Theatre Company** (952-979-1111, www.stagestheatre.org), a wonderful training ground for young actors, as well as an art gallery that showcases local artists and students. Across the street, a former car dealership is the western suburbs' favorite movie theater, with several screens and $2 tickets ($1 on Tuesdays). Several restaurants have been added around this core, and the accompanying throngs of customers are bringing a tangible vibrancy and exuberance to Hopkins' streets.

The old-style city has even gone trendy with mixed-use Marketplace Lofts on Main Street, which won a 2004 Smart Growth Design Award. Another Smart Growth Award went to the city for turning an abandoned defense plant into a mixed business and residential neighborhood of row houses and town-homes, thus bringing housing and jobs together and turning a blighted indus-trial property into a community amenity.

Other amenities are also typical of a real town: sidewalks, a downtown library, grocery store, city hall, post office, and banks and office complexes. A large ballfield, arena, and Katherine Curren elementary school are also located in the heart of downtown.

While most housing runs to small bungalows, larger homes, including new condos, can be found in the vicinity of Oak Ridge Country Club north of Highway 7, and around Meadowbrook Golf Course, on the east side of town. In addition to its varied and affordable housing, possibly the best thing going in Hopkins is good schools. The Blake School (www.blakeschool.org) is an out-standing college-preparatory day school, and Hopkins School District #270, which serves the entire city, comes enthusiastically recommended. (See **Childcare and Education**.)

Public transportation is good here as well, with bus routes along all the major corridors.

Hopkins is the trailhead for the Southwest LRT biking and hiking trail, which continues west past Lake Minnetonka, or south to Chaska. At one time the center of a thriving truck farming community, it still calls itself the Raspberry Capital and hosts a 10-day Raspberry Festival every July. Highlights include a fun run, Little League Tournament, fireworks, and human and canine royalty (www.hopkinsraspberryfestival.com).

City of Hopkins, 1010 S First St, 55343; 952-935-8474, www.hopkinsmn.com

EDEN PRAIRIE

Boundaries: North: 62 Crosstown; **West**: Chanhassen at Chanhassen Rd and Dell Rd; **South**: Minnesota River; **East**: City of Bloomington, Town Line Rd; **Area**: 36 square miles; **Population**: 60,000

Eden Prairie was the fastest-growing city in Minnesota for ten straight years from 1980 to 1990. Along the way, the farmhouses and barns were bulldozed and the cropland paved, leaving only one farmhouse still standing.

Fortunately for the chai tea and caramel skim latte lovers among us, the 130-year-old farmhouse on Eden Prairie Road (Highway 4) just south of Highway 5 has been converted into a Dunn Bros. Coffeehouse (www.dunn bros.com). In a city that is without a downtown, it has become the commu-nity's gathering place.

Rated by *Money Magazine* as one of the best places in the United States to live and work, and named by *Parents Magazine* as 2005's "Best Place to Raise Kids," this city has made a commitment to "balance" that includes development of life cycle and affordable housing. (Life cycle housing is housing that meets people's needs through all the different stages of life.) That has meant a goal of having 25% rental housing stock by the year 2010, and a total of 43% multiple family housing—both goals that appear to have been met already. Still, one of the city's most interesting developments is one of its first: **The Preserve**, located in southeast Eden Prairie off Highway 169 and Anderson Lakes Parkway. This was the metro's first successful master-planned community. Another interesting neighborhood is **Bearpath**, off Dell Road on the city's western edge, an exclusive, gated golf course development. Less lavish digs can be found near Eden Prairie Center and in the vicinity of Flying Cloud airport. This busy general aviation airport already sees more than 160,000 take-offs and landings each year, and is due for expansion. To meet the ground transportation needs of its residents and the city's workforce, Eden Prairie has joined with Chaska and Chanhassen to develop Southwest MetroTransit (www.swtransit.org or www.metrotransit.org), a system that offers express service to Minneapolis and several other popular destinations (see the **Transportation** chapter).

Eden Prairie School District #272 (www2.edenpr.org/wps/portal) serves most of the city, although some areas along the northern edge are in the Minnetonka or Hopkins school districts. The **Community Center/Round Lake Park** sports complex, on Valley View Road (next to the high school), is the focal point of park and rec activities. It includes skating rinks, a fitness center, athletic fields, and even a beach and fishing pier.

City Hall, 8080 Mitchell Rd, 55344; 952-949-8300, TDD 952-949-8399
24-Hour Prairie Line, 612-949-856; www.ci.eden-prairie.mn.us or www.edenprairie.org

GOLDEN VALLEY

Boundaries: North: Medicine Lake Rd, City of New Hope, City of Crystal, 34th Ave North, 26th Ave, City of Robbinsdale; **West**: Hwy 169, City of Plymouth; **South**: I-394, City of St. Louis Park; **East**: Xerxes, City of Minneapolis; **Area**: 10.2 square miles; **Population**: 20,281

Located roughly along the 45th parallel, exactly halfway between the equator and the North Pole, Golden Valley is served by major freeways I-394 and I-694, and bisected by Highway 55, making it attractive to big corporate employers such as General Mills, as well as those looking for older custom-built homes with large lots and mature trees. Some of its neighborhoods, such as **North Tyrol Hills**, have such wide expanses of green lawns, they might even be described as pastoral. With very little room for new housing, the emphasis here is on invigorating the existing housing stock through remodeling and infill development (the demolition of existing housing and replacement with new).

Golden Valley is home to the **Perpich Center for Arts Education**, a public arts-oriented high school, located on Olson Memorial Highway, www.pcae.k12.mn.us; and to **Breck** (www.breckschool.org), a private Episcopal K–12 college preparatory school. It is also served by two public school districts: Hopkins Independent School District #270 (www.hopkins.k12.mn.us), which operates Meadowbrook Elementary, 5430 Glenwood Avenue; and Robbinsdale Independent School District #281 (www.rdale.k12.mn.us), which has two schools here, an elementary and middle school. Download the school district attendance maps from the city's web site.

Parks include **Theodore Wirth Park** (www.minneapolisparks.org), with its golf course, wildflower garden, trails, and other recreation amenities too long to list.

One other perk—Golden Valley is smoke-free. Not only are restaurants smoke-free indoors and out, but the city has banned smoking in public parks and on the city-owned golf course.

City of Golden Valley, 7800 Golden Valley Rd, Golden Valley, 55427; 763-593-8000, www.ci.golden-valley.mn.us

ST. LOUIS PARK

Boundaries: North: Interstate 394; **West**: Hwy 169 and Hopkins; **South**: Edina and Hopkins; **East**: Minneapolis at France Ave; **Area**: 10.8 square miles; **Population**: 44,102

Restaurants, shopping, watering holes where you can grab a drink after work, major medical facilities, top-notch schools—St. Louis Park has something for everyone, including easier access to such Minneapolis amenities as the Chain of Lakes than many Minneapolis residents have.

The array of housing here is probably the most diverse in the Twin Cities, ranging from single-family homes in tree-shaded, often hilly neighborhoods to large apartment complexes and the region's hottest new "smart growth" community, Excelsior & Grand (www.excelsiorandgrand.com). With a high proportion of single-family and multi-family rental units, the median rent is on the low side for the Twin Cities market. North of Cedar Lake Road, **Westwood Hills** is a 1960s and newer development of executive homes located between the **Minneapolis Golf Club** (www.minneapolisgolfclub.com) and 150-acre **Westwood Hills Nature Center**, a great place to bike or bird watch. Across town, in the city's southeast corner, **Minikahda Vista** borders yet another golf course, the Minikahda Club (www.minikahdaclub.org), which is actually in Minneapolis. Houses here were built in the 1920s and '30s, about the same time as neighboring Linden Hills in Minneapolis. Though this is one of St. Louis Park's oldest neighborhoods, it is still one of the most desirable, especially for those looking for houses with character. Still, only about 25% of St. Louis Park's houses have more than three bedrooms and a bath and a half, which means that many families eventually move out to find more space. In an effort to encourage residents to stay and "supersize" their homes, the city has made a "rehab advisor" available at no cost, and will even pay the cost of a two-hour consultation with an architect. The city also holds remodeling workshops throughout the year and helps homeowners obtain low-interest loans.

SLP is equally innovative when it comes to providing utilities, and expects city-wide high-speed wireless Internet to be available by the end of 2006.

St. Louis Park is served by nationally recognized St. Louis Park School District #283, www.slpschools.org, as well as by several private schools, including Minneapolis Jewish Day School, www.mjds.net; and Benilde-St. Margaret's Catholic junior high and high school, www.bsm-online.org.

Major employers include Methodist Hospital and Park Nicollet Health Center, one of the country's largest multi-specialty clinics, which are both located on Excelsior Boulevard near Highway 100.

Bus transport is easy from the Louisiana Avenue Transit Station to downtown Minneapolis, and there are many routes that run through Knollwood Shopping Center, Methodist Hospital, or along Minnetonka Boulevard and Excelsior Boulevard.

City of St. Louis Park, 5005 Minnetonka Blvd, St. Louis Park, 55416; 952-924-2500, www.stlouispark.org

LAKE MINNETONKA COMMUNITIES

Communities Immediately Surrounding the Lake
Deephaven (see pp. 96–98)
Excelsior (see pp. 96–98)
Greenwood (see pp. 96–98)
Long Lake (see pp. 98–99)
Minnetonka (has a small amount of footage on Gray's Bay) (see pp. 90–91)
Minnetonka Beach (see pp. 96 and 148)
Minnetrista (see pp. 148)
Mound (see pp. 95–98)
Orono (see pp. 96–98)
Shorewood (see pp. 96–98)
Spring Park (see p. 148)
Tonka Bay (see p. 148)
Victoria (see p. 148)
Wayzata (see pp. 96–98)
Woodland (see p. 96)
Communities Nearby
Chanhassen (see p. 105)
Independence (see pp. 98–99)
Maple Plain (see pp. 98–99)
Medina (see pp. 98–99)
Plymouth (see pp. 99–100)

WAYZATA
ORONO/LONG LAKE/MEDINA/MAPLE PLAIN/INDEPENDENCE
DEEPHAVEN AND WOODLAND
EXCELSIOR/GREENWOOD/SHOREWOOD
MOUND
PLYMOUTH

Lake Minnetonka (the "Big Water" in the native Dakota language) is located 20 miles west of Minneapolis. The granddaddy of metro-area lake living, it is 11 miles long, from east to west, and 6 miles wide, with nearly 150 miles of mostly developed shoreline.

It runs from Wayzata and Excelsior in the east to Mound in the west, and generally contains the metro's priciest real estate.

The late 1800s were boom years for Lake Minnetonka. Rail lines reached Wayzata in 1867, bringing visitors from all over the country. To accommodate the sightseers, grand hotels were built in Wayzata, Deephaven, Excelsior, Minnetonka Beach, Mound, and Tonka Bay. The summer visitors played tennis, sailed, and participated in amateur theatricals. Excelsior put on pageants at the Excelsior Commons that featured galloping horses and wagons, and included nearly every person and animal who lived in the village. Turn-of-the-century steamboats, among them the *City of Saint Louis,* a 160-foot sidewheeler that is said to have carried 1,000 passengers, ferried visitors on tours of the lake. Excelsior even had a casino overlooking the lake, and Big Island was the site of an amusement park.

Within a quarter of a century, however, most of the resorts had burned down and the summer cottage era had begun.

Today, 100 years later, Lake Minnetonka is still a playground. Cruise boats offer tours of the lake. Day-trippers visit the antique stores, dine at the many restaurants, and swim at the beaches. The lake provides world-class sailing, scuba diving, bass fishing, power-boating and water-skiing. In winter, ice a couple of feet thick is safe for cross-country skiing, ice boating, ice fishing, and snowmobiling.

Connected by a ring of state highways and county roads, the picturesque villages that encircle "The Lake" feature countless multi-million-dollar homes, a shrinking number of cottages and older houses—most of which are destined to be torn down and replaced with "Starter Castles"—and a growing number of multi-family options such as townhomes, twin homes, and condos. With regular real estate, two-thirds of a property's value is in the buildings; with lake property, two-thirds of the value is in the land—hence builders' willingness to tear down lovely old homes and replace them with "McMansions."

Lake homes in the eastern (Lower) Lake Minnetonka communities of **Deephaven, Greenwood, Excelsior, Wayzata, Orono, Minnetonka Beach,** and **Woodland** boast some of the highest price tags in the metro area. Look in Excelsior, if you'd like to find a house with a garden in a cute, small town. Wayzata also offers in-town living, but mostly in condominiums. Properties at the west end of the lake, around **Mound,** which is less conveniently located and has lower water quality, are more reasonably priced. Homes back from the lake fetch lower prices and don't pay lakeshore taxes, while still offering lake access and, sometimes, water views.

On the south side of Highway 7, near Excelsior, spring-fed Christmas Lake (in Shorewood and Chanhassen) is another premier Twin Cities address. Clean, cold, and clear, it is small enough that it doesn't have the big boat traffic of the larger lake, making it by far the better place to live if your family likes to swim and water ski, or just putt around. **Shorewood,** which strings along Highway

7 for about six miles, has all manner of housing, including relatively affordable houses and plenty of new "villas." With big new multi-family complexes springing up all over the lake area, it's easy to find low-maintenance housing and rentals here. Expect to pay the least for apartments and condos near Mound.

Families with school-age children are drawn to this area by more than the desire to live at a good address—Wayzata School District #284 gets five stars from parents for its academic and sports programs, and for how well it succeeds at integrating new students. Nearby Orono School District #278 is small and personal with an excellent music program. Minnetonka School District #276 has a reputation for working well with gifted students. (See **Childcare and Education**.)

Shopping is conveniently located in Excelsior, Wayzata, Mound, and Navarre, and at several locations in Shorewood. Restaurants are plentiful throughout the area.

Area Code: 952

Community Resources: *Chanhassen Dinner Theatres*, 501 W 78th St, Chanhassen, 952-934-1500, www.chanhassentheatres.com; *Gray Freshwater Biological Institute*, 2500 Shadywood Rd (County Rd 19), Navarre, 952-471-9773, www.freshwater.org; *Lake Minnetonka Conservation District*, www.lmcd.org; *Minnetonka Center for the Arts*, 2240 North Shore Drive, Orono, 952-473-7361, www.minnetonkaarts.org; *Minnetonka Yacht Club*, www.mycsailing.org; *Museum of Lake Minnetonka and Steamboat Minnehaha*, 952-474-2115, www.steamboat minnehaha.org; *Music Association of Minnetonka/ArtsCenter Minnetonka*, 952-401-5954, www.musicassociation.org, presents 60 free concerts a year in the western suburbs; *Old Log Theater*, 5175 Meadville, Excelsior, 952-474-5951, www.oldlog.com; *Twin Cities Polo Club*, www.twincity polo.com; *University of Minnesota Landscape Arboretum*, 3675 Arboretum Dr, Chaska, 952-443-1400, www.arboretum.umn.edu; *Upper Minnetonka Yacht Club*, www.umyc.org; Wayzata Yacht Club, www.wyc.org

Parks: *Lake Minnetonka Regional Park*, 4610 County Rd 44, Minnetrista, *Morris T. Baker Regional Park Reserve and Golf Course*, and *Noerenberg Memorial Gardens*, 2840 North Shore Dr, Orono, are operated by the Three Rivers Park District, www.threeriversparks.org. *Lake Minnewashta Regional Park*, Highway 41 south of Highway 7, includes a swimming beach, boat launch, trails, www.co.carver.mn.us/parks/minne washta_park.htm. *The Depot*, 402 E Lake St, Wayzata, has picnic tables with great water views and is the setting for Wednesday night concerts in summer. *Excelsior Commons*, Lake St, offers a tennis court, playground, baseball diamond, two beaches, plus a wide green that is popular for Frisbee throwing, kite flying, and pick-up soccer games. *Wosfeld Woods Scientific and Natural Area* (www.wolsfeldwoods.org), located in Orono and Medina, off County Rd 6, is one of the last remaining examples of the original "Big Woods" that once covered this part of Minnesota. This land is owned and managed by the Minnesota Department of Natural

Resources. A map of the area is posted at www.dnr.state.mn.us/snas/sna00985/index.html.

Local Events: Apple Days, Excelsior (September); Art on the Lake, Excelsior Commons (June); Chilly Open Golf Fundraiser, Wayzata Bay (February); Holiday Open House Tours, Excelsior and Wayzata (November/December); James J. Hill Days, Wayzata (September)

City of Orono, 2750 Kelley Pkwy, Crystal Bay, 55323; 952-249-4600, www.ci.orono.mn.us

City of Wayzata, 600 Rice St, Wayzata, 55391; 952-404-5300, www.wayzata.org

City of Deephaven, 20225 Cottagewood Rd, Deephaven, 55331; 952-474-4755, www.cityofdeephaven.org

City of Excelsior, 339 3rd S, Excelsior, 55331; 952-474-5233, www.ci.excelsior.mn.us

City of Greenwood, 20225 Cottagewood Rd, Deephaven, 55331; 952-474-4755

City of Shorewood, 5755 Country Club Rd, Shorewood, 55331; 952-474-3236, www.ci.shorewood.mn.us

City of Mound, 5341 Maywood Rd, Mound, 55364; 952-472-0600, www.cityofmound.com

LONG LAKE, MEDINA, MAPLE PLAIN, INDEPENDENCE

Long Lake, just west of Wayzata Country Club, is the commercial center of the north shore area, offering restaurants, bars, a bank, and other businesses. While it does have a few smaller, older, more affordable houses, and some apartments and new condo complexes, most homes are single-family detached, and very "silver spoon."

Medina is the place to look for homes with real acreage, especially if you want to have a horse. With all the parks and trails here, there's plenty of room to ride. Of course, you'll pay for it. Many of the homes are 10,000 square feet or more, and sell for millions. Though Medina's population is expected to rise to nearly 6000 by 2010 (and double that by 2030), a portion of it is still designated "diversified rural," which means a density of no more than one house per ten acres. Other areas, mostly along Highway 55, have been designated "developing," and can (will) have at least three houses per acre.

Maple Plain and the **City of Independence** are located another five miles west on U.S. Highway 12. Largely rural, they are both loaded with plenty of attractive amenities. The **Twin City Polo Grounds** is located here, as is beautiful Lake Independence. **Pioneer Creek Golf Course** is considered one of the metropolitan area's best golfing bargains, and private **Windsong Farm Golf Club** was ranked by the *Minneapolis Star Tribune* as one of Minnesota's top five courses. Long Lake and Maple Plain are entirely within the Orono School District (K–12). Children in Medina and Independence attend schools in four districts: Westonka District 277, Orono District 278, Delano District 879, and Rockford District 883.

City of Long Lake, 450 Virginia Ave, Long Lake, 55356; 952-473-6961,
www.ci.long-lake.mn.us
City of Medina, 2052 County Rd 24, Medina, 55340; 763-473-4643,
www.ci.medina.mn.us
City of Maple Plain, PO Box 97, Maple Plain, 55359; 763-479-0516,
www.mapleplain.com
City of Independence, 1920 County Rd 90, Independence, 55359; 763-479-
0527, http://independence.govoffice.com

PLYMOUTH

Boundaries: North: Maple Grove; **West**: Ferndale Rd/Brockton Ln; **South**:
Ridgemont Ave, Luce Line Hiking and Biking Trail; **East**: Hwy 169; **Area**: 36
square miles; **Population**: 70,000

Plymouth, 10 miles northwest of Minneapolis, maintained its rural character
well into the 1970s—much longer than most Twin Cities suburbs. Today agriculture is a thing of the past, however, and the city has a diverse economic base
that provides the Twin Cities with over 50,000 jobs.

Plymouth's stated goal is to provide its residents with a strong economic
base, preserve the natural environment, and foster respect for individuals, and
it has taken a number of actions to enable it to meet this goal. Resources have
been committed to preserving open space, and the city now has 70 miles of
trails and about 40 parks. Year-round recreation programs at the **Plymouth
IceCenter/Life Time Fitness Center** (763-509-0909, www2.ci.
plymouth.mn.us) have something to offer all ages, from ballroom dance to
community garden plots to rock climbing. Other public amenities include a
walking-jogging track and ballroom.

Plymouth has been involved in a planned development process since
1973, and thus has been able to limit its industrial/commercial development to
locations along main roads. It has also been able to create a wide range of
housing, owner-occupied and rental, single-family detached and multi-family.
Though Plymouth is essentially built-out in the south, new development is still
taking place in the north/northwest, where you will find higher-end, single-
family homes and townhomes. Older neighborhoods, in the southern part of
the city near Wayzata, contain a mix of ramblers, bungalows, 1970s split-levels,
and two-story colonials.

Interstate-494, highways 169 and 55, and county roads 6 and 9 run
through the city, making it attractive to both corporations and commuters. The
city operates its own public transit service, and offers express bus service
between Plymouth and downtown Minneapolis. Many residents don't need to
commute, however, because they work at businesses headquartered in the city.
Shopping is scattered throughout the city or located minutes away at
Ridgedale (on 394) or in Wayzata.

Plymouth is served by four school districts: Wayzata #284
(www.wayzata.k12.mn.us), Robbinsdale #281 (www.rdale.k12.mn.us/dist),

Osseo #279 (www.district279.org), and Hopkins #270 (www. hopkins.k12.mn.us). (For more information, see **Childcare and Education**.) City of Plymouth, 3400 Plymouth Blvd, Plymouth, 55446; 763-509-5000, www2.ci.plymouth.mn.us

NORTH/NORTHWEST SUBURBS

BROOKLYN PARK/CHAMPLIN
CORCORAN, DAYTON, HASSAN/ROGERS
MAPLE GROVE

BROOKLYN PARK AND CHAMPLIN

Boundaries: *Brooklyn Park:* **North**: 109th Ave N; **West**: Osseo/Maple Grove, Jefferson Hwy, Hwy 169; **South:** Brooklyn Center, Crystal, New Hope; **East**: Mississippi River; **Area**: 26.1 square miles; **Population**: 68,000; *Champlin:* **North**: Mississippi River; **West**: Dayton; **South**: 109th Ave N, Brooklyn Park, Maple Grove; **East**: Mississippi River; **Area**: 8.2 square miles; **Population**: 23,300

Brooklyn Park is located on the banks of the Mississippi River, 12 miles from downtown Minneapolis. The sixth largest city in the state, it is a still-growing second-ring suburb expected to top out at 85,000 by 2030. In 2005, the city had about 16,000 single-family homes and nearly 11,000 multi-family units. New homes here, though similar to all the other new houses going up throughout the Twin Cities, are somewhat more moderately priced.

Next-door neighbor **Champlin** is divided roughly down the middle, with older, 1950s and '60s ramblers on the east side of Highway 169, and 1970s split levels and newer homes on the west. Numerous townhouses have sprung up near Highway 169, filling out the middle. Recently constructed executive-level homes can be found along the Mississippi River, off West River Road.

Recreation is close at hand for residents of both Brooklyn Park and Champlin. Topping the list are 4900-acre Elm Creek Park Reserve (www.three riversparks.com), on the western side of Champlin, and nationally recognized Edinburgh USA (www.edinburghusa.org) golf course in Brooklyn Park. Children in Brooklyn Park attend schools operated by Anoka-Hennepin School District #11 (www.anoka.k12.mn.us), Osseo School District #279 (www.district 279.org), or Robbinsdale School District #281 (www.rdale.k12.mn.us). Children in Champlin attend Anoka-Hennepin Schools (www.anoka. k12.mn.us). Hennepin Technical College (www.hennepintech.edu) and North Hennepin Community College (www.nhcc.mnscu.ed) are both located here.

Because population in this area is expected to grow by a third in the near future, and congestion is already very bad, Hennepin County is undertaking a major redesign and renovation of Highway 81. In addition, MetroTransit is planning a busway that will provide "Bus Rapid Transit" service along the Highway 81 corridor from downtown Minneapolis through Robbinsdale, Crystal, Brooklyn Park, Osseo, Hassan Township, Dayton, Maple Grove and Rogers.

Other main roads that serve this area are I-94, and highways 252, 610, and 169.

City of Brooklyn Park, 5200 85th Ave N, Brooklyn Park, 55443; 763-424-8000,
www.ci.brooklyn-park.mn.us or www.brooklynpark.org
City of Champlin, 11955 Champlin Dr, Champlin, 55316; 763-421-8100,
www.ci.champlin.mn.us

CORCORAN, DAYTON, AND HASSAN TOWNSHIP/ROGERS

The western Hennepin county cities of Corcoran, Dayton, and Hassan
Township are expected to quadruple in population by 2030. At this time, developers are literally creating residential communities out of farm fields. To see
what sort of homes they are putting up, look online at the Builders Association
of the Twin Cities Parade of Homes, www.paradeofhomes.org. To find out
what the future holds, ask to see a copy of the city's Comprehensive Plan.

City of Corcoran, 8200 County Rd 116, Corcoran, 55340; 763-420-2288,
www.ci.corcoran.mn.us
City of Dayton, 12260 South Diamond Lake Rd, Dayton, 55327; 763-427-
4589, www.ci.dayton.mn.us
Hassan Township, 25000 Hassan Pkwy, Rogers, 55374; 763-428-4100,
www.townofhassan.com
City of Rogers, 12913 Main St, Rogers, 55374; 763-428-2253, http://
rogers.govoffice.com

MAPLE GROVE

Boundaries: North: 109th Ave N; **West**: Hwy 101; **South**: 62nd Ave N;
East: Hwy 169; **Area**: 36 square miles; **Population**: 64,000

Nearly everything in Maple Grove is new. Since 1999, the city has gone from
open land and gravel pits, with half a dozen residential neighborhoods along
I-494, to insta-community, with a newly created town center and mile after mile of
great room/three-car-garage/granite countertop housing built by all the region's
major builders. Townhomes have the same open-plan layouts and trendy finishes, and some of the more expensive units also feature three-car garages. To see
examples of what's being built look online at www.paradeofhomes.org. The
city's much-ballyhooed new downtown has a government center, new library,
movie theater, retail shops, townhomes, and the Arbor Lakes "lifestyle" mall.
Located just north of interstates 94 and 694, Arbor Lakes has quickly become a
popular shopping destination. (See **Shopping for the Home.**)

The community is served by two school districts. Osseo district #279
(www.district279.org) covers most of the Maple Grove area and serves almost
22,000 students, making it one of the largest school districts in Minnesota. The
district provides transportation for kindergartners who live over 1/2 mile from
their school, and for children in grades 1–12 who live over 1 mile from school.
Wayzata district #284 (www.wayzata.k12.mn.us) provides service to the south-

ernmost part of the city. Attendance area maps can be downloaded from each school's web site.

Maple Grove Transit, 763-494-6010, www.ci.maple-grove.mn. us/administration/transit/overview.htm, provides commuter express service to and from downtown Minneapolis.

City of Maple Grove, 8001 Main St, Maple Grove, 55369; 763-494-6000, www.ci.maple-grove.mn.us

OUTER WESTERN SUBURBS

Ten years ago, the properties along Interstate Highway 94 between Maple Grove and St. Cloud weren't suburbs—they were working farms. Today cheap land and easy access to interstates and major highways have turned the west/northwest fringe of the Twin Cities into one of the fastest growing areas in the state—and into a driver's nightmare, as well, putting great pressure on roads whose designs are insufficient for the amount of traffic they are being asked to carry. Interstate-94, which carries the heaviest and fastest traffic, is known for its fatal cross-median crashes and long delays in the vicinity of Highway 101.

WRIGHT COUNTY

Boundaries: North: Mississippi River, Sherburne County; **West**: Stearns and Meeker counties; **South**: McLeod County; **East**: Crow River, Hennepin County; **Area**: 716 square miles (31 miles north/south, 36 miles east/west); **Population**: 106,734

Wright County, just west of Hennepin, is another of the fastest growing counties in the country. Its population is estimated to have increased nearly 20% between 2000 and 2004, with some of its cities even tripling in size.

Though over 70% of Wright County is currently classified agricultural, once Highway 55 is made four lanes from Annandale to I-494, it is expected that this corridor, at least, will become very densely developed. Many new developments are already clustered around the county's 298 lakes.

For the latest on what sort of homes are being built and where, check out www.paradeofhomes.org.

Web Site: Wright County Government Center, 10 2nd St NW, Buffalo, 55313, 763-682-3900, 800-362-3667, www.co.wright.mn.us
Police: Wright County Sheriff, 10 2nd St NW, Buffalo, 55313-1197; Emergency, 911; 24-hour Non-emergency, 763-682-1162
Emergency Hospital: Monticello–Big Lake Community Hospital, 1013 Hart Blvd, Monticello, 55362, 763-295-2945, www.hospitalsoup.com/ ExternalWebFrame.asp?HospitalID=11912
Library: Great River Regional Library System, www.griver.org

Parks: 3000 acres of parks, 31.5 miles of trails, 17 miles of ski trails, six fishing piers, a 12-hole disc golf course, seven playgrounds; five swimming beaches; two campgrounds; parks along the North Fork and main branch of the Crow River offer access to one of the region's most scenic and accessible state canoe routes. Ney Nature Center near Maple Lake, is an environmental education facility for local schools and the public.

SHERBURNE COUNTY

BIG LAKE
ELK RIVER
ZIMMERMAN

Boundaries: North: Benton and Mille Lacs counties; **West**: Stearns County; **South**: Mississippi River and Wright County; **East**: Isanti and Anoka counties; **Area**: 431 square miles; **Population**: 70,000

Sherburne County consists of ten townships and the City of Elk River. Early on, it was hoped that the proposed Northstar Commuter Rail line would extend from Minneapolis to St. Cloud along the I-94 corridor and relieve some of the congestion in this area. The general feeling now is that the currently anticipated route (from Minneapolis, through Fridley, Coon Rapids, Anoka, Elk River, and ending at Big Lake) will not accomplish that objective. What the line is expected to do, however, is to increase demand for property around the terminals along its route, and to attract investment in large-scale developments. To see what is being built and how much it will cost, keep your eye on www.paradeofhomes.org.

Web Site: Sherburne County Government Center, 13880 Hwy 10, Elk River, 55330-4601, 763-241-2701, 800-433-5229, www.co.sherburne.mn.us
Police: Sherburne County Sheriff's Department: Emergency, 911; Nonemergency, 763-241-2500, 800-433-5245
Emergency Hospital: Fairview Northland Regional Hospital, 911 Northland Dr, Princeton, 763-389-1313
Library: Great River Regional Library System, branches in Becker, Big Lake, Elk River, St. Cloud, www.griver.org
Public Schools: Children here attend schools of Big Lake Independent School District 727 (www.biglake.k12.mn.us), one of the fastest growing districts in the state; or Elk River Area District 178 (www.elkriver. k12.mn.us), already one of the state's 10 biggest school districts
Parks: 30,600-acre Sherburne National Wildlife Refuge, managed by the U.S. Fish and Wildlife Service (www.midwest.fws.gov/Sherburne), consists of wetlands, prairie, and oak savanna, and is home to sandhill cranes, trumpeter swans, bald eagles, hawks, a variety of ducks and geese, and other wildlife. The Refuge provides a variety of opportunities for experiencing nature including hiking and cross-country ski trails, a wildlife drive, fishing,

and hunting. Sand Dune State Forest (www.dnr.state.mn.us/ state_forests/index.html), managed by the Minnesota Department of Natural Resources, includes more than 18 miles of groomed trails for snowmobiling and horseback riding. The Blue Hill and Mahnomen trails, located along County Rd 9, provide nine miles of hiking and cross-country skiing. Golf courses: Elk River Country Club, 20015 Elk Lake Rd NW, Elk River, 763-441-4111, is semi-private and relatively flat; Pinewood Golf Course, 14000 182nd Ave NW, Elk River, 763-441-3451, has rolling greens, medium-width fairways, and some shots over water.

Community Publications: *West Sherburne Tribune*, 29 Lake St, Big Lake, 55309, 763-263-3602, www.westsherburnetribune.com; published weekly

Public Transportation: The Northstar Coach provides weekday express service between park and ride locations in Elk River and Coon Rapids and the downtown Minneapolis 5th Street transit station, 1-888-528-8880, www.commutercoach.org.

City of Big Lake, 160 Lake St N, Big Lake, 55309; 763-263-2107, www.biglakemn.org

Township of Big Lake, 21960 County Rd 5, Big Lake, 55309; 763-263-8111, www.biglaketownship.com

City of Elk River, 13065 Orono Pkwy, Elk River, 55330; 763-635-1000, www.ci.elk-river.mn.us.

City of Zimmerman, 12980 Fremont Ave, Zimmerman, 55398; 763-856-4666, www.zimmerman.govoffice.com

CARVER COUNTY

CHANHASSEN
CHASKA

Boundaries: North: Shorewood; **West**: McLeod and Sibley counties; **South**: Minnesota River; **East**: Eden Prairie; **Area**: 376 square miles; **Population**: 82,000

In 2005, Carver County surveyed its residents asking them to rate nine community characteristics. Coming out on top were air quality and recreational opportunities. Affordable childcare, water quality, job opportunities, and affordable housing received the lowest ratings. Download the complete survey from the county's web site, and compare the residents' other responses with what you're looking for in a new home.

Web Site: Carver County Government Center, 600 East 4th St, Chaska, 55318, 952-361-1500, www.co.carver.mn.us

Carver County License Center: 418 Pine St, Chaska, 55318, 952-361-1900

Police: 606 East 4th St, Emergency: 911; Non-emergency, 952-361-1212

Emergency Hospital: Ridgeview Medical Center, 500 South Maple St, Waconia, 952-442-2191, www.ridgeviewmedical.org; St. Francis Regional

Medical Center, 1455 St. Francis Ave, Shakopee, 952-403-3000, www.Stfrancis-shakopee.com

Library: Carver County Library System, www.carverlib.org

Community Resource: The Minnesota Landscape Arboretum, 3675 Arboretum Dr, 952-443-1400, www.arboretum.umn.edu, is part of the Department of Horticultural Science at the University of Minnesota. Its mission is to serve as a resource for horticultural and environmental information, and to develop and evaluate plants and horticultural practices for cold climates.

Parks: Carver County operates three regional parks: 200-acre Baylor Park and Onan Observatory on Eagle Lake in the western part of the county; 340-acre Lake Minnewashta Park off Hwy 41; and 8-acre Lake Waconia Regional Park on the south shore of the lake. The parks offer swimming beaches, picnic facilities, trails, playgrounds, boat accesses, and campgrounds, www.co.carver.mn.us/parks.

Public Transportation: SouthwestTransit, 952-949-2BUS, www.swtransit. org, provides commuter and reverse-commuter service between Minneapolis and Eden Prairie, Chanhassen, and Chaska.

CHANHASSEN

Boundaries: North: Shorewood; **West**: Victoria, Chaska; **South**: Minnesota River; **East**: Eden Prairie; **Area**: 24 square miles; **Population**: 20,321

Conveniently located 20 miles from Minneapolis, along Highway 5, Chanhassen grew from a population of 11,000 in 1990 to over 20,000 in 2000, and is expected to reach 38,000 in just a few years. About one-third of its housing consists of multi-family units built since 1990. Some of the city's prettiest neighborhoods have been built around its lakes, Christmas and Lotus lakes in the north, and Lake Riley in the south, all of which are surrounded by custom-built houses.

Shopping is conveniently located along the city's West 78th Street main drag, which extends in an unbroken line of strip malls from the Chanhassen Dinner Theatre (www.chanhassentheatres.com), at the east end of the street, to Byerly's grocery store and Target at the west. In between you will find a movie theater, hotel (www.countryinns.com/chanhassenmn), banks, medical offices, Cub Foods, the library, and several restaurants. Children in the northern part of Chanhassen attend Minnetonka District 276 schools (www. minnetonka.k12.mn.us). The rest of the city is in the Chaska school district (www.district112.org). Two private schools (K–8) are located in or near downtown: St. Hubert Catholic School, (www.sthubert.org/school.html); and Chapel Hill Academy, (www.chapel-hill.org). Many students in this area are home-schooled.

City of Chanhassen, City Hall, 7700 Market Blvd, Chanhassen, 55331; 952-227-1100, www.ci.chanhassen.mn.us/

CHASKA

Boundaries: North: Victoria, Chanhassen; **West**: Laketown and Dahlgren Townships; **South**: Minnesota River; **East**: Chanhassen; **Area**: 45 square miles; **Population**: 21,694

The old yellow brick buildings in the historic river city of Chaska sit in marked contrast to the ecru and beige tract-house suburbia that surrounds them. Another contrast: the name "Jonathan" painted on a silo across Highway 41 from a Super Target. Jonathan (www.jonathaninchaska.com) was an early sub-division in Chaska, conceived as an alternative to the sprawling, sterile suburbs that began sprouting in cornfields all over the country in the 1960s. The idea behind it was that people should be able to live, work, and play within a single, ecologically healthy, pedestrian-friendly city. This new urban environment even had amenities (a concept new for its time) like tot-lots, backyards that melted into parks and greenbelts, and groomed ski trails. The houses, too, were wildly experimental. Some were modular, intended to grow or shrink with a family. Many contained such futuristic gadgets as trash-compactors and a community information system (think early Internet) that allowed residents to be "seen" by doctors at nearby Waconia hospital! The community was so famous in the early 1970s that the *Washington Post* and *Newsweek* covered its construction, and people moved from all over the country to live in it. Then the recession hit and it fizzled. Intended to become a city of 50,000, it topped out at 1500. "Ah, Jonathan, you were such a big, beautiful test-tube baby," wrote *Newsweek,* "but you may never make it to 1990."

Fast-forward to 2006 and Carver County is one of the 100 fastest-growing counties in the nation. Its population nearly doubled from 47,000 to 82,000 between 1990 and 2004, and is expected to nearly double again by 2030. Most of the growth is taking place in Chaska and its neighbors, Chanhassen and Victoria, where large developments now dominate the landscape. In Chaska proper, new condos are being built along the Minnesota River. Farther out, expensive single-family homes are springing up surrounding **the Chaska Town Course**, a municipal 18-hole golf course near Lake Bavaria (www. chaskatowncourse.com). Older homes and apartments surround **Hazeltine National Golf Club** (www.hngc.com), east of Highway 41.

For non-golfers, recreation revolves around the **Community Center**, www.chaskacommunitycenter.com, which has a walking/running track, pool, gym, and skating arena.

Children here attend Chaska Independent School District #112, www. district112.org. At the present time, the commute into Minneapolis takes approximately 45 minutes, but the conversion of Highway 212 to a freeway-style four-lane roadway is expected to save about 15 minutes, once it is completed in 2008. In the meantime commuters also have the option of taking SouthWest Transit (952-949-2BUS, www.swtransit.org) into town. Express buses operate all day and into the night.

City of Chaska, 1 City Hall Plaza, Chaska, 55318; 952-448-2851, www.ci.
chaska.mn.us

NORTH/NORTHWEST METRO SUBURBS
ANOKA COUNTY

ANDOVER
CITY OF ANOKA
BLAINE
COON RAPIDS
FRIDLEY
LINO LAKES
RAMSEY

Boundaries: North: Isanti County; **West**: Hennepin and Sherburne counties; **South**: Ramsey and Hennepin counties; **East**: Chisago and Washington
counties; **Area**: 424 square miles; **Population**: 316,830

The traditional image of Anoka County is one of blue-collar burgs and right-
wing politics: a place where there's very little to do beyond snowmobiling,
hunting, and fishing. That's changing—rapidly. Upscale new housing, "smart
growth" town centers, the anticipated construction of the Northstar
Commuter Rail Line, and the possibility of a Vikings stadium/entertainment
complex in Blaine all add up to a county on the brink of a new era. According
to the Minnesota State Demographer, the area surrounding the Northstar
Commuter Rail Corridor is the single fastest growing region in Minnesota.
    Even without the Vikings and the Northstar Commuter Line, this fourth
most populous county in Minnesota has exploded! From 1990 to 2000, it
grew almost twice as fast as the rest of Minnesota, and is expected to increase
its population by another third by 2030. Unfortunately, for a region that des-
perately needs entry-level housing, most of the development so far has con-
sisted of move-up, single-family homes. That may be remedied soon, as an
increasing number of multi-family dwellings are being planned, or are already
under construction in the cities along the proposed Northstar Commuter Rail
Line. Using existing tracks owned by the Burlington Northern Santa Fe (BNSF)
Railway, the first phase of the Northstar Line is expected to provide service on
a 40-mile route from Minneapolis to Big Lake. Six stations are proposed:
Minneapolis, Fridley, Coon Rapids, Anoka, Elk River, and Big Lake. It is
expected that the Northstar Line will cut the commute between Elk River and
Minneapolis from well over an hour to 35 minutes. Along the way, new town
centers are already under construction in Ramsey and Anoka. The projects will
add hundreds of thousands of square feet of shopping and thousands of units
of transit-oriented housing, including lofts, single- and multiple-family housing, and rentals. Until that time, rentals are in short supply, although some can

be found in the parts of the county closest to Minneapolis and along major highways and I-35W.

What Anoka County may lack with respect to major highway access, it more than makes up with abundant natural resources. The gorgeous Rum River flows through the west side of the county, and 16 regional and county parks offer a variety of recreation, including swimming, fishing, horseback riding, hiking, biking, canoeing, boating, golfing and cross-country skiing. They include **Bunker Hills Regional Park** (Coon Rapids), **Carlos Avery Wilderness Area** (Columbus Township), **Coon Rapids Dam Regional Park**, **Rice Creek Chain of Lakes Regional Park Reserve** (Centerville/Lino Lakes), **Sandhill Crane Nature Area** (East Bethel), **Springbrook Nature Center** (Fridley), and **Wargo Nature Center** (Lino Lakes).

Web Site: www.co.anoka.mn.us
Area Code: 763; 651 in the eastern part of the county
Anoka County Government Center: 2100 3rd Ave, Anoka, 55303; 763-421-4760, www.co.anoka.mn.us
Driver's Licenses: State Exam Station, 530 West Main St, Anoka, 763-422-3401; North Metro Exam Station, Arden Hills, 651-639-4057; Anoka License Center, 6111 Hwy 10, Ramsey, 763-576-5768; Blaine License Center, 11000 Hwy 65 NE, Blaine, 763-767-3889; Columbia Heights License Center, 3982 Central Ave NE, Columbia Heights, 763-789-7202; Coon Rapids License Center, 3026-1/2 111th Ave, Coon Rapids, 763-712-4102; Ham Lake License Center, 17565 Central Ave NE, Ham Lake, 763-413-9717
Post Office: Anoka Post Office, 2168 7th Ave North, Anoka, 55303
Emergency Hospitals: Mercy Hospital, 4050 Coon Rapids Blvd, Coon Rapids, 763-236-6000; Unity Hospital, 550 Osborne Rd, Fridley, 763-236-5000; www.mercyunity.allina.com
Library: Anoka County Library, 707 County Rd 10 NE, Blaine, 763-785-3695, www.co.anoka.mn.us
Parks: www.co.anoka.mn.us/departments/park_rec/index.htm; Parks Info Line, 763-767-2820
Transportation: 612-373-3333, www.metrotransit.org; Anoka County "Traveler" bus system, Anoka County Transit Office, 763-422-7075, www.co.anoka.mn.us/departments/transportation/index.htm; Northstar Commuter Coach, www.commutercoach.org
Community Publications: *Anoka County Union, Blaine-Spring Lake Park Life,* and *Coon Rapids Herald,* www.abcnewspapers.com
Community Resources: Lyric Arts Theater, Anoka, 763-422-1838, www.lyricarts.org; Anoka County History Center, Anoka, 763-421-0600, www.ac-hs.org; Banfill-Locke Center for the Arts, Fridley, 763-574-1850, www.banfill-locke.org; Anoka-Hennepin Technical College, 1355 West Main St, Anoka, 763-576-4700, www.ank.tec.mn.us; National Sports Center, 1700 105th Ave NE, Blaine, http://nscsports.org

ANDOVER

Boundaries: North: 181st Ave NW; **West**: Rum River, City of Anoka; **South**: Coon Rapids; **East**: Ham Lake; **Area**: 34.1 square miles; **Population**: 30,000

You can still find Minnesota's traditional mix of Norwegians, Swedes, and Germans in this little piece of Midwest paradise that residents describe as "not quite in the cities, but not too far out." There, for the price of a 35-minute commute, the locals say they get a "not-overpopulated" feeling at the same time that they are still close to shopping at all the big chains, from Rainbow Foods to Home Depot and Menard's, which are just off Highway 10 in nearby Coon Rapids. And though most of the houses are quite new, there are still enough old farmhouses, set back from the roads across long front lawns, to give the area a visual connection with its agricultural roots. Development has been steady here since the 1970s, so housing offers a variety of single-family, owner-occupied, family-sized homes whose architecture is typical of each era. Andover is expected to grow to a population of 40,500 by 2030.

Children in a small section in the northern part of the city attend St. Francis District 15 schools (www.stfrancis.k12.mn.us), while Anoka-Hennepin School District #11 (www.anoka.k12.mn.us) serves the rest.

City of Andover, 1685 Crosstown Blvd NW, Andover, 55304; 763-755-5100, www.ci.Andover.mn.us

CITY OF ANOKA

Boundaries: North: Ramsey, Andover; **West**: Ramsey; **South**: Mississippi River; **East**: Coon Rapids; **Area**: 6.7 square miles; **Population**: 18,000

Located at the confluence of the Rum and Mississippi rivers, in the southwest corner of the county, Anoka (the county seat) is one of the designated stops along the proposed Northstar Commuter Rail Line. Since the rail route was proposed, Anoka has been working to develop a residential and commercial Transit Village around the (potential) Northstar station site. Apart from the new multi-family housing, most homes in Anoka are older, "city-style" properties, with houses built close together on small lots. Garrison Keillor, host of radio's *A Prairie Home Companion,* was born in Anoka and graduated from Anoka High School. His fictional Lake Wobegone is presumed to be based on this town.

City of Anoka, 2015 First Ave North, Anoka, 55303-2270; 763-576-2700, www.ci.anoka.mn.us

BLAINE

Boundaries: North: 133rd Ave NE; **West**: University Ave NE; **South**: 85th Ave NE; **East**: Sunset Ave NE; **Area**: 34 square miles; **Population**: 52,000

If you or your children are into sports, you might save yourself hours of driving time by living in Blaine, home of the **National Sports Center**. The NSC (http://nscsports.org) is a 660-acre campus with 52 soccer fields, four Olympic sheets of ice, an outdoor stadium with a 400-meter track, cycling velodrome, indoor sports hall, and the National Youth Golf Center (www.golfnygc.org), an 18-hole golf course, built specifically for youth and families. Most of the metro's major tournaments are held here, from soccer and lacrosse to the state high school track and field championships. The facility's biggest annual event, the **Schwan's USA CUP** soccer tournament (www.usacup.org), is the largest youth sporting event in the Western Hemisphere. For serious adult golfers, the community is home to the **Tournament Players' Club** (www.tpc.com/private/twin_cities), a private 7146-yard, par-72 layout that is the site of the 3M PGA Champions Tour Championships. It is the upper-bracket housing surrounding the TPC that has put Blaine on the map as one of the metro's fancier addresses. Blaine led the metro in housing starts in 2002, and anticipates that rate will remain constant over the next decade. While some of the new housing will consist of townhomes, most of the projects are single-family homes.

Some children here attend Centennial School District #12 (www.isd12.org), but most attend Spring Lake Park #16 (www.splkpark.k12.mn.us), which has several schools in the city. Some children are bused as a way of maintaining a similar socioeconomic composition in all the schools.

The city has bus service that ranges from regular route local buses and all-day expresses in the more densely populated areas, to peak-only service elsewhere.

City of Blaine, 10801 Town Square Dr NE, Blaine, 55449-8101; 763-784-6700, www.ci.blaine.mn.us

COON RAPIDS

Boundaries: North: Andover; **West**: Anoka, Mississippi River; **South**: Mississippi River, Fridley; **East**: Blaine; **Area**: 23 square miles; **Population**: 62,721

Another stop on the proposed Northstar line, Coon Rapids is a quiet, older suburb located three miles north of I-694 up University Avenue (Highway 47). It is about a thirty-minute drive from downtown Minneapolis. Available housing includes single- and multi-family homes, condominiums, townhomes, waterfront homes, riverfront homes, luxury homes, and rentals. Since the housing boom started here in the 1950s, you can find homes from every era, but the greatest number date from the mid-1980s forward. The 500-acre **Bunker**

Hills Regional Park (www.anokacountyparks.com), is home to highly rated **Bunker Hills Golf Course** as well as a waterpark that features a wave pool and variety of water slides. **Bunker Park Stable** offers trail rides, hay and sleigh rides, lessons, and even a walking pony ride for small children. Abundant shopping is centered on Highway 10. The entire city of Coon Rapids is located in the Anoka-Hennepin School District #11 (www.anoka.k12.mn.us). In February, the community turns out for Snowflake Days, a ten-day celebration that includes sporting events, dances, dog sled races, a medallion hunt, and the Miss Coon Rapids Pageant.

City of Coon Rapids, 11155 Robinson Dr, Coon Rapids, 55433; 763-767-6493, www.ci.coon-rapids.mn.us

FRIDLEY

Boundaries: North: Coon Rapids, Blaine, Spring Lake Park; **West**: Mississippi River (Brooklyn Park, Brooklyn Center); **South**: Columbia Heights, Minneapolis; **East**: Mounds View, New Brighton; **Area**: 10.89 square miles; **Population**: 27,000

Fridley is known for two things—the World Headquarters of Medtronic, and the 1965 Fridley Tornado. A city of 27,000 people, it is located mostly north of I-694 along highways 47 (University Avenue NE) and 65 (Central Avenue NE). While its industries are high-tech, its neighborhoods are modest and affordable. The majority of the city's housing stock was built during the 1960s, after the city was flattened by the tornado, and consists of single-family detached ramblers and split-levels on fairly small cul-de-sac lots. Several small apartment complexes and other multi-unit housing were built about ten years later. Some redevelopment is beginning to take place, especially in the area west of University Avenue. Designated as a stop on the Northstar Commuter Rail Line, the city has developed a 2020 Comprehensive Plan that calls for the eventual conversion of many existing single-family detached homes into multiple-family high-density housing.

While a lot of the city has something of a "Rustbelt" appearance, attractive, well-kept homes are to be found along its wetlands and beside the river, and in the **Innsbruck** neighborhood in the southeastern corner. The city's crowning glory is 127-acre **Springbrook Nature Center** (www.springbrooknaturecenter.org). The largest park in Fridley, the nature center offers three miles of hiking trails, walkways over wetlands, a Halloween Pumpkin Walk, and summer day camps.

The Fridley School District (www.fridley.k12.mn.us) serves the central area of the city. Children in the northern part of the city attend Spring Lake Park schools (www.splkpark.k12.mn.us). The South Innsbruck area is in the Columbia Heights school district (www.colheights.k12.mn.us). **Banfill-Locke Center for the Arts**, on East River Road, is the focal point for the city's cultural life, providing classes for adults and children as well as a life-drawing co-op and juried art shows. Shopping is conveniently located along University Avenue or 15 minutes away at Rosedale.

City of Fridley, 6431 University Ave NE, Fridley, 55432; 763-571-3450, www.ci-fridley.mn.us

LINO LAKES

Boundaries: North: Ham Lake; **West**: Blaine; **South**: County Road J; **East**: Centerville; **Area**: 33 square miles; **Population**: 19,123

Located along a chain of 13 lakes in the North Metro, Lino Lakes is committed to the concept of "conservation development," which is intended to provide high-density housing while permanently preserving natural features and open space. Recreation includes one of the most scenic of all the region's public golf courses, **Chomonix** (www.chomonixgolf.com), in the **Rice Creek Chain of Lakes Regional Park Reserve**.

Lino Lakes is served by three school districts: Centennial School District #12, 763-792-6000, www.centennial.k12.mn.us; White Bear Lake Area School District #624, 651-773-6000, www.whitebear.k12.mn.us; and Forest Lake School District #831, 651-982-6000, www.forestlake.k12.mn.us. You can download a map of their attendance areas from the city's web site.

City of Lino Lakes, 600 Town Center Pkwy, Lino Lakes, 55014; 651-982-2400, www.ci.lino-lakes.mn.us

RAMSEY

Boundaries: North: 181st Ave North; **West**, Sherburne County; **South**: Mississippi River; **East**: Rum River; **Area**: 28.8 square miles; **Population**: 20,735

A bedroom community in the far western reaches of the county, about 25 miles north of Minneapolis, Ramsey contains a mixture of single-family homes on larger parcels of land, golf communities, and numerous townhouses. Its population is expected to reach 45,000 by 2030. Bus service for commuters consists of peak-only express service from the southern end of the city. Not to worry, though—Ramsey is located along the proposed Northstar Commuter Rail Line. Recreation revolves around the city's wetlands and natural areas, including **Rum River Central Regional Park** and **Mississippi West Regional Park**, as well as **The Links at Northfork**, a true Scottish links-style golf course, which is open to the public. Take a virtual tour of the course at www.golfthelinks.com. Children here attend schools operated by Elk River District 728 (www.elkriver.k12.mn.us) or Anoka-Hennepin District 11 (www.anoka.k12.mn.us).

City of Ramsey, 7550 Sunwood Dr (as of October 2006), Ramsey, 55303; 763-427-1410, www.ci.ramsey.mn.us (until October 2006: 15153 Nowthen Boulevard NW)

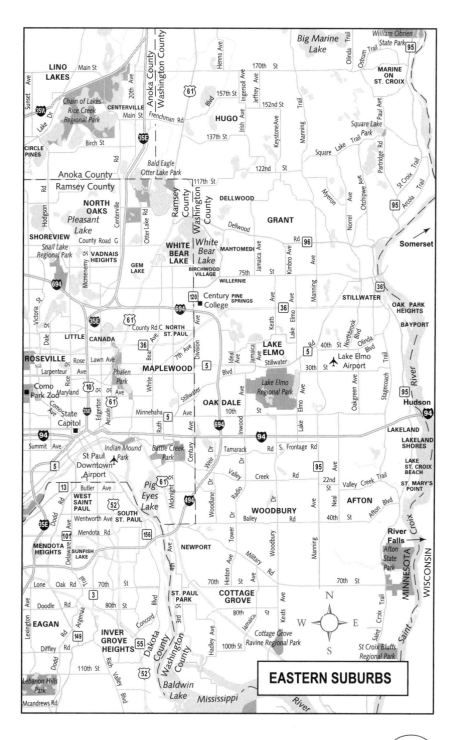

EASTERN SUBURBS

NORTHEAST METRO SUBURBS
RAMSEY COUNTY

ARDEN HILLS (*See western suburbs map*)
MAPLEWOOD
MOUNDS VIEW (*See western suburbs map*)
NEW BRIGHTON (*See western suburbs map*)
NORTH OAKS
NORTH ST. PAUL
ROSEVILLE
SHOREVIEW
VADNAIS HEIGHTS
WHITE BEAR LAKE/DELLWOOD

Boundaries: North: County Rd J; **West**: Silver Lake Rd; **South**: Mississippi River; **East**, Hwy 120; **Area**: 156 square miles; **Population**: 511,035

Ideally situated for easy access to interstate highways 35E, 35W, and 694, these suburbs are only a short commute from the core cities, particularly from downtown St. Paul. Many residents don't have to commute, however, because of all the national companies that have large corporate facilities here: SYSCO and Medtronic are in Mounds View; Guidant and Land O'Lakes are in Arden Hills; and international business giant 3M employs 11,000 people at its headquarters in Maplewood.

These suburbs aren't all business though. They are thick with recreation amenities as well. Nine county and five regional parks, extensive bike and cross-country ski trails, golf courses, ice arenas, swimming beaches, and boating facilities combine to give some parts of this region an almost rural flavor. Community centers help to make them like small towns. North St. Paul actually is a small town, and even has a downtown.

What is known as the "Livability Factor" is high here, and residents enjoy a wide range of housing styles and prices, as well as nearby shopping in Roseville and at Maplewood Mall. Roseville alone has one of the largest concentrations of shopping centers in the entire upper Midwest.

Web Site: Ramsey County Government Centers, 50 Kellogg Blvd West, St. Paul, 55102-1664; 160 East Kellogg Blvd, St. Paul, 55101; 651-266-8500, www.co.ramsey.mn.us

Area Code: 651

Emergency Hospitals: Fairview-University Medical Center, 2450 Riverside Ave, Minneapolis, 612-672-6000, www.fairview.org; Mercy & Unity Hospitals, 4050 Coon Rapids Blvd, Coon Rapids, 763-236-6000, www.mercyunity.allina.com

Libraries: www.ramsey.lib.mn.us

ARDEN HILLS

Boundaries: North: North Boundary of Twin Cities Army Ammunition Plant; **West**: I-35W; **South**: County Rd D; **East**: Lexington; **Area**: 9 square miles; **Population**: 9500

Eight miles north of downtown St. Paul, the City of Arden Hills is small and neighborly, with rolling hills, lakes, excellent parks, well-kept houses, and a vibrant commercial and industrial sector. Over half the population 25 and older hold bachelor's degrees, and nearly 20% hold graduate or professional degrees. Housing here is overwhelmingly single-family detached and owner-occupied, with only a small proportion of multi-family and rental units. In the 1970s, Arden Hills was one of the fastest growing cities in the state, and those '70s styles (split-levels, colonials, ramblers) still account for approximately one-third of the city's housing stock. Most are in the moderate to executive price range, and many are situated on scenic wooded lots. The northern third of the city is occupied by the old Twin Cities Army Ammunition Plant, which is being cleaned up and redeveloped into mixed-use and pedestrian-friendly housing.

City Hall, 1245 West Hwy 96, Arden Hills, 55112; 651-634-5120, www.ci. arden-hills.mn.us

MAPLEWOOD

Boundaries: North: County Rd D, I-694; **West**: St. Paul, Roseville, Little Canada; **South**: St. Paul at Larpenteur Ave and Newport at Bailey Rd; **East**: North St. Paul at Ariel St and Oakdale, and Woodbury at Century Ave; **Area**: 19 square miles; **Population**: 35,000

Maplewood wraps around the east and north sides of St. Paul like a puzzle piece. It has developed constantly since World War II, so housing styles vary greatly. You'll find examples of every era's popular housing types, most of which have been well preserved, some updated. Many are ramblers, dating from the 1950s and '60s, and are smaller than 1500 square feet. Approximately one-third of Maplewood's housing units are townhouses and condominiums. The city's newest, most upscale neighborhoods are located in a six-mile-long, one-mile-wide leg that extends southward alongside Woodbury and Oakdale.

Bracketed by interstates 94, 694, 494, and 35E, and by major state highways 61 and 36, Maplewood is all about shopping and big business. Maplewood Mall is the center of an extensive commercial area; 3M, which has about 11,000 employees at its Maplewood headquarters, is one of Minnesota's largest employers and best-known international corporations.

Maplewood has numerous neighborhood parks and playgrounds as well as the **Maplewood Nature Center**, **Keller Golf Course**, **Goodrich Golf Course**, and **Aldrich Arena**. The **Community Center** has a track, racquetball and basketball courts, performing arts theater, and an aquatics center with a 120-foot water slide. The **Gateway Trail** bike path can be easily accessed from the community center's parking lot. Mountain bikers should head for **Winthrop Street Mountain Biking Area** in **Battle Creek Park**, with its 5.5 kilometers of challenging mountain biking trails in hilly, wooded terrain. This is also a thrilling cross-country ski trail in the winter. (See **Sports and Recreation**.) Maps and directions to Maplewood's parks are available online at www.co.ramsey.mn.us/parks.

Children in Maplewood have some interesting choices of schools: Tri-District Community Cultures/Environmental Science year-round magnet school (www.emid6067.net/TriDistrict), Roseville (www.isd623.org), and North St. Paul/Maplewood/Oakdale (www.isd622.org). Hill-Murray, a private Catholic school for grades 7–12, is located on Larpenteur Avenue (www.hill-murray.org).

City of Maplewood, 1830 County Rd B East, Maplewood, 55109; 651-249-2000, www.ci.Maplewood.mn.us

MOUNDS VIEW

Boundaries: North: Blaine; **West**: Spring Lake Park; **South**: New Brighton; **East**: Shoreview, Arden Hills; **Area**: 4 square miles; **Population**: 12,360

The city of Mounds View is conveniently located between highways 35W on the east and 65 on the west. It is home to Medtronic, Liberty Enterprises, SYSCO Minnesota, and Multi-Tech Systems. Housing is a mix of post-1960 apartments, duplexes, and townhouses, and single-family detached homes on large wooded lots. The section of the city known as **Knollwood Park** features 1930s-era houses.

City of Mounds View, 2401 Hwy 10 NE, Mounds View, 55112; 763-717-4000, www.ci.mounds-view.mn.us

NEW BRIGHTON

Boundaries: North: Mounds View; **West**: Stinson Blvd; **South**: St. Anthony Village; **East**: I-35W; **Area**: 7 square miles; **Population**: 22,000

Twenty minutes from the downtowns of both Minneapolis and St. Paul, New Brighton is an old town with a lot of new housing options. Originally incorporated in the 1880s, it is primarily residential, offering a range of housing from owner-occupied single-family detached homes on culs-de-sac to rental apartments. The town is split into northern and southern halves by I-694. Most housing dates from the 1970s, but **Wexford Heights**, along Silver Lake Road, just south of the freeway, is comprised of custom homes built in the mid-1990s. **Innsbruck**, located both north and south of I-694, boasts homes that were considered luxury houses when they were built in the 1970s and '80s, and affordable "manor homes" built in the early 1990s. Fast forward to 2006, and the current action centers on the **Northwest Quadrant** (north of I-694, along the west side of Old Highway 8), where the city is going forward with a multi-phased, mixed-use development of 750 townhomes, condos, and lofts linked to Long Lake Regional Park by a broad central greenway.

Children in New Brighton attend either Mounds View (www.moundsview schools.org) or St. Anthony/New Brighton (www.stanthony.k12.mn.us) district schools (see **Childcare and Education**). Recreation amenities include a par 30 executive golf course (with Sunday night family golf!), and a network of trails for walking, biking, and blading. The community's principal festival is **Stockyard Days**, held annually in August to celebrate its heyday as the rail-head for the region's cattle industry.

City of New Brighton, 803 Old Hwy 8 NW, New Brighton, 55112; 651-638-2100, www.ci.new-brighton.mn.us

NORTH OAKS

Boundaries: North: County Rd I to County Rd J; **West**: Hodgson Rd; **South**: Hwy 96; **East**: Centerville Rd; **Area**: 7.3 square miles; **Population**: 4128

If you're looking for a quiet wooded setting, you will probably like North Oaks, a private planned community of 6500 acres of open fields and heavily wooded hillsides, private trails, meandering roads, and a community-owned private golf course. Though the average list price here runs well over a million dollars, some older houses have sold for much less. Not a gated community, it is private property, and is run by the North Oaks Home Owners' Association. Though many children here attend private schools, those who wish to attend public school have a choice of Moundsview District 621 (www.moundsviewschools.org) or White Bear Lake (www.whitebear.k12.mn.us).

City of North Oaks, 100 Village Center Dr, Ste 150, North Oaks, 55127; 651-484-5777, www.cityofnorth-oaks.com

NORTH ST. PAUL

Boundaries: North: Radatz St/Beam Ave/Lydia Ave; **West**; Ariel St; **South**: Holloway; **East**: Hwy 120; **Area**: 2.9 square miles; **Population**: 11,600

There may be more to North St. Paul than a snowman, but he's the thing that everybody remembers when they think about this city. Forty-four feet tall and made out of steel and stucco, this landmark grew out of the community's tradition of building a huge snowman every winter. He's has been standing at his present location at Highway 36 and Margaret Street (Central Park) since 1990, and has been adopted as the city's official logo. There are actually a lot of interesting things about this city, including its affordable housing, and the fact that here, in a place where the closest thing most suburbs have to a downtown is a city hall complex, North St. Paul has a real downtown. Like a real town, North St. Paul also distributes its own electricity, offering its customers a chance to

"Go Green" by buying power from renewable energy sources. Housing here is overwhelmingly single-family detached. About a third dates from the 1950, with another third from the 1970s. Most homes have three bedrooms. Recent development consists of a few small condo and townhome redevelopments of existing properties. Homes here are less than 75% owner-occupied. North St. Paul is expected to grow by only 10% by 2030, so for those looking for a fairly stable place that is more small town than suburb, on the north side of metro, this town may be worth a look. Children here attend North St. Paul–Maplewood–Oakdale schools (www.isd622.org). Residents have access to the **Gateway Trail**, which cuts through North St. Paul on its way to and from St. Paul and Stillwater.

City of North St. Paul, 2400 Margaret St, North St. Paul, 55109, 651-747-2400, www.ci.north-saint-paul.mn.us

ROSEVILLE

Boundaries: North: County Rd D; **West**: Highcrest Rd; **South**: Roselawn Ave, Hamline, Larpenteur; **East**: Rice St; **Area**: 13.2 square miles; **Population**: 33,000

With 82 square feet of retail per person (five times the state average), residents sometimes feel that they live in a giant shopping mall. Starter homes are also plentiful here, but there is a serious lack of step-up housing. The city is working on that problem by offering low-interest loans for home improvement projects, and by subsidizing first-time homebuyers. The parks and recreation amenities are another incentive for families to live here: 34 parks, indoor and outdoor skating facilities (including a speedskating track and what the city claims to be the largest skating party in the state on New Year's Eve), an arboretum, par-3 golf course—the list goes on and on.

City of Roseville, 2660 Civic Center Dr, Roseville, 55113-1899; 651-792-7000, www.ci.roseville.mn.us

SHOREVIEW

Boundaries: North: Hwy 1 (Blaine and Lino Lakes); **South**: County Rd D; **East**: Lexington Ave and I-35W; **West**: Rice St, Hodgson St (North Oaks, Vadnais Heights, and White Bear Lake); **Area**: 11.2 square miles; **Population**: 27,000

Three broadcast towers on the north side of I-694 are the tallest structures in Minnesota, and mark the entrance into Shoreview. This city appeals to those looking for easy access to Minneapolis and St. Paul, a range of housing options, and close proximity to recreation. Located both north and south of I-694, Shoreview has all of that, including 11 lakes, 1400 acres of parkland and a basic housing stock that dates from the 1960s, but has recently been updated with the addition of apartments and modern single-family detached houses and villas. Turtle Lake, one of the larger lakes in the city, has a public park, beach, and boat launching facility, as well as a mixture of smaller/older and large/new houses. The city also boasts what residents say is the best community center in the Twin Cities. A focal point for community life, this facility includes a fitness center and library, skate park, and **Tropics Indoor Waterpark**, www.ci. shoreview.mn.us/CommunityCenter/CommunityCenter.html.

Major employers in the area include Deluxe Corporation, Medtronic, and Wells Fargo. Most students in Shoreview attend Mounds View schools, www.moundsviewschools.org; but the children in the southernmost part of the city are in the Roseville School District, www.isd623.org.

City of Shoreview, 4600 Victoria St N, Shoreview, 55126; 651-490-4600, www.ci.shoreview.mn.us

VADNAIS HEIGHTS

Boundaries: North: Hwy 96; **East**: Rice St; **West**: Centerville Rd; **South**: County Rd D; **Area**: 7.3 square miles; **Population**: 13,000

Because one-third of Vadnais Heights consists of lakes and wetlands, many of the neighborhoods of 1970s–'90s houses back up to open space, giving them a rural, end-of-the-road feel, even though they're only minutes from I-35E, I-694, and Highway 61. You will find duplexes, townhouses in the $200,000 range, apartments and condominiums here as well. The gem of Vadnais Heights' parkland is **Vadnais–Sucker Lake Regional Park**, which boasts 1200 acres of woods and lakes. Home for many years to numerous small truck farms, Vadnais Heights is now home to the Agricultural and Food Sciences Academy (www.agacademy.com), a charter school. Two public school districts serve this city: White Bear Area Schools (www.whitebear.k12.mn.us) and Mounds View (www.moundsviewschools.org).

City of Vadnais Heights, 800 East County Rd E, Vadnais Heights, 55127; 651-204-6000, www.ci.vadnais-heights.mn.us

WHITE BEAR LAKE

DELLWOOD

Boundaries: North: Hugo; **East**: Washington County (Mahtomedi); **South**: I-694; **West**: Centerville Rd; **Area**: 12 square miles; **Population**: 22,000

White Bear Lake has a racy past. A turn-of-the-century haven for wealthy families from St. Paul, it became a hideout for gangsters in the 1930s, and Zelda and Scott Fitzgerald boozed it up here during Prohibition. In fact, they created such a rumpus, they were asked to leave! Fitzgerald, a St. Paul native, is said to have used it as the setting for his story, *Winter Dreams*.

Following renovation in the 1990s, the pedestrian-friendly downtown looks more like Fitzgerald's turn-of-the century summer resort than ever. Ornate lamps and old-fashioned storefronts evoke images of those indolent years and invite visitors to linger and browse in the unique shops. (See **Shopping for the Home.**)

White Bear Lake is to the East Metro what Lake Minnetonka is to the West. Over the past 50 years this one-time summer resort has developed into a bedroom community with a mix of housing, from those that rival Summit Avenue's mansions to others that are modest and cottagey. The lakeshore is where you'll find the most lavish homes, and while the historic lakeside retreats designed by Cass Gilbert and other famous architects have been protected, other less famous houses have been razed and replaced. Back from the shore, White Bear Lake is also home to many tracts of 1960s split-levels and ramblers; about one-third of its housing is rental or multi-family. Though seemingly fully developed for a long time, several large redevelopments are in the works, including the redevelopment of entire blocks of the city.

Many newcomers, attracted by golf and sailing, choose to live close to the **Dellwood Golf Club** (www.dellwoodhillsgc.org) or the **White Bear Yacht Club** (www.wbyc.com), both of which are located in neighboring **Dellwood**, which is on the northeastern shore of White Bear Lake in Washington County (www.co.washington.mn.us/info_for_residents/communities/cities_townships/ city_of_dellwood). With a median income in excess of $130,000, Dellwood has the distinction of being the state's wealthiest city. Among its residents are members of some of the state's oldest families, as well as former governor Jesse Ventura. Strictly residential, there is no commercial property here except the golf club and apple orchard—not even a city hall! About half its homes are suburban in character and the rest are rural, including a number of farms.

Other lakeshore communities include **Mahtomedi** (see East Metro Suburbs/Washington County), **Birchwood** (http://birchwood.govoffice.com), and **White Bear Township** (www.ci.white-bear-township.mn.us), which is notable for its unique annual town meeting form of government, where residents vote on all issues including taxes and expenditures.

White Bear's early reputation as a health and recreation resort persists with relaxation and amusement still revolving around the water. The 2500-acre **White Bear Lake** is famous for its sailing and fishing. Within ten miles of White Bear there are five public golf courses, including **Manitou Ridge** (www.co.ramsey.mn.us/PARKS/golf/manitou_ridge.asp), which features long holes with panoramic views of the metropolitan area. Swimming beaches and two public launches are located at **White Bear Lake County Park**. White Bear is also home to the **Lakeshore Players** (www.lakeshoreplayers.com), the oldest continuously operating community theater in the state.

Children who live in White Bear attend School District #624 (www.white bear.k12.mn.us). School District #832 (www.mahtomedi.k12.mn.us) serves students from Dellwood. Post-secondary education is available nearby at Century College (www.century.mnscu.edu).

Unlike so many areas of the Twin Cities, White Bear has abundant transportation. The city is served by several major roads: I-35, I-694, State Highway

61, County Highway 96, and Highway 49. Its Lake Area Bus Line (612-373-3333, www.metrotransit.org) provides transportation between stops in Mahtomedi, Birchwood, White Bear Township, Vadnais Heights, and the City of White Bear Lake. During morning and evening commuter hours, the bus line also connects with Metro Transit buses at Maplewood Mall.

City of White Bear Lake, 4701 Hwy 61, White Bear Lake, 55110; 651-429-8526, www.whitebearlake.org

EAST METRO SUBURBS
WASHINGTON COUNTY

AFTON
COTTAGE GROVE
DELLWOOD (SEE P. 120)
FOREST LAKE
HUGO
LAKE ELMO/BAYTOWN TOWNSHIP
MAHTOMEDI/GRANT
OAKDALE
STILLWATER/MARINE ON ST. CROIX
WOODBURY

Boundaries: North: Chisago County; **West**: Ramsey County; **South**: Mississippi River; **East**: St. Croix River; **Area**: 424 square miles; **Population**: 201,000. It consists of six townships and 24 cities.

The projected growth for this county is staggering: a gain of 150,000 households by 2030. Hugo, for example, is expected to grow from a population of 4,000 to 25,000; Woodbury will quadruple from 20,000 to 84,000. Looking for places that are not expected to change so much? Try Afton, Dellwood, Lake St. Croix Beach, Landfall, and Lakeland Shores.

For a long time this has been one of the fastest growing counties in Minnesota. Ironically, it developed from farmland to suburb at breakneck speed not only because of its proximity to downtown St. Paul, but also because of its rural, open-to-the-skies landscape, of which nearly three-fourths was still vacant in 1990. That makes most of the housing here quite new, compared to the other close-in suburbs. The county is made up overwhelmingly of single-family and owner-occupied detached houses, though new townhomes are literally popping up everywhere. In fact, most new construction is multi-family. Older homes are generally set on expansive lots, necessary for private septic systems in a county that had limited access to the metropolitan sewer (MUSA) line until recently. The extension of the sewer line, however, has forced some cities such as Lake Elmo to accept more growth and higher population density than they had previously planned. In spite of all the new houses, these undulating hills, lakes, and forests are still home to hunting, horseback riding, biking, bird watching, and record-book fishing. There are even a few farms left. That said, very few of the county's residents work in agriculture, though many of them work at the small- and mid-sized medical and high-tech companies nearby, or at one of Minnesota's largest employers, 3M, which is headquartered in Maplewood.

One perennial complication of suburban sprawl is education: Keep in mind that attendance boundaries are sometimes redrawn as populations change.

With 83 miles of frontage on the **St. Croix National Scenic Riverway** and the Mississippi River, as well as over 4000 acres of parks, Washington County offers opportunities for diverse experiences: boating; scuba diving in the clear waters of **Square Lake**; and horseback riding at **Lake Elmo Park Reserve**, to name just three. In addition to county and regional parks, Washington County also has two state parks, **William O'Brien** and **Afton**, as well as a portion of the **Gateway State Trail**.

Washington County Government Center: 14949 62nd St N, Stillwater, 55082-0006; 651-430-6000, TTY 651-430-6246; www.co.washington.mn.us; **Washington County License and Service Centers**: open weekdays and Saturdays until noon: Forest Lake License Center, Northland Mall, 651-430-8280; Stillwater License Center, Valley Ridge, 651-430-6176; Woodbury License Center/Washington County Service Center, 2150 Radio Dr, Woodbury, 651-275-8600

Washington County Law Enforcement Center: 15015 62nd St N, Stillwater, 55082-3801, non-emergency telephone 651-439-9381

Fire: each city contracts for its own fire protection, often with volunteer fire departments

Hospital: Lakeview Hospital, 927 West Churchill St, Stillwater, 651-439-5330, www.lakeview.org

Washington County Library System: www.co.washington.mn.us/info_for_residents/library

Community Resources: *Historic Courthouse,* 101 West Pine St, Stillwater; *Washington County Fairgrounds,* Lake Elmo, is host to numerous dog shows and horse shows; equestrian center, www.washingtoncountyfair.org.

Community Publications: St. Paul Pioneer Press, www.twincities.com

Parks: www.co.washington.mn.us/info_for_residents/parks_division; Cottage Grove Ravine Regional Park; Hardwood Creek Trail; Lake Elmo Park Reserve; Pine Point Regional Park; Square Lake Park

Public Transportation: 612-373-3333, www.metrotransit.org

AFTON

Boundaries: North: I-94; **West**: Hwy 18 (formerly Hwy 95); **South**: 60th St; **East**: St. Croix River; **Area**: 36 square miles; **Population**: 2800

If you dream of living in a small village, Afton may be the spot for you. It's the best of all worlds—friendly neighbors, a broad range of housing styles set in a village-like atmosphere, and only a 30-minute commute to St. Paul. The charm here is natural: the St. Croix River, the lush floodplain forest, the rolling fields and country meadows. Like the song, "Roll on Sweet Afton," it's enough to make your heart sing.

Afton's small business district lines Highway 21 (St. Croix Trail). There are no shopping centers, no strip malls, just marinas, restaurants, ice cream parlors, and other small shops, many housed in buildings left over from the 19th century. New development is being carefully planned to preserve the area's rural feeling. Five-acre lots are the minimum and all subdivisions are required to have contiguous open space. Because of this, Afton's population is expected to grow by only about 500 people by 2030.

Afton is a major recreation area, offering the **Afton Alps Golf and Ski Area**, 651-436-1320, one of the largest ski hills in Minnesota, and **Afton State Park**, 651-436-5391, located along the St. Croix River flyway—a great place to hike, camp, and watch hawks, bald eagles, and other birds of prey.

Web Site: Afton City Hall, 3033 S St. Croix Trail, 651-436-5090, www.cityof afton.net (office hours 9 a.m.–2:30 p.m. Monday–Thursday)
Area Code: 651
Zip Code: 55001
Post Office: 30333 St. Croix Trail
Police Non-emergency: Washington County, 651-439-9381
Fire Non-emergency: Lower St. Croix Volunteer Fire Department, 651-436-7033
Hospital: Lakeview Hospital, 927 W Churchill St, Stillwater, 651-439-5330, www.lakeview.org
Schools: South Washington County District #833, 651-458-6300; Stillwater District #834, 651-351-8340

COTTAGE GROVE

Boundaries: North: Woodbury; **West:** St. Paul Park and Grey Cloud Township; **South:** Mississippi River; **East:** Hwy 95 (Manning); **Area:** 34.6 square miles; **Population:** 32,000

Cottage Grove is said to be the birthplace of Minnesota agriculture, and a few descendants of the original settlers still farm here. Early surviving landmarks include two "old villages"—Old Langdon School Village, at Jamaica Avenue and West Point Douglas Road, and Old Cottage Grove, at 70th and Lamar—that date back to the 1850s.

Cottage Grove was a quiet place until the 1960s, when Orrin Thompson Homes started the bedroom-community development that brought the population to nearly 30,000 by 1999. Those original houses sold in the 1960s and '70s for as little as $10,000; now they sell for twenty times that, but given the cost of housing in the Twin Cities, they still qualify as good starter homes. Recent construction, however, tends to be much more pricey. And if you decide to move here, expect to see a lot of new building! The expansion of the MUSA (sewer) line will open vast stretches of Cottage Grove's land to development, nearly doubling the city's population by 2030.

While the fertile soil sustains working farms in Cottage Grove, it is the Mississippi and St. Croix River scenery that is attracting new residents. The river valleys also provide space in which to hike, ski, and ride horses. **River Oaks Municipal Golf Course** boasts splendid views of the Mississippi River. Most commercial development in Cottage Grove is in the downtown portion of the city along Highway 61, where you'll find Rainbow Foods, Cub Foods, Snyder Drug, Kmart, and Target. 3M is among the city's largest employers.

Web Site: www.cottage-grove.org
Area Code: 651
Zip Code: 55016
Post Office: 7130 E Point Douglas Rd
City Hall: 7516 80th St S, Cottage Grove, 651-458-2800, TDD 651-458-2897
Police Non-emergency: 651-458-2811
Fire Non-emergency: 651-458-2809
Hospital: United, 333 N Smith Ave, St. Paul, 651-241-8000; Woodwinds Health Campus, 1925 Woodwinds Dr, Woodbury, 651-232-6880, www.healtheast.org
School: South Washington County District #833, 651-458-6300, www.sowashco.k12.mn.us
Public Transportation: 612-373-3333, www.metrotransit.org; express buses run to downtown St. Paul. Park & Ride lots are on Hwy 61.

FOREST LAKE

Boundaries: North: 240th St N; **West**: Anoka County; **South**: 180th St N; **East**: New Scandia; **Area**: 36 square miles; **Population**: 16,000

Forest Lake used to be considered "Up North" but now, since it's less than thirty miles from the Twin Cities, it has come to be viewed as a reasonable commute. Located just north of the point at which I-35 splits into 35W (heading for Minneapolis) and 35E (heading for St. Paul), it has easy access to both cities. A fast-growing community, it spreads over parts of Washington, Anoka, and Chisago counties. The City of Forest Lake serves as the hub for the area, with shopping malls, major grocery chains, churches, a radio station, and a newspaper, the *Forest Lake Times* (www.forestlaketimes.com).

Another city whose population is expected to double by 2030, it is designated as a "developing community" (higher density housing) in its southwestern corner, where the MUSA (sewer) line has been extended, and "diversified rural" (one house per ten acres) in the east. Homebuilders have a wide variety of choices, including city lots or rural acreage, lake homes, hobby farms, or estates. Prices are generally lower than they would be for properties closer to the Cities.

A quick peek at the city's calendar of events shows that there's always something to do here—Fourth of July parade, ice fishing contest, Chamber of

Commerce Golf Tournament, water sports on Forest Lake, as well as hunting, fishing and cross-country skiing in 23,800-acre **Carlos Avery Wildlife Management Area**, www.dnr.state.mn.us. Downhill skiing is close by at **Wild Mountain** at Taylors Falls, 651-465-6315, 800-447-4958, www.wild mountain.com, and at **Trollhagen** in Dresser, Wisconsin, 800-826-7166.

Area Code: 651
Zip Code: 55025
Post Office: 78 6th Ave SW
Forest Lake City Hall: 220 N Lake St, 651-464-3550, http://www.ci. forest-lake.mn.us
Police Non-emergency: 651-464-5877; after 4:30 and weekends, 651-439-9381
Fire Non-emergency: 220 N Lake St, 651-464-2244
Hospital: Fairview Lakes Regional Medical Center, 5200 Fairview Blvd, Wyoming, 55092, 651-982-7000, www.fairview.org
Library: 220 N Lake St, 651-464-4088
School: Forest Lake Area District #831, 651-982-8100
Public Transportation: 612-373-3333, www.metrotransit.org; very limited

HUGO

Boundaries: North: 180th St; **West**: Elmcrest; **South**: 120th St; **East**: Keystone; **Area**: 36 square miles; **Population**: 9000

While Hugo may or may not be named for French writer Victor Hugo, this rural community located fifteen miles north of St. Paul is still one of the fastest-growing cities in Washington County, expected to reach a population of 24,000 by 2030.

The lakes and fields have historically attracted outdoorsmen, hunters and fishermen, and horse and cattle ranchers. To preserve the country look, the city has adopted policies that encourage cluster housing and field preservation. Post-MUSA (sewer) zoning designates the highest density for the west side of the city, and one house per ten acres on the east side. Most development at this time is occurring in the southwest corner, near the freeway, with builders emphasizing master-planned communities that feature open space, multi-housing, and amenities such as pools. Most of the housing is for sale; rentals are scarce. New housing is weighted about 2-to-1 multi-family units over single-family homes. Most older homes are single-family detached, largely owner-occupied, and have been built since 1970. By metro standards, Hugo's housing is considered affordable and therefore attractive to young families. There are also executive-level developments, particularly around Bald Eagle Lake. Municipal sewer and water service are only available in the southwest quadrant of the city at this time. The entire sewer project is due to be completed by 2020.

Hugo's children are split among four school districts. Forest Lake District 831 serves the north; White Bear Lake District 624, the southwest; Mahtomedi District 832, the south central; and Stillwater District 834 serves the southeast corner. You can download a map of the school districts' attendance areas off the City of Hugo web site.

As for shopping, the downtown has the basic necessities, a hardware store, and several restaurants. Major retail stores are located nearby in White Bear Lake and Forest Lake. And a downtown redesign is in the works, with a new park on Egg Lake as its focal point. Other plans include senior housing and a more high-profile life for historic buildings such as the old feed mill.

Web Site: www.ci.hugo.mn.us
Area Code: 651
Zip Code: 55038
Post Office: 5615 150th St
City Hall: 14669 Fitzgerald Ave North, Hugo, 55038; 651-762-6300
Police Non-emergency: Washington County, 15015 62nd St N, Stillwater, 651-439-9381
Fire Non-emergency: 5323 140th St N, Hugo, 651-429-6366
Hospitals: HealthEast St. John's Hospital, 1575 Beam Ave, Maplewood, 651-232-7000, www.healtheast.org; Fairview Lakes Regional Medical Center, 5200 Fairview Blvd, Wyoming, 55092, 651-982-7000, www.fairview.org
Schools: Forest Lake District #831, 651-982-8100; Mahtomedi District #832, 651-407-2000; Stillwater District #834, 651-351-8340; White Bear Lake District #624, 651-415-5657
Parks: Bruce Vento–Hardwoods Creek Regional Trail; Paul Hugo Farm Wildlife Management Area, www.dnr.state.mn.us.
Community Resources: Hugo Animal Farm, www.hugoanimalfarm.com, offers a taste of farm and country life through tours and hayrides.
Community Publications: *Neighborhood News & Report*, www.your neighborhoodnews.net; *The Hugonian*, www.hugonian.com
Public Transportation: Peak-only express bus service

LAKE ELMO

BAYTOWN TOWNSHIP

Boundaries: North: Hwy 36; **West**: Ideal Avenue and Oakdale; **South**: I-94; **East**: Manning; **Area**: 26 square miles; **Population**: 7700

Lake Elmo and its neighbor Baytown Township are either an egregious example of urban sprawl or sublime havens that preserve the rural lifestyle, depending on how you look at large houses spaced far apart on acreage. Things are changing, however. **Baytown**, where most of the houses have been built since 1990, had grown from a population of under a thousand in 1990 to 1500 in 2000, and is expected to reach 3400 by 2030. In Lake Elmo, where land-use ordinances tried to preserve the city's rural character by requiring 50% of the land to be set aside as permanent open space, the city has been forced by the advent of sewer service to allow higher density homes and businesses to be built in the southern section of the city along Interstate Highway 94.

Water contamination has become another issue in the area. Perfluoro-chemicals (PFCs) and trichloroethylene (TCE) have been detected in water in Lake Elmo, Baytown, and West Lakeland townships. The largest concentration of TCE appears to be under the Lake Elmo airport, and is spreading eastward toward the St. Croix River—and nobody knows where's it's coming from. A different kind of contamination, PCFs, has been detected in wells south of Highway 6 in an area centering on Inwood Avenue. That source has been identified—an old landfill—and cleanup is under way. In the meantime, private wells in several areas have been sealed and municipal water has been extended to some of the neighborhoods in Lake Elmo. In Baytown/West Lakeland townships, older homes that still depend on wells have been fitted with whole-house granular activated carbon (GAC) filter systems, and new developments are required to provide water from a deeper aquifer that has not been contaminated. Download a copy of the Baytown/West Lakeland Townships Special Well Construction Area from the Minnesota Department of Health web site, www.health.state.mn.us/divs/eh/wells/baytownmap.html.

Lake Elmo, long a leader in encouraging housing development designed to preserve its rich landscape of prairies, woodlands, open water, and swamps, is home to several "conservation" developments. Its **Fields of St. Croix** development on Highway 5, between the Washington County Fairgrounds and Stillwater High School, was built in the 1990s, but is still considered one of the most successful cluster housing conservation communities in the country.

Three school districts serve Lake Elmo, but an elementary school and a junior high school are within the city limits. City park facilities include baseball fields, skating rinks, and playgrounds. **Lake Elmo Park Reserve**'s two-acre chlorinated swimming pond is a family favorite with a sandy bottom and gradual drop-off. The state record tiger muskie was caught in Lake Elmo in 1999. Several parks allow deer hunting.

Web Site: www.lakeelmo.org
Area Code: 651
Zip Code: 55042
Post Office: 3469 Lake Elmo Ave
City Hall: Lake Elmo, 3800 Laverne Ave N, 651-777-5510; Baytown Township, 4220 Osgood Ave N, Stillwater, 55082, 651-430-4992
Police Non-emergency: Washington County, 651-439-9381
Lake Elmo Volunteer Fire Department Non-emergency: 3510 Laverne Ave, 651-770-5006
Baytown Fire Service: supplied by Bayport Fire Department, 651-439-6992
Schools: Stillwater District #834, 651-351-8340; Mahtomedi District #832, 651-407-2000; Maplewood–North St. Paul–Oakdale District #622, 651-748-7622
Hospital: Lakeview Hospital, 927 West Churchill St, Stillwater, 651-439-5330, www.lakeview.org
Parks: Lake Elmo Park Reserve; Star Trail snowmobile trail, www.startrail.org/maps.html; Demontreville Wildlife Area

Community Resources: Ramsey Center for the Arts, 3585 Laverne Ave, 651-486-4883, RamseyCFA.org; The Children's Farm School, 651-439-7745, www.childrensfarm.org; Animal Inn dog training facility, Hwy 5, 1 mile east of 694, 651-777-2317, www.animalinnboardingkennel.com.

Public Transportation: 612-373-3333, www.metrotransit.org; express buses go to downtown St. Paul; service is available along Hwy 5 to Stillwater and Oakdale

MAHTOMEDI

GRANT

Boundaries: North: Dellwood and Grant; **West**: Hwy 120; area: **South**: I-694 and Pine Springs; **East**: Ideal Ave; **Area**: 2500 acres; **Population**: 8000

Mahtomedi (pronounced "Ma Toe Mee Die") is a turn-of-the-century resort town on the east shore of White Bear Lake. With its streetcar line and amusement park, it was to St. Paul what Excelsior was to Minneapolis: a summer resort for escapees from the heat of the cities. But the merry-makers had such a good time dancing in the pavilion that they decided to winterize their cottages and stay year 'round. A few of the old buildings are still standing.

Their presence has preserved Mahtomedi's summer resort ambiance despite the rapid growth and development that took place in the 1970s. Because the whole city has municipal sewer and water, it is fully built out, though it is expected to reach a population of 9200 by 2030, due mostly to in-fill construction of townhomes and condominiums. Some residential developments are centered on small parks.

The City of **Grant** calls itself "A Home in the Country," and it is. Located just east of Mahtomedi and west of Stillwater, a mile from the Highway 36–I-94 interchange, most of its 17,000 acres are agricultural, with a few commercial farms and a lot of hobby farms. The minimum lot size is five acres. With good access to the **Gateway Trail**—and neighbors who won't complain about animal smells—it is a great place to have a horse.

Area Code: 651
Zip Code: 55115, 55090
Post Office: 2223 Fifth St, White Bear Lake
City Hall: Mahtomedi: 600 Stillwater Rd, 651-426-3344, www.ci.Mahtomedi.mn.us; Grant, 11 Wildwood Rd, Willernie, 55090, 651-426-3383, www.ci.grant.mn.us
Police Non-emergency: Washington County, 651-439-9381
Fire non-emergency: Call City Hall, 651-426-3344
School: Mahtomedi District #832, 651-407-2000; Stillwater District #834, 651-351-8340
Library: Wildwood Branch/South Washington County Library System, 651-426-2042, www.co.washington.mn.us/info_for_residents/library
Hospital: HealthEast St. John's, 1575 Beam Ave, Maplewood, 651-232-7000, www.healtheast.org

Parks: Gateway Trail; parks and beaches on White Bear Lake
Public Transportation: 612-373-3333, www.metrotransit.org; buses
   travel along Hwy 120 to Century College and Sunray Transit Hub

OAKDALE

Boundaries: North: I-694; **West**: Geneva Ave (also known as Trunk Hwy 120
and Century Ave); **South**: I-94; **East**: Lake Elmo; **Area**: 11.1 square miles;
Population: 27,500

Ten minutes east of St. Paul, along both I-94 and I-694, this city near 3M's headquarters was among the fastest-growing municipalities in the metropolitan
area during the 1990s. Now, with about 8000 owner-occupied properties, and
2000 rental units, the city is essentially fully developed, but it still retains something of a small-town feel. Neighborhoods include snug ramblers laid out on
suburban-style curbless streets, and plenty of children. In fact, nearly a third of
the population is under the age of 18.

Web Site: www.ci.oakdale.mn.us
Area Code: 651
Zip Code: 55128
Post Office: 1175 Gershwin Ave
City Hall: 1584 Hadley Ave N, 651-739-5086
Police Non-emergency: 1584 Hadley Ave N, 651-738-1022
Fire Non-emergency: 651-739-5086
Library: 1010 Heron Ave N, 651-730-0504
Hospital: HealthEast St. John's, 1575 Beam Ave, Maplewood, 651-232-7000,
   www.healtheast.org
School: District #622 Maplewood–North St. Paul–Oakdale, 651-748-7622
Community Publication: *Oakdale/Lake Elmo Review*, 651-777-8800
Parks: Tanners Lake; Oakdale Park Nature Center; Richard Walton Park
Community Resources: Marcus Ultrascreen (3-story screen) Cinema, 5677
   Hadley Ave; Globe College, 7166 10th St North, www.globecollege.com
Public Transportation: 612-373-3333, www.metrotransit.org; buses
   travel along Stillwater Blvd, Hadley, 10th St, and Century

STILLWATER

MARINE ON ST. CROIX

Boundaries: North: Hwy 96; **West**: Manning; **East**: St. Croix River; **South**:
Hwy 36; **Area**: 7 square miles (the Stillwater vicinity encompasses a much
larger area); **Population**: 17,000

On the way to **Stillwater** via Highway 36, you'll pass fast-food joints, chain
stores, and innumerable cul-de-sac developments. Who would guess that at
the end of the four-lane highway lies an entire town that is on the National

Register of Historic Places—Victorian "painted ladies," with cupolas, gazebos, leaded glass windows and all.

This old lumber town, which bills itself as the birthplace of Minnesota, celebrates its 19th-century past with antique shops, romantic bed and breakfasts, Lumberjack Days, and paddle-wheeling up and down the St. Croix. But be advised, if it's one of the old houses you want you'll probably have to get in line. Tourists are always knocking on residents' doors saying, "If you ever want to sell. . . ."

Fortunately, there are a lot of other not-quite-so-old homes on Stillwater's streets, though the number of rental and affordable housing units, both in town and farther out, continues to decline, and in 2006 the average home price was about $350,000.

Newer construction includes everything from 1970s houses built on pleasant culs-de-sac to brand-new luxury condos in the heart of downtown, www.stillwatermills.com. Other new developments include "New Urbanist" developments such as **Liberty on the Lake**, off Highway 36, which has houses built in styles that reference the older homes of Stillwater; and **The Fields of St. Croix**, near the high school, which has a distinct New England feel.

Local sporting events and cultural opportunities are well attended by area residents, and the Stillwater high school orchestra has been ranked #1 in the state; and then there is football . . .

Twelve miles upriver from Stillwater, there is another historic town, **Marine on St. Croix**, founded in 1839, and site of the first commercial sawmill along the St. Croix River. This village is one of the few places in the Midwest where the word "quaint" seems to apply. The 1872 jail has been preserved and turned into a museum. Other historic buildings, the 1870 General Store and 1888 Village Hall, are still in use for their original purposes. In fact, the village hall is the oldest village hall in the state still being used for governmental purposes—and it can be rented for weddings. Yet even Marine is not without more modern development—albeit development that is still in touch with the past. **Jackson Meadow** (www.jacksonmeadow.com), the village's new neighborhood is a 336-acre conservation development that features 64 simple white frame custom homes clustered near the road like an old-fashioned village. All together, the houses only take up 30% of the land, leaving the remaining 230 acres in woods and open prairie. All the houses have been designed by Duluth architect David Salmela, who received the 2005 American Institute of Architects Honor Award for Regional and Urban Design for his work on the project.

Marine is a great place to go for a Sunday afternoon or weekend. The 1856 **Asa Parker House** bed and breakfast, 651-433-5248, is within walking distance of both **William O'Brien State Park** and the **Marine Landing**.

Web Site: www.ci.stillwater.mn.us
Area Code: 651
Zip Codes: 55082, 55083, 55407 (Marine on St. Croix)
Post Office: 102 3rd St N
City Hall: 216 N Fourth St, 651-430-8800

Marine on St. Croix City Hall: 121 Judd St, 651-433-3636, http://marine. govoffice.com (Office Hours: Mon–Thurs 8:00 a.m.–4:30 p.m.)

Police Non-Emergency: Washington County Law Enforcement Center, 15015 62nd St N, 651-351-4900

Fire: Emergency only, 911

Hospital: Lakeview Hospital, 927 West Churchill St, 651-439-5330, www.lakeview.org

School: Stillwater District #834, 651-351-8340

Library: 223 N Fourth St, 651-439-1675; Marine on St. Croix Village Hall, 651-433-2820

Community Publications: *Stillwater Courier News* (weekly), 651-439-4366; *Stillwater Gazette* (daily), 651-439-3130, www.stillwatergazette.com

Community Resources: Washington County Historic Courthouse; Minnesota Zephyr historic dining train, www.minnesotazephyr.com; numerous bed-and-breakfasts, www.ilovestillwater.com; Lumberjack Days, www.lumberjackdays.com; historic buildings in Marine on St. Croix; Marine Restoration Society

Stillwater License Center: Valley Ridge shopping center, 651-430-6176; driver's license tests: written test, Wednesdays only; road tests by appointment, 651-639-4058.

Parks: Gateway Trail; Lowell Park and Pioneer Park are popular places to take wedding photographs and have reservable parking; William O'Brien State Park

Public Transportation: MetroTransit, 612-373-3333, www.metrotransit. org: express buses from Stillwater to St. Paul; buses travel along Hwy 5/Stillwater Blvd, Pine St, 4th St, Curve Crest; Park & Ride, County Rd 5 at Orleans St

WOODBURY

Boundaries: North: I-94; **West**: I-494, I-694; **South**, Cottage Grove; **East**: St. Croix River; **Area**: 36 square miles; **Population**: 50,000

If you've lived in Woodbury for ten years, you're an old-timer; and if you've lived here since the late 1970s, when the first developer struck out across the farm fields, you can call yourself a founding father, or mother.

Since the 1970s, when the upscale **Evergreen** development was built to lure 3M executives over from Maplewood, Woodbury, located a mile southeast of St. Paul, has been transformed from a sleepy rural township into Minnesota's fastest growing city, and is expected to grow to a population of 84,000 by 2030. In 2005, Woodbury ranked No. 1 on *Money Magazine*'s list of the most desirable places to live in the Central United States for cities under 100,000 in population.

Development is ongoing, with active projects that are almost exclusively large, multi-phased master-planned communities. It is the city's goal to provide flexible housing options that will enable citizens to live here throughout their lives. Consequently, housing runs the gamut from rental apartments and townhomes to large-lot estates, and includes hard-to-find three- or four-bedroom apartments. Woodbury does not have an established downtown, but it is creating one in the area surrounding City Hall, along Pioneer Road and Valley Creek Road. There they have connected the Southeast Area YMCA at one end and the Washington County library at the other, through an indoor park. Called Central Park, it includes "Lookout Ridge," a children's interactive playground, and is home to School District 833's Early Childhood Family Education program.

Interestingly, for a city that already has 38 parks, 2800 acres of dedicated parkland, and 75 miles of trails, voters in 2005 overwhelmingly approved a referendum for the city to purchase and preserve even more open space. Woodbury's population growth was touched off by a parallel explosion in jobs. Major employers include 3M, State Farm Insurance, The Hartford, TARGET.DIRECT, and other high tech and manufacturing companies. Combined, these companies have made Woodbury into a place where you can both live and work—unusual in a region where so many experience long commutes.

Web Site: www.ci.woodbury.mn.us
Area Code: 651
Zip Codes: 55125, 55129
Post Office: 7595 Currell Blvd
City Hall: 8301 Valley Creek Rd, 651-714-3500; License Center: 2150 Radio Dr, 651-275-8600; renew a Minnesota driver's license here or purchase automobile tags, but if you're moving from another state, you must take a written test administered in Stillwater on Wednesdays; call 651-430-6176. The test is also administered at the license substation at 1600 University Ave in St. Paul, 651-642-0808.
Police: Woodbury Public Safety, Non-emergency, 651-739-4141
Fire: Non-emergency, 651-714-3700
Hospital: Woodwinds Health Campus, 1925 Woodwinds Dr, Woodbury, 651-232-6880, www.healtheast.org
Library: Washington County Library–Woodbury Branch, 8595 Central Park Pl, Woodbury, 651-731-1320, www.co.washington.mn.us/info_for_residents/library
Schools: South Washington County District #833, 651-458-6300, www.sowashco.k12.mn.us; Stillwater District #834, 651-351-8340, www.stillwater.k12.mn.us; North St. Paul/Maplewood/Oakdale District #622, 651-748-7622, www.isd622.org
Community Publications: *The Woodbury Bulletin*, 651-730-4007; *Woodbury/Maplewood Review*, 651-777-8800
Public Transportation: MetroTransit, 612-373-3333, www.metrotransit.org

WESTERN WISCONSIN

Living in Western Wisconsin appeals to those who want to live in the country but still have access to the Twin Cities. It is considered a reasonable commute for those who work in the East Metro: Somerset is 27 miles from 3M, in Maplewood, and the popular Troy Burne area, south of Hudson, is 18. Hudson, itself, is twenty minutes from downtown St. Paul.

Though Minnesotans make fun of Wisconsin, with its cheeseheads and fiendish native sons like Jeffrey Dahmer, Twin Citians are pulling up stakes and relocating to Pierce, Polk, and St. Croix counties as fast as they can sign with a builder.

There are lots of reasons. For one: Wisconsin is beautiful. With rolling hills and vast stretches of green grass and trees, it's pure eye candy. Then there are the wholesome small towns, straight out of central casting. Finally, there are the prices. At least for now, you can get a three-acre lot in Wisconsin for much less than you'd have to pay for a half-acre lot in Minnesota.

So what will it be like in five years? The bridges over the St. Croix River (the dividing line between the two states) are key. Already the Vertical Lift Bridge between Stillwater and Houlton, Wisconsin, and the I-94 freeway bridge between Woodbury and Hudson carry thousands of commuters across the river every day. As Wisconsin Highway 64 is upgraded to four lanes, and if (when) plans go through to build another bridge south of downtown Stillwater linking Minnesota highways 36 and 95 with Wisconsin highways 35 and 64, it can only be imagined how many Twin Citians will suddenly find it feasible to live there.

As in any place that is transitioning from agricultural to residential, most people who move here will have to have their own wells, contract for heating oil, and maintain their own septic systems. (For well and septic system information, see the **Getting Settled** chapter.) Because of the need for septic systems, many townships have a 3-acre or more minimum lot size. Look online at the University of Minnesota extension service web site for suggestions for making septic systems blend in: www.extension.umn.edu/distribution/horticulture/DG6986.html and www.extension.umn.edu/info-u/plants/BG442.html.

Heating is another issue. While houses "in town" might have access to natural gas, most homeowners in the country heat with propane. Buy before winter on contract, to lock in the price. While consumption will depend on many factors, such as insulation and whether heat is turned up during the day, expect a three-bedroom house to use at least 1200 gallons each winter.

Childcare is generally offered in the same level of facilities as in Minnesota, but is about $50 per week cheaper for one child. For information about schools, see the **Childcare and Education** chapter. Both Hudson and Stillwater offer all the usual activities for children—gymnastics, dance, skating, art, basketball, and hockey, etc. The downside, of course, is the drive.

ST. CROIX COUNTY

HUDSON
SOMERSET
RIVER FALLS

Boundaries: North: Polk County; **West**: St. Croix River; **South**: Pierce County. **East**: Dunn County; **Area**: 722 square miles; **Population**: 73,400

St. Croix County, which includes Somerset, Hudson, and parts of River Falls, is just over the state line (the St. Croix River) on I-94. It is already the fastest growing county in Wisconsin, and one of the 100 fastest growing counties in the nation. Its county seat is Hudson.

St. Croix County Government Center: 1101 Carmichael Rd, Hudson, 54016-0000, 715-386-4600, www.co.saint-croix.wi.us
Emergency Hospital: Hudson Hospital, 405 Stageline Rd, Hudson, 54016, 715-531-6000, www.hudsonhospital.org; River Falls Area Hospital, 1629 E Division St, River Falls, 715-425-6155, www.allina.com/ahs/riverfalls.nsf
Police: St. Croix County Sheriff, 1101 Carmichael Rd, Hudson; Emergency, 911; Non-emergency, 715-381-4320
Parks: www.co.saint-croix.wi.us/Departments/CountyPark/; Willow River State Park, 5 miles east of Hudson, offers beautiful scenery, camping, picnic grounds, nature trails, and winter cross-country ski trails.
Community Resources: For tourist information for the entire St. Croix River Valley, visit www.saintcroixriver.com.
Public Transportation: 612-373-3333, www.MetroTransit.org: the bus system can also be accessed at Guardian Angels Park & Ride at I-94 and Inwood Rd in Woodbury. The Stillwater Park & Ride is off Highway 5 near Orleans Street.

HUDSON

Hudson, with its marina and picturesque Victorian houses, is one of the prettiest towns on the St. Croix river.

Many who move here first came to play golf. There are five golf courses nearby: **Troy Burne** (www.troyburne.com), **Clifton Hollows** (800-487-8879), **Clifton Highlands** (www.cliftonhighlands.com), **Kilkarney Hills** (www.kilkarneyhills.com), and **River Falls Golf Club** (www.riverfalls golfclub.com). Greens fees at the other courses are among the lowest in the metro area ($25–$35). The locals' favorite: Clifton Highlands. Municipal water/sewer service is available within the city limits of the City of Hudson and the Village of North Hudson.

City of Hudson, 505 3rd St, Hudson, 54016, 715-386-4765, www.ci.hudson.wi.us

SOMERSET

Somerset, founded in 1856, has been known in more recent times for tubing on the Apple River, outdoor summer rock concerts, and camping. One of the fastest growing areas in the fastest growing county in Wisconsin, it is an affluent area being built out by established Twin Cities builders.

Village of Somerset, 110 Spring St; PO Box 356; Somerset, 54025, 715-247-3395, www.vil.somerset.wi.us

RIVER FALLS

Thirty miles east of Minneapolis and St. Paul, this college town is home to the University of Wisconsin–River Falls. Many commute from here to the eastern metro.

Rich with recreational activities, you'll find some of the best trout fishing in the Midwest right in the middle of downtown.

Another highlight: the Kansas City Chiefs football team holds its summer training camp here, www.uwrf.edu/chiefs.

City of River Falls, 123 E Elm St, River Falls, 54022, 715-425-0900, www.rfcity.org

PIERCE AND POLK COUNTIES

Though not profiled in this book, Pierce (south of Hudson) and Polk (north of Hudson) counties are both starting to grow with Twin Cities commuters. For information about them, look on their web sites:

Polk County, Wisconsin
County Courthouse
100 Polk County Plaza, Suite 170
Balsam Lake, WI 54810-9082
715-485-9226
www.co.polk.wi.us

Pierce County, Wisconsin
County Courthouse
414 West Main Street
Ellsworth, WI 54011-0119
715-273-3531
www.co.pierce.wi.us

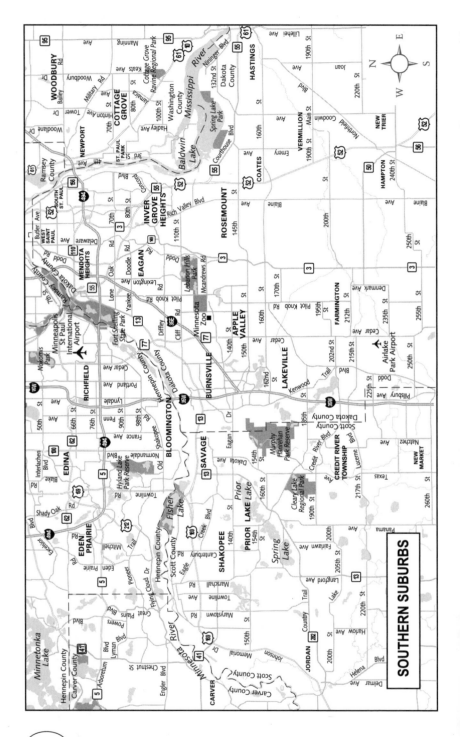

SOUTHERN SUBURBS

SOUTH METRO SUBURBS
DAKOTA COUNTY

APPLE VALLEY
BURNSVILLE
EAGAN
FARMINGTON
INVER GROVE HEIGHTS
LAKEVILLE
MENDOTA HEIGHTS
ROSEMOUNT
SOUTH ST. PAUL

Boundaries: North: Minnesota River; **East**: Mississippi River; **West**: Scott County; **South**: Goodhue, Rice counties; **Area:** 593 square miles; **Population**: 380,000; projected: 413,510 (2010), 504,270 (2030)

Just across the river from Minneapolis and St. Paul, Dakota County feels far away from the hustle and bustle—at least in some places. One-third suburban and two-thirds rural—and hoping to stay that way, it offers residents a wide variety of bedroom communities ranging from intensely urban Burnsville and Apple Valley, to rural Vermillion, collegiate Northfield, and small town Hastings, the county seat. As is the case all over the Twin Cities, it's all about growth. The county had a population of 275,000 in 1990, and by 2005 was already pushing 380,000. Much of the growth has occurred in Lakeville, Rosemount, and Farmington, which have easy access to the rest of the metro via I-35 and Highway 52.

The word "easy," in this case, means easy to get onto the highways, not necessarily easy to get somewhere. For example, the 13-mile trip on I-35W from Burnsville (the northernmost of Dakota County's cities) to Best Buy's headquarters on I-494 in Richfield can take anywhere from 20 minutes to more than an hour. Problems are the result of insufficient highway capacity, congestion-causing interchanges and rush-hour carpool lanes that are often half empty because most commuters in this automobile-centered county go solo. The Minnesota Department of Transportation (MNDOT) says that it will be at least 20 years before it can undertake necessary improvements, though it has discussed the possibility of turning I-35's carpool lanes into toll lanes for solo drivers. (See MN-PASS in the **Transportation** chapter to see how this system works.) In the meantime, there is commuter bus service from Apple Valley, Burnsville, Eagan, and Rosemount. The county is also studying the feasibility of providing commuter rail on existing railroad tracks from Hastings, through Saint Paul and into Minneapolis. This proposed line is known as the Red Rock Corridor, and you can download information about it from the county's web site.

In other transportation-related news, a new north-south runway was put into service at Minneapolis–St. Paul International Airport in October 2005. Approximately 37% of departing flights and 17% of arrivals use this new runway. While residents of Minneapolis have felt some relief from their overhead noise, the new flight path now impacts Eagan, Apple Valley, Lakeville, Farmington, Burnsville, Inver Grove Heights, Sunfish Lake, and Rosemount in Dakota County, as well as parts of Bloomington along the Minnesota River bluffs that had no noise before and now have 65-decibel (very loud) noise levels. The runway's opening coincided with a lawsuit brought by the cities of Minneapolis, Eagan, Bloomington, and Richfield claiming that the Metropolitan Airports Commission (MAC) is not providing the noise mitigation it promised. For information about the MAC's noise abatement programs, look online at www.macnoise.com.

In recent years Dakota County has attracted the attention of national developers such as Toll Brothers, who have purchased thousands of homesites and put pressure on property owners to sell increasingly more ecologically fragile lands. To combat this, the county has developed a program that pays landowners for agreeing not to subdivide their land. It is hoped that, in this way, some Dakota County farmers will be able to keep farming, and that nearly 80,000 acres with cultural, ecological, or historical significance will be preserved. So far, this program has been used to preserve **Pilot Knob** (see Mendota Heights below), the **Caponi Art Park** in Eagan, and **Wiklund Wildlife Preserve** in Rosemount. The county's long-range goal is to create contiguous areas of protected properties. Hence the Caponi project is part of a proposed greenway that will eventually link Eagan City Hall with **Lebanon Hills Park**, about three miles away. With a diverse natural landscape that includes lakes, rivers, bluffs, wooded hillsides, and prairies, Dakota County offers particularly high quality recreation opportunities. It also offers jobs. Job growth in Dakota County is consistently better than the state and the national rates, and the county is expected to have 214,150 jobs by 2030, compared with 148,261 in 2000.

For the latest update on home styles, pricing, and where developments are being built in Dakota County, check out the Builders Association of the Twin Cities Parade of Homes, www.paradeofhomes.org.

Dakota County Government Center: 1590 Hwy 55, Hastings, 55033-2372, 651-438-4418, www.co.dakota.mn.us
Service Centers: Dakota County Western Service Center, 14955 Galaxie Ave, Apple Valley, 55124, 952-891-7570; Dakota County Northern Service Center, 1 Mendota Rd W, West St. Paul, 55118, 651-554-6600
Police: Dakota County Sheriff Department, Law Enforcement Center, 1580 Hwy 55, Hastings, 55033, 651-438-4700
Emergency Hospitals: Fairview Ridges Hospital, 201 E Nicollet Blvd, Burnsville, 952-892-2462, www.fairview.org; Regina Medical Center, 1175 Nininger Rd, Hastings, 651-480-4100, www.reginamedical.org
Library: www.co.dakota.mn.us/library
Community Resources: Pilot Knob Preservation Association, www.pilot knobpreservation.org; Sibley House Historic Site, Mendota, www.dakota history.org/county/mendota.asp; Mendota Historic Sites Walking Tour, www.mendotamn.org/maptable.html; UMORE Park Master Gardener

Demonstration and Display Garden, Rosemount, www.mggarden.
umn.edu; Caponi Art Park and Learning Center, www.caponiartpark.org;
Minnesota Zoo, Apple Valley, www.minnesotazoo.org

Parks: www.co.dakota.mn.us/parks; Big Rivers Regional Trail; Lake Byllesby
Regional Park; Lebanon Hills Regional Park; Miesville Ravine Park Reserve;
Dakota County Mississippi River Regional Trail

Public Transportation: *MetroTransit*: 612-373-3333, www.metro
transit.org; buses travel along Highways 13, 55 and 52, County Rd 42,
Johnny Cake Ridge Rd, Yankee Doodle Rd, Pilot Knob Rd, Blackhawk Rd,
Cliff Rd, I-35W, I-35E; transit hubs are located in Eagan at Yankee Doodle
and Pilot Knob rds, and in Burnsville at Highway 13 and Nicollet. Park &
Ride lots are scattered throughout the area. *Minnesota Valley Transit
Authority*, 952-882-7500, www.mvta.com, provides commuter bus service from Apple Valley, Burnsville, Eagan, Rosemount, and Savage to
downtown Minneapolis, downtown Saint Paul, Mall of America, and to
the Minneapolis/St. Paul International Airport.

APPLE VALLEY

Boundaries: North: Eagan; **West**: Burnsville; **South**: Lakeville, Rosemount;
East: Rosemount; **Area**: 18 square miles; **Population**: 45,500

Apple Valley, located 12 miles south of Minneapolis and St. Paul, has quiet
streets and low crime. Its nighttime population is over 45,000, but it tends to
empty out during the day as people go to other cities to work. Nearly 60% of
the city's houses were built between 1970 and 1990, and another 30% have
been built since 1990. The city has numerous rental apartments. According to
the city's web site, in 2006, 90% of the homes had a market value under
$250,000, and a third were under $150,000. Look in the area abutting the
Minnesota Zoo for the city's more luxurious neighborhoods.

The city has a number of sports and recreation facilities, including an outdoor aquatic center, ice arena, and the **Minnesota Zoo**. Most of the city's children attend schools operated by Rosemount-Apple Valley-Eagan Independent
School District 196, www.isd196.k12.mn.us. A small portion of the city, in the
northwestern corner, is in the Burnsville-Eagan-Savage district, www.
isd191.org.

City of Apple Valley, 7100 W 147th St, Apple Valley, 55124, 952-953-2500,
www.ci.apple-valley.mn.us

BURNSVILLE

Boundaries: North: Minnesota River; **West**: Savage; **South**: Lakeville, Scott
County; **East**: Eagan, Apple Valley; **Area**: 24.9 square miles; **Population**: 60,220

Those who watched the 2006 Winter Olympics will have heard many references to Burnsville, home of Buck Hill Ski Area and U.S. Ski Team members

Lindsey Kildow and Kristina Koznick. With a vertical drop of only 300 feet, **Buck Hill** (www.buckhill.com) operates a nationally acclaimed ski racing program, and has put many racers on the U.S. Ski Team. That isn't a bad metaphor for Burnsville, itself, which, while not a glamorous city, still gets the job done with a large stock of entry-level housing, including numerous townhouse and apartment complexes. There are a few luxurious neighborhoods, too, especially west of I-35 in the vicinity of 150th and 155th streets, where new single-family homes are priced from $500,000 to just under a million. Though rumors go around every year that Buck Hill is going to be sold for development, they are not true. In fact, in 2004 the city rezoned the Buck Hill property from single-family residential to Commercial Recreation District, expressly to preserve it. So, if you have children who like to ski, rest assured that the little ski hill that *SKI Magazine* calls the "Legendary capital of American ski racing" will be around to send a few more generations of Minnesotans to the Olympics—maybe even a child of your own. Other recreation facilities include **Burnsville Ice Center**, a skate park, and soccer dome. **The Garage** (www.thegarage.net) offers teens a gathering and performance space.

Positioned where I-35 splits to become I-35W (heading to Minneapolis) and I-35E (which goes to St. Paul), Burnsville has easy access to both those cities and the airport—on a good day. Throw in a little wet weather or a simple fender-bender, and 35W, in particular, becomes a parking lot. Shopping is conveniently located at Burnsville Mall (www.burnsvillecenter.com) and for miles along County Road 42.

Burnsville is served by three public school districts: Burnsville-Eagan-Savage Independent School District 191 serves approximately 70% of residences in the city, www.isd191.org; Rosemount-Apple Valley-Eagan Independent School District 196 serves approximately 20% of residences in Burnsville, www.isd196.k12.mn.us; and Lakeville Area Public Schools Independent School District 194 serves the southernmost residences, www.isd194.k12.mn.us.

City of Burnsville, 100 Civic Center Pkwy, Burnsville, 55337, 952-895-4400, www.ci.burnsville.mn.us

EAGAN

Boundaries: North: Mendota Heights; **West**: Minnesota River, Burnsville; **South**: Apple Valley, Rosemount; **East**: Inver Grove Heights; **Area**: 34.5 square miles; **Population**: 64,000

Eagan, in northern Dakota County, has easy access to I-494 and Highway 77 (Cedar Avenue), and ranks high on *Money Magazine*'s list of best places to live. One of the fastest-growing cities in the state, its population of 10,000 in 1970 is expected to top out at 69,000 within the next decade. A city with owner-occupied homes of every type and price range, it is also home to a number of major industries including Thomson West, Lockheed Martin, UPS, Northwest Airlines, Blue Cross/Blue Shield of Minnesota, and Midwest Coca-Cola Bottling.

Eagan contains over 1000 acres of the **Minnesota Valley Wildlife Refuge**, as well as **Cascade Bay,** which has been named one of the top ten public outdoor aquatic facilities in the US. Children here attend schools in three districts: Burnsville-Eagan-Savage District 191, www.isd191.org; Rosemount–Apple Valley–Eagan District 196, www.isd196.k12.mn.us; and West Saint Paul/Mendota Height/Eagan District 197, www.isd 197.k12.mn.us. Local post-secondary institutions include Argosy University (www.argosyu.edu), Embry-Riddle Aeronautical University (www.ec. erau.edu), and Rasmussen Community College (www.rasmussen.edu).

City of Eagan, 3830 Pilot Knob Rd, Eagan, 55122, 651-675-5000, www.ci. eagan.mn.us

FARMINGTON

Boundaries: North: Rosemount; **West**: Lakeville; **South**: Randolph, Hampton; **East**: Vermillion; **Area**: 12.5 square miles; **Population**: 19,000

Farmington is one of those rare things in the metro—a traditional town. One of Dakota County's oldest communities, it was shown on maps even before Minnesota became a state. A number of buildings from those early days survive, including the Oak Street historic preservation area, which is home to a large collection of houses built between the 1870s and the 1930s, www.ci.farmington.mn.us/HPC/HeritageLandmarks.htm. New growth suburbs surrounding the town offer a full range of life-cycle options, including high-density, lower-priced townhouses and single-family homes. Children here attend Farmington District 192 Schools, www.farmington.k12.mn.us.

City of Farmington, 325 Oak St, Farmington, 55024, 651-463-7111, www.ci. farmington.mn.us

INVER GROVE HEIGHTS

Boundaries: North: South St. Paul, Sunfish Lake; **West**: Eagan; **South**: Rosemount; **East**: Mississippi River; **Area**: 28.6 square miles; **Population**: 32,000, projected 46,000 (2025)

If you're looking for a home with a small amount of acreage that's within twenty minutes of downtown St. Paul, Inver Grove Heights may be the place for you. A wooded community with rolling hills and bluffs that overlook the Mississippi River, it is only two-thirds developed—at least so far. Since part of it has been designated "rural residential," (one house per 2.5 acres), it can be expected to retain some semblance of an open "rural" look, at least for a while. IGH has been part of every era's building boom, and has a stock of '50s-forward houses to prove it. While 40% of the housing is valued at $150,000 or less, new construction tends to fall into the $300,000–$1,000,000 range.

Once a community of farms, it still boasts a few agricultural properties, including **Triple-S Ranch** riding stable (www.triple-sranch.com) and **Gerten's Greenhouses** (www.gertens.com). The city operates two public marinas, which provide access to the Mississippi River. Children here attend Inver Grove Heights Community Schools, District 199, www.invergrove. k12.mn.us. Post-secondary schools include Inver Hills Community College, www.ih.cc.mn.us.

City of Inver Grove Heights, 8150 Barbara Ave, Inver Grove Heights, 55077, www.ci.inver-grove-heights.mn.us

LAKEVILLE

Boundaries: North: Burnsville, Apple Valley; **West**: Scott County; **South**: New Market; **East**: Farmington, Rosemount; **Area**: 38 square miles; **Population**: 49,023

Strategically located 20 miles south of Minneapolis on I-35, Lakeville bills itself as "The Southern Gateway to the Metro Area." That's because, as you're driving north on I-35, it's the place where farmland suddenly gives way to townhouses. As a designated "developing community" in the metro area regional plan, its population is expected to reach 86,000 by 2030. To accommodate all these new residents, the city has in recent years issued twice as many building permits for townhouses as for single-family homes. Most recently, it has received a lot of publicity for its 2100-unit **Spirit of Brandjten Farm** masterplanned community (http://homesofspirit.com), which includes custom-built homes in the near-million-dollar price range. Children here attend schools in three school districts: Farmington School District 192 (www. farmington.k12.mn.us) serves the eastern side of the city; the Lakeville Area Public Schools (www.isd194.k12.mn.us) serve most of the city; and Rosemount–Apple Valley–Eagan District 196 (www.isd196.k12.mn.us) serves the northeastern corner. You can download the school districts' boundaries from the city's web site.

One local issue of note: Airlake Airport, which is used now as a general aviation "reliever" for Minneapolis–St. Paul International Airport (MSP), is expected at some point to start getting overflow traffic from MSP that will include "light" jets. The airport has already been approved for a new crosswind runway and new hangars, although they have not been built yet due to lack of funds.

For those who have heard rumors of a "Downtown Lakeville," but have never known where it is, it can be found at the intersection of County Road 50 and Holyoke Avenue in the southern reaches of the city, directly south of the growing commercial district of Heritage Commons.

City of Lakeville, 20195 Holyoke Ave, Lakeville, 55044-9177, 952-985-4400, www.ci.lakeville.mn.us

MENDOTA HEIGHTS

Boundaries: North: Minnesota River; **East**: Delaware Avenue; **West**: Highway 13; **South**: Eagan; **Area**: 9.4 square miles; **Population**: 11,378

The most beautiful view of the Twin Cities is from **Pilot Knob** in Mendota Heights. From this bluff at the end of the Mendota Bridge you can see across the confluence of the Mississippi and Minnesota rivers to historic Ft. Snelling and the skyscrapers of Minneapolis beyond. This is the place where the Dakota tribes buried their dead on scaffolds, so they could overlook the river, and where the Dakota signed the Treaty of 1851, which ceded all the land that is now Minnesota to the U.S. government. The name Pilot Knob derives from the promontory's use as a navigation guide by old-time riverboat pilots, and it is featured in one of the most famous paintings of Minnesota, *Distant View of Fort Snelling*, painted in 1846 by Seth Eastman.

Primarily a residential community, with curvy streets built around woods and wetlands, Mendota Heights has an industrial area in its southern quarter that is home to Ecolab and Northland Insurance. Most housing consists of owner-occupied single-family homes dating from the late 1970s to mid-1980s. The city is short on rental and multi-family housing, but is adding a new town center off Dodd Road called **The Village at Mendota Heights** (www.villagemh.com/the-village.cfm), which will include retail and office space as well as row houses and lofts. Children here attend West Saint Paul/Mendota Heights/Eagan School District 197, www.isd197.k12.mn.us. Private schools include Convent of the Visitation School (www.visitation.net) and St. Thomas Academy (www.cadets.com).

City of Mendota Heights, 1101 Victoria Curve, Mendota Heights, 55118, 651-452-1850, www.mendota-heights.com

ROSEMOUNT

Boundaries: North: Inver Grove Heights; **East**: Mississippi River; **West**: Apple Valley; **South**: Vermillion; **Area**: 36 square miles; **Population**: 17,997 (2004); projected, 36,700 (2030)

Located approximately 15 miles south of the Minneapolis–St. Paul International airport, the western part of Rosemount boasts an expanding residential community with single-family homes, townhomes, condominiums, and low-income housing, while the city's eastern third is heavily industrial, with an oil refinery and an industrial waste containment facility.

A major portion of the city is in Rosemount-Apple Valley-Eagan Independent School District #196 (www.isd196.k12.mn.us), which is the second largest district in the state. Other students attend Hastings schools (www.isd196.k12.mn.us), or Inver Grove Heights (www.invergrove.k12.mn.us).

The city is also served by twelve non-public schools and Dakota County Technical College (www.dctc.mnscu.edu).

City of Rosemount, 2875 145th St W, Rosemount, 55068-4997, 651-423-4411, TTY 651-423-6219, www.ci.rosemount.mn.us

SOUTH ST. PAUL

Boundaries: North: St. Paul; **West**: West St. Paul; **South**: Inver Grove Heights; **East**: Mississippi River; **Area**: 5.7 square miles; **Population**: 20,167

Ten minutes from downtown St. Paul, this old stockyard district is sometimes called the East Metro's version of Northeast Minneapolis, a section of the cities where ethnic eateries blend with fern bars and upscale shops and condos. There is also an active regional airport, South St. Paul Airport (Fleming Field). Owned and managed by the city, it is the home of the Southern Minnesota Wing of the Commemorative Air Force (www.cafsmw.org) and the famous Miss Mitchell B-25 bomber.

Major employers include Sportsman's Guide mail-order house, Dakota Premium Foods (meatpacking), and American Bottling. Shopping is conveniently located in the neighborhood or along South Robert Street in West St. Paul.

City of South St. Paul, 125 3rd Ave North, South St. Paul, 55075, 651-554-3200, www.southstpaul.org

SCOTT COUNTY

CREDIT RIVER TOWNSHIP
JORDAN
PRIOR LAKE
SHAKOPEE

Boundaries: North: Minnesota River, Carver County; **West**: Minnesota River, Sibley County; **South**: Le Sueur and Rice Counties; **East**: Dakota County; **Area**: 365 square miles; **Population**: 89,498

The extension of sewer service and a new, high bridge over the Minnesota River are fueling a building boom in Scott County that has made it one of the fastest growing places in the nation. Its population increased from 57,846 in 1990 to almost 90,000 in 2000, for a gain of 55%, and is expected to hit 220,940 by 2030.

So far, two-thirds of the county's residents live in its three northernmost cities: Shakopee, Savage, and Prior Lake. Another 15% live in upscale master-planned communities in Elko, New Market, and Credit River, in the eastern part of the county, down I-35. The rest of the county has been able to remain somewhat agricultural. That's changing, however, and land is being consumed at a fast pace as the construction of high-amenity developments is following

Highway 169 west to Jordan and Belle Plaine, and Highways 21 and 13 south to New Prague. About 70% of the new housing is single-family, with 30% multi-family units. The multi-family homes are located primarily in the northernmost cities, although a number of townhomes have been built in golf course developments in Elko. Rentals, too can be found primarily in the northern cities, where rents are generally slightly lower than in next-door neighbor Burnsville, and significantly lower than in Eden Prairie, which is just across the river over the Highways 101 and 169 bridges. Bridges are of major importance here, in part because the Minnesota River is prone to spring flooding, and in part because of the way traffic backs up over them during rush hours and busy Renaissance Fair and Valley Fair weekends. Be sure to take them into consideration when contemplating your commute. Four-lane bridges are located on I-35 at Burnsville and Highway 169 at Savage, and two-lane bridges are located on Highway 101 at Shakopee, Highway 41 at Chaska, County Road 45 between Jordan and Carver, and in Belle Plaine. While most commuters here drive solo in their cars, the county does offer commuter transit service five days a week using Minnesota Valley Transit Authority (MVTA) express buses.

Scott County Government Center: 200 Fourth Ave W, Shakopee, 55379, 952-445-7750, www.co.scott.mn.us

Police: Scott County Sheriff's Office: Emergency, 911; Non-emergency: 952-496-8300

Emergency Hospitals: Ridgeview Medical Center, 500 S Maple St, Waconia, 55387, 952-442-2191, www.ridgeviewmedical.org; St. Francis Regional Medical Center, 1455 St. Francis Ave, Shakopee, 55379, 952-403-3000, www.Stfrancis-shakopee.com

Library: Scott County Library System, www.scott.lib.mn.us

Attractions: Canterbury Park Racetrack and Card Club, 1100 Canterbury Rd, Shakopee, www.canterburypark.com; Raceway Park (NASCAR), One Checkered Flag Blvd, Shakopee, www.goracewaypark.com; Historic Murphy's Landing, 2187 E County Rd 101, Shakopee; Valleyfair! Amusement Park, One Valleyfair Dr, Shakopee, 952-445-7600 or (800) FUN-RIDE, www.valleyfair.com; Minnesota Renaissance Festival, 3 miles south of Shakopee on Highway 169, www.renaissancefest.com; Trail of Terror, 3 miles south of Shakopee on Highway 169, www.trailofterror fest.com

Parks and Recreation: 2400-acre Murphy-Hanrehan Park Reserve, near Savage, off County Road 75, has trails for walkers, bikers, horses, snowmobiles, and cross-country skiers. In 2004, the park was designated as an "Important Bird Area" by the National Audubon Society. Cleary Lake Regional Park, near Prior Lake on Scott County Road 27, has a 9-hole golf course and driving, and facilities for swimming, boating and fishing. Winter activities include cross-country skiing on groomed trails. Both parks are part of the Three Rivers Park System, www.threeriversparks.org. Golf courses include: Stonebrooke Golf Club, 2693 County Rd 79, Shakopee, 952-496-3171, www.stonebrooke.com; The Wilds Golf Club, 3151 Wilds Ridge, Prior Lake, 952-445-3500, http://golfthewilds.com, which was named "Minnesota's #1 Public Course" by *Golf Digest*; and The Ridges at Sand Creek, 21775 Ridges Dr, Jordan, 952-492-2644, www.ridgesatsandcreek.com, which was nominated for "Best New Course" by *Golf Digest* in 2001. Meadows at Mystic Lake, off County Road 83, is a new course adjacent to Mystic Lake Casino, www.ccsmdc.org/meadows/index.html. The Legends Golf Club, 8670 Credit River Blvd, Prior Lake, was one of *Golf Digest*'s 2002 Top Ten Upscale New Golf Courses, www.legendsgc.com.

Public Transportation: Minnesota Valley Transit Authority, 952-882-7500, www.mvta.com, provides commuter bus service from Savage. The Savage Park & Ride is located at 141st St and Huntington Ave, one block north of County Rd 42 (behind McDonald's).

CREDIT RIVER TOWNSHIP

Located in the eastern part of the county off I-35W, this is the fastest growing township in what has been the fastest growing county in Minnesota. Children here attend Lakeville Area Public Schools, www.isd194.k12.mn.us.

Credit River Township City Hall, Credit River Township Hall, 7450 Credit River Blvd (on Highway 68 half a mile east of the intersection of Highways 27 and 68), Credit River, 952-440-5515, www.creditrivertownship.com. The Township Clerk maintains regular office hours on Tuesday and Thursday mornings from 8:30 a.m. until noon.

JORDAN

Located 8 miles south of Shakopee and 25 miles southwest of the major regional intersection of Interstate 494 and Highway 169, Jordan is a place to look for homes on acreage as well as golf course developments. Children here attend Jordan School District #717 schools, www.jordan.k12.mn.us.

City of Jordan, 210 1st St East, Jordan, 55352, 952-492-2535, www.jordan.govoffice.com

PRIOR LAKE

Prior Lake (the lake) is known for its waterskiing, while Prior Lake (the city) is known for being home to Scott County's biggest landowner, the Shakopee-Mdewakanton Sioux Indian tribe, whose reservation is located entirely within the city. This tribe of about 200 members operates the Mystic Lake casino (www.mysticlake.com), which is said to be the second-most profitable Indian casino in the nation. Traffic around Mystic Lake is not inconsequential, as the casino gets over 18,000 visitors every day. To learn more about the tribe, check out the Minnesota Indian Affairs Council's web page at www.cri-bsu.org/IA_web/htdocs/tribes/shakopee.html.

Here you will find housing here of every type, with many multi-family options, as well as luxurious homes surrounding the lake and **The Legends** golf course. Recreation, of course, centers on the lake, and the **Shakopee–Prior Lake Water Ski Association** (www.priorlake waterski.org) is one of the oldest and largest water ski clubs in the country. Buried as Prior Lake is, away from major highways, the commute is no picnic. But the Laker Lines, the city of Prior Lake's transit service (www. cityofpriorlake.com/transit.shtml), does run express commuter buses each day. Prior Lake/Savage Area School District (www.priorlake-savage.k12.mn.us) serves all of Prior Lake.

City of Prior Lake, 16776 Fish Point Rd SE, Prior Lake, 55372-1714, 952-447-4230, www.cityofpriorlake.com

SHAKOPEE

Shakopee, population 20,568 in 2000, is expected to grow to more than 50,000 by 2030. The Scott County seat, it is located 23 miles from Minneapolis, at the intersection of Highways 169 and 101. Home to **Canterbury Park**, **Valley Fair Amusement Park**, **Murphy's Landing**, and **Raceway Park**, it bills itself as "The Definition of Fun." Along with all the nearby "attractions," it has shopping on Main Street and a regional hospital. Recreation centers around a 920-acre park and open space system which includes a community center, ice arena, skate park, and outdoor aquatic park. The city also operates **Enigma Teen Center** (www.enigmateencenter.com), which gives local young people a place to hang out. Children here attend schools operated by Shakopee School District 720, www.shakopee.k12.mn.us.

City of Shakopee, 129 S Holmes St, Shakopee, 55379, 952-233-9300, www. ci.shakopee.mn.us

OTHER SUBURBAN COMMUNITIES

Today, the Twin Cities are much more than just the metropolitan boundaries of Minneapolis and St. Paul. The post–World War II baby boom, followed by the rapid expansion in the 1960s of the interstate highway system, led to enormous migration of new families into what had been farms and forests. In fact, over the past fifty years or so the metro area has grown into an amorphous expanse that includes more than 188 distinct suburban communities within the seven-county metro area, alone. If we jump to the 13-county metro area, the suburbs become too numerous to count.

Virtually all of the Twin Cities' growth has been in the suburbs, with seven counties in the 13-county metro statistical area among the 100 fastest growing in the nation: Scott, Sherburne, Wright, St. Croix (Wisconsin), Chisago, Carver, and Isanti.

The attraction of these exurbs is obvious: larger lots, new buildings with floor plans that meet the needs and desires of today's families, and amenities such as private community centers, trails, and pools. For the latest on what sort of homes are being built and where, there is no better source than the Builders' Association of the Twin Cities Parade of Homes, www.paradeofhomes.org.

Below are web addresses for some of the suburban communities not profiled in this book:

WESTERN SUBURBS

- Buffalo, www.ci.buffalo.mn.us
- Greenfield, www.greenfield.govoffice.com
- Minnetonka Beach, www.ci.minnetonka-beach.mn.us
- Minnetrista, www.ci.minnetrista.mn.us
- Monticello, www.ci.monticello.mn.us
- Spring Park, http://springpark.govoffice.com
- Tonka Bay, http://cityoftonkabay.net
- Victoria, www.ci.victoria.mn.us
- Waconia, www.waconia.org

SOUTHWESTERN SUBURBS

- Belle Plaine, www.belleplainemn.com
- New Prague, www.ci.new-prague.mn.us

NORTHERN SUBURBS

- Brooklyn Center, www.ci.brooklyn-center.mn.us
- Cambridge, www.ci.cambridge.mn.us
- Circle Pines, www.ci.circle-pines.mn.us
- Columbia Heights, www.ci.columbia-heights.mn.us
- Crystal, www.ci.crystal.mn.us
- Ham Lake, www.ci.ham-lake.mn.us
- Little Canada, www.ci.little-canada.mn.us
- New Hope, www.ci.new-hope.mn.us
- Robbinsdale, www.ci.robbinsdale.mn.us
- St. Anthony, www.ci.saint-anthony.mn.us

SOUTHERN SUBURBS

- Elko, www.ci.elko.mn.us
- Hastings, www.ci.hastings.mn.us
- New Market, www.newmarketcity.com
- Northfield, www.ci.northfield.mn.us
- Savage, www.ci.savage.mn.us
- West St. Paul, www.ci.west-saint-paul.mn.us

THE TWIN CITIES USED TO BE CONSIDERED ONE OF THE MOST AFFORDABLE metro areas in the country, but with home values that have appreciated 60% in Minneapolis and St. Paul in the past five years—and up to five times that in the most desirable suburbs—the National Association of Home Builders no longer honors us with that designation. Still, if you're moving here from such cities as San Francisco and New York City, where median home prices can be three times as high as ours, buying a home in the Twin Cities area can look quite feasible.

That said, the new lofts and condos in the downtowns, and the grandiose developments that sprawl along the interstate highways, are unabashedly aimed at more affluent buyers, leaving very little actually "affordable" housing to be found. That's true for renters, as well as buyers. Although vacancy rates tend to be higher in the East St. Paul suburbs and lower in Minneapolis, rents can still be quite pricey, and there is stiff competition for the most desirable units.

Consequently, if you are looking for a starter home, you may need to be flexible about your choice of neighborhood—and you may need to get creative about how you're going to pay for it, too. One popular strategy: buy an income-producing duplex in your chosen neighborhood as your first home, then sell it after a few years and use the appreciation on your investment to finance your dream house up the block. To do that, you need to find a neighborhood that has a wide range of housing such as NE or South Minneapolis, or the west side of St. Paul. St. Louis Park (www.stlouispark.org) is another popular get-your-foot-in-the-door town. It has apartments, condos, duplexes (often called double bungalows up here) and a vast number of homes under 1500 square feet. They're ideal for starter homes, but—even better—the city is actively engaged in trying to keep people from having to move away to find family-size housing and has developed a number of programs to help residents enlarge their homes, including help with architects and loans.

Beyond the not-so-well-kept secret of St. Louis Park, the piece of advice most often dished out by locals is this: if you're single, stick with the cities and avoid the 'burbs. Except for St. Louis Park, which counts many young singles among its residents and is closer to the Minneapolis Chain of Lakes than some parts of Minneapolis, the suburbs are almost universally family-oriented. The downtowns of both cities, however, are exploding with tony new lofts in refurbished factories that are only suitable for singles or couples. Of course, sophisticated downtown digs can be pretty pricey, which brings us to another urban option—the Hiawatha Light Rail and its transit-oriented housing.

HOUSING OPTIONS
TRANSIT-ORIENTED HOUSING

An unfortunate consequence of our existing planning and policy environment is that it is often much cheaper to build on undeveloped farmland in the exurbs than it is to build within existing communities. But the **Hiawatha Light Rail Transit Line** is changing that. Often characterized as "smart growth," transit-oriented housing along the LRT is making it possible for people to drive less at the same time it is revitalizing the neighborhoods along its route. Condos and apartment complexes have already begun rising, and Bloomington is planning a whole new downtown around its two LRT stops. Similarly, north of the cities, the **Northstar Commuter Rail** (if/when built) will begin in Minneapolis and travel out 40 miles through Fridley, Coon Rapids, Anoka, and Elk River to Big Lake (www.mn-GetOnBoard.com). Keep your eye on these cities, as they offer a variety of homes and apartments already, and expect to see strong property value appreciation with the advent of their own transit-oriented development.

ATTACHED OR MULTI-FAMILY HOUSING

For years, most housing in the Twin Cities was either single-family detached or apartments, with relatively few options in between. That is no longer the case. In fact, multi-family and attached housing accounted for more than half of the building permits in the metro in 2005, according to the Builders Association of the Twin Cities. Consequently, twin homes and townhouses now span the region from Shakopee to Princeton, and can even be found within the cities of Minneapolis and St. Paul. Lofts are less widespread, and more concentrated in the two downtowns. Those thinking about buying a loft should be sure to catch the annual **Loft and Condo Living Tour** (www.loftlivingtour.com). You'll be able to check out amenities and views, pick up new decorating ideas— and see what different developers have to offer. Those looking for twin homes and townhouses will be able to see a number of models on the **Builders Association of the Twin Cities Parade of Homes**, www.parade ofhomes.org (check the web site for dates and times).

HOUSE-HUNTING

ONLINE RESEARCH

The Internet has completely changed how people find their homes. Thanks to the **Regional Multiple Listing Service**'s "broker reciprocity" agreement, you can now sit back home in New Jersey and use the MLS's sophisticated search engine to view all the Greater Metro MLS real estate listings, including property in Wisconsin. Just click on www.TheMLSonline.com, put in your city choices, price range, and amenities, and in a few minutes you'll have pictures of all the listings that meet your criteria, plus clickable links that allow you to take virtual tours of the properties and links for contacting the listing agents online. You'll also gain a realistic idea of how much the kind of home you're interested in might cost, and be able to identify agents who specialize in the neighborhoods you'd like to look at. Don't worry that you'll be looking at properties that are long gone—the MLS database is updated every 15 minutes. Of course, property that isn't listed with an agent won't be on the MLS web site, so for "For Sale by Owner" listings, check out the *St. Paul Pioneer Press HomeSeller* (http://newspaperads.twincities.com/Sections.aspx?sec=16393), the *Minneapolis Star Tribune* (www.startribune.com/homes), or **Home Avenue** (www.homeavenue.com/fsbo/info/default.aspx).

A different sort of search engine, **www.MNrealty.com**, bills itself as "Your Independent Guide to Minnesota Real Estate On-Line." Not a brokerage, this site lists property for sale and links to information such as schools and sports.

For those looking for apartments, see the section on **Renting**, below.

OTHER HOMEBUYING RESOURCES

- **Accessible Space, Inc.**, 651-645-7271, 800-466-7722, www.accessible space.org., is a nonprofit that provides accessible and affordable housing and supportive living services for adults who have mobility impairments, brain injuries, and physical disabilities.
- **Chrysalis Women's Center**, 4432 Chicago Ave, Minneapolis, 612-871-0118, www.chrysaliswomen.org, offers classes on homebuying, credit repair, and managing finances.
- **The Home Ownership Center**, 651-659-9336, 1-866-462-6466, www.hocmn.org, provides services to low-income people.
- **Parade of Homes**, www.paradeofhomes.org, is the Builders Association of the Twin Cities' four-times-a-year-showcase of new and remodeled construction throughout the metro area.

GETTING TO KNOW THE NEIGHBORHOOD

The **Minneapolis Neighborhood Revitalization Program** (612-673-5140, www.nrp.org) is an excellent resource for information about Minneapolis, offering profiles of neighborhoods, listings of community events and, sometimes, even home tours. You should also call the police precinct that patrols your neighborhood of interest. The numbers are listed at the end of each neighborhood profile.

The best advice when house or apartment hunting, however, is to visit prospective neighborhoods—have breakfast at a local restaurant and walk around, don't just drive. Find out if services and conveniences you are accustomed to having are available nearby, and pay attention to your comfort level. Check on traffic and noise levels at different times of the day and night. If you are put off by the noise of airplanes taking off and landing (as in South Minneapolis, Richfield, East Bloomington, Eagan, Mendota Heights, and western St. Paul) or by strangers roller-blading on your street (around the city lakes), factor these into your decision about where to live. There isn't much you can do about crowds of exercise enthusiasts, but for information about airplane noise and possible abatement programs check out the **Metropolitan Airports Commission**'s (**MAC**) web site (www.macnoise.com).

Also consider the commute. According to the Texas Transportation Institute, the Twin Cities metropolitan area is the fifth most congested area in the nation for its size. That means that Twin Citians spend an average of 43 hours per year just sitting in traffic. If you're a fan of Books on Tape, that might not be so bad, but you should still test drive your route at rush hour, morning and night, to be sure of what you're getting into. Lastly, some people are able to commute by bus, but the usefulness of buses depends entirely upon where you live, where you need to go, and at what time. Information about Twin Cities bus routes can be accessed on the Internet at **www.metrotransit.org**. See **Transportation** for more details.

RENTING

Renting for a while is a great way to get to know the town before you commit to a permanent address, and you can easily find an apartment on your own. First check this guide's neighborhood descriptions to learn about the types of housing in different parts of town—then, if possible, use Minnesota's climate to assist your apartment search: many people choose not to move in winter, creating more vacancies in the summer. Begin looking around the first of June, and you might even be lucky enough to find a handsome, turn-of-the-century brick apartment with hardwood floors and tall windows near Uptown or Summit/Grand, two of the most popular neighborhoods for newcomers.

ONLINE AND NEWSPAPER RESOURCES

Numerous online resources such as **www.rentnet.com** are available. Locally, **www.apartments-in-minneapolis.net/Minneapolis** is free and covers the entire metro area. A national service, **www.sublet.com** has up-to-date listings from all over the metro. Browse it for free, and when you find something of interest, register (for a fee) and they will give you the contact information. Since the same company that owns that site also owns **www.City leases.com** and **www.Metroroommates.com**, you'll gain access to those sites at no extra cost. **Craigslist** (www.craigslist.com, and click on Minneapolis, or http://minneapolis.craiglist.org) also maintains extensive free listings of rental housing, with new postings each day.

Free neighborhood newspapers can be found at businesses and newsstands throughout the Twin Cities. Other papers to watch:

- **The *Minneapolis Star Tribune*** has the most comprehensive metro-area listings. You can access the classifieds online at www.startribune.com/homes. This web site has a searchable database and clickable links to connect you with *Apartments Magazine, New Construction Magazine,* an apartments tour, and more.
- ***St. Paul Pioneer Press*** is the better resource for St. Paul and the eastern metro area. Access the classifieds at www.twincities.com.
- ***City Pages*** is a free alternative weekly, available at businesses metro-wide. The listings are not extensive, but worth checking, and it also lists sublets; www.citypages.com.
- ***Minnesota Daily*** is the University of Minnesota newspaper. To place your own "roommate wanted" ad, call 612-627-4140 or check www.mn daily.com.

APARTMENT SEARCH FIRMS

Many landlords contract with rental agents or apartment search firms to find tenants for their units. A search firm can be very convenient if you have a limited amount of time to find a place. Agents will fax you information and arrange appointments for you to view available units. When talking to a rental agent, be specific about your needs; this way you will not waste time considering places that aren't right for you. The following are some of the largest and most well-known apartment search firms. The property owners typically pay their fees, so the service to the tenant is usually free:

- **Apartments.com**, www.apartments.com, has apartments plus short-term listings as well as video tours and a furniture rental center.
- **Apartments by Rent Net**, www.rent.net, offers 360-degree online visuals.
- **Apartment Search**, 800-APARTMENT, www.apartmentsearch.com.
- **HousingLink**, 612-522-2500, www.housinglink.org, is a nonprofit service that maintains a directory of affordable housing properties. Property owners and managers may list their affordable vacancies here for free.
- **Park Avenue of Wayzata**, 952-475-1700, www.parkavenueof wayzata.com, lists townhouses and condominiums in the western suburbs.
- **Relocation Central**, 952-881-9298, 651-636-3860, 763-537-2866, 800-989-8780, www.relocationcentral.com/minneapolis-apartments.html, is part of the Cort Furniture rental empire and has several offices in the metro.

TEMPORARY HOUSING/SUBLETS/SHARING

If finding a long-term place to live is proving difficult, you may want to consider taking a short-term sublet. Many such sublets are available in May, when students begin to leave town with time remaining on their leases, or during the winter when the "snowbirds" move to warmer climates. But remember, most leases say that a tenant can sublet only if the landlord agrees to it—and that permission should be in writing. (The original tenant remains responsible for unpaid rent and damage done to the apartment by the new tenant.) The *Minneapolis Star Tribune* lists corporate/relocation short-term rentals in its classified section, and *City Pages* has ads for sublets and roommates. Check the **Temporary Lodgings** chapter for additional temporary alternatives and see **Online Research** and **Online and Newspaper Resources** above.

CHECKING IT OUT

Your apartment search will be easier if you keep a few things in mind. First, ask yourself how much space you really want to pay for. If you're alone, a studio or efficiency might be most cost-effective. Studios generally are found in downtown Minneapolis and St. Paul and, in 2005, the average monthly rent was about $595. A one-bedroom generally will cost $150–$200 more than a studio, a second bedroom adds anywhere from $150 to $500. Add a third bedroom and you're looking at an approximate total cost of $1200 to $1300. The bulk of the larger units can be found in the eastern, southern, and western suburbs.

In Minnesota, an important question to ask is: who will be paying for heat? If it's you and not the landlord, you could be adding a substantial amount to your cost of living during the cold months. You can find out the average cost of heating for an apartment by calling the gas or electric company that provides service to that building (most likely CenterPoint and Xcel—see the **Getting Settled** chapter). Another consideration when choosing a place to live is the availability of parking. Off-street, indoor parking is especially desirable in the winter—your car will start in the morning, you won't have to scrape off ice and snow, and you won't have to move your car for the city snowplow. City streets are plowed according to several different plans, but no matter the schedule, if your car is parked on a street in the way of the snowplow, it will be towed, and be assured it will be expensive and time-consuming to get your car out of the impound lot. (See **Snow Emergency Parking** in **Getting Settled**.)

Also be sure to check with your city's housing inspection department for a property's past code violations and current citations. Minnesota law requires that landlords disclose any outstanding inspection orders for which a citation has been issued for violations that threaten the health or safety of tenants. However, the law has many loopholes. Better to trust your city's inspections department for current status information. Landlords who rent units built before 1978 also must disclose any known lead-based paint and include a warning in the lease. The **National Lead Information Center** (800-424-5323) can provide information and a copy of the Environmental Protection Agency's pamphlet "Protect Your Family from Lead in Your Home."

Finally, watch for discrimination. In Minnesota, it's illegal to deny housing based on race, religion, age, or any other personal basis. Minneapolis specifically prohibits discrimination based on sexual orientation. However, Fair Housing laws may not apply to owner-occupied complexes of four or fewer units. If you're in Minneapolis and believe you are a victim of discrimination, call the **Minneapolis Department of Civil Rights**, at 311.

STAKING A CLAIM

When viewing prospective apartments, take along appropriate documentation. That includes job and bank account information, personal references, the name and telephone number of your previous landlord, and your checkbook. Many landlords use tenant screening services and the information they receive is used to approve or deny your tenancy. If a landlord uses the service's information to deny rental, increase your security deposit, or increase your rent, he/she must give you written notice of the adverse action and you have a right to add an explanation of the problem to your file.

LEASES, SECURITY DEPOSITS, AND TAX REFUNDS

The terms of a rental agreement are stated in a lease. Lease agreements should be in writing. Be sure you understand everything in a written lease before you sign it, and get a copy for your files. Remember that a lease is a legally binding agreement and that a tenant does not have the right to break a lease, even for good reasons like moving or buying a home. Following are some clauses you should challenge before signing, or avoid:

- Unannounced entry—Minnesota has enacted a law forbidding a landlord to enter an apartment without permission or reasonable notice (24 hours) except in emergencies.
- Responsibility for repairs without compensation. If you agree to perform any maintenance on your apartment, you can negotiate a rent decrease. Make sure it's in writing.
- Escalation and acceleration clauses—some leases permit an owner to raise the rent during a lease period (escalation). Other lease language may state that upon missing a month's rent, you are immediately liable for the rest of the lease amount, which could be thousands of dollars (acceleration). These kinds of clauses are legal, but you may not want to rent from someone who proposes them. Pay attention and read the fine print.
- Late charges—if your lease does not include information about late charges, then your landlord may not impose them, except for the filing and service fees related to unlawful detainer that are permitted by law.

As for security deposits, a landlord may require a deposit of any amount in order to pay for damage the tenant might do to the unit. The amount of this deposit may be increased at any time during a month-to-month lease. However, the security deposit must be returned with interest within 21 days after the end of the tenancy, or the landlord must provide a written explanation as to why it is being withheld. If a landlord does not refund the deposit, with interest, the tenant can take the matter to court. Minnesota law also gives tenants the chance to get some of their money back in the form of a partial refund of the property taxes they pay indirectly through their rent. To claim your credit, file a property tax refund form and certificate of rent paid (which your landlord must give you by January 31 of each year) with the Minnesota Department of Revenue. (See **Money Matters**.)

LANDLORD PROBLEMS

The **Minnesota Attorney General**'s office offers several free booklets for consumers, including "Landlords and Tenants: Rights and Responsibilities." Download them from the internet at www.ag.state.mn.us, or request a hard copy from the Attorney General's office at 651-296-3353 or 800-657-3787.

Other sources of assistance include:

- **First Call for Help** (24 hours), 211; funded by the United Way, this is a general information number that can provide housing assistance with respect to lists of available rental housing, advice on landlord issues, loan programs, transitional housing, and referrals to other resources.
- **HOME Line**, 3455 Bloomington Ave, Minneapolis, 612-728-5767, 1-866-866-3546 (Greater Minnesota), www.homelinemn.org, provides free legal, organizing, education, and advocacy services so that tenants throughout Minnesota can solve their own rental housing problems. HOME Line serves the entire state of Minnesota except the cities of Minneapolis and St Paul.

RENTER'S INSURANCE

Get it. Generally a building owner's insurance covers damage to the building, not your personal possessions. Renter's insurance, however, does provide relatively inexpensive protection against theft, water damage, fire, and, in many cases, personal liability. Insurance companies that sell homeowner's insurance also sell renter's insurance.

BUYING

Minnesota loves homeowners! Yes, property taxes are high, but if you live in the home you buy, the state will offset some of your tax burden by giving you a **homestead property tax credit** and by allowing you to deduct mortgage interest payments from your taxable income, thereby reducing the amount of income taxes you have to pay. The state even allows you to deduct interest from other loans if you are willing to use your home as collateral.

Homes come in many forms, from traditional, **single-family detached** houses to multiple ownership situations: cluster homes, condos, townhouses, patio homes, and co-ops. **Cluster homes** are detached houses built close together with shared outdoor grounds, recreational facilities, and maintenance costs. **Condominiums** are buildings in which you purchase a unit, but all the land and other facilities are jointly owned by the entire condo community. In a **townhouse**, you purchase both the structure and the land under it. A **patio home** is similar to a townhouse; however, in addition to purchasing the unit and the land under it, it will also come with a small yard. **Cooperatives** are buildings in which you own a share in the corporation that owns the building, with a housing unit reserved for each shareholder's use. A multiple housing complex, sometimes referred to as **association housing**, is managed by a board of the homeowners, which collects dues and assessments for maintenance and repairs.

Good questions to ask about association housing are:
- What percentage of the units are owner-occupied?
- How much are the association dues and projected assessments?
- What are the rules and regulations?
- Is the development professionally managed?
- Have there been any lawsuits involving the association in the past five years?

When scouting for any home, don't forget the cold climate! Energy costs are high here for both heating and cooling. And, while houses built since the energy crisis of the 1970s may have very tight, energy-efficient construction, they may also have problems with moisture and poor indoor air quality (carbon monoxide, radon). The newest houses solve this problem with balanced mechanical ventilation systems and sealed-combustion appliances that do not draw air from inside the home.

Older houses can be remodeled and/or made more energy-efficient to meet modern families' needs. Two locally produced books have been created to assist those with older homes. *The Longfellow Planbook: Remodeling Plans for Bungalows and Other Small Urban Homes* can be purchased from the Longfellow Community Council (4151 Minnehaha Avenue South, Minneapolis 55406, 612-722-4529) for $18.50, $10 for Longfellow residents. *Cape Cods and Ramblers: A Remodeling Planbook for Post-WW II Houses* will help you time-tune houses from the 1940s, '50s and '60s. Residents of Blaine, Brooklyn Park, Columbia Heights, Coon Rapids, Crystal, Fridley, Golden Valley, Hopkins, Mounds View, New Brighton, New Hope, Robbinsdale, Richfield, Roseville, and St. Louis Park can purchase the book for $10 from their city halls. Those who live outside those communities can get a copy for $15 from the City of Brooklyn Park (763-424-8000).

A 2004 law requires sellers of residential property to disclose all material facts—of which they're aware—that could significantly or adversely affect an ordinary buyer's use or enjoyment of the property. This not only covers environmental hazards such as lead and mold but also includes information that a prospective buyer would want to know that is not directly associated with the physical condition of the property, such as the expansion of a road that is adjacent to the property, or the expansion of an airport runway that would allow air traffic to fly over the property. Despite this statutory protection, when viewing a prospective home be sure to keep your eyes open. One important thing to look for: roof and structural damage caused by ice dams (see **Local Lingo** in the **Introduction**), which may form if a house is not adequately insulated and ventilated, a common problem in Minnesota. And, since homes often have defects that are not easily visible, it is wise to protect yourself by having a professional roof/mechanical systems inspection prior to purchase. Professional residential inspectors can be found in the Yellow Pages under "Home and Building Inspection," or ask your realtor for a recommendation. The **American Society of Home Inspectors'** web site (www.ashi.com) includes information about what's involved in a home inspection and what to do if your inspection report reveals a problem.

WORKING WITH REALTORS

Even if an agent takes you to see a home, he or she is actually representing the seller, not you. If you want an agent who will act on your behalf, you will need to hire a buyer's broker. This person will not give information about you and what you can afford to the seller and will negotiate the lowest possible price for you. There are thousands of real estate agents of both types working in the Twin Cities area, and you can get information about them from the **Minneapolis Area Association of Realtors** (952-933-9020, www.mpls realtor.com). However, according to the Real Trends 500 Report for 2003 (the latest year for which data were available), these are the region's top four real estate brokerage offices by sales. They all have numerous offices throughout the metro:

- **Edina Realty,** 800-328-4344, relocation@edinarealty.com, www. edinarealty.com.
- **Coldwell Banker Burnet,** 952-820-HOME (4663) or 877-879-7505, www.cbburnet.com.
- **Re/Max Results**, 952-829-2900, 800-878-2901, www.minnesota homes.com.
- **Counselor Realty**, 763-786-0600, Fax: 763-786-4312, www.counselor-realty.com.

PURCHASE AGREEMENTS, CREDIT, MORTGAGES, INSURANCE

The purchase agreement is a legally binding document between the buyer and seller that states the price and all terms of a sale. It is the most negotiable and variable document produced in the homebuying process. It is also the single most important, since it is the document to which a buyer may attach contingencies. Such contingencies can protect you, the buyer, from being legally bound by the purchase agreement if, for example, you cannot sell the house you live in now, the house you are buying does not pass its mechanical and structural inspection, the seller is not able to give you possession by a certain date, or you cannot qualify for a loan.

Speaking of which, lenders suggest that you prequalify for your loan. To that end, meet with your potential lender to determine the amount of possible financing. Go prepared with documents that pertain to your finances and check your credit report to make sure it is accurate before meeting with a loan officer. You can check your credit report with all three national credit bureaus listed here. You are entitled to one free copy of your report each year, or a new report if you've been denied credit based on your credit report within the last 30 days. For more information about your rights concerning your credit report, contact the **Federal Trade Commission,** at 1-877-FTC-HELP, or check out the Federal Trade Commission's web site at www.ftc.gov.

The National Credit Bureaus are:

- **Equifax**, PO Box 105851, Atlanta, GA 30348-5851, 800-685-1111, www.equifax.com
- **TransUnion**, PO Box 1000, Chester, PA 19022, 800-916-8800, www. transunion.com
- **Experian**, PO Box 2104, Allen, TX 75013-9595, 1-888-397-3742, www. experian.com

When qualifying for a mortgage, the rule of thumb is that most people (depending on their existing debt load) can afford a home that is two and one-half times their annual gross income, or monthly payments of about 28% of their gross income. (Known as the 28/36 Rule, the other part of this rule states that no more than 36% of your income should be spent on *all* your monthly debt payments, including mortgage expenses, auto loans, credit cards, and utility payments.) In recent years, however, the rise in home prices has far out-paced wage increases, making affordable housing hard to find and threatening to drive middle-income buyers out of the real estate market entirely. To prevent that, lenders have developed several "creative" alternatives to the standard home loan, including low down payment loans, "interest-only" mortgages, and negative amortization mortgages. All these loans have the advantage of helping buyers to get into more home than they would normally qualify to buy; but they also carry the disadvantage that buyers who use these tools are not building equity in their homes and are exposing themselves to financial ruin should the real estate market collapse, leaving them with a house that is worth less than they still owe on it.

The **Minnesota Attorney General's Home Buyer's Handbook** (651-296-3353, 800-657-3787, or available online at www.ag.state.mn.us) contains information about more conventional solutions to the homebuying conun-drum including Veterans Administration (VA) and Federal Housing Administration (FHA) loans, the most popular loans for first-time homebuyers. It also contains a Loan Qualification Worksheet to help you figure out what you can afford.

Banks and mortgage-lending institutions also have web sites that can help you to prequalify for a mortgage. Wells Fargo (www.wellsfargo.com) adver-tises a "Relocation Mortgage Program," which they say is designed specifically for corporate transferees.

Of course, no lender's loans are unique. Most, if not all, lenders offer a variety of fixed-rate and adjustable-rate mortgage products and participate in government-insured VA and FHA loan programs, both of which require low down payments and have flexible qualifying guidelines. The thing to watch for, while you're shopping, is for sellers who quote you one price if you place your mortgage with their "preferred provider," and a higher price if you don't. It's illegal, but it's still been done—a lot.

Housing assistance is available for those in need. The **U.S. Department of Housing and Urban Development (HUD),** 920 Second Avenue South, Suite 1300, Minneapolis, 55402-4012, (612-370-3000, TTY 612-370-3186, Fax 612-370-3220, www.hud.gov), can help consumers buy homes, find Section 8 rentals, access HUD properties that are for sale, and figure out how much they can afford to spend on housing. The **Minnesota Housing Finance Agency (MHFA)** (651-296-8215, or 800-710-8871, TTY 651-297-2361, www.mhfa. state.mn.us) is sometimes able to make loans at below-market interest rates to first-time buyers or those with moderate incomes. For other resources for financial assistance, contact your city hall.

Once your loan is approved, your lender will require you to buy homeowner's insurance to protect their investment (your home). A basic homeowner's policy includes liability insurance to protect you if someone is injured on your property, property protection to insure your house and personal belongings against damage or loss, and living expense coverage to pay for you to live elsewhere while repairs are being made. You may also be required to buy mortgage insurance, which pays your lender if you default on your loan, and title insurance, which protects the lender in case the legal title to the property isn't clear. It doesn't protect you, though, so, in addition, you may want to buy an owner's title insurance policy, or get an attorney's opinion on your title. If the seller has purchased title insurance in recent years you may be able to get the same title company to issue you a new policy at a lower cost, so be sure to ask about a re-issue credit. Other consumer tips for buying insurance are available on the **Minnesota Attorney General**'s web site (www.ag.state.mn.us). Advice includes starting to shop as soon as you have signed a purchase agreement, and to purchase a policy with a high deductible in order to lower your cost. A deductible of $1000 to $2500 is often recommended. You may also be able to save money by buying your home and auto coverage from the same company. In addition, subtract the value of the land from the value of the property and only buy insurance to cover the value of your home. After all, your house can burn down, but your land will remain.

Some of the major insurance companies in the area are:

- **Allstate**, www.allstate.com
- **American Family Insurance**, www.amfam.com
- **Farmers Insurance Group**, www.farmersinsurance.com
- **St. Paul Fire and Marine Insurance Company**, www.stpaul.com/fire-and-marine
- **State Farm**, www.statefarm.com

CLOSING ON YOUR HOME

This is panic time! Most homes close the last week of the month because buyers want to avoid having to pay interest on their monthly loan payment, so underwriters, appraisers, and title companies are always in a mad scramble. Then, once you get to the actual closing you will probably be asked to sign the tallest stack of papers you have ever seen. How to avoid problems? There are a few things you can do. First, schedule your closing at least six weeks from the date your purchase agreement was signed. Then keep in contact with your lender to see if additional information is required. The week you close, ask your closer for a copy of the completed **Settlement Statement** (the HUD-1 form). You have the right to see this form one business day before the closing. It will contain a list of all your closing costs. Compare it to the good faith estimate of closing costs your loan officer gave you when you applied for the loan. The actual closing costs should not differ much from the estimate. If they do, you may be getting scammed. There are some costs, however, such as insurance premiums, the loan origination fee, and mortgage registration, that can only be nailed down after your loan is approved because they are based on the amount of your loan and the final value of the property. Finally, at the closing, be sure you've brought everything necessary: calculator to check addition, your homeowner's insurance binder and receipt showing this has been paid, a photo ID, your addresses for the last ten years, and a cashier's check to pay the balance of your down payment and unpaid closing costs. For more information on closing, including an explanation of all those papers you'll be asked to sign, download the **Closing Checklist** from the Minnesota Attorney General's website (www.ag.state.mn.us).

BUILDING

For those who are thinking of building, "location, location, location" is everything. Land prices within the Twin Cities are skyrocketing, and property near water sells at a premium. You also pay higher property taxes to live on it. For those willing to live a 40-minute drive away from the Twin Cities, in communities where the culs-de-sac meet the cornfields, such as Waconia, Chisago City, Northfield, or Hudson, Wisconsin, land prices are more reasonable—though the environmental costs associated with the loss of farmland and long car commutes are high.

Building a new home in the Twin Cities may require the additional expense of drilling a well and putting in a septic system. While there is a lot of water around, many municipalities do not provide it. Be sure to check this out even in established suburbs. (An example: the cities around Lake Minnetonka have sewer service, but they don't all have municipal water.) Well water here, by the way, is likely to be full of iron, requiring the installation of water softeners and high-tech filter systems, all of which add to the cost of a house, as will radon protection (see **Helpful Services**).

MINNESOTA ENERGY CODE REQUIREMENTS

"Build It Tight and Ventilate It Right" is the motto here. Because of our tight air sealing and insulation requirements, a single-family home built after April 2000 must have a mechanical ventilation system. Most builders use either an air exchanger or continuously exhausting fans to meet this energy code requirement. To learn more, call the **Builders Association of the Twin Cities** (651-697-1954, www.paradeofhomes.org) or the **Builders Association of Minnesota** (651-646-7959, www.bamn.org). They can provide general information about building a new home as well as state building code details. Your city clerk or building inspector will also be able to provide building code information, as well as give you a copy of local zoning ordinances. Free information on conservation and renewable energy is available from the **Minnesota**

Department of Commerce Energy Information (651-296-5175, 800-657-3710, www.state.mn.us/portal/mn/jsp/home.do?agency=Commerce).

FINDING AN ARCHITECT AND BUILDER

For a listing of local architects, go to the **American Institute of Architects** (www.aia-mn.org/home.cfm). This web site also includes information about working with an architect and questions to ask.

If you're here in the spring or fall, the **Parade/Preview of Homes**, sponsored by the Builders Association of the Twin Cities (see above), is the perfect opportunity to scout locations, check out the latest home designs and construction techniques, and connect with local architects and builders.

Once you collect a few names, be sure to check them out with the **Minnesota Department of Labor and Industry, Residential Builders and Contractors Unit** (443 Lafayette Road North, St. Paul, 651-284-5065, www.doli.state.mn.us/contractor.html). The department's web site contains a directory of licensed contractors, a consumer guide to hiring a contractor, complaint information, Contractor Recovery Fund application package, and annual enforcement action listings. The **Contractor Recovery Fund** compensates owners or renters of residential property in Minnesota who have lost money due to a licensed contractor's fraudulent, deceptive or dishonest practices. However, the Recovery Fund will only pay out a total of $75,000 in claims against any one contractor, so you should request that your contractor obtain a performance bond, thus assuring a specific level of protection for your project. For more information, the Minnesota Attorney General's **"The Citizen's Guide to Home Building and Remodeling"** is downloadable off the AG's web site (www.ag.state.mn.us).

MAXIMIZING POTENTIAL RESALE

In 1970, just 10% of new homes were 2400 square feet; but by 2004, 39% of new homes had at least 2400 square feet. In 1970, a bath and a half and two-car attached garage were standard; by 2004 multiple bathrooms and a three-car garage were a given.

The challenge when buying or building a house is always to find a property that meets your needs while maximizing your potential resale price. So while you think about what you want, keep these construction trends in mind: new construction at nearly every price point seems to include high ceilings, ballroom-sized living spaces, and high-tech kitchens. "Green" features such as high-efficiency insulation and energy-efficient appliances are often talked about, but, in general, prospective buyers are unwilling to pay extra for them. While attached three-stall garages are standard in new construction, buyers also seem willing to pay extra for a fourth stall, so that they will have room to store a snowmobile or a boat. Along with a big garage, mudrooms, fireplaces, a minimum of two bathrooms, and flat driveways (or steep driveways with built-in heating coils to melt the ice) are usually deemed essentials in this market. This being Minnesota, where the mosquito is considered the "state bird," add a screened porch to that list. For the same reason, plus the shortness of the summer season, swimming pools are often, though not always, considered a detriment.

HOME WARRANTIES

Builders usually offer new home warranties, but if your builder does not, you are still protected under state law, and the coverage is basically the same, though it is not "bumper-to-bumper" as we have come to expect with our cars. There is a one-year warranty on workmanship and defective materials that are not in compliance with building standards, but you must notify the builder within six months of discovering the problem or the builder is not liable. There is a two-year warranty on installation of cooling, plumbing, and electrical systems. Major construction defects are covered for ten years, but your idea of a major construction defect and The Law's may differ widely, as people who have had stucco and mold problems and cracks in their foundations have discovered. Basically, "major structural damage" appears to be limited to the load-bearing walls of the house and to damage that makes a house uninhabitable. For remodeling projects, work is generally covered for a one-year period. Check **Minnesota Statute Chapter 327A** (www.revisor.leg.state.mn.us/stats/327A/02.html) for the good news/bad news.

Should you discover a defect in your new home, notify your builder immediately by registered letter and also notify your local building inspector. At the very least, the building inspector can give you a copy of your city's building codes and, if you're lucky, a building inspector can be a valuable ally in getting the work done properly. If your contractor ignores you, or if his corrections to the problem are unsatisfactory, you can file a complaint against the contractor with the **Department of Labor and Industry, Enforcement Division** (651-284-5005, 800-DIAL-DLI (800-342-5354), TTY 651-297-4198, www.doli.state.mn.us). You might also want to file a report with the **Better Business Bureau** (651-699-1111). If you think you might need to get a lawyer, contact one early in the process because there is a statute of limitations on home defect lawsuits. Suing is very expensive, but if you win and are still unable to collect from the contractor, you may be eligible to have part of your judgment paid to you from the Minnesota Contractor Recovery Fund (see above).

HOME WARRANTY SERVICE PLANS

It is a common misconception that your homeowner's insurance policy will cover breakdowns of your home's mechanical systems. Unfortunately, it won't. Standard homeowners' policies only cover theft and specific disasters. A home warranty service plan, on the other hand, covers repairs or replacement of your property's mechanical systems and all appliances including the heating system, water heater, plumbing, wiring, central air conditioning, and more. It doesn't matter whether your home is one year old or a hundred; it only matters that the covered items were in good working order at the start of the home warranty contract. Home Protection Plans are available through many realtors. According to Bob Vila, formerly on *This Old House,* "Home warranties make great sense when the house and its appliances and systems start to wear, perhaps after 10 years." To find out how long appliances can be expected to last, check out Vila's web site (www.bobvila.com).

MECHANICS' LIENS

Every contractor, subcontractor, or material supplier who has been involved in your construction project is entitled to a mechanic's lien on your property. This means that they may go to court and try to take possession of your property if they are not paid. To avoid this problem, you may pay any subcontractor directly or withhold from your contractor whatever amount is necessary to pay subcontractors until the contractor has provided you with lien waivers signed by the subcontractors. (A lien waiver is a written statement signed by a subcontractor acknowledging receipt of payment and giving up his right to file a lien against your property.) If you obtain valid lien waivers from the subcontractors, or if you pay the general contractor in full before receiving notice from a subcontractor that he intends to file a lien against your property, you cannot be forced to pay for the services or material a second time, even if the contractor fails to pay the subcontractor. For further information, contact the **Minnesota Attorney General's Office, Consumer Protection** (1400 NCL Tower, 445 Minnesota Street, St. Paul, 55101, Hotline 651-296-3353, 800-657-3787, TTY 651-297-7206, TTY Toll-free 800-366-4812, www.ag.state.mn.us).

EFORE YOU CAN START YOUR NEW LIFE IN THE TWIN CITIES, YOU AND your worldly possessions have to get here. How difficult that will be depends on how much stuff you've accumulated, how much money you're willing or able to spend on the move, and where you're coming from.

But first, a word of caution: watch out for shakedown schemes that begin with a lowball bid off the Internet and end with the mover holding your belongings hostage for a high cash ransom. Despite the fact that federal law says that movers cannot charge more than 10% over any written estimate, it is not unusual for unscrupulous movers to charge you several times their written estimates—and with your possessions in their possession, you may find yourself paying anyway, since companies that operate this way also won't tell you where they're holding your stuff. It's fraud. It's extortion. And sometimes there isn't a lot the police can do to help you. So help yourself first. Check out the **MovingScam** web site (www.movingscam.com) for help finding a reputable mover. MovingScam.com is dedicated to providing solid, impartial consumer education and to working for better consumer protections in the moving industry. Its featured articles include "Understanding Estimates," "Phony Internet Moving Brokerages Take Consumers for a Ride," and "Planning an International Move." It also maintains a "Blacklist." Its message boards are staffed around the clock with experienced volunteers who answer moving-related questions promptly and at no cost to the consumer.

A similar web site, run by the **Federal Motor Carrier Safety Administration (FMCSA)**, is www.protectyourmove.com. This web site provides one-click checking to make sure that an interstate mover is properly registered and insured. It also posts news of recent criminal investigations and convictions, and offers links to local Better Business Bureaus, consumer protection agencies, state attorneys general, state moving associations, and the **FMCSA Safety Violation and Consumer Household Goods Complaint Hotline** (888-DOT-SAFT [888-368-7238], www.1-888-dot-saft.com). Don't expect much from this hotline, however. It is essentially just a database and you will only hear from the DOT if it looks at your complaint and determines that enforcement action is warranted.

TRUCK RENTALS

The first question you need to answer: am I going to move myself, or will I have someone else do it for me? If you're used to doing things for yourself, by all means, rent a vehicle and head for the open road. It may well be the best way to get your belongings where you're going. As one web page says, "U-Haul has never held any family's belongings hostage." So look in the Yellow Pages under "Truck Rental," then call around and compare. Below, we list four national truck rental firms and their toll-free numbers and web sites, but for the best information you should call a local office. Note that most truck rental companies now offer "one-way" rentals (don't forget to ask whether they have a drop-off/return location in or near your destination) as well as packing accessories and storage facilities. Of course, these extras are not free and, if you're cost-conscious, you may want to scavenge boxes from liquor stores or purchase them from discounters and arrange for storage yourself. (See **Moving Supplies** and **Storage** sections below.)

Finally, if you're planning on moving during the peak moving months (May through September), call well in advance of when you think you'll need the vehicle—a month at least. And consider timing your move for the middle, rather than the end, of the month, because the prices might be slightly cheaper.

Speaking of price: cheapest is not always best, and some companies in this industry do have a history of unresolved complaints with the **Better Business Bureau**, so be sure to contact your local BBB and request a report (www.bbb.org, or in Minnesota call 651-699-1111, www.minnesota.bbb.org). The following are national truck rental companies with offices in the Twin Cities:

- **Budget**, 800-428-7825, www.budget.com
- **Penske**, 800-222-0277, www.penske.com
- **Ryder**, 800-467-9337, www.ryder.com
- **U-Haul**, 800-468-4285, www.uhaul.com

Not sure that you want to drive the truck yourself? Commercial freight carriers such as ABF (www.upack.com) and PODS (888-776-PODS, www.PODS.com) offer an in-between service: they deliver a trailer or container to your home, you pack and load as much of it as you need, and they drive the vehicle or deliver your container to your destination.

MOVERS

Surveys show that most people find movers through the **Yellow Pages**. If that's too random for you, probably the best way to find a mover is through a personal recommendation. If someone recommends a mover to you, though, get names (the salesperson or estimator, the drivers, and the loaders). To paraphrase the NRA, moving companies don't move people, people do. Absent a friend or relative who can point you to a trusted moving company, you can try the Internet; just be careful. For long distance or interstate moves, the **American Moving and Storage Association**'s site (www.moving.org) is useful for identifying member movers both in Minnesota and across the country. Members of **AAA** have a valuable resource at hand in **Consumer Relocation Services**, which will assign the member a personal consultant to handle every detail of the move, free of charge, and which offers discounts of up to 60% on interstate moves as well as replacement valuation coverage of up to $50,000 at no charge. Call 800-839-MOVE or check online at www.consumers relocation.com/aaa-benefits.htm.

But beware! Since 1995, when the federal government eliminated the Interstate Commerce Commission, the interstate moving industry has degenerated into a largely unregulated industry with thousands of unhappy, ripped-off customers annually. In fact, the Council of Better Business Bureaus reports that complaints against moving and storage companies rank near the top of all complaints received by Bureaus every year. And there's more bad news—since states do not have the authority to regulate interstate moving companies, and since the federal government basically won't, you're really pretty much on your own in your dealings with an interstate mover.

Therefore Better Business Bureaus and Attorneys General around the country urge you to take precautions before hiring a mover by doing the following things:

- Make sure the mover is licensed and insured. For intrastate moves, call the **Department of Transportation Office of Freight and Commercial Vehicle Operations** (651-405-6060) to see if a mover is licensed. If yours is an interstate move, make sure the carrier has a Department of Transportation MC ("Motor Carrier") or ICC MC number; it should be displayed on all advertising and promotional material as well as on the truck. With the MC number in hand, contact the **Department of Transportation's Federal Motor Carrier Safety Administration** at 888-368-7238 or 202-358-7028 (offers the option of speaking to an agent), or check online at www.fmcsa.dot.gov or www.protectyourmove.gov, to see if the carrier is licensed. If the companies you're interested in appear to be federally licensed, the next step is to contact the Better Business Bureau (www.bbb.org) and find out if the Bureau has a record of any complaints against them.

- Get several written estimates from companies that have actually sent a sales representative to your home to do a visual inspection of the goods to be moved. Don't worry about cost here; estimates should always be free. And don't do business with a company that charges for an estimate or wants to give you an estimate over the telephone. Do, however, make sure each company is giving you an estimate for approximately the same poundage of items to be moved, and the same services. Finally, only accept estimates that are written on a document that contains the company's name, address, phone number, and signature of the salesperson. Note that estimates can be either binding or non-binding. A binding estimate guarantees the total cost of the move based upon the quantities and services shown on the estimate. A non-binding estimate is what your mover believes the cost will be, based upon the estimated weight of the shipment and the extra services requested. With a non-binding estimate the final charges will be based upon the actual weight of your shipment and services provided. If you accept a mover's non-binding estimate, you must be prepared to pay 10% more than the estimated charges at delivery (110 Percent Rule).

- Follow-up with your State Department of Transportation to find out if the estimate the mover gave you is based on the hourly rate they have filed with the Department of Transportation. Some movers may *quote* below this rate and then, at your destination, attempt to *charge* the higher rate they filed with the state. Also follow up with your mover to find out how the unloading will be handled at the destination end, and ask for references—then check them.
- Be sure you understand the terms of the moving contract. Get everything in writing, including the mover's liability to you for breakage or loss. Consider whether to buy additional replacement insurance to cover loss or damage. Check your homeowner's or renter's insurance policy to see what, if any, coverage you may already have for your belongings while they are in transit. If the answer is none, ask your insurer if you can add coverage for your move. You can purchase coverage through your mover. A mover's coverage, however, is normally based on the weight of the items being insured, not on their value. So if you want to cover the actual value of your belongings, you will need to purchase "full value" or "full replacement" insurance. Though it's expensive, it's worth it—and you can lower the cost by increasing your deductible. Better yet, consider packing and moving irreplaceable, fragile or sentimental items, documents, and jewelry yourself. That way you can avoid the headache and heartache of possible loss or breakage of your most valuable possessions.
- Compile an inventory of all items shipped and their condition when they left your house, take pictures, and be present for both the loading and unloading of your things. Since checking every item as it comes off the truck is probably impossible when you're moving the contents of an entire house, write "subject to further inspection for concealed loss or damage" on the moving contract to allow for damage you may discover as you unpack.
- File a written claim with the mover immediately if any loss or damage occurs—and keep a copy of your claim, as well as all the other paperwork related to your move. If your claim is not resolved within a reasonable time, file complaints with the Better Business Bureau and appropriate authorities, as well. (See **Consumer Complaints—Movers,** below.) To learn more about your rights and responsibilities with respect to interstate moving, check out the United States Department of Transportation (USDOT) publication "Your Rights and Responsibilities When You Move," which is downloadable off the www.protectyourmove.gov web site.

Some general advice, if you've followed the steps above and succeeded in hiring a reputable mover:
- Listen to what the movers say; they are professionals and can give you expert advice about packing and preparing. Also, be ready for the truck on

both ends—don't make them wait. Understand, too, that things can happen on the road that are beyond a carrier's control (weather, accidents, etc.) and your belongings may not get to you at the time, or on the day, promised.
- Treat your movers well, especially the ones loading your stuff on and off the truck. Offer to buy them lunch, and tip them if they do a good job.
- Be prepared to pay the full moving bill upon delivery. Cash or a cashier's check may be required. Some carriers will take VISA and MasterCard but it is a good idea to get it in writing that you will be permitted to pay with a credit card since the delivering driver may not be aware of this and may demand cash.
- Finally, before moving pets, attach tags to their collars with your new address and phone number in case your pets accidentally wander off in the confusion of moving. For more help in this area, you might want to look into *The Pet-Moving Handbook* (First Books, www.firstbooks.com).

INTRASTATE MOVES

When hiring a local mover, follow all the steps above for dealing with interstate movers: check that they are licensed and insured, check with the Better Business Bureau, check estimates, check contracts, and check references. It's a whole lot easier when the company is local! Here are a few Twin Cities–based movers:
- **Fisher Transfer**, 181 James Ave North, Minneapolis, 612-377-5112, is a family-owned company that has been in business in the Twin Cities since 1939.
- **Good Stuff Moving & Delivery**, St. Paul, 651-488-4808
- **Local Motion**, 612-929-6683, 763-476-6683, 651-776-6683, 952-474-6683, is one of the area's largest moving and storage companies.
- **Rose's Daughters** provide concierge-type moving services, 612-330-3772 or 651-373-1323, www.rosesdaughters.com
- **Two Men and a Truck**, www.twomen.com, advertise that they will also pick up and deliver appliances and large pieces of furniture. A national franchise, there are four offices in the metro area: Bloomington, 500 American Blvd West, 612-341-2800; Robbinsdale, 3758 West Broadway, 763-478-0100; Burnsville, 14217 Ewing Ave South, 952-894-8606; and Eden Prairie, 14500 Martin Dr, 952-942-4949.

MOVING SUPPLIES

Movers' boxes, while not cheap, are usually sturdy and the right size. Sometimes a mover will give a customer free used boxes—it doesn't hurt to ask. But if you need to buy them yourself, UPS stores sell boxes, shipping tape, bubble cushioning, foam peanuts, markers, and labels, as do the office megastores. If your move is within the metro area, a good source for new and used boxes is **A Bargain Box Company** (2800 Winter Street NE, 612-331-3355 and 6870 Shingle Creek Parkway, Minneapolis, 763-503-3518).

ROAD RESTRICTIONS

A special consideration when you're timing a move or building a house in Minnesota is road restrictions. From March 1 to May 1, when the roads are heaving and thawing, the state, counties, and cities all restrict the weight of the vehicles that may drive here. Many residential streets are closed to vehicles weighing more than four tons per axle. This affects both construction equipment and moving vans. Local contractors are accustomed to working around the road restrictions, but if you're moving from out of state be sure to bring this to your mover's attention. For more information, refer your mover to the **Department of Transportation** (651-747-2253 or toll free at 800-723-6543 [in season], www.mrr.dot.state.mn.us/research/seasonal_load_limits/sllindex.asp) and/or call your (new) city hall.

STORAGE

Probably the easiest way to find storage close to your new home is to look online at your new city's web site or at www.move.com, where you can put in your zip code and be linked to nearby local businesses, including storage facilities. You can also check the **Yellow Pages** in the phone book or online at Verizon's http://yellowpages.superpages.com and Qwest's www.dexonline.com. Check under "Household Goods Moving and Storage" or "Real Estate, Moving and Storage" for complete listings. Given our wild weather swings, units with climate controls are often preferred. Keep in mind that demand for storage surges in the prime moving months (May through September), so try not to wait until the last minute to look for something to rent. Also, if you don't care about convenience, your cheapest storage options may be outside the Twin Cities. You just have to figure out how to get your stuff there and back.

A word of warning: unless you no longer want your stored belongings, pay your storage bill and pay it on time. Storage companies may auction the contents of delinquent customers' lockers.

A few area storage companies for you to compare:

- **Great Plains Mini-Storage**, 505 Shimmcor St, Mayer, 952-657-1019, www.storagecentermn.com
- **Minikahda Mini-Storage**, www.minikahda.com; 1441 Hunting Valley Rd, 651-641-0101 (U of M and Midway) and other locations throughout the metro.
- **Shurgard Mini-Storage**, www.minnesotaministorage.com, 866-866-6199 (24-hour line); I-494 and France Ave, Edina/Bloomington, 952-835-0580, and numerous other locations.
- **Public Storage**, 1-800-44-STORE, www.publicstorage.com, 9640 Hudson Rd, Woodbury, 651-731-0807, and other locations.

CONSUMER COMPLAINTS—MOVERS

To file a complaint concerning a Minnesota mover, contact the **Minnesota Department of Transportation, Office of Freight and Commercial**

Vehicle Operations (1110 Centre Pointe Curve, Mendota Heights, 55120, 651-405-6060, www.dot.state.mn.us). If yours was an interstate move, your options are limited in terms of government help. The Federal Motor Carrier Safety Administration (www.fmcsa.dot.gov) recommends that you contact the Better Business Bureau in the state where the moving company is licensed as well as that state's consumer protection office to register a complaint. You can also file a complaint with FMCSA in one of two ways: use their complaint web site: www.1-888-dot-saft.com, or call their Hotline, toll free: 888-DOT-SAFT (888-368-7238), TTY 800-877-8339, from 10:00 a.m. to 6:00 p.m., Eastern time, Monday–Friday.

If satisfaction still eludes you, start a letter-writing campaign: to the state Attorney General, to your congressional representative, to the newspaper, to the Internet—the sky's the limit. Of course, if the dispute is worth it, you can hire a lawyer and seek redress the all-American way.

TAXES

If your move is work-related, and you're not being reimbursed for moving costs by your employer, some or all of your moving expenses may be tax-deductible—so you need to keep your receipts. Though eligibility varies depending, for example, on whether you have a job or are self-employed, generally the cost of moving yourself, your family, and your belongings is tax deductible, even if you don't itemize. The criteria: in order to take the deduction, your move must be employment-related, your new job must be at least 50 miles farther away from your former residence than your old job location, and you must be here for at least 39 weeks during the first 12 months after your arrival.

In general, this is what you can deduct:
- The cost of transportation and hauling from your old residence to your new one.
- The cost of storage-in-transit (limited to 30 consecutive days).
- The cost of shipping your car.
- The cost of moving your household pets.
- The cost of your family's trip to your new residence (this includes lodging, but not meals).

If you take the deduction and then fail to meet the requirements, you will have to pay the IRS back, unless you were laid off through no fault of your own or transferred again by your employer. Consulting a tax expert for guidance about the IRS's rules with respect to moving is probably a good idea. However, if you're a confident soul, get a copy of **IRS Form 3903** (www.irs.gov) and do it yourself!

CHILDREN

Studies show that moving, especially frequent moving, can be hard on children, but there are things you can do to help your children through this stressful time:
- Talk about the move with your kids and, to the extent possible, involve them in the process.

- Make sure your children have their favorite possessions with them on the trip; don't pack "blankey" in the moving van.
- Make sure you have some social life planned on the other end. Your child may feel lonely in your new home and such activities can ease the transition.
- Maintain links to the important people you have left behind.
- If your children are of school age, take the time to involve yourself in their new schools and in their academic life. Don't let them fall through the cracks.

For younger children, there are dozens of good books on the topic. Just a few include *Max's Moving Adventure: A Coloring Book for Kids on the Move* by Danelle Till, illustrated by Joe Spooner; *Alexander, Who's Not (Do You Hear Me? I Mean It!) Going to Move* by Judith Viorst; *Goodbye/Hello* by Barbara Hazen; *The Leaving Morning* by Angela Johnson; *Little Monster's Moving Day* by Mercer Mayer; *Who Will Be My Friends?* (Easy I Can Read Series) by Syd Hoff; *I'm Not Moving, Mama* by Nancy White Carlstrom, illustrated by Thor Wickstrom; and *The Berenstain Bears' Moving Day* by Jan and Stan Berenstain.

For older children, try *The Moving Book: A Kid's Survival Guide* by Gabriel Davis; *Amber Brown is Not a Crayon* by Paula Danziger; *The Kid in the Red Jacket* by Barbara Park; *Hold Fast to Dreams* by Andrea Davis Pinkney; *Flip Flop Girl* by Katherine Paterson; and *My Fabulous New Life* by Sheila Greenwald.

For general guidance, read *Smooth Moves* by Ellen Carlisle; *Will This Place Ever Feel Like Home?, New and Updated Edition, Simple Advice for Settling in After You Move* by Leslie Levine; and Clyde and Shari Steiner's *How To Move Handbook.*

ONLINE RESOURCES—RELOCATION

- **American Car Transport**, www.American-car-transport.com
- **Apartments.com**, www.apartments.com, includes short-term rentals and furniture rental, as well as moving information.
- **Best Places**, www.bestplaces.net, compares quality-of-life and cost-of-living data of US cities.
- **www.firstbooks.com**; relocation resources and information on moving to Atlanta; Boston; Chicago; Los Angeles; New York; San Francisco; Seattle; Washington, D.C.; and London, England. Also publisher of the *Newcomer's Handbook for Moving to and Living in the USA; The Moving Book: A Kids' Survival Guide; Max's Moving Adventure: A Coloring Book for Kids on the Move;* and the *Pet-Moving Handbook.*
- **www.homestore.com**; relocation resources, including a handy salary calculator that will compare the cost of living in US cities.
- **www.moving.org**; members of the American Moving and Storage Association.
- **The Riley Guide**, www.rileyguide.com/relocate.html; online moving and relocation clearinghouse, including Moving/Relocation Guides, Cost of Living and Demographics, Real Estate Links, and School and Health Care Directories.
- **www.usps.com**; relocation information from the United States Postal Service.

O PENING A BANK ACCOUNT IS ONE OF THE FIRST THINGS YOU WILL
need to take care of upon arriving. Many landlords and rental agents will
not accept a tenant who does not have a checking account, so it's probably wise to keep your old bank account for at least a short time after moving.

BANK ACCOUNTS AND SERVICES

Both "big" national banks and "little" local banks offer Internet and telephone
banking, mortgages, and ATM and debit cards that you can use anywhere in
the world. "Little" locally based banks, however, often specialize in personal
service. The first three institutions on this list are the "Big Banks" in this region,
including homegrown Twin City Federal; the rest are community banks. Many
other local banks/savings and loans can be found in the Yellow Pages.

- **Twin Cities Federal (TCF) Savings and Loan**, 612-823-2265, www.tcf
  bank.com, has branches or ATMs in the Minneapolis skyway system, col-
  leges and public buildings, and innumerable gas stations, markets, and
  grocery stores.
- **US Bank**, 612-US BANKS, 612-872-2657, 800-US BANKS, www.
  usbank.com, has branch offices and ATMs in several grocery stores, Wal-
  Marts, and Targets.
- **Wells Fargo**, 800-869-3557, www.wellsfargo.com, has ATMs in some
  Rainbow Foods and Cub Foods stores.
- **Anchor Bank**, www.anchorlink.com, has branches throughout the
  metro.
- **Bremer Financial**, 800-908-BANK, www.bremer.com, is employee-
  owned and has over 100 locations in the Upper Midwest, including 25
  offices in the Twin Cities metropolitan area and several in Wisconsin.
- **Cherokee State Bank**, 651-227-7071, www.bankcherokee.com, has sev-
  eral branches, mostly in St. Paul.
- **First National Bank,** 715-386-5511 or 651-436-8441, www.ibank
  fnb.com, has branches in Hudson, Wisconsin; and Woodbury, Stacy, and
  North Branch, Minnesota.

- **Franklin National Bank**, www.franklinbankmpls.com: 525 Washington Ave North, Minneapolis, 612-874-6000; 2100 Blaisdell Ave South, Minneapolis, 612-874-6000.
- **KleinBank**, 877-KLEINET (553-4638), www.kleinet.com, has 18 branches located in the north metro and western suburbs.
- **Premier Banks**, www.premierbanks.com, has numerous branches, as well as surcharge-free ATMs.
- **The River Bank**, www.theriverbank.com: 880 6th St North, Hudson, 715-386-8700, 877-592-5559 (toll free); 712 Rivard St, Somerset, 715-247-4995.
- **State Bank of Long Lake**, 1964 W Wayzata Blvd, 952-473-7347, 888-311-3880, www.sblonglake.com.
- **University Bank**, 200 University Ave West, St. Paul, 651-265-5600, www.universitybank.com.
- **Western Bank**, 651-290-8100, www.western-bank.com; centered both physically and philosophically on University Ave in Frogtown in St. Paul, Western Bank has been involved in community development since 1935. It has offices in Edina, Maplewood, Minneapolis, Oakdale, St. Paul, and Mounds View.

CHECKING AND SAVINGS ACCOUNTS

Although debit cards are quickly becoming the way to bank and transact business, you might be pleasantly surprised at how readily most Twin Cities merchants still accept personal checks. To open an account, most banks require a minimum deposit (depending on the type of account you want, some have minimums as low as $50), current photo identification, and your Social Security number.

ONLINE BANKING

Virtually every bank offers online banking, making it easy to track your account activity, pay your bills, or even apply for a loan—all from the comfort of your own home. Services vary from bank to bank, and some charge a fee for automatic bill-paying features. See above, under **Bank Accounts and Services,** for area banks' web addresses. Two national Internet banks that may be worth investigating are **www.netbank.com** and **www.presidential.com**. Both advertise significantly higher interest rates than their so-called "brick and mortar" competitors.

CREDIT UNIONS

Your place of work or neighborhood may offer membership in a credit union—which could be your best banking deal of all. These nonprofit, cooperative financial institutions offer almost all the same products that banks do, usually with fewer fees and higher interest rates. Your employer will be able to tell you if you are eligible for membership in any credit unions through your work. To find other ways of becoming eligible for membership in a credit union, call the Minnesota Credit Union Network (800-477-1034, www.mncun.org) and a representative will help you find credit unions in your area that you are eligible to join. Or use the Credit Union Match Up service (www.howtojoinacu.org). For links to all the local credit unions that have web addresses, visit Credit Unions Online (www.creditunionsonline.com). The National Credit Union Administration (www.ncua.gov), an independent federal agency that supervises and insures credit unions, maintains a searchable database. You can also use this site to file a complaint. Here are two credit unions nearly any Twin Cities resident can join:

- **U.S. Federal Credit Union**, 2535 27th Ave South, Minneapolis, and other locations, 952-736-5000 or 800-345-2733, www.usfed.org; you are eligible for membership if you live, work, worship, volunteer, or attend school in Anoka, Carver, Dakota, Hennepin, Ramsey, Scott or Washington County, or Northfield.
- **The Twin Cities Co-ops Federal Credit Union**, 866-JOIN-TCU, 651-215-3500, www.tcuconnect.com; membership is open to Minnesota and Wisconsin residents who meet certain criteria or who make a $5 tax-deductible contribution to the credit union's foundation. This credit union has nine branch locations in the Minneapolis/St. Paul metropolitan area, and a branch in Princeton.

CONSUMER PROTECTION—BANKING

If you have a problem with your bank, first try to resolve the matter by bringing it to the attention of a senior bank officer. If the problem is still not taken care of to your satisfaction, you can file a complaint with the **Board of Governors of the Federal Reserve System, Division of Consumer and Community Affairs** (20th and C Streets NW, Stop 801, Washington, DC 20551; 202-452-3693; www.federalreserve.gov/pubs/complaints/default.htm). This is really the only number you need—complaints about financial institutions that are not supervised by the Federal Reserve System will be forwarded by the Fed to the appropriate agency.

CREDIT CARDS

Department store credit cards are good to use to establish a credit history if you have none. Applications can often be obtained at the checkout counter, and stores frequently offer immediate discounts when you apply for a card. **Macy's** and **Target**, with their numerous locations metro-wide, are particularly good credit cards for this area—they are easy to qualify for, and they're cards you can use often enough to establish a good history. While it's only good at one store, the **Von Maur Department Store** (Eden Prairie Center, 952-829-0200, www.vonmaur.com) offers its customers an interest-free credit card with no fees and flexible payments. Search for low-rate, no annual fee, etc. cards on the Internet at **CardWeb** (www.cardweb.com).

Call to request a credit card application or apply online:

- **VISA**, www.usa.visa.com, and **MasterCard**, www.mastercard.com, are available from banks. The **Northwest Airlines WorldPerks VISA** card earns frequent flyer miles with every purchase, 800-327-2881.
- **American Express**, 800-THE-CARD, www.americanexpress.com
- **Discover Card**, 800-347-2683 (or apply at a Sears store), www.discover card.com

IDENTITY THEFT, CREDIT CARD FRAUD, AND CREDIT REPORTS

Following a steady stream of disclosures of security breaches affecting major banks, credit card companies, and businesses that collect and sell personal data, as well as the vulnerability of the State of Minnesota's own e-business, it seems nearly impossible to do anything to protect yourself from either credit card fraud or identity theft—and yet, if you're a victim, a fraud such as identity theft can nearly ruin your life. Victims spend an average of 600 hours trying to repair their credit; it's a daunting task. For more information, contact the **Identity Theft Resource Center** at 858-693-7935 or www.idtheftcenter.com.

That said, there is some good news: by Minnesota law you are not liable for more than $50 improperly charged to your credit card. Industry standards are even tougher and, in practice, consumers are not held responsible for any unauthorized charges on their credit cards. Industry standards are even tougher and, in practice, consumers are not held responsible for any unauthorized charges on their credit cards. The trick is to check your monthly statements carefully and notify your credit card company immediately when the charges are incorrect. So what else can you do to protect yourself? Security experts recommend several things. Don't print your full name and Social Security number on your checks, and don't carry your Social Security card in your wallet. Don't let your mail sit in your mailbox any longer than absolutely necessary, and shred personal documents before putting them into the trash. Finally, think twice before you make a financial transaction over the Internet. Convenient though it may be, security failures have been identified even on web sites you might reasonably expect to be secure, such as those of the State of Minnesota. In fact, at the time of this writing, several of Minnesota's agencies' online services are shut down pending security improvements, and legislators are calling for audits of others. Finally, check your credit rating periodically. You are entitled to one free credit report per year from each of the three major credit reporting companies, so if you request a report every four months from a different credit reporting company, you'll be able to keep tabs on your credit rating—for free. You can also visit **www.annualcredit report.com** for online access to all three.

The national credit bureaus are:

- **Equifax**, P.O. Box 105873, Atlanta, GA 30348, 800-685-1111, www.equifax.com
- **Experian**, P.O. Box 2104, Allen, TX 75002-2104, 888-397-3742, www.experian.com/

- **TransUnion Corporation,** P.O. Box 390, Springfield, PA 19064-0390, 800-916-8800, www.transunion.com

TAXES

Is Minnesota really a high-tax state? It depends. According to a January 2005 tax system overview posted on the Minnesota Department of Revenue web site (see below), if you make 0 to $10,235, your total state and local tax rate is 17.5%; but if you make $116,126 or more, your total tax rate is only 10.1%.

For questions about individual income tax, contact the **Minnesota Department of Revenue** (www.taxes.state.mn.us, email: indinctax@ state.mn.us, or call 651-296-3781, 711 for Minnesota Relay). For questions regarding other tax types, go to the department's tax information page (www.taxes.state.mn.us/taxes/all_tax_types.shtml) and select a tax type.

HISTORY OF TAXATION IN MINNESOTA

Nine years before Minnesota became a state in 1858, the territorial assembly established a property tax levy to support the schools. Property taxes remained the primary source of revenue until the hardships of the Great Depression made property taxes hard to collect. Then the need for dependable government funding, combined with the call for tax relief by property owners, led the legislature to establish the state individual and corporate income tax systems in 1933. Since that time, Minnesota has relied somewhat more on the income tax, and somewhat less on sales and property taxes, than most other states. That weighting toward the income tax, however, has left Minnesota open to the charge of being a high tax state. It also opened the door for the election, in 2002, of a governor and legislature who immediately signed a "No New Taxes" pledge, then proceeded to cut taxes for the state's wealthiest residents at the same time that they began shifting the burden of paying for essential services away from the state and income taxes and onto local governments (school districts, cities, and counties) whose only sources of funding are sales and local property taxes.

That's why your property taxes will most likely be higher than your home's previous owner's.

So what can you do about it?

Be proactive. Check with your city hall and find out how much of a tax increase you might reasonably expect before you buy. The **Minnesota Department of Employment and Economic Development**'s community profiles web site lists property tax information for every city (www.mnpro.com). Be sure that you make yourself eligible for all possible tax deductions. If you're moving within Minnesota, be sure that your new main job location is at least 50 miles farther from your former home than your old job was, so that you will be eligible to deduct moving expenses from your federal return. For additional information, refer to the Form 3903 Instructions (PDF) and Publication 521, Moving Expenses, both posted on the **IRS** web site (www.irs.gov/), or call 800-829-1040. See **Moving and Storage** for more information.

INCOME TAXES

As a resident here, you will have to pay both federal and state income taxes. For federal forms and information contact:

- **Federal Tax Forms**, 800-829-FORM, or pick them up at a public library or post office, or download them from the Internet, www.irs.ustreas.gov.
- **Federal Tax Help**, 800-829-1040, www.irs.ustreas.gov
- **Federal Teletax Information System**, 800-829-4477, TTY 800-829-4059 (for recorded federal tax information), or www.irs.ustreas.gov
- **Internal Revenue Service**, 316 North Robert St, St. Paul, 800-829-4477, www.irs.ustreas.gov
- **IRS Tax Help Line**, 800-829-1040, www.irs.gov

The state income tax is based on federal adjusted income minus 85 exemptions, deductions and credits. In 2005, there were three rates that increased with income: 5.35%, 7.05% and 7.85%. To obtain Minnesota state income tax forms or ask questions call the **Minnesota Department of Revenue** (10 River Park Plaza, St. Paul, 651-296-3781). Forms are also available at libraries and post offices during tax season or online at www.taxes. state.mn.us, where you can also file your return online.

Free tax help is available to seniors and others with low incomes through the **American Association of Retired Persons (AARP) Tax-Aide** program (http://www.aarp.org/money/taxaide/). In Minneapolis, volunteers are available on Tuesdays and Wednesdays in Room 11, Minneapolis City Hall, 350 South Fifth Street (use the Fourth Street entrance). If you need more information, check the **Department of Revenue's Tax Information** index (www.taxes.state.mn.us/taxes/individ/index.shtml). If you can't find the answer you need, you can call the department's **Individual Income Tax Help Line** at 651-296-3781 or 711 for Minnesota Relay. Hours of operation are Monday–Thursday, 9:00 a.m. to 4:45 p.m., Friday, 9 a.m. to noon. You can also email your tax questions to indinctax@state.mn.us.

SALES TAX

The state sales tax (on most goods except food and clothing) is 6.5%, with an additional amount collected within certain cities including Minneapolis and St. Paul. Due to cuts in state aid to cities, other metro area cities may soon need to resort to sales taxes as well. In addition, the legislature has authorized Hennepin County to charge an additional sales tax to pay for a new Twins Stadium.

PROPERTY TAXES

First-half Minnesota property taxes are due May 15th. Owners whose taxes are not included in their mortgage payments can pay in person or by mail or credit card. In Anoka, Dakota, Hennepin, Ramsey and Washington counties, property owners can go online to pay their bills. Second-half taxes are due October 15th. For more information, call your county's assessor:

- **Anoka**: 763-323-5400, www.co.anoka.mn.us/v1_departments/div-property-rec-tax/index.asp
- **Carver**: 952-361-1980 or 952-361-1500, www.co.carver.mn.us
- **Dakota**: 651-438-4200 or 800-247-1056, www.co.dakota.mn.us
- **Hennepin**: 612-348-3011, www.hennepin.us
- **Isanti**: 763-689-3859, www.co.isanti.mn.us
- **Ramsey**: 651-266-2000, www.co.ramsey.mn.us
- **Scott**: 952-496-8150, www.co.scott.mn.us
- **Sherburne**: 763-241-2590 or 800-438-0575, www.co.sherburne.mn.us
- **Washington**: 651-430-6100, www.co.washington.mn.us
- **Wright**: 763-682-7367, www.co.wright.mn.us

Property taxes are different for each city and county and include levies to support school districts, watershed districts, mosquito control, and other services. Several factors determine how much tax is paid, including the market value and type (class) of property, and the amounts levied by each of the taxing authorities. Taxes change each year, but the previous year's taxes for property you are considering buying will always be stated on the property's listing sheet. Property taxes are expected to increase by an average of 10.2% in 2006, according to the Minnesota Department of Revenue. To find out about anticipated property tax changes in the community you are considering, call the city hall or, since school district levies account for the bulk of property taxes, call your local school district (see **Childcare and Education** chapter).

There is also a state general property tax on commercial, industrial and public utility property, and on seasonal residential recreational property, including cabins. Included in your local property tax statement, the state property tax is paid to the county treasurer along with local property taxes, but the money raised from the state general tax does not go to local governments (i.e., counties, cities, school districts, etc.). Instead, it is deposited in the state general fund.

STATE PROPERTY TAX REFUNDS

Minnesota has two property tax refund programs for homeowners: the regular refund for those who own and reside in their homes on January 2 (Homestead Credit), and the special property tax refund for those whose property taxes have increased by more than 12% from the previous year. To apply for either or both of these refunds, use Form M1PR, Minnesota Property Tax Refund. For a fee, you can file your M1PR electronically online at the **Minnesota Department of Revenue**'s web site (www.taxes.state.mn.us). Otherwise, forms and instructions are available at many libraries, or you can order them by calling the Department of Revenue's 24-hour forms order service (651-296-4444). Minnesota also offers tenants a renter's property tax refund. Your landlord is required to send you the Certification of Rent Paid (CRP) form no later than January 31. You then have nearly seven months (until August 15th) to fill out your half—the M1PR form—and send both to the state for a refund of the portion of your rent that went to property taxes. The refund averages $554, so it is well worth filing. Keep an eye on this program, however, because our "No

New Taxes" governor and legislature keep eyeing it as a way of raising state revenue without "raising" taxes.

WISCONSIN TAXES

Wisconsin collects income, property, and sales (excise) taxes. Tax information is posted on the **Department of Revenue (DOR)**'s web site (www.dor.state.wi.us). You may also email questions from the web page or call the DOR's headquarters in Madison (608-266-2772). The Hudson DOR office (2100 O'Neil Road, Suite 200, 54016-8195, 715-381-5060) offers tax help on Mondays only, from 7:45 a.m. to 1:00 p.m. The state encourages its residents to order forms and file electronically.

MONEY ORDERS

Western Union services are available at a number of Twin Cities locations including most Snyder Drug stores, Kmarts, and Twin City Federal and other banks. There are several Western Union/TCF sites in the Minneapolis skyway system. For other **Western Union** locations, use their online worldwide agent locator (www.westernunion.com).

STARTING A BUSINESS IN MINNESOTA

The **Department of Employment and Economic Development (DEED)** publishes "A Guide to Starting a Business in Minnesota" that is available free of charge. Order it online (www.deed.state.mn.us), or by calling the publications order line (651-296-3871, 800-310-8323). DEED offers a wide range of technical assistance tailored to the needs of small and medium-sized businesses in the areas of startup, expansion, or relocation. So does the federal **Small Business Administration** (www.sba.gov) and its corps of business volunteers at **SCORE** (100 North 6th Street, Minneapolis, 612-370-2324, www.scoremn.org; 176 North Snelling Avenue, St. Paul, 651-632-8937). SCORE is an organization of active and retired business people with a wide range of expertise, who volunteer to provide free business counseling—they're well worth a call.

NOW THAT YOU'VE LANDED A PLACE TO LIVE AND OPENED A CHECKING account, you're probably wondering: what will it take to get life back to normal? This chapter covers most of the services you will need: electricity, gas, telephone, water, and garbage and recycling, as well as those essentials of modern life—cable (or digital) and Internet. There is also automobile-related information including how to obtain a Minnesota driver's license and register your car, and specifics about getting a library card, voting, and subscribing to the local papers.

UTILITIES

Minnesota's utility industry is comprised of 126 municipal electric utilities, 31 municipal gas utilities, a number of small cooperatives, five large investor-owned gas/electric companies, one garbage/electric company, and practically countless telecommunications providers. Sound complicated? It is and it isn't. In fact, most electricity and gas are provided by either **Xcel Energy** or **Reliant/CenterPoint Energy** (even in Wisconsin), and most telecommunications services are provided by **Qwest**. Furthermore, one of the real joys of our computer age is that now you can sign up for all your utilities with just a couple of clicks. You can do this in two ways. One: sign up to connect or transfer all your utilities online at a single web site, **Twin Cities Utility Connect** (www.moveminneapolis.com). Just put in your address and the web site will automatically locate the providers that serve your area. Then you can compare their packages and prices side-by-side, and order the services that work best for you. Or, easier still, go to your **new city's home page**, choose **New Resident Information**, and then set up your utilities through the clickable links the city provides. For those establishing service from afar, be sure to have your new address handy when you're ready to set up your new accounts.

Note: Before you dig in your new yard call **Gopher State One Call** (651-454-0002, www.gopherstateonecall.org); they will come out and locate and mark all your buried cables and gas lines. This service is free.

To report gas and electric service problems, call:

- **Electric Outages**: 800-895-1999, TTD/TTY 651-639-4481
- **Gas Odor or Gas Leak Emergency**: 800-895-2999, 612-372-5050

TELEPHONE

CONVENTIONAL AND LOCAL LONG DISTANCE

Getting a telephone used to be something you had to do weeks in advance of moving into your new home—now you don't really need a land line at all, unless you just want your name in a phonebook. On the other hand, you do still need a local phone number, not just so your new friends won't have to call you long distance, but because the newspaper and most other services keep track of your account based on your phone number. Moreover, more often than not these days, land line service comes bundled with cell phones, high-speed Internet, and cable or satellite TV, so it's convenient, when you're shopping, to buy the whole package. Nearly every company listed below offers bundled packages, no matter how they're categorized.

Qwest is the dominant player in this market. It provides hardwire local and long distance phone service, high-speed Internet, wireless, and digital television throughout most of the Twin Cities area. You can order new residential service online at www.qwest.com/homeservice, or call 866-375-6683 (MOVE), 800-244-1111, 800-223-3131 or TTY 711, 7:00 a.m.–9:00 p.m., Monday–Friday and 8:00 a.m.–4:30 p.m., Saturday. For more information on establishing your phone service, as well as other utilities, check online at the web address above for **Qwest Mover's Services**. If you choose to go with a land line, the one-time charge for installing or changing your service will depend on the amount of work required, including inside wire work and additional jacks. If you do not have a previous credit history with Qwest, a service deposit will be required, but the deposit will be refunded to you, with interest, after 12 months if your phone bills have been paid on time. (Consumer tip: save yourself some money; the phone company's charges for work inside your residence are steep, but doing inside wiring yourself is easy, so even if you have to buy a few tools and some materials, you're going to come out way ahead if you do the work yourself. Directions are only a Google search away.)

Other providers licensed to do business in the Twin Cities include:

- **AT&T**, 800-222-0300, TTY/TTD 800-833-3232, www.att.com
- **Comcast Phone of Minnesota**, 651-222-3333, www.Comcast.com
- **Frontier Communications**, 800-921-8101, www.frontieronline.com
- **Global Crossing**, 800-414-1973, 800-236-1009, www.globalcrossing.com
- **MCI**, 800-444-3, 1-877-777-6271, 800-444-3333, http://consumer.mci.com
- **McLeodUSA**, 800-500-3453, www.mcleodusa.com
- **Sprint**, 800-788-3500 (Billing and New Accounts), www.sprint.com/local
- **Verizon**, 800-256-4646, www22.verizon.com

To compare long distance pricing and plans, go to the **Telecommunications Research Action Center (TRAC)** web site (www.trac.org). The TRAC web site also includes information about how to file a complaint with the

FCC, wireless tips, and links for directory assistance via the Internet. (For more about TRAC see **Cell Phones** below.)

AREA CODES

The Twin Cities metropolitan area uses a 10-digit calling system and has four local area codes:

- **612** is assigned to Minneapolis, Richfield, Fort Snelling, and St. Anthony.
- **651** belongs to St. Paul and the East Metro, including Washington County, Eagan, and Dakota County.
- **763** serves suburbs to the north and northwest of Minneapolis and I-394, including Anoka, Sherburne, and Wright counties, and the cities of Becker, Blaine, Brooklyn Center, Buffalo, Cambridge, Circle Pines, Coon Rapids, Delano, Elk River, Fridley, Golden Valley, Isanti, Lexington, Medina, Monticello, Mounds View, Plymouth, Princeton, St Francis, and Waverly.
- **952** includes Apple Valley, Bloomington, Burnsville, Chanhassen, Eden Prairie, Edina, Hopkins, the Lake Minnetonka area, St. Louis Park, Waconia, and other communities south of I-394.

Outside the metro, northern Minnesota uses Area Code **218**; western Minnesota is **320**; southern Minnesota is **507**; and Pierce, Polk, and St. Croix counties in Wisconsin, which are considered collar counties of the Twin Cities metro region, use **715**.

WIRELESS

The big news in Minnesota is that **Wireless Fidelity (Wi-Fi)** is expanding beyond coffee shops and libraries! It moved into the fast lane in 2005 when tiny Chaska became one of the first cities in the world to offer citywide Wi-Fi wireless Internet service to its residents. Now the rest of the metro is getting together to create a metro-wide Wi-Fi network, with service expected to be in place by late 2007 or early 2008. But even as Wi-Fi is breaking clear of the starting gate, it is quickly being overtaken by the next generation of service, 6.5 million-bit-per-second **WiMax**. Already in use at some businesses and colleges in the cities, WiMax is also available in the Western Metro exurbs along the I-94 corridor. For Wi-Fi information, check with your city hall. WiMax is available through Implex.net and StoneBridge Wireless Broadband (www.sbwireless.net) but it's expensive: a modem still costs about $800.

VOIP

Most of the companies listed in the "Telephone" section above also offer **Voice over Internet Protocol (VoIP),** which allows those who have high-speed internet to use computers to make calls for free or a flat monthly fee. The biggest players in this market are **Skype** (www.skype.com) and **Vonage**, (1-VONAGE-HELP, www.vonage.com). With Vonage, you can even keep your current phone number and transfer it to a Vonage account. (Consumer tip: don't cancel your old service until your new service is in place; if you let go of your number, you may not get it back!)

VoIP isn't without its problems, however. Chief among them is the fact that VoIP cannot be used to dial 911. For this reason alone, having a conventional land line or cell phone for emergencies is advisable.

CELL PHONES
Cell phones—with their reach-you-anytime-anywhere capability—are taking the place of hardwire telecommunications. Many consumers have dropped their long distance service and are taking advantage of in-network and family cell phone plans. Others have given up having a home phone entirely. That said, since Minnesota has only recently converted from analog to digital, there are issues with the towers and consequent black holes where there is no reception, particularly in the western suburbs. It's more of an annoyance than a problem, but just to be sure you're not stuck at home with a cell phone that won't work there, you should try to arrange to return the phone if it doesn't work where you need to use it.

But just as cell phones have become more popular, buying them has become more confusing. Pricing plans, phone models . . . the choices can be boggling. But there is help for making an informed decision: the **Telecommunications Research & Action Center (TRAC)** web site (www.trac.org). The TRAC staff researches telecommunications issues and publishes rate comparisons and consumer tips. One of their tips: subscribers to Verizon Local Digital Choice plans can switch to the national America's Choice plan for up to 30 days, when traveling, in order to avoid paying roaming charges when they are outside their local calling area. You'll find lots more of the same on this very interesting web site.

The following are the metro area's largest cellular providers:

- **Cingular**, 866-CINGULAR, www.cingular.com; formerly AT&T, Cingular has stores in the Mall of America, Eden Prairie Center, Maplewood Mall, Ridgedale, Rosedale, Riverdale Commons in Coon Rapids, Southdale, at 132 Second St in St. Cloud, and 7060 Valley Creek Rd in Woodbury.
- **Sprint PCS**, 800-480-4PCS, www.sprintpcs.com, has numerous stores throughout the Twin Cities. Check its web page or the White Pages for the store nearest you.
- **T-Mobile**, 800-TMOBILE, www.t-mobile.com, sells through dealers at all the major malls as well as Office Depot and COMP USA.
- **Verizon**, 800-256-4646, www.verizonwireless.com, is located at all the major malls, at Circuit City and Radio Shack, and at numerous other locations throughout the Twin Cities.

PREPAID CELLULAR SERVICES AND LONG DISTANCE CARDS
With only slightly higher rates and no year-long contracts or monthly service charges, prepaid cellular is easily worth the small amount of inconvenience of having to continually replenish minutes. Available at numerous stores in the Twin Cities, phones come with a card representing a certain financial value ranging from $15 to $100. Activate the card and, when the money runs out,

replenish it with another payment. This is called "topping up." **T-Mobile Prepaid Mobile To Go** starter kits are available locally at T-Mobile outlets, 7-Eleven stores, and CVS/Pharmacies, online at www.t-mobile.com, or by calling 1-877-677-5505. **Verizon's** pay-as-you-go plan, **FreeUp**, includes text messaging (www.verizonwireless.com). Target stores offer several pay-as-you-go phones including **Cingular's GoPhones,** which are also available at Cingular stores and online (1-866-CINGULAR or www.cingular.com/gophone). Also online, **Amazon.com** offers pay-as-you-go phones as well as "top-up" cards. Locally, "top-up minutes" can be purchased from many retailers or at U.S. Bank ATMs. Prepaid long distance cards are sold at retailers throughout the area, including those mentioned above, and at gas stations, pharmacies, and grocery stores, as well.

CONSUMER PROTECTION—DO NOT CALL LISTS
Minnesota's Do Not Call law will not stop all your telemarketing calls, but it will stop a lot. Unfortunately for the sanctity of your dinner hour, certain organizations such as nonprofits and political parties are exempt from the law. To put some limits on your phone traffic, however, be sure sign up for both state and national Do Not Call lists online (www.ftc.gov/donotcall) or call toll-free (1-888-382-1222, TTY 1-866-290-4236). You must call from the number you wish to register. Registration is free. If your number has been on the registry for at least three months, and a telemarketer calls, complain to the FTC online (www.donotcall.gov) or call (1-888-382-1222, TTY 1-866-290-4236). You'll need to provide the date of the call and the phone number or name of the company that called you, so don't just yell at the caller and hang up.

CONSUMER PROTECTION—CRAMMING
"Cramming" used to be what you did before an exam, but the word, when applied to your telephone bill, has a much more sinister meaning now: it's the practice of third parties placing unauthorized charges on your phone bill. So always check your statements thoroughly, and if you do find a problem, remember this: under the Truth in Billing Act, you cannot lose your phone service for failure to pay a disputed "miscellaneous" charge. That said, be sure to call your carrier's customer service the minute you spot an unauthorized charge in order to ensure your rights. (See **Consumer Protection—Utility Complaints** below.)

DIRECTORY ASSISTANCE
Dial **411** for directory assistance. Qwest only gives you one free directory assistance call per month, but you can find numbers for free through the Internet via these web sites:
* **www.anywho.com**
* **www.switchboard.com**
* **www.dexonline.com**
* **www.twincities.citysearch.com**

ONLINE SERVICE

LOCAL PROVIDERS

Minnesota has many local Internet service providers, most of which have been in business since the mid-1990s. Popular with locals, they offer access to the Internet as well as web hosting, authoring, consulting, and networking services, and receive frequent accolades for their "Minnesota-nice" friendly and helpful tech support:

- **CP Telecom**, 612-236-1000, 800-942-8169, www.cpinternet.com
- **Minnesota WaveTech**, www.wavetech.net
- **Southern Minnesota Internet Group**, 1-866-GET-SMIG, www.smig.net
- **Twin Cities Internet**, 612-377-8707, www.tcinternet.net
- **US Internet**, 800-US-Internet (800-874-6837), www.usinternet.com, offers Wi-Fi and WiMax.
- **Vector Internet Services**, www.visi.com

NATIONAL PROVIDERS

When considering a national Internet service provider, be sure to find one that will connect you through a local call instead of long distance. Getting connected during peak demand hours is often a problem, particularly with cable service. The following are our principal providers:

- **America Online**, 800-827-6364, 800-273-1647, www.aol.com, or www.free.aol.com/welcome, for a free trial
- **AT&T WorldNet**, 800-967-5363, www.consumer.att.com
- **Comcast**, 800-COMCAST, www.comcast.net
- **Earthlink/MindSpring Enterprises**, 800-719-4332, www.earthlink.net; also offers Wi-Fi
- **Mediacom**, www.mediacom.com, www.mchsi.com
- **Microsoft Network**, 800-426-9400, www.msn.com

CABLE

Twin Cities cable service is divided geographically:

- **Time Warner**, 612-522-2000, www.timewarnercable.com, provides cable TV and Road Runner Internet access for all of Minneapolis and most of the South and West Metro.
- **Comcast**, 651-222-3333, 800-255-4640 or 800-266-2278, www.comcast.net, serves St. Paul and the North Metro, and western Wisconsin.
- **MediaCom**, 800-332-0245, www.mediacomcc.com, serves parts of the metro including the Lake Minnetonka area; put in your zip code to see if they serve your area.

SATELLITE SERVICE

Check out **DishMinnesota** (www.dishminnesota.com) for comprehensive information about this fast-changing business and the latest deals.

- **DISH Network**, 800-942-4713, 1-866-451-DISH, http://dishtv.com
- **Direct TV**, 800-directv, www.directtv.com; sold locally at Best Buy, Blockbuster, and Circuit City

ELECTRICITY AND NATURAL GAS

You can call the companies listed below to see if your new home is in their service area, or save yourself a lot of trouble and ask at your new city hall. Better yet, look online at your city's web page and use its clickable links.

Xcel Energy (612-330-5500, 800-895-4999 Billing and New Accounts, 800-895-1999 Electrical Outage, www.xcelenergy.com) is both an electric and gas utility. Because Xcel's business is regulated by the state, the products and services they are allowed to sell vary in different zip codes. To determine what service they provide in your area, go to their web site and type in your zip code.

In many areas, residents get their electricity from Xcel, but buy their natural gas from **Reliant/CenterPoint Energy**. You can arrange for both services with one telephone call to 612-372-4727 or 800-245-2377, or online at www.centerpointenergy.com. Service can be connected with only a few days' notice, but it is recommended that you put in your order two weeks in advance. Reliant/CenterPoint offers "Budget Helper," a 12-month plan to help even out your monthly energy payments. Call 612-372-5050 for emergency gas leaks, 612-333-6466 or 800-722-6821 for emergency furnace repair.

Some cities have their own municipal utilities, including South St. Paul, Circle Pines, Anoka, Elk River, Buffalo, Delano, Chaska, Shakopee, and North St. Paul. Of these, Anoka's is by far the largest, serving more than 11,000 customers. Links to those municipalities are found at the ends of the sections about them, and on the **Minnesota Municipal Power Agency**'s web site (www.mmpa.biz). One thing this collective does that Xcel and Reliant/CenterPoint do not do is offer customers a **Green Power** program that enables retail customers to purchase hydro power and wind power. The following are municipal utilities:

- **Anoka Electric**, 763-576-2903, www.ci.anoka.mn.us, serves parts of Ramsey County.
- **Dakota County Electric**, 651-463-7134, www.dakotaelectric.com, serves Eagan, Apple Valley, and Burnsville.
- **Elk River Municipal Utilities and Great River Energy**, 763-441-2020, www.ci.elk-river.mn.us, purchases wind energy from a wind farm in Chandler, Minnesota. Retail purchasers can purchase wind power in blocks of 100 kilowatt-hours.
- **Minnesota Valley Electric Cooperative**, 952-492-2313, www.mvec.net, serves the southwestern suburbs in Carver, Hennepin, and Scott counties.
- **North St. Paul, Utility Billing**, 651-747-2413, www.ci.north-saint-paul.mn.us, pushes wind power and offers Energy Rebates on energy-efficient appliances.
- **Shakopee Public Utilities**, 952-445-1988, www.shakopeeutilities.com.

HEATING ASSISTANCE/COLD WEATHER RULE

In Minnesota there is a **Cold Weather Rule** that says residential customers who cannot pay their bills in full cannot have their heat cut off between October 15 and April 15—but there are certain procedures that must be followed for you to qualify, including contacting your utility and trying to work out a payment plan. For more information about cold weather shut-off, call your local utility or, in the Excel service area, call 800-895-4999.

The state also has some money to help pay for weather-proofing or fixing broken heating equipment. Contact the **Minnesota Energy Assistance Office** (800-657-3805) to request help.

CONSUMER PROTECTION—UTILITY COMPLAINTS

Try to resolve any billing or other disputes with your phone, gas, or electric company on your own. But if a problem persists, the people to call depend on what you're complaining about. If you have a complaint or inquiry about cellular or mobile phone service, contact the **Attorney General's Office** (651-296-3353, 800-657-3787, www.ag.state.mn.us). For issues related to investor-owned gas and electric utilities, Dakota Electric Cooperative, and local and in-state long distance telephone, call the **Minnesota Public Utilities Commission Consumer Affairs Office** (651-296-0406, 800-657-3782, www.puc.state.mn.us).

SEWER AND WATER

If you are renting an apartment, sewer and water are probably included in your rent. If you are a homeowner or renting a house, call your local city hall to establish service. In Minneapolis, call the **Utility Billing Office** (311 or 612-673-1114), or request service online (www.ci.minneapolis.mn.us); a budget plan is available. For water emergencies, call 612-673-5600. St. Paul residents should call 651-266-6350 for billing and general information. Water emergencies are handled at 651-266-6868. If the house you are buying has a private well, be sure to have it inspected and tested for bacteria and hardness. A rotten egg smell may indicate that you have iron bacteria growing in your well and plumbing, a common problem, but one that can be hard to solve. In such circumstances, chances are good that the water is safe to drink but you will need a water softener and pre-filter.

Okay. That was the short version of water and sewer. It will work for you if you plan to live in the city or an established suburb. If you're moving to the suburban fringe, however, there's a lot more you need to know.

SEWER

Sewer service is no less complicated than Minnesota's other utilities, and at the same time, equally simple: if your city provides sewer service, sign up for it by calling your city hall. If it doesn't, then you will need to have your own system. Whether your property has—or doesn't have—sewer will be detailed on your Multiple Listing Service (MLS) listing sheet. If you're moving here from a region where everybody has sewer, though, you're probably wondering what's up.

Here's the explanation.

Sewer service is relatively new to Twin Cities suburbs. It started in the early 1970s when the cities surrounding Lake Minnetonka agreed to put in sewer in order to clean up the lake. Since then, the regional sanitary sewer system known as **MUSA (Metropolitan Urban Service Area)** has been expanded twice. Today the suburbs of Eagan, Woodbury, Eden Prairie, Chanhassen, and Maple Grove all lie within the MUSA line. Soon it will expand to include White Bear Lake, White Bear Township, Columbus Township, Centerville, Lino Lakes, Rosemount, Inver Grove Heights, Hugo, Forest Lake, the northern half of Blaine, Ramsey, Corcoran, Medina, Shakopee, Orono, Lakeville, and Farmington.

So what does that mean to you, a new person in town? If you're looking at houses in a densely developed area, probably nothing; but if you're looking at homes or property on the developing edge, get ready to pay an assessment when sewer is extended to your property. Call your city hall and find out what they are projecting for the cost—it will be thousands. (But don't get too excited, the cost will simply be added to your property taxes and paid off over a number of years.) If you will need to have a septic system, don't worry. Taking care of it isn't difficult as long as you follow a few basic guidelines, such as keeping trees at least 100 feet away from it, and not overloading it. If you have a big party, rent portable toilets for guests to use. And be careful what you flush. Never flush tampons, cat litter, or large quantities of toilet tissue. Compost kitchen waste, and never pour grease down the drain. For more information, order "Taking Care of Your Septic System" from the University of Minnesota Extension Store (http://shop.extension.umn.edu/Default.aspx).

WATER

Of the 187 municipalities in the Twin Cities seven-county metropolitan area, 123 have municipal water supply systems. St. Paul and Minneapolis both supply their residents with treated water from surface sources such as the Mississippi River and the St. Paul chain of lakes. Most of the other cities use water supplied from the groundwater system via municipal wells. Some municipalities, such as Shorewood, provide water to some residents, but not to all. Others, including some as close-in as Lake Minnetonka in the west and White Bear Lake in the east, require that people get water from their own private wells. To find out about your water situation, look on your MLS listing sheet and/or contact your city hall.

According to the Metropolitan Council—the agency charged with keeping track of these kinds of things—the average charge for water in the region is $1.92 for 1000 gallons, or 83 cups for 1 penny. The cost of water from a private well, however, depends upon a number of factors, including its depth and whether the water from it will need to be filtered and softened before you can use it (and it probably will). To find out how deep the wells are in your vicinity, put in your address on the Department of Health's online County Well Index (www.health.state.mn.us/divs/eh/cwi/index.html). To find a licensed well contractor, check the directory at www.health.state.mn.us/divs/eh/wells.

Keep in mind, though, that even here in the Land of 10,000 Lakes, water is still a threatened resource.

At the time of the writing of this book, finding water isn't difficult. However, it is suspected that the increase in roads and roofs (impervious surfaces) from the building boom we are experiencing may be depleting groundwater supplies. Rain and snowmelt now rush off the paved landscape and into the storm sewers rather than slowly seeping down through the soil and recharging our underground aquifers. That's one reason cities are encouraging rain gardens and limiting the percentage of a property that can be covered by hardscape. Another is the presence in the groundwater of contaminants from run-off that are potential threats to human health. Nitrates from nitrogen fertilizer and herbicides and pesticides have recently been found in residential wells in Dakota County in the South Metro (not to single them out, since so far Dakota is the only county that is testing for them). Other toxins have been detected in groundwater in Brooklyn Center to the north and Lake Elmo and Baytown Township to the east. But don't make the mistake of thinking that those are the only places where's there's a problem. It is reasonable to assume, since we all drink from the same underground aquifers, that the same substances are present in all our well water—and in surface sources, too.

If your city has a municipal system, you can get information about the water's quality from the city's public works department or from the city's annual report. Consumers can also request a water report online (www.epa.gov/safewater/dwinfo.htm), or by calling the **Environmental Pollution Agency's (EPA's) Safe Drinking Water Hotline**, 800-426-4791. If you have a private well, you'll have to take care of water-testing yourself. The Health Department suggests that well water be tested once a year for bacteria and every other year for nitrates. Wells should also be tested at least once for arsenic. The Health Department maintains a list of certified testing labs at www.health.state.mn.us/divs/eh/wells/#labs. The list includes:

- **Engel Water Testing**, Minnetrista, 952-955-1800, www.engelwatertesting.com
- **Minneapolis Health Department**, 612-673-2160
- **St. Paul–Ramsey County Department of Public Health**, St. Paul, 651-266-1321
- **Twin City Water Clinic**, Hopkins, 952-935-3556
- **Water Laboratories, Inc.**, Elk River, 763-441-7509

Most private well water needs to be filtered and softened. The principal local water softener companies include:
- **Commers**, 9150 W 35W Service Dr NE, Blaine, 763-252-7707, www.commers.com
- **Culligan Water Conditioning**, Toll Free 1-888-Hey-Culligan; www.culligan.com; North Metro, 763-421-5512; West Metro, 952-933-7200; Northern Dakota and Southern Washington counties, 651-451-2241
- **Eco Water System**, 61 7th Ave, Hopkins, 952-935-5105, www.ecowater.com
- **Haferman Water Conditioning, Inc.**, Kinetico, 952-894-4040, www.hafermanwater.com
- **Lindsay Water Conditioning**, Minneapolis, 952-941-2117

Many of the companies above also supply drinking water, but for home delivery of bottled water, see Drinking Water in Shopping for the Home.

STORMWATER UTILITY FEE

This fee is discussed early in the Minneapolis section of the **Neighborhoods** chapter.

FROZEN PIPES

Even temperatures in the teens can freeze unprotected pipes, but there are steps you can take to keep it from happening to you. Disconnect and drain all outdoor hoses before cold weather hits. Inside, try to keep your pipes warm. On a really cold night, open cabinets under your kitchen and bathroom sinks to get warm air to exposed pipes. If you have just one problem pipe, turn the cold water on there so that it just trickles, and leave it running continuously during extremely cold weather. Wrap water pipes near outside walls with insulation tape. If you leave home for a winter vacation, don't turn the heat off. But if your precautions fail and a pipe does freeze, acting quickly but carefully is key. Place a space heater near the pipe to warm the surrounding air and/or use a blow dryer to warm it at the point of the freeze. Don't use a blowtorch! If water starts leaking from the frozen pipe, it means the pipe has burst, so turn off the water to it and turn it off fast. Once you have the water turned off, you can solder or replace the broken pipe yourself, or call for a plumber. If you don't know a plumber already, companies like **Roto-Rooter** (800-GET-ROTO, www.roto-rooter.com) usually offer 24-hour plumbing and drain service. You can also find plumbers in your area through the Yellow Pages, or online at a directory such as **www.plumbingnetworks.com**. After the pipe is repaired, make sure it's properly insulated before next winter.

GARBAGE AND RECYCLING

If you're in an apartment, you can probably skip this section, but if you're renting or buying a house, you'll need to arrange for garbage pick-up, and possibly recycling.

Some cities contract to haul garbage for you. If, however, you have to do it yourself, be sure to check your city's web page for a list of their approved haulers. That said, **Waste Management** (952-890-1100, www.wmtwincities.com) covers nearly the entire metropolitan area, and **Ace Solid Waste** (763-427-3110, 800-964-4281, www.acesolidwaste.com) covers the North/Northwest Metro including Anoka, Sherburne, and Wright counties, and parts of Chisago, Hennepin, and Washington counties.

In **Minneapolis**, the city hauls residential garbage and recyclable materials and provides trash containers for each house. Haulers will take yard waste as well as large items, such as discarded furniture. The base fee for garbage is $22.25 per dwelling plus a rental fee for the disposal cart, tax, and an environmental services fee. Part of this is offset by a monthly recycling credit. For more information look on the city's web page (www.ci.minneapolis.mn.us/utility-billing), or call 311.

In **St. Paul** (www.stpaul.gov) recycling pick-up is provided, but each household must hire a garbage service. (If you are renting, the landlord may already have made arrangements.) Rates vary from company to company and depend on the volume of the trash container you choose. City officials believe this system cuts down on waste, and it does get you to root out those recyclables in order to reduce your load. Disposal of large objects must be arranged separately with your hauler.

For specific information about what can be recycled and when to put it out, call your city hall. **Eureka Recycling**, St. Paul's official recyclers, also has a very helpful A-Z online guide (www.eurekarecycling.org/reu_guide.cfm) that tells you how and where to recycle or safely dispose of everything. Wondering what happens to the materials you recycle? Recycling is a $3 billion business in Minnesota, and Anchor Glass in Shakopee is one of the big dogs in the industry. Each year it recycles 46,000 tons of glass into bottles for Budweiser, La Choy soy sauce, A1 steak sauce, Snapple, and lots of microbrews.

APPLIANCE AND ELECTRONICS RECYCLING

If old computers and appliances are still usable, consider giving them away via **The Twin Cities Free Market** (www.twincitiesfreemarket.org). Created by **Eureka Recycling** (Solid Waste Hotline, 651-633-EASY, www.eureka recycling.org), which keeps track of all exchanges, the Internet-based Free Market exchange has kept over 4 million pounds of still-useful items out of the landfills to date.

If electronics and appliances are not usable, either ask the retailer you're buying your replacements from to haul the old equipment away, or drop them off at a county recycling center. **Hennepin County** has two: 8100 Jefferson Highway, Brooklyn Park, or 1400 West 96th Street, Bloomington. There is no charge for most electronics. Before going, call 612-348-3777 for directions, fees, and to verify that they will accept the item you wish to dispose of, or check online at www.hennepin.us. The **Carver County Environmental Center** (116 Peavey Circle, Chaska, 952-361-1835 or 952-361-1800, www.co.carver. mn.us/Divisions/LandWaterServices/EnviroServices/EnviroCenter.html) charges $10 for a refrigerator, and recycles many items for free. **Asset Recovery Corp** in St. Paul (651-602-0789, www.assetrecoverycorp.com), and **Waste Management Recycling** (www.wm.com) are private companies that accept consumer electronics for a fee, and have drop sites statewide. For a complete list of household recyclers, go to www.moea.state.mn.us/plugin/ recyclers-household.cfm.

RECYCLING CLEAN UP, PAINT UP, FIX UP PRODUCTS

Whenever possible, leftover latex paint should be allowed to dry out and may then be disposed of along with the regular trash. Unopened full gallons or larger containers of paint are a welcome—and tax-deductible—donation to the **Reuse Center** (2216 East Lake Street, Minneapolis, 612-724-2608).

Oil-based paint, paint thinner, paint remover, primers, stains and varnishes, wood preservatives, furniture stripper, glue with solvents, adhesives, roofing tar, driveway sealers, and concrete cleaners should be disposed of at a Hazardous Waste Disposal site such as the **Carver County Environmental Center** (see above). Consider donating unopened containers to the Reuse Center.

Construction debris can be disposed of at **Dem-Con**, south of Shakopee (952-445-5755), for $4.50 per yard. There is a 4-yard minimum to use this facility.

Still usable building materials and tools may be donated, for a tax deduction, to any of the following organizations: the Reuse Center (see above); **PPL (Project for Pride in Living) S.H.O.P.** (850 15th Avenue NE, Minneapolis, 612-789-3322); or **Habitat for Humanity** (3001 4th Street SE, Minneapolis, 612-331-4090 ext 630).

COMPOSTING SITES

Take your grass, leaves, and small brush to the following locations:
- **Ramsey County**: North side of Pierce-Butler Route at Pryor; Pleasant Ave just south of St. Claire; corner of Frank and Sims; Winthrop just south of London Ln
- **Hennepin County**: 630 Malcolm Ave, Minneapolis, 612-331-4610; Maple Grove Yard Waste, west of County Rd 121 on 101st Ave N, 763-420-4886

DRIVER'S LICENSES, STATE IDs, AND AUTOMOBILE REGISTRATION

DRIVER'S LICENSES AND STATE IDs

You have 60 days from the date you move to Minnesota to obtain a Minnesota driver's license. The minimum age to receive a driver's license is 16. If you have a valid out-of-state license, only a written test and eye exam are required. Take your current driver's license and another form of ID such as a passport or birth certificate with you to the licensing station (a county service center). If you changed your name when you got married, take your marriage certificate as well. If your current license is no longer valid, or you are not a licensed driver yet, you will be required to pass a behind-the-wheel driving test. The cost for a license is $37.50. State identification cards are also available at county service centers (see below). The cost is $12.50.

Information regarding vehicle and driver licenses and state ID cards may be obtained from the **Minnesota Department of Public Safety** (445 Minnesota Street, Suite 168, St. Paul, MN 55101, 651-296-6911, TTY 651-282-6555, www.dps.state.mn.us/dvs). Examining stations are located throughout the metro area; call to schedule a driving test.
- **Anoka County**, www.co.anoka.mn.us, State Exam Station, 530 W Main St, Anoka, 763-422-3401; North Metro Exam Station, Arden Hills, 651-639-4057
- **Carver County**, Chaska Exam Station: 418 Pine St, Chaska, 952-448-3740, www.co.carver.mn.us

- **Dakota County**, www.co.dakota.mn.us; 14955 Galaxie Ave, Apple Valley, 952-891-7570; 1 Mendota Rd W, West St. Paul, 651-554-6600; Burnsville Transit Station Hub, 100 E Hwy 13, Burnsville, 952-707-6436; 20085 Heritage Dr, Lakeville, 952-891-7878
- **Hennepin County**, 612-348-8240, www.co.hennepin.mn.us; Hennepin County Government Center, 300 S 6th St—Public Service Level, Minneapolis; Brookdale Service Center, 6125 Shingle Creek Pkwy, Brooklyn Center; Ridgedale Service Center, 12601 Ridgedale Dr, Minnetonka; Southdale Service Center, 7009 York Ave S, Edina; Maple Grove Service Center, 9325 Upland Ln N, Maple Grove; Eden Prairie Service Center, 479 Prairie Center Dr, Eden Prairie; Minnesota Driver's License Exam Station, 2455 Fernbrook Ln, Plymouth, 952-476-3042
- **Ramsey County**, www.co.ramsey.mn.us, 445 Minnesota St, St. Paul, 651-296-6911; St. Paul/Midway Written Exam Station, 651-642-0808
- **Scott County**, www.co.scott.mn.us, Customer Service Center, Government Services Building, located at 200 W Fourth Ave, Shakopee, 952-496-8150
- **Sherburne County**, www.co.sherburne.mn.us, Department of Motor Vehicles, 600 Railroad Dr, Elk River; 763-422-3401, to schedule a road test appointment
- **Washington County**, www.co.washington.mn.us: Forest Lake License Center, Northland Mall, 1432 S Lake St, Forest Lake, 651-430-8280; Stillwater License Center, Valley Ridge, 1520 W Frontage Rd, Stillwater, 651-430-6176; Woodbury Service Center, 2150 Radio Dr, Woodbury, 651-275-8600
- **Wright County**, www.co.wright.mn.us, 10 Second St NW, Buffalo, 763-682-3900, 800-362-3667

WISCONSIN
- **Driver's License Information**, 608-266-2353, www.dot.wisconsin.gov/drivers/drivers/apply/drivrlic.htm
- **Vehicle Registration**, www.dot.wisconsin.gov/drivers/vehicles/veh-forms.htm
- **Department of Motor Vehicles**, 2100 O'Neil Rd (near Carmichael Rd), Hudson; open Wednesday, 7:45 a.m.–5:45 p.m., Thursday, 8:15 a.m.–6:15 p.m., and Friday, 7:45 a.m–5:00 p.m. There is no direct phone number to that location, but the automated phone system number is 800-924-3570. Register vehicles at the St. Croix County Government Center, 1101 Carmichael Rd, Hudson, in the Clerk's office, 715-386-4609, www.ci.Hudson.wi.us.

AUTOMOBILE REGISTRATION

You have 60 days from the time you move here to register your car with the state of Minnesota. After two months you can be hit with a fine, so it pays to get this done as quickly as possible. You can register your vehicle at one of the county service/licensing centers (above) or at an **Automobile Association of America (AAA)** office (952-927-2600) if you are a member. Take your car's certificate of title, proof of insurance, and your personal identification. Motor vehicle licenses must be renewed each year. The registration tax depends on the value of your car; it will be no less than $35 a year, and could be as much as several hundred dollars (ouch!). To determine your registration tax, contact the Minnesota Department of Public Safety's central office. Once you're registered, you should receive an annual renewal notice several weeks before your registration expires. You may renew license tabs online at the Department of Public Safety web site, www.dps.state.mn.us/dvs, 651-296-6911.

Wisconsin vehicle registration information is posted online at www.dot.wisconsin.gov/drivers/vehicles/veh-forms.html. Those living in the Hudson can register their vehicles at the St. Croix County Government Center, 1101 Carmichael Road, Hudson; register in the Clerk's office, 715-386-4609.

AUTOMOBILE SAFETY

In Minnesota, approximately one-third of all traffic deaths involve alcohol. Consequently, the state has strengthened its intoxication laws and judges have toughened their sentencing. On August 1, 2005, Minnesota became the last state in the union to lower the legal limit for alcohol concentration in a driver's blood to 0.08%. We now have "zero tolerance" for underage drinking and driving, as well. A first conviction for DWI (Driving While Impaired) is punishable by a maximum fine of $3000 and maximum jail time of a year, or both; a second offense can result in the forfeiture of your car. A fourth drunken-driving arrest in 10 years is a felony carrying mandatory prison time and a very stiff fine. For more information, visit the **Department of Public Safety**'s web site (www.dps.state.mn.us) and click on Office of Traffic Safety.

Another law to promote public safety is mandatory seat belt use by all front-seat occupants and all children under the age of 11 years regardless of where they are sitting. Children under four must be secured in a safety seat that meets federal safety standards. That means the car safety seat must bear a stamp of approval from the Federal Department of Transportation.

CONSUMER PROTECTION—AUTOMOBILES

If you are looking for a new car, Minnesota has a lemon law that covers new vehicles that have been purchased or leased in the state. The law defines a "lemon" as a vehicle that continues to have a serious defect which substantially impairs its use, value, or safety, after a reasonable number of attempts to repair it. A car that you have been unable to use, due to warranty repairs, for 30 or more cumulative business days may also be covered by this law. In any case, if you report the defect within the warranty time period, the manufacturer must repair, refund, or replace the defective vehicle. If, after a reasonable number of attempts, the manufacturer is unable to repair the defect, you may go to court or go through a manufacturer's arbitration program to seek a full refund of the car's purchase price.

For those interested in purchasing a used car, Minnesota has a used car warranty law requiring used car dealers (not private sellers) to provide basic warranty coverage for cars that cost more than $3000. The terms of this warranty vary according to the age and mileage of the car. A car that does not meet the warranty guidelines will be marked "as is" on the window sticker, meaning that the seller has no obligation to fix any problems that arise.

For a guide to Minnesota's Lemon Law, Used Car Warranty Law, and Truth in Repairs Law, look online at the **Minnesota Attorney General**'s web site (www.ag.state.mn.us), or call 651-296-3353 or 800-657-3787, TTY 651-297-7206 and 800-366-4812.

AUTOMOBILE INSURANCE

The Minnesota No-Fault Act requires owners of motor vehicles to maintain No-Fault insurance. Violation of the law can result in fines or imprisonment and revocation of driving privileges. Another law requires that proof of insurance be in the vehicle at all times and shown to a peace officer upon demand. Some of the major insurance companies in Minnesota include **AAA** (952-927-2518, www.aaa.com); **Allstate** (www.allstate.com); **American Family** (www.amfam.com); **Farmers Insurance Group** (www.farmers.com); and **State Farm** (www.statefarm.com). Check the Insurance listings in the Yellow Pages to locate agents near you.

PARKING

Parking in Minneapolis is tight, and you might have to look for a while to find parking at the price you want to pay. The city operates 20 parking ramps (structures) and 9 lots. A map of the facilities is available on the city's web site (http://parking.ci.minneapolis.mn.us/parking_facilities.htm). Printable maps and parking information can be found on the web site of the **Minneapolis Downtown Council** (www.downtownmpls.com). Ramps tend to be clustered around Target Center and the Warehouse District, the courthouse, and Orchestra Hall. For those needing to prioritize cost over convenience, you can expect cheaper rates on the city's periphery. If you're determined to commute into downtown every day by car, consider purchasing a monthly ramp pass. The costs at this writing ranged from $127.50 at the Hawthorne Transportation Center, 31 North 9th Street on the downtown fringe, to $250 a month at 10th and Lasalle. I-394 (which comes into downtown Minneapolis from the western suburbs) goes directly into three parking ramps in the Warehouse District. Monthly parking rates can be found at http://parking.ci.minneapolis.mn.us/parking_rates.php. A number of office buildings offer parking underneath, including the IDS building, Hennepin County Government Center, and Marquette Plaza.

Minneapolis also has about 7000 parking meters. For those who find a parking space on the street, take the meter seriously. An expired meter will get you a ticket and may get your car towed. Confusion often arises because meters in different parts of town have different time restrictions and rates. Meters accept only quarters and U.S. dollar coins, or parking cards that work in meters the same as money. Cards are sold from parking card dispenser machines located in parking ramps and at City Hall. For further information, call 612-673-AUTO (2886) or look online at www.ci.minneapolis.mn. us/parking.

The same parking cards work in St. Paul, where much of the parking is on-street and metered. For information about ramps in St. Paul, there is a clickable map posted on **St. Paul's Transportation Management Organization**'s **(TMO**'s) web site (www.saintpaulparking.com). Click on any facility and see its monthly and hourly rates. Convenient ramps are attached to RiverCentre, the St. Paul Hotel, Science Museum, and the Minnesota History Center. Parking is harder to find around the state capitol. For information on parking at the University of Minnesota, including rates and maps, contact the **University Parking Services** office (612-626-PARK). For information about parking in the downtowns call:

- **Minneapolis Parking Information**, 612-673-2411; Monthly & Event Parking, 612-338-7275; Permits, Critical Areas, 612-673-2411
- **St. Paul Parking Information**, 651-266-6200

RESIDENTIAL PARKING PERMITS

In Minneapolis, St. Paul, and most of the surrounding suburbs, there are desig-nated **Critical Parking Areas**. Residents in these areas are given, or can buy, stickers that permit them to ignore the parking restrictions on their streets. In Minneapolis, stickers cost $25 a year and can be obtained at City Hall. Some cities, such as Deephaven, give one free parking permit to each household and charge for second and third permits. Apply for permits at your own city hall.

SNOW EMERGENCY PARKING

Those moving here from more southerly climes should pay particular attention to yet another peculiar aspect of life in the North: the "snow emergency." This is when Minneapolis, St. Paul, and many of the suburbs restrict on-street park-ing in order to accomplish necessary plowing. Snow emergency rules require that you move your car from one side of the street to the other in some munic-ipalities, or stay off certain streets entirely in others. Residents are expected to pay attention to the weather and take steps to know when Snow Emergencies have been declared. There are several ways to do this, including checking the local media. *Every* station broadcasts the snow emergency news. You won't miss it! You can also sign up for email alerts with virtually every TV station. Just register on their web pages.

In Minneapolis, residents may call the **24-hour Snow hotlines**: English, 612-348-Snow (7669); TTY 612-673-2116. Minneapolis residents may also sub-scribe to the city's own **Email Snow Alert** service (at www.ci.minneapolis. mn.us). The city also sends email alerts to mobile devices such as cell phones and PDAs, and has been testing an automated voice messaging alert service. The **Snow Emergency Phone Alert** system has the capability of calling all listed numbers in the city automatically. For those who have caller ID, the phone number displayed is 612-348-7669, which is the **Minneapolis Snow**

Emergency Hotline number, and the "caller" will appear as "MPLS SNOW EMERG." The system will leave a recorded message on your answering machine if you're not home. To add or remove a listed phone number, or add an unlisted phone number (cell phone, direct work line, unlisted land line) to the system, visit www.ci.minneapolis.mn.us/snow/phone-alert/. The city cannot guarantee that you will receive a telephone call alerting you of a Snow Emergency, so it's important that people keep an ear to the news or call **612-348-SNOW** whenever snow falls and you think a Snow Emergency might be declared. Minneapolis is also working to make parking less of a concern by opening some of its ramps for free or reduced-price overnight and first day of the emergency parking. The city uses the word "snOasis" to describe these garages, which have, in the past, included ramps in downtown and at the university. Check the city's web site (www.ci.minneapolis.mn.us) for this year's ramp locations.

In St. Paul, watch for "Night Plow Route" signs. These are the sides of streets that will be plowed between 9 p.m. and 6 a.m. the first night after a snowfall. The unsigned sides of streets are usually plowed the next night. St. Paul snow emergency information can be obtained by calling **651-266-PLOW** or visiting the city's web site (www.stpaul.gov/depts/publicworks/senews.html). Sign up for email notification of snow emergencies on the city's web site.

Don't worry that you might somehow miss the relevant information—it's all over the airwaves. But do take it seriously. Parking restrictions are strictly enforced and cars are tagged and towed quickly and unceremoniously. One last piece of advice: don't go off on vacation and leave your car parked on a street— any street. Standing in a three-hour line at the impound lot is not a fun way to end a vacation. See **Surviving the Weather** for more winter-related tips.

TOWED VEHICLES

Hope you never need these numbers. The **Minneapolis Impound Lot** is at **51 North Colfax Avenue**. For directions and information call 612-673-5777, or go to www.ci.minneapolis.mn.us/impound-lot. Have your license plate number ready, or be able to provide the last four numbers of your car's serial number. The impound lot is open 6 a.m. to 3 a.m., daily. The regular towing fee is $138. The heavy-duty towing fee is $175. Storage costs $18 per day, and is assessed at midnight. The impound lot will accept a check, cash, or a credit card. Identification is required.

St. Paul has two impound lots: **830 Barge Channel Road** (651-266-5630) for vehicles tagged and towed from locations south of Interstate 94; and **1129 Cathlin Street,** a few blocks west of Snelling and across the street from the State Fairgrounds, for vehicles tagged and towed from locations north of Interstate 94. It will cost $163.36 to get your vehicle out of the impound lot if you pick it up before midnight the day it is towed. A $15 storage fee is added to that amount for each additional day the vehicle is left there. And, of course, you must also pay $45 for your parking ticket. The impound lot is open 24 hours a day. If you have questions about a towed vehicle, call 651-603-6895. For maps to the impound lots and other information, go to www.stpaul.gov/depts/public works/senews.html. Payment may be made in cash, by check or credit card.

VOTER REGISTRATION

Minnesota has a colorful political tradition that went neon in 1998, when we elected former professional wrestler and Brooklyn Park mayor Jesse "The Body" Ventura to be our governor. Perhaps you caught him in his purple boa singing "Werewolves of Minnesota" at his inaugural party? Unfortunately, he had a somewhat controversial tenure as governor and wound up in an adversarial relationship with both the state legislature and local newspeople. Nevertheless, if you're riding the Hiawatha LRT to work everyday, it's Jesse you should thank. After leaving office, he did a number of things including acting in movies, teaching at Harvard, and speaking all over the country encouraging people to vote. Speaking of which . . .

To register to vote, you must be a United States citizen, 18 years old, and neither legally incompetent nor a convicted felon deprived of rights. You must have lived in Minnesota for at least 20 days. It is easiest to register when you apply for your driver's license. Otherwise, you can also register in person at your city hall, county or government center, or by mail using a **Minnesota Voter Registration Form.** Download it from the **Secretary of State**'s web site (www.sos.state.mn.us) or pick one up at any library or city hall. Mail it to the Secretary of State at the address shown on the form. After the Secretary of State processes your registration, you will be sent a postcard confirming your eligibility and telling you where to vote. It will also tell you in which congressional, legislative, school, or other special districts you live. Keep this card and take it with you when you go to vote the first time. If you have your card, you'll be ahead of the game if you are challenged.

ELECTION DAY REGISTRATION

If you don't have time to register in advance, you can still register at your polling place on Election Day. First call your city hall and find out where you're supposed to vote, or look it up online at http://pollfinder.sos.state.mn.us, or on the **League of Women Voters** web site (www.lwvmn.org). Then go to your polling place, taking with you a Minnesota driver's license or other photo identification card that shows your new address in the precinct. You may also wish to ask a neighbor who can vouch for your residency to accompany you. If your Minnesota license shows a former address, you must take a recent utility bill with you to prove your current address. (The utility bill must have your name and current address, and be due within 30 days of the election. Utility bills may be for electric service, gas, water, solid waste, sewer, telephone, or cable TV.) College students may use a student fee statement, student picture ID card, or registration card showing their address in the precinct. You need not register a party affiliation, and primaries are open.

ABSENTEE VOTING

If you're going to be unable to vote in your precinct on Election Day—or just want to avoid the crowds—you can vote by absentee ballot. Get an absentee ballot application from your municipal clerk, then vote in the clerk's office, or mail your ballot back in plenty of time to arrive before the deadline.

Finally, if you're sick or injured, or for some reason unable to go into your polling place on election day, you have the right to ask the election judges to come out to you. To find out what else you are entitled to, read this Voters' Bill of Rights:

MINNESOTA VOTERS' BILL OF RIGHTS
For all persons residing in this state who meet federal voting eligibility requirements:
1. You have the right to be absent from work for the purpose of voting during the morning of Election Day.
2. If you are in line at your polling place any time between 7:00 a.m. and 8:00 p.m., you have the right to vote.
3. If you can provide the required proof of residence, you have the right to register to vote and to vote on Election Day.
4. If you are unable to sign your name, you have the right to orally confirm your identity with an election judge and to direct another person to sign your name for you.
5. You have the right to request special assistance when voting.
6. If you need assistance, you may be accompanied into the voting booth by a person of your choice, except by an agent of your employer or union or a candidate.
7. You have the right to bring your minor children into the polling place and into the voting booth with you.
8. If you have been convicted of a felony but your civil rights have been restored, you have the right to vote.
9. You have the right to vote without anyone in the polling place trying to influence your vote.
10. If you make a mistake or spoil your ballot before it is submitted, you have the right to receive a replacement ballot and vote.
11. You have the right to file a written complaint at your polling place if you are dissatisfied with the way an election is being run.
12. You have the right to take a sample ballot into the voting booth with you.
13. You have the right to take a copy of this Voter's Bill of Rights into the voting booth with you.

POLITICAL PARTIES

You won't be here long before you'll notice references in the news to the "DFL" and the "IR," which are the Democratic Farmer-Labor and Independent Republican parties. These aren't upstart third parties; they're the state's

Democrats and Republicans. (Actually, the Republicans dropped the "Independent" from their name in 1995, but people still talk about the IRs, so you may as well know what they're talking about.) The DFL was formed in the 1940s, when Minnesota's Democrats, led by Hubert Humphrey, merged with the populist Farmer-Labor Party. At about the same time, Minnesota's Republicans added "Independent" to their name in the hope of attracting more independent voters. Truly independent parties here have included the Green Party, the Reform Party, and the Independence Party. In 1998, Jesse Ventura ran as a candidate for the Reform Party and, as he said, "shocked the world" when he unexpectedly beat the major party candidates. As a result of those elections in the 1990s, the Independence Party (then the Reform Party) fulfilled Minnesota's statutory requirements and became a major party. In the last few elections the Constitution and Green Parties have also won—and lost— major party status. As of the writing of this book, the third party movement in Minnesota seems to have collapsed for the time being, though the Green Party does have a few current office holders. Some statistics: as of 2005, the Republicans have held the governorship for 12 of the last 16 years. At the time of the writing of this book, they are in the majority in the Minnesota House of Representatives, but in the minority in the state Senate by five seats. The result is that the House passes one version of a piece of legislation, the Senate passes something different, and then the bill is resolved in conference committee where, in recent years, things the legislature never voted on have often been added, and in that way passed into law. For more information about Minnesota's principal political parties, contact them at the addresses below. For TDD service to contact the parties, call (metro) 651-297-5353, or (Greater Minnesota) 800-657-3529.

- **Democratic Farmer-Labor State Office**, 651-293-1200 or 800-999-7457, www.dfl.org
- **Green Party**, www.mngreens.org
- **Independence Party**, www.mnip.org
- **Republican State Office**, 651-222-0022, www.mngop.com

For non-partisan information about Minnesota's candidates and issues, look online at www.e-democracy.org and the League of Women Voters web site (www.lwvmn.org). The **Minnesota Public Interest Research Group (MPIRG)** (612-627-4035, www.mpirg.org) is an advocacy group for the public interest on issues of the environment, consumer protection, and social justice.

CAUCUS SYSTEM

As de Tocqueville observed a couple hundred years ago, the principle that distinguishes the United States from all other societies is the belief that good government leadership, the kind that represents and serves people best, starts at the grassroots (local) level. In Minnesota we serve that principle through our caucus system.

A caucus is a meeting of local members of a political party to nominate candidates and plan policy. Held in every voting precinct in the state on Caucus

Night (the first Tuesday in March) by all the major parties, caucuses give voters a voice in the political process at the absolute grassroots level. They are an opportunity for you and your neighbors to discuss issues that are important to you and to influence the selection of your party's candidates and political platform. At the caucus you can introduce resolutions and can offer to serve as a delegate to the next level of your party's meetings—district, state, and national conventions. Everyone who is a qualified voter (or will be by the next election) may participate in one party's precinct caucus in any one year. (Older children are encouraged to attend, though not participate in the voting.) Each party determines its own specific procedures. For example, in the DFL party, there must be equal numbers of men and women on every committee, at every level. So how do you decide which party's caucus to attend? Well, which party's policies and candidates do you generally support? It's that easy. For detailed information about participating in caucuses, see the **League of Women Voters of Minnesota** web site (www.lwvmn.org).

POLITICAL CONTRIBUTION REFUND PROGRAM

Minnesota voters who contribute gifts of money to candidates for state office or to state political parties are eligible to apply for a refund of all or a portion of the contributions they have made during the calendar year. The maximum refund is $50 for an individual and $100 for a married couple. The political committee you contributed to will automatically send you a refund form along with a receipt. All you have to do is fill it out and send it in. Each individual may apply for only one refund per year. The underlying goal of the program is to make it unnecessary for candidates to accept large contributions from individual donors or lobbying groups by providing candidates with enough small contributions to adequately finance their campaigns.

LIBRARY CARDS

Minneapolis, St. Paul, and surrounding counties all have separate library systems, but they are connected: once you get a card at one library system, you can use it to get a card at another one, search for a book and have it delivered from one system to the other, and even check out a book from one system and return it to the other. The library systems are online, so you can scan for titles, place requests, and check your borrowing records from home. To get a card, you'll need to visit a library in person with identification and, if you don't yet have a Minnesota driver's license, a piece of mail with your new address. Check the **Neighborhoods** chapter of this book for the library nearest you. Call the following libraries if you have questions:

- **Anoka County Library System**, www.anoka.lib.mn.us
- **Carver County Library System**, 952-448-9395, www.carverlib.org; Chanhassen Library, 7711 Kerber Blvd, Chanhassen, 952-227-1500; Chaska Library, 3 City Hall Plaza, Chaska, 952-448-3886
- **Dakota County Library System**, 651-688-1547, www.co.Dakota.mn.us/library

- **Hennepin County Libraries**, 12601 Ridgedale Dr, Minnetonka, 952-847-8800, www.hclib.org
- **Minneapolis Central Public Library**, 300 Nicollet Mall, 612-630-6000, www.mpls.lib.mn.us
- **Ramsey County Library**, 4570 Victoria St, Shoreview, 651-486-2200, www.ramsey.lib.mn.us
- **Scott County Library System,** 13090 Alabama Ave S, Savage, 952-707-1760, www.scott.lib.mn.us
- **St. Paul Central Public Library**, 90 W 4th St, 651-266-7000, New Cards, 651- 266-7030, www.sppl.org
- **Washington County Public Library**, 2150 Radio Dr, Woodbury, 651-275-8500, www.co.washington.mn.us/library

PASSPORTS

Getting a passport can take as long as six weeks, so be sure to give yourself plenty of time. If your need is urgent, you can pay a fee and receive two-week expedited service; if you need even faster service, look on the Internet for passport expediting services.

Apply in person at one of the county service centers listed above, if you're applying for a passport for the first time. Take with you two identical, full-face photographs of yourself, proof of U.S. citizenship (an original or certified birth certificate, an expired passport or a naturalization certificate), and a valid form of photo identification such as a driver's license. To find the facility nearest you, do a zip code, state, or city search at the **Passport Acceptance Facility Search Page** (http://iafdb.travel.state.gov).

Simple renewals can be handled by mail. Download application forms and get complete information from the **U.S. Department of State Bureau of Consular Affairs National Passport Office Information Service**, http://travel.state.gov/passport/passport_1738.html, 1-877-487-2778. General travel information and advisories are available at http://travel.state.gov/travel/travel_1744.html.

Minnesotans often travel to **Canada**—Voyageurs National Park is half in Minnesota and half in Canada, and Winnipeg is a popular long-weekend destination. U.S. citizens must show either a U.S. passport or other proof of U.S. citizenship, such as an original or certified birth certificate together with photo identification. A single parent traveling with children, or grandparents or other guardians traveling with children, should carry proof of custody or letters from the non-accompanying parent/s authorizing travel. (This is in addition to proof of the child's citizenship.) Hunters may take ordinary rifles and shotguns into Canada, but fully automatic and assault-type weapons are prohibited. A complete list of prohibited firearms can be found at the **Canada Border Services Agency** web site (www.cbsa-asfc.gc.ca/). In addition, anyone with a criminal record (including a Driving While Impaired charge) should contact the Canadian Embassy or nearest consulate before going. For complete information about traveling to Canada, check the **U.S. Consular Services** web page (www.amcits.com/travel.asp).

PRINT AND BROADCAST MEDIA

TELEVISION

For old-fashioned broadcast (free) TV, the Twin Cities offer the national networks, plus a few independents. Of course, if you've ordered cable, the channels will differ from those given here. These are the major local affiliates:

- **Channel 2** KTCA-TV PBS (aka Twin Cities Public television, TPT), www.tpt.org
- **Channel 4** WCCO-TV CBS
- **Channel 5** KSTP-TV ABC, www.kstp.com
- **Channel 9** KMSP-TV FOX, www.kmsp.com
- **Channel 11** KARE11-TV NBC, www.kare11.com
- **Channel 17** KTCI-TV PBS, www.tpt.org
- **Channel 23** KMWB-TV CW, www.kmwb23.com
- **Channel 29** WFTC-TV Fox, www.fox29.com
- **Channel 41** KPXM-TV Independent, www.ionline.tv
- **Channel 45** KSTC TV (UHF), Independent, www.kstc45.com

RADIO

Here's a brief guide to what's available on the radio airwaves in the Twin Cities:

ADULT CONTEMPORARY
- **KQRS** 92 FM
- **KSTP** 94.5 FM (also known as KS95)
- **CITIES 97** 97.1 FM is one of the local Clear Channel stations.
- **DRIVE 105** 105.1, 105.3, 105.7 FM

ALTERNATIVE ROCK
- **KUOM**, Radio K, Real College Radio, 770 AM, 106.5 FM, and 100.7, is possibly the oldest station in the state, and plays an eclectic mix of music that includes many local artists.
- **KVSC** 88.1 FM, St. Cloud State University
- **KXXR** 93.7 FM (93X) plays hard rock and sponsors the 93X Fest (formerly EdgeFest) every summer in Somerset, Wisconsin.

CHILDREN'S PROGRAMMING
- **KDIZ** 1440 AM

CHRISTIAN/RELIGIOUS
- **KTIS** 900 AM, 98.5 FM
- **WLOL** 1330 AM

COUNTRY
- **KEEY** 102.1 FM—2005 Country Music Association Station of the Year

EASY LISTENING
- **WLTE** 102.9 FM

ETHNIC
- **KFAI** 90.3, 106.7 FM, "Fresh Air" plays a wide variety of music, airs programming in 13 different languages, and allows members of the public to use its broadcast facilities for their own programs.
- **KMOJ** 89.9 FM broadcasts an adult urban format.
- **WDGY** 630 AM is a Spanish-language station.
- **WMIN** 740 AM is a Spanish-language station.

JAZZ, TALK, TRAFFIC REPORTS
- **KBEM** 88.5 FM also partners with the Minnesota Department of Transportation to provide traffic reports.
- **KJZI** 100.3 FM

NEWS, TALK, WEATHER, COMMUNITY UPDATES
- **WCCO** 830 AM has been one of the area's top-rated stations since the 1920s, and is probably the area's most trusted station for weather reports and school closings.
- **KSTP** 1500 AM broadcasts nationally syndicated and local programs.
- **KTNF** 950 AM broadcasts progressive talk radio.

OLDIES
- **KQQL** 107.9 FM, KOOL 108 plays music from the 60s and 70s.

POP, TOP 40S
- **KDWB** 101.3 FM
- **KZJK** 101.4 FM Jack

PUBLIC RADIO
- **KSJN** 99.5 FM broadcasts classical, talk, and world music formats simultaneously over the same radio frequency in a digital technique called "multicasting." A digital radio receiver is required to pick up these broadcasts.
- **KNOW** 91.1 FM, Minnesota Public Radio, news and talk radio.
- **KCMP** The Current 89.3 FM broadcasts an iPOD eclectic mix, including many local musicians.

SPORTS
- **KFAN** 1130 AM

WEB
- **www.misplacedmusic.org** broadcasts local artists on the web.

NEWSPAPERS & MAGAZINES

Whether your interest is in theater, restaurants, or parenting, there is a local (and probably free) newspaper or magazine for you. The **Star Tribune** (612-673-4000, www.startribune.com) and **St. Paul Pioneer Press** (651-222-5011, www.twincities.com) are the two major news dailies. For an edgier read, try **City Pages** (612-375-1015, www.citypages.com), a free alternative weekly available online and at businesses metro-wide, which covers the local arts/entertainment scene, offering its own take on everything from politics to the personals. The **Minnesota Daily** (www.mndaily.com) covers the University of Minnesota's news and sports. The **Sun** community newspapers (www.mnsun.com), and a number of other neighborhood and special-interest, feature-driven weeklies, are always available next to grocery store entrances. Latest editions usually hit the newsstands on Wednesdays.

Two local glossies, **Mpls/St. Paul Magazine** (www.mspmag.com) and **Minnesota Monthly** (www.minnesotamonthly.com), which is published on behalf of Minnesota Public Radio (MPR), are great guides to life in the Twin Cities. They include reviews about area restaurants, trends, recreation, environmental issues, music, the arts, people profiles, shopping, lifestyles, getaways, and children's activities. *Minnesota Monthly* also contains MPR's program guide. The Twin Cities offer a multitude of parenting magazines and newspapers; probably the most popular is **Minnesota Parent** (www.mnparent.com), which describes itself as an "eclectic journal of family living" and contains essays as well as useful parenting information. A relative newcomer to the TC scene is **Pulse of the Twin Cities**, "Locally Grown Alternative Newspaper" (www.pulsetc.com). Two publications specializing in news for "minorities" are **Insight News** (612-588-1313, www.insightnews.com), a free newspaper serving Minnesota's growing African-American community, and **Minnesota Women's Press** (651-646-3968, www.womenspress.com), also free, and published every other Wednesday. Both of these can be found at co-ops and coffee shops. The **Utne Lens** (www.utne.com) is the online version of the *Utne Reader*, which reprints articles from over 2000 media sources.

For those interested in the moves and shakes of local finance and commerce, **MinnesotaBusiness Magazine** (www.minnesotabusiness.com) will keep you informed about the whos and the whats, as will **Women's Business Minnesota** magazine (www.womensbizmn.com) whose particular focus is helping Minnesota women achieve success (subscribe online). A subscription to **Politics in Minnesota** (www.politicsinminnesota.com) will keep you on top of Minnesota politics. And for local consumer information you can't beat **Twin Cities Consumer Checkbook**, a magazine that rates local service providers. Pick up an issue at your local bookstore, download articles for $10 to $15, or subscribe (651-646-2057, www.checkbook.org). Finally, if you're looking for local GLBT information, check out **Lavender Magazine** online, at www.lavendermagazine.com (see the **Helpful Services** chapter for more GLBT information and publications).

KNOWING WHERE TO GO FOR A SPECIFIC SERVICE IS PARTICULARLY important when you first move. The following information, which includes particulars about renting furniture, hiring a house cleaner, pest control, shipping services, and consumer protection, might make your life a little easier. Also included in this chapter is a section on services for the disabled, one to assist new residents from abroad, and information about gay and lesbian life in the Twin Cities.

RENTAL SERVICES

If you don't own everything you need to set up housekeeping, have no fear—someone has it and they're ready to rent.

FURNITURE, APPLIANCES, COMPUTERS, AND TELEVISIONS

Most rental stores now rent everything—including electronics and appliances. When you go shopping, take a list of what you need and a floor plan drawing; staff at the showroom will be able to help you figure out what will fit.

- **Cort Furniture Rental**, 8925 Lyndale Ave S, Bloomington, 952-884-5622; 1279 Trapp Rd, Eagan, 651-405-0009, www.cortfurniture.com
- **Quality Furniture Rental**, 916 Rice St, St. Paul, 651-487-2191; 9125 Lyndale Ave S, Bloomington, 952-884-4741
- **Rent-A-Center**, www.rentacenter.com; 523 W Broadway, Minneapolis, 612-521-3540; 2208 E Lake St, 612-724-6663; 4041 Central Ave NE, Columbia Heights, 763-788-7970

COMPUTER RENTAL

- **Audiovisual and Video Resources**, 3994 Cedarvale Dr, Eagan, 651-456-9033, www.avvr.com
- **FedEx Kinko's Copy Centers** have PCs and Macs available for in-store use; numerous locations, http://fedex.kinkos.com.

- **First Choice Computer Rental**, 7600 W 27 St, St. Louis Park, 952-975-9926, www.1stchoicecomputerrent.com
- **University of Minnesota**, 612-624-2713, www.ebc.umn.edu; you can rent an entire computer lab from the University of Minnesota.

DOMESTIC SERVICES

HOUSE CLEANING

In addition to taking care of routine chores on a regular basis, most cleaning services also offer a one-time cleaning service, including a once-over after moving day (or after your house-warming party). This list is just to get you started, and recommendation should not be implied. Before you employ any cleaner or cleaning service, be sure to check references, and hire only those services that are insured. Check the Yellow Pages for additional services or ask your friends or co-workers for recommendations.

- **1-800-GOT-JUNK,** junk removal service, does office, moving, and estate clean-ups, 1-800-468-5865, www.1800gotjunk.com.
- **Coit Services** has been in business for over fifty years. They clean carpet, upholstery, draperies, air ducts, tile, and grout, and can handle fire and flood restorations, as well. Call 1-800-FOR-COIT, www.coit.com. Appointments can be scheduled online.
- **Distinctive Cleaning**, 6139 Kellogg Ave, Edina, 952-922-2457, 952-922-2461, 651-225-1214, 866-813-6232
- **Jack Pixley Sweeps,** fireplace cleaning and repair, 763-422-0481, 651-646-3872
- **Junk Squad** specializes in estate, moving, and garage clean-ups, 952-828-9999, ext. 60.
- **Maid Brigade**, 651-294-0019, www.maidbrigade.com
- **Merry Maids**, 952-472-7531, www.merrymaids.info, advertises "short notice cleaning."
- **Molly Maid**, 952-401-1890, 952-345-0190, www.mollymaid.com
- **Sedgwick,** furnace and air duct cleaning, 952-881-9000
- **Stanley Steamer,** carpet cleaning, www.stanleysteamer.com: East Suburbs, 651-224-1646; North Suburbs, 763-421-9109; South/West Suburbs, 952-888-7340

PEST CONTROL

Apart from mosquitoes, Minnesota pests tend to run to squirrels and bats that move into your attic, and raccoons and wood ducks that fall down your chimney. With that in mind, your first line of defense should be to make sure that all your chimneys and air vents are properly screened. Carpenter ants can also be a problem, so trim shrubbery back away from your foundation. Should you develop a problem that requires a professional solution, here are some local services:

- **ADIOS Bugs and Critters**, 952-445-8127, www.adiosbugs.com
- **Diversified Mosquito Spraying**, 952-934-7064

- **Metropolitan Mosquito Control**, 651-645-9149
- **Orkin**, 1-888-ORKINMAN, www.orkin.com
- **Plunkett's Pest Control**, 651-487-2000, 763-571-7100, 952-884-8382, 877-571-7100, www.plunketts.net
- **Professional Mosquito Control**, 800-240-4262, www.professional mosquitocontrol.com
- **Terminix**, 800-TERMINIX, www.terminix.com
- **Wildlife Management Services**, 612-926-9988

MAIL SERVICE

Minneapolis' main post office is located downtown at 100 South First Street. Hours of operation are: Monday–Friday, 7 a.m.–11 p.m., Saturday, 9 a.m.–1 p.m. St. Paul's main post office at 180 East Kellogg Boulevard is open Monday–Friday, 6 a.m.–6 p.m., Saturday, 8 a.m.–1 p.m.; 800-ASK-USPS (800-275-8777), www.usps.com. For mail that needs to go out immediately, the Eagan post office (3145 Lexington Avenue South) is open 24 hours a day.

JUNK MAIL

To curtail the onslaught of mail newcomers always receive after relocating, make a written request—including name and address—asking to be purged from the Direct Marketing Association's list (Direct Marketing Association Mail Preference Service, P.O. Box 9008, Farmingdale, NY 11735). Another option is to call the "Opt-out" line (888-567-8688), requesting that the main credit bureaus not release your name and address to interested marketing companies.

MAIL RECEIVING SERVICES

- **UPS Stores**, 1360 University Ave, St Paul, 651-642-5972; 5115 Excelsior Blvd, St. Louis Park, 952-927-8137; and numerous other locations metro-wide. Call 800-PICK-UPS, or search by zip code for the nearest location at www.ups.com.

SHIPPING SERVICES

Most shipping services offer freight service for large items as well as package and same day delivery.
- **DHL Worldwide Express**, 800-225-5345, www.dhl-usa.com
- **Federal Express**, 800-238-5355, www.fedex.com
- **Roadway Package Systems** (RPS), 800-257-2837, www.roadway.com
- **United Parcel Service** (UPS), 800-PICK-UPS (742-5877), www.ups.com
- **US Postal Service Express Mail**, 800-ASK-USPS or 800-275-8777; Domestic Package Tracking, 800-222-1811; International Package Tracking, 800-222-1811, TDD/TTY 877-877-7TDD (877-877-7833), www.usps.com

CONSUMER PROTECTION–RIP-OFF RECOURSE

The best defense against fraud and consumer victimization is to avoid it. So read all contracts down to the smallest print, save all receipts and canceled checks, get the names of telephone sales and service people with whom you deal, date every paper you sign, and check with the Attorney General's office or the Better Business Bureau for complaints.

- **Minnesota Attorney General's Office Consumer Division**, 651-296-3353, 800-657-3787, TTY 651-297-7206, TTY 800-366-4812, www.ag. state.mn.us/consumer
- **Better Business Bureau of Minnesota**, 2706 Gannon Rd, St. Paul, 651-699-1111, www.mnd.bbb.org
- **Minnesota Department of Human Rights** is the state agency charged with protecting people from discrimination. Write them at 190 E 5th St, St. Paul, MN 55101, or call 651-296-5663, 800-657-3704, TTY 651-296-1283, www.humanrights.state.mn.us.

IDENTITY FRAUD

Identity fraud is on the increase and since it can take years for the victims of such fraud to clear their names, the best defense is to avoid becoming a victim in the first place. That said, it's hard to do when the State of Minnesota sells your driver's license data to anybody willing to plunk down $1000 for the list and $450 for monthly updates—even though virtually nobody checks the box giving the state permission to do so. There are some aspects of data privacy over which you do have control, however. Don't have your Social Security number printed on your checks. Shred undesired pre-approved credit offers. Don't carry credit cards, social security cards, birth certificates or passports, except when you need them. Cancel all unused credit card accounts. Always take credit card and ATM receipts away with you and never toss them in a public trash container. Keep a list of all your credit cards, including information on customer service and fraud department telephone numbers. And never give out credit card or social security information over the phone unless you initiated the call.

If you have been a victim of identity fraud, call the three major credit reporting bureaus immediately.

- **Equifax**, 800-525-6285, www.Equifax.com
- **TransUnion**, 800-916-8800, www.transunion.com
- **Experian (TRW)**, 888-397-3742, www.experian.com

Also call the Minnesota Attorney General's office (see address and phone number above). Every year they successfully help many people recover their losses—and someday they may even be able to get the state to stop selling our data!

SAFETY ISSUES

HANDGUNS

Probably the first thing you noticed upon arriving in Minnesota was the conspicuous "Guns Prohibited On These Premises" signs posted on the doors of many buildings, including grocery stores and libraries, and you're probably wondering what's going on. If it's any consolation, so are most of the rest of us! The fact is that the signs are there because they are the only way to ban guns from public premises under a 2005 Minnesota law called the Minnesota Personal Protection Act (conceal-and-carry law). This law threw out Minnesota's previous statutory provisions with respect to granting handgun permits, and replaced them with an expedited application process at the same time that it prohibited the barring of firearms from public facilities such as city halls, parks, recreation centers, and municipal liquor stores.

RADON

Most people understand that outdoor air pollution can harm their health, but may be unaware that indoor air pollution from radon can be every bit as dangerous. In fact, the Surgeon General has warned that radon is the second leading cause of lung cancer in the United States, next to smoking. For non-smokers, radon is the number one cause of lung cancer. So what is radon? It's a colorless, odorless, tasteless radioactive gas produced by the breakdown of minerals such as uranium and radium in the soil. Because of our geology and the way our homes are built to be airtight and negative pressured, radon can be a serious problem here. Indeed, the Minnesota Department of Health estimates that one in three homes in Minnesota has a high enough radon level to pose a risk to the occupants' health. One important factor is that many homes in Minnesota have basements that are used as living spaces, and that radon levels are often highest in the level of a building in closest contact with the soil. So what do you do about it? First, test for it. There are short-term and long-term radon test kits. The short-term test kit takes four to seven days to complete, offering a snapshot of radon levels during those days; the long-term test kit takes 91 days to a year to complete, producing a time-averaged picture of radon levels. Test kits cost between $5 and $25, and the price includes laboratory analysis. Buy them at hardware and home supply stores, or get one free from the **American Lung Association (ALA)** (651-227-8014, www.alamn.org, or order online at http://mn.radon.com). Hennepin County has both kinds of kits, which you can order online (www.co.hennepin.mn.us), or by calling **Public Health** (952-351-5200). Their short-term test kit costs $9; the long-term kit, $20.

If your levels are high, you can reduce exposure by using mitigation techniques. According to the ALA, most homes can be fixed for between $800 and $2500 (simple caulking and painting are NOT a fix). If you're building a new home, you can reduce the amount of radon coming in by using radon-resistant construction techniques. The ALA Health House builder guidelines include radon-reduction strategies. For more information on these builder guidelines, call the **Health House program** (877-521-1491, or look online at www.alamn.org). For complete information, look online at the **Minnesota Department of Health** web site (www.health.state.mn.us/divs/eh/indoorair/radon), which includes a list of certified and trained radon mitigation contractors. Minnesota residents can also call 800-798-9050 for general radon information.

Wisconsin residents can access general radon information, get a map of radon test results by zip code, and learn about radon-resistant construction at the **Wisconsin Radon Program** web site (www.dhfs.state.wi.us/dph_beh/RadonProt), or by calling 888-569-7236 (888-LOW-RADON).

Nationally, the U.S. **Environmental Protection Agency** (EPA) also maintains a radon web site which includes scientific findings and links to discounted tests (www.epa.gov/radon/, 800-SOS-RADON [800-767-7236]).

SMOKING BANS

Smoking bans are a bit of a patchwork here:

- **Hennepin County** bans smoking in indoor areas of restaurants, bars, and private clubs, including those serving only alcohol. **Golden Valley**, in Hennepin County, takes the ban one step further and bans smoking in all indoor areas of all workplaces, and within 25 feet of entrances and open windows. **Bloomington**, also in Hennepin County, bans smoking from all indoor areas of workplaces and within 25 feet of a door or open window, but allows smoking in up to one-half of an outdoor dining area.
- **Minneapolis**, also in Hennepin County, bans smoking in all indoor areas of all restaurants and bars, bowling alleys, pool and billiard halls, and private clubs, but allows smoking outside.
- **Ramsey County** bans smoking in all restaurants, but allows it in some bars.
- **Anoka County** does not ban smoking.

KEEPING THE BUGS AWAY

Mosquitoes are so common in Minnesota that they're facetiously referred to as our state bird. In fact we are home to roughly 50 species of them. We are also home to 13 species of ticks, including deer ticks. The bites of most of these insects are usually only a minor annoyance. On rare occasions, though, they can cause serious illness and even death. Mosquitoes can carry encephalitis and West Nile virus, and deer ticks can transmit Lyme disease. The **Centers for Disease Control (CDC)** strongly recommends that people who live in Minnesota use a repellent to lower the danger of insect-borne diseases. DEET, which is the active ingredient found in Deep Woods Off, Skintastic, Ultrathon, and many other repellents, is highly effective against both mosquitoes and ticks, and is a popular choice. For those who dislike DEET's strong odor or the damage it can do to some synthetic fabrics, two new products have recently appeared on store shelves. Picaridin, found in Cutter Advanced, has tested effective against mosquitoes, but is still being tested to see if it repels ticks. Oil of lemon eucalyptus is widely available in products like Off Botanicals, Repel, and Fite Bite. It repels mosquitoes about as effectively as 7% DEET (two hours' protection), but is still being tested on ticks, and is not recommended for children under three. Many DEET products contain much higher concentrations than 7%, however, and therefore last longer. Ultrathon, a 3M product, contains an additive that inhibits absorption, so that it lasts eight to twelve hours, making it the repellent of choice for many serious gardeners or those who go camping in the Boundary Waters.

And while you're protecting yourself, don't forget to protect your pets. Mosquitoes spread heartworms in dogs, so dogs here need to be tested for heartworm every spring and given a heartworm preventative. Dogs can also catch Lyme disease. There are vaccines to prevent Lyme disease in dogs, as well as topical insecticides such as fipronil (Frontline) that are applied to the skin between the dog's shoulder blades once a month. Horses in Minnesota need to be vaccinated against mosquito-borne diseases, too, including West Nile virus and Eastern (EEE) and Western (WEE) encephalitis. Potomac fever, which may be transmitted by ticks from horses to people, has also occurred here. It is currently recommended that horses be vaccinated in April or May and then again in the latter part of the summer, i.e., August. This schedule is a change from earlier recommendations, and is timed to offer the greatest protection during the time of the year when infection is most likely to occur.

SERVICES FOR PEOPLE WITH DISABILITIES

The slogan for a disabled advocacy program on community radio station KFAI is "Disabled and Proud—Not an Oxymoron!" This slogan could also describe the supportive environment for the disabled in the Twin Cities. Here the physically challenged will find visibility (a reporter for one of the local TV stations works from a wheelchair), organization, communication, and reliable mobility. Of course, the reviews are mixed, and the past several years of state budget deficits have resulted in changes to eligibility and service delivery for many programs used by people with disabilities. MinnesotaCare and home and community waiver programs to keep people out of institutional care have been favorite legislative targets of budget cutting proposals, as have services to the mentally ill.

On the other hand, in accordance with the 1990 Americans with Disabilities Act, public buildings are handicapped-accessible, and every parking lot has handicapped spaces. Non-disabled people who park in them face fines of up to $200, and police are generally tough on enforcement. Most city sidewalks have curb cuts, and in the downtowns, with ramp parking and skyways, it is possible to go for miles without stepping outside, although parking spaces for over-sized vans are still hard to come by. On the cultural front, theaters and concert halls set aside special sections for people in wheelchairs, and many facilities offer hearing augmentation devices or signed performances.

By state law, Minnesota schools are required to offer special needs students a full range of services. Contact the **Department of Education** (651-

582-8200, http://education.state.mn.us/mde) for more information. The library systems offer services for the hearing and vision impaired, such as books-on-tape and high-magnification lenses. Call 952-847-8850 for **At Home Services of Hennepin County libraries**; Minneapolis, 612-630-6170; Ramsey County, 651-486-2200; St. Paul, 651-632-5089; and Washington County, 651-430-6000, TTY 651-430-6246 (www.co.washington.mn.us).

There is an active community of animal lovers who train service dogs in several programs: **Helping Paws of Minnesota** (952-988-9359, www.helping paws.org) and **Hearing and Service Dogs of Minnesota**, in Minneapolis (612-729-5986, TTY and Fax 612-729-5914, email: info@hsdm.org, www.hsdm.org) are among them.

The area also offers a multitude of sports and outdoor recreation opportunities for the physically challenged (see **Adapted Athletics** in **Sports and Recreation**). The Power Hockey league allows anyone in a power wheelchair to participate. If you want to sign up, call the **US Electric Wheelchair Hockey Association** (www.usewha.org). If it's camping or canoeing you like to do, **Wilderness Inquiry** creates outdoor adventures for people of all ages, abilities, and backgrounds (612-379-3858, 800-728-0719, or online, www.wilderness inquiry.org/trip). For those who love horses, Minnesota has a **We Can Ride** chapter, offering therapeutic horseback riding and cart driving for children and adults at several locations. Call 952-934-0057 to sign up or volunteer.

On the downside, although all MetroTransit buses are equipped with wheelchair lifts, winter weather can make it hard to get to them. Winter plowing, un-shoveled walks, and the process of freezing and thawing may make it impossible to get around for days or weeks at a time. And, though the downtown has an extensive skyway system, most downtown parking ramps will not accommodate large vans.

For the latest disability information, be sure to read **Access Press** (www.accesspress.org), a monthly tabloid newspaper available free at over 200 locations or on disk. Subscriptions are available for $25 a year; to subscribe call 651-644-2133.

GETTING AROUND

DISABLED CERTIFICATES AND CAR LICENSE PLATES

To apply for a Minnesota disability certificate or disabled car license plates call **Driver and Vehicle Services** (651-296-6911, TDD/TTY 651-282-6555), or download the application from the web site (www.mndriveinfo.org). You may apply after a physician or chiropractor certifies that you meet the state requirements for a disabled person. If your disability is permanent and you are the owner/primary driver of a vehicle, you may apply for disabled plates at the time of vehicle registration.

In Wisconsin, download applications for temporary parking certificates or plates from the **Wisconsin Department of Transportation** web site (www.dot.wisconsin.gov/drivers/vehicles/personal/special/#disabled), or go in person to a DMV office. The office in Hudson (2100 O'Neil Road, 800-924-3570) is handicapped-accessible (many are not).

BUS TRANSPORTATION

Buses are lift-equipped, and all Metro Transit drivers are trained to recognize "bus identifier cards" used by the vision- or hearing-impaired to display the bus route number they are waiting for. Call **Metro Transit Customer Relations** (612-373-3333, www.metrocouncil.org/transit/access) for information about these cards. **Metro Mobility certification** takes three weeks, but once certified, participants receive door-through-door public transportation. Reservations should be made in advance. This is a shared-ride system structured to transport multiple passengers to multiple destinations. It works well to get disabled people to and from work. To apply, you must complete an Americans with Disabilities Act (ADA) application. Call **Metro Mobility Customer Services** (651-602-1111, TTY 651-221-9886 between 8 a.m. and 4:30 p.m., Monday–Friday, or email mmscmail@metc.state.mn.us) for an application form, or with questions. The off-peak fare is $2.00 per one-way trip; the peak hour fare is $2.50 per one-way trip. ADA-certified customers also are entitled to use regular route transit for $.50.

MOBILITY AND SPECIAL CARE EQUIPMENT

If you need to rent or purchase a scooter or motorized wheelchair, specially outfitted van, or other medical devices and supplies, here are some places to start looking:

- **Ability Solutions Showroom**, 6311 Cambridge St, St. Louis Park, 612-253-5438, www.abilitysolutions.net
- **Accessible Van Rentals**, 888-256-5807, www.wheelchair-getaways.com
- **Complete Mobility Systems**, 1915 County Rd C, St. Paul, 651-635-0655 or 800-788-7479, www.completemobility.com
- **Jackson Medical**, 651-645-6221
- **Mobility for Independence**, 621 W Lake St, Ste 305, Minneapolis, 55408, 612-825-1845, www.mobilityforindependence.org, gives grants toward the purchase of mobility equipment.
- **R.C. Sales and Manufacturing**, 14726 Wake St NE, Ham Lake, 763-786-6504, is a specialized builder of wheelchair-accessible vans.
- **RollX Vans**, 2200 Hwy 13, Savage, 952-890-7851, sells new and previously owned handicapped-accessible vans and minivans, power openers, ramps and lifts, transfer seats, and driving controls.
- **Waldoch**, 13821 Lake Dr, Forest Lake, 651-464-3215, 800-328-9259, www.waldoch.com

COMMUNICATIONS

DEAF AND HARD OF HEARING

Minnesota's Deaf and Hard of Hearing Services operates eight regional offices. The Metro office is located at 130 East Seventh Street, in Downtown St. Paul (mailing address: Department of Human Services, 444 Lafayette Road, St. Paul, MN 55155-3814, telephone 651-297-1316, TTY 651-297-1313, Fax 651-215-6388). You can email this office at dhhs.metro@state,mn.us. For more information, look online at the **Department of Human Services** web site (www.dhs.state.mn.us).

BLIND AND VISUALLY IMPAIRED

Minnesota offers a special homestead tax credit as well as providing many adaptive services to the blind and visually impaired. To find out about either, make your first call to the **Minnesota Department of Economic Security, Services for the Blind** (651-642-0500, TTY/TDD 651-642-0506, or toll free Voice/TDD 800-652-9000, www.mnssb.org). The main Services for the Blind office is located at 2200 University Avenue, Suite 240, St. Paul. Office hours are 8:00 a.m.–4:30 p.m., Monday–Friday. This office offers job and independent living rehabilitation classes and services, including group classes for the blind elderly. Its communications center provides Radio Talking Books and voice-edition newspapers. It also has a store that sells adaptive aids at cost. Transportation is provided to group classes. Additional resources to consider:

- **BLIND Inc**. (Blindness Learning In New Dimensions) is a nonprofit training facility where people learn to live independently, use Braille, cook, clean, and sew. It also teaches industrial arts and job readiness skills, 100 E 22nd St, Minneapolis, 612-872-0100, www.blindinc.org.
- **Minnesota Library for the Blind**; order books online at telnet://lbph.lib.mn.us. To access the service, you must first call the library at 800-722-0550 to obtain a library code and password.
- **Vision Loss Resources Inc**., www.visionlossresources.com, provides services to people who are out of school. Their **West Metro** facility houses a rehab and community center, 1936 Lyndale Ave S, Minneapolis, Voice/TTY 612-871-2222. Their **East Metro** facility is located at 216 S Wabasha, St. Paul, Voice/TTY 651-224-7662. This organization provides services for visually impaired seniors and those with chronic illnesses including diabetes. Email, Internet access, and computer training for blind people also are available here.

HEALTH CARE

Medical Assistance for Employed Persons with Disabilities ("MA-EPD") is a buy-in program which allows the working disabled to pay a premium and retain their Medical Assistance coverage. For more information, contact your county human service agency.

HOUSING

There is a critical shortage of affordable housing in the Twin Cities, so it may take a long time to locate an acceptable apartment. Start your search early.

Minnesota law requires that a disabled person and his/her family must be given priority with respect to handicapped-equipped rental housing. This means that if a family without a disabled member is living in handicapped-equipped housing, they can be asked to move to another unit in the same rental complex to make way for a family that does include a disabled person. For help finding barrier-free housing or housing assistance programs for the disabled, call the **National Handicapped Housing Institute** (651-639-9799), or the

United Way's First Call for Help (211), a comprehensive information referral for any social service need.

For information about accessible hotels and motels in the Twin Cities area check the **Temporary Lodgings** chapter in this book.

INDEPENDENT LIVING

The **Metropolitan Center for Independent Living** (MCIL) is one of eight such centers in Minnesota. It offers up-to-date information about community resources related to people with disabilities, including housing and benefits referral. This organization is an amazing resource. It lists job openings, provides peer mentoring, accessible conference space, a computer lab for consumer use, advocacy, subsidized personal assistance, and classes for people with disabilities to acquire the skills they need for independent living. The **Senior Companion** program provides necessary support to seniors wanting to stay in their own homes. The **Ramp Project** assists those needing ramps. The **Transition Program** assists students and young adults with disabilities, ages 14 through 24, to make a successful transition from high school to post-secondary education, to employment and adult independent living. Call 651-646-8342, TTY 651-603-2001, or visit www.mcil-mn.org.

ADDITIONAL RESOURCES

Following is a variety of resources, both governmental and nonprofit, that may be of use to those with special needs:

- **Accessible Space** is a nonprofit corporation that provides disability-adaptive housing, 651-645-7271 or 800-466-7722, www.accessible space.org.
- **ADA Minnesota**, 651-603-2015, TTY 651-603-2001, is the Minnesota resource for information about the Americans with Disabilities Act.
- **Advocating Change Together** (ACT), 651-641-0297
- **ARC Minnesota**, www.arcminnesota.com, provides advocacy, referrals for services, and educational materials, 800-582-5256, 651-523-0823.
- **City Housing and Redevelopment Authorities** (HRA) take applications for Section 8 subsidized housing. For information, call the St. Paul HRA, 651-298-5459, or Minneapolis HRA, 612-342-1400. Applications for subsidized units are actually processed by building managers. It's a good idea to have your name added to the waiting list at all of the buildings in which you'd like to live.
- **Closing the Gap**, www.closingthegap.com, provides a technology forum for children and adults with special needs.
- **Courage Center**, 3915 Golden Valley Rd, Golden Valley, is Minnesota's most famous rehabilitation center. For service and program information, call 763-588-0811, 888-8INTAKE, TTY 763-520-0245, www.courage.org
- **Disability Linkage Line** (DLL), 866-333-2466, www.minnesotahelp.info
- **"Disabled and Proud"** airs on Tuesday nights at 7:30 p.m. on KFAI, 90.3 FM in Minneapolis and 106.7 FM in St. Paul.

- **Lutheran Social Services**, 612-879-5205, www.lssmn.org; services include transitional housing and permanent supportive housing.
- **Minnesota Disability Law Center,** 612-332-1441, 800-292-4150, TDD 612-332-4668, www.mndlc.org, provides free civil legal assistance to individuals with disabilities.
- **Minnesota State Council on Disability**, Voice/TTY, 651-296-6785, 800-945-8913, 711, www.disability.state.mn.us; whatever your disability, this is the agency to contact when you are looking for any kind of assistance.
- **National Handicapped Housing Institute** (NHHI), 651-639-9799, rents apartments to the handicapped and disabled.
- **Public housing** is available through the local **Public Housing Authority** (PHA). To apply, contact the individual county or city you prefer and complete and return the application, even if there are no vacancies. Then have your name added to the waiting list at all of the buildings in which you'd like to live. Public Housing Authorities include S St. Paul, 651-451-1838; St. Louis Park, 952-924-2500; Minneapolis, 612-342-1413; Hopkins, 952-939-1329; St. Paul, 651-298-5158; Plymouth, 952-509-5410.

INTERNATIONAL NEWCOMERS

A variety of helpful information can be found online at the **US Citizen and Immigration Services** web site: http://uscis.gov. If you have specific questions, you can also contact the USCIS national customer service center (800-375-5283, TTY 800-767-1833). Once you know what you need to do, you'll undoubtedly have to fill out paperwork. To get the proper forms call 800-870-3676 or look on the USCIS web site (listed above).

For further assistance, you can schedule an appointment with US Citizen and Immigration Services by calling 800-375-5283. Below are the addresses of local USCIS district and satellite offices:

- **St. Paul District Office** (serving Minnesota, North Dakota, South Dakota, and parts of Wisconsin): 2901 Metro Dr, Ste 100, Bloomington, MN 55425
- **Asylum Office**: 401 S La Salle St, 8th Flr, Chicago, IL 60605
- **Nebraska Service Center**: processes most forms filed in this area. Forms are available through the USCIS web site or by calling 800-870-3676 to have forms mailed to you.
- **Duluth Application Support Center**—515 W 1st St, Ste 208, Duluth, MN 55802; 218-720-5208

PUBLICATIONS

You can download a useful guide, "Welcome to the United States: A Guide for New Immigrants" free at http://uscis.gov/graphics/citizenship/imm_guide.htm. The booklet includes information on your rights and responsibilities as well as the steps to take to become a US citizen.

International newcomers experiencing culture shock can get a quick overview of American culture, etiquette, expectations, and quirks in the

Newcomer's Handbook for Moving to and Living in the USA by Mike Livingston, published by First Books (www.firstbooks.com).

LOCAL CONSULATES

Some local consulates in the Twin Cities are:

Canadian Consulate General
701 4th Avenue South
Minneapolis, MN 55415-1600
612-333-4641
www.dfait-maeci.gc.ca/can-am/minneapolis/menu-en.asp

Royal Danish Consulate
1417 East River Parkway
Minneapolis, MN 55414
612-338-7283
www.ambassade.dk/dkusaminc.php3

Finnish Consulate
2429 Girard Ave S
Minneapolis, MN 55405-2537
612-374-2718
www.minnesotafinnish.org

Consulat of Iceland
6428 Nordic Circle
Edina, MN 55439-1140
952-942-5745
www.iceland.org/us

Consul of Mexico
797 East 7th Street
Saint Paul, MN 55106
Tel: 651-771-5494
http://portal.sre.gob.mx/saintpaul/

Norwegian Consulate General
821 Marquette Avenue
Minneapolis, MN 55402-2929
612-332-3338
www.norway.org/Minneapolis

Swedish Consulate General
706 2nd Avenue South
Minneapolis, MN 55402–3003
612-332-6897
www.swedenabroad.com

MOVING PETS TO THE USA

- **The Pet-Moving Handbook** (First Books) covers domestic and international moves, via car, airplane, ferry, etc. Primary focus is on cats and dogs.
- **Cosmopolitan Canine Carriers** out of Connecticut, 800-243-9105, www.caninecarriers.com, has been shipping dogs and cats all over the world for over 25 years. Contact them with questions or concerns regarding air transportation arrangements, vaccinations, and quarantine times.

GAY AND LESBIAN LIFE

With the second-largest per capita Gay/Lesbian/Bisexual/Transgender (GLBT) population in the U.S., Minnesota—and Minneapolis, in particular—has long been a leader in extending gay rights to its citizens. Openly gay people serve on city councils and, years ago, one of St. Paul's council members went through well-accepted gender reassignment. Many of the largest companies in our private sector also support the GLBT community by extending domestic partner benefits to their employees; and, since 1991, same-sex couples have been able to register as domestic partners at Minneapolis City Hall.

For years we lived complacent in the thought that our state had some of the strongest civil rights protection laws in the country for gays, lesbians, bisexuals, and transgender people. However, Minnesota politics have recently taken a hard right turn, and those protections are under attack.

Nevertheless, we still have a well-established GLBT community, and it has created a service center, clearinghouse, and information line that is the envy of non-gays, called **OutFront Minnesota** (www.outfront.org). The Info Line (612-822-0127 or 800-800-0350) provides over two hours of recorded information about gay life in Minnesota. For visitors to the Twin Cities, OutFront can make hotel reservations and supply an itinerary for a three-day visit.

ENTERTAINMENT

The Metro doesn't have one gay neighborhood or "strip," but we do have some traditionally "gay" bars that have been around for a long time, as well as new places opening up in Northeast Minneapolis along East Hennepin. We are also home to the **Twin Cities Gay Men's Chorus**, which performs six times a year at the Ted Mann Concert Hall at the University of Minnesota. For tickets call 612-339-SONG, or purchase tickets online (www.tcgmc.org).

- **19 Bar**, 19 W 15th St (east of Loring Park), 612-871-5553, is the oldest gay bar in the Twin Cities.
- **Gay 90s Theatre Cafe and Bar**, 408 Hennepin Ave, Minneapolis, 612-333-7755, has been voted the Twin Cities' best gay bar many, many times, although its drag shows and three dance floors probably attract at least as many straight college students and bachelorette parties as gays.
- **Town House**, 1415 University, St. Paul, 651-646-7087, www.townhouse bar.com

HOUSING

If you're looking for like-minded GLBT neighbors, you can cast a wide net. Gays are integrated into neighborhoods throughout the Twin Cities. Some places to start your search in Minneapolis: Lowry Hill, Uptown, Stevens Square, Powderhorn, Longfellow, East Isles, anywhere in South Minneapolis, and downtown or in the Near Northside. Gays are also leading the way to gentrify Northeast and the Camden area of North Minneapolis. However, Loring Park, traditional center of gay activity in the Twin Cities, is becoming less of a rental community than it used to be, as many of the apartments are being converted into condominiums. In St. Paul, consider Como, anywhere on the west side, or the new lofts downtown. In the suburbs there are well-established GLBT communities in St. Louis Park and Golden Valley.

OTHER GLBT RESOURCES

- **District 202 Community Center**, 1601 Nicollet Ave S, Minneapolis, is a drug-free, alcohol-free, "safe space" for young people, many of whom are from minority communities, 612-871-5559.
- **KFAI-FM Community Radio**, 90.3 FM and 106.7 FM, www.kfai.org, broadcasts several GLBT-themed shows: "Fresh Fruit," "Womanist Power Authority," and "This Way Out."
- **Lavender Magazine** is a biweekly publication covering culture, arts, news, and the local bar scene. It is free at bookstores, coffee shops, restaurants and bars, or available by subscription, 612-871-2237, www.lavender magazine.com.
- **Minneapolis Public Schools: Out 4 Good**, 612-668-0180
- **Minnesota AIDS Project**, 1400 Park Ave, Minneapolis, 612-373-2437, www.mnaidsproject.org
- **Northern Lights Women's Softball League**, www.nlwsl.org
- **PFLAG (Parents & Friends of Lesbians & Gays)** sponsors monthly programs and discussions; call 612-825-1660, or check www.pflag.org.
- **Power Pages**, www.powerpagesonline.com
- **Quatrefoil Library**, 1619 Dayton Ave, St. Paul, 651-641-0969, www.qlibrary.org
- **Query Booksellers**, 520 E Hennepin, Minneapolis, 612-331-7701, www.querybooks.com, specializes in GLBT reading matter.
- **Rainbow Families**, 711 W Lake St, Ste 210, Minneapolis, 612-827-3118, www.rainbowfamilies.org
- **St. Paul Public Schools: Out for Equity**, 651-603-4942, provides support to students, staff, and families.

MOVING TO A NEW PLACE MEANS RUNNING LOTS OF ERRANDS—FROM buying new curtains to replacing mops and brooms that didn't make it into the moving truck. The Twin Cities present you with many shopping choices, from major national department stores to flea markets. If you're looking for something trendy, start in Uptown; if sophisticated is your style, try 50th and France; and if it's toilet bowl brushes, school supplies, or a good price on a small appliance, beat feet to Target. If your passion is fashion, there are choices from Ragstock's vintage jeans to designer boutiques—and there is no sales tax on clothing!

Partly because of our climate and partly because of the massive urban sprawl and resultant car culture, indoor malls dominate retail shopping here, with Southdale Mall in Edina said to be the first indoor retail center built in the United States (1955). There are dozens more now and the list below will help guide you. In the meantime, if you can't get out, try shopping the local businesses listed at ShopMinnesota (http://pd.startribune.com/shoppingportal/index.jsp).

SHOPPING MALLS AND DISTRICTS

MALLS

Planes full of shoppers fly in from all over the world to spend their yen at the 4.2-million-square-foot **Mall of America** (Highways 77 & I-494 in Bloomington, 952-883-8800, www.mallofamerica.com). This is the largest fully enclosed shopping and entertainment complex in the United States, as well as one of the nation's most visited tourist attractions. Easily accessible from downtown Minneapolis via the Hiawatha LRT line, the mall's anchor stores are **Bloomingdale's, Macys, Nordstrom**, and **Sears**, but you can find over 500 other stores there, including a wedding chapel and The Nap Store, a place to lie down and rest when you get shopped out. The Twin Cities retail scene is also home to the latest trend in buzz-word shopping, the "Lifestyle Mall," which features upscale retailers in Disney-esque storefront-on-Main-Street settings. We have two, so far: the **Shoppes at Arbor Lakes**, I-94 and 694 in Maple Grove (www.shoppesatarborlakes.com) and **Woodbury Lakes** at I-94 and Radio Drive (www.woodburylakes.com). Stores at these malls include **Ann Taylor, Banana Republic, Coldwater Creek, Gap** and **Baby Gap,** as well as some independents you won't find elsewhere.

Given our weather, enclosed malls are still the standard, and most of the ones below offer a mix of practical and pricey shopping. The four "Dales" and Burnsville Center were our mega-malls before the Mall of America came to town, and they are still hubs for a vast array of surrounding shopping. They are generally where you'll find Macy's, JC Penney, and Sears.

- **Brookdale Center**, off Brooklyn Blvd in Brooklyn Center, 763-566-3373, www.brookdaleshoppingcenter.com
- **Burnsville Center**, County Rd 42, Burnsville, 952-435-8181, www.burnsvillecenter.com
- **Eden Prairie Center**, I-494 and Hwy 212, Eden Prairie, 952-941-7650, edenprairiecenter.com, is anchored by Sears, Target, a mutiplex movie theater, Kohl's, and the only Twin Cities branch of Iowa-based Von Maur. Though you can practically see the mall from the freeway, getting to it is a real test of navigational skills, even for locals. Follow signs for Hwy 212 or Prairie Center Dr, and you won't stray too far off course.
- **Galleria**, 69th St and France Ave, Edina, 952-925-4321, www.galleria edina.com, includes upscale shopping at Gabbert's Furniture and Design Studio, Tiffany's, Laura Ashley, and Sonnie's women's fashions, as well as several restaurants and a Rocco Altobelli Salon and Spa.
- **Maplewood Mall**, I-694 & White Bear Ave, St. Paul, 651-770-5020, www.simon.com
- **Ridgedale**, I-394 and Ridgedale Dr, Minnetonka, 952-541-4864, www.ridgedalecenter.com
- **Rosedale**, Hwy 36 and Fairview Ave, Roseville, 651-633-0872, www.myrosedale.com.
- **Southdale**, 6601 France Ave S, Edina, 952-925-7885, www.southdale. com, includes numerous restaurants, a huge theater complex, and a Mini-Cooper showroom.

SHOPPING DISTRICTS

- **Uptown (Lake Street and Hennepin Avenue)**, www.uptown minneapolis.com, is as urban and edgy as Minnesota gets. Besides the numerous cafés, bars, and art galleries, close to a hundred trendy clothing, housewares, furniture, and home decorating stores are located here. North of Lake on Hennepin there are a number of antique and specialty shops. A few blocks east, the Lyn-Lake intersection is packed with global restaurants, shops, and more. (See **Cultural Life** for more information). Check out the massive **Uptown Art Fair** in August.
- **Grand Avenue, St. Paul**, www.grandave.com, is a treasure trove of interesting bars and restaurants and unique specialty retail shops. During

Grand Old Days in June, the whole street becomes one long block party with bands and beer and games for the children.

- **Minneapolis Midtown Exchange**, at the east end of Lake St (intersection of Chicago and Lake), is the place to look for small ethnic businesses.
- **Warehouse District, Minneapolis**, dubbed "The Design District," the old warehouses clustered around Washington Ave have been rehabbed and turned into chic lofts, galleries, design studios, and restaurants. There is an LRT station on Hennepin, and many Warehouse District establishments will even provide an LRT ticket for you if you stop in for a drink or meal before a Target Center game.
- **Northeast Minneapolis/Historic St. Anthony**, across the river from downtown via the Hennepin Ave and 3rd Ave bridges, "Nordeast," one of the oldest parts of Minneapolis, has recently blossomed with a lot of trendy new lofts—and a lot of trendy new shopping to serve them.
- **Nicollet Mall, Minneapolis**, www.downtownminneapolis.com; the city's famous downtown pedestrian mall is home to sophisticated housewares, home furnishings, and department stores such as **Target, Macy's**, and **Williams-Sonoma**. Getting around from store to store in winter is made easier by the second-story skyway system. There is an on-the-mall farmers' market in summer, and the **Holidazzle Parade** enlivens shopping between Thanksgiving and Christmas. Shop for bargains at **Marshall's** and **Nieman's Last Call**. Target has everything, including groceries.
- **Linden Hills**, 43rd St and Upton Ave S, Minneapolis, www.linden-hills.com, just west of Lake Harriet, is home to several first-rate, locally owned shops, including two especially good stores for children: **Wild Rumpus** children's bookstore (2720 43rd St, 612-920-5005, www.wildrumpusbooks.com) and **Creative Kidstuff** (4313 Upton, www.creativekidstuff.com).
- **50th and France Avenue, Edina**, www.50thandfrance.com, has a hundred classy boutiques, trendy accessories, an indie movie theater, bakeries, restaurants, and a Lund's grocery. In June, this crossroads and its surrounding streets are transformed into an exotic bazaar by the Edina Art Fair.
- **Midway**, centered on University Ave at Snelling, midway between Minneapolis and St. Paul, provides the necessities: grocery stores, banks, warehouse and discount department stores, second-hand furniture, and clothing retailers. Farther down University Ave, past Lexington, the neighborhood known as **Frogtown** is home to countless Asian markets.
- **South Robert Street**, West St. Paul, transcends nationality with ethnic groceries and national department and discount stores such as Menard's, Lowe's Home Store, and Target.
- **Stillwater** (See **Quick Getaways** chapter)
- **Wayzata on Lake Minnetonka**, about 20 minutes west of Minneapolis out I-394; the sign on the **Wayzata Home Center** at 1250 Wayzata Blvd says it all: "London, Paris, Wayzata." Antique shops here have something for everyone. When exploring Wayzata in warm weather months, park your car and walk or use the trolley.
- **West Seventh, St. Paul**; those who think that shopping in St. Paul is tatty and dull, haven't been to West 7th, a major commercial artery which heads

west/southwest out of downtown through the city's few remaining intact Victorian Romanesque commercial blocks, and is home to many antique shops and interesting restaurants.

- **White Bear Lake** features one-of-a kind shops clustered in a friendly downtown that has cobblestone streets and a turn-of-the-century resort quality. Make this a day trip, especially if you like to knit, sew, or quilt. The local summer festival, **Manitou Days**—held in late June—includes a Lake Shore Art Fair, "Then and Now" walking tour, sailboat regatta, 5K run, water ski show, and beach dancing.

OUTLET MALLS

- **Albertville Premium Outlets**, about forty minutes west of the metro area on I-94 in Albertville, 763-497-1911, www.premiumoutlets.com, is the highest-quality outlet in the state. Tenants include Carter's, Waterford, Brooks Bothers, Coach, BCBG, and many, many more. The San Antonio Shoes factory store carries shoes for wide feet.
- **Medford Outlet Center**, 45 miles south of the metro on I-35 at exit 48, 1-507-455-2042, has Payless Shoes and Columbia—but nothing high fashion.
- **Tanger Outlet Center**, I-35 North, Exit 147, North Branch, 651-674-5886, 800-409-3631, www.tangeroutlet.com, is home to Gap, Old Navy, Bass, Liz Claiborne, Toy Liquidators, and a General Nutrition Center. Check its web site before you go, and download the coupons.

DEPARTMENT STORES

If you'd have trouble living without Bloomingdale's or some other top-of-the-line department store, you can breathe easier—most of the national one-stop shopping giants are here. But before you settle down and become a regular customer at one of the more familiar stores, pay a visit to **Von Maur** at Eden Prairie Center (952-829-0200, www.vonmaur.com). This family-owned, Iowa-based department store carries the same brands of clothing and gifts as the other higher-end department stores, but they'll give you free hemming, an interest-free credit card with no fees and flexible payments, and their shoe salesroom is legendary. Von Maur doesn't have "sales," as such, but moves this season's merchandise to sale racks every week as newer merchandise comes in. For an easy way to find weekly specials at all the local stores, check online atwww.shoplocal.com.

- **Bloomingdale's**, Mall of America, Bloomington, 952-883-2500, www. Bloomingdales.com
- **Herberger's**, 952-886-2900, www.herbergers.com: Rosedale and 4 other metro locations
- **JC Penney**, 952-920-8101, www.jcpenney.com
- **Kmart**, www.kmart.com, has numerous locations.
- **Kohl's**, 952-881-8861, www.kohls.com; 10 metro locations, Kohl's runs sales almost continuously on everything from clothing to coffee makers.
- **Macy's**, www.macys.com, 612-375-2200; carries name brands such as Liz Claiborne and Coach.

- **Neiman-Marcus**, 505 Nicollet Mall, Minneapolis, 612-339-2600, www. neimanmarcus.com
- **Nordstrom**, Mall of America, Bloomington, 952-883-2121, www.nordstrom. com; this chain has built its reputation on excellent service and great shoes for both men and women. Check out the clearance items at Nordstrom's Rack, 952-854-3131, on the third floor, as well as its "Half-Yearly" sale in June.
- **Sears, Roebuck & Co.**, www.sears.com

DISCOUNT STORES

Costco (www.Costco.com) and **Sam's Club** (www.samsclub.com) are membership discounters. Costco is a little more polished, and generally preferred, but only has three stores here, all on the western side of town: 5801 16th St W, St. Louis Park, 763-582-9603; 12011 Technology Dr, Eden Prairie, 952-943-4801; and 12547 Riverdale Blvd, Coon Rapids, 763-712-7768. Sam's Club has many more locations, and they're conveniently scattered throughout the metro area. Though it is not generally advertised, both Sam's Club and Costco sell liquor to non-members; and while both chains offer the standard mix of food, electronics, and pharmacies, etc., some locations also have gas stations. Sam's Club's parent company, **Wal-Mart** (www.walmart.com) is also represented in the Twin Cities with half a dozen stores.

Dwarfing these chains, however, is our homegrown trendsetter, **Target** (www.Target.com). There may not be a Target on every street corner, but with 64 stores in the state, it certainly seems like it. Known for its huge selections of cheap chic wares, it is a one-stop shopping mecca for everything from groceries and prescription drugs to designer housewares, clothing, toys, and electronics. Target's flagship store is in downtown Minneapolis at 900 Nicollet Mall, 612-338-0085. If you spend a certain amount, they will validate your parking at the nearby LaSalle ramp. And while you're there, sign up to be notified about the Target Direct warehouse sale. This is the e-commerce division of Target, and when it unloads its inventory, it is one of the best sales around.

Other local discount stores include:

- **5-Day Furniture**, 9056 Penn Ave S, Bloomington, 952-884-5555
- **China and Crystal Center**, 256 Water St, Excelsior, 952-474-2144
- **DSW Shoe Warehouse**, www.dswshoe.com: 8236 Hwy 7, St Louis Park, 952-931-9077; Mall of America, 952-876-0991
- **H&M (Hennes & Mauritz)**, Mall of America, sells designer knockoff fashions at bargain basement prices.
- **Nordic Ware Factory Outlet Store**, Hwys 7 and 100, St. Louis Park, 952-924-9672, www.nordicware.com, manufactures bundt pans and other cooking equipment. If you ever find you need a krumkake iron, this is the place to go, but call first for open dates and times.
- **Sportsman's Guide**, 411 Farwell Ave in South St. Paul, 651-552-5248, 888-844-0667, http://shop.sportsmansguide.com, is both a liquidation showroom and mail-order house. It sells name brand shoes, hunting gear, and outdoor apparel.

- **Tuesday Morning**, www.tuesdaymorning.com, is open for a few weeks at a time, several times a year, to sell seasonal merchandise at 50-80% off. It always has good deals on towels and bedding. Check their web site or the White Pages for locations nearest you.

HOUSEHOLD SHOPPING

APPLIANCES, COMPUTERS, AND ELECTRONICS

The Twin Cities are well-supplied with all the larger appliance and electronics vendors, such as **Circuit City** (800-284-4886, www.circuitcity.com), **Sears** (www.sears.com), **Radio Shack** (www.radioshack.com), and homegrown **Best Buy** (www.bestbuy.com). If you can't find the equipment or service you require there, try one of the following vendors:

- **Apple Stores**, www.applestore.com: Mall of America, Bloomington, 952-854-4870; Southdale, 952-920-8260; Ridgedale, 952-486-4861
- **ApplianceSmart,** www.appliancesmart.com, is a factory-authorized liquidation outlet for Whirlpool, Maytag, Jenn-Air, Kitchen Aid, GE, and Frigidaire: Como Ave and Hwy 280, St. Paul, 651-645-3614, and several other locations.
- **Audiophile Hi-Fi Sound Electronics**, 1226 Harmon Pl, Minneapolis, 612-339-6351, www.hifi-sound.com; besides the seriously high-tech new stuff, this store sells refurbished electronics and repairs old equipment as well.
- **CompUSA**, www.CompUSA.com: 2480 Fairview Ave, Roseville, 651-635-0770; 8320 Tamarack Village, Woodbury, 651-578-0078
- **Excelsior Appliance Sales and Service**, 237 Water St, Excelsior, 952-474-7200, is just one example of a locally owned store that will give you good prices and great service.
- **FirstTech**, 2640 Hennepin Ave S, Minneapolis, 612-374-8000 (main), 612-374-8050 (service), www.firsttech.com; sells and services Macintosh Apple computer products.
- **Guyer's**, www.guyers.com, 13405 15th Ave N, Plymouth, 763-553-1445, and other locations; check prices here first for major appliances, cabinets, carpets, and fireplaces.
- **Micro Center**, "The Ultimate Computer Store," 3710 Hwy 100 S, St. Louis Park, 952-285-4040
- **Stereoland**, 2325 Hennepin Ave S, Minneapolis, 612-377-1772, and other locations, www.stereoland.com
- **Warner's Stellian**, www.warnersstellian.com, has been in business for 50 years. The odd name "Stellian" comes from the combination of the founders' names, Steve and Lillian. The stores' kitchen displays feature working appliances that customers are urged to try before they buy: 1711 N Snelling Ave, St. Paul, 651-645-3481, and several other locations.

BEDS, BEDDING & BATH

MATTRESSES

A good selection of mattresses can be found at most major department stores or at specialty retailers such as **Mattress Giant** (www.mattressgiant.com), but for those who'd rather buy from the source, the places listed below are local manufacturers. For consumer bed-buying tips, check out www.consumersearch.com, which rates the big brands by budget and body-type.

- **ComfoRest Adjustable Beds**, 5019 University Ave NE, Columbia Heights, 763-572-8361, www.comforest.com
- **Original Mattress Factory**, www.originalmattress.com: Minnesota Factory and Store, 261 E Hwy 36, Maplewood, 651-482-9338, and several other locations.
- **Restwell Mattress Company**, 8229 Hwy 7, St. Louis Park, 952-908-3348, www.restwellmattress.com
- **Sleep Number Bed by Select Comfort**, 888-637-8167, www.Select Comfort.com: Ridgedale and other major malls.
- **Slumberland Furniture**, www.slumberland.com, 7801 Xerxes Ave S, Bloomington, 952-888-6204, and other locations; clearance stores are located at 1925 Suburban Ave, St. Paul and 4140 Excelsior Blvd, St. Louis Park. Carries major brands plus their own private label mattress, which is made by King Coil.

BEDDING

Department stores, **Linens 'n Things** (www.lnt.com), and **Ikea** (www.ikea.com) can handle all your bedding needs, from the beds themselves to shams and comforters; but if you don't want to spend a bundle, check out **Tuesday Morning** (www.tuesdaymorning.com), which always has some designer linens on sale at closeout prices. Also try **F & B Linen Shoppe**, 1085 Grand Ave, St. Paul, 651-602-0844, 800-268-2993, www.fblinen.com, which specializes in fine linens.

FURNITURE AND HOUSEWARES

Gabbert's Furniture and Design Studio (3501 Galleria, Edina, 952-927-1500, www.gabberts.com) is the Gold Standard here for furniture and decorative accessories. Shop their Odds and Ends room for high-style bargains. **International Market Square** (275 Market St, Minneapolis, 612-339-6003, www.asidmn.org) is the local to-the-trade designers' showroom. Go there with a designer or catch the twice-a-year sample sales in April and September. For everyday housewares, **Target** (www.target.com) is always a good choice, as is **Tuesday Morning** (www.tuesdaymorning.com), which sells everything at 50%–80% off. Other local favorites:

- **Becker Furniture**, 13150 First St, Becker (Hwy 10 at Becker between the Twin Cities and St. Cloud), 800-261-4188, 763-262-9000, www.becker furnitureworld.com, has the largest selection of any furniture showroom in the Twin Cities. Clearance items are sold in both the main store at Becker and in the **Becker Outlet**, 261 W Division St, Waite Park (near St. Cloud), 877-251-4200; Metro, 320-251-4200.

- **Cooks of Crocus Hill**, www.cooksofcrocushill.com; 877 Grand Ave, St. Paul, 651-228-1333; 3925 W 50th St, Edina, 952-285-1903; and in Macy's stores; loved by avid cooks—both for its classes and for its top-of-the-line cooking equipment.
- **Designer Marketplace**, 160 Glenwood Ave N, Minneapolis, 612-381-8508, www.dmpmn.com, is an outlet for the designers at International Market Square. Every item is marked down at least 50% from retail showroom prices.
- **DESQ**, www.desqus.com:Yorktown Mall, Edina, 952-830-1010; Woodbury Village, 651-222-0290; sells modular office and home office furniture including wall beds that make even the most cramped space look roomy.
- **Macy's Interior Design**, 800-480-1623, www.macys.com: 700 On the Mall, Minneapolis, 612-375-2200; Southdale, Edina, 952-896-2160; Rosedale, 651-639-2040; warehouse store (open every day) at 701 Industrial Blvd NE, Minneapolis, 612-623-7111; offers medium to higher quality furniture, accessories, and carpeting of all styles.
- **IKEA**, 8000 Ikea Way (adjacent to the Mall of America), Bloomington, 952-858-8088, www.ikea.com
- **Marketplace Furniture Outlet**, 8001 Bass Lake Rd, New Hope, 763-535-3404, sells closeout new items as well as furniture that has been used in model homes.
- **Room and Board**, www.roomandboard.com; 7010 France Ave S, Edina, 952-927-8835, and other locations; sells contemporary and children's furniture. The outlet store, 4680 Olson Memorial Hwy, Minneapolis, 763-529-6089, is open Saturdays and Sundays only.
- **Rosenthal Furniture**, 22 N 5th St, Minneapolis, 612-332-4363, www.rosenthalfurniture.com, is a warehouse-type showroom which special-orders from hundreds of manufacturers.
- **Scratch N' Dent Furniture Warehouse**, 3900 Louisiana Circle, St. Louis Park, 952-924-1061
- **USA Baby and Childspace Galleries**, 515 W 77th St (northeast corner of 494 and Lyndale), Richfield, 612-798-0055
- **Williams-Sonoma**, www.williams-sonoma.com; Mall of America, Bloomington, 952-854-4553; Galleria, Edina, 952-285-1338; IDS Center, Minneapolis, 612-376-7666

LAMPS AND LIGHTING

- **Citilights**, 1619 Hennepin Ave, Minneapolis, 612-333-3168, www.citilights.com
- **Creative Lighting**, I-94 at Snelling Ave (on the south frontage road just west of Snelling), St. Paul, 651-647-0111, www.creativelights.com, has the Twin Cities' best selection of lighting fixtures, and runs a great Bargain Room sale every fall.

- **Muska Lighting Center**, 700 Grand Ave, St. Paul, 651-227-8881, www.muskalighting.com

CARPETS AND RUGS

- **American Rug Laundry**, 4222 E Lake St, Minneapolis, 612-721-3331, is the local favorite for rug cleaning.
- **Carpet One Hopkins**, 907 Hopkins Center, 952-933-9097 (see the White Pages for other locations), offers nearly next-day installation.
- **Cyrus Carpets**, Galleria, Edina, 952-922-6000, deals in fine Oriental rugs.
- **Gabberts**, 3501 Galleria, Edina, 952-927-0725, www.gabberts.com, carries medium to expensive carpeting and Oriental rugs.
- **Macy's**, 800-480-1623, www.macys.com: 700 On the Mall, Minneapolis, 612-375-2200; Southdale, Edina, 952-896-2160; Rosedale, 651-639-2040; warehouse store (open every day) at 701 Industrial Blvd NE, Minneapolis, 612-623-7111; often offers deep discounts to those opening new accounts.

HARDWARE, PAINT, AND WALLPAPER

Hirshfield's (www.hirshfields.com), with over a dozen stores dispersed throughout the metro, has been the TC's go-to paint and wallpaper store for over a hundred years. Now, of course, even the Big Box retailers such as **Menard's** (www.menards.com) and **Home Depot** (800-425-3376, www.homedepot.com) carry paint and match colors as well, but for best quality, you may still want to try a paint and wallpaper specialty store. The same is true for hardware. In addition to many **Ace Hardware** (www.acehardware.com) and **True Value** (www.truevalue.com) stores, the metro has a number of other neighborhood hardware stores that are staffed with seasoned associates capable of giving you all the help you need:

- **Beisswenger's Do It Best Hardware**, 1360 Old Hwy 8 NW, New Brighton, 651-633-1271, www.beisswengers.com, has a small engine repair shop.
- **Frattalone's**: 650 Grand Ave, Saint Paul, 651-292-9800, and many other locations
- **Guse Hardware**, 4602 Bryant Ave S, Minneapolis, 612-824-7655
- **Mills Fleet Farm**, 8400 Lakeland Ave N, Brooklyn Park, 763-424-9668, www.fleetfarm.com (check the White Pages for other locations), is a locally owned small chain that sells hardware, paint, and building materials in addition to housewares, toys, and auto parts.
- **Rockler Woodworking and Hardware Stores**, www.rockler.com: 2020 W County Rd 42, Burnsville, 952-892-7999; 1935 Beam Ave, Maplewood, 651-773-5285; 12995 Ridgedale Dr, Minnetonka, 952-542-0111; 3025 Lyndale Ave S, Minneapolis, 612-822-3338; the Minneapolis store offers classes, some on a walk-in basis.
- **Seven Corners Ace Hardware**, 216 W 7th St, St. Paul, 651-224-4859, www.7corners.com, also repairs power tools.

These two stores are best known for their decorative hardware:

- **The Brass Handle**, 3605 Galleria Mall, Edina, 952-927-7777, www.brass-handle.com
- **Nob Hill Decorative Hardware**, 3027 Holmes Ave, Minneapolis (Uptown), 612-824-7424, www.nobhillhardware.com, is a showroom that special orders from a number of manufacturers.

GARDEN CENTERS AND NURSERIES

One of the biggest problems for any gardener is choosing the right plants for his/her hardiness zone. The Twin Cities metro is in hardiness zone 4a, which means that our average minimum temperature is in the minus 25–30 degrees Fahrenheit range. Unfortunately, summer temps often climb into the 90s (and occasionally over 100), creating a climate that is inhospitable to many popular garden plants. Good advice: start cultivating a fondness for hostas, peonies, shrub roses, and daylilies—four plants that actually thrive here. Get your questions answered online by a U of M Master Gardener at www.extension.umn.edu/projects/yardandgarden/askmgintro.html. (For more gardening information, see the **Sports and Recreation** chapter.)

- **Ambergate Gardens**, 8730 County Rd 43, Chaska, 952-443-2248, www.ambergategardens.com, specializes in vigorous, cold-hardy perennials. Call for directions or a catalogue.
- **Bachman's**, 612-861-7311 (phone orders), www.bachmans.com, with locations throughout the Twin Cities, is the longtime go-to garden center for the entire area.
- **Holasek's Nursery**, 8610 Galpin Blvd, Chanhassen, 952-474-6669, grows the plants that are sold by many local retail garden stores, but home gardeners can shop their greenhouses, too.
- **Minnesota Nursery Landscape Association**, www.GardenMinnesota.com
- **Plants and Things USA**, US Hwy 10 & Sunfish Lake Blvd, Anoka, 763-427-4103, www.plantsandthingsusa.com, specializes in lightweight boulders, waterfalls, lawn furniture, etc. . . . and they deliver! Their clearance center at 15660 Cleveland Ave, Elk River, 763-323-9056, is worth the trip.
- **Prairie Restorations**, Princeton, Minnesota, 800-837-5986, www.prairieresto.com
- **Linder's Greenhouse & Garden**, 270 W Larpenteur, St. Paul, www.linders.com, is another all-inclusive garden center.
- **Otten Bros. Nursery and Landscaping**, 2350 W Wayzata Blvd, Long Lake, 952-473-5425, www.ottenbros.com
- **Sam Kedem Nursery/Town & Country Roses**, 12414—191st St E, Hastings, 651-437-7516, toll free 877-340-2304, www.kedemroses.com, specializes in roses, vines, and shrubs suitable for our climate.
- **Savory's Gardens**, 5300 Whiting Ave, Edina, 952-941-8755, www.savorysgardens.com; founded by a former president of the Hosta Society, this nursery offers its own hosta introductions in addition to other shade-tolerant plants.

- **University of Minnesota Landscape Arboretum**, 3675 Arboretum Dr, Chanhassen, 952-443-1400, www.arboretum.umn.edu, is the local expert on winter-hardy plants. Become a member and enjoy unlimited access to "The Arb's" 1000 acres of public gardens and classes that will teach you everything you need to know to be a successful gardener here.

SECOND-HAND SHOPPING

For those of you whose idea of a good deal is something free, check out the **Twin Cities Free Market** (www.twincitiesfreemarket.org), a listing service that allows local residents to get or give away still-useable goods. You'll find appliances, sports equipment, computers, and furniture among the many offerings here, but no live animals, firearms, or cars. Created by St. Paul–based Eureka Recycling, which keeps track of all exchanges, Twin Cities Free Market has kept over 4 million pounds of still-useful items out of the landfills to date—and that's none too trashy!

ARCHITECTURAL SALVAGE AND RESTORATION

- **Art and Architecture**, 3338 University Ave SE, Minneapolis, 612-904-1776
- **Bath Fitter—one-day bathroom resurfacing**, 651-645-1100, www.bathfitter.com
- **Bath Wizards—tub, shower, and sink refinishing**, 763-571-5667, www.bathwizards.com
- **Building Materials Outlet, Midwest, Inc.**, 2795 Hwy 55 E, Eagan, 651-454-8840, www.cannonrecovery.com, sells liquidation merchandise, overruns, and extra inventory; most items are at least half off retail.
- **John's Antiques**, 261 7th St W, St. Paul, 651-222-6131, is a good place to look for vintage lights.
- **Lumber Liquidators**, 8899 Hastings St NE, Blaine, 763-784-3440, www.lumberliquidators.com, advertises that it has the lowest prices on hardwood flooring and will meet competitors' prices.
- **Luxury Bath Systems**, 8555 Lyndale Ave S, Bloomington, 952-885-0042, 800-A-NEW-TUB, www.luxurybath.com, creates custom tub liners and wall systems designed to fit over existing tubs and wall surfaces.
- **The Reuse Center**, 2801 21st Ave S (enter and park on 29th St), Minneapolis, 612-724-2608, www.greeninstitute.org, or www.thereuse center.com, markets high-quality salvaged and green building products and provides living wage jobs for residents of Phillips and surrounding neighborhoods. Because they are called in to dismantle and salvage reusable building materials from many older homes in the area, your chances are good for finding a match for your own old doors here—plus they'll even show you how to hang them in one of their many do-it-yourself classes.
- **Surface Renew**, www.surfacerenew.net, resurfaces bathtubs, wall tile, and kitchen counters; Southwest suburbs, 952-946-1460; North suburbs, 763-253-2300; Minneapolis, 612-869-7242; St. Paul, 651-251-2100.

ANTIQUE SHOPS AND FLEA MARKETS

The Twin Cities' multitude of antique and junk shops tend to be clustered together in places such as West 7th Street in St. Paul, or the cities of Excelsior, Hopkins, Wayzata, Stillwater, and Buffalo. In Minneapolis, venerable dealers are found in the warehouse district along 1st and 3rd Avenues North. The **Decorative Arts Council of the Minneapolis Institute of Arts** also brings in some of the nation's premier dealers for their **Antiques Show and Sale** every October (612-870-3039, www.artsmia.org/antiques-show). The weekend includes a preview party and lectures and is used as a fundraiser for the Institute. There are also many interesting shops and flea markets to be found off the beaten path. So hitch up the U-haul, and happy hunting!

- **Antiques Riverwalk**, 210 3rd Ave N, Minneapolis, 612-339-9352, antiquesriverwalk.com, is home to nearly thirty dealers.
- **Elko Traders Market Antique Show and Flea Market**, www.traders-market.us, off I-35 at Elko/New Market exit: Memorial Day, 4th of July, Labor Day weekends.
- **JunkMarket**, 2345 Daniels St, Long Lake, 952-249-9151, www.junkmarket.com, sells junk transformed—or suitable to be transformed—at three sales each year. They also offer do-it-yourself seminars.
- **Medina Flea Market**, in the Medina Ballroom parking lot on Hwy 55 west of Minneapolis, Sunday mornings from 6 a.m. to noon.
- **Osowski's Flea Market**, Orchard Rd, Monticello, claims to be the state's biggest flea market. It's open Saturdays and Sundays year-round.
- **Rose Galleries**, 3180 Country Dr, Little Canada, 651-484-1415 or 888-484-1415, www.rosegalleries.com, is an auction house where you can sometimes find very fine pieces.
- **Sister Fun**, www.sisterfun.net (formerly in Uptown); sells new stock that pertains to things from your long-lost youth—Scooby Doo lunch boxes, etc.
- **US Postal Service auctions of unclaimed and undeliverable goods,** www.usps.com/auctions, are held every eight weeks in St. Paul at the Mail Recovery Center, 443 Fillmore Ave E. Auction information and directions are posted in the post offices and on their web site.

GARAGE SALES, THRIFTS, AND VINTAGE SHOPS

If your idea of the perfect Saturday afternoon is spending a few hours poking through tempting tubs of other people's flotsam, then rejoice—you have moved to the right place. The Twin Cities are garage sale heaven, with a season that runs every weekend from April to September. Some swank sales draw thousands of customers year after year, especially the **Benilde–St. Margaret School Sale** in the Spring (www.bsm-online.org); the **Wayzata Community Church Sale** in August (www.wayzatacommunitychurch.org); and the **American Cancer Society World's Largest Garage Sale** in the fall (800-227-2345, www.cancer.org). To find out about these and all the other garage sales in between, look in the papers on Wednesdays and use the ads as a guide to map out your route. Estate sales are also held on weekends, and are often the better place to look for nice furnishings; Edina and Minnetonka are considered the ultimate hunting grounds. Also posh: the **Goodwill** boutique where they stockpile all the good stuff. Called **Second Debut** (www.goodwilleaster seals.org), it's at 4300 West 36½ Street in St. Louis Park, next door to the Opitz Outlet, so you can easily make a day of it, bargain shopping in St. Louis Park.

Finally, for those who are looking for a funky outfit, or gently used designer clothing, the vintage and consignment stores included in this list have been vetted by some serious local shoppers, and while it is in no way comprehensive, they say it should get you off to a good start:

- **ARC Value Village Thrift Stores**: 6330 Brooklyn Blvd, Brooklyn Center, 763-503-3534; 6528 Penn Ave S, Richfield, 512-861-9550; 2751 Winnetka Ave N, New Hope, 763-544-0006
- **Bears Repeating**, 85th and Zane Ave N, Brooklyn Park, 763-493-4002, stocks gently used children's items.
- **Big Lots**, 763-503-9833, www.biglots.com, sells name brand closeouts (including frozen food, wine and beer, and furniture) for up to 70% off retail; several locations.
- **Hope Chest for Breast Cancer Retail Store**, 3850 Shoreline Dr, Navarre/Orono, 952-471-8700, www.hopechest.us, is rich with ritzy items.
- **Lula's**, www.lulasvintagewear.com; 1587 Selby Ave, St. Paul, 651-644-4110; 710 W 22nd St, Minneapolis, 612-872-7090
- **Nu Look Consignment**, 4956 Penn Ave S, Minneapolis, 612-925-0806, www.nulookconsignment.com, stocks women's, men's, and children's clothing, including designer maternity fashions.
- **Plato's Closet**, www.platoscloset.com; is strictly for teens; several locations throughout the Twin Cities.
- **Plums Plus Size**, 1213 Randolph Ave, St. Paul, 651-698-PLUS, www.plumsplussize.com
- **PPL Shop**, 850 15th Ave NE (in the historic Northrup King Bldg), Minneapolis, 612-789-3322, www.ppl-inc.org; Project for Pride in Living is a nonprofit whose mission is to help low- and moderate-income people become self-sufficient. They accept donations of good used household and office equipment from local companies and homeowners, and sell them together with new imported home décor, clothing, jewelry, and gift items; most items are priced 50%–70% off retail.
- **Ragstock Clothing**, www.ragstock.com: many locations; is tops with teens and college kids.
- **Salvation Army**, www.thesalarmy.com: 900 4th St N, Minneapolis, 612-332-5855, and other locations
- **Tatters Clothing**, 2928 Lyndale Ave S, Minneapolis, 612-823-5285, has men's and women's vintage clothing, as well as new versions of vintage stuff.
- **Turn Style consignment shops**, 651-690-3438, www.turnstyle consign.com, sell clothing for the whole family, and some home furnishings; several locations in the Twin Cities including Highland Park at Cleveland, and Ford Pkwy, St. Paul.

- **Unique Thrift Stores**, 2201 37th Ave NE, Columbia Heights, 763-788-5250; 1657 Rice St, St. Paul, 651-489-5083; 4471 Winnetka Ave N, New Hope, 763-535-0200

FOOD

GROCERIES

Locally based **Cub Foods** (www.cub.com) and **Rainbow** (www.roundy's.com) are warehouse food stores. Their aisles are lined with formidable towers of boxes, cans, and produce, but they also include some ethnic foods and feature highly regarded bakeries and delis. Both are 24-hour enterprises, enabling you to go on late-night shopping sprees. Some Cub stores have begun using fingerprint technology, so once you've set up your account, you'll be able to run in and shop even if you're not carrying your checkbook or credit card. Many of the stores in these chains also offer in-store banking, full-service pharmacies, and MinuteClinics (see **Health Care** chapter for pharmacies and MinuteClinics). With over 60 Cubs and 30 Rainbows spread throughout the metro, there is bound to be at least one near you, no matter where you choose to live.

National warehouse stores **Costco** (www.Costco.com) and **Sam's Club** (www.samsclub.com) also have a presence in this market, though you will need to become a member if you want to shop there for anything other than liquor (see **Discount Stores** above).

Just getting started in the Twin Cities is another low-cost chain, **Aldi** (1311 E Franklin Avenue, Minneapolis, and other locations, www.aldifoods.com). This group of smaller grocery stores carries a limited assortment of private label products and holds down overhead by charging for shopping bags, requiring a deposit for carts, and not accepting credit cards. Aldi does not publish its phone numbers, so to find an Aldi store near you, check the store locator on their web page. Also new to the Twin Cities is **Trader Joe's**, which offers an array of high-quality foods, plus beer and wine, at reasonable prices (4500 Excelsior Boulevard, St. Louis Park, 952-285-1053, www.traderjoes.com).

And don't forget **Target**, Minnesota's homegrown retail chain, which has numerous stores throughout the metropolitan area. (See **Discount Stores** above.) Though they have relatively small grocery departments, they, too, boast highly regarded bakeries and delis, and many who shop there praise them for the quality of their produce. The downtown Target is located at 900 Nicollet Mall, and if you spend a certain amount, they will validate parking for you at a nearby ramp. (Check the White Pages or online at www.target.com for other locations.)

For fancier shopping, **Lund's** (www.lundsmarket.com), **Byerly's** (www.byerlys.com), and **Kowalski's** (www.kowalskis.com) are all gourmet supermarket chains that charge premium prices but offer first-rate service, specialty products, restaurants, catering, cooking schools, pharmacies, and wine shops. There isn't much difference between them, though Kowalski's tends to be preferred for some of the local products they carry. Each of these enterprises has stores throughout the metro area. **Jerry's Foods** is also in this category but limits its stores to Edina and Eden Prairie (9625 Anderson Lakes Parkway, Eden Prairie, 952-941-9680; 5101 Vernon Avenue S, Edina, 952-929-2685).

Somewhere in the middle, between the cut-rate and gourmet chains are the last few remaining neighborhood supermarkets: **Knowlan's/Festival Foods** (www.festy.com/), **Rick's Markets**, **Coburn's**, and **SuperValu**. SuperValu is actually the major food distributor in this area, so no matter where you shop, you're likely to be buying Super Valu's food.

FOOD CO-OPS AND NATURAL FOODS

Besides offering unsprayed produce and the gamut of "free" foods (wheat-free, free-range, etc.), co-ops sell many foods in bulk, allowing you to buy the exact one tablespoon of celery seed that you need to make your favorite rib rub. Most stores also feature take-out delis offering good-for-you gourmet fare. Co-ops sell shares and distribute dividends to members, and some allow you to volunteer at the store for a discount on groceries. Following are well-known grocery co-ops in the metro area:

- **Eastside Food Co-op**, 2551 Central Ave NE, 612-788-0950
- **Hampden Park Co-op**, 928 Raymond Ave, St. Paul, 651-646-6686, www.hampdenparkcoop.com
- **Lakewinds Natural Foods**, www.lakewinds.com: Hwy 101 and Minnetonka Blvd, Minnetonka, 952-473-0292; 1917 2nd Ave S, Anoka, 763-427-4340; Chanhassen, 435 Pond Promenade, off Great Plains Blvd
- **Linden Hills Co-op**, 2813 W 43rd St, Minneapolis, 612-922-1159, www.lindenhills.coop
- **Mississippi Market**, www.msmarket.coop; 1810 Randolph St, St. Paul, 651-690-0507; 622 Selby Ave, St. Paul, 651-310-9499
- **North Country Co-op**, 1929 S 5th St, Minneapolis, 612-338-3110, www.northcountrycoop.com
- **River Market**, 221 N Main St, Stillwater, 651-439-0366, www.rivermarket.coop
- **Seward Co-op Grocery and Deli**, 2111 E Franklin Ave, Minneapolis, 612-338-2465, www.seward.coop
- **Valley Natural Foods**, 13750 County Rd 11, Burnsville, 952-892-1212, www.valleynaturalfoods.com
- **Wedge Community Co-op**, 2105 Lyndale Ave S, Minneapolis, 612-871-3993, www.wedge.coop

In a class of their own are Tao Natural Food and Books, Whole Foods, and the new make-and-take meal assembly stores. **Tao Foods** (2200 Hennepin Avenue in Minneapolis, 612-377-4630) is a small shop that combines food and medicine, offering homeopathic remedies, herbal tonics, and a juice bar. **Whole Foods** (3060 Excelsior Boulevard, Minneapolis, 612-927-8141, and 30 Fairview Avenue South, St. Paul, 651-690-0197, www.wholefoods.com) is a national chain offering organic and health foods as well as gourmet treats and a bakery. This is not a place to shop for bargains.

MAKE-AND-TAKE MEAL ASSEMBLY

An option that might be more of a bargain than you'd expect is **Make-and-Take meal assembly**, where the store does the prep and all you do is the assembly. Some offer ready-made meals to pick up. Meals generally cost less than $3 a serving.

- **Let's Dish**, www.letsdish.net; several locations
- **Mix It Up**, www.mixitupmeals.com; several locations
- **Sociale**, 651-994-9000, www.socialegourmet.com, offers meal pick-up in the Minneapolis Skyway system and will deliver to Edina and southwest Minneapolis for a small fee.

FARMERS' MARKETS AND HOME GROWN PRODUCTS

Corn, raspberries, apples, Christmas trees . . . nothing beats buying them directly from the growers, and it's easy to do. Seasonal garden produce, flowers, and farm-raised meat are sold at scores of farmers' markets, vegetable stands, orchards, and farms throughout the metro area. You can get a free copy of the full directory from **Minnesota Grown** (Minnesota Department of Agriculture, 651-296-4939, www.minnesotagrown.com).

- **Minneapolis Farmers' Market**, www.mplsfarmersmarket.com: one block south of Hwy 55 on Lyndale Ave N, open daily, 6 a.m.–2 p.m., April 24 to December 24; Nicollet Mall, Thursdays, 6 a.m.–6 p.m., May to November; Midtown Public Market, E Lake St at 22nd Ave S
- **St. Paul's Farmers' Market** has locations in St. Paul and its suburbs. Call the hotline at 651-227-6856 or visit www.stpaulfarmersmarket.com for locations and hours. The largest market is at Fifth and Wall St, St. Paul: Saturday and Sunday mornings, and Wednesday afternoons, April to November.

COMMUNITY GARDENS

Many neighborhoods have community gardens, particularly in Minneapolis. These are available for free or for a nominal rental fee to people who want to grow vegetables and flowers. Check with your own neighborhood organization for possibilities for you (311), or contact the **Sustainable Resources Center** (www.src-mn.org) or the **Minnesota State Horticultural Society** (Minnesota Green: 651-643-3601, 800-676-6747, www.norrtherngardener.org).

HOME DELIVERY

- **Meyer Brothers Dairy**, 105 E Lake St, Wayzata, is the last of the original home delivery dairies in the Twin Cities. Started in 1936 by the Meyer Brothers (Bob milked the cows, Cliff bottled, Herb drove the Lake Minnetonka route, and Ted took the Minneapolis route), the company is still going strong—but now offers eggs, juice, meat and deli meats, bakery products, and fruits and vegetables, too. Order online at www.meyerbros

dairy.com, or call customer service at 952-473-7343.
- **Milkman Delivers**, www.milkmandelivers.com, is a network of independently owned delivery routes that serves most of the metro area. They offer dairy products, meat, bread, desserts, juice, and even household cleaning products.
- **Schwan's** has been delivering ice cream and other frozen products to Minnesota homes for over 50 years, Call 888-SCHWANS or order online, www.theschwanfoodcompany.com.
- **Simon Delivers**, 763-656-5600, www.simondelivers.com, delivers food and wine throughout the Twin Cities—and to your cabin Up North, as well!

ETHNIC MARKETS

The foods available in the Twin Cities' ethnic markets and restaurants reflect the growing diversity of our state. In Minneapolis, take a walk down "Eat Street," the 17-block stretch of restaurants along Nicollet Avenue north of Lake Street, and you will smell and hear the world. In the same spirit, the Mercado (1515 East Lake Street) and Cesar Chavez Street in West St. Paul, are centers for the Hispanic community. University Avenue east of Lexington and Rice Street in St. Paul serve that purpose for members of several Asian communities. Other ethnic markets are scattered throughout the Twin Cities. Even though many of the local supermarkets and co-ops offer a selection of foods for ethnic cooking, try some of these below for a more authentic experience—and, remember, in no way is this a complete list:

AFRICAN
- **Afrik Grocery and Halal Meat**, 410 Cedar Ave, Minneapolis
- **Makola African Market**, 1218 Thomas Ave, St. Paul, 651-644-5344

GREEK, MIDDLE EASTERN
- **Abu Nader**, 2095 Como Ave, St. Paul, 651-647-5391
- **Bill's Imported Foods**, 721 W Lake St, Minneapolis, 612-827-2891
- **Holy Land Bakery & Deli**, 2513 Central Ave NE, Minneapolis, 612-781-2627
- **Sinbad Mideastern Grocery, Bakery and Deli**, 2528 Nicollet Ave, Minneapolis, 612-871-6505

INDIAN
- **Patel Grocery and Video**, 1835 Central Ave NE, Minneapolis, 612-789-8800

ITALIAN
- **Broder's Cucina Italiana**, 2308 W 50th St (50th and Penn), Minneapolis, 612-925-3113; delivers.
- **Buon Giorno Italia**, 981 Sibley Memorial Hwy, Lilydale, 651-905-1080; **Buon Giorno Express**, 335 University Ave E, St. Paul, www.buongiorno italia.biz; considered by most to be the best Italian shops in the Twin Cities.
- **Cossetta's**, 211 W 7th St, St. Paul, 651-222-3476, www.cossettaventi. com; catering.

- **Delmonico's Italian Foods**, 1112 NE Summer St, Minneapolis, 612-331-5466, has been operating in "Nordeast" since most of the people who lived here were Italian immigrants.

LATINO/MEXICAN
- **El Burrito Mercado and Cafeteria**, 175 Cesar Chavez St, St. Paul, 651-227-2192; www.elburritomercado.com
- **Joseph's Mexican & Lebanese Market**, 736 Oakdale Ave, St. Paul, 651-228-9022
- **La Cosecha Market**, 1515 E Lake St (at the corner of Lake and Bloomington), Minneapolis, 612-728-5457
- **Marissa's Bakeries**, 2750 Nicollet Ave S, 612-871-4519, Minneapolis; and 3733 Nicollet Ave S, Minneapolis, 612-822-0448
- **Morgan's Mexican and Lebanese Foods**, 736 S Robert St, St. Paul, 651-291-2955

ASIAN
- **Phil Oriental Foods**, 789 University Ave W, St. Paul, 651-292-1325
- **United Noodles**, 2015 E 24th St, Minneapolis, 612-721-6677, www.united noodles.com, is the largest oriental grocery in the Midwest.

SCANDINAVIAN/RUSSIAN/EASTERN EUROPEAN
- **Ingebretsen's**, 1601 E Lake St, Minneapolis, 612-729-9331 (food), 612-729-9333 (gifts), 800-279-9333 (to order a catalogue), www.ingebretsens.com
- **Kramarczuk Sausage Co.**, 215 Hennepin Ave E, Minneapolis, 612-379-3018
- **Olsen Fish**, 2115 N 2nd St, Minneapolis, 612-287-0838, www.olsen fish.com, has been processing lutefisk and pickled herring on the north side of Minneapolis since 1910. For those who've never heard of this delicacy, lutefisk is gelatinous lye-soaked cod which Scandinavians eat with copious amounts of melted butter, especially at Christmas. To order, call their Lutefisk Hotline, 800-882-0212.
- **Taste of Scandinavia**, www.tasteofscandinavia.com, 845 Village Center Dr, North Oaks, 651-482-8285; 2900 Rice St, Little Canada, 651-482-8876; both a traditional bakery and a café that serves breakfast, lunch, and dinner.

DRINKING WATER

Minneapolis and St. Paul supply municipal water to their residents and some suburbs from surface sources, principally the Mississippi River. Others drink groundwater from municipal or private wells. Increasingly, people here have become concerned about the quality and taste of their water. As a result, sales of bottled drinking water (which may or may not, depending on the supplier, be any better than your own water) have soared. Grocery stores sell bottled water, and there are a number of drinking water delivery services that rent coolers as well. Those who wish to collect their own spring water can do so from a natural spring located at the Richard T. Anderson Conservation Area in the

southwest corner of Eden Prairie (18700 Flying Cloud Drive). The following companies provide home delivery:
- **Premium Waters**, 2125 Broadway NE, Minneapolis, 612-379-4141 www.premiumwaters.com
- **Culligan**, 7165 Boone Ave N, Brooklyn Park, 763-535-4545, or 1001 Marie Ave S, St. Paul, 651-451-2241, www.culliganbottledwater.com
- **Glenwood Inglewood Co.**, 225 Thomas Ave N, Minneapolis, www.glenwoodinglewoodwater.com
- **Great Glacier, Inc.**, Princeton, 763-389-9555, www.greatglacier.com; covers the entire metro area.

EATING OUT

The Twin Cities has restaurants for every taste, many clustered in the Minneapolis warehouse district and around Uptown. Nicollet from Lake Street North is even called "Eat Street" because of its blocks of ethnic eateries. More rainbows of restaurants line Selby, University, Como, W 7th, and Grand Avenues in St. Paul. Look for restaurant listings, plus reviews, online at **www.sourceguides.com** and **www.twincities.citysearch.com**. One quick tip: If you're looking for a place to celebrate a special occasion, **La Belle Vie** (510 Groveland, Minneapolis, 612-874-6440, www.labellevie.us) is generally regarded as the best restaurant in the state.

OTHER SHOPPING

AUTOMOBILES

A list of metro area new car and truck franchise dealerships (with clickable links) can be found on the **Greater Metropolitan Automobile Dealers Association of Minnesota, Inc.** web site (www.gmada.com/). But don't limit your choices to dealerships that are close to home—you may well get a better deal and enhanced customer service from a dealer located on the metro fringe. For more information about shopping for a car, Minnesota laws, and consumer protection, see the **Getting Settled** chapter of this book.
- **AAA**, www.a.a.a.com; besides offering emergency road service and license tab renewal, AAA can help you find a car, negotiate the deal, arrange the financing, and perform the diagnostics and service for the vehicle during the time you own it. AAA can also help you sell your car or find a car for you online!
- **Andrews Saab and Subaru,** www.andrewsofprinceton.com; in Princeton, about an hour northwest of Minneapolis, 763-631-Saab, 800-882-7220; Minneapolis/St. Paul Metro Line: 763-633-Saab (763-633-7222); sends trucks to the Cities on a regular schedule to pick up vehicles that need repair or maintenance—and leaves you with a loaner to drive for the day.
- **Hourcar** car-sharing, www.hourcar.org, is managed by the nonprofit **Neighborhood Energy Consortium (NEC)**, 651-221-4462, and has car hubs in Uptown, the Wedge, the Minneapolis Riverfront district,

Loring/Stephens Square, Minneapolis Depot, University of Minnesota, and Lowertown, St. Paul. Members include individuals, families, and businesses. They offer pay-as-you-go and flat rate plans.

- **U-Pull R Parts Salvage Yard**, www.upullrparts.com: 2875 160th St W, Rosemount, 651-322-1800; 20418 Hwy 65 NE, E Bethel, 763-434-5229. Special events include the Spring Stockup (where they're buying) and the July Courage Center Pullathon, when you can buy all the parts you can lift and carry 20 feet for $29.05.
- **Victoria AutoHaus**, 1900 W 80th St (Hwy 5), Victoria, 952-443-3000, handles new, used, imported, and domestic cars, vans, and trucks. They will find the car you're looking for and deliver it.

ART

Artists who live and work in Northeast Minneapolis and Lowertown in St. Paul periodically open their studios for public sales. Keep an eye on the paper for time and details, or check out the **Art-A-Whirl** web site (www.art-a-whirl.org). The spring **St. Croix Valley Pottery Tour and Sale** is a similar event, except that it's spread out over a 75-mile route northeast of the Twin Cities, along Highway 95, from Stillwater to Cambridge. Check their web site for a map and details (www.minnesotapotters.com). There are also numerous galleries, especially in Uptown and the Minneapolis warehouse district. And don't forget the art schools. **The Minneapolis College of Art and Design** (612-874-3654, www.mcad.edu) holds a students' art sale early every December, and the **Minnetonka Center for the Arts** (2240 North Shore Drive, Orono, 952-473-7361, www.minnetonkaarts.org) has frequent shows and sales.

ART SUPPLIES AND COSTUMES

- **Art Cellar and Bookstore at the Minneapolis College of Art and Design**, 2501 Stevens Ave S, Minneapolis, 612-874-3775, www.mcad.edu, is a nonprofit shop whose proceeds go to cash-strapped students.
- **Artstarts' Art Scraps**, 1459 St. Clair Ave, St. Paul, 651-698-2787, www.artscraps.org, stocks surplus goods and manufacturing scraps, and sells them at starving artist prices.
- **Dick Blick Art Materials,** 2501 26th Ave S, Minneapolis, 612-721-6421, www.dickblick.com
- **Mosaic on a Stick**, 595 N Snelling, St. Paul, 651-645-6600, www.mosaiconastick.com, is where the serious crafters shop and take classes.
- **Teener's Theatrical Department Store**, 1517 Central Ave NE, 612-339-2793, www.teenerstheatricals.com, carries thousands of theatrical, costume, and party items.
- **Wet Paint**, 1684 Grand Ave, St. Paul, 651-698-6431, www.wetpaintart.com, has been selected City Pages' "Best Art Supply" store several years running.

FOR CHILDREN

Superstore children's retailers such as **Toys "R" Us, Kids "R" Us**, and **Babies "R" Us** can be found in the major mall shopping areas throughout the Twin Cities. You won't have trouble seeing them from the freeways, but you can always use the web page store locator to find them (www.toysrus.com). **Gymboree** (www.gymboree.com), a local favorite in new moms' gift registries, also has a number of stores throughout the metro. Finally, **Target**, of course, carries toys and children's clothing and equipment, along with everything else. We are also well-outfitted with many independent children's specialty retailers:

- **Baby Grand**, 1137 Grand Ave, St. Paul, 651-224-4414, www.babyon grand.com
- **Cribz**, 3545 Galleria, Edina, 952-922-0109
- **Creative Kidstuff**, 651-222-3255, 800-353-0710, www.CreativeKid stuff.com
- **The Glasses Menagerie**, 3142 Hennepin Ave (Uptown), Minneapolis, 612-822-7021, www.Kidseyes.com
- **Peapods Natural Toys & Baby Care**, 251 Snelling Ave S, St. Paul, 651-695-5559, www.peapods.com
- **www.MySchoolSupplyStore.com**, is an online store where you can buy your child's school supplies and have them delivered to your door. School districts' supplies lists are posted on their web site.

MUSIC, CDS, AND RECORDS

Local independent record stores sell a variety of music—including local artists'—that you can't find at the chain stores. Here are just a few:

- **Cheapo**, www.cheapodiscs.com, 1300 W Lake St, Minneapolis, 612-827-0646 (records), 612-827-8238 (CDs); several other locations.
- **Electric Fetus**, 2000 4th Ave S, Minneapolis, 612-870-9300, www.electricfetus.com; this is *the* place to go for music by local bands.
- **Urban Lights Music**, 449 University Ave W, St. Paul, 651-647-9650, is another good place to go if you're looking for local artists.

WINTERWEAR

In the introduction, we warned you about the winter months and the need for warm clothes. No kidding, even with global warming, winters here are no joke. If you arrived without the right winter gear, the following are a few places where you can get the coats and boots you'll need to stay warm and happy from Thanksgiving to Easter. Don't forget the department stores.

- **Burlington Coat Factory**, www.burlingtoncoatfactory.com; several locations including 3700 S Hwy 100, St. Louis Park, 952-929-6850
- **Hoigaard's**, 3550 S Hwy 100, St. Louis Park, 952-929-1351, www.hoigaards.com

- **L.L. Bean Catalogue**, 800-341-4341, www.llbean.com; L.L. Bean not only guarantees its merchandise, it also rates it. Buy a 50-below coat and you'll be dancing comfortably on the ice in February.

HARD-TO-FIND GOODS AND SERVICES

Angie's List (612-339-6600, www.angieslist.com) advertises itself as a list of plumbers, auto mechanics, painters, etc., recommended by "neighbors," but you still need to check references. There is a fee to join.

FURNITURE RESTORATION AND CONSERVATION

- **American Society of Appraisers**, www.appraisers.org
- **Anthony's Furniture Restoration**, 4553 Bryant Ave S, Minneapolis, 612-824-1717; 3406 Lyndale Ave S, Minneapolis, 612-822-9057; offers French polishing and cleaning for your fine antiques, as well as refinishing and repair.
- **Randy Bohn and Associates**, 651-437-1785, specializes in European and early American antique finishes and repair.
- **Upper Midwest Conservation Association**, Minneapolis Institute of Arts, 2400 Third Ave S, Minneapolis, 612-870-3120, www.preserveart.org/
- **Minnesota Historical Society**, 651-297-3896, www.mnhs.org, offers workshops on "Preserving Your Treasures."

SHOE REPAIR

- **Bob's Shoe Repair**, Wayzata Bay Center, Wayzata, 952-473-8248, stays open until 9 p.m.
- **George's Shoe & Leather Repair**, 672-1/2 Grand Ave, St. Paul, 651-227-8258

SHOES FOR HARD-TO-FIT FEET

- **Schuler Shoes**, www.schulershoes.com, Har Mar Mall, Roseville, 651-631-8344, and other locations.

DAYCARE

PROBABLY THE BEST WAY TO FIND A GOOD DAYCARE PROVIDER IS BY referral from someone you know and trust. You'll want to look for daycare centers that are accredited by the **National Academy of Early Childhood Programs** (www.naeyc.org) or the **Minnesota Association for the Education of Young Children** (651-646-8689, www.mnaeyc.org). In addition, various agencies and centers may be helpful:

- **Minnesota Child Care Resource and Referral Network**, 651-665-0150, www.mnchildcare.org, is a statewide information service, 866-807-6021 or 888-291-9811. Call with your zip code and they will transfer you to the agency that provides childcare referrals in your area. Their listings include nanny services.
- For University of Minnesota–affiliated families, the **University of Minnesota Child Care Center** operates year-round in a state-of-the-art facility on the East Bank, 612-627-4014, http://education.umn.edu/ChildCareCenter/.
- In St. Paul, the **University of St. Thomas Child Development Center** at Grand and Finn (651-962-5040, www.stthomas.edu/childdevelopment) accepts infants as young as six weeks. The waiting time is long—one to two years—but you can put your child on the waiting list before he or she is born.
- Another option: **YWCA** (www.ywcampls.org) and **YMCA** (www.ymca twincities.org) childcare centers. The Y is the largest nonprofit provider of childcare in the United States. They offer before and after school care, school release care, half-day programs for preschoolers, and full-day care for age 6 weeks to kindergarten. A full-time kindergarten program is offered at their Downtown location, 1130 Nicollet Mall, Minneapolis, 612-332-0501. Check out other locations (which are spread throughout the Twin Cities and even include Hudson, Wisconsin). **YMCA of Greater St. Paul**, 612-465-0450; **YMCA of Minneapolis**, 612-371-8700.

When searching for the best place for your child, be sure to visit prospective providers—and make an appointment. Security-conscious providers should not allow you on their premises unless you have an appointment and can be accompanied by a staff member at all times. In general, look for safety, cleanliness and caring attitudes on the part of the providers. Check that the kitchen, toys, and furniture are clean and safe. Ask for the telephone numbers of other parents who use the service and talk to them. It's a good idea to request a daily schedule—look for both active and quiet time, and age-appropriate activities. In this part of the country, four to five months of the year are spent indoors, so you should ask about active time in the winter.

Keep in mind that being licensed does not necessarily guarantee quality. If you think a licensed provider might be acceptable, be sure to call your county's childcare licensing bureau. They will be glad to tell you if there are any complaints against the provider in their files. The numbers to call are **Hennepin County** (Minneapolis), 612-348-3883; **Ramsey County** (St. Paul), 651-266-3779; **Washington County**, 651-430-6488. For further information, contact the **Minnesota Department of Human Services**, 651-296-2588, www.dhs.state.mn.us.

For drop-in childcare while you go shopping or to a movie, **Clubkid** is a popular choice. It accepts children age 16 months to 10 years at two locations: Edina, 952-831-1055; and Minnetonka, 952-545-1979. In 2005–06, rates were $7.50 per hour for a toddler, 16–30 months; and $6.50 for a child age 30 months to 10 years.

ONLINE RESOURCES

The **Minnesota Child Care Resource and Referral Network**, 1-888-291-9811, www.mnchildcare.org, maintains a free online database of over 10,000 local providers. This database is updated monthly. Parents can search for childcare by vacancy, location, hours, type of care, children's ages, or languages. The web site also lists possible resources for financial aid and tax credits. Other tax information is available from the **Internal Revenue Service (IRS)**, www.irs.gov/taxtopics/tc600.html. Articles posted here include information about how to apply for federal tax credits such as the Child and Dependent Care Tax Credit, Child Tax Credits, and Earned Income Credit (EIC).

NANNIES AND AU PAIRS

In the Twin Cities you can expect to pay at least $500–$600 per week for a live-in nanny, more for a nanny with more experience, and more if housekeeping is expected. The **Greater Minneapolis Day Care Association** (612-341-1177, www.gmdca.org) and **Ramsey County Resources for Childcaring** (651-641-6601, www.resourcesforchildcare.org) provide referrals to nanny agencies. You can look in the Yellow Pages under "Nanny Services" for a complete list of area businesses or look online at **www.nannylocators.com/minnesota.htm**. Local nanny referral services include the following:

- **HomeBuddies**, 4205 Brunswick Ave S, St. Louis Park, 612-812-4081, www.homebuddiesonline.com, is a member of the American Childcare Association. This agency also handles referrals for housekeepers and personal assistants.
- **Midwest Nannies**, 1614 Garfield Ct, St. Cloud, 320-654-9330
- **Nannies from the Heartland**, 5490 Balsam Ln N, Minneapolis, 763-550-0219
- **Nanny Professionals**, 245 E 8th St, Suite 703, St. Paul, 651-221-0587

Minnesota State Southeast Technical College in Red Wing (1-877-853-TECH, www.southeastmn.edu) offers an **Associate in Applied Science Professional Nanny/Family Child Care** degree-granting program. They do not run a placement agency, but contact the school and any interested graduates will call you back. These graduates are *much* in demand.

Be sure to check all references given to you by applicants. Do-it-yourselfers may visit the **Bureau of Criminal Apprehension** office, 1430 Maryland Avenue East, St. Paul, to view public criminal history information for no charge. A printed copy costs $4. Call 651-793-2420 for information. You may also search online at the **Minnesota Public Criminal History Search**, https://cch.state.mn.us/Common/BCAHome.aspx. This web site contains public data on criminal convictions. Be aware that convictions for driving while intoxicated may not always be reported to the state. If you prefer a professional background check, **Verified Credentials** (952-985-7200, 800-473-4934, www.verifiedcredentials.com) is a Minnesota firm that specializes in pre-employment screening. A check of criminal history, credit history, driving record and employment history costs an average of $200. **California Trustline**, an agency of the state of California, conducts fingerprint searches through the FBI for high misdemeanors and felonies in all states. This service is available to prospective childcare employers who live in any state, and requires three or four weeks to complete. Call 800-822-8490 or check www.trustline.org.

If you are contracting directly with your nanny for his or her services (rather than through an agency), there are certain taxes that will have to be paid, such as social security, Medicare, federal and state unemployment and income taxes. These obligations apply to both full- and part-time in-home workers. You will also need to carry workers' compensation, which you may be able to purchase through either your homeowner's or automobile insurance provider. For assistance call the **Minnesota Department of Labor and Industry**, 651-284-5005, www.doli.state.mn.us. For more information about Minnesota taxes, download *Hiring An In-Home Childcare Giver, Your Tax Responsibilities As An Employer,* produced by Resources for Childcaring, and available from Redleaf Press, 651-641-6675, redleafinstitute.com/pdf/nannymn.pdf. Also check the **HomeWork Solutions** web site, www.4nannytaxes.com, **800-NANITAX**, whose web site features a free online payroll tax calculator.

AU PAIRS

Au pairs are young adults between the ages of 18 and 26 who provide a year of in-home childcare and light housekeeping in exchange for airfare, room and board, and a small stipend. The program offers a valuable cultural exchange between the host family and the (usually European) au pair, as well as a flexible childcare schedule for parents. The downside is that the program only lasts one year (at most, two), and that an au pair doesn't have the life or work experience of a career nanny. **European Au Pair**, 952-476-4236, www.euraupair.com, located in Wayzata, brings over au pairs from western Europe, South Africa, and Japan. The weekly stipend is only $139.05, but there are other fees, including a $300 application fee, $5950 annual program fee (covers liability, life, and medical insurance, training, and an international roundtrip airline ticket), and $250 for a domestic airline ticket.

SCHOOLS

Families moving to Minnesota with school-age children have four choices for their children's education: public schools; private schools; charter schools; and homeschooling.

Public schools, operated by elected school boards and paid for with a combination of state funding and property taxes, must accept any and all students who live within their geographic boundaries. Unlike some other states, Minnesota's districts do not necessarily correspond to city or county lines. Thus Hennepin County (in which Minneapolis is located) has 16 autonomous public school districts, as well as some that offer special shared services. Overall, the state has 417 public school districts, which served 842,915 students in 2003–2004 (the most recent year for which figures are available). With a long-standing reputation for providing quality education, the public schools offer a variety of programs including magnet schools, English as a Second Language programs, special education, and birth to age 21 services for the disabled. (For more information, see **Public Schools** below.)

Private schools are operated by parent boards and paid for through tuition and fundraising. They are free to set their own standards for admission and decide what sort of program they wish to provide. The Twin Cities' private schools include several nationally acclaimed institutions such as Breck, Blake, and St. Paul Academy. (See **Private Schools** below.)

Charter schools—regarded by proponents as a way for parents to become more involved in their children's education, and by detractors as an interim measure for destroying the public schools—are something of a hybrid. They are paid for with public money, but organized and run by groups of parents. They are exempt from many regulations relating to public schools, and are free to organize curricula around the needs of the students they intend to serve. Minnesota's 125 currently operating charter schools served over 17,000 students in 2004–2005, and include institutions as diverse as the four **Sobriety Highs** (www.sobrietyhigh.org), **High School for Recording Arts**

in St. Paul (www.hsra.org), and **Minnesota Agricultural and Food Science Academy** in Vadnais Heights (www.agacademy.org.

The **University of Minnesota's Center for School Change** has used a multi-million-dollar grant from the Bill and Melinda Gates Foundation to help found several charter schools including the **St. Paul Conservatory for Performing Arts** (www.spcpa.org) and the **Great River School** (www.greatriverschool.org), a St. Paul high school based on the Montessori philosophy.

Curriculum control, good teachers, and greater opportunity for parental involvement are touted as positive aspects of charter schools; the cons include difficulties with transportation, financial accounting issues, and charges that charter schools take the best students away from struggling school districts. For more information, contact the **Minnesota Association of Charter Schools**, 1295 Bandana Blvd. #165, St. Paul, MN 55108, Fax: (651) 644-0433, Voice/TTY: (651) 644-0432, www.mncharterschools.org. Consumer tip: Since several charter schools have been forced to close during the school year, primarily because of financial mismanagement, if you are interested in this concept, you might want to look for schools that are overseen by school districts. They seem to have the best track records, both academically and financially.

Homeschooling is defined as the education of children under the supervision of their parents. According to the Minnesota Department of Education, about 17,000 children were homeschooled in the state in 2004–2005. Parents wishing to homeschool their children must meet minimum standards, including a bachelor's degree or a passing score on the state's Pre-Professional Skills Test. The test is administered twice a year at St. Cloud State University. For further information about homeschooling, contact the Minnesota Homeschoolers' Alliance, 612-288-9662, 1-888-346-7622, www.homeschoolers.org, email: mha@homeschoolers.org.

PUBLIC SCHOOLS

Minnesota's public schools face many challenges including rapid growth in districts on the urban fringe, declining enrollments in the inner cities and older suburbs, and the increasing diversity of the student population.

At the same time, years of cuts in state funding have left cash-strapped public schools hustling homeowners for new property tax levies and asking parents to fundraise for program essentials such as books, buses, and heat. And because each student comes with at least some state funding, school districts have started advertising to recruit students away from other districts, as well.

It hasn't always been this way.

Prior to 1971, schools in Minnesota were financed solely through property taxes. As a result, there were huge disparities between property-tax–rich and property-tax–poor districts. By 1970, property taxes had risen so high in some places that those on fixed incomes were selling their homes because they couldn't pay the taxes. And even that high level of taxation couldn't make up for the growing inequality between rich and poor communities. Finally, in 1971, the Democratic governor and Republican legislature got together and revised the tax structure, shifting the burden of paying for education away from the localities and onto the state, i.e., away from property taxes and onto income taxes. In that way, they sought to ensure that everyone would receive adequate public services at similar property tax rates throughout the state. This collection of laws became known as the **Minnesota Miracle**. It provided a stable source of funding for more than 30 years until 2002, when a "tax-cutting" governor and legislature renounced the Miracle and shifted the burden of paying for schools back toward local residential property taxpayers.

So that's where we stand now. Property taxes are rising—sometimes by astronomical amounts. (According to the *Minneapolis Star Tribune,* at the time of the writing of this book, Belle Plain is looking at a property tax increase of 242%.) But since homeowners can only bear so much, school districts have had to put everything on the chopping block. Districts have closed buildings, cut bus transportation, laid off teachers, shortened the length of the school day, and reduced the number of credits required for graduation. Expect more cuts to come: Minneapolis, for example, expects to close 21 schools in 2006.

That's the bad news. The good news is that Minnesota's 417 public school districts have fought to save the programs that set them apart, and still offer a wide range of options: year-round programs; magnet schools, Early Childhood Family Education; college credit for high school students, language immersion; adaptive athletics; half-day and full-day kindergartens, and extended-day childcare. One notable program is the **Northwest Suburban Integration School District** #6078 (www.nws.k12.mn.us), which operates 10 multicultural arts, science, and **International Baccalaureate** magnet schools in the Northwest Metro area. And, so far, the budget cutting hasn't done away with our public, residential arts high school, the **Perpich Center for Arts Education** in Golden Valley (www.mcae.k12.mn.us). Likewise, the **Fine Arts Interdisciplinary Resource School** (www.wmep.k12.mn.us/fair) in Crystal is going strong. This inter-district school serves grades four through eight, and integrates the arts into core subjects such as science and math. Several year-round schools are going strong as well, including St. Paul's **Four Seasons A Plus School** (http://fourseasonsspps.org), **Valley Crossing K–6 Community School** in Woodbury (www.vc.k12.mn.us); **Harambee Community Cultures/Environmental School** in Maplewood (www.emid6067.net/Harambee); and **Crosswinds East Metro Arts and Science Middle School** in Woodbury (www.emid6067.net/Crosswinds). And we still have **Open Enrollment**, so that if the schools in your district don't meet your needs, your children may still be able to attend public school outside the district in which you live. To learn more about the districts you're considering, call for a copy of *Schoolhouse Magazine*, 952-475-5496, 800-224-3642, www.school-house.com/. The price is $7.95 per single copy. Updated annually, this publication contains general information provided by the public school districts and private and charter schools. It also provides comparative data covering everything from age of the buildings to test scores. Another resource you may want to try is **SchoolMatch**, a firm that maintains a database on public and private schools, including student-teacher ratios, test scores, and per-pupil spending; call 614-890-1573 or look online at www.schoolmatch.com. They'll fax you reports about requested schools at prices ranging from $10 for a basic "snapshot" of a school system's national ranking to $49 for a "school system report card." Please keep in mind, however, that no amount of number crunching can tell you as much about whether a school is right for your child as your own gut feeling when you walk through the door.

That said, if you are determined to try to quantify your school-selection process, there are a few figures that teachers believe really do help to tell a school's story. The turnover rate, the percentage of students who move in or out of the district in any given year, can have a huge effect on a school. Too few new kids and the schools might become cliquish; too many and there may be problems with teachers having to spend most of their time getting new students up to speed. Other figures worth looking at include size of student body, what percentage of students participate in extracurricular activities, and how many of a school's graduates go on to graduate from college or technical school. But, please, don't get too hung up on test scores—they may mean nothing more than that teachers in that school are doing a good job of teaching to the tests. Or, as pointed out by administrators of some of the schools listed below, one class of students, such as special education, can make what is deemed to be insufficient progress and cause a whole school to fail.

MAKING YOUR PRESENCE KNOWN IN THE DISTRICT

Even if your oldest child is not yet in school, call your school district's administration office to assure your child's inclusion in the district's database, and to ensure that you will be notified about early childhood screening and kindergarten registration. It will also connect you with the district's **Early Childhood Family Education (ECFE)** services. All school districts provide ECFE programs for infants and preschoolers. These include parent education and support as well as child learning experiences. School districts also provide free **Early Childhood Health Screening** for children ages three and four. This includes a check for vision, hearing, developmental and growth status, and an immunization review.

VISITING A SCHOOL

Most of the literature tells you to compare costs per pupil, graduation rates, and test scores. While these objective measures may support your choice, there really is only one way to choose a school: visit.

When visiting a school, your gut reaction will probably tell you everything you need to know. Ask yourself these questions: Am I comfortable here? Are elementary-age students moving around naturally, but staying on task? What are the halls like in junior high and high schools when classes change? Are students engaged in discussions or projects? Is student work displayed? Ask elementary teachers about reading and math groups and if children move up as they build skills. Find out if there are any special programs offered to assist new students with the transition into a new school. Ask if parents are encouraged to volunteer in the classroom. Finally, look at the facility and equipment. Are the computer labs up-to-date with enough computers? Are instructional materials plentiful and new? Do you see opportunities for your child to do things he/she likes to do— art, music, science, etc.? If all passes muster, then the next step is registering.

SCHOOL REGISTRATION

Register in person at the school your child will attend, and call first to make sure the staff member you need to see will be available. If you are registering a kindergarten student, you will be asked to bring proof of birthday—children need to be five by September 1st in order to enter kindergarten. You don't need to bring anything to register students who are in first grade or higher, but you will be asked to sign a form allowing the district to request records from your child's previous school. Take medical records with you, if possible, because you will have to provide proof of vaccinations at the beginning of the school year.

IMMUNIZATIONS

Minnesota's School Immunization Law requires documentation of students' immunizations before entering school. Requirements vary by grade. All **kindergartners** must have written proof, either from their doctor or from their parents' records, of the following immunizations: five DPT (diphtheria, pertussis, tetanus); four polio; two MMR (mumps, measles, rubella); varicella (chickenpox) or history of having the disease; and Hepatitis B series (3 immunizations given over a minimum period of 4–6 months). All **seventh graders** are required to show proof of: a second MMR (measles, mumps, and rubella), Hepatitis B series immunizations, varicella (chicken pox) or history of having the disease, and TD (tetanus booster).

PARENT COMMUNICATION

"Parent portals" are the latest wrinkle in the dialogue between schools and parents. With names like "Schoolview" and "ParentConnect," these computer software programs allow parents to track their children's school attendance, class schedules, assignments, and grades by logging onto a web page or receiving email alerts.

EDUCATIONAL STANDARDS AND GRADUATION REQUIREMENTS

Tests are usually given the last two weeks of April and the first week of May. Beginning with the graduating class of 2010, students will be required to complete 21.5 course credits and pass the **Minnesota Comprehensive Assessments-II/Graduation-Required Assessments for Diploma (MCA-II/GRAD)** in Reading and Mathematics and Written Composition. The written composition test is given in Grade 9. Students in Grade 10 take the MCA in reading and students in Grade 11 take the MCA in mathematics. Students who do not pass the MCA-II tests are given opportunities to retake the tests until they pass. Most schools offer remediation in the form of test-preparation courses. While first-time tests require both multiple-choice and constructed-response answers, retests require only multiple-choice answers.

The **Minnesota Comprehensive Assessments** are a snapshot measurement of students' achievement compared to Minnesota's academic standards. They chart the progress of schools and districts (not students) over time, presumably generate information for school improvement and school account-ability, and allow for comparison of schools and districts throughout the state. All students in grades 3–8, 10 and 11 are required to take the MCAs. Student performance on the MCAs is charted using 5 achievement levels. Student sub-groups scoring in levels 1 and 2 are considered to be non-proficient and stu-dent subgroups scoring in levels 3, 4 and 5 are considered to be proficient. The state then reports the results for each school on the **Minnesota Department of Education** web site: www.education.state.mn.us.

Called the **Minnesota State Report Cards**, these reports are issued by the Department of Education on the first day of the State Fair. Schools that have even one subgroup of students who have not made **Adequate Yearly Progress (AYP)** earn two stars. If all subgroups in a school make AYP, the school earns three stars. Up to two additional stars may be earned by having superior performance when compared to schools of similar size or with a simi-lar percentage of students eligible for free lunch.

School districts contend that the state report cards do not report the full picture, however, because a school is tagged AYP-underperforming when even one subgroup of students (out of the nine subgroups) does not score in the proficient range on the test, even if all the other eight subgroups scored well above the state average.

NO CHILD LEFT BEHIND
The federal No Child Left Behind Act of 2001 requires that schools—not students—show evidence of "Adequate Yearly Progress" (AYP). Schools that don't make the mark must provide transfer options for their students and sup-plemental services, including tutoring. Schools that still fail to improve risk being closed. For parents, the most visible effect of NCLB is that children will now have to take standardized tests nearly every year. Here's a summary of what to expect:

For students: Annual testing in grades 3–8, in math and English, began in 2005. By 2007, states must begin testing students in science as well. *For teach-ers:* By the end of the 2005–2006 school year, your child's teachers had to be rated "highly qualified" in the subjects they teach. Becoming "highly qualified" could have entailed earning a degree in the subject they teach or taking extra training. *For schools:* Each year schools must increase the number of students who achieve state standards. The goal is that at the end of 12 years, all students in all schools will be able to pass all the tests.

But will they? The **Minnesota State Office of Educational Accountability (Legislative Auditor**) ran a computer simulation to see, and came to the disturbing conclusion that "between 80 and 100% of Minnesota's elementary schools (will) fail to make AYP by 2014 . . . even if there are large, sustained improvements in student achievement (as measured by these tests) . . ." and, furthermore, anywhere from 35% to 76% of Minnesota's elementary schools will "be subject to NCLB-prescribed restructuring within the next decade." You can read the Legislative Auditor's entire report on the costs associated with No Child Left Behind online at www.auditor. leg.state.mn.us/Ped/2004/pe0404.htm.

Those wishing to learn more about education issues in the state should check out the **League of Women Voters** web site (www.lwvmn.org) for non-partisan information, or the **Education Minnesota** homepage (www. educationminnesota.org), for the teachers' view. Education Minnesota is an affiliate of the National Education Association, the American Federation of Teachers, and the AFL-CIO.

QUESTIONS TO ASK ABOUT TESTING AT YOUR CHILD'S SCHOOL
• How has this testing changed the nature of teaching and learning at your school?
• Is this one of the at-risk schools?
• Do your school's test results fairly describe the education that's taking place here?
• How much time is spent practicing test-taking skills and memorizing lists?
• What is being sacrificed to make time for test-prep activities?
• How does your school make use of test results?
• What do you do about students or subgroups of students who consistently score below grade level?

WRITTEN CURRICULUM STANDARDS
The state's written standards for the arts, language arts, math, science, and social studies are posted online at the **Department of Education's** web site, http://education.state.mn.us/mde/index.html. There are no standards for health or PE.

ADVANCED PLACEMENT (AP) VS. INTERNATIONAL BACCALAUREATE (IB)
Parents in some school districts have been lobbying against the International Baccalaureate program, a demanding curriculum taught at many levels in schools across the metro. The principal charge appears to be the IB curriculum's international focus. Conversely, they characterize Advanced Placement (AP) courses as "homegrown American." Students who have taken both AP and IB courses say they have found nothing "un-American" in the IB curriculum, but that the two programs do constitute very different approaches to advanced work: AP courses move swiftly through a large body of material so that students will be able to do well on the long AP tests; and the IB program moves slowly, exploring topics in depth, with emphasis placed on students conducting their own inquiry, as in science classes, where students conduct their own experiments. The IB program also allows internationally mobile students to transfer from one IB Diploma Program school to another—a real boon to the families of Minnesota's numerous international businesses. For more information, visit the International Baccalaureate Organization's web site, www.ibo.org. For AP information, check with your local school district.

ADAPTIVE ATHLETICS
In 1992, the ***Minnesota State High School League*** became the first association in the nation to sanction interscholastic sports for kids with disabilities. With one division for cognitively impaired athletes (CI) and another for the

physically impaired (PI), kids with disabilities have, since that time, been able to earn varsity letters and participate in state tournaments, just like their able-bodied counterparts. Adaptive athletics are, however, unlike other sports in that they are usually co-ed, not organized along school district lines, and players using walkers, wheelchairs and prosthetic limbs all share the same field or floor. So far, there are four adapted sports—soccer, floor hockey, bowling, and softball. For information contact the **Metro Association for Adapted Athletics (MAAA)**, www.mnadaptedathletics.com. Rules, teams, and schedules can also be found on the Minnesota State High School League web site, www.mshsl.org.

METRO AREA PUBLIC SCHOOLS

ANOKA-HENNEPIN #11
11299 Hanson Blvd NW
Coon Rapids, MN 55433
763-506-1000
www.anoka.k12.mn.us/
Cities Served: Anoka, Champlin, Dayton, Ramsey, parts of Brooklyn Park, Coon Rapids, and Andover

If you have a budding astronomer in your family, you might want to check out this school district, which has an observatory at its Jackson Middle School in Champlin that is outfitted with one of the state's biggest telescopes. Robotic remote controls allow students at the district's other 44 schools to tune in to the scope's celestial views. With over 42,000 students, this is the state's largest school district, and it's still growing.

BLOOMINGTON #271
1350 West 106th St
Bloomington, MN 55431
952-681-6400
www.bloomington.k12.mn.us
Cities Served: Bloomington

Bloomington has ten elementary schools (K–5), three middle schools (6–8), two high schools, and three alternative learning centers. Its special programs and services include an after-school program for middle school youth and a fee-based school-aged childcare program. This district earned the 2005 "What Parents Want" Award from SchoolMatch. The award recognizes school districts for meeting the needs of the families they serve.

BROOKLYN CENTER #286
6500 Humboldt Ave North
Brooklyn Center, MN 55430
763-561-2120
www.brookcntr.k12.mn.us
Cities Served: Brooklyn Center

One of the state's smallest districts, with only two schools, Brooklyn Center's very existence has been threatened by a failed bond referendum in 2005. That said, at the time of the writing of this book, the district is still serving about 1700 students. Because of its geographic proximity to Anoka and Minneapolis, and because of its small schools, many families choose to open enroll their children into this district.

BUFFALO, HANOVER, MONTROSE #877
214 NE First Ave
Buffalo, MN 55313
763-682-5200
www.buffalo.k12.mn.us
Cities Served: Buffalo, Hanover, Montrose, and the surrounding townships

District #877, located 40 miles west of Minneapolis in Wright County, covers a 157-square-mile area and serves approximately 5000 students housed in five elementary schools, a middle school (grades 6–8), high school (grades 9–12) and an alternative high school. Upgrading Highway 55 to four lanes is expected to bring a huge building boom to this area in the near future, so expect many changes.

BURNSVILLE #191
100 River Ridge Ct
Burnsville, MN 55337
952-707-2000
www.isd191.org
Cities Served: Portions of Burnsville, Eagan, Savage, Apple Valley and Shakopee

District 191 serves 10,500 students at ten elementary schools (K–6), three junior highs (7–9), one traditional senior high school, and one alternative senior high. It was named one of the Twin Cities' best public school systems by the book *Going to Work: A Unique Guided Tour Through Corporate America*, and has also received a "What Parents Want Award" from SchoolMatch. Like many "older" districts, enrollment is declining, and there have been discussions about closing one of the district's elementary schools.

CHASKA #112
11 Peavey Rd
Chaska, MN 55318
952-556-6100
www.district112.org
Cities Served: Carver, Chanhassen, Chaska, and Victoria

District 112 has been hard hit by state education funding cuts, but as a growing district, with a 2005 enrollment of 8400, it decided not to make teacher cuts, but instead to increase class sizes. All kindergarten children attend the Early Childhood Center (ECC) in Chaska.

CENTENNIAL #12
4707 North Rd
Circle Pines, MN 55014
651-792-6000
www.isd12.org
Cities Served: Blaine, Centerville, Circle Pines, Lexington and Lino Lakes

Because of pending development in this area, this school district is expected to experience major changes. Successive years of budget reductions and failed operating levy referenda have forced the district to lay off teachers and consider closing a school.

CHISAGO LAKES #2144
13750 Lake Blvd
Lindstorm, MN 55045
651-213-2000
www.chisagolakes.k12.mn.us
Cities Served: Chisago City, Lindstrom, Taylor's Falls

This district operates schools in Chisago City and Lindstrom. The high school offers several unique programs including agri-science and American Sign Language.

COLUMBIA HEIGHTS #13
1400 49th Ave NE
Columbia Heights, MN 55421
763-528-4500
www.colheights.k12.mn.us

Cities Served: Columbia Heights, Hilltop, and the southern third of Fridley
This district offers 10-week enrichment sessions for 6th graders and some 7th and 8th graders.

DELANO #879
700 Elm Ave
Delano, MN 55328
763-972-3365
www.delano.k12.mn.us
Cities Served: Delano, Corcoran, Independence, Loretto, Maple Plain, Medina, Minnetrista, Montrose, Watertown, and parts of Franklin, Rockford, and Woodland townships

All schools are located on a 100-acre campus in Delano. With new or remodeled schools, this district's facilities are probably the best in the area.

EDEN PRAIRIE #272
8100 School Road
Eden Prairie, MN 55344-2292
952-975-7000
www2.edenpr.org/wps/portal
Cities Served: Most of Eden Prairie (some areas along the northern edge of the community are in the Minnetonka and Hopkins school districts)

Named one of the nation's "Top Ten Districts Overall," Eden Prairie led the metro with 21 National Merit Semifinalists in 2003.

EDINA #273
5701 Normandale Rd
Edina, MN 55424
952-848-3900
www.edina.k12.mn.us
Cities Served: Edina

In Minnesota, Edina's schools are the standard by which all other schools are judged. It has consistently been rated among the top school districts in the nation, and in 2005, SchoolMatch named it a Parents' Choice winner for schools that most match what parents want in a school district. When house hunting, be aware that some neighborhoods have Edina addresses, but the children attend Richfield or Hopkins schools.

ELK RIVER AREA SCHOOL DISTRICT (ERASD) #728
327 King Ave
Elk River, MN 55330
763-241-3400
www.elkriver.k12.mn.us
Cities Served: Albertville, Dayton, Elk River, Otsego, Ramsey, Rogers, St. Michael, Zimmerman, townships of Big Lake, Baldwin, Burns, Hassan, Livonia, Nowthen, Orrock, and Stanford

This large and growing district of nearly 11,000 students and 17 schools stretches 20-some miles from Zimmerman in the north to Rogers and Hassan in the south.

FARMINGTON #192
421 Walnut St
Farmington, MN 55024
651-463-5000
www.farmington.k12.mn.us
Cities Served: Farmington

With enrollment approaching 6000 students, schools are expected to be over capacity by 2008–09. The district hopes to open a new 2000-student high school in fall 2008, but its selection of a site on land the city's development plan designates as open space until 2020 has created a legal dispute that is unresolved at the time of the writing of this book. Click on their web site for individual school profiles.

FOREST LAKE #831
6100 210 St North
Forest Lake, MN 55025
651-982-8100
www.forestlake.k12.mn.us
Cities Served: Forest Lake, Marine on St. Croix, Wyoming, Columbus, Linwood, Lino Lakes, New Scandia, East Bethel, Ham Lake, Hugo, Stacy

This district is known for the way it integrates art and writing and experiential activities into its curriculum, and its teams have won state and world Odyssey of the Mind championships. And yet the schools have not fared well in No Child Left Behind (NCLB) scoring. The district feels that that scorecard unfairly represents its schools, and that sentiment is echoed by parents.

FRIDLEY #14
6000 W. Moore Lake Dr
Fridley, MN 55432
763-502-5000
www.fridley.k12.mn.us
Cities served: Fridley

The Fridley School District serves the central area of the City of Fridley. It offers an International Baccalaureate program, which it expects to become authorized in 2007. One unusual course taught here: horticulture.

HASTINGS #200
1000 11th St West
Hastings, MN 55033
651-437-6111
www.hastings.k12.mn.us/
Cities Served: Hampton, Hastings, Miesville, New Trier, and Vermillion, and portions of Denmark, Douglas, Hampton, Marshan, Nininger, Ravenna, and Vermillion townships

This 170-square-mile district is, geographically, one of the largest school districts in the Twin Cities metropolitan area, but at 5200 its K–12 enrollment is relatively small.

HOPKINS #270
1001 Highway 7
Hopkins, MN 55305
952-988-4000
www.hopkins.k12.mn.us
Cities Served: Hopkins, Minnetonka, Golden Valley, Eden Prairie, Edina, Plymouth, St. Louis Park

Many of you have probably seen the miracle last-second game-tying basketball shot that Hopkins senior Blake Hoffarber made while lying on his back, but neither he nor his school district is a one-shot wonder. Hopkins, in fact, is nearly everybody's favorite school district, as evidenced by the huge number of students trying to enroll there. Hopkins, in fact, is so popular that it can't accept all the students who apply, and has to maintain an open enrollment waiting list.

Among its excellent course offerings is one of the most extensive music programs in the state. Diverse co-curriculars include a LEGO league and robotics.

INVER GROVE #199
2990 80th St East
Inver Grove Heights, MN 55076
651-306-7800
www.invergrove.k12.mn.us
Cities Served: Inver Grove Heights

This district serves about 3700 students who live in the community, as well as almost 300 students from neighboring communities who open enroll here. The district's 2004 Minnesota Comprehensive Assessment test scores were pulled down by its special ed students, but as a spokesperson for the district has written, "If all students were at a proficient level, there would not be a need for special education." The administration's opinion is mirrored by district parents, who are quite indignant and quick to point out that most of the classes scored well above the state average.

JORDAN #717
500 Sunset Dr
Jordan, MN 55352
952-492-6200
www.jordan.k12.mn.us
Cities Served: Jordan

Jordan has a single campus that houses all of the district schools. High school juniors and seniors may take classes at the Carver-Scott Vocational Cooperative. Located on Highway 169, just seven miles south of Shakopee, this small town has easy access to the metro area, and is attracting a lot of new development.

LAKEVILLE #194
8670 210th St West
Lakeville, MN 55044
952-232-2000
www.isd194.k12.mn.us
Cities Served: Lakeville, a portion of the City of Burnsville, the City of Elko, and Credit River, Eureka, and New Market townships

With approximately 10,900 students in 2005–2006, the enrollment in the Lakeville Area Public School District has doubled in the past ten years, making it one of the most rapidly growing districts in Minnesota. The district opened a second high school in 2005 and expects to need a third around 2010. Channel 22, the Lakeville School District local access channel, broadcasts board meetings, sporting events, concerts, and school information.

MAHTOMEDI INDEPENDENT SCHOOL DISTRICT #832
1520 Mahtomedi Ave
Mahtomedi, MN 55115
651-407-2000
www.mahtomedi.k12.mn.us
Cities Served: Dellwood, Mahtomedi, Pine Springs, Willernie, Grant, Hugo, Lake Elmo, Oakdale, and White Bear Lake

Mahtomedi, whose motto is "individual attention with a world view," is a small suburban school district of 3000 students. Its language arts curriculum is literature-based and multidisciplinary. Science classes emphasize experimentation. While this area is growing, the schools are still small and have an intimate atmosphere, as well as very involved teachers and parents.

MINNEAPOLIS PUBLIC SCHOOLS
807 N.E. Broadway
Minneapolis, MN 55413
612-668-0000
www.mpls.k12.mn.us
City Served: Minneapolis

This district's 38,000-member student population is highly diverse, with students speaking more than 90 languages. Having to teach such a multiplicity of cultures has turned into a challenge that, combined with declining enrollment and decreasing revenues, has thrown this district into crisis. Teachers have been fired, programs dismantled, schools closed. Yet when, in 2003, Eden Prairie had the most National Merit Scholarship Semifinalists (21) in the metro, Minneapolis was second with 19. The magnet schools, in particular, are well regarded by parents. Visit the district's School Choice Center online at http://schoolchoice.mpls.k12.mn.us.

MINNETONKA
5621 County Rd 101
Minnetonka, MN 55345
952-401-5000
www.minnetonka.k12.mn.us
Cities Served: Minnetonka, Chanhassen, Deephaven, Eden Prairie, Excelsior, Greenwood, Shorewood, Tonka Bay, Victoria, and Woodland

This high-performing district has approximately 7700 students. Its high school partnered with the city of Minnetonka to build an outstanding rehearsal and performance space that is used jointly by the school and community orchestras and choral groups. As a cost-cutting measure, the length of the high school's day has been reduced from seven periods to six, and the district has changed its graduation requirements by decreasing social studies and electives credits. While the district has a long-standing reputation for academic excellence, it has an equally long-standing reputation for being extremely cliquish, and it can be difficult for teenagers to transfer here.

MONTICELLO #882
302 Washington St
Monticello, MN 55362
763-271-0300
www.monticello.k12.mn.us
City Served: Monticello

Monticello's high school features one of the finest indoor field houses in the state. Because of its location (with good access to the freeway and near Big Lake, which is expected to be the terminus of the Northstar light rail transit line), this school district will undoubtedly experience great growth in the near future.

MOUND WESTONKA PUBLIC SCHOOL DISTRICT
(see Westonka Public School District #277, below)

MOUNDS VIEW #621
2959 Hamline Ave North
Roseville, MN 55113
651-639-6118
www.moundsviewschools.org
Cities Served: Arden Hills, Mounds View, New Brighton, North Oaks, Roseville, Shoreview, Vadnais Heights and portions of Spring Lake Park and White Bear Township

Mounds View is one of the larger districts in Minnesota, serving more than 10,000 students, several hundred of whom open enroll into the district. It offers adaptive physical education, physical and occupational therapy, and many other special services.

NORTH ST. PAUL-MAPLEWOOD-OAKDALE #622
2520 East 12th Ave
North St. Paul, MN 55109
651-748-7622
www.isd622.org
Cities Served: Lake Elmo, Landfall, Maplewood, North St. Paul, Oakdale, Pine Springs, Woodbury

Those who like to watch halftime at the football bowl games may have seen this district's North High School band performing at the Orange Bowl or the Hall of Fame game. They've also marched in the Macy's Thanksgiving Day Parade, making this one of the most high-profile districts around. A large district, it serves more than 11,630 students in 16 school buildings, and it offers year-round options.

ORONO INDEPENDENT SCHOOL DISTRICT #278
PO Box 46
Long Lake, MN 55356
952-449-8300
www.orono.k12.mn.us
Cities Served: Independence, Long Lake, Maple Plain, Medina, Minnetonka Beach, Orono

The district operates four schools on a 120-acre central campus nestled against 2000 feet of lakeshore in Long Lake. The campus is also home to a first-class childcare facility, swimming pool, ice arena, nature study area, stadium, multiple tennis courts, four campus gymnasiums, two auditoriums, and ample fields for football, soccer, baseball, softball, and other outdoor activities. Most teachers in this district have advanced degrees, and parents are so anxious to be involved, the schools practically have to run a lottery to select volunteers. That said, a November 2005 levy referendum failed after a group of parents hired an out-of-state consultant to help them defeat the district's proposals for increased operating revenues and new boilers at three of the schools.

OSSEO SCHOOL DISTRICT #279
11200 93rd Ave North
Maple Grove, MN 55369
763-391-7000
www.district279.org
Cities Served: Brooklyn Park, Maple Grove, Plymouth, Brooklyn Center, Osseo, Corcoran, Hassan, and Dayton

The Osseo School District serves an extensive and rapidly developing area of the northwestern suburbs of Minneapolis. It has about 22,000 students who attend 19 elementary schools (grades K–6), four junior highs (grades 7–9), three senior highs (grades 10–12), and a special education transition center for young adults. French, German, Spanish, and additional languages are offered through a cooperative arrangement with the local technical college. High school programs also include studio courses in art, early graduation, and mentorships. A number of elective courses are available through online instruction.

PERPICH CENTER FOR ARTS EDUCATION
6125 Olson Memorial Hwy
Golden Valley, MN 55422
763-591-4700
www.mcae.k12.mn.us
Cities Served: Statewide

This is a residential, tuition-free, public high school for 310 artistically talented 11th and 12th grade students from all across Minnesota. Majors include Music, Dance, Theater, Visual Arts, Media Arts, and Literary Arts. Students are selected for admission based on demonstrated ability in the arts and/or potential for growth in an art area. Information sessions about the Arts High School are held throughout the year. Applications are due each February for the upcoming school year.

PRIOR LAKE–SAVAGE #719
5300 Westwood Dr SE, Box 539
Prior Lake, MN 55372
952-226-0000
www.priorlake-savage.k12.mn.us
Cities Served: Prior Lake, Savage

This is another rapidly growing school district, which welcomed nearly 500 new kindergarten students in 2005—the district's largest entering class ever. With a large local Native American population, it is no surprise that one of the things that sets this district apart is its commitment to environmental education, which is integrated throughout the curriculum.

RICHFIELD #280
7001 Harriet Ave South
Richfield, MN 55423
612-798-6000
www.richfield.k12.mn.us
Cities served: Richfield, part of Edina

This district has about 4400 students who attend two (K–2) elementaries, one 3–5 intermediate school, one middle school (grades 6–8), and one high school (grades 9–12). Middle school offerings include classes at Richfield's Wood Lake Nature Center. French, German, and Spanish begin in middle school. With 1400 students at the high school, parents feel it is big enough to have a wide variety of class offerings, but small enough that students receive individual attention.

ROBBINSDALE AREA SCHOOLS #281
4148 Winnetka Ave North
New Hope, MN 55427
763-504-8000
www.rdale.k12.mn.us/dist
Cities Served: Brooklyn Center, Brooklyn Park, Crystal, Golden Valley, New Hope, Plymouth, and Robbinsdale

District 281, which draws students from north Minneapolis as well as the seven cities within its boundaries, serves approximately 13,000 K–12 students. It is known for its Spanish Immersion School for grades K–5, as well as for its sports programs, which even include croquet. Sandburg Middle School offers the only authorized Middle Years IB Program in the state.

ROSEMOUNT–APPLE VALLEY–EAGAN #196
14445 Diamond Path
Rosemount, MN 55068
651-423-7700
www.isd196.k12.mn.us
Cities Served: Rosemount, Apple Valley, Eagan, Burnsville, Coates, Inver Grove Heights, and Lakeville, and rural Empire and Vermillion townships

Rosemount–Apple Valley–Eagan has seen a slight decrease in enrollment—down to 28,269 students. As Minnesota's fourth largest school district, it covers 110 square miles, and consists of 18 elementary schools (K–5), six middle schools (6–8), four high schools (9–12), the School of Environmental Studies optional high school (11–12), an alternative high school (9–12) and Dakota Ridge Special Education School, which serves all ages. It has six National Blue Ribbon Schools of Excellence and numerous state and nationally recognized programs in academics, the arts and athletics.

ROSEVILLE INDEPENDENT SCHOOL DISTRICT #623
1251 West County Rd B2
Roseville, MN 55113
651-635-1600
www.roseville.k12.mn.us
Cities Served: Roseville, Falcon Heights, Little Canada, Lauderdale, Shoreview, Maplewood, and Arden Hills

This district of 6278 students uses more than 1450 miles of toilet tissue each year, owns 2376 computers and 250 acres of schoolyards and playgrounds, and must have a really fun math program for its students to have generated those and all the other statistics that it publishes in its monthly newsletter! Though they are proud of the strong showing their students make on standardized tests, district officials say they prefer to emphasize long-term learning.

SHAKOPEE SCHOOL DISTRICT #720
505 South Holmes St
Shakopee, MN 55379
952-496-5006
www.shakopee.k12.mn.us
Cities Served: Shakopee, Savage, Prior Lake and Jackson, Louisville, and Sand Creek

This district, which already serves 5400 students, is experiencing rapid growth and will be opening a new high school in the fall of 2007. A growing number of this district's classes offer college credit, including Composition, Democracy in a Changing World, Microeconomics, AP Calculus, AP Music Theory, and AP Psychology. Language choices include Japanese, Spanish, and German. The senior high also offers a program in the construction trades.

SOUTH ST. PAUL SPECIAL SCHOOL DISTRICT #6
104 5th Ave South
South St. Paul, MN 55075
651-457-9400
www.sspps.org
City Served: South St. Paul

"Where the school and community are one" is the motto of this city and school district, whose boundaries are nearly the same. Both elementary schools have begun the process of becoming certified with the International Baccalaureate Primary Years Program, the junior high school has been approved to start the process of certification for the IB Middle Years Program, and the high school already participates in the IB program. In 2004, the Educational Foundation presented the graduating seniors with more than $166,000 in college scholarships.

SPRING LAKE PARK #16
8000 Hwy 65 NE
Spring Lake, MN 55432
763-786-5570
www.splkpark.k12.mn.us
Cities Served: Spring Lake Park, parts of Fridley, parts of Blaine

At 4500 students, Spring Lake Park is roughly one-tenth the size of its "Big Brother" neighbor, Anoka-Hennepin. It has four elementary schools, a middle school, and a high school, with an average of 300 students in each grade. That compares to about 3000 students per grade at Anoka-Hennepin. As the district superintendent says, "We like to think that our school district is the perfect size. We've been described as 'small in size, extra-large in opportunity,' and we're proud of that description."

ST. ANTHONY-NEW BRIGHTON #282
3303 33rd Ave NE
St. Anthony Village, MN 55418
612-706-1000
www.stanthony.k12.mn.us
Cities Served: New Brighton, St. Anthony Village

This district's highly regarded academic program utilizes the area's urban cultural resources such as nearby art and science museums.

ST. LOUIS PARK #283
6425 West 33rd St
St. Louis Park, MN 54426
952-928-6000
www.stlpark.k12.mn.us
City Served: St. Louis Park

In November 2005, St. Louis Park was named one of the 100 Best Communities for Young People in America by America's Promise, an organization founded by retired General Colin Powell. The district's schools are a big part of the reason. All seven St. Louis Park schools have been designated Schools of Excellence by the U.S. Department of Education, and the high school was ranked number 305 among the top 1000 public high schools in America by *Newsweek* magazine. In addition, SLP eighth grade students ranked first in the nation in math proficiency, and tied for seventh in reading, on the 2003 National Assessment of Education Progress.

ST. PAUL #625
360 Colborne Ave., St. Paul, MN 55102
651-293-5100
www.spps.org
Cities Served: St. Paul

With more than 42,000 students and 256 program sites, St. Paul Public Schools (SPPS) is Minnesota's second-largest school district. Its student population is diverse, consisting of students who hail from countries throughout the world, speak more than 95 languages and dialects, and have arrived in the district with a wide range of educational experiences and skills. To meet the incredible variety of needs, the school district has developed a large array of choices including traditional neighborhood schools, magnets, year-round schools, language immersion, and extended-day school-age childcare. Languages offered include Latin, Russian, Swahili, Vietnamese and American Sign Language.

SOUTH WASHINGTON COUNTY SCHOOLS #833
7362 East Point Douglas Rd
Cottage Grove, MN 55016
651-458-6300
www.sowashco.k12.mn.us
Cities Served: Cottage Grove, St. Paul Park, Newport, Woodbury, Afton, and
Denmark

South Washington County School District 833 is a rapidly growing district that
covers 84 square miles and serves 16,400 students. New elementary schools
opened in 2001, 2002, and 2003. It offers a wide variety of elective courses,
including Air Force Junior ROTC.

STILLWATER AREA SCHOOL DISTRICT #834
1875 South Greeley St
Stillwater, MN 55082
651-351-8340
www.stillwater.k12.mn.us/
Cities Served: Afton, Bayport, Baytown Township, Grant, a portion of Hugo,
Lake Elmo, Lakeland, Lakeland Shores, Lake St. Croix Beach, Marine on St.
Croix, May Township, Oak Park Heights, St. Mary's Point, Stillwater, Stillwater
Township, West Lakeland Township, Withrow, and a portion of Woodbury

The high school is the core of the Stillwater community, and many who don't
have children in the schools turn out for its concerts, games, and other events.
They're good, too! Stillwater's music program is nationally recognized and its
"Ponies" have won numerous state championships in every sport.

WACONIA PUBLIC SCHOOLS #110
504 Industrial Blvd
Waconia, MN 55387
952-442-0600
www.waconia.k12.mn.us
Cities Served: Waconia, St. Bonifacius, New Germany

Although 2605 students may sound like a small district, this is actually one of
the fastest growing districts in the state. Its enrollment nearly doubled between
1995 and 2005, and is expected to nearly double again by 2012.

WAYZATA #284
210 County Rd 101 North
763-745-5000, www.wayzata.k12.mn.us
Cities Served: Corcoran, Maple Grove, Medicine Lake, Medina, Minnetonka,
Orono, Plymouth, and Wayzata

Students in Wayzata schools consistently score at the highest levels on standardized tests, including college entrance exams. Though this is an extremely

affluent and well-educated community, the test scores are, at least in part, due to the fact that Wayzata High School has the most rigorous graduation requirements in the state.

WEST ST. PAUL #197
1897 Delaware Ave
West St. Paul, MN 55118
651-681-2300
www.isd197.org
Cities Served: West St. Paul, Mendota Heights, Eagan, Inver Grove Heights, Lilydale, Mendota, Sunfish Lake

In response to having some of its schools tagged as racially isolated, this district is turning its elementaries into magnet schools. Garlough is the first, and is being reorganized as an environmental magnet in cooperation with the Dodge Nature Center, which is across the street from the school.

WESTONKA PUBLIC SCHOOL DISTRICT #277
5901 Sunnyfield Rd East
Mound, MN 55364
952-491-8000
www.westonka.k12.mn.us
Cities Served: Mound, Minnetrista, Spring Park, Shorewood, Lyndale, Navarre, Independence, Orono

Westonka is seen by parents as an improving district. All its schools have successfully met the requirements of the federal No Child Left Behind Act, and three of them have been recognized as five star schools, meaning that they have outperformed similar schools in the state (see **Standards** above).

WHITE BEAR LAKE #624
4855 Bloom Ave
White Bear Lake, MN 55110
651-407-7500
www.whitebear.k12.mn.us
Cities Served: Birchwood, Gem Lake, Hugo, Little Canada, North Oaks, Vadnais Heights, White Bear Lake, White Bear Township

This district's elementary program emphasizes basic skills and writing and includes gifted programs in communications and math. The high school curriculum includes advanced courses offered through College in the Schools, a program in conjunction with the University of Minnesota.

WRIGHT COUNTY SCHOOLS
District 876: Annandale, South Haven, Silver Creek; www.annandale.k12.mn.us
District 877: Buffalo, Hanover, Montrose; www.buffalo.k12.mn.us (see above)
District 466: Cokato, Dassel; www.dc.k12.mn.us
District 879: Delano; www.delano.k12.mn.us (see above)
District 2687: Howard Lake, Waverly, Winsted; www.hlww.k12.mn.us
District 885: St. Michael, Albertville; www.stma.k12.mn.us
District 881: Maple Lake; www.maplelake.k12.mn.us
District 882: Monticello; www.monticello.k12.mn.us (see above)
District 728: Otsego (Elk River); www.elkriver.k12.mn.us (see above)
District 883: Rockford; www.rockford.k12.mn.us

WESTERN WISCONSIN SCHOOLS
Like Minnesota, Wisconsin has a set of state academic standards for public education. Read them at /www.dpi.state.wi.us/standards.

SCHOOL DISTRICT OF HUDSON
1401 Vine St
Hudson, WI 54016
715-386-4900
www.hudson.k12.wi.us

This is one of the fastest growing school districts in Wisconsin.

SCHOOL DISTRICT OF RIVER FALLS
852 East Division St
River Falls, WI 54022
715-425-1800
www.rfsd.k12.wi.us

River Falls has three elementary schools, one middle school, one high school, and two charter academies. River Falls Montessori Charter School (www.rfsd.k12.wi.us/montessori) served grades K–2 in 2005–06, but will add a grade each year through grade 5. Renaissance Alternative Academy charter school (www.rfacademy.us) serves grades 9–12 with an emphasis on computer science and technology.

SCHOOL DISTRICT OF SOMERSET
645 Sunrise Dr
Somerset, WI 54025
715-247-3313
www.somerset.k12.wi.us

Road upgrades and the new Stillwater bridge are expected to encourage more people to move to this district in the near future.

PRIVATE SCHOOLS

The metropolitan area is home to many excellent private and parochial schools. Here are just a few of the best known. For information about all of them, including Montessori schools, check out **Private School Review**, www.private schoolreview.com/state_high_schools/stateid/MN.

BLAKE
110 Blake Rd
Hopkins
952-988-3420
www.blakeschool.org

BENILDE–ST. MARGARET (BSM)
2501 Hwy 100 South
St. Louis Park
952-927-4176
www.bsm-online.org

BRECK
123 Ottawa Ave North
Golden Valley
763-381-8100
www.breckschool.org

INTERNATIONAL SCHOOL OF MINNESOTA (ISM)
6385 Beach Rd
Eden Prairie
952-918-1840, 952-918-1800
www.ism-sabis.net

MINNEAPOLIS JEWISH DAY SCHOOL
4330 Cedar Lake Rd South
St Louis Park
952-381-3500
www.mjds.net

ST. PAUL ACADEMY AND SUMMIT SCHOOL
1150 Goodrich Ave
1712 Randolph Ave
St. Paul
651-698-2451
www.spa.edu

THE TWIN CITIES METROPOLITAN AREA IS HOME TO OVER A DOZEN COLLEGES and universities, and an equal number of technical schools. Oldest among them is **Hamline**, founded in 1854. The land grant **University of Minnesota** followed soon after. Five of the colleges, Hamline, Macalester, Augsburg, University of St. Thomas, and The College of St. Catherine, have joined together to form the **Associated Colleges of the Twin Cities (ACTC)** (www.associatedcolleges-tc.org). Students at these schools may sign up for courses at any of the ACTC campuses, and parents whose children are enrolled in some of these schools may audit courses there for free.

REDUCED OUT-OF-STATE TUITION OPTIONS

Minnesota has agreements with several neighboring states to provide lower tuition for Minnesota residents who attend public colleges and universities in those states. Called **reciprocity**, the agreements cover **Wisconsin, North Dakota, and South Dakota**. The state also has an agreement with the Canadian province of **Manitoba**, and a limited agreement with **Iowa Lakes Community College** in Iowa. State students wishing to attend colleges in **Kansas, Michigan, Missouri, and Nebraska** may also be eligible for tuition reductions through the **Midwest Student Exchange Program** (http://msep.mhec.org). More information about Tuition Reciprocity is available online from The **Minnesota Office of Higher Education** www.ohe. state.mn.us.

Those interested in attending a public Minnesota college should visit the **Minnesota State Colleges and Universities'** (MnSCU) web page (www.mnscu.edu). It has links to campus profiles, a searchable program index, and transfer and financial information; you can also call them at 651-296-8012, 888-667-2848, or TTY 651-282-2660. The **Minnesota Private Colleges'** homepage (www.mnprivatecolleges.org) has links to 17 private colleges as well as financial and admissions information and *US News and World Report*'s ranking of schools in our region. (Newsflash! The **Minneapolis College of Art and Design** has been named one of the **Best 10 Design Schools**;

Macalester and **Carleton** are in the **Top Ten Best Value**; **Hamline** is **Top Ten Best University** and **Carleton** is **Top 5 Best National Liberal Arts Colleges**!)

For those who can't get away to take classes, **Minnesota Online** (www.mnonline.org) makes it possible for you to access over 1500 online courses from the state's 25 two-year public colleges and seven public universities.

Finally, many people have graduated from high school and immediately started to work, finding it impossible to attend any of the state's four-year degree-granting colleges or universities. For them, the two-year community college system is starting to offer four-year degree programs. Near the metro area, **Anoka-Ramsey Community College** (www.an.cc.mn.us) offers four-year degree programs in education, nursing, and public administration, and graduate-level education and informational media classes. Check the **Minnesota State Colleges and Universities** System website (www.mnscu.edu) for information about this and other community college programs as well.

TWIN CITIES UNIVERSITIES AND COLLEGES

- **Augsburg College**, 2211 Riverside Ave, Minneapolis, 612-330-1001 (Admissions), 800-788-5678, www.augsburg.edu; known for its ability to work with special needs students, it also offers Weekend College, where adult students can earn a college degree or develop a job-related skill. Enrollment: about 3000.
- **Bethel University**, 3900 Bethel Dr, Arden Hills 55112; 651-638-6400, 800-255-8706, www.bethel.edu; a four-year, liberal arts Baptist college located about 15 minutes from downtown St. Paul and Minneapolis, Enrollment: about 3000.
- **College of St. Catherine**, 2004 Randolph Ave, St. Paul, 55105; 651-690-8850, 800-656-KATE, www.stkate.edu; this Catholic liberal arts college for women admits men to its master's programs and its two-year campus in Minneapolis. Enrollment: about 3500.
- **Concordia University-St. Paul**, 275 N Syndicate St, St. Paul, 55104; 651-641-8230, 800-333-4705, www.csp.edu; a private Lutheran liberal arts college. Enrollment: about 1700.
- **Dunwoody College of Technology**, 818 Dunwoody Blvd, Minneapolis 55403-1192; 612-374-5800, 800-292-4625, www.dunwoody.edu, is one of the top technical schools in the US in automotive, electronics, and tool and die manufacturing.
- **Hamline University**, 1536 Hewitt Ave, St. Paul, 55104; 651-523-2207, 800-753-9753, www.hamline.edu; a nationally recognized coeducational Methodist liberal arts college with a School of Law and several graduate programs. Enrollment: undergraduate, 1800; graduate, 1000.
- **Hennepin Technical Colleges**, 9000 Brooklyn Blvd, Brooklyn Park, 763-488-2450; 13100 College View Dr, Eden Prairie, 952-995-1452; Customized Training Services, 1820 Xenium Ln N, Plymouth, 763-550-7159, 800-345-4655, TTY 763-488-2571, www.HennepinTech.edu; educate people for

careers that do not require a baccalaureate degree for entry, such as computer science and nursing. Enrollment: over 13,000.

- **Macalester College**, 1600 Grand Ave, St. Paul, 55105; 651-696-6357, 800-231-7974, www.macalester.edu; has a reputation for producing dedicated social activists. Enrollment: about 2500.
- **Metropolitan State University**, 730 Hennepin Ave, Minneapolis; 700 7th St E, St. Paul; www.metrostate.edu; offers vocationally oriented bachelor's degrees. Enrollment: about 10,000. Register through their online catalogue.
- **Minneapolis College of Art and Design**, 2501 Stevens Ave S, Minneapolis, 55404, 612-874-3760, 800-874-6223, www.mcad.edu; located adjacent to the Minneapolis Institute of Art, this four-year private liberal arts college is one of the top art schools in the country. Enrollment: approximately 650.
- **Minneapolis Community and Technical College** (MCTC), 1501 Hennepin Ave, Minneapolis 55403; 612-659-6000, www.mctc.mnscu.edu; a non-residential two-year community college located near downtown by Loring Park. Its motto is, "If you don't chase your dreams, who will?" This is the most ethnically diverse campus in the state, with a large English as a Second Language (ESL) program and state-of-the-art technical equipment. Enrollment: 10,500.
- **Normandale Community College**, 9700 France Ave S, Bloomington 55431, 952-487-8200, 866-880-8740, TTY 952-487-7032, www.normandale. edu, offers 2-year associate degrees; its engineering and health sciences departments, in particular, are highly regarded by graduates who started there and continued to higher degrees in other institutions. Enrollment: over 11,000.
- **University of Minnesota**, Washington Ave at E River Rd, Minneapolis 55455; Como Ave at Cleveland Ave, St. Paul, 612-625-5000, www1. umn.edu/twincities/; "the U" Twin Cities campus has a student body of over 51,000, making it the second-largest campus in the nation behind Arizona State. One of the top public universities in the country, it is highly regarded as a major research institution, particularly with respect to agriculture, business, medicine, and public service. The heart-lung machine, cardiac pacemaker, flight recorder (black box) for aircraft, and retractable seat belt for cars were all invented by University researchers. It is also the world's leading kidney transplant center.
- **University of St. Thomas**, 2115 Summit Ave, St. Paul, 55105; 651-962-6150, 800-328-6819, www.stthomas.edu; the largest private school in Minnesota, this coeducational Catholic university has satellite campuses in Anoka, Chaska, Mall of America, Woodbury, Owatonna, Rochester, Downtown Minneapolis. Enrollment: approximately 11,000.
- **William Mitchell College of Law**, 875 Summit Ave, St. Paul, 55105; 651-227-9171, 888-WMCL-LAW, www.wmitchell.edu; founded in 1900, this 1100-student private law school set among the mansions of Summit Ave boasts two Chief Justices among its alumni. Entering classes of about 375.

NEARBY COLLEGES

- **Carleton College**, 100 S College St, Northfield, 55057; 507-646-4190, 800-995-CARL, www.carleton.edu; regarded as one of the country's best small liberal arts colleges. Enrollment: 1935.
- **College of Saint Benedict**, 37 College Ave S, St. Joseph, 320-363-5308, 800-544-1489, www.csbsju.edu; "St. Ben's" is a Catholic four-year liberal arts college for women. It shares a common undergraduate curriculum, identical degree requirements, and a single academic calendar with neighboring St. John's University, Catholic school for men. Enrollment: 4000.
- **Gustavus Adolphus College**, 800 W College Ave, St. Peter, Minnesota 56082; 507-933-7676, 800-GUSTAVUS, www.gustavus.edu; this private, residential liberal arts college of Swedish heritage is located in a small town about an hour and a half from the Twin Cities. Enrollment: about 2500.
- **St. John's University**, Collegeville, 320-363-2196, 800-544-1489, www.csbsju.edu; a Catholic college for men. Enrollment: about 4000.
- **St. Olaf College**, 1520 St. Olaf Ave, Northfield, 55057; 507-646-3025, 800-800-3025, www.stolaf.edu; a four-year, coeducational, residential, Lutheran liberal arts college with a beautiful campus and nationally recognized music and mathematics programs. The St. Olaf College Christmas Festival is the hottest holiday ticket in Minnesota. Check it out online at www.stolaf.edu/publications/christmas. Enrollment: about 3000.

Other notable institutions:
- **Art Institutes International Minnesota**, Minneapolis, 612-332-3361, www.aim.artinstitutes.edu
- **Century College**, 3300 Century Ave N, White Bear Lake, 651-779-3200, www.century.edu
- **College of St. Scholastica**, Duluth, 800-447-5444, www.css.edu
- **College of Visual Arts**, St. Paul, 651-224-3416, www.cva.edu
- **Concordia College**, Moorhead, 800-699-9897, www.goconcordia.com
- **Minnesota State University–Mankato**, 800-722-0544, www.mnsu.edu
- **Minnesota State University–Moorhead**, 800-593-7246, www.mnstate.edu
- **Southwest Minnesota State University**, Marshall, 800-642-0684, www.southwest.msus.edu
- **St. Cloud State University**, St. Cloud, 877-654-7278, www.stcloudstate.edu
- **St. Mary's University of Minnesota**, Winona, 800-635-5987, www.smumn.edu
- **University of Minnesota–Crookston**, 800-862-6466, www.crk.umn.edu
- **University of Minnesota–Duluth**, 800-232-1339, www.d.umn.edu
- **University of Minnesota–Morris**, 800-992-8863, www.mrs.umn.edu
- **Winona State University**, Winona, 800-342-5978, www.winona.edu

AREA COMMUNITY COLLEGES

- **Anoka-Ramsey Community College**, Coon Rapids, Cambridge, 763-427-2600, www.anokaramsey.mnscu.edu, offers four-year degree programs and some graduate-level classes.
- **Inver Hills Community College**, Inver Grove Heights, 651-450-8391, www.inverhills.mnscu.edu
- **North Hennepin Community College**, Brooklyn Park, 763-424-0702, www.nh.cc.mn.us
- **Anoka-Hennepin Technical College**, Anoka, 763-576-4850, www.ank.tec.mn.us
- **Dakota County Technical College,** Rosemount, 651-423-8301, www.dctc.mnscu.edu, offers the nation's only wood-finishing technology program.
- **St. Paul Technical College**, St. Paul 651-846-1600, www.sptc.tec.mn.us

HEALTH CARE PLANS

As recently as 2003, Minnesota was the state with the highest percentage of residents with some kind of health care coverage—nearly 90%. Following a number of state budget cuts, that may no longer be the case. On paper, though, we still look pretty good. We *are* home to the world-famous **Mayo Clinic**, which was named the second-best hospital in the nation by *U.S. News and World Report* in 2005. And we do have some of the highest life expectancies in the nation—81.5 years for females and 76.5 years for males according to the State Demographer's most recent figures.

That's the good news. The bad news is that the cost of health care is becoming prohibitively expensive, even in this state where Health Services is the biggest industry.

Most solutions seem to revolve around "tiered service" health care plans. A Minnesota company, Patient Choice, which was formed by a coalition of large employers operating under the name of Buyer's Health Care Action Group, launched and managed the first tiered service network program in the country back in 1997. Since then, tiered networks have taken off. Blue Cross and Blue Shield, Health Partners, and Medica have all adopted tiered systems that are essentially based on cost. Blue Cross's plan divides the state's hospitals into two tiers. Making the cut for Tier I (cheapest) designation are the Fairview system, Health East system, Lakeview Memorial, North Memorial, Methodist, Ridgeview, Hennepin County Medical Center (HCMC), and Woodwinds hospitals. Some of the state's top providers, however, such as the Mayo Clinics, Abbott Northwestern, and Children's in Minneapolis and St. Paul, have been designated Tier II, and it will cost Blue Cross members more out-of-pocket to be treated at them.

According to Medica, these tiered plans show patients "the real value of provider performance." If you're young and healthy, have no known health conditions, no family—and don't expect to start one any time soon—the most cost-effective provider might be just fine for you. However, if you have—or plan to start—a family, you may want to think twice before cutting yourself off from high-quality specialty providers such as the Children's hospitals, with their neonatal intensive care and child-friendly surgical departments.

You can check data for the hospitals you're considering by going to www.minnesotahealthinfo.org and clicking on "Adverse Health Events in Minnesota." You can also do a quality check on hospitals and clinics by name or zip code through the **Joint Commission on Accreditation of Healthcare Organizations** web site (www.jcaho.org/). Please note that some hospitals are "Accredited with requirements for improvement," and you will have to download the full report to learn what those requirements might be.

Finding objective information about physicians is infinitely harder, but **Health Grades** (www.healthgrades.com) does rate hospitals, nursing homes, and doctors. You can research a doctor by name and find out his or her board certifications, education, training, and disciplinary actions, but not malpractice suits. **Public Citizen** also maintains a list of doctors who have been disciplined (www.questionabledoctors.org). To determine if a doctor is board certified in a specialty area, check with the **American Board of Medical Specialties** (866-275-2267, www.abms.org). In the state of Minnesota, complaints against health care providers—physicians, technicians, psychiatrists, etc.—are handled by the **Minnesota Board of Medical Practice** (www.bmp.state.mn.us). Contact them at University Park Plaza, 2829 University Avenue SE, Suite 400, Minneapolis 55414, 612-617-2130, webmaster@bmp.state.mn.us.

Of course, where choosing a physician is concerned, there is no substitute for word of mouth . . . Lacking that, however, the **Neighborhood Health Care Network** (651-489-CARE, 866-489-4899 toll-free outside the metro area, or www.nhcn.org) provides medical and dental referrals. Or buy the **Mpls/StPaul Magazine**'s annual special issue that lists the top docs in the Twin Cities (www.mspmag.com). Their information is usually pretty good. The trouble is that the physicians you're most interested in may not be part of your own provider network—which brings us to information about insurers and provider networks.

SERVICE PLANS

The following provide services to the majority of Minnesota residents:
- **Allina Health System**, 5601 Smetana Dr, Minnetonka, 55343, 952-992-2000, www.allina.com, owns Abbott Northwestern, Mercy, Unity, and United hospitals, Phillips Eye Institute, and Sister Kenny Rehabilitation Institute.
- **Blue Cross and Blue Shield of Minnesota**, 3535 Blue Cross Rd, Eagan, 55122, 651-662-8000, 1-800-382-2000, TDD 1-888-878-0137, www.bluecrossmn.com
- **Cigna**, www.cigna.com, has a growing presence in Minnesota, offering service through **Preferred One** and **Cigna Behavioral Health**. It also offers coverage for expatriate employees and travelers visiting outside the U.S., through **CIGNA International**, www.cigna.com/intl.

- **HealthPartner**s, Member Services, P.O. Box 1309, Minneapolis, 55440-1309, 952-883-5000, 800-883-2177, TTY 952-883-5127, www.health partners.com, operates a network of 22 clinics, primarily on the east side of the metro. It owns Regions Hospital and a large specialty center in St. Paul, and has affiliations with Abbott Northwestern, North Memorial, St. John's, Fairview Ridges, Children's, Mercy, and several hospitals in Wisconsin.
- **Mayo Health Plan**, 21 1st St NW, Rochester, 55902, 507-287-3329, www.mayo.edu, offers a full range of health services through a network of community-based providers, primarily in southern Minnesota; check out your health concerns on their web page.
- **Medica Health Plans**, P.O. Box 9310, Minneapolis, 55440-9310, 952-945-8000, 800-952-3455, TTY 952-992-3190 or 800-841-6753, www. medica.com, is Minnesota's largest Health Maintenance Organization (HMO) and Preferred Provider Organization (PPO), and second-largest insurer, and includes 96% of metro area physicians and hospitals/clinics in its plans.
- **Metropolitan Health Plan**, Member Services, 822 S 3rd St, Ste 140, Minneapolis, 55415, 612-347-8557, or 612-347-6308, www.mhp4life.org, is Hennepin County's licensed HMO. It provides care through Hennepin County Medical Center and a number of community clinics.
- **Patient Choice**, 952-992-1700, www.patientchoice.com, offers what it terms "value-based purchasing programs," which differentiate physicians and hospitals on measures of quality, cost, and service.
- **UCare Minnesota**, 2550 University Ave W, Ste 201-S, St. Paul, 55114, 651-647-2632, 612-676-3200, 800-203-7225, www.ucare.org, administers Medical Assistance, MinnesotaCare, and plans for seniors, and adults who have physical disabilities.
- **UnitedHealth**, 9900 Bren Rd E, Minnetonka, 55343, 800-328-5979, www.unitedhealthgroup.com, offers health savings accounts, "gap" coverage, and an AARP-branded Medicare drug plan.

COMPLAINTS

If you have a health care concern or complaint, contact the **Minnesota Attorney General's Office Consumer Division** (1400 NCL Tower, 445 Minnesota Street, St. Paul, MN 55101, 651-296-3353, TTY 711, www.ag.state. mn.us).

HEALTH CARE ASSISTANCE PROGRAMS

In addition to private health insurance, government plans cover some people. The plans are described in detail at www.dhs.state.mn.us. Here is a brief overview:
- **Medical Assistance** pays for medical care for low-income senior citizens, children and families, and people with disabilities. For information, contact your county human services agency, 651-296-7675 or TTY 711.
- **Medicare** is the federal government's health insurance program for people 65 and older and qualified disabled individuals of any age. For information

about Medicare eligibility or to apply for Medicare benefits, call the **Social Security Administration** at 800-772-1213, TTY 800-325-0778.

- **MinnesotaCare** is a minimal program for Minnesotans who do not have access to other health care insurance: 651-297-3862, 800-657-3672, www.dhs.state.mn.us.
- **Minnesota Prescription Drug Program** helps pay for prescription drugs for people who are age 65 and older or certified disabled. For information contact the Senior Linkage Line (800-333-2433) or call your county human services agency.
- **Minnesota RxConnect Online** enables people to order prescription medications from Canada; go to www.state.mn.us and click on MN RxConnect.

AREA HOSPITALS AND SPECIALTY CLINICS

The Attorney General's web site includes a downloadable copy of a Minnesota-legal "Advanced Health Care Directive," (www.ag.state.mn.us).

Below is a list of TC-area hospitals and special clinics, all in Minnesota unless otherwise noted:

- **Abbott Northwestern Hospital**, 800 E 28th St, Minneapolis, 55407, 612-863-4000, www.abbottnorthwestern.com
- **Anoka-Metro Regional Behavioral Treatment Center**, 3301 7th Ave N, Anoka, 55303, 763-712-4000
- **Bethesda Rehabilitation Hospital**, 559 Capitol Blvd, St Paul, 55103, 651-232-2300, www.bethesdahospital.org
- **Buffalo Hospital**, 303 Catlin St, Buffalo, 55313, 763-682-1212, buffalohospital.org
- **Cambridge Medical Center**, 701 S Dellwood St, Cambridge, 55008, 763-689-7700
- **Children's Hospitals and Clinics of Minnesota**, 2525 Chicago Ave S, Minneapolis, 55404, 612-813-6100, www.childrenshc.org
- **Children's Hospitals and Clinics of Minnesota—St. Paul, MN**, 345 N Smith Ave, St Paul, 55102, 651-220-6000, www.childrenshc.org
- **Fairview Northland Regional Hospital and Clinic**, 911 Northland Dr, Princeton, 55371, 763-389-1313, www.fairview.org
- **Fairview Ridges Hospital**, 201 E Nicollet Blvd, Burnsville, 55337, 952-892-2462, www.fairview.org
- **Fairview Southdale Hospital**, 6401 France Ave S, Edina, 55435-2199, 952-924-5000, www.fairview.org
- **Fairview-University Medical Center**, 2450 Riverside Ave, Minneapolis, 55455, 612-672-6000, www.fairview.org
- **Gillette Children's Specialty Healthcare**, 200 E University Ave, St Paul, 55101, 651-291-2848, www.gillettechildrens.org
- **Hennepin County Medical Center**, 701 Park Ave, Minneapolis, 55415, 612-873-3000, www.hcmc.org
- **Hudson Hospital**, 405 Stageline Rd, Hudson, WI 54016, 715-531-6000, www.hudsonhospital.org

- **Lakeview Memorial Hospital**, 927 W Churchill St, Stillwater, 55082, 651-439-5330, www.lakeview.org
- **Mayo Clinic**, 200 First St. SW, Rochester, 55905, 507-284-2511, www.mayoclinic.org/rochester
- **Mercy & Unity Hospitals**, 4050 Coon Rapids Blvd, Coon Rapids, 55433, 763-236-6000, www.mercyunity.allina.com
- **Methodist Hospital Park Nicollet Health Services**, 6500 Excelsior Blvd, St Louis Park, 55426, 952-993-5000, www.parknicollet.com (To reach the after-hours nurse line, call the number for your regular Park Nicollet clinic; the call will roll over to the nurse line if it's after 5 p.m.)
- **Monticello–Big Lake Community Hospital District**, 1013 Hart Blvd, Monticello, 55362, 763-295-2945, www.mblch.com
- **North Memorial Health Care**, 3300 Oakdale Ave N, Robbinsdale, 55422, 763-520-5200, www.northmemorial.com
- **Phillips Eye Institute**, 2215 Park Ave S, Minneapolis, 55404, 612-775-8800, www.phillipseyeinstitute.com
- **Regina Medical Center**, 1175 Nininger Rd, Hastings, 55033, 651-480-4100, www.reginamedical.org
- **Regions Hospital**, 640 Jackson St, St Paul, 55101, 651-254-2191, www.RegionsHospital.com
- **Ridgeview Medical Center**, 500 S Maple St, Waconia, 55387, 952-442-2191, www.ridgeviewmedical.org
- **River Falls Area Hospital**, 1629 E Division St, River Falls, WI 54022-1571, 715-425-6155
- **Shriners Hospitals for Children–Twin Cities**, 2025 E River Pkwy, Minneapolis, 55414, 612-596-6100, www.shrinershq.org
- **Sister Kenny Rehabilitation**, 800 E 28th St, Minneapolis, 55407, 612-863-4466, www.allina.com
- **St Cloud Hospital**, 1406 Sixth Ave N, St Cloud, 56303, 320-251-2700, www.centracare.com
- **St. Francis Regional Medical Center**, 1455 St. Francis Ave, Shakopee, 55379, 952-403-3000, www.Stfrancis-shakopee.com
- **St. John's Hospital**, 1575 Beam Ave, Maplewood, 55109, 651-232-7000, www.healtheast.org
- **St. Joseph's Hospital**, 69 W Exchange St, St Paul, 55102, 651-232-3122, www.healtheast.org
- **TRIA Orthopaedic Center**, 8100 Northland Dr, Edina, 55431, 952-831-TRIA (8742), www.tria.com
- **United Hospital**, 333 N Smith Ave, St Paul, 55102, 651-241-8000, www.allina.com
- **VA Medical Center–Minneapolis**, One Veterans Dr, Minneapolis, 55417, 612-725-2000, www.va.gov
- **Woodwinds Health Campus**, 1925 Woodwinds Dr, Woodbury, 55125, 651-232-6880, www.healtheast.org

MAKING HEALTH CARE AFFORDABLE

COMMUNITY CLINICS

Many community clinics use sliding fee scales based on income.

- **Annex Teen Clinic** (North Suburban Youth Health Clinic), 4915 N 42nd Ave, Robbinsdale, 763-533-1316, www.teenhealth411.org
- **Cedar-Riverside People's Center**, 425 20th Ave S, Minneapolis, 612-332-4973; this University of Minnesota clinic offers free or affordable primary care services to the community with the help of medical student volunteers.
- **Central Avenue Clinic**, 2610 Central Ave NE, Minneapolis, 612-781-6816; **Fremont Clinic**, 3300 Fremont Ave N, Minneapolis, 612-588-9411; Sheridan Women's and Children's Clinic, 612-362-4111, www.fremonthealth.org
- **Hennepin County Medical Center**, 701 Park Ave, Minneapolis, 612-873-3000, www.hcmc.org
- **Midwest Health Center for Women**, 33 S Fifth St, Fourth Floor, Minneapolis; 612-332-2311, Emergency 612-332-2314, 800-998-6075, www.midwesthealthcenter.org
- **Planned Parenthood of Minnesota/South Dakota**, 800-230-PLAN, www.ppmns.org, offers services to both men and women: 1200 Lagoon Ave, Minneapolis (Uptown), 612-823-6300; 6900 78th Ave N, Brooklyn Park, 763-560-3050; 2530 Horizon Dr, Burnsville, 952-890-0940; Centro de Salud, 1921 Chicago Ave S, Minneapolis, 612-813-8050, www.centromn.org; 451 E St. Germain St, Ste 100, St. Cloud, 320-252-9504; 1965 Ford Pkwy, St. Paul (Highland), 651-698-2406; 1700 Rice St (Crown Plaza), 651-489-1328. Emergency contraception, 888-NOT-2-LATE.
- **Red Door**, 525 Portland Ave S, Minneapolis, 612-348-6363, TTY 612-348-4729, www.co.hennepin.mn.us, provides confidential treatment for sexually transmitted diseases.
- **Robbinsdale Clinic**, P.A., 3819 W Broadway, Robbinsdale, 763-533-2534, is a primary care medical clinic that also offers first trimester abortion services. Note: check the address as people often confuse this clinic with the Robbinsdale Women's Center, which is located directly across the street.
- **St. Paul STD Clinic**, 555 Cedar St, Room 111, St. Paul, 651-266-1352, www.co.ramsey.mn.us/ph
- **TAMS (Teen Age Medical Service)**, 2425 Chicago Ave S, Minneapolis, 612-813-6125, www.childrenshc.org (click on "Clinics and Departments," then choose "Teen Age Medical Service" [TAMS]), is an adolescent outpatient program of Children's Hospitals and Clinics. TAMS also operates a school-based clinic at Southwest High School in Minneapolis.
- **Uptown Community Clinic (Neighborhood Involvement Program)**, 2431 Hennepin Ave S, Minneapolis, 612-374-4089
- **West Side Health Center**, 153 Concord St, St. Paul, 651-222-1816
- **West Suburban Teen Clinic**, 478 Second St, Excelsior, 952-474-3251, www.teenhealth411.org

- **Youth Emergency Service (Y.E.S.)**, 608 20th Ave S, Minneapolis, 612-339-7033

"MINUTECLINICS"

If you don't have time to sit in a doctor's waiting room, try the MinuteClinic at your local grocery store. Staffed by certified nurse practitioners and physicians' assistants, MinuteClinics provide quick, walk-in care for simple ailments such as strep throat, female bladder infections, or sinus infections. They also give flu shots. The charge for most services is $44. MinuteClinics are located adjacent to the pharmacies at select **Cub Foods**, **Target**, and **CVS** stores (952-929-1233, www.minuteclinic.com).

LOW-COST DENTAL

The **University of Minnesota School of Dentistry's Dental Clinics** provide general and special dental care in **Moos Health Sciences Tower**, 515 Delaware Street SE, Minneapolis, on the East Bank Campus. Fees vary based on the type of program in which you receive care, and are lowest in the predoctoral and dental hygiene programs where services typically cost 35% to 50% less than they would in the general community. To become a patient in the **Pre-doctoral D.D.S. clinical program**, call 612-624-8400 to schedule an initial appointment or 612-625-2495 for additional information. Treatment in the **Family Dentistry Clinic** generally costs 20% to 35% less than in the general community (612-625-5441). The U also has a **Faculty Practice Clinic**, where consultative and second-opinion services are provided by faculty specialists who are engaged in dental education and research (612-626-3233). Even those who are not already patients, but have a dental emergency during regular clinic hours, can call for help.

PRESCRIPTIONS

Minnesota Rx Connect Online is the State of Minnesota's web site that provides information on obtaining prescription drugs from Canada. Go to www.state.mn.us and click on Rx Connect (on the right-hand side of the page).

PRESCRIPTION ALERT

Recently some pharmacists have refused to fill prescriptions for emergency contraception and other birth control pills and devices. Minnesota law does not directly address the issue of a pharmacist's obligation to fill prescriptions, so in the interest of saving yourself a lot of trouble, be sure to ask the pharmacist if he/she will fill your prescription before you hand it over. If that pharmacist says no, most drug stores have policies that require that the pharmacist transfer the prescription to another nearby pharmacy or pharmacist, so that your prescription can be filled the same day. Be aware that this procedure has not always been followed, however, so it's better to find out up front.

PHARMACIES

Most large clinics have pharmacies. So do most **Cub** (www.cubpharmacy.com), **Target** (http://target.com/pharmacy), **Rainbow**, and **Byerly's** (www.byerlys.com) stores. Finding a pharmacy that's open at night, however, can be a challenge. The following locations have 24-hour pharmacies, and sometimes drive-up windows or home delivery.

- **Walgreens** stores, 1-800-WALGREENS, www.walgreens.com, offer drive-through service, and are open 24 hours at the following locations:
  - **Apple Valley**, Cedar Ave and County Rd 42, 952-432-5557
  - **Bloomington**, 9800 Lyndale Ave S, 952-884-8246
  - **Brooklyn Park**, Corner of Zane and Brooklyn Blvd, 763-566-8350
  - **Champlin**, 11401 Market Pl Rd, 763-427-6389
  - **Coon Rapids**, Corner of University and Egret, 763-755-1259
  - **Eden Prairie**, Northeast corner of Eden Prairie Rd and Hwy 5, 952-937-2934
  - **Edina**, 6975 York Ave, 952-920-3561
  - **Hopkins/St. Louis Park**, 540 Blake Rd and Hwy 7, 952-938-1168
  - **Minneapolis**, 4547 Hiawatha, 612-722-4249
  - **Plymouth**, Vinewood Ln and Rockford Rd, 763-553-9731
  - **Savage**, Northwest corner of County Rd 13 and County Rd 42, 952-226-1283
  - **West St. Paul**, Robert St at Butler Ave, 651-455-5590
  - **White Bear Lake**, Hwy 96 and Centerville Rd, 651-426-9225
  - **Woodbury**, Northeast corner of Donegal and Valley Creek, 651-735-0722
- **CVS/pharmacy**, 1-800-SHOPCVS, www.cvs.com, has in-store MinuteClinics, and will deliver prescriptions to your door. They operate an online pharmacy as well as about a dozen stores in the Twin Cities, most of them north of I-94.
- **Snyder Drugs**, 952-935-5441, 888-248-8880, www.snyderdrug.com, which was founded in Minneapolis in the 1920s, has numerous stores scattered throughout the Twin Cities. They offer home delivery for a small fee, and many locations have drive-up windows.

HEALTH LAW—PROTECTING PRIVATE INFORMATION

Minnesota has a number of state laws that restrict the use and dissemination of personal health information by health care providers. The general rule is that a provider cannot share your health information with a third party unless you have given written consent or there is a law that authorizes the provider to share your information. If you believe your right to privacy has been violated, contact the **Minnesota Attorney General's Office** (651-296-3353) for assistance with your complaint.

D OGS (AND, SOMETIMES, CATS) IN THE TWIN CITIES METRO AREA must be licensed and vaccinated. Call your city hall for information about your city's pet ordinances.

VETERINARY CARE

If you don't have any personal recommendations, look in the Yellow Pages or call the **Minnesota Veterinary Medical Association** (651-645-7533), whose membership includes 900 licensed veterinarians throughout the state. For emergency needs, check the **Useful Numbers** chapter of this book under **Veterinarians, Emergency**. When in doubt, call the **University of Minnesota 24-hour line** (612-625-9711).

In Minnesota, heartworm medication is given May–November, following a blood test by your veterinarian. To control ticks and fleas, many pet owners use an externally applied systemic flea and tick medication such as Top Spot or Bio-Spot. Those who intend to take their pets to Wisconsin or rural areas or Up North should consider vaccinating them against Lyme disease.

PET ADOPTION

For those who want to adopt a pet, a local animal shelter is a good place to begin. Kittens and puppies will come with their first vaccinations and a discount coupon to have them spayed or neutered. Area shelters include:

- **Animal Humane Society**, 845 N Meadow Ln, Golden Valley, 763-522-4325; Lost and Found, 763-522-7130; Boarding, 763 489 2222; email: boarding@animalhumanesociety.org
- **Humane Society of Ramsey County**, 1115 Beulah Ln, St. Paul (by the Como Park Zoo), 651-645-7387
- **Minnesota Valley Humane Society**, 1313 E Hwy 13, Burnsville, 952-894-5000
- **St. Croix Animal Shelter**, 9785 Hudson Rd, Woodbury, 651-730-6008

For those who want to adopt a purebred dog, most breed clubs include rescue groups that are dedicated to finding loving homes for abandoned dogs of their specific breed. A good place for the Internet-inclined is the **American Kennel Club**'s web site (www.akc.org/breeds/rescue), which provides links to the national breed clubs' rescue organizations. Those looking to buy a purebred puppy can connect with breeders at local dog shows, or contact the **Minnesota Purebred Dog Breeders Association**, www.geocities.com/mpdba.

PET STORES

- **Manitou Mutts Antiques, Pet Grooming and Gear**, 5413 Manitou Rd (Hwy 19), Tonka Bay, 952-380-1364; buy some jewelry for yourself, a jeweled collar for your dog, a T-shirt for your cat, a four-poster, a couple of bags of fresh-baked treats, and get your pet a manicure . . . it's unique!
- **Bone Adventure**, http://boneadventure.com: 726 E Lake St, Wayzata, 952-473-0227; 5045 France Ave S, Edina, 612-920-2201; 312 E Hennepin Ave, Minneapolis, 612-378-0211
- **PETCO**, www.petco.com, 13691 Ridgedale Dr, Minnetonka, 952-541-1981 (check White Pages for other locations); stores offer pet food and supplies plus veterinary, grooming, dog training, pet photography, and doggie day camp.
- **PetSmart**, www.petsmart.com: 1640 New Brighton Blvd, Minneapolis, 612-788-7045; 5640 Cedar Lake Rd, St. Louis Park, 952-797-9798; 1410 University Ave W, St. Paul, 651-641-1256; 5660 Main St NE, Fridley, 763-502-0102; 1100 W 78th St, Richfield, 612-798-3665; 4190 Vinewood Ln, Plymouth, 763-551-8999 (check the White Pages for other locations). Stores feature pet foods and supplies, grooming, and veterinary services.
- **Petstuff**, 14665 Excelsior Blvd, Minnetonka, 952-930-9383, is a locally owned non-chain store.

DOGS

About the same number of people own dogs in the Twin Cities as have children, approximately 33%. As a result, the number of dog parks and dog-related businesses in the area has exploded. Those listed below will give you a start at finding the services you need for your pet.

DOG WALKERS, BOARDING AND DAYCARE

What to do when going out of town without Fido? Call a pet service. Those in the Southwest Metro might try **Pampered Paws** (952-906-0303). Other boarding kennels that have good word-of-mouth are **Paws, Claws and Hooves Pet Boarding** (10500 Great Plains Boulevard, Chanhassen, 952-445-7991) and **The Dog House Boarding Kennels** (3505 W Wayzata Boulevard, Orono, 952-473-9026). In the North Metro, **Armstrong Ranch Kennels** (8404 161st Avenue NW, Anoka, 763-427-1777, www.armstrongkennels.com) is the largest boarding and training facility in the Midwest. On the edge of Minneapolis, the **Animal Humane Society** (845 Meadow Lane North,

Golden Valley, 763-489-2222, www.ahshc.org, email: boarding@animal
humanesociety.org) boards dogs, cats, rabbits, ferrets, and other small animals.
In Hopkins, daycare, obedience, and agility can be found at **Cloud Nine
Training and Daycare for Dogs** (8 12th Avenue South, 952-939-9174,
http://cloudninetraining.com). For other boarding/daycare suggestions, check
with your vet and other pet owners. Pet sitters and boarding facilities are
found under "Pet Boarding and Sitting" and "Kennels" in the Yellow Pages.
Local online resources include **www.pet-net.net/usa/minnesota.htm**,
www.dogromp.org, and **www.petsittersmn.org**. Be sure to ask for and
check references.

DOG TRAINING

For beginners through experts, for those who want to compete, or who want
to participate in activities like flyball, agility or tracking, the training clubs listed
below will help you train your dog—and be there to commiserate with you
when he/she stops in mid-course to smell the hotdogs. Those interested in flyball should check out the www.flyballdogs.com web site for team information.
For a listing of most of the breed and training clubs in the area, check out
BarkBytes (www.barkbytes.com).
- **Animal Inn**, 651-777-2317, www.animalinnboardingkennel.com, has
  facilities in Golden Valley, Eagan, and Lake Elmo.
- **Bloomington Obedience Training Club**, 8127 Pleasant Ave S, 952-
  888-4998, www.botcmn.org
- **Canine U** classes are specifically designed for family pets. Classes start every
  few weeks at the Minnesota Valley Humane Society, 1313 Hwy 13 E in Burnsville
  and other South Metro locations; 952-894-5000, www.mvhspets.com.
- **Cloud Nine Training and Daycare for Dogs**, 8 12th Ave S, Hopkins,
  952-939-9174, http://cloudninetraining.com
- **Dog Works** teaches obedience but specializes in agility, 6338 Carlson Dr,
  Eden Prairie, 952-949-0099, www.dogworksinc.com.
- **Total Recall**, 17285 Forest Blvd, Hugo, 651-464-1799, www.trdogs.com
- **Training Camp Inc.**, Heavenwood Farm, Stillwater, 612-922-1114; herd-
  ing classes.
- **Twin Cities Obedience Training Club**, 2101 NE Broadway St,
  Minneapolis, 612-379-1332, www.tcotc.com

DOG PARKS

It's getting easier to find a place to exercise your dog off-leash, as more parks (and
even some new subdivisions) are fencing in spaces in which people may exercise
their pets. The **Responsible Owners of Mannerly Pets (ROMP)** web site,
www.dogromp.org, lists dog parks in the metro area, and provides pictures,
directions, and downloadable permit forms. Indoor dog play areas for small dogs
are still scarce, but can often be found in doggy daycare facilities. There is a fee for
indoor play. Outdoor play areas usually require either a park pass or permit.

INDOOR PLAY AREAS FOR SMALL DOGS

- **Dog Days,** 1752 Grand Ave, St. Paul, 651-696-1817, has both indoor and outdoor play space.
- **Downtown Dogs,** 821 2nd Ave N, Minneapolis, 612-374-DOGS, www.downtowndogsminneapolis.com, offers daycare, training, and trainer-supervised play.
- **Pet Junction,** 157 W County Rd E, Shoreview (roughly 694 & Rice St), 651-490-0026, www.petjunctiononline.com, offers training classes and open small dog playtimes.

OUTDOOR PLAY AREAS

- **Dakota County**:
    - **Burnsville Alimagnet Dog Park**, 1200 Alimagnet Pkwy (off County Road 11), 952-895-4500, http://www.alimagnetdogpark.org/; 7 acres, fenced; open daily, 5 a.m. to 10 p.m.
- **Hennepin County:**
    - **Bloomington Dog Park** on 111th St between Nesbitt and Hampshire Aves; approximately 25 acres including a swimming hole; partially fenced; pet license required; open daily, dawn to 10 p.m.
    - **Lake of the Isles Park**, 2845 E Lake of the Isles Pkwy (Lake of the Isles Pkwy and W 28th St); 2.6 acres. Fully fenced.
    - **Minnehaha Park**, 5399 S Minnehaha Ave (east of the intersection of Hiawatha Ave S and 54th St); 4.2 acres along the Mississippi River. Partially fenced. Beach.
- **Ramsey County**: All parks open daily from sunrise to sunset; permits not required; 651-266-8500, www.co.ramsey.mn.us/parks
    - **St. Paul, ArlArk**—Arlington/Arkwright Off-Leash Dog Area (on the corner of Arlington Ave and Arkwright St); 4.5 acres. Fully fenced. Open daily from sunrise to 9 p.m.; permit not required.
    - **White Bear Lake, Otter Lake** (Otter Lake Rd); 10 acres. Partially fenced. 1 separate acre is fully fenced for small dogs. The dog park entrance is next to the boat launch.
- **Three Rivers Park District**; Park permit required (1 per dog), 763-559-9000, www.threeriversparkdistrict.org:
    - **Osseo** (Hennepin County): **Elm Creek Park Reserve**, 13351 Elm Creek Rd; over 30 acres. Fenced. Swimming.
    - **Prior Lake** (Scott County): **Cleary Lake Regional Park** (near Prior Lake on Scott County Rd 27); 35 acres with pond. Fenced. Trails are mowed in summer, packed in winter.

DOG SHOWS

Watch for notice of the following major shows in the newspaper: **Land O'Lakes Kennel Club**: January, RiverCentre, St. Paul; **Lake Minnetonka Kennel Club**: June at the Waconia Fairgrounds; **St. Croix Valley Kennel Club**: August at the Washington County Fairgrounds; **Minneapolis Kennel Club**: November, Canterbury Downs, Shakopee, www.minneapoliskc.org

MINNESOTA'S CLIMATE MAY BE COLD, BUT LOCAL CULTURE IS ON *fire*—and it isn't all polka bands and *A Prairie Home Companion*, either. It's three Tony Award–winning theater companies—the Guthrie, Children's Theater, and Theatre de la Jeune Lune—and other arts and entertainments are as diverse as the calligraphed St. John's Bible and the always-quirky **Fringe Festival** (www.fringefestival.org), eleven days of live stage performances in a variety of neighborhood venues throughout Minneapolis. Then there's Walker Art Center, internationally famous for its contemporary exhibits, and its venerable traditional counterpart, the Minneapolis Institute of Art. The Minnesota Orchestra and St. Paul Chamber Orchestra are held in high regard by classical music aficionados everywhere, and the Grammy Award–winning group Sounds of Blackness got its start at Macalester College in St. Paul. Popular music acts from Bob Dylan to Soul Asylum to Prince, Atmosphere, Har Mar Superstar, and Marcy Playground (named for the Marcy Open School in Minneapolis) originated in the thriving club scene here. Did we mention the hundreds of small galleries, ballet troupes, and avant-garde theater stages? By some measures, the arts activity is hotter here than it is in New York. And while Minnesotans don't dance in the aisles, they nearly always show their appreciation for performers with a standing ovation.

TICKETS

Ticket prices are lower than New York's, but you can still drop a bundle on a good seat. The best prices come with series tickets, but if you take training as an usher you can often enjoy performances for free. Many venues have their own box offices, and most organizations sell tickets online. **Ticketmaster** (651-989-5151, www.ticketmaster.com) has a user-friendly web site as well as ticket centers located at Macy's Twin Cities stores and Coburn's Super Store in Elk River. Pick up discount "Treatseats" at the ticket centers and you'll save on performances, museums, and many events. For community-level events such as Designers' Showhouses and the Fringe Festival, check out www.ticketworks.com

or **Uptown Tix** (612-604-4466, www.uptowntix.com). Finally, season ticket holders often turn in tickets they can't use, so sometimes a last-minute call to the box office will net you the best seats in the house.

MUSIC–SYMPHONIC, CHORAL, OPERA, CHAMBER

The level of artistry in the Twin Cities is extraordinary. For classical music, start with the **Minnesota Orchestra** (www.minnesotaorchestra.org) and **St. Paul Chamber Orchestra** (www.thespco.org), or take your pick from the following:

- **American Composers' Forum**, 332 Minnesota St, #E145, St. Paul, 651-228-1407, www.composersforum.org, presents concerts that showcase emerging composers.
- **Minnesota Boychoir**, 651-292-3219, www.boychoir.org; this concert choir, made up of 48 boys ages 8–14 from all over the Twin Cities, performs at churches, the Minnesota Orchestra, and the Guthrie Theater—when they're not away on tour.
- **Minnesota Chorale**, 612-333-4866, www.mnchorale.org; this 150-voice chorus performs regularly with the Minnesota Orchestra and the St. Paul Chamber Orchestra.
- **Minnesota Opera**, 620 N 1st St, Minneapolis, 612-333-6669, www.mnopera.org; this professional opera company has achieved an international reputation for originating opera productions. The company offers four main-stage productions each season at the Ordway Music Theatre, as well as an acclaimed educational touring production.
- **Minnesota Orchestra**, Orchestra Hall, 1111 Nicollet Mall, Minneapolis, 612-371-5656, 800-292-4141, www.minnesotaorchestra.org; courtesy parking is available in front of Orchestra Hall while you are visiting the Box Office. For those who aren't too sure about "highbrow" music, be sure to catch **Sommerfest**, a four-week festival of food, dancing, and some free concerts presented every summer from July into August.
- **Minnesota Youth Symphonies**, 790 Cleveland Ave S, Ste 203, St. Paul, 651-699-5811, www.mnyouthsymphonies.org, provides preprofessional orchestral training for children, elementary through college levels. Three major concerts are presented each season at Orchestra Hall, Minneapolis and O'Shaughnessy Auditorium, St. Paul.
- **VocalEssence** is an arts outreach program of the Plymouth Congregational Church in Minneapolis. This innovative series hosts world-famous orchestral and choral performers and assists emerging composers. Call 612-624-2345 for tickets or visit their web site at www.vocalessence.org, where you can read their concert previews.
- **The Saint Paul Chamber Orchestra**, Hamm Building, Ste 500, 408 St. Peter St, St. Paul, 651-291-1144, www.thespco.org; for a newcomer's kit that includes a voucher for two tickets for the price of one, call 651-291-1144. Order tickets online on its web page.
- **The Schubert Club**, 302 Landmark Center, 75 W Fifth St, St. Paul, 651-292-3268, www.schubert.org

COMMUNITY MUSIC

There are over a hundred community bands in the state, according to the Minnesota Community Band Resource Center. There are also nearly innumerable community choral societies, orchestras, and musical theaters, ranging from ensembles of professionals to volunteer organizations whose purpose is simply to give people who love music a chance to participate. So if you're interested in playing, this list of organizations will give you a place to get started. If you're only interested in listening, these groups are a treat—and their concerts are usually free! For a comprehensive listing of community bands and links to bands that have web pages as well as a calendar of local band concerts, visit the **Community Band Resource Center** web page at www.visi.com/~diazwalby/band.html.

- **Apollo Male Chorus**, Eisenhower Community Center, Hwy 7, Hopkins, 952-933-6322, www.apollomalechorus.com; this is ranked one of the top ten male choruses in the world.
- **Greater Twin Cities Youth Symphonies**, 528 Hennepin Ave, Minneapolis, 612-870-7611, www.gtcys.org
- **Medalist Concert Band**, www.medalistband.com; this 70-member adult concert band has been described by the National Band Association as "one of the foremost community bands in the nation." It presents over 20 concerts each year throughout the area at venues including the Lake Harriet Bandshell.
- **Metropolitan Boys Choir**, Minneapolis, 612-827-6501, www.mbchoir.com
- **Minneapolis Pops Orchestra**, www.mplspops.org; this group of professional musicians play together only in July at Lake Harriet in the Bandshell, in a concert tradition that started over 100 years ago.
- **Music Association of Minnetonka**, 18285 Hwy 7, Minnetonka, 952-401-5954, www.musicassociation.org
- **Star of the North Concert Band**, www.starofthenorth.org, performs locally at parks all over the metro area, and their international credits include Australia and New Zealand, Wales and England.
- **Twin Cities Gay Men's Chorus**, 528 Hennepin Ave, Ste 701, Minneapolis, 612-339-SONG, www.tcgmc.org

MUSIC—CONTEMPORARY

The Twin Cities have a long, rich history of great popular music. From Bob Dylan, who started out playing the coffeehouses of Cedar-Riverside, to Brother Ali, Prince, and Har Mar Superstar rocking the house at First Avenue, to garage-rock bands such as the Jayhawks, the Replacements, and Soul Asylum, and country-blues stars like Little Jonny Lang, the Twin Cities have been and continue to be a place to catch great gigs and perhaps experience music history in the making.

Little known fact: the disco-era hit "Funkytown" was written by Minneapolis ad man Steven Greenberg and sung by Cynthia Johnson, a secretary at the Maplewood Police Department. It topped the charts for four weeks back in May 1980, and went platinum again in 2005 on the "Shrek 2" soundtrack. You can see Funkytown's original gold record at The Minneapolis Hard Rock Cafe, 600 Hennepin Avenue, which also displays Prince memorabilia.

The following venues are best known for the category under which they're listed, although many of them book acts of every genre. Tickets for almost all the venues can be purchased from **Ticketmaster** (www.ticketmaster.com).

BLUES

- **Famous Dave's Blues and BBQ**, 3001 Hennepin (Uptown), Minneapolis, 612-822-9900, www.famousdaves.com
- **Minnesota Music Café**, just off the corner of 7th St E and Payne, on the edge of downtown St. Paul near Metropolitan State University, 651-776-4699, www.minnesotamusiccafe.com; this is where Little Blues Brother Jim Belushi, Mick Jagger, Jonny Lang, and Keb' Mo' go to jam when they're in town.

COUNTRY, BLUEGRASS

- **Dulono's**, 607 W Lake St, Minneapolis, 612-827-1726; this family-style restaurant/biker/police hangout is home to jam sessions on the first and third Wednesdays of every month, and live music with no cover charge on weekends.
- **Homestead Pickin' Parlor**, 6625 Penn Ave S, Richfield, 612-861-3308, www.homesteadpickinparlor.com

DINNER AND DANCING

- **Babalu**, 800 Washington Ave N, Minneapolis, 612-746-3158, www.babalu.us, offers authentic Caribbean cuisine and live Latin jazz on weekends.

FOLK

- **Cedar Cultural Centre**, 416 Cedar Ave S, Minneapolis, 612-338-2674, www.thecedar.org
- **Ginkgo Coffeehouse**, 721 N Snelling Ave, St. Paul, 651-645-2647, www.ginkgocoffee.com

IRISH AND CELTIC

- **The Liffey**, 175 W 7th St, St. Paul, 651-556-1420, www.theliffey.com
- **The Local**, 931 Nicollet Mall, Minneapolis, 612-904-1000, www.the-local.com
- **O'Gara's Irish Pub and Restaurant/O'Gara's Garage**, 164 N Snelling Ave, St. Paul, 651-644-3333, www.ogaras.com

JAZZ

- **Dakota Jazz Club and Restaurant**, 1010 Nicollet Ave S, Minneapolis, 612-332-1010, www.dakotacooks.com
- **Dixie's**, 695 Grand Ave, St. Paul, 651-222-7345, www.dixiesongrand.com
- **Fine Line Music Cafe**, 318 First Ave N, Minneapolis, 612-338-8100, www.finelinemusic.com

POLKA, LOUNGE MUSIC

- **Nye's Polonaise Room**, 112 Hennepin Ave E, Minneapolis, 612-379-2021, www.nyespolonaise.com; the only place you're likely to hear "The World's Most Dangerous Polka Band."

ROCK/HIP HOP/R&B

- **Bunkers Music Bar and Grill**, 761 Washington Ave N, Minneapolis, 612-338-8188, www.bunkersmusic.com, features homemade gravy and local bands.
- **First Avenue and 7th St Entry**, 701 1st Ave N, Minneapolis, 612-338-83885, www.first-avenue.com; parking nearby in lots and ramps.
- **The Quest Club**, 110 5th St N (Wyman Building), Minneapolis, 612-338-3383, www.thequestclub.com
- **Station 4**, 201 E 4th St (at Sibley St in Lowertown), St. Paul, 651-298-0173, www.station-4.com
- **Triple Rock Social Club**, 620 Cedar Ave, Minneapolis, 612-333-7399, www.triplerocksocialclub.com
- **Turf Club**, 1601 University Ave, St. Paul, 651-647-0486, www.turfclub.net

SPORTS BARS

- **Mac's Industrial**, 312 Central Ave SE (University and Central, where Southeast turns into Northeast), Minneapolis, 612-379-3379, www.macsindustrial.com
- **Alary's**, 139 7th St E, St. Paul, 651-224-7717, www.alarys.com, runs a shuttle over to the Excel Center and allows smoking.

TEEN/ALL-AGES CLUBS

- **The Garage**, 75 Civic Center Pkwy, Burnsville, 952-895-4664, www.thegarage.net; open weekdays from 2:30 p.m. to 5:30 or 6:00 p.m., and on Fridays and Saturdays until 11:30 p.m. Staffed by paid employees and volunteers and featuring local teen performers.

NIGHTCLUBS AND DISCOS

- **Bryant-Lake Bowl**, 810 W Lake St, Minneapolis, Ticketline 612-825-8949, www.bryantlakebowl.com
- **Gay 90s**, 408 Hennepin Ave, Minneapolis, 612-333-7755, www.gay90s.com
- **Loring Pasta Bar and Kitty Kat Klub**, 315 14th Ave SE, Minneapolis, 612-331-9800, www.loringcafe.com
- **The Myth Nightclub**, 3090 Southlawn Dr; for tickets call Ticketmaster, 651-989-5151, www.mythnightclub.com
- **Star Central**, 4005 Central Ave, Columbia Heights, 763-788-6673, http://starcentrallive.com
- **Varsity Theater and Café des Artistes**, 1308 Fourth St SE (Dinkytown), Minneapolis, 612-604-0222, www.varsitytheater.org

CONCERT HALLS, ARENAS

- **Benson Great Hall, Bethel College**, 3900 Bethel Dr, Arden Hills, 651-638-6333, www.bethel.edu
- **Fitzgerald Theater**, 10 E Exchange St, St. Paul, 651-290-1221, www.fitzgeraldtheater.publicradio.org; home base for Garrison Keillor's long-running nationally broadcast *A Prairie Home Companion* radio show.
- **Guthrie Theater**, 818 Second St S, Minneapolis, 612-377-2224, www.guthrietheater.org
- **Landmark Center**, 75 W 5th St, St. Paul, 651-292-3233, www.landmarkcenter.org
- **Northrop Auditorium**, 84 Church St SE, Minneapolis, 612-624-2345, www.northrop.umn.edu
- **Orchestra Hall**, 1111 Nicollet Mall, Minneapolis, 612-371-5656 or 800-292-4141, www.minnesotaorchestra.org
- **Ordway Music Theater**, 345 Washington St, St. Paul, 651-224-4222, www.ordway.org
- **O'Shaughnessy Auditorium**, 2004 Randolph Ave, St. Paul, 651-690-6700, www.stkate.edu/oshaughnessy
- **RiverCentre/Roy Wilkins Auditorium/XCEL Energy Center**, 175 Kellogg Blvd, St. Paul, 651-726-8240, www.xcelenergycenter.com
- **Target Center**, 600 1st Ave N, Minneapolis, 612-673-0900, www.targetcenter.com; the 5th and 7th St ramps are connected to the center by skyways.

MUSIC LESSONS

- **Homestead Pickin' Parlor**, 6625 Penn Ave S, Richfield, 612-861-3308, www.homesteadpickinparlor.com
- **MacPhail Center for the Arts**, 1128 LaSalle St, Minneapolis, 612-321-0100, www.macphail.org
- **Rymer-Hadley Center for the Arts**, 1910 County Rd B W, Roseville, 651-604-3750, www.rymerhadley.org

- **West Bank School of Music**, 1813 S 6th St, Minneapolis, 612-333-6651, www.westbankmusic.org

DANCE

PERFORMANCE GROUPS

Some of the following groups are cross-listed below as organizations that also offer dance lessons:
- **Ballet Arts Minnesota**, 528 Hennepin Ave, Minneapolis, 612-340-1071, www.balletartsminnesota.org
- **Ballet of the Dolls**, 820 18th Ave NE, Minneapolis, 612-623-7660, www.balletofthedolls.org
- **Ethnic Dance Theater**, 2337 Central Ave NE, Minneapolis, 612-782-3970, www.ethnicdancetheatre.com
- **Minnesota Dance Theater**, 528 Hennepin Ave, Minneapolis, 612-338-0627, www.mndance.org
- **Zenon Dance Company**, 528 Hennepin Ave, Minneapolis, www.zenon dance.org

LESSONS

- **Attitude Dance** teaches group and private classes in swing, waltz, tango, etc., 651-245-6670, http://attitudedancing.com.
- **Ballet Arts Minnesota**, 528 Hennepin Ave, Minneapolis, 612-340-1071, www.balletartsminnesota.org
- **Ballet of the Dolls**, 820 18th Ave NE, Minneapolis, 612-623-7660, www.balletofthedolls.org
- **Ballet Minnesota/Classical Ballet Academy of Minnesota**, 249 E 4th St, St. Paul, 651-222-7199, www.balletminnesota.org
- **Foster's DanceSport Studio**, 816 1/2 Main St, Hopkins, 952-938-0048, www.fostersdancesport.com
- **Tapestry Folk Dance Center**, 3748 Minnehaha Ave S, Minneapolis, 612-722-2914, www.tapestryfolkdance.org
- **Zenon Dance Company**, 528 Hennepin Ave, Minneapolis, 612-338-1101, www.zenondance.org

THEATERS

The Twin Cities have something for everyone—from Broadway musicals to avant-garde experiments, plus all the new shows that preview here before opening on Broadway.
- **Brave New Workshop**, 2605 Hennepin Ave S, Minneapolis, and 17 W 7th Pl, St. Paul, 612-332-6620, www.bravenewworkshop.com, is the nation's oldest ongoing satiric theatre.
- **Cedar Cultural Center**, 416 Cedar Ave S, Minneapolis, 612-338-2674, www.thecedar.org

- **Chanhassen Dinner Theatres**, 501 W 78th St, Chanhassen, 952-934-1500, www.chanhassentheatres.com
- **Children's Theatre Company**, 2400 3rd Ave S, Minneapolis, 612-874-0400, www.childrenstheatre.org
- **Great American History Theatre**, 30 E 10th St, St. Paul, 651-292-4323, www.historytheatre.com
- **Guthrie Theater**, 818 Second St S, Minneapolis; and **Guthrie Lab**, 700 N 1st St, Minneapolis, Box Office 612-377-2224, 877-44STAGE, TTY 612-377-6626, www.guthrietheater.org
- **Jungle Theater**, 2951 Lyndale Ave S, Minneapolis, 612-822-4002, www.jungletheater.com, presents both contemporary and classic plays as well as numerous community outreach/education programs for all ages. This is a great place to volunteer!
- **Old Log Theater**, 5175 Meadville St, Excelsior, 952-474-5951, www.old log.com, is the oldest continuously operating dinner theater. It stages comedies and British farces.
- **Ordway Music Theatre**, 345 Washington St, St. Paul, 651-224-4222, www.ordway.org
- **Orpheum, Pantages, and State Theatres**, 910, 710, and 805 Hennepin Ave, Minneapolis, 612-339-7007, www.hennepintheatre district.com
- **Penumbra Theatre Company**, 270 Kent St, St. Paul (Selby-Dale), 651-224-3180, is Minnesota's only African-American professional theater company.
- **Plymouth Playhouse**, 2705 Annapolis Ln (I-494 and Hwy 55), Plymouth, 763-553-1600, www.plymouthplayhouse.com, is home of the long-running musical, "How to Talk Minnesotan."
- **Stages Theatre Company**, 1111 Main St, Hopkins, 952-979-1111, www.stagestheatre.org
- **Theatre de la Jeune Lune**, 105 N 1st St, Minneapolis, Box Office 612-333-6200, www.jeunelune.org

MOVIE THEATERS

If it's first run, major studio blockbusters you enjoy, the Twin Cities can offer you a mega-multiplex in downtown Minneapolis or practically any major mall. But if your taste runs to classics, documentaries, or little gems given limited release, ah . . . , then you have really moved to the right place: the Uptown, Lagoon, and Parkway all show independent releases; the University of Minnesota Film Society (Minnesota Film Arts) shows a combination of international movies and genre-based retrospectives and documentaries at the Bell Auditorium and Oak Street Theater; the Walker Art Center and Minneapolis Institute of Art host film screenings in conjunction with other programs; and the Science Museum of Minnesota and Minnesota Zoo each have theaters designed to make you feel like you're part of the action. For all the local listings, check the newspapers or look online at www.startribune.com/movieguide, or twincities.citysearch.com/section/movies

COMEDY

Some clubs feature comics on certain nights only. Call for schedules.
- **The Brave New Workshop**, www.bravenewworkshop.org, 2605 Hennepin Ave S, Minneapolis, 612-332-6620, and 17 W 7th Pl, St. Paul, 612-332-6620
- **Bryant-Lake Bowl Show Lounge**, 810 W Lake St, Minneapolis, 612-825-8949, www.bryantlakebowl.com

CULTURE FOR KIDS

- **Children's Theatre Company**, 3rd Ave S, Minneapolis, 612-874-0400, www.childrenstheatre.org, is the Twin Cities' premier children's theatre.
- **The Flint Hills International Children's Festival**, Rice Park, St. Paul, www.ordway.org; sponsored by the Ordway Center for the Performing Arts and Flint Hills Resources, this celebration of arts from around the world includes performances, food, and take-home projects.
- **MacPhail Center for the Arts**, 1128 LaSalle St, Minneapolis, 612-321-0100, www.macphail.org; music, theater, and dance lessons for children (and adults).
- **Minnetonka Center for the Arts**, 2240 N Shore Dr, Wayzata, 952-473-7361, www.minnetonkaarts.org, offers numerous classes for kids (and adults).
- **Minnesota Children's Museum**, 10 W 7th St, Downtown St. Paul, 651-225-6000, www.MCM.org; buttons, gizmos, interactive make-believe, a theater, and hands-on exhibits that change frequently make every trip an adventure. Admission is free on the third Sunday of every month.
- **Minnesota Orchestra**, www.minnesotaorchestra.org, presents "KinderKonzerts" to school groups and special family concerts for the general public.
- **Stages Theatre**, 1111 Main St, Hopkins, Box Office 952-979-1111, Administration 952-979-1123, www.stagestheatre.org, is a professional theater environment that offers terrific classes for even very young children who are interested in theater.
- **Stepping Stone Theatre for Youth Development**, Landmark Center, 75 W 5th St, St. Paul, 651-225-9265, www.steppingstonetheatre.org, offers numerous classes and performing arts camps. Street parking is limited, but ramp parking is available nearby.

ART

"Gallery crawls"—nights when all the studios are open—are popular in both Minneapolis and St. Paul warehouse districts. Call a gallery and they'll tell you where and when these fun events take place. In Spring, keep your eyes open for ads announcing **Art-A-Whirl**, the six-square-mile, free-floating studio party/art sale presented by the Northeast Minneapolis Arts Association, www.nemaa.org.

EVENTS AND MUSEUMS

- **Minneapolis Institute of Arts**, 2400 S 3rd Ave, Minneapolis, 612-870-3131, www.artsmia.org
- **Minnesota Museum of American Art**, 50 W Kellogg Blvd, St. Paul, 651-266-1030, www.mmaa.org; check out the museum's Art Here First Fridays, which are single night exhibitions of art and music designed to introduce and celebrate communities of artists in the Twin Cities.
- **The Museum of Russian Art**, 5500 Stevens Ave S, Minneapolis, 612-821-9045, www.tmora.org, is the only institution in the United States dedicated to Russian art.
- **The Northrup King Building** is home to over a hundred artists, www.northrupkingbuilding.com.
- **St. Paul Art Crawl**, Lowertown and Downtown St. Paul, 651-292-4373, artcrawl.org
- **Walker Art Center**, 1750 Hennepin Ave, Minneapolis, 612-375-7560, www.walkerart.org
- **Frederick R. Weisman Art Museum**, 333 E River Rd, U of Minnesota, Minneapolis, 612-625-9494, is best known for its collection of American art from the first decades of the twentieth century.

HISTORY AND CULTURAL MUSEUMS

- **American Swedish Institute**, 2600 Park Ave, Minneapolis, 612-871-4907
- **Bell Museum of Natural History**, U of Minnesota, Minneapolis, 10 Church St SE, Minneapolis (the corner of 17th and University), 612-624-7083, www.bellmuseum.org. Fun for kids—a slumber party at the Bell: bring your sleeping bags, explore the museum by flashlight, and fall asleep to a spooky animal bedtime story.
- **Historic Fort Snelling State Park**, Hwy 5 at Hwy 55, Minneapolis, 612-726-1171; costumed guides present demonstrations, give tours, and talk to you like it's still 1827.
- **Mill City Museum**, 704 S Second St, Minneapolis, 612-341-7555, www.mnhs.org; built within the ruins of the Washburn A Mill, this river-front museum chronicles the flour milling industry that dominated world flour production for roughly a half-century, thus fueling the growth of Minneapolis, which is known around the world as the "Mill City." The museum's "Ruin Courtyard" is often used for summer concerts.
- **Minnesota History Center and Minnesota Historical Society**, 345 W Kellogg Blvd, St. Paul, 651-296-6126, TTY 651-282-6073, or 800-657-3773, www.mnhs.org
- **Science Museum of Minnesota and Omnitheater**, 120 W Kellogg, St. Paul, 651-221-9444, www.smm.org; the Science Museum is a multi-level extravaganza of hands-on exhibits and creative demonstrations, with a 3D multimedia laser-theater and 180 degree screen Omnitheater that shows science-related films.

LITERARY LIFE

BOOKSTORES

The Twin Cities are home to many excellent new and used bookstores. They include chains such as **Barnes & Noble** (www.barnesandnoble.com) and **Borders** (www.borders.com), which have many locations. But, as befits the #2 Most Literate place in the country, we are rich with independent booksellers, as well. They survive by virtue of their customer service and erudition, tend to be tucked away in neighborhoods where they are harder to find—and these are but a few of them listed below:

- **Amazon Bookstore Cooperative**, 4755 Chicago Ave S, Minneapolis, 612-821-9630, www.amazonfembks.com, is the oldest independent feminist bookstore in North America.
- **Big Brain Comics**, 81 10th St S, Minneapolis, 612-338-4390, www.big braincomics.com
- **Birchbark Books,** 2115 W 21st St, Minneapolis, 612-374-4023, www.birchbarkbooks.com, is owned by author Louise Erdrich.
- **Excelsior Bay Books**, 36 Water St, Excelsior, 952-401-0932, www.excelsior baybooks.com, is a real neighborhood bookstore known for its children's books and fiction.
- **Half Price Books**, www.halfpricebooks.com/minnesota.html, has several locations around the Twin Cities.
- **The Loft Literary Center** (and Open Book, below), 1011 Washington Ave, 612-215-2575, www.loft.org, is where emerging writers hone their craft and readers can listen to outstanding writers discussing their literary influences.
- **Magers & Quinn Booksellers**, www.magersandquinn.com, 3038 Hennepin Ave S, Minneapolis, 612-822-4611; 608 2nd Ave S, Minneapolis, 612-822-4611; for the friendly atmosphere, scholarly staff, and a sense that there are treasures to be found here, this bookstore is a favorite among the Twin Cities' many excellent used book stores.
- **Micawber's Books**, 2238 Carter Ave, St. Paul, 651-646-5506, www.micawbers.com, is tucked away in the St. Anthony neighborhood near Muffuletta Restaurant.
- **Open Book**, 1011 Washington Ave S, Minneapolis, 612-215-2650, www.openbookmn.org, is home to the Minnesota Center for Book Arts, The Loft Literary Center (above), and local publisher Milkweed Editions.
- **Query Booksellers**, 520 E Hennepin, Minneapolis, 612-331-7701, www.querybooks.com, specializes in gay and lesbian reading matter.
- **The Red Balloon**, 891 Grand Ave, St. Paul, 651-224-8320, www.red balloonbookshop.com, is a fantastic children's bookstore that stages many fun family events throughout the year.
- **Uncle Edgar's Mystery Bookstore and Uncle Hugo's Science Fiction Bookstore**, 2864 Chicago Ave, Minneapolis, 612-824-9984, 612-824-6347, www.unclehugo.com
- **Wild Rumpus**, 2720 W 43rd St, Minneapolis, 612-920-5005, www.wild rumpusbooks.com, in Linden Hills, has a kid-sized door and pet animals. The ambiance alone is certain to turn children into bookworms.

LIBRARIES

Local library systems are all part of MELSA, the **Metropolitan Library Service Agency**, an alliance of metropolitan libraries (651-645-5731, www.melsa.org). With MELSA, as its motto says, "Your library card is good at over 100 locations!"

The **Hennepin County Library System** (www.hclib.org) serves suburban Hennepin County residents through 26 libraries and extensive outreach services. All branches offer free wireless Internet. The Ridgedale Library also has a bookstore where discarded and donated books are sold. These main libraries, which boast larger collections and bigger computer labs, are open longer hours and on weekends:

- **Brookdale Library**, 6125 Shingle Creek Pkwy, Brooklyn Center, 952-847-5600
- **Eden Prairie Library**, 565 Prairie Center Dr, Eden Prairie, 952-847-5375
- **Maple Grove Library**, 8351 Elm Creek Blvd, Maple Grove, 952-847-5550
- **Ridgedale Library**, 12601 Ridgedale Dr, Minnetonka, 952-847-8800
- **Southdale Library**, 7001 York Ave S, Edina, 952-847-5900

The **Minneapolis Public Library System** (www.mplib.org) consists of the new Central Library on the Nicollet Mall, 14 community libraries, two tech centers, and a literacy center. It has developed special collections to serve the area's many immigrant populations, as well as an extraordinary African-American history and culture collection at the **Sumner Library** (611 Van White Memorial Boulevard) in North Minneapolis. Many of the libraries are designated "Homework Helper" locations. **The St. Paul Public Library** (651-266-7073, www.sppl.org) includes its own **Central Library** (90 Fourth St W, St Paul, 651-266-7000) and branches in most St. Paul neighborhoods. Call 651-642-0379 for Bookmobile Service.

Other county libraries are as follows:

- **Ramsey County Library System**, 651-486-2200, www.ramsey.lib.mn.us
- **Anoka County Library System**, www.anoka.lib.mn.us
- **Dakota County Library System**, 651-688-1547, www.co.Dakota.mn.us/library
- **Washington County Library**, 651-275-8500, www.co.washington.mn.us/library
- **Carver County Library System**, www.carverlib.org, operates two libraries: **Chanhassen Library**, 7711 Kerber Blvd, Chanhassen, 952-227-1500, and **Chaska Library**, 3 City Hall Plaza, Chaska, 952-448-3886. When the reserved list is long for a book in the Hennepin County system, you can usually get it here, with a much shorter wait.
- **The Scott County Library System**, 13090 Alabama Ave S, Savage, 952-707-1760, www.scott.lib.mn.us, is another place to locate materials that are on long reserve lists elsewhere.

B OB HOPE ONCE SAID, "IF YOU WATCH A GAME, IT'S FUN. IF YOU PLAY IT, it's recreation. If you work at it, it's golf." You'll have plenty of occasion for all three here, and many other sports besides. To the hale and hearty, this climate is not an impediment but an opportunity. Ice boating, anyone?

If it's spectator sports you're after, a calendar of Twin Cities sporting events is posted online at www.twincitiessports.com, or pick up a free copy of *Twin Cities Sports* at your local grocery or sporting goods store. Tickets for most games and events can be purchased through **Ticketmaster**, 612-989-5151, www.ticketmaster.com, or **TicketKing**, http://twincitiestickets.com.

The three major sports venues are: **Hubert H. Humphrey Metrodome**, 900 South 5th Street, Minneapolis: 612-332-0386, TTY Relay Service: 800-627-3529, www.msfc.com; **Target Center**, First Avenue North between 6th and 7th Streets, Minneapolis, 612-673-8333, www.targetcenter.com; and **Xcel Energy Center**, on the corner of Kellogg Boulevard and West Seventh Street in downtown St. Paul, 651-265-4800, www.xcelenergycenter.com. The Metrodome is on the **Hiawatha LRT** line, and there are parking ramps that connect to Target Center through the skyway system. Parking for the Xcel Center is located in the **River Center Ramp**, which has an entrance off of Kellogg, across the street from the arena. (See **Transportation** for more information.)

PROFESSIONAL SPORTS

Sports fans in Minnesota teeter between ecstasy and frustration. They remember with pride the performances of hometown heroes like **Kirby Puckett**, who helped the Twins win the World Series in 1987 and 1991. The same goes for Hopkins High School's ESPY winner, **Blake Hoffarber**, who scored the winning point in the 2005 Minnesota Class 4A state basketball title game from flat on his back, with the clock about to run out. But fame is fleeting and recent lackluster seasons as well as pro athletes' brushes with the law and the **Twins'** and **Vikings'** constant threats to move if they don't get new stadiums have caused some football fans to take down their purple mailboxes, and persuaded some baseball fans to exchange their "Homer Hankies" for pigs' snouts and head over to St. Paul for **Saints** games and cheaper beer. Basketball, however, is a sport where the picture is getting brighter. The NBA's **Timberwolves** and the WNBA's **Minnesota Lynx** are packing in the crowds. Hockey is on the upswing, too, as the **Minnesota Wild** professional hockey team is back on the ice at Xcel Energy Center following the NHL lockout.

BASEBALL

The American League's **Minnesota Twins** play 80 or so games a year in the Hubert H. Humphrey Metrodome in Minneapolis. For tickets, call 612-33-TWINS (338-9467). For game stats, schedules, player information, and daily ticket specials visit the Twins' web site at http://minnesota.twins.mlb.com. To reserve a space in what is advertised as "The Closest Parking to the Metrodome," call 612-673-7470. A new stadium—with a grass playing field—will be located just north of the Target Center and is expected to open in 2010. Across town, the **St. Paul Saints**, a professional minor league team, plays dozens of home games at the tiny Municipal Stadium in St. Paul's Midway. Off-diamond sideshows include grandstand massages, fat-suit races, a pig mascot that carries out the ball, lots of giveaways, and affordable tickets, food and drink. Call 651-644-6659 for ticket information or buy tickets online at www.saintsbaseball.com.

BASKETBALL

The **WNBA's Minnesota Lynx** play at **Target Center** in Minneapolis. Tickets are available at the Target Center Box Office or Ticketmaster (see above). For team updates visit www.wnba.com/lynx. The NBA's **Minnesota Timberwolves** also play at the Target Center. For game tickets, call Ticketmaster (see above). For Timberwolves statistics check www.nba.com/timberwolves.

FOOTBALL

Perennial contenders in the National Football League, the **Minnesota Vikings** play eight regular season home games at the **Humphrey Metrodome** each year, as well as several pre-season games. The NFL schedule comes out in May. In July, when single-game tickets go on sale, die-hards camp out in front of the Vikings ticket office at the Metrodome to be first in line. For those who don't know already, the Minnesota version of the Hatfields and McCoys is the Vikings' rivalry with **Green Bay**, whose fans wear "cheese heads"—in comparison, the Minnesota fans' Viking horns and milkmaid braids don't look half bad. For season tickets, call 612-33-VIKES (338-4537). For team information check www.vikings.com.

HOCKEY

The **Minnesota Wild** drop their pucks on the ice at state-of-the-art Xcel Energy Center in downtown St. Paul. Check www.wild.com for details or call 651-222-WILD. Minnesota is also home to the **U.S. Hockey Hall of Fame**, about three hours north of the Twin Cities in Eveleth, www.ushockeyhall.com.

LACROSSE

The National Lacrosse League **Minnesota Swarm** (www.mnswarm.com) play indoors at the Xcel Energy Center. Their 16-game regular season schedule begins in December and runs through April. Buy tickets online or call 1-888-MN-SWARM.

SOCCER

The fast action of soccer can readily be appreciated when you watch the professional **Minnesota Thunder** at James Griffin Stadium, 275 North Lexington Parkway (St. Paul Central High School), St. Paul, 651-917-TEAM (8326), www.mnthunder.com. The Thunder put on pre-game clinics for kids and post-game parties at local bars for adults.

COLLEGE SPORTS

The biggest college draw is, of course, the **University of Minnesota**, which plays in the Big Ten Conference, www.gophersports.com. "**Golden Gopher**" basketball and hockey each have a particularly large following. In football, the U's biggest rival is **Iowa**, which they play for a bronze pig known as "**Floyd of Rosedale.**" Their other big rivalry is with nationally ranked **University of Michigan**, over **The Little Brown Jug**. Finally, in 2005, after 16 consecutive years of losing, they brought that venerable trophy home to Minnesota, as fans of both teams sat there and watched the game in disbelief. To learn about this historic moment and get the latest (unofficial) word on all Gopher sports, read The **GopherHole**, online at www.gopherhole.com. For schedules and tickets to any U of M event, contact the **Minnesota Athletics Ticket Office** at **Mariucci Arena**, 4 Oak Street SE, Minneapolis; 612-624-8080 or **1-800 U-GOPHER**. You can also purchase tickets by e-mail at **go4tix@umn.edu**. Home games are held at the **Metrodome**, so neither teams nor spectators have to worry about hypothermia.

PARTICIPANT SPORTS AND RECREATION

Minnesota is all about sports. From babies to grannies, everybody participates in something. People moving into the area who want to play team sports should call their local Community Services or the **Cities Sports Connection**, 612-929-9009, www.cscsports.com. Sign up on their web site for social outings as well as adult recreation. Sports include broomball, volleyball, kickball, basketball, football, softball, bowling and soccer. Games are played at locations throughout the Twin Cities, all year round.

AUTOMOBILE RACING

- **Brainerd International Raceway and Resort,** www.brainerdraceway andresort.com. For tickets call 218-824-7220 or 1-866-444-4455.
- **Donnybrooke Performance Driving School** offers racecar driving lessons at Brainerd International Raceway. Lessons are open to any licensed driver 16 years old or older, 952-249-7223, www.donnybrooke.com.
- **Elko Speedway**, 26350 France Ave, Elko, 952-461-7223
- **Minnesota Street Rod Association** meets monthly to talk cars and sponsors a "Back to the '50s" car show at the Minnesota State Fairgrounds, www.msra.com.
- **Raceway Park**, 1 Checkered Flag Boulevard, Shakopee, 952-445-2257

BICYCLING

From the **National Sports Center's Velodrome** bike track in Blaine, 763-785-5614, www.nscsports.com/velo) to the interconnected web of trails that stretches from the western suburbs to Stillwater, the Twin Cities are blessed with an abundance of places to bike. Recreational biking has exploded, and bike commuting has also taken off. It's not unusual to see bikers wheeling to and from work dressed in suits, with important papers stowed in backpacks—even in the winter! Minneapolis, in particular, promotes bike commuting by offering low-cost bike lockers at numerous locations in downtown and at the University, and by providing guaranteed rides home in bad weather. (See **Transportation** for more information.)

Throughout the rest of the Metro, increasing numbers of off-street bike routes have either been built or are under construction. Download a regional **Twin Cities Bike Map and Commuter Guide**, www.metrocouncil.org/transportation/bikemap/bikemap.htm. An excellent map published by the University of Minnesota Extension Service, "**Bicycle Guide and Commuter Map**" is available at area bike shops or from the Commuter Connection, located on the Pillsbury Center skyway level.

The Twin Cities have been named one of *Bike Magazine's* 15 best cities in North America for mountain biking. Try these popular and scenic routes, many of which are also used for walking and skating, and cross-country skiing in winter:

- **Afton Alps Mountain Bike Area**, Hastings, www.aftonalps.com/mtbike.html.
- **Gateway Trail** begins just south of Wheelock Pkwy and east of I-35E in St. Paul, and extends 18 miles to Pine Point Park in Stillwater, www.dnr.state.mn.us/statetrails/gateway.

- **Luce Line Trail** from Plymouth west to Cosmos, www.luceline.com/.
- **"Minneapolis Grand Rounds,"** 50-mile National Scenic Byway loops around the Minneapolis Chain of Lakes, www.minneapolisparks.org/grandrounds.
- **Mississippi Gorge** trails on both sides of the Mississippi River between the Franklin Avenue Bridge and Ford Parkway Bridge create an 8-mile loop, www.nps.gov/miss/tug/segments/seg12.html.
- **Southwest Regional LRT Trail** from Hopkins west to Victoria or southwest to Chanhassen; or from Hopkins east to Minneapolis, to connect with the Midtown Greenway, www.fbiw.org/Trail/trailguide.htm.
- **Theodore Wirth Park** has an off-road cycling trail north of Highway 55, between Twin Lakes and Wirth Parkway, www.minneapolisparks.org.

For out-of-town biking, the trails below are just a sampling. Most of them are also open for horseback riding, cross-country skiing, and snowmobiling. **The Bicycle Vacation Guide, Minnesota and Wisconsin**, www.little transport.com/bicycle_vacation_guide.htm, is a good guide to help you plan your trip.

- **Cannon Valley Trail** from Cannon Falls to Red Wing, www.cannon valleytrail.com.
- **Gandy Dancer** is a 98-mile trail from St. Croix Falls to Superior in northwestern Wisconsin, www.nps.gov/sacn.
- **Heartland State Trail** is a 49-mile multiple-use route between Park Rapids and Cass Lake about 200 miles north of Minneapolis,www.dnr. state.mn.us/state_trails/heartland.
- **Lutsen Mountain Bike Park**; on the North Shore, www.lutsen.com.
- **Root River Trail** from Fountain to Houston in the far southeastern corner of Minnesota is a 42-mile paved multiple-use trail that offers outstanding views of the Red River Valley, www.trailsfromrails.com/root_river_trail.htm.

ONLINE RESOURCES

The **Twin Cities Bicycling Club**, www.mtn.org/tcbc, organizes scheduled rides and provides long lists of clickable links. For more places to ride, trails and maps (and there are many more) check out the following numbers and web sites:

- **East Metro**: Maps and up-to-date information about the condition of trails can be found on the **Friends of the Parks and Trails of St. Paul and Ramsey County** web site, www.friendsoftheparks.org.
- **Explore Minnesota**, www.exploreminnesota.com, offers an excellent guide called **Biking Minnesota** that lists trails and mountain-biking locations as well as lodging and trail pass requirements.
- **GORP Minnesota Maps** offers detailed regional maps, http://gorp. away.com/gorp/location/mn/mn.htm.
- **Hennepin County Bikeways & Trails**, www.threeriversparkdistrict.org.
- **Minneapolis Department of Public Works**, www.ci.minneapolis.mn. us/citywork/public-works/transportation/bicycles/maps/index.html, posts maps and information about locker locations and bike-friendly buses on its

web page. The maps are also available in print from the City.

- **Minneapolis Parks and Recreation Board**, www.minneapolis parks.org, is the place to look for Grand Rounds National Scenic Byway route information.
- **Minnesota Bike Trails & Rides**, www.mnbiketrails.com, is the **Minnesota Department of Natural Resources**' online trails magazine.
- **Minnesota Bike Map & Twin Cities Bicycle Map and Commuter Guide** (published in 2001) lists every street in the core cities and rates the routes (good, fair, poor) for bike commuters. It can be ordered from the **Minnesota Department of Transportation**, MnDOT Map and Manual Sales, www.dot.state.mn.us/mapsales.
- **Rehbeins Arena**, Lino Lakes, year-round BMX racing, www.rehbeins bmx.com.
- **Trails from Rails/Minnesota Bicycle Trails**, includes maps for Cannon Valley Trail, Glacial Lakes Trail, Paul Bunyan Trail, Root River Trail, Sakatah Singing Hills Trail, and Willard Munger Trail, and links to places to stay along the way, www.trailsfromrails.com/minnesota.htm.
- **Trail Source** keeps tabs on trails throughout the world, www.trail source.com.
- **Twin Cities Bike Map and Commuter Guide**, www.metrocouncil. org/transportation/bikemap.
- **Two Wheel View/Trips for Kids—Twin Cities**, coordinates environmental stewardship with local, regional, and international biking programs, www.twowheelview.org/.

LOCAL BICYCLING CLUBS
- **Minneapolis Bicycle and Pedestrian Alliance** posts a complete list of local riding clubs and clickable links to commuter information and bike shops, www.bikeped.org.
- **Minneapolis Off-Road Cycling Advocates** (MOCA) designed and built the Wirth Park trail, www.mocatrails.com.
- **Rovers**: This club emphasizes quiet sports such as hiking, canoeing, climbing, bicycling, and skiing. Trip costs (day/weekend/extended) are shared and coordinated by members. Hotline: 612-782-7139, www.MN Rovers.org.
- **Ski Hawks Sport and Social Club**: This more social club sponsors bike, ski, and snowboarding trips, rollerblading, and happy hours, www.Ski HawksMN.org.
- **Twin Cities Bicycling Club**: TCBC is the largest recreational bicycling club in the Minneapolis–St. Paul area, www.mtn.org/tcbc.
- **The Wheelmen** is a national organization whose mission is to promote the restoration and riding of pre-1918 cycles. Early Wheelmen pushed the Twin Cities to pave their streets and create the Chain of Lakes system that we all enjoy today. You won't have any trouble recognizing the members—they ride funny-looking cycles and wear funny-looking clothes and are usually surrounded by curious onlookers. Check the national web site, www.thewheelmen.org, for current local contact information.

BILLIARDS AND POOL

- **City Billiards Bar & Cafe** is the see-and-be-seen pool hall of the Twin Cities, 25 N 4th St, Minneapolis, 612-338-2255, www.citybilliards.com.

BIRDING

Located along the **Mississippi River flyway**, the Twin Cities are home to eight unique birding habitats, and it is possible to see nearly 300 species of birds here without ever venturing far from home. To find out where to go and when, get a copy of **The Twin Cities Birding Map**, ISBN 0-9641238-9-4. It is available at bookstores, birdseed outlets, and interpretive centers throughout the Metro. For those who'd rather explore the world of birds in comfort with a cold drink in their hands, the **Mississippi National River & Recreation Area**, www.nps.gov/miss/features/birding/birdboat.html, sponsors occasional cruises down the Mississippi on "**The Birding Boat**." Cruises depart from Harriet Island, St. Paul. For tickets, contact the Padelford Packet Boat Company, 651-227-1100, www.riverrides.com. Guided van tours through the **Minnesota Valley National Wildlife Refuge** will also net glimpses of bald eagles, great blue herons and wild turkeys, close enough for even the nearsighted to see. Tours are run by volunteers and available on a reservation-only basis, www.friendsofmnvalley.org, 952-858-0740. Online, sign up for email updates about bird and butterfly migrations at **Journey North**, www.learner.org/jnorth, an educational web site for school children, teachers, scientists, and nature lovers. The **Minnesota Ornithologists' Union** web site posts recently sighted bird photos as well as a ton of local birding information, www.moumn.org.

BOATING

Minnesota isn't called the **Land of Ten Thousand Lakes** for nothing. There are hundreds of lakes within the metro area alone, and most of them are host to boats of some kind. **Lake Minnetonka**, the **St. Croix River**, and the **Mighty Mississippi** are the most popular big boat waters and have numerous public launch sites. In the East Metro, **White Bear Lake** is home to world-class sailors. In the South Metro, **Prior Lake** is loved by water-skiers for its calm waters. (Water-skiing was actually born at **Lake City**, Minnesota, on the Mississippi River, www.lakecity.org.)

If you've got a craft already, you'll need a **license**. A boat license is good for three years, and the cost depends on the type of boat. For a license application, call the **Department of Natural Resources**, 651-296-6157, www.dnr. state.mn.us. Its web site includes the **Minnesota Boating Guide**, a downloadable booklet that summarizes Minnesota's boating laws and regulations.

If you're looking for a loaner, you can rent small sailboats, canoes and paddleboats at most parks. Call one of the following for bigger boat rental. Most of the popular lakes Up North offer plenty of rentals for those on vacation.

- **Excel Boat Club**, Excelsior, is a membership boat club that rents a variety of power boats, 952-401-3880, www.excelboatclub.com.
- **Rockvam Boat Rental**, Spring Park, rents fishing boats and pontoons by the day, 952-471-9515,www.rockvamboatyards.com.

If you're looking for a boat to buy, you won't have to travel far. Minnesota seems to have as many boat dealers as it has car lots, and they sell everything from fishing boats to luxury yachts. If it's a fine vintage boat you're looking for, though, try **Mahogany Bay** in Mound, which sells, services, restores and stores classic boats, 952-495-0007, www.mahoganybay.com.

Once you have a boat, finding a place to keep it can be difficult and expensive, though many cities offer good deals on dockage to their residents. Check with your city hall about waiting lists and fees. Most facilities require that boat owners remove their boats for the winter, but **French Regional Park** on Medicine Lake in Plymouth rents slips for sailboats under 20 feet in length, and offers winter storage, too. Slips and storage spaces are available on a first-come, first-served basis, 763-694-7750, www.threeriversparkdistrict.

Contact the local Power Squadrons for courses in how to operate a boat safely:
- **Minnetonka Power Squadron**, 612-253-2628, www.sb.usps.org/minn
- **St. Paul Sail and Power Squadron**, Mound, 952-472-9300

BOWLING

You betcha! Bowling is making a comeback. And even though it's a sport that requires concentration, it's also a fun, casual night out. Several local bowling alleys offer other entertainment as well: The **Bryant Lake Bowl** even offers a wine and espresso bar and performance space!
- **Bryant Lake Bowl**, 810 W Lake St, Minneapolis, 612-825-3737
- **Elsie's Bowling Center**, 729 NE Marshall St, 612-378-9701, www.elsies.com

BRIDGE

The **Twin Cities Bridge Center** teaches lessons and sponsors duplicate tournaments, 6020 Nicollet Ave, Minneapolis, 612-861-4487, www.district14.org/Minnesota/Minneapolis.

CASINOS

Indian gaming is one of Minnesota's biggest industries, and most casinos remain open all night. You have to be 18 to gamble, though most establishments have some kind of facility for children, such as an arcade. For more information on casinos in Minnesota check www.midwestcasinoguide.com/minnesota.
- **Grand Casino**, Mille Lacs and Hinckley, www.grandcasinomn.com

- **Little Six**, 2354 Northwest Sioux Trail, Prior Lake, 952-445-8982, www.littlesixcasino.com
- **Mystic Lake Casino**, Prior Lake, 800-262-7799, www.mysticlake.com
- **Treasure Island Casino**, Hwy 61 and 316, Red Wing, 800-222-7077, www.treasureislandcasino.com

CHESS

The **Chess Club of Minnesota** (www.mnchess.com) offers coaching, mini-camps, and tournaments for all ages from kindergarten up. **The Minnesota State Chess Association** (www.minnesotachess.org) sponsors tournaments, including the state championships and other events.
- **North Suburban Chess Club** meets at 6 p.m. on Wednesdays at the Har Mar Mall Barnes and Noble Bookstore, Roseville
- **South Suburban Chess Club**, 952-890-2644, holds monthly tournaments at Thunderbird Hotel, Bloomington.
- **West Suburban Chess Club** meets to play at several locations, including 6:30–9:30 every Monday night at Borders Books, 1501 S Plymouth Rd, Minnetonka

CURLING

If you've always wanted to bowl outdoors in the winter, the closest you'll come to fulfilling your dream is this old-fashioned game that uses "curling stones" and is played on polished ice. Contact the **St. Paul Curling Club**, 470 Selby Ave, St. Paul, 651-224-7408, www.stpaulcurlingclub.org.

DANCE

Dancing is in again! Twin Cities dance clubs offer lessons, host dances, participate in competitions and perform at festivals and fairs. For Square Dance lessons in the Minneapolis–St. Paul area, visit www.squaredanceminnesota.com. For regular ballroom dancing, check the Yellow Pages under "Dance Instruction." Local dance clubs include:
- **Dakota Grand Squares**, South St. Paul, give square dance lessons at several St. Paul locations. All square dancers and round dancers are welcome at their events, www.grandsquares.com.
- **Tapestry Folkdance Center** offers beginner instruction in International Folk Dancing, Contra, and Swing, and features live music on weekends, 3748 Minnehaha Ave, Minneapolis, 612-722-2914, www.tapestryfolkdance.org.

For professional lessons try these (see **Cultural Life** chapter for more):
- **Arthur Murray**, 5041 France Ave, Edina, 612-920-1900, www.arthurmurraympls.com.
- **Four Seasons Dance Studio** is a dancers' co-op that offers instruction in a number of partner dances and a four-week Saturday-morning crash

course for wedding couples, 1637 Hennepin Ave S, Minneapolis, 612-342-0902, www.4seasonsdance.com.

DISABLED ATHLETES

In 1992, the **Minnesota State High School League** became the first association in the nation to sanction interscholastic sports for kids with disabilities (see **Adapted Athletics** in the **Childcare and Education** chapter).

The **Power Hockey** league allows anyone in a power wheelchair to participate. If you want to sign up, call the **US Electric Wheelchair Hockey Association**, 763-535-4736, www.usewha.org.

DISC (FRISBEE) GOLF

Disc golf is played at a growing number of metro-area parks. The **Minnesota Frisbee Association** (MFA) maintains an up-to-date clickable map on its web site, http://users.spacestar.net/bogie6/metro.html. Get information about Minnesota leagues and tournaments at www.corediscgolf.com and www.pdga.com.

DOG-RELATED RECREATION

DOG SLEDDING
Many resorts and dogsled outfitters offer opportunities to mush across the frozen tundra behind a line of powerful huskies. For a complete list, look online at www.exploreminnesota.com. Here are a just few:
* **Boundary Country Lodge to Lodge Adventures**, Grand Marais, 218-388-4487, 800-322-8327, www.boundarycountry.com.
* **Cragun's Resort**, 11000 Craguns Drive, Brainerd, 218-825-2700, 800-272-4867, www.craguns.com
* **Outward Bound Wilderness**, Ely, 866-467-7651, www.outwardboundwilderness.org
* **Wilderness Inquiry**, Minneapolis, 612-676-9400, 800-728-0719, www.wildernessinquiry.org; can take you on safari in Africa, too!
* **Wintergreen Dogsled Lodge**, Ely, 218-365-6022, www.dogsledding.com

SLED DOG RACES
Check out **www.sleddogcentral.com** for race dates and locations. Here are a couple, not too far away, where you can watch the Big Dogs run:
* **John Beargrease Sled Dog Marathon**, Duluth, 800-438-5884, www.beargrease.com
* **Pine River Sled Run**, Merrill, Wisconsin, 1-715-536-9474

GAME FAIR

Minnesota Game Fair, www.gamefair.com, is held at **Armstrong Ranch Kennels**, between Anoka and Elk River on Highways 10 and 169, www.armstrong kennels.com. This late August weekend event is a family affair where there are activities for the whole family, including your dog.

FISHING AND HUNTING

You are now in hunting and fishing country! Everything stops for the season openers, spring and fall. Really! Including homebuilding! Though many go "Up North," you barely have to leave your neighborhood to fish here, because the **Department of Natural Resources (DNR)** stocks lakes in the metro, as well as waters Up North. Don't forget **ice fishing**, either. Most who fish in summer enjoy "hardwater fishing" in winter, too—sometimes in two-story houses outfitted with amenities such as stoves, televisions, underwater cameras, and enough beds to sleep a crowd. In fact, whole communities of ice houses, complete with plowed roads and street signs, spring up every winter on otherwise desolate frozen lakes. Ice houses can be homemade, purchased, or rented. Rent a 4-holer on **Lake Minnetonka**—with a heated restroom— from **Pike Dreams** (952-470-880, www.pikedreams.com/ice.htm) for about $200/day. To rent an ice house on famed **Lake Mille Lacs**, look online at www.millelacs.com. The latest craze: **darkhouse angling**. That's when you spearfish through a hole in the ice that is enclosed in a darkened space. For information and help getting started, contact the **Minnesota Darkhouse and Angling Association**, www.mndarkhouse.org. For anything else you want to know about ice fishing, visit **The Ice Fishing Home Page**, http://hickorytech.net/~jbusby/iceangler.html.

Remember that all forms of fishing and hunting require a **license**. You can purchase hunting and fishing licenses and apply for hunting lotteries through the state's **Electronic License System (ELS)**. ELS gives you three options for buying licenses: online, phone, or in person. **Online**, buy your licenses through the DNR's web page, www.dnr.state.mn.us/licenses. Purchase licenses **by phone** at 1-888-665-4236 (1-MN-LICENSE). Call any time of day or night, seven days a week. This toll-free call provides immediate licensing by way of a license identification number, which will be issued at the time of the call. Finally, you can buy your licenses **in person** from a state licensing agent. Agents include bait shops, marinas, sporting goods stores, hardware stores, gas stations, and county license centers. Search the DNR web site by county to find a licensing agent near you, www.dnr.state.mn.us/licenses/agents.html. Though noted metro-area lakes are often surrounded by homes, they are still crowded with walleye, bass, and crappies (people up here say "croppies"). Hang your hook in **Lake Minnetonka, Lake Elmo, Lake Waconia,** or **Forest Lake** and you might come home with a record-winner. Or cast your jig in the waters of the **Mississippi River,** just below the **Coon Rapids Dam** or the **Ford Dam** near downtown St. Paul. On the hottest days of summer, big carp are attracted to the oxygen-rich shallows along the dams' concrete spill-ways, and the deeper holes are home to more traditional game fish, including smallmouth bass and walleye.

For those who want to travel, **Lake Mille Lacs (www.millelacs.com)** and **Leech Lake** are home to big walleye and muskie. **Lake of the Woods** bills itself as the "**Walleye Capital of the World**." Call 800-382-FISH or visit www.lakeofthewoodsmn.com for resort information. **Plastic-coated maps** that show the good fishing spots on each lake are sold at bait and sporting goods stores. Data on fish stocking and water quality, as well as consumption advice guidelines, are searchable by lake on the **Department of Natural Resources Lake Finder** web site, www.dnr.state.mn.us/lakefind/. Sadly, the increase in impervious surfaces and agricultural and industrial run-off has not only made consumption of fish an iffy proposition but has actually wiped out several area fisheries. Trout that once swam in suburban waters like **Golden Valley Creek**, **Purgatory Creek**, and **Trout Brook** no longer exist. Both **stocked and native trout**, however, can still be found in the **Rush River**, about an hour east of the Twin Cities, in Wisconsin. A **Wisconsin fishing license** is required for anyone 16 or older. Licenses can be purchased online at http://dnr.wi.gov.

To learn about the best hunting grounds and fishing holes, tune in to **Ron Schara** and his black Labrador retriever Raven on **Minnesota Bound** on **KARE11** television weekends, or listen to Ron on **WCCO** radio (AM 830) at 5:30 on Saturday mornings. Schara has also written numerous books on hunting and fishing, and authors a monthly newsletter. Sign up for it on his web site, www.mnbound.com. Learn about local events, as well as the best fishing holes and places to hunt, by reading **Minnesota Sportsman** magazine, www.minnesotasportsmanmag.com.

GARDENING

The **University of Minnesota Landscape Arboretum** (www.arboretum.umn.edu), otherwise known as "The Arb," is located on Highway 5 west of Chanhassen. It features over 1000 acres of public gardens, natural and native areas, and its **Master Gardeners** (www.mg.umn.edu) will answer all your gardening questions, 952-443-1400.

As long as you choose plants that are hardy in our zone (4a, minimum temperatures of minus 30 degrees Fahrenheit), you'll find Minnesota gardening quite enjoyable. Check out the Master Gardeners' list of their top 25 plants for Minnesota at http://www.extension.umn.edu/extensionnews/2002/MasterGardenersChooseTop25.html. If you need to over-winter non-hardy plants, you'll want to use the **Minnesota Tip** method (see http://www.extension.umn.edu/projects/yardandgarden/ygbriefs/h112rose-mntip.html).

For nurseries and more gardening resources, see **Gardening** in the **Shopping** chapter. For a peek at what other people are growing, check with the **Arboretum Auxiliary** about its annual bus tour of private gardens. The information will be advertised in the papers and listed on the Arboretum's web site (see address and phone number above). In addition, many neighborhoods and members of plant societies open their garden gates for fundraising events. Keep an eye out for them in the local papers or get a subscription to the **Northern Gardener**, www.northerngardener.org. Other resources include:

- **Minnesota Native Plant Society**, www.mnnps.org
- **Northscaping**, an internet community of northern gardeners and landscapers, www.northscaping.com

GOLF

Having just moved, you may not be quite ready to join a country club, but don't worry, many public courses here are as good as the clubs—in fact, many are better! The **Minnesota Golf Association**, 952-927-4643, www.mngolf.org, can give you lots of information but for a unique Minnesota experience, try these: **Walker in the Rough, Baker National**, and **The Legends Club**. Okay. So Walker in the Rough is mini-golf—it was designed by area artists and architects, and it's definitely unique. Located at the north end of the **Minneapolis Sculpture Garden** in front of the Walker Art Museum, its hazards include a mirrored labyrinth, and the sculpture garden's signature spoon-and-cherry fountain. For information, look on the museum's web site, www.walkerart.org. (Please note that you must be present in person to get on the wait list.)

Now for the real golf. Play **Baker National** in **Medina** if for no other reason than to see what the Twin Cities used to look like before they got so built up. Set amidst lakes and rolling fields, this challenging course is owned and operated by the **Three Rivers Park District**, www.threeriverspark district.org. On the other side of the metro, **The Legends Club** in **Prior Lake** is #3 on Golfweek's Top 10 Minnesota Public Courses, www.golfweek.com; and #12 on Golf Digest's Top Twenty Minnesota Courses, www.golfdigest.com.

A little farther afield, but well worth the trip, is **The Quarry** at Giant's Ridge, Biwabik, a new course which debuted #16 on Golf Digest's list of 100 Greatest Public Courses, and was also named Best New Upscale Public Course. Nearby are **The Legends**, also at Giant's Ridge, and **The Wilderness at Fortune Bay** on Lake Vermillion. All three were designed by the great modern course architect **Jeffrey Brauer**, who refers to this collection of northern Minnesota courses as his "Pinehurst." In the opposite direction, try **Willinger's** in Northfield, 952-440-7000, www.willingersgc.com. For information about these and all the other golf courses in Minnesota, complete with a clickable map, check out **www.minnesotagolf.com**. For reviews of approximately 35 golf courses, visit **www.mnsportspage.com**. To reserve tee times at most courses, call **Teemaster** at 952-525-1100, or make your reservations online at www.teemaster.com. Teemaster and the **Minnesota Chapter** of the **Professional Golfers' Association (PGA) of America** also team up to offer a free-golf package to those who order a PGA card. Check Teemaster's web site for details. Here are some of the public courses that Twin Cities golfers say rank with the best:

- **Baker National**, 2935 Parkview Dr, Medina, www.threeriverspark district.org/golf/baker.

- **Bunker Hills**, Hwy 242 & Foley Blvd, Coon Rapids, 763-755-4141, www.bunkerhillsgolf.com.
- **Chaska Town Course**, 3000 Town Course Dr, Chaska, 952-443-3748, www.chaskatowncourse.com; #5 on *Golfweek's* list of Top Ten Minnesota Public Courses.
- **Edinburgh USA**, 8700 Edinbrook Crossing, Brooklyn Park, 763-493-8098, www.edinburghusa.org.
- **Keller Golf Club**, 2166 Maplewood Dr, St. Paul, 651-484-3011, www.co. ramsey.mn.us/parks/golf/keller.asp.
- **Meadowbrook**, 201 Meadowbrook Rd, Hopkins, 952-929-2077, www. minnesotagolf.com/link_outs/meadowbrook.html.
- **Rush Creek**, 7801 Troy Ln, Maple Grove, 763-494-8844, www. rushcreek.com; #7 on *Golfweek's* Top Ten Minnesota Public Courses.
- **St. Croix National**, 1603 32nd St, Somerset, Wisconsin, 715-247-4200, www.wpgolf.com/stcroix/index.html.
- **Troy Burne**, 295 Lindsay Rd, Hudson, Wisconsin, 715-381-9800, or Toll Free 877-888-8633, www.troyburne.com.
- **The Wilds**, 3151 Wilds Ridge, Prior Lake, 952-445-4455, www.golf thewilds.com; #8 on *Golfweek's* Top Ten Minnesota Public Courses.

For those interested in private clubs, both **Interlachen** in Edina (www. www.interlachencc.org) and **Hazeltine**, in Chaska (www.hngc.com), have made *Golf Digest's* list of 100 Greatest Golf Courses, and are ranked 1 (Interlachen) and 2 (Hazeltine) on the magazine's list of Top 20 Minnesota Courses. Ranked 15th on this list is another interesting course, the **Tournament Players Club** of the Twin Cities (www.tpc.com/private/ twin_cities/), a private course off 35W in Blaine/Circle Pines. Owned and built by the Professional Golfers Association, the TPC, which opened in the spring of 2000, is used once a year for a Champions Tour event; the rest of the time it is available to members. It is occasionally open to the public for charity events.

And don't forget—this *is* Minnesota, and we also play **snow golf** here. For a quick getaway, work out your winter kinks on Breezy Point's links, near Brainerd. Their 9-hole course on the lake has tree-lined fairways and interesting hazards. Participants use regular golf clubs and tennis balls. Contact **Breezy Point Resort** online at www.breezypointresort.com or call 800-432-3777. Closer to home, **Wayzata** hosts its Chilly Open fundraiser each year on **Lake Minnetonka**, and golf is sometimes played on other lakes, as well.

HEALTH CLUBS AND GYMS

If you work for a larger organization, ask human resources about a health or fitness club benefit or membership discount. Many of the centers listed below have locations throughout the Twin Cities. Note that the health club business is one without fixed prices: the dripping person on the treadmill next to you may have paid twice as much or half as much as you. Also, a big caveat emptor: it pays to read the fine print on any agreement . . . for example, "annual membership" and "no fees" may not mean what you think they do.

- **Bally Total Fitness**; St. Louis Park, Fridley, Bloomington, Richfield, Eagan, St. Paul, Little Canada; 800-515-CLUB, www.ballyfitness.com.
- **Calhoun Beach Club Inc.**, 2925 Dean Pkwy, Minneapolis, 612-927-9951, www.calhounbc.com.
- **Flagship Athletic Club**, 755 Prairie Center Dr, Eden Prairie, 952-941-2000, www.flagshipac.com.
- **Life Time Fitness** health clubs and family recreation facilities; about a dozen locations throughout the Twin Cities; 952-380-0303, www.lifetimefitness.com.
- **Lonna Mosow's Center for Mind and Body Fitness**, 6409 City West Pkwy, Eden Prairie, 952-941-9448; www.lonnamosow.com.
- **Northwest Athletic Clubs**; 10 locations: Bloomington; Brooklyn Center; Burnsville; Eden Prairie; Edina; Fridley; Maple Grove; Minnetonka; St. Louis Park; Target Center (Minneapolis); 952-525-CLUB, www.northwestac.com.
- **Regency Athletic Club and Spa**; 1300 Nicollet Ave, Minneapolis; 711 W Lake St, Minneapolis; 612-343-3131; www.regencyclubspa.com.
- **The Gym Training Center**, 2855 Glacier Ln, Plymouth, 763-553-0171, www.thegymusa.net.
- **The Marsh**, 15000 Minnetonka Blvd, Minnetonka; this peaceful, affirming exercise facility has a yoga tower and two pools along with the normal equipment rooms and aerobics classes. Physical therapy is available here as well. The restaurant serves gourmet food and is open for lunch and dinner, 952-935-2202, www.themarsh.com.
- **The University Club**, 420 Summit Ave, St. Paul, 651-222-1751, www.universityclubofstpaul.com.
- **The Ys**—YWCA and YMCA—have locations throughout the Twin Cities and western Wisconsin. A monthly membership may cost much less than for a private club, and volunteering at the Y can earn you a discount. Call 612-371-8700, 612-465-0450, or look online at www.ymcatwincities.org, www.ywcampls.org, www.ywcaofstpaul.org.

HIKING

The amount of green you see on the Minnesota State map speaks for itself—a good part of the northern third of the state is either state or national forest, and there are dozens of interconnected local, regional, and state parks and trails that wind throughout the metro. Four national parks are within a day's drive. For detailed information about trails, including ratings, look online at **www.trails.com**, or buy one of the numerous excellent hiking/biking guidebooks written about Minnesota, such as *60 Hikes within 60 Miles: Twin Cities* by Tom Watson. For more hiking opportunities see the **Quick Getaways** and **Lakes and Parkways** chapters. Here are a few suggestions to get you started:
- **Afton State Park**, Hastings, 651-436-5391, www.dnr.state.mn.us/state_parks/afton; hike the rolling bluffs along the St. Croix River.
- **Carver Park Reserve**, west of Chanhassen off Highway 5, www.threeriversparkdistrict.org, has 12.2 miles of turf hiking trails and another 8.5 miles of paved trails.

- **Fort Snelling State Park**, Hwys 5 & 55, St. Paul, 612-725-2390, www. dnr.state.mn.us/state_parks/fort_snelling, is a historic site with trails that connect to the metro parkways.
- **North Hennepin Trail Corridor**, www.threeriversdistrict.org; 5.6-mile paved trail connecting Coon Rapids Dam Regional Park in Brooklyn Park to Elm Creek Park Reserve in Maple Grove.

    Local hiking clubs include:
- **Minnehikers**, 612-230-6475, www.minneapolisparks.org; sponsored by the Minneapolis Park and Recreation Board.
- **St. Paul Hiking Club**, 651-793-4412; posts its events in the *St. Paul Pioneer Press* Outdoors Events Calendar, www.twincities.com/ mld/twincities/entertainment/events/13014729.htm.
- **Thursday Night Hikers**, www.northstar.sierraclub.org or www.angel fire.com/mn/thursdaynighthikes, is an aggregation of hiking enthusiasts from the Minnesota Rovers, the North Star Ski Touring Club, the Sierra Club, and others, who hike every Thursday night throughout the year, except Thanksgiving. After the hike, they go to a restaurant for dinner/ dessert and further conversation.
- **Ullr Ski, Bike and Social Club**, www.ullr.org; also hikes.

HORSEBACK RIDING

Hennepin County used to have the most horses per capita of any county in the U.S. Now, if you want to keep horses, you really need to move farther out. Washington County toward **Forest Lake, Medina/Maple Plain/ Independence** in western Hennepin County, **Jordan, Lakeville**, and **western Wisconsin** still have room—and zoning friendly to horses. **Baker Park Reserve** in Medina has just over nine miles of trails to ride; and **Murphy-Hanrehan Park Reserve** in Savage has 13.9 miles of horse trails plus a 20-horse camping spot, 763-559-9000, www.threeriversparkdistrict.org. The **Minnesota Valley National Wildlife Refuge** (http://midwest.fws.gov/ MinnesotaValley) allows riding on 13 miles of trails that cross the **Louisville Swamp** (off Highway 169 near **Jordan**) and connect with the **State Corridor Trail**. Pick up a trail brochure at the kiosk near the parking lot for more details. Be aware that trails can be flooded during spring and summer, and are used by hunters in the fall. Call the Visitor Center at 952-854-5900 for an update. A trail map is posted at this address: www.fws.gov/midwest/ MinnesotaValley/louisville.html. Washington County allows horses in **Lake Elmo Park Reserve** and **Pine Point Park** (www.co.washington.mn.us/ info_for_residents/parks_division). The **Minnesota Trail Riders Association** (www.mntrailriders.com) can also help you find places and horses to ride.

    For a comprehensive list of Minnesota stables with some clickable links, look online at www.polocenter.com/stable/stableusmnm.htm. Here are some of the larger boarding and training facilities:

- **Alpine Farms**, 2182 Homestead Trail, Long Lake, 763-473-1361
- **Aux Chevaux Equestrian Center**, 8305 W Broadway Ave, Forest Lake, 651-464-7692
- **Bob Jensen Stables**, 19650 Judicial Rd, Lakeville, 952-435-6374; saddlebreds
- **Bunker Park Stables**, 550 Bunker Lake Blvd (between State Hwy 65 and Hansen Blvd in Bunker Hills Regional Park in Andover), 763-757-9445, www.bunkerparkstable.com; is north of the twin cities about a 25-minute drive from both downtowns. It offers guided trail rides, hay rides, sleigh rides, boarding and lessons.
- **Center Line Riding School**, 6795 County Rd 26, Maple Plain, 763-479-6126; boarding, lessons, dressage, combined training
- **Hardwood Creek Farm**, 2306 80th St E, Hugo, 651-429-4900; saddlebreds
- **River Bend Stables**, 8680 Rebecca Park Trail, Rockford, 763-477-6640; hunters, jumpers, boarding
- **Triple S Ranch**, 108th St at Barnes Ave, Inver Grove Heights, 651-452-5964; boarding, training, and lessons (hunt seat, Western, equitation, dressage, combined)
- **Twin City Polo Club**, West End Farm, 6755 Turner Rd, Maple Plain (one mile south of Hwy 12 off County Rd 90), 763-479-4307, www.twincity polo.com
- **Valient Stables**, 11755 Partridge Rd, Stillwater, 651-430-1763; saddlebreds
- **Westwind Stables**, 22365 Inga Ave, Hastings, 651-480-1124; boarding, lessons, dressage and equitation, camps, hundreds of acres of trails
- **Woodloch Stable**, 5676 170th St N, Hugo, 651-429-1303, www.bunker parkstable.com/woodloch.html; boarding, training, lessons, summer youth day camps

If *watching* the ponies is closer to what you have in mind, **Canterbury Park** (952-445-7223 or 800-340-6361, www.canterburypark.com) in Shakopee runs thoroughbred and quarterhorse races throughout the summer months.

HORSE SHOWS AND EVENTS
- **Animal Humane Society Hunter and Jumper Show**, June, at Alpine Farms (see above)
- **Polo Classic**, first Sunday in August, West End Farm, Maple Plain; polo match benefiting the Children's Home Society of Minnesota, www.poloclassic.org
- **Tanbark Cavalcade of Roses**, for saddlebreds, held at the Minnesota State Fairgrounds Coliseum, St. Paul, in June; www.statefair.gen.mn.us.

ICE SKATING/HOCKEY/BROOMBALL

If slip-sliding and gliding across a smooth lake surface under the stars is your idea of Heaven, you've come to the right neck of the woods. Nearly every lake in the Twin Cities has a rink and warming house in winter. Some lake rinks are small and neighborhood-maintained, but **Centennial Lakes Park** in Edina (www.ci.edina.mn.us) is ten full acres, and groomed daily. They'll rent you skates for under $5 a day, if you don't have your own, and the warming house has both indoor and outdoor fireplaces. **Lake of the Isles** and **Powderhorn Park** are even more scenic. The following ice arenas are inside and are open year 'round, except for a week or two in summer when they replace their ice. Most of them participate in the **United States Figure Skating Association**'s "Learn How to Skate" program (www.usfsa.org), are home to competitive skating clubs and hockey leagues, and also offer open skating for the general public. To find the rink nearest you, visit **Rinkfinder** (www.rinkfinder.com), a service of the **Minnesota Ice Arena Manager's Association**, or **ArenaMaps.com**, which includes clickable links. Here are some of the main arenas:

- **Aldrich Arena**, 18850 White Bear Ave, Maplewood, 651-748-2511, www.co.ramsey.mn.us/parks/ice_arenas/aldrich.asp
- **Augsburg College Arena**, 2323 Riverside Ave, Minneapolis, 612-330-1163, www.augsburg.edu/athletics/facilities.html
- **Braemer Arena**, 7501 Hwy 169, Edina, 952-941-1322, www.ci.edina.mn.us
- **Breck School Ice Arena**, 5800 Wayzata Blvd, Minneapolis, 763-545-1614, www.breckschool.org
- **Burnsville Ice Center**, 251 Civic Center Pkwy, Burnsville, 952-895-4651, www.Burnsville.org
- **Dakotah Arena**, 2100 Trail of Dreams NW, Prior Lake, 952-496-6888, www.ccsmdc.org/Dakotah/index.html
- **The Depot**, Minneapolis, 225 Third Ave, 612-375-1700, 612-339-2253, www.thedepotminneapolis.com/rink.htm
- **Eagan Civic Arena**, 3870 Pilot Knob Rd, 651-675-5590, www.cityofeagan.com
- **Highland Arena**, 800 Snelling Ave S, St. Paul, 651-695-3766, www.co.ramsey.mn.us/parks
- **Maple Grove Community Center**, 12591 Weaver Lake Rd, Maple Grove, 763-494-6500, www.ci.maple-grove.mn.us
- **Minnetonka Ice Arena**, 3401 Williston Rd, Minnetonka, 952-939-8310, www.eminnetonka.com
- **Parade Ice Garden**, 600 Kenwood Pkwy, Minneapolis, 612-370-4846, www.minneapolisparks.org
- **Plymouth Ice Arena**, 3650 Plymouth Blvd, Plymouth, 763-509-5250, www.ci.Plymouth.mn.us
- **Roseville Skating Center**, 2660 Civic Center Dr, Roseville, 651-792-7006, www.ci.roseville.mn.us/parks/index.php; has indoor and outdoor facilities

- **Schwan's Super Rink**, 1850 105th Ave NE, Blaine, 763-717-3880, www.superrink.org
- **White Bear Lake Sports Center**, 1328 Highway 96, White Bear Lake, 651-429-8571, www.whitebearlake.org

HOCKEY

Minnesotans bleed hockey—it's in their genes. It used to be only boys, but now it's girls, too. It starts with kids so little they take breaks from skating to lick the ice and rises to the level of the NCAA champion men's and women's **University of Minnesota Hockey Gophers** (www.gophersports.com) and the legendary **1980 U.S. Olympic Team** and its **"Miracle on Ice."** The sport is mythic here, and a lifestyle. There's lesson hockey, league hockey, school hockey, summer-camp hockey, traveling hockey, park hockey, and pick-up hockey. There's even **Power Hockey** for people in power wheelchairs. To sign up, call the **US Electric Wheelchair Hockey Association**, 763-535-4736 or look online at www.usewha.org.

If you have a child who wants to play hockey, it will take over your life—and most coaches and the other parents will expect you to accept that fact without complaint and schedule Christmas, weddings, and family vacations accordingly. To learn more about it, for both men and women, visit **www.life timehockey.com**. Then make your first hockey-themed vacation a trip to Eveleth, on the Iron Range, to visit the **United States Hockey Hall of Fame** (www.ushockeyhall.com). Adults who'd like to learn to play hockey can sign up for **Adult Beginning Hockey**, which guarantees "no checking/no fighting," Augsburg Arena, 800-4-HOCKEY, www.hna.com. For everything there is to know about every hockey program in the state, including camps and summer camps, go to **ArenaMaps.com**, which includes clickable links.

We also play **broomball** here, which is like hockey, but played with a broom instead of a stick. Check it out or, if you're brave, go ahead and invite your new friends over for a broomball party or join one of the many co-ed, post-college teams. For information about either sport, check with your local park and recreation department or your local school district's Community Services—or simply ask at your favorite bar. **Lord Fletcher's** in Spring Park on Lake Minnetonka is where many of the broomball leagues play, 952-471-8513.

MARCH MADNESS

Kentucky has the Derby, but Minnesota has the **State High School Hockey Tournament.** Held every year in **March** in **St. Paul**, it's the state's biggest event after the state fair. For days, kids and parents wearing high school hockey jerseys clog the concourses at **Xcel Arena**, and every hotel room in St. Paul is transformed into a fire marshal's nightmare. Then there's usually a blizzard. Life can't get much more Minnesota than that! For everything you need to know to talk hockey tournament around the water cooler, visit the **Minnesota State High School League**'s web site, www.mshsl.org.

IN-LINE SKATING AND SKATEBOARDING

It is fitting that here in the home of **Rollerblade®**, one of the most popular warm-weather activities is to strap on in-line skates and cruise the marvelous trail system. Heavily used lake routes, such as along **Lake Calhoun** and **Lake of the Isles**, have separate paths for people on and off wheels, so in-line skaters can mix it up with bikers. The **Summit Avenue bike lane** and **Mississippi River parkways** are popular in-line routes as well. In winter, the hallways of the **Metrodome**, 612-825-3663, are regularly opened to in-line skaters. It's spacious, warm, and home to the Vikings and Twins; what more could you ask? Or try the **Roller Garden**, 5622 West Lake Street, St. Louis Park, 952-929-5518, www.rollergarden.com; lessons are available. The cost of each session includes roller skate rental, but in-line skates are extra. The **Minnesota Inline Skate Club**, www.skateminnesota.org, reviews trails, giving them one to four wheels depending on how worthwhile they are to skate. Here are a few skate parks to try:

- **Ollie and Company Indoor Skate Park**, 13835 Aberdeen St, Ham Lake, 763-767-5757, www.ollieindoorskatepark.com
- **Roseville Aggressive Skate Park**, 2661 Civic Center Dr, Roseville, 24-hour Skate Line: 651-792-7191, www.ci.roseville.mn.us
- **Southdale YMCA "Tri-City Skate Park,"** 7355 York Ave S, Edina, 952-835-2567, www.ymcatwincities.org/locations/southdale.asp
- **3rd Lair Skate Park & Skate Shop**, 850 Florida Ave S, Golden Valley, 763-79 SKATE (75283), www.3rdlair.com
- **White Bear Lake YMCA "Wheel Park,"** 651-777-8103, 2100 Orchard Ln, www.ymcatwincities.org/locations/northeastSP.asp

JUST FOR KIDS

In addition to **Playgrounds and Amusement Parks**, below, you might be interested in:

- **Bounce On Air**, moonwalk and bouncers to rent for parties, 612-961-6580, www.bounceonair.com.
- **Gymboree Play and Music**, for children newborn to 5 years, several locations, www.playandmusic.com
- **My Gym Children's Fitness Center**, 956 Prairie Center Dr, Eden Prairie; serves ages three months to nine years, and is available for birthday parties; 952-906-0028, www.my-gym.com

LACROSSE

Look on the **Minnesota Lacrosse Association** web site (www.mn-lacrosse.com) for everything you need to know about how to get involved in this sport.

PAINTBALL

Paintball is all the rage for parties these days. You can go out to a farm or arena to play it, or some companies will bring their paintball equipment to you. Here are a few places to play. The **Minnesota Paintball Internet Guide** (www.mnpig.com) will net you many, many more.

- **Action Packed Paintball Games**, 8200 Old Hwy 169, Jordan, 952-492-6776, www.actionpackedpaintball.com
- **FSL Paintball Arena**, 6651 141st Ave, Ramsey, 763-780-8461, www.fsl paintball.com
- **Joes Paintball Platoon**, 22202 County Rd 15, Elk River, 612-964-6829, www.joespaintballplatoon.com
- **Northside Sports Park**, 14622 Ferret St NW, Ramsey, 763-427-3892, www.northsidesports.com
- **Special Forces Paintball**, Buffalo, 763-682-0582, www.specialforces paintball.com; has its own field as well as a mobile unit they can bring to your backyard for parties
- **Splat Tag**, 854 Rice Street, St. Paul, 651-488-7700, www.splattag.com
- **St. Croix Paintball**, 1810 Webster Street, Hudson, Wisconsin 715-377-0441, www.stcroixpaintball.com

PLAYGROUNDS AND AMUSEMENT PARKS

- **Chutes and Ladders**, Hyland Park Reserve, Bloomington, has climbing options and slides suitable for almost any skill level, www.threerivers parkdistrict.org.
- **Lake Minnetonka Regional Park**, Minnetrista, www.threerivers parkdistrict.org
- **Valley Fair Amusement Park and Whitewater Country Waterpark**, Shakopee, www.valleyfair.com; purchase discounted tickets online

RACQUET SPORTS

The courts listed here are either public courts or private institutions that offer daily rates for non-members. Keep in mind that most health clubs contain racquetball and indoor tennis courts; see listings below under **Health Clubs**. The following are indoor courts. Outdoor courts can be found at parks and school-yards throughout the region. Don't overlook the school district community services catalogues as sources for lessons, leagues, and partners.

- **Daytona Club**, 14740 N Lawndale Ln, Dayton, 763-427-6110, www. daytonagolfclub.com
- **Ft. Snelling Tennis and Learning Center**, 100 Federal Dr, Minneapolis, near the junction of 62 and 55, 612-252-8367, www.tennisandlearning.org
- **Nicollet Tennis Center**, 4005 Nicollet Ave, Minneapolis, 612-825-6844, www.nicollettennis.com

ROCK AND ICE CLIMBING

The granite bluffs of the Upper Midwest offer some worthy challenges to climbers. The best rock climbs nearby are the quartzite bluffs at **Devil's Lake State Park** near Baraboo, Wisconsin, about a four-hour drive southeast. It's a beautiful hiking area, too. Climbers also like the sheer basalt walls on the banks of the **St. Croix River at Interstate State Park** in Taylors Falls and the ice along Highway 61 out of **Duluth**. For more information about Minnesota climbing, look online at www.mnclimbing.org. To practice on indoor walls and sign up for indoor and outdoor lessons, visit the following places:

- **Carnival Thrillz**, 329 S Lake Ave, Canal Park, Duluth, 218-279-9980
- **Midwest Mountaineering**, 309 Cedar Ave S, Minneapolis, 612-339-3433
- **P.J. Asch Otterfitters**, 413 E Nelson St, Stillwater, 651-430-2286, www.pjaschotterfitters.com
- **REI Recreational Equipment**, 750 W 79th St, Bloomington, 952-884-4315, www.rei.com
- **Vertical Endeavors**, 855 Phalen Blvd, St. Paul, 651-776-1430, www.verticalendeavors.com

RUNNING/WALKING

Even in the glacial cold of January you see hardy Minnesotans jogging along the streets and parkways. For those who are trying to rack up miles, the **Minneapolis Chain of Lakes** provides a flat and scenic way to achieve your goals. Here, according to the Minneapolis Park and Rec Board, are the walking distances around each lake: **Cedar**, 1.68 miles; **Lake of the Isles**, 2.6 miles; **Lake Calhoun**, 3.1; **Lake Harriet** 2.75; and **Lake Nokomis** 2.7.

For route suggestions, race information, and running mates, call the following numbers. Also listed is an annual event that (briefly) transforms distance running here into a spectator sport, the **Twin Cities Marathon**. For more local clubs visit www.twincitiessports.com.

- **Active Life and Running Club (ALARC)**, www.alarc.com
- **All-American Trail Running Association**, www.trailrunner.com, gives the run-down on trails and clubs all over the country
- **Get in Gear 10K**, April, www.getingear10K.com
- **James Page Brewery 5K**, September, also known as the Blubber Run, ends with pizza and beer on Peavey Plaza in front of Orchestra Hall in downtown Minneapolis, www.pagebrewing.com.
- **Lifetime Fitness Triathlon**, July. Billed as The Battle of the Sexes, there are cash prizes worth half a million dollars for the professionals who compete in this event, but thousands of local athletes also compete for the fun (and chance of being seen on national television), www.ltftriathlon.com.
- **Minnesota Distance Running Association**, 952-927-0983, www.runmdra.org

- **Northwest Athletic Clubs Club Run**, 612-673-1282, www.north westac.com
- **Team Run N Fun**, 651-290-2747; informal running group, meets twice a month, sponsored by Run N Fun stores, St. Paul and Eden Prairie, www. runnfun.us
- **Twin Cities Marathon**: this 26-mile road race winds around the lakes of Minneapolis and along the Mississippi River to the finish line at the state capitol. Held in crisp October, it is billed as the most beautiful marathon in America and attracts thousands of runners and cheering spectators who line every foot of the way, www.twincitiesmarathon.org. If you want to run in this race, enter early and train hard—the entries fill fast, and just so you know, there's a punishing uphill late in the race.
- **Twin Cities Race for the Cure**, www.racecure.org

ONLINE TRAINING
- **Cool Running**, www.coolrunning.com/engine/3/3_5/400.shtml
- **Lake Superior College**'s virtual 13-week training courses for marathons and half-marathons are prepared by Grandma's Marathon record holder Dick Beardsley, www.lsc.edu/online/Degrees/grandmas.cfm
- **Grandma's Marathon**, www.grandmasmarathon.com
- **Training Peaks**, www.trainingpeaks.com

WALKING TO GET TO KNOW THE NEIGHBORHOOD
There are innumerable places in the Twin Cities where you can get your exercise and learn something at the same time. Here are just a few:
- **Eloise Butler Wildflower Garden and Bird Sanctuary**, off Theodore Wirth Pkwy, Minneapolis; naturalist-led nighttime walks on the nights just before the full moon are truly beautiful. Reservations are required, 612-370-4903.
- **F. Scott Fitzgerald Walking Tour of St. Paul**: The tour begins at 481 Laurel, where Fitzgerald was born, and continues down Summit Avenue to the Romanesque brownstone apartment building (593–599) Fitzgerald once described as, "A house below the average on a street above the average." This is where he was living when his first novel was accepted for publication, and it's reported that he ran down the street stopping traffic and telling drivers his news. For a printable map of the complete tour, click on http://caudle2.home.comcast.net/fscotwlk.htm.
- **Historical walking tours** are led by staff of the **Minnesota Historical Society,** year 'round at many state historic sites. Call 651-296-6126 or check the Society's calendar of events posted on the Internet at www.mnhs.org/calendar.
- **Minneapolis Riverfront** tours are offered most weekends. They begin and end at the Mill City Museum, 612-341-7555, www.millcity museum.org.
- **French Regional Park in Plymouth** is a particular favorite because its ten miles of trails meet the needs of those who have difficulty walking as

well as those of serious runners. One particularly gentle paved trail has rest stops every quarter of a mile. Other trails eventually lead to the **Luce Line State Trail**. Morning and evening walks are led by YMCA staffers, www.threeriversparkdistrict.org. (See also **Biking** and **Skiing—Cross-country** in this chapter, and **Dog Parks** in the **Pets** chapter.)

- The **Minnesota Valley National Wildlife Refuge** offers numerous guided wildlife walks, including summer solstice, prairie-in-bloom, bird-watching, and full-moon hikes. Walks start at the visitors' center, 3815 American Blvd E in Bloomington, across from the Airport Hilton Hotel. Check the refuge's online calendar for times and dates; www.fws.gov/midwest/minnesotavalley/calendar.html or call 952-854-5900.

SAILING/WINDSURFING/ICE BOATING

Minnesota waters are known to boaters across the country. **Lake Minnetonka** and **White Bear Lake** in the Twin Cities suburbs and **Lake Calhoun** in the shadows of Minneapolis' skyscrapers are home to nationally competitive yacht clubs and experienced sailing schools. **Lake Superior** is one of the finest sailing grounds in the world. Online, tack over to **www.ussailing.com** for answers to all your questions as well as programs for sailors with special needs. Locally, contact:

- **Calhoun Yacht Club and Sailing School,** 612-285-5963, www.lakecalhoun.org
- **Lake Harriet Yacht Club,** 612-920-9420, www.lhycsailing.com
- **Lake Minnetonka Sailing School,** 952-404-1645, www.lakeminnetonkasailingschool.org
- **Minneapolis Parks and Recreation Board**, www.minneapolisparks.org, offers beginner-level evening lessons for adults at Lake Harriet.
- **Minnetonka Yacht Club and Sailing School,** 952-474-4457, www.mycsailing.org
- *Northern Breezes* is the free local sailing news magazine, www.sailingbreezes.com.
- **Sailboats, Inc.,** Lake City, Minnesota; and Bayfield and Barker's Island, Wisconsin, 800-826-7010 or www.sailboats-inc.com offers instruction and charters on Lake Pepin and Lake Superior.
- **Upper Minnetonka Yacht Club**, 4165 Shoreline Dr, Spring Park, www.umyc.org
- **Wayzata Yacht Club and Sailing School,** 1100 E County Rd 16, Wayzata, 952-473-0352, www.wyc.org
- **White Bear Yacht Club and Sailing School**, Clubhouse 651-429-4567, www.wbycsail.org

Ice boating and windsurfing are not as organized as sailing, but there are some races and there are plenty of guys out there experimenting with their "sleds," particularly on **Lake Minnetonka, Lake Calhoun,** and **Lake Waconia**. Those interested should contact one of the yacht clubs listed above, or just show up where you see a group of ice boaters gathered, often on

Wayzata Bay of Lake Minnetonka. For windsurfing, these places can outfit you with equipment and arrange for lessons:

- **The House Boardshop**, located at the junction of 35E and I-694 at 300 S Owasso Blvd, St. Paul, 651-482-9995, 800-992-7245, www.the-house.com
- **Scuba Center Windsurfing**, 5015 Penn Ave S, Minneapolis, 612-925-4818, www.scubacenter.com

SCUBA DIVING

Diving is a year-round sport in Minnesota—no kidding. They just cut holes in the ice. Good dives are found at **Square Lake Park** in Washington County and in **Lake Superior**. There is also diving in the **Crosby-Ironton mines** "Up North." The following places can get you certified and equipped, but also check with your school district's Community Services.

- **Scuba Center Windsurfing**, 5015 Penn Ave S, Minneapolis, 612-925-4818, www.scubacenter.com
- **Scuba Daddy's Dive Shop**, 13761 Nicollet Ave S, Burnsville, 952-892-1444, www.scubadaddys.com
- **Scuba Dive and Travel**, 4741 Chicago Ave S, Minneapolis, 612-823-7210, www.scubadiveandtravel.com

SKIING—CROSS-COUNTRY

Once it snows, cross-country ski tracks seem to magically appear on all the lakes, parks, and golf courses. You can follow them or, if you want to get out into the woods, try just about any of the Regional or State Parks listed in the **Lakes and Parkways** chapter or the trails listed in **Biking** or **Hiking** above. To ski public land, anyone over age 16 will need a **Great Minnesota Ski** pass, available from the **Department of Natural Resources (DNR)**, 1-888-MNLICENSE or 1-888-665-4236, www.dnr.state.mn.us/licenses/skipass. An annual pass is $15 plus an issuing fee. Ski passes may also be purchased using Minnesota's **Electronic Licensing System (ELS)**. There are 1800 locations around the state where you can use ELS. For a list of these, go to the ELS homepage, www.dnr.state.mn.us/licenses/agents.html, or call the **DNR Information Center** at 651-296-6157 or 1-888-646-6367, TTY: 651-296-5484 or 800-657-3929. Day passes can be purchased at most parks. Money from the ski passes is used to maintain the trails.

Many county parks groom trails for skiing, and some of them offer other amenities as well. Try **Baker Park Reserve**, Maple Plain, which also offers a sliding hill and cozy chalet. The short (6.1K) trail at **French Regional Park** is lighted. For more information about these parks and many others, visit the www.threeriversparkdistrict.org web site. In town, **Wirth Park Winter Recreation Area**, Minneapolis, provides space for tubing and snowboarding, as well as cross-country skiing, www.wirthwinter.com.

To find more places to ski, order free maps of groomed ski trails throughout the state, as well as information about lodging, online from the **Minnesota Office of Tourism**, www.exploreminnesota.com. The

Minnesota Nordic Ski Association's web site, www.mnnordicski.org, includes trail maps and snow conditions as well.

For an invigorating winter getaway, rent a cabin on the **North Shore** (the arrowhead-shaped part of the state, north of Duluth), and tour the area's granite bluffs and woods on cross-country skis. For a more isolated experience, the **Boundary Waters Canoe Area** is open to cross-country skiers in winter. You can even ski yurt-to-yurt if you want to! For full details call **Boundary Country Lodge to Lodge Adventures**, Grand Marais, 218-388-4487, 800-322-8327, www.boundarycountry.com.

Neighboring Wisconsin has skiing too! In fact, it is host to the country's most famous cross-country ski race, the **American Birkebeiner**. Starting at **Hayward, Wisconsin**, about a three hours' drive from the Twin Cities, this 51-kilometer race is held every February. The "Birkie," as it's affectionately known, is open to world-class competitors and well-conditioned amateurs. Call 800-872-2753 or 715-634-5025 for information; pick up entry forms at local ski shops, or enter online at www.birkie.org. Even if you're not interested in racing, this region's 858,400-acre **Chequamegon National Forest** is always a beautiful place to ski. For Wisconsin travel information look online at **www.travelwisconsin.com**.

LEARN TO SKI
The park districts offer free cross-country ski lessons, as do Community Services programs through the schools. In the cities, call the following numbers for more information:
- **Minneapolis Parks and Recreation Board**, www.minneapolis parks.org
- **St. Paul Division of Parks and Recreation**, www.stpaul.gov/depts/ parks

For rentals, sales, and advice, try the following (among others):
- **Aarcee Rentals**, 2910 Lyndale Ave S, Minneapolis, 612-827-5746, www. aarceerental.com
- **Hoigaard's**, 3550 S. Hwy 100, St. Louis Park, 952-929-1351, 800-266-8157, www.hoigaards.com
- **Midwest Mountaineering**, 309 Cedar Ave S, Minneapolis, 612-339-3433, www.midwestmtn.com
- **REI,** 750 W American Blvd, Bloomington, 952-884-4315; 1955 County Rd B2 W (Schneiderman's Plaza), Roseville, 651-635-0211; www.rei.com

SKIING–DOWNHILL

While Minnesota is not mountainous, it is hilly, and its short runs have turned out some of the top U.S. Ski Team racers in the country—**Cindy Nelson** grew up at **Lutsen** and **Kristina Koznick** learned to race at **Buck Hill**. For the rest of us, the nearby slopes offer a fun day out, with more of our time spent skiing than riding lifts. Snowboarding is allowed at most areas. All ski areas offer rentals. For snow conditions in Minnesota, Wisconsin, and the Upper Peninsula of Michigan, check out **www.mnsnow.com**. To find the perfect pair of skis, try **Joe's Ski Shop's Demo Center at Wild Mountain** ski area in **Taylor's Falls**. By purchasing a Demo Pass, you can try up to five pairs of the latest skis. **Joe's Ski Shop** is located at 33 County Road B, St. Paul, 651-488-5511, 888-GO-TO-JOES, www.joesskishop.com. The **Minnesota Skiing Guide** (www.minnesotamonthly.com) will clue you in on local downhill skiing and snowboarding areas, cross-country trails, snowshoeing, dogsledding, and even winter getaways.

These are the region's most popular ski areas:

- **Afton Alps**, 6600 Peller Ave S, Afton, 651-436-5245, 800-328-1328, www.aftonalps.com
- **Buck Hill**, 15400 Buck Hill Rd, Burnsville, 952-435-7174, www.skibuck.com
- **Hyland Hills Ski Area and School**, 8800 Chalet Rd, Bloomington, 952-835-4604, www.threeriversparkdistrict.org
- **Indianhead Mountain**, Wakefield, Michigan, 800-3-INDIAN, www.indianheadmtn.com; in the Michigan Upper Peninsula (UP) 225 miles northeast of St. Paul; gets a lot of snow; other ski areas and cross-country trails nearby.
- **Lutsen Mountain Ski Area**, Lutsen, www.lutsen.com; the closest Minnesota comes to mountain skiing, beautiful views of Lake Superior; cross-country trails as well.
- **Spirit Mountain**, Duluth, 800-642-6377, www.spiritmtn.com
- **Welch Village**, North of Red Wing off Highway 61 on County Road 7, 651-222-7079, www.welchvillage.com
- **Wild Mountain Ski and Snowboard Area**, Taylor's Falls, 651-465-6315, 800-447-4958, www.wildmountain.com

For certified ski and snowboard instruction or race coaching contact:

- **Afton Ski Racing**, 651-436-7652, www.teamafton.com
- **Blizzard Ski and Snowboard School**, 952-945-9192, http://snowbliz.com
- **Buck Hill Ski Racing**, 952-435-7174 or www.skibuck.com
- **Mt. Gilboa Alpine Racing Inc.**, 952-930-9422, www.teamgilboa.com
- **SkiAway**, Sports Hut, 952-546-3622, www.skiaway.net, offers lessons for women taught by women.
- **SkiJammers Ski and Snowboard School**, 952-473-1288, www.skijammers.com
- **Tonkawood Ski School**, for ages 4-8, 763-473-1141, www.sportshut.com
- **Otto Hollaus Ski School**, 651-436-5528, www.ottohollaus.com

SNOWMOBILING

In winter, this is the state "sport" for Minnesotans who love their motorized vehicles. Minnesota has 20,385 miles of snowmobile trails. More than 18,000 of those miles are managed and maintained by local snowmobile clubs. A

Snowmobile Vacation Guide is published in the December issue of *Snowgoer* magazine, 601 Lakeshore Parkway, Minnetonka, 952-476-2200. Also call the DNR, 651-296-6157, www.dnr.mn.us, for locations of trails. For snowmobile rentals contact **Bay Rentals Inc.**, Minnetonka, 952-474-0366.

Anyone planning to ride on a state or groomed trail in Minnesota must purchase a **Minnesota Snowmobile State Trail Sticker**. Those who ride only on private land or on lakes do not need the sticker. Purchase permits when you register your vehicle or from any of the 1800 electronic licensing (ELS) agents throughout Minnesota. For a list of these, go to the ELS homepage, www.dnr.state.mn.us/licenses/agents.html, or call the **DNR Information Center** at 651-296-6157 or 1-888-646-6367, TTY: 651-296-5484 or 800-657-3929. Minnesota residents born after December 31, 1976, must also complete a DNR snowmobile safety training course before they can legally ride a snowmobile anywhere in Minnesota, including private land. Those 16 or older may order the **Snowmobile Safety CD-ROM** from the DNR by calling (651) 296-6157, toll free 1-888-MINNDNR (646-6367) or by email info@dnr.state.mn.us. Study the information at home and print-out the forms/tests and send them in along with the $10.00 fee to receive your safety certification.

SNOWSHOE HIKING

For a fun, naturalist-led snowshoe hike, nothing beats **North Mississippi Regional Park**, off Interstate 94 and 49th Avenue North, Minneapolis. Call 612-370-4865 to schedule a tour for your own group, or 763-694-7693 for information about scheduled events, www.minneapolisparks.org.

SOCCER

Soccer is rapidly becoming Minnesota's most popular youth sport, with approximately 76,000 players ages 6 to 19. It's an exciting spectator sport as well. The 50 fields at the 172-acre **National Sports Center** in **Blaine** have been home to the professional **Minnesota Thunder** and also the site of the **USA Cup**, the premier youth soccer tournament in the country, www.usacup.com. Local soccer associations offer recreational, competitive, and Olympic development programs, and summer coaching and player camps. For information about soccer programs in your community check your school community services guide or contact the **Minnesota Youth Soccer Association**, 11577 Encore Circle, Minnetonka, 55343, 952-933-2384, 800-366-6972, www.mnyouthsoccer.org. In the South Metro, Soccer Blast MN, 3601 West 145th Street, Burnsville, 952-895-1962, www.soccerblastmn.com, offers ISSE soccer training, year-round youth and adult recreational and competitive leagues—and you can rent a field and party room for your own private soccer party.

SWIMMING BEACHES

Rising mercury sends sweaty Minnesotans straight to the beaches—and there are hundreds from which to choose. Most are open from early June to mid-

August. If you sign your children up for beach swimming lessons, be advised that June is often stormy. On the other hand, the beaches are sometimes closed on summer's hottest days because of parasites in the water that cause swimmers' itch. Consequently, pool lessons are often preferred.

In the **Three Rivers park system** (www.threeriversparkdistrict.org), **Baker** (Maple Plain), **Bryant Lake** (Eden Prairie), **Cleary Lake** (Prior Lake), **Elm Creek** (Maple Grove), **Fish Lake** (Maple Grove), **French Regional** (Plymouth), **Lake Minnetonka Regional** (Minnetrista), and **Lake Rebecca** (Rockford) all have really nice swimming beaches with picnic facilities and playgrounds. **Lake Minnetonka Regional Park** and **Elm Creek Park Reserve** feature swimming ponds with filtered and chlorinated water. Lake Minnetonka Regional Park's nearly two-acre swimming pond also has a handicapped-accessible ramp that extends into the pool. **"De-Bug" Beach Wheelchairs**, designed to allow access to areas that would normally be inaccessible for people who use wheelchairs, are available free of charge at both Elm Creek and Lake Minnetonka Regional Parks.

Another chlorinated, sandy-bottomed swimming pond can be found at **Lake Elmo Park Reserve**, 1515 Keats Avenue North, Lake Elmo, in **Washington County**, as can one of the area's best scuba diving lakes, **Square Lake**, 15450 Square Lake Trail North, Stillwater. For information, call 651-430-8370 or look online at www.co.washington.mn.us/info_for_residents/parks.

Ramsey County operates public beaches on several lakes. For facility information look online at www.co.ramsey.mn.us/parks/parks/swimming.asp.

There are a number of beaches available throughout **Anoka County**, including **Bunker Beach Water Park** in Bunker Hills Regional Park, Coon Rapids, 763-767-2895 infoline & group reservations, 763-757-3920 general park system line, www.co.anoka.mn.us/departments/park_rec/index.htm.

Back in the cities—**Minneapolis'** most popular beach is on **Lake Nokomis**, although the beaches on **Cedar**, **Calhoun** and **Harriet** are also heavily used. In 2004, Minneapolis developed **LAURI**, the **Lake Aesthetic and User Recreation Index**, an online reference that rates Minneapolis lakes for water quality and aesthetics (that would be color and odor of the water, not the quality of the tattooed-topless at Cedar Lake's Hidden Beach). The online guide reports data for all the city's public swimming lakes: **Lake Calhoun, Cedar Lake, Lake Harriet, Lake Hiawatha, Lake of the Isles, Loring Pond, Lake Nokomis, Powderhorn Lake**, and **Wirth Lake**. Check out LAURI and the beaches' hours of operation, facilities, lessons, directions and parking, etc., on the **Minneapolis Park and Recreation Board** web site, www.minneapolisparks.org.

St. Paul operates beaches on **Lake Phalen** and **Lake Como**. For directions, hours of operation, etc., look online at **St. Paul Parks and Recreation**, www.stpaul.gov/depts/parks.

In the western suburbs, **Shady Oak Lake** on Shady Oak Road just outside of **Hopkins** is so heavily used, unless you get there early it's difficult to find a parking spot, www.hopkinsmn.com/parkrec/shadyoakbeach.html. While many **Lake Minnetonka** cities maintain beaches for their residents, the primary public beach is at the **Excelsior Commons**.

SWIMMING LESSONS

Given the amount of water we have in Minnesota, every child should learn to swim. Most schools and Community Services programs offer swimming lessons, but there are several private swimming schools as well. Among them:

- **Foss Swim Schools**: Chanhassen, 952-906-5942; Knollwood Mall, St. Louis Park, 952-935-8732; Maple Grove, 763-416-8993; www.foss swimschool.com
- **Martha Burns Swimming School**, 160 N Blake Rd, Hopkins, 952-945-0346, www.mbswimschool.com
- **YMCA** (ages 6 months to 16 years) 612-375-YMCA, www.ymca twincities.com

SWIMMING POOLS AND WATER PARKS

You can hit the beach all winter long at the Twin Cities' indoor water parks:

- **Anoka Aquatics Center**, 155 17th Ave, Anoka, has a 200-foot water slide and 1- and 3-meter diving boards, 763-421-7730, www.ci.anoka.mn. us/parksandrec/aquatic_center.html
- **Apple Valley Family Aquatic Center**, 14421 Johnny Cake Ridge Rd, Apple Valley; four-story water slide; 952-953-2300, www.ci.apple-valley.mn.us/Parks/Facilities/Aquatic_Center/main.html
- **Eko Backen Waterslides**, 22570 N Manning Trail, New Scandia Township (near Forest Lake), offers snow-tubing in winter; 651-433-2422, http://ekobacken.com
- **Maplewood Community Center Aquatic Park**, 2100 White Bear Ave, has a 120-foot waterslide, and spraying water toys; 651-249-2100, www.ci.maplewood.mn.us
- **Marriott Depot Waterpark**, 225 Third Ave S, Minneapolis; indoor water park, open to the public Thursday–Sunday; 612-375-1700, www.the depotminneapolis.com/courtyard.htm
- **St. Louis Park Aquatic Park**, 3700 Monterey Dr, St. Louis Park; outdoor municipal facility with water playground, 2 drop slides, 2 twisting slides, zero-depth pool, lap pool; 952-924-2567, http://www.stlouispark.org/experience/aquatic_park.htm
- **Tropics Indoor Water Park**, 4580 N Victoria St (Shoreview Community Center), Shoreview; 651-490-4700, www.ci.shoreview.mn.us/Tropics/Tropics.htm
- **Valleyfair Amusement Park & Whitewater Country Waterpark**, County Rd 101, Shakopee; included in Valleyfair's general admission: Ripple Rapids lazy river, Panic Falls slides, Raging Rapids flume ride; 800-FUN-RIDE, ww2.valleyfair.com
- **Water Park of America at the Grand Hotel Mall of America**, Bloomington, billed as "America's Biggest Water Park and Resort;" 70,000-square-foot indoor water park features a 10-story water slide tower and arcade with on-site redemption center, www.waterparkofamerica.com

- **Wild Mountain/Taylor's Falls Recreation Area**, 37200 Wild Mountain Rd (7 miles north of Taylor's Falls), 651-465-6315, 800-447-4958, www.wildmountain.com; a waterpark at a ski resort; attractions include the Big Country innertube ride, Black Hole speed slide, a lazy river, dedicated children's area

WALKING

See **Running/Walking**, above.

SPORTING GOODS STORES

For those in need of gear, we offer the following list of places to start shopping. If you're not sure whether you want to buy an expensive item, inquire about testing or renting—or investigate the second-hand sporting goods stores.

- **Aarcee Recreation,** 2910 Lyndale Ave, Minneapolis, 612-827-5746, www.aarceerental.com, provides outdoor goods and services, including canoes, cross country skis, and camping equipment.
- **Alternative Bike and Board Shop**, 2408 Hennepin Ave S, Minneapolis, 612-374-3635, http://altbikeboard.com
- **Cabela's**, 800-237-4444, www.cabelas.com, 3900 Cabela Dr, Owatonna, Minnesota, off I-35 south of the cities, 507-451-4545; Rogers, at the intersection of I-94 and Minnesota Hwy 101, 218-773-0282; Cabela's superdome-sized stores are a tourist attraction as well as the definitive sports equipment shopping experience.
- **Erik's Bike Shops**, Minnetonka Blvd at Texas Ave, St. Louis Park, and other locations, 952-920-1790, www.eriksbikeshop.com
- **Freewheel Bike**, 1812 S Sixth St, Minneapolis (U of Minnesota—West Bank), 612-339-2219 (sales), 612-339-2235 (service), http://freewheel bike.com, is one of the largest bike shops in the nation. It offers bike maintenance classes and group rides.
- **The House Boardshop**, located at the junction of 35E and 694 at 300 S Owasso Blvd, St. Paul, 800-992-7245, 651-482-9995, www.the-house. com, has a great selection—and equally great prices—on windsurfing equipment and lessons, snowboards, and more.
- **Hoigaard's**, 3550 S Hwy 100, St. Louis Park, 952-929-1351, www. hoigaards.com, can outfit you for almost any sport. This is also a good place to look for a winter coat and patio furniture. Don't miss Hoigaard's annual tent sale.
- **Joe's Ski Shop**, 33 County Rd B, St. Paul, 651-488-5511, 1-888-GO-TO-JOES, www.joesskishop.com
- **Midwest Mountaineering**, 309 Cedar Ave S, Minneapolis (near the U of M), 612-339-3433, www.midwestmtn.com, carries outdoor equipment and clothing, and holds a spectacular fall sale.
- **Northstar Lacrosse**, 774 Main St, Hopkins, 952-938-0399, northstar lacrosse.com, is the place to go for lacrosse equipment.

- **Pierce Skate and Ski**, 208 W 98th St, Bloomington, 952-884-1990, www.pierceskateandski.com, has been Ski Magazine's Gold Medal Shop for a decade.
- **REI**, www.rei.com, 750 W 98th St, Bloomington, 952-884-4315, and 1995 W County Rd B2, Roseville, 651-635-0211, has bikes, skis, canoes, and camping gear—and a monster climbing wall.
- **Run N Fun**, www.runnfunshoes.com, 6405 West City Pkwy, Eden Prairie, 952-944-RFUN, and 868 Randolph Ave, Saint Paul, 651-290-2747, is the racing headquarters for many high school and college track teams, and includes a Nike women's "concept shop."
- **SCUBA Dive and Travel**, 4741 Chicago Ave, Minneapolis, 612-823-7210, www.scubadiveandtravel.com; this full-service dive shop rents dry suits, wet suits, regulators, lift bags, tanks, weights, and all accessories needed for diving. Classes are also available.
- **2nd Wind Exercise**, 6819 Wayzata Blvd, St. Louis Park, 952-544-2540, www.2ndwindexercise.com, has several locations throughout the Twin Cities and at the Outlets at Albertville. They sell new and used better-grade exercise equipment.
- **Soccer Express USA**, www.soccerexpressusa.com, 653 S Snelling Ave, St. Paul, 651-698-8092, and 10116 Cedar Lake Rd, Minnetonka, 952-544-6662
- **Sportsman's Guide Outlet**, 490 Hardman Ave S, St. Paul, 651-552-5248, www.sportmansguide.com, sells overstocks, returns, discontinued items, and special purchases at 5 to 50% discounts.
- **Twin City Tennis Supply**, 4747 Chicago Ave S, Minneapolis, 612-823-9285, www.tctennis.com; this is where the champions shop.
- **West Marine**, 13889 Ridgedale Dr, Minnetonka, 952-545-5540, 800-BOATING, www.westmarine.com

WITH 11,842 LAKES, AND 16.7 MILLION ACRES OF FORESTS, YOU could consider all of Minnesota one big park if you wanted to—and many people do! Approximately ten thousand years ago, when the most recent ice age ended, the receding glaciers left behind a landscape filled with lakes, marshes, bogs, and fens. When European settlers arrived they found this wet land difficult to develop, so thousands of acres were preserved, quite accidentally. Today, many of these wetlands are parks where thousands of people congregate for recreation and relaxation. Amazingly though, the wetlands almost didn't become parks.

By the 1880s, Twin Cities' lakes had become popular locations for resorts and houses, and while state officials coveted the prime waterfront areas as regional parks, their plan was not well received. Citizens were afraid it was a speculation scheme by conspiratorial insiders. Park proponents prevailed, though, by citing the success of New York's Central Park. Soon, **Theodore Wirth**, in the persistent manner of New York City's Robert Moses, was tearing down houses on the east shore of Lake Calhoun and marshaling the park system into what it is today. Wirth Park is named after him.

Thanks to him, 99% of the residents of Minneapolis live within six blocks of a park. And thanks to his template for development, parks are an integral part of all our other cities as well. Consequently, you can expect that anywhere you choose to live, there will be parks and trails nearby. The biggest plus, though, is the interconnectedness of the system. While there are gaps, and the linkages aren't perfect, every city, county, and regional planning agency within the metro area has as its goal the establishment of contiguous green space. Thanks to them we can easily bike from the western suburbs to the Mississippi Riverfront in Minneapolis and, with just a little more trouble, continue on to north of Stillwater. Thanks to the planners, too, there is public access to every lake and river—quite often, handicapped access, as well!

The following is a brief sampling of some of the metro's 136,900 acres of parks and open space. The highlighted parks were chosen because they offer very different experiences of this region. By visiting them, you will quickly be able to develop a broad perspective on your new home. For many more places to go and things to do, look under your specific interests in **Sports and Recreation**. Download Twin Cities park, bike, and trail maps from the Metropolitan Council web site, www.metrocouncil.org. You will find clickable links to county, city, and regional parks there as well.

MISSISSIPPI RIVER

A place that never ceases to delight is the narrow corridor that the Mississippi River carves from Itasca through Minneapolis and St. Paul. This 72-mile route is one of the most diverse and complex ecosystems on earth. Shallow and narrow at its upper end, by the time the Mississippi reaches its confluence with the Minnesota River at Fort Snelling, it has become a wide and powerful feature of the largest inland navigation system on earth. At this point, it "becomes what the Mississippi is," a symbol of our nation, a critical migration and transportation corridor at the heart of America's history, and one of the planet's most identifiable features when observed from outer space.

Within the 54,000-acre riverfront, dozens of state and local parks provide outstanding recreation opportunities. For those who feel the river is best experienced by watercraft, be sure to plan ahead and obtain navigational charts, particularly if you are boating on the section of the river that is part of the inland waterway system. (The U.S. Army Corps of Engineers posts downloadable **navigation charts** and revisions on its web site, www.mvr.usace.army.mil/NavCharts/UMRNavCharts.asp.) Not only are there locks, dams, and shoals to navigate, but you will also be sharing the channels with commercial barges that cannot maneuver out of your way. If that thought is enough to make you take back your captain's hat, try the Padelford tour boats, 651-227-1100 or 800-543-3908, www.riverrides.com. Their daily sightseeing cruises, running Memorial Day to Labor Day, also include lunch or dinner.

The parkways along either bank are lovely for walking and biking. The **St. Anthony Falls Heritage Trail** is a self-guided tour from the Stone Arch Bridge (built for trains 150 years ago and now the exclusive domain of pedestrians and bicyclists) to Nicollet Island and back to SE Main Street. Interpretive markers and kiosks along the way describe the birth of Minneapolis. If your mood is romantic, stroll here on a moonlit evening and enjoy the skyline reflected in the black river. If you're in a hurry, take a segway tour of this area, www.humanonastick.com. For longer tours, you can follow **West River Parkway** and eventually reach **Minnehaha Park** on the city's far south side. Alternatively, follow **East River Parkway/East Mississippi River Boulevard** south, going through the University of Minnesota campus, to **Hidden Falls Park**, a picnic area on the riverbank. A little farther along the parkway is **Fort Snelling State Park**, the place where the Minnesota and Mississippi Rivers meet and the site of a stone fort built in the 1820s. The parkway ends at **Crosby Farm Nature Area**, off Gannon Road at Shepard Road, St. Paul. This secluded preserve of Mississippi River estuaries and marshes features a boardwalk through the marsh and is one of the few places in the metro area where nesting warblers can be found. The entrance to Fort Snelling State

Park is off Post Road, south of State Highway 5. A day-use park with no camping allowed, it boasts a swimming beach, handicapped-accessible fishing pier, and boat access.

CITY PARKS

Every city has a park system, but the biggest is that of **Minneapolis** (www. minneapolisparks.org), which encompasses 18 lakes and nearly 6400 acres of parkland, including over 170 neighborhood parks and 49 year-round recreation centers. Because the city dedicates 15% of its land to parks, it has been named one of the top 10 green cities in the nation by *The Green Guide*. It has also been called the "closest thing to park nirvana" by the Trust for Public Land.

St. Paul (www.stpaul.gov/depts/parks) has more miles of shoreline along the Mississippi than any other municipality along the entire length of the river. Its series of 16 public parks provides over 3500 acres of floodplain and bluff-top wildlife habitat and opportunities for recreation. Though these incredible parks have, until recently, been viewed as individual sites, the city is in the process of consolidating and connecting them, and forming a new park that will be known as "**The National Great River Park**." You can access the river in many places along Mississippi River Boulevard. Unique to St. Paul are the city's elegant public squares, such as **Rice Park**, where the locals sit to relax and people-watch. In winter the squares twinkle with holiday lights—and, during St. Paul's Winter Carnival, with ice sculptures.

CITY PARK HIGHLIGHTS

- **Big Island Veteran's Camp** in Lake Minnetonka, www.ci.orono.mn.us; has rustic campsites and hiking trails, and is only accessible by boat.
- **Minneapolis Chain of Lakes,** www.minneapolisparks.org; walk, bike, drive, or paddle around these lakes, which run north to south along the western edge of Minneapolis. **Cedar Lake** has a quiet public swimming beach. **Lake of the Isles** offers walking paths, canoe rentals, and skating rinks (with a warming house) in the winter. **Lake Calhoun** has a large public beach and offers boat rentals and lessons. **Lake Harriet** has swimming, boat rentals, a bandshell that hosts summer concerts, and the second oldest public rose garden in the United States.
- **Minnehaha Creek** connects with the above lakes. When the water is high enough, you can start at Gray's Bay in Minnetonka and canoe all the way through South Minneapolis to Minnehaha Park, via the creek.
- **Como Park Zoo, Conservatory, Amusement Park, and Golf Course**, 1431 N Lexington Pkwy, St. Paul, www.stpaul.gov/depts/parks, has something for everyone; in winter, the golf course becomes Como Ski Center. (See **Gardens** below.)
- **Minnehaha Park and Falls**, 4801 Minnehaha Ave S, Minneapolis, www.minneapolisparks.org, is one park you can get to on the Hiawatha LRT. This 171-acre sports and nature area surrounds Minnehaha Falls, where Minnehaha Creek empties into the Mississippi River. On summer

afternoons and weekends, the park is packed with family reunions and company picnics. There are well-marked paths for hiking and nature viewing. A particularly dramatic prospect is the frozen falls in mid-winter, as seen from the ski trails below.

- **Indian Mounds Park** (www.stpaul.gov/depts/parks/userguide/indian mounds.html), is situated atop Dayton's Bluff east of downtown St. Paul. It was established in 1893, making it one of the oldest parks in the region. The six mounds here are thought to be burial sites for at least two American Indian cultures. At the north end of the park there is an overlook from which you can gaze down on Minnesota's capital city, and upon the transportation network that has given it life—the river, the railroad, the freeways, and the St. Paul Airport—all laid out before you like a map.
- **Springbrook Nature Center**, 100 85th Ave NE, Fridley, www.ci.fridley. mn.us/parksrec/snc/sncmain.htm, has been voted the number one park/nature center to take families in the greater metropolitan area by readers of *Parents* magazine. Check out their seasonal events such as Halloween Walk, Winterfest, and Spring Fling, which are appropriate even for very small children.
- **Woodlake Nature Center**, 6710 Lakeshore Dr, Richfield, www.woodlake naturecenter.org, is a 150-acre natural area dedicated to environmental education, wildlife observation, and outdoor recreation. Its three miles of trails are wheelchair accessible in summer, and one of the best places to go for a quick cross-country ski in winter.

COUNTY PARKS

While all the counties have their own park systems, the most extensive is Hennepin County's **Three Rivers Park District**, www.threeriversparks.org. The name "Three Rivers" derives from the fact that all park properties are located in watersheds that flow into one of three rivers: the Mississippi, Minnesota, or Crow. The district includes nearly 27,000 acres of park reserves, regional parks, regional trails and special-use facilities such as beaches, boat launches, interpretative centers, campsites, stables, and ski hills.

- **Elm Creek Park Reserve**, Maple Grove, www.threeriversparks.org, is the largest of all the Three Rivers Parks. With over 4900 acres, this park offers everything, including long hiking/biking loops through miles of mostly unspoiled Minnesota countryside. It also has a chlorinated upland swimming pond, massive children's play area, and off-leash pet exercise area. In winter, the park offers cross-country skiing, snow-tubing, a beginner downhill and snowboarding hill, and provides lighted trails for evening skiing.
- **Hyland Lake Park Reserve**, Bloomington, www.threeriversparks.org, is a winter downhill ski and snowboard area, and a summer hiking/ biking/golf practice center. Home to one of the metro's most popular creative play areas, the park also includes a 6-mile grass loop dog-walking trail, and fishing pier on Hyland Lake.

- **Lake Elmo Park Reserve**, Lake Elmo, www.co.washington.mn.us/ info_for_residents/parks_division/parks_and_trails/lake_elmo_park_reserve, is 2165 acres in size (3 1/2 square miles) with 80% of its acreage set aside for preservation and protection. This 80% will eventually resemble the land as it was prior to the arrival of the settlers in the mid-1800s. The park offers eight miles of turf trails for horses and mountain bikers, as well as an equestrian campground, swimming beach, and orienteering course. Trails are groomed for skiing in winter.

REGIONAL PARKS

The immediate metro includes 46 regional parks and park reserves, 22 regional trails, and six special recreation areas. Visit www.metrocouncil.org/parks/ parks.htm for an online, clickable map and parks directory.

- **Battle Creek Regional Park**, off Lower Afton Road, is an 1840-acre active recreation area with an off-leash dog park and tough mountain biking course. Internet surfers can check www.co.ramsey.mn.us/parks for rules and trail maps.
- **Bunker Hills Regional Park**, Bunker Lake Blvd, www.anokacounty parks.com/qlinks/Parks/BunkerHills/bunker.htm, is situated at the city borders of Ham Lake, Andover, Coon Rapids, and Blaine. Covering 1600 acres, this park has everything from stables where you can rent a horse for a guided trail ride to a wavepool waterpark and top-rated golf course. In winter, take a sleigh ride or hitch up your dog and try skijoring (being pulled by your horse or dog) over the park's 12-kilometer skijoring course.
- **Lake Minnetonka Regional Park**, Minnetrista, www.threerivers parks.org, features a boat launch, fishing piers, creative play area and handicapped-accessible chlorinated lake water swimming pond.
- **Square Lake Regional Special Recreation Feature**, Stillwater, www.co.washington.mn.us/info_for_residents/parks_division/parks_and_ trails/square_lake_park, has some of the clearest water in Minnesota, and is a favorite of scuba divers from throughout the region.

REGIONAL TRAILS

One of the finest regional trail systems in the country is right here in the Twin Cities, where an extensive network of 22 regional trails connects local communities to park reserves and regional parks. Download trail maps from the Metropolitan Council's web site, www.metrocouncil.org/parks/r-pk-map.htm. Routes designated **"Trails . . . At Your Pace"** are generally a mile or less and have flat or gentle terrain, rest stops every 1/4 mile, restrooms, and staffed facilities. Look for these trails at Baker and Hyland Park Reserves, Fish Lake, and French and Lake Minnetonka Regional Parks, www.threeriversparks.org.

- **Big Rivers Regional Trail**, from Mendota Heights through Eagan to Lilydale, is a four-mile flat trail with spectacular views of Fort Snelling, the Minnesota River Valley, and the confluence of the Minnesota and Mississippi Rivers, www.co.dakota.mn.us/parks/index.htm.

- The **Southwest LRT Regional Trail** runs west-east from Carver Park Reserve in Victoria, along the shore of Lake Minnetonka, and eventually to Minneapolis, where it connects with the Midtown Greenway. The southern fork of this trail begins in Chanhassen and runs through St. Louis Park, where it connects to the Minneapolis trails, www.threeriversparks.com.

STATE PARKS

Minnesota has 72 state park and recreation areas, a number of which are located within the metro area. Vehicle permits are required. They can be purchased at REI Outdoor Recreation stores in the Twin Cities, at any state park, and from the DNR, 651-296-6157 or toll free 1-888-MINNDNR (646-6367), www.dnr.state.mn.us. Check availability and make **campsite reservations** online at **www.stayatmnparks.com**. Links to information about all Minnesota's state parks, including maps, fees, reservations, events and activities, and rules can be found at www.dnr.state.mn.us. This web site also includes the "**Lake Finder**," which contains data for more than 4500 lakes and rivers throughout Minnesota, including lake surveys, depth maps, water quality and clarity, stocking reports, and fish consumption advice (from the Department of Health).

- **Afton State Park**, on the banks of the St. Croix River near Hastings, offers over 20 miles of trails across roller-coaster terrain of grassy ridges and deep wooded ravines. Though many of the paths are quite challenging, part of the trail system is handicapped accessible. You can backpack camp here year-round in very private campsites—one so secluded, it's only accessible by canoe. The Afton Alps downhill ski area is open to mountain bikers in summer. Fishing and swimming are also available within the park.
- **Blue Mounds State Park**, in the southwestern corner of the state near Luverne, has 100-foot-tall quartzite cliffs that loom over the surrounding tall-grass prairie. Rock climbing and bird watching are popular here, and the park is home to a herd of bison. As long as you're in the vicinity, be sure to visit nearby Pipestone National Monument and the fascinating Jeffers Petroglyphs, near Windom.
- **Fort Snelling State Park**, 101 Snelling Lake Rd, St. Paul (by the airport): Located in the heart of the Twin Cities, where the Mississippi and Minnesota rivers converge, this park offers extensive hiking, bike and ski trails that link to Minnehaha Park and the Minnesota Valley National Wildlife Refuge. You can canoe here, swim, or play golf. Trails allow visitors to hike up to historic Fort Snelling for a view of military life in the 1820s. Ski alongside ice floes in the river in winter.
- **Hill Annex Mine State Park**, between Grand Rapids and Hibbing on U.S. Hwy 169, offers boat, bus, or fossil tours of this historic iron-ore mine.
- **Interstate State Park**, on Hwy 8, just south of Taylors Falls, was formed by earthquakes and lava flows a billion years ago. Then, for another half a million years, the entire region was washed by advancing and retreating seas. Evidence of this fascinating geologic history can be seen in the rock formations found here as well as in the fossil remains of ancient animals.

Both sides of the river offer rugged trails and spectacular views of the St. Croix River Valley. Taylors Falls Scenic Boat Tours (www.wildmountain. com/boat/boat_home) offers narrated cruises daily from May through mid-October. Taylors Falls Canoe Rental (www.wildmountain.com/canoe/ canoe_home.html) specializes in one-way canoe and kayak trips, which start in the park and continue downstream to either the Osceola Landing (7 miles) or William O'Brien State Park (17 miles). A shuttle takes you back to your car.

- **Itasca State Park**, 21 miles north of Park Rapids, is where the Mississippi River begins its 2552-mile journey to the Gulf of Mexico. Wading across the river at this point is a long-standing Minnesota tradition. Overnight lodging is available, as is a full-service restaurant.

- **Jay Cooke State Park**, about two and a half hours north of Minneapolis, east of Carlton on the St. Louis River, is the place to go for kayaking and whitewater rafting. Linked to the **Willard Munger State Trail**, it is also perfect for backpackers, bikers, hikers, horseback riders, and cross-country skiers. There are a number of drive-in camping sites, some of which stay open in winter, and some of which are handicapped accessible. For rafting information contact Superior Whitewater Raft Tours, 218-384-4637, www.minnesotawhitewater.com. For kayaking lessons and information about group trips, contact the University of Minnesota–Duluth Outdoor Program, 218-726-7128, www.umdrsop.org.

STATE TRAILS

Maps for these and other state trails are available online at www.dnr. state.mn.us/state_trails/index.html.

- The **Gateway State Trail** is part of the ambitious **Willard Munger State Trail**, planned to connect St. Paul with Duluth. Eighteen miles long, it goes from north of Stillwater at **Pine Point Park**, to St. Paul, where it dead-ends northeast of the capitol area at Cayuga St, by 35E. Along the way, the paved, multiple use track cuts through a cross-section of urban areas, parks, lakes, and even some rural landscapes that are a surprise to most first-time trail users.

- Biking the **Luce Line**, from Plymouth west to Cosmos, is like taking a jaunt down a quiet country road. A 63-mile-long former railroad grade, it is paved for 30 miles, from Plymouth west to Winsted, with a parallel path for horseback riding.

- The **Minnesota River Valley State Trail** stretches for over 40 miles along the south bank of the Minnesota River, from Fort Snelling to Belle Plaine. It is ideal for hiking, cross-country skiing, mountain biking, horseback riding, and snowmobiling, but be very careful if you use this trail during hunting season.

- **Root River State Trail/Harmony–Preston State Trail** is a 42-mile-long multiple-use trail through the quaint and picturesque rural communities of southeastern Minnesota.

- The 63-mile paved **Willard Munger State Trail**, from Hinckley to Duluth, is a favorite of the in-line skating crowd.

SCENIC BYWAYS

Minnesota has 23 designated Scenic Byways, ranging from the Waters of the Dancing Sky in the northwestern corner of the state to the Minneapolis Grand Rounds. Here are just two highlights. For complete information, look online at the state's tourism web site, www.exploreminnesota.com, or at the federal Highways Administration site, www.byways.org.

- The **Minneapolis Grand Rounds** (www.minneapolisparks.org/grandrounds) is the nation's only urban scenic byway. As it makes its 50-mile circuit of the city, it offers impressive views of the downtown skyline, the Mississippi Riverfront, and Minneapolis Chain of Lakes. Human-made attractions along this route include the historic Stone Arch Bridge, the Walker Arts Center Sculpture Garden, and the city's historic mill district. Download a map of the route from the web site, or simply follow the signs.
- **The Great River Road Scenic Byway** begins at the headwaters of the Mississippi in Itasca State Park and follows the river all the way through the state. The northern portion of the route runs through the magnificent forests of Minnesota's "Lake Country," an area which is also known for its unsurpassed fishing and hunting. Attractions along this leg include 18-foot-high statues of legendary Paul Bunyan and Babe his Blue Ox in Bemidji, and the Little Falls home of Charles Lindbergh. The Forest History Center in Grand Rapids shows visitors life as it was in a 1900-era logging camp. The southern portion runs from the Twin Cities to Winona. On this portion of the route, Hwy 61 hugs the riverbluffs for some of the most stunning scenery and best bird watching in the state. (See **Quick Getaways**.)

REGIONAL LAKES

Fishing seasons for walleye, muskellunge, and large- and small-mouth bass are generally mid-May to mid-February. Fishing for lake trout runs mid-May through September. For more information on fishing, see **Fishing** in the **Sports and Recreation** chapter and check the DNR's web site, www.dnr.state.mn.us. For information about whether the ice is safe, or to find out about rules and regulations on various Hennepin County lakes and rivers, including Lake Minnetonka, the Mississippi River and the Minnesota River, look online at the Hennepin County Water Patrol's web site, www.waterpatrol.org. Speaking of ice—the average ice-out date on Lake Minnetonka is April 15, although, in fact, the ice has never actually gone out on that date. The earliest the ice has ever gone out was March 11, 1878; the latest was May 8, 1856. The most common ice-out dates have been April 17 and 18th (9 times each). A list of all the ice-out dates since 1855 can be found on the Freshwater Society's web site, www.freshwater.org.

- At over 14,000 acres, **Lake Minnetonka**, west of Minneapolis between highways 12 and 7, is the largest body of water in the Twin Cities area, and the ninth largest lake in the state. With over 120 miles of shoreline, it is accessible at numerous public boat ramps. The closest public launch site to

Minneapolis is at Gray's Bay off Hwy 101 in Minnetonka. Several national bass fishing contests are held here each year. Water skiers gravitate to St. Alban's Bay and the quieter waters at the west end of the lake. Those who wish to see and be seen head for the north side of Big Island, between Excelsior and Wayzata, or Lord Fletcher's at Spring Park. Families will enjoy Lake Minnetonka Regional Park, west of Excelsior, which features a swimming pond, boat ramp, and extraordinary playground.

- **White Bear Lake**, east of Hwy 61 at White Bear, is to the East Metro what Minnetonka is to the west. A shallow lake with a sandy bottom, it is a favorite for swimming, sailing, windsurfing, ice boating, and fishing for carp, bluegills, and bullheads.

FORESTS

Less than 1% of the oak, maple, and basswood Big Woods that spanned the middle of the state in the 1850s has survived into the 21st century.

- However, a pristine, 43-acre Big Woods remnant does lie within **Eden Prairie's Riley Creek Conservation Area**, off Dell Rd, between Pioneer Trail and Flying Cloud Drive. The area is ideal for nature study and photography, but there are no trails. Unfortunately, it is severely pressured by surrounding development.
- Another old growth forest, **Wolsfeld Woods**, Hwy 6 at Brown Rd, Long Lake, has fared better, and is home to 185 acres of trees so old and tall that sunlight pierces them like arrows.
- Another tiny remnant of the Big Woods, 14-acre **Wayzata Cenacle Big Woods**, is located on Wayzata Blvd, in the heart of downtown Wayzata, next door to Colonial Square Shopping Center.

Finally, a cautionary note to hikers and nature lovers: The woods and fields, even fairly close to houses, are not 100% safe during **deer hunting season**. Generally, bow season begins in mid-September and firearm season begins in early November. If you feel the need to take a late fall walk in the woods, be sure to wear hunter's "blaze" orange. And if you are taking Fido with you, put an orange vest on him as well. And make plenty of noise. For more information on hunting seasons and regulations check www.dnr.state.mn.us.

NORTH COUNTRY NATIONAL SCENIC TRAIL

The nation's longest hiking trail, the **North Country National Scenic Trail** (www.nps.gov/noco), is a work in progress. Viewed on a map, it looks like the path of an ant, beginning at Crown Point State Historic Site on the Vermont–New York border and meandering over 4000 miles through New York, Ohio, Pennsylvania, Michigan, Wisconsin, and Minnesota, and ending at Lake Sakakawea in North Dakota. Information, updates and brochures can be obtained from the North Country National Trail Association, www.northcountry trail.org; or access the National Park Service homepage, www.nps.gov.

GARDENS

Out-of-town visitors and locals alike delight in Minnesota's public gardens. Here are just a few:

- The **Eloise Butler Wildflower Garden and Bird Sanctuary** in Theodore Wirth Park in Minneapolis (www.minneapolisparks.org), is a peaceful place to learn about and enjoy nature. The oldest public wildflower garden in the U.S., it was originally a botany lab for Minneapolis school teachers. Naturalist tours and programs are offered on weekends. Try the blindfolded sensory walks, "Pond Critters for Kids," and moonlight walks. MetroTransit buses stop at Glenwood Ave and Theodore Wirth Pkwy, just a short two-block walk to the garden's gate (follow the signs).
- **Lyndale Park Gardens**, also in Minneapolis, on the east side of Lake Harriet, www.minneapolisparks.org, is another peaceful urban oasis in the midst of the busy city. It has four distinctive gardens: the Rose Garden, the Perennial Garden, Peace (Rock) Garden, and the Perennial Trial Garden. Immediately adjacent to the Peace Garden is the Thomas Sadler Roberts Bird Sanctuary. MetroTransit buses stop at the intersection of W 40th St and Bryant Ave S. The gardens are just a two-block walk west of the bus stop.
- Located in popular Como Park in St. Paul, the glass-domed Victorian-era **Marjorie McNeely Conservatory**, 651-487-8200, www.comozoo conservatory.org, with its large collection of tropical palm trees and orchids, is a lovely escape on a minus 30° day. In summer, the park's outdoor Japanese garden is the perfect place to sit and enjoy a meditative cup of tea.
- **Noerenberg Memorial Gardens**, on County Rd 51 (North Shore Dr), overlooking Lake Minnetonka, www.threeriversparks.org, features a variety of unusual plantings, as well as an antique boathouse with a deck where you can sit and enjoy the peace and beauty of the lake. Combine a trip to this garden with lunch at the Minnetonka Art Center, practically across the road, www.minnetonkaarts.org.
- The **University of Minnesota Landscape Arboretum**, 3675 Arboretum Dr, Chaska, 952-443-1400, www.arboretum.umn.edu, is, at over a thousand acres, the largest and most diverse of Minnesota's horticultural sites. Special focus areas include a Japanese garden and restored prairie. There is a three-mile drive through the Arboretum that takes visitors past many of the collections. A guided tour follows this route as well.

WISCONSIN PARKS

- **The Apostle Islands National Lakeshore**, off the south shore of Lake Superior near Bayfield, Wisconsin, www.nps.gov/apis, boasts attractions for everyone from amateur naturalists to lighthouse lovers. For sea kayakers, this 21-island freshwater archipelago is a paddler's paradise of sandstone caves, beaches, lighthouses, and big water. Others can visit the islands via public excursion boats. Camping and hiking are allowed on most. There are hotels, bars, and restaurants on Madeline Island, which is not part of the park. Madeline Island is served several times a day by a ferry from Bayfield harbor, three miles away. Read more about this area in **Quick Getaways**.

- The **Chequamegon-Nicolet National Forest**, www.fs.fed.us/r9/cnnf, covers over a million and a half acres in Wisconsin's Northwoods. It has five designated Wilderness Areas that are open for fishing, hunting, hiking, canoeing, and "no-trace" camping. The North Country National Scenic Trailruns the length of the Rainbow Lake Wilderness, north of Drummond. For more information about the North Country Scenic Trail, see above).
- The **National Freshwater Fishing Hall of Fame and Museum**, 10360 Hall of Fame Dr, Hayward, Wisconsin, http://freshwater-fishing.org, is housed inside a giant concrete, steel, and fiberglass Muskie sculpture.

V OLUNTEERING FOR AN ORGANIZATION IS A SATISFYING WAY TO MAKE A difference in your new community while at the same time meeting people who share similar interests. Area schools, sports teams, hospitals, and museums are always in need of volunteers.

VOLUNTEER PLACEMENT SERVICES

The following organizations coordinate many volunteer activities in the Twin Cities. Call them and they will help you find a place in need of your special talents:

- **Community Volunteer Service of the St. Croix Valley Area (CVS)**, 2300 Orleans St W, Stillwater, 651-439-7434, www.volunteercvs.org; serves Washington and St. Croix counties.
- **Junior League of Minneapolis**, 763-545-9423, www.jlminneapolis.org
- **Junior League of St. Paul**, 651-291-7377, www.jlsp.org
- **United Way First Call for Help**, 211
- **Volunteer Match**, www.volunteermatch.org; just put in your zip code and be matched with a local nonprofit that's looking for volunteers
- **Volunteer Resource Center**, 2021 E Hennepin Ave, Ste 420, Minneapolis, 612-379-4900, www.handsontwincities.org
- **Volunteers of America**, Minnesota Office, 5905 Golden Valley Rd, Golden Valley, 763-546-3242, www.voamn.org.

AREA CAUSES

The following are some of the Twin Cities service organizations that need volunteers:

AIDS

- **AIDS Project Minnesota**, 1400 S Park Ave, Minneapolis, 612-341-2060, www.mnaidsproject.org

- **The Aliveness Project**, 730 E 38th St, Minneapolis, 612-822-7946, www.aliveness.org

ANIMALS

- **Animal Humane Society**, 845 N Meadowbrook Ln, Golden Valley, 763-522-4325; 14–18 youth program and adult program, www.ahshc.org
- **Como Park Zoo**, St. Paul, 651-487-8200, www.comozoo conservatory.org
- **Humane Society of Ramsey County**, St. Paul, 651-645-7387, ext.124, www.hsca.net; needs volunteers to walk dogs and clean cages.
- **Minnesota Zoo**, AppleValley, 952-431-9200, www.mnzoo.com
- **Raptor Center at the University of Minnesota**, 1920 Fitch Ave, St. Paul, 612-624-4745, www.raptor.cvm.umn.edu. Established in 1974, The Raptor Center specializes in the medical care of eagles, hawks, owls, and falcons; volunteer manager 612-624-3928, trcvol@umn.edu.
- **We Can Ride** (see **Disability Assistance,** below)

ART AND MUSIC

- **Minneapolis Institute of Art**, 2400 3rd Ave S, Minneapolis, 612-870-3013, www.artsmia.org
- **Minnesota Orchestra Volunteer Association**, 1111 Nicollet Mall, 612-371-5654, www.wamso.org
- **Walker Art Center**, 612.375.7574, http://learn.walkerart.org/guide.wac; request a Tour Guide Training application online or email tours@walkerart.org

BUSINESS

- **SCORE**, www.scoremn.org; 100 N 6th St, Minneapolis, 612-370-2324; 176 N Snelling Ave, St. Paul, 651-632-8937; sponsored by the Small Business Administration, this organization of active and retired business people provides free business counseling.

CHILDREN/YOUTH

- **Big Brothers Big Sisters of the Greater Twin Cities**, 2550 University Ave, St. Paul, 651-789-2400, www.bigstwincities.org
- **Boys and Girls Club Twin Cities**, 651-999-0600, www.boys andgirls.org; **Boys and Girls Club of Minneapolis**, 2323 11th Ave S, 612-870-7570
- **Boy Scouts of America**, 5300 Glenwood Ave, Golden Valley, 763-545-4550, www.northernstarbsa.org
- **Girl Scout Council of Greater Minneapolis**, 5601 Brooklyn Blvd, Brooklyn Center, 763-535-4602, www.girlscoutsmpls.org

- **Meld**, 219 N Second St, Ste 200, Minneapolis, 612-332-7563, www. meld.org; is a peer self-help parenting education program
- **Pillsbury United Communities/Pillsbury House**, 3501 Chicago Ave S, Minneapolis, 612-824-0708, www.puc-mn.org
- **Youthlink**, 212 2nd Ave N, Minneapolis, 612-252-1200, www.youthlink mn.org
- **Teens Alone**, helps homeless teenagers in the West Metro, 952-988-TEEN, www.teensalone.org.
- **The Garage**, 75 Civic Center Pkwy, Burnsville, 952-895-4664, www.the garage.net; open weekdays from 2:30 p.m. to 5:30 or 6:00 p.m., and on Fridays and Saturdays until 11:30 p.m. Staffed by paid employees and volunteers. Local teen performers.
- **Twin Cities Underground**, 405 W Lake St, Minneapolis, 612-824-2612, www.tcunderground.com. Co-sponsored by Allina Hospitals and Clinics, the Cities 97 radio station, Southside Community Health, and others, TC Underground is a teen club that features student performers. It's run by both kids and parent/community volunteers. To volunteer, email tcvolunteer@gmail.com.
- **Two Wheel View/Trips for Kids—Twin Cities**, serves youth ages 12 years and older, teaching them the principles of environmental stewardship and coordinating local, regional, and international biking programs, 866-858-2453, www.twowheelview.org.

DISABILITY ASSISTANCE

- **Adaptive Recreation Office**, City of St. Paul, 651-266-6375, www.stpaul.gov/depts/parks/adaptiverecreation/volunteeropps.html
- **Alliance for the Mentally Ill**, 800 Transfer Rd, St. Paul, 651-645-2948, http://mn.nami.org
- **ARC of Minnesota**, 651-523-0823, www.arcminnesota.com
- **Courage Center**, 3915 Golden Valley Rd, Golden Valley, 763-520-0214, www.courage.org, is always looking for people with strong communications skills to volunteer with youth and adults who have physical disabilities. The ski program is especially fun, but they also have need for martial arts instructors, archers, aquatic therapy—and that's just the A's. Download an application off the web site.
- **People Incorporated**, 317 York Ave, St. Paul, 651-774-0011, TTY 612-521-2116, www.peopleincorporated.org
- **Sister Kenny Institute**, 800 E 28th St, Minneapolis, 612-863-4466, www.allina.com
- **We Can Ride**, 952-934-0057, www, wecanride.org, offers therapeutic horseback riding and cart driving for children and adults at four locations: Hennepin County Home School in Eden Prairie, Carver Scott Educational Cooperative in Waconia; Shriner's Ranch in Independence, and Pine Meadow Farm in Delano. Volunteer training begins each February.

ENVIRONMENT

- **Clean Water Action**, 308 E Hennepin Ave, Minneapolis, 612-623-3666, www.cleanwateraction.org/mn
- **Land Stewardship Project**, 2200 4th St, White Bear Lake, 651-653-0618, www.landstewardshipproject.org
- **Minnesota Environmental Action Network**, www.mnaction.org
- **Minnesota Center for Environmental Advocacy**, 26 E Exchange St, St. Paul, 651-223-5969, www.mncenter.org
- **Minnesota League of Conservation Voters**, 1101 W River Pkwy, Ste 250, Minneapolis, www.mnlcv.org
- **Nature Conservancy**, 1101 W River Pkwy, Ste 200, Minneapolis, 612-331-0750, http://nature.org/wherewework/northamerica/states/Minnesota
- **Sierra Club**, North Star Chapter, 2327 E Franklin, Minneapolis, 612-659-9124, www.northstar.sierraclub.org; this very active organization saved Pilot Knob (sacred to the Dakota and best vantage point from which to see the Twin Cities) in Mendota Heights from developers, and sponsors numerous fun outings and events such as the Cool Cities Hybrid Car Tour and Scavenger Hunt.
- **Two Wheel View/Trips for Kids—Twin Cities** (see **Children/Youth**, above)
- **University of Minnesota Landscape Arboretum**, Hwy 5 and Arboretum Dr, Chanhassen, 952-443-1400, www.arboretum.umn.edu

EVENTS

- **Minneapolis Aquatennial**, www.aquatennial.org; this event is always looking for volunteers to work the numerous events, and it's a great way to feel like you're part of the community. Volunteers get a T-shirt, invitations to parties, and a chance to ride on the Volunteers' float in the Torchlight Parade. Check online to volunteer.
- **St. Paul Winter Carnival**, St. Paul Festival and Heritage Foundation, 429 Landmark Center, St. Paul, 651-223-4700, http://volunteer.winter-carnival.com

GAY, LESBIAN, BISEXUAL, TRANSGENDER

- **OutFront Minnesota**, 310 38th St E, Minneapolis, 612-822-0127, www.outfrontminnesota.org; this comprehensive resource will connect you to wherever you wish to volunteer.

HEALTH AND HOSPITALS

Most hospitals welcome volunteers—see the **Health Care** chapter in this book for a list of local institutions, and give the nearest one a call. For specific health issues, try one of the following:

- **American Cancer Society**, 2520 Pilot Knob Rd, Mendota Heights, 651-255-8100, www.cancer.org
- **American Heart Association**, 4701 W 77th St, Edina, 952-835-3300, www.americanheart.org
- **American Lung Association**, 490 Concordia Ave, St. Paul, 800-642-LUNG, 651-227-8014, www.alamn.org
- **Association for Nonsmokers—Minnesota**, 2395 University Ave W, Ste 310, St. Paul, 651-646-3005, www.ansrmn.org
- **NARAL Pro-Choice Minnesota**, 550 Rice St (Minnesota Women's Building), St. Paul, 651-602-7655, www.prochoiceminnesota.org
- **Planned Parenthood of Minnesota**, St. Paul: 1965 Ford Pkwy, 651-698-2406, 1700 Rice St, 651-489-1328; Minneapolis: 1200 Lagoon Ave, 612-823-6300; www.ppmns.org

HISTORY

- **Minnesota Historical Society**, 651-296-6126, www.mnhs.org/about/volunteers

HOMELESS SERVICES

- **People Serving People**, 612 S Third St, Minneapolis, 612-332-4500, www.peopleservingpeople.org
- **St. Stephen's Shelter**, 2211 Clinton Ave, Minneapolis, 612-874-9292, www.ststephensmpls.org
- **Salvation Army**, 2727 Central Ave NE, Minneapolis, 612-789-2858; 401 W 7th St, St. Paul, 651-224-4316; www.redshield.org

HOUSING

- **Twin Cities Habitat for Humanity** is an organization of 20,000 volunteers, 10,000 donors, and a staff of 65 dedicated employees. Over the past years, Twin Cities Habitat has helped nearly 600 families become owners of quality, affordable housing. To volunteer, call 612-331-4090, or sign up online at www.tchabitat.org/volunteer.asp.

HUMAN SERVICES

- **American Red Cross**, 1201 W River Pkwy, Minneapolis, 612-871-7676; Blood Services, St. Paul: 651-291-4600, www.mplsredcross.org
- **Amicus**, 100 N 6th St #347B, Minneapolis, 612-348-8570, www.amicususa.org, provides services for ex-inmates.
- **Emergency Food Shelf Network**, 8501 54th Ave N, New Hope, 763-450-3860, www.emergencyfoodshelf.org
- **Food Perspectives**, 763-553-7787, www.foodperspectives.com
- **House of Charity Soup Kitchen and Learning Center**, 510 S Eighth St, Minneapolis, 612-594-2000, www.houseofcharity.org

- **Metro Meals on Wheels**, 612-789-5007, www.meals-on-wheels.com; every community participates in this program.
- **Neighborhood Involvement Program**, 2431 Hennepin Ave S, Minneapolis, 612-374-3125
- **Phyllis Wheatley Community Center**, 1301 Tenth Ave N, Minneapolis, 612-374-4342, www.pwccenter.org, is the oldest African-American agency in the Twin Cities.
- **Second Harvest Food Bank**, many locations, 651-209-7939, www.2harvest.org
- **Sharing and Caring Hands**, 525 N 7th St, Minneapolis, 612-338-4640, www.sharingandcaringhands.org
- **VEAP (Volunteers Enlisted to Assist People)**, 9731 James Ave S, Bloomington, 952-888-9616, www.veapvolunteers.org, is a grassroots agency founded in 1973 by thirteen churches in Richfield for the purpose of neighbors coming together to help other neighbors. VEAP volunteers help residents in Bloomington, Edina, Richfield, and a small portion of South Minneapolis.

LITERACY

- **English Learning Center for Immigrants and Refugee Families**, 2315 Chicago Ave S, Minneapolis, 612-874-9963, www.englishlc.org
- **House of Charity Soup Kitchen and Learning Center**, 510 S Eighth St, Minneapolis, 612-594-2000, www.houseofcharity.org
- **Minnesota Literacy Council**, 756 Transfer Rd, St. Paul, 651-645-2277, www.themlc.org

MEN'S SERVICES

- **Resource Center for Fathers and Families**, 430 Oak Grove St, Minneapolis, 612-874-1509, www.resourcesforfathers.org

POLITICS–PARTIES

- **Democratic Farmer Labor State Office,** www.dfl.org
- **Green Party**, www.mngreens.org
- **Independence Party**, www.mnip.org
- **Republican State Office**, www.mngop.com

POLITICS–PUBLIC INTEREST

- **Association of Community Organizations for Reform Now (ACORN)**, 757 Raymond Ave, St. Paul, 651-642-9639, www.acorn.org
- **Friends for a Nonviolent World**, 1050 Selby Ave, St. Paul, 651-917-0383, www.fnvw.org

- **League of Women Voters of Minnesota**, 550 Rice St, St. Paul, 651-224-5445, www.lwvmn.org, is a non-partisan political organization that encourages the informed and active participation of citizens in government.
- **Minnesota Common Cause**, www.commoncause.org
- **Minnesota Public Interest Research Group (MPIRG)**, 2414 University Ave SE, Minneapolis, 612-627-4035, www.mpirg.org
- **Minnesota Women's Political Caucus**, 550 Rice St, St. Paul, 651-228-0995, www.mnwpc.org
- **Veterans for Peace**, 612-821-9141, www.twincitiesvfp.org

SENIOR SERVICES

- **Little Brothers Friends of the Elderly**, 612-721-6215, www.little brothers.org/twincities

WOMEN'S SERVICES

- **Minnesota Coalition for Battered Women**, www.mcbw.org
- **Minnesota Women's Press**, www.womenspress.com
- **Sojourner Domestic Violence Project**, Hopkins, 952-933-7433, www.sojournerproject.org

WHILE THE LARGEST ACTIVE LUTHERAN CONGREGATION IN THE U.S. can be found in south Minneapolis at the Mount Olivet Lutheran Church (www.mtolivet.org), not everybody in Minnesota is Lutheran. In fact, Lutherans may be outnumbered by Catholics—and those two religious traditions may well be outnumbered by everybody else!

Obviously there are too many active houses of worship in the Metro area to list here but we offer the following as a place to start. For a complete listing look in the Yellow Pages under "Churches" and "Synagogues."

CHURCHES

AFRICAN METHODIST EPISCOPAL

- **St. Peter's AME Church**, 401 E 41st St, Minneapolis, 612-825-9750, stpetersame.org; daycare, 612-823-3009
- **St. James AME Church**, 624 Central Ave W, St. Paul, 651-227-4151, stjamesamec-stpaul.org

ANGLICAN

- **Anglican Church of St. Dunstan**, 4241 Brookside Ave S, St. Louis Park, 952-920-9122, http://huey.cc/dunstan

APOSTOLIC

- **Rehoboth Church of Jesus Christ**, 916 31st Ave N, Minneapolis, 612-529-2234

ASSEMBLIES OF GOD

- **Bethel Assemblies of God**, Nicollet Ave & 57th St, Minneapolis, 612-866-3227

- **Summit Avenue Assembly of God**, 854 Summit Ave, St. Paul, 651-228-0811, summitag.org

BAPTIST

- **Bethesda Baptist Church**, 1118 S 8th St, Minneapolis, 612-332-5904, bethesdamnonline.com
- **First Baptist Church**, 10936 Foley Blvd NW, Coon Rapids, 763-755-3748, www.fbccr.net
- **Progressive Baptist Church**, 1505 Burns Ave, St. Paul, 651-774-5503, www.progressivebptchurch.org
- **Wooddale Church**, 6630 Shady Oak Rd, Eden Prairie, 952-944-6300, www.wooddale.org

CHRISTIAN SCIENCE

- **First Church of Christ, Scientist**, 2315 Highland Pkwy, St Paul, 651-291-7640, www.mtn.org/csreadingroom
- **Second Church of Christ, Scientist**, 228 S 12th St, Minneapolis, 612-332-3368, www.mtn.org

CHURCH OF CHRIST

- **Minneapolis Central Church of Christ**, 1922 4th Ave N, Minneapolis, 612-374-5481, www.churches-of-christ.net
- **Spirit of the Lakes United Church of Christ**, 2930 13th Ave S, Minneapolis, 612-724-2313, www.spiritucc.org
- **Summit Avenue Church of Christ**, 10 S Grotto, St. Paul, 651-222-0872

CHURCH OF JESUS CHRIST OF LATTER-DAY SAINTS

- **Latter-Day Saints Institute**, 1205 University Ave SE, Minneapolis, 612-331-1154
- **Church of Jesus Christ of Latter-Day Saints Family History Centers**, 2801 Douglas Dr N, Minneapolis, 763-544-2479; 4700 Edinbrook Pkwy, Minneapolis, 763-425-1865; and 9700 Nesbitt Ave S, Bloomington, 952 893-2393

CONGREGATIONAL

- **First Congregational Church of Minnesota**, 500 8th Ave SE, Minneapolis, 612-331-3816, www.firstchurchmn.org
- **Plymouth Congregational Church**, 1900 Nicollet Ave, Minneapolis, 612-871-7400, www.plymouth.org
- **Woodbury Community Church**, 2975 Pioneer Dr, Woodbury, 651-739-1427, wccmn.org

DISCIPLES OF CHRIST

- **First Christian Church**, 2201 First Ave S, Minneapolis, 612-870-1868, www.disciples.org

EASTERN ORTHODOX

- **Russian Orthodox Church**, 1201 Hathaway Ln NE, Fridley, 763-574-1001, www. stgeorgeroc.org
- **St. George Greek Orthodox Church**, 1111 Summit Ave, St. Paul, 651-222-6220, stgeorgegoc.org
- **St. Mary's Greek Orthodox Church**, 3450 Irving Ave S, Minneapolis, 612-825-9595, www.stmarysgoc.org
- **St. Michael's Ukrainian Orthodox**, 505 4th St NE, Minneapolis, 612-379-2695, www.uocofusa.org

EPISCOPAL

- **Cathedral Church of St. Mark**, 519 Oak Grove St, Minneapolis, 612-870-7800, www.st-marks-cathedral.org
- **Christ Episcopal Church-Woodbury**, 7305 Afton Rd, Woodbury, 651-735-8790, www.christchurch-woodbury.org
- **Episcopal Diocese of Minnesota**, 1730 Clifton Pl, Minneapolis, 612-870-3300, www.episcopalmn.org
- **St. Alban's**, 6716 Gleason Rd, Edina, 952-941-3065, stalbanschurch.org
- **St. David**, 13000 St. David's Rd, Minnetonka, 952-935-3336, www.nathannetwork.org
- **St. Martin's by-the-Lake**, County Rd 15 and Westwood Rd, Minnetonka Beach, 612-471-8429, www.stmartinsbylake.org
- **St. Paul's**, Franklin and Logan at Lake of the Isles, 612-377-1273, www.stpaulsmpls.org
- **St. Paul's Church on the Hill**, 1524 Summit Ave, St. Paul, 651-698-0371, www.stpaulsonthehillmn.org
- **Trinity Episcopal Church**, 322 2nd St, Excelsior, 952-474-5263, www.trinityexcelsior.org
- **University Episcopal Center**, 331 17th Ave SE, Minneapolis, 612-331-3552, www.uec-mn.org

EVANGELICAL

- **Brookdale Covenant Church**, 5139 Brooklyn Blvd, Brooklyn Center, 763-535-6305, www.covchurch.org
- **Chinese Evangelical Free Church**, 1021 Hennepin Ave, Minneapolis, 612-332-5484, www.tccefc.net
- **Community Covenant Church**, 901 Humboldt Ave N, Minneapolis, 612-374-3935, www.cccminneapolis.org

- **Russian Evangelical Christian Church**, 1205 Tenth Ave, Shakopee, 952-496-0578

FRIENDS (QUAKERS)

- **Minneapolis Friends Meeting**, 4401 York Ave S, Minneapolis, 612-926-6159, www.quaker.org
- **Twin Cities Friends Meeting**, 1725 Grand Ave, St. Paul, 651-699-6995, www.tcfm.org

INDEPENDENT//MULTIPLE AFFILIATIONS

- **Colonial Church of Edina**, 6200 Colonial Way, Edina, 952-925-2711, www.colonialchurch.org
- **Japanese Fellowship Church**, 4217 Bloomington Ave, Minneapolis, 612-722-8314, www.japanesefc.org
- **Living Waters Christian Church**, 1002 2nd St NE, Hopkins, 952-938-4176, www. www.livingwaterschurchmn.com
- **Wayzata Evangelical Free Church**, 705 County Rd 101 N, Plymouth, 763-473-9463, www.wayzatafree.org

JEHOVAH'S WITNESSES, WWW.WATCHTOWER.ORG

- **Riverview Congregation** (with Spanish), 1545 Christensen Ave, West St. Paul, 651-457-7139

LUTHERAN

- **Beautiful Savior**, 5005 Northwest Blvd, Plymouth, 763-550-1000, www.beautifulsaviorlc.org
- **Bethlehem Lutheran Church**, 4100 Lyndale Ave S, Minneapolis, 612-312-3400, www.bethlehem-church.org
- **Calvary Lutheran Church**, 7520 Golden Valley Rd, Golden Valley, 763-545-5659, www.calvary.org
- **Como Park Lutheran Church**, 1376 W Hoyt Ave, St. Paul, 651-646-7127, www.comoparklutheran.org
- **Den Norske Lutherske Mindekirke** (The Norwegian Lutheran Memorial Church, Mindekirchen), 924 E 21st St, Minneapolis, 612-874-0716, www.mindekirchen.org; just off Franklin Ave in Minneapolis, this old Norwegian-heritage church sponsors Norwegian classes and sometimes holds bilingual services.
- **Evangelical Lutheran Church Association**, 612-870-3610, www.elca.org
- **Hosanna Lutheran Church**, 9600 163rd St W, Lakeville, 952-435-3332, www.hosannalc.org

- **Holy Trinity Lutheran Church**, 2730 E 31st St, Minneapolis, 612-729-8358, www.htlcmpls.org
- **Luther Memorial Church LCA**, 3751 Sheridan Ave N, Minneapolis, 612-522-3639, www.hmonglutheranministry.org
- **Luther Seminary**, 2481 Como Ave, St. Paul, 651-641-3456, www.luthersem.edu
- **Mt. Calvary**, 301 County Rd 19, Excelsior, 952-474-8893, www.mountcalvary.org
- **Mt. Olivet Lutheran Church**, 5025 Knox Ave S, Minneapolis, 612-926-7651, www.mtolivet.org
- **Prince of Peace Lutheran Church**, 13901 Fairview Dr, Burnsville, 952-435-8102, www.princeofpeaceonline.org

MENNONITE

- **Faith Mennonite Church**, 2720 E 22nd St, Minneapolis, 612-375-9483
- **St. Paul Mennonite Fellowship**, 576 S Robert St, St. Paul, 651-291-0647

METHODIST

- **Hamline United Methodist Church**, 1514 Englewood Ave, St. Paul, 651-645-0667
- **Hennepin Avenue United Methodist Church**, 511 Groveland at Lyndale Ave, Minneapolis, 612-871-5303, www.haumc.org
- **North United Methodist Church**, 4350 Fremont Ave N, Minneapolis, 612-522-4497
- **Walker Community United Methodist Church**, 3104 16th Ave S, Minneapolis, 612-722-6612, www.mumac.org
- **Wesley United Methodist Church**, Marquette Ave & Grant St, Minneapolis, 612-871-3585, www.thewesleychurch.org
- **Woodbury United Methodist Church**, 7465 Steepleview Rd, Woodbury, 651-738-0305, www.woodburyumc.org

METROPOLITAN COMMUNITY CHURCHES

- **All God's Children Metropolitan Community Church**, 3100 Park Ave S, Minneapolis, 612-824-2673, www.agcmcc.org; a consciously inclusive Christian faith community, reaching out to all with a primary focus to the GLBT community.

NON-DENOMINATIONAL

- **The Rock** meets in Uptown Minneapolis on Friday nights; check their web site for details, www.rockthechurch.com
- **Cedarcrest Church**, 1630 E 90th St, Bloomington, www.cedarcrestchurch.org

PRESBYTERIAN

- **Aldrich Avenue Presbyterian Church**, 3501 Aldrich Ave S, Minneapolis, 612-825-2479, www.aldrichchurch.org; sometimes holds services at the Lake Harriet Bandshell.
- **Arlington Hills Presbyterian**, 1275 Magnolia Ave E, St Paul, 651-774-6028, www.arlingtonhillspresbyterian.org
- **Bryn Mawr Presbyterian Church**, 420 S Cedar Lake Rd, Minneapolis, 612-377-5222, www.brynmawrchurch.org
- **Macalester-Plymouth United Church**, 1658 Lincoln Ave, St. Paul, 651-698-8871, www.macalester-plymouth.org
- **Presbyterian Church Synod of Lakes & Prairies**, 8012 Old Cedar Ave S, Minneapolis, 952-854-0144, www.lakesandprairies.org
- **Presbytery of the Twin Cities**, 122 W Franklin Ave, Minneapolis, 612-871-7281, www.ptcaweb.org
- **Stadium Village Church**, 501 Oak St, SE, Minneapolis, 612-331-1632, www.stadiumvillagechurch.org
- **St. Luke**, 3121 Groveland School Rd, Minnetonka, 952-473-7378, www.stlukeweb.org
- **Westminster Presbyterian Church**, Nicollet Mall & 12th St, Minneapolis, 612-332-3421, www.wpc-mpls.org

ROMAN CATHOLIC

The web site for the Archdiocese of St. Paul and Minneapolis, www.arch spm.org, provides information about St. Paul's majestic cathedral and offers links to other Catholic resources.

- **Archdiocese of St. Paul and Minneapolis**, 226 Summit Ave, St. Paul, 651-291-4400, www.archspm.org
- **Basilica of St. Mary**, 88 N 17th St, Minneapolis, 612-317-3400, www.mary.org
- **Cathedral of St. Paul**, 239 Selby Ave, St. Paul, 651-228-1766, www.cathedralsaintpaul.org
- **Dignity Twin Cities** is a community of Catholic GLBT people, their families and friends, 612-827-3103, www.dignitytwincities.org
- **Liberal Catholic Church of St. Francis**, 3201 Pleasant Ave, Minneapolis, 612-823-4276, www.liberalcatholic.org
- **NET** (National Evangelization Teams) **Ministries** is an international Catholic youth ministry based in the Twin Cities. It holds monthly masses for teens, www.netusa.org.
- **Our Lady of Guadalupe**, 401 Concord St, St. Paul, 651-228-0506, www.ourladyoflourdes.com
- **Our Lady of Lourdes Church**, One Lourdes Place NE, Minneapolis, 612-379-2259, www.ourladyoflourdes.com, is the oldest continuously used church in the city. It was designated a U.S. historic landmark in 1934.

- **Pax Christi**, 12100 Pioneer Trail, Eden Prairie, 952-941-3150, www.pax christi.com
- **Presentation of the Blessed Virgin Mary**, Larpenteur Ave at Kennard St, St. Paul, 651-777-8116, www.presentationofmary.org
- **St. Joan of Arc Church**, 4537 3rd Ave S, Minneapolis, 612-823-8205, www.stjoan.com
- **St. Olaf Catholic Church**, 215 S 8th St, Minneapolis, 612-332-7471, www.saintolaf.org
- **St. Patrick's**, 6820 Saint Patrick's Ln, Valley View and Gleason Rds, Edina, 952-941-3164, www.st-patricks.org
- **St. Stephens Catholic Church and Shelter**, 2211 Clinton Ave S, Minneapolis, 612-874-0311, www.ststephensmpls.org
- **St. Victoria Catholic Church**, 8228 Victoria Dr, Victoria, 952-443-2661, www.stvictoria.net

UNITARIAN UNIVERSALIST

- **First Unitarian Society of Minneapolis**, 900 Mt. Curve Ave, Minneapolis, 612-377-6608, www.firstunitariansociety.org
- **Nora UU Church**, 12333 155th Ave, Hanska (about an hour and a half southwest of Minneapolis), 507-439-6240, mankatofellowship.org/nora; organized in 1881, this tiny country church is the only remaining Norwegian liberal congregation and the only existing rural church that was actually built to be a Unitarian church. The grounds, church, cemetery, log cabin museum filled with immigrant artifacts, and parsonage are well-kept and beautiful in their simplicity. The church's early October Smorgasbord fundraiser is an opportunity to enjoy a beautiful drive through Minnesota's farmlands at harvest time as well as an authentic Norwegian meal.
- **Unity Unitarian Church**, 732 Holly Ave, St. Paul, 651-228-1456, www.unityunitarian.org
- **Unitarian Universalist Association**, 122 W Franklin Ave, Minneapolis, 612-870-4823, www.psduua.org
- **White Bear Unitarian Universalist Church**, 328 Maple St, Mahtomedi, 651-426-2369, www.whitebearunitarian.org

UNITED CHURCH OF CHRIST

- **First Congregational Church of Minnesota**, 500 8th Ave SE, Minneapolis, 612-331-3816, www.firstchurchmn.org
- **Mayflower Congregational Church**, 106 E Diamond Lake Rd, Minneapolis, 612-824-0761, www.mayflowermpls.org
- **Macalester Plymouth United Church**, 1658 Lincoln Ave, St. Paul, 651-698-8871, www.macalester-plymouth.org
- **St. Anthony Park United Church of Christ**, 2129 Commonwealth Ave, St. Paul, 651-646-7173, www.sapucc.org
- **St. Paul's United Church of Christ**, 900 Summit Ave, St. Paul, 651-224-5809, www.cherokeeparkunited.org

- **Wayzata Community Church**, 125 W Wayzata Blvd, Wayzata, is the largest UCC church in town, 952-473-8877, www.wayzatacommunity church.org.

WESLEYAN

- **Oakdale Wesleyan Church**, 6477 N 10th St, Oakdale, 651-739-2940, www.oakdalechurch.org

SYNAGOGUES

The web site of the **Minneapolis Jewish Federation/St. Paul United Jewish Fund and Council** (www.jewishminnesota.org) contains links to local synagogues, arts and Jewish culture. Sign up on their web page and they will welcome you with a packet of information about the Jewish communities in the Minneapolis and St. Paul areas. This site also has links for singles and newcomers. Newcomers should also check in at the **Jewish Community Center–Greater Minneapolis** (4330 Cedar Lake Road South, St. Louis Park, 952-381-3400, www.sabesjcc.org), as well as **Shalom Minneapolis** at the same address (952-381-3432).

JEWISH–CONSERVATIVE

- **Adath Jeshurun Congregation**, 10500 Hillside Ln W, Minnetonka, 952-545-2424, www.adathjeshurun.org, is one of the most beautiful buildings and settings in the Twin Cities.
- **Beth El Synagogue**, 5224 W 26th St, St. Louis Park, 952-920-3512, www.bethelsynagogue.org
- **Temple of Aaron Congregation**, 616 S Mississippi River Blvd, St. Paul, 651-698-8874, www.templeofaaron.org

JEWISH–ORTHODOX

- **Adath Israel Synagogue**, 2337 Edgcumbe Rd, St. Paul, 651-698-8300, www.adath.com
- **Bais Yisroel**, 4221 Sunset Blvd, St. Louis Park, 952-926-7867, www.baisyisroel.org
- **Kenesseth Israel**, 4330 W 28th St, St. Louis Park, 952-920-2183, www.kennessethisrael.org

JEWISH–RECONSTRUCTIONIST

- **Mayim Rabim**, 44th and York Ave S, Minneapolis, 612-922-5983, www.mayimrabim.org

JEWISH—REFORM

- **Mount Zion Temple**, 1300 Summit Ave, St. Paul, 651-698-3881, www. mzion.org
- **Temple Israel**, 2324 Emerson Ave S, Minneapolis, 612-377-8680, www.templeisrael.com

ISLAM

The **University of Minnesota's Muslim Students Association** (300 Washington Avenue SE, Minneapolis) has developed an extensive list of resources including community centers, Islamic organizations, and Islamic businesses (www.tc.umn.edu/~muslimsa). Many Muslim restaurants, groceries, and fabric stores are concentrated along Central Avenue, north of downtown Minneapolis, and near the University.

- **Abuubakar As-Sadique Islamic Center**, 325 Cedar Ave S, Minneapolis, 612-333-2341, www.somalitalk.com/abubakar/
- **Islamic Center of Minnesota**, 1401 Gardena Ave NE, Minneapolis, 763-571-5604, www.icmorg.com

EASTERN

BAHA'I

- **Baha'i Faith**, 1680 Bellows St, West St. Paul, 651-455-7169
- **Baha'i Faith**, 4 Pine Tree Dr, Arden Hills, 651-482-9455
- **Baha'i Faith**, 426 Fairview Ave N, St. Paul, 651-641-0336
- **Baha'i Faith**, 3644 Chicago Ave, Minneapolis, 612-823-3494, www.pluralism.org
- **Baha'i Faith**, 1350 Nicollet Ave, Minneapolis, 612-872-1846

BUDDHIST

- **Clouds in Water Zen Center**, 308 Prince St, St. Paul, 651-222-6968, www.cloudsinwater.org
- **Compassionate Ocean Dharma Center**, 3206 Holmes Ave, Minneapolis, 612-825-7658, www.oceandharma.org
- **Dharma Field Zen Center**, 3118 W 49th St, Minneapolis, 612-928-4868, www.dharmafield.org
- **Karma Kagyu Minneapolis**, 4301 Morningside Rd, Edina, 952-926-5048, www.ktcminneapolis.org
- **Minnesota Zen Meditation Center**, 3343 E Lake Calhoun Pkwy, Minneapolis, 612-822-5313, www.mnzenctr.com; posts information on the practice of Buddhism and activities of the Twin Cities Buddhist community on its web site

- The **Shambhala** tradition has attracted interest because of its music and art. Visit www.shambhala-mn.org for more information.
- **Soka Gakkai International USA**, 1381 Eustis St, St. Paul, 651-645-3133, www.sgi-usa.org

HINDU

- **Geeta Ashram Church**, 10537 Noble Ave N, Brooklyn Park, 763-493-4229, www.geetaashram.org
- **Hindu Mandir**, 1835 Polk St NE, Minneapolis, 612-788-1751; New Temple, 10530 Troy Ln, Maple Grove (corner of 105th Ave and Troy Ln), www.hindu mandirmn.org; the New Temple is a 42,000-square-foot building on a 40-acre property with landscaping designed to make it "a place of peace."
- **Meditation Center**, 631 University Ave NE, Minneapolis, 612-379-2386, www.hindunet.org

For more information about Hinduism in the Twin Cities, check www.hindu mandir.org. This site is associated with the Hindu Society of Minnesota, where many events take place.

SIKH

- **Sikh Society of Minnesota**, 5831 University Ave NE, Fridley, 763-574-0886, mnsikhs.com

OTHERS

If you're an "eclectic practitioner," e.g., a Wiccan, Druid, tolerant Pantheist, etc., the multitraditional **Wiccan Church of Minnesota** (www.wiccan churchmn.org) may be for you. In addition, the **Minnesota Atheists Online** (www.mnatheists.org) have a site that explains this oft-misunderstood belief system.

NEW AGE

- **Eckankar Spiritual Center**, Temple of Eck, 1200 W 78th St, Chanhassen, (952) 380-2200, www.eckankar.org
- **Lake Harriet Community Church**, 4401 Upton Ave S, Minneapolis, 612-922-4272, www.www.lhscweb.org, describes itself as "a spiritually diverse community that honors and explores all sacred beliefs and empowers the unique connection to the Divine Spirit within each of us."

I F YOU WANT TO KNOW WHAT MINNESOTA IS LIKE IN THE WINTER, RENT the movie *Grumpy Old Men.* You'll see that Minnesotans don't just endure the winter, we revel in it! As the mercury plunges, our spirits soar! When snow blankets the landscape and residents of states "Down Below" bundle in blankets and huddle in front of roaring fires, Minnesotans head outside. It's time for us to ski, skate, sled, snowboard, snowmobile, ice fish, or maybe even try our hands at clattering across "hard water" at 50 miles an hour in an iceboat. In fact, there's even more to do here in winter than in summer—and there are no mosquitoes!

With snow cover on the ground continuously for several months, it's no surprise that snowmobiles were invented right here in Minnesota. Originally developed as a serious way to get around in inclement weather, snowmobiles quickly became Minnesotans' preferred recreation vehicle. There are now over 20,000 miles of snowmobile trails in the state. Free snowmobile trail maps and license information are available from the Minnesota **DNR Information Center** (651-296-6157 or 1-888-646-6367, TTY: 651-296-5484 or 1-800-657-3929, 1-888-665-4236, www.dnr.state.mn.us). (See **Snowmobiling** in the **Sports and Recreation** chapter.)

Winter, which sets in here by November and lasts into April, is usually brought down by bitter cold weather systems that dip south from Canada. Be prepared for week-long periods of sub-zero (that's sub-zero, not sub-freezing) temperatures, and for the possibility of an April blizzard. Sign up with any local television station for email notification of snow emergencies, school closings, and late openings.

Take winter seriously: if you don't stay active in the cold weather months, cabin fever and shortness of daylight can result in malaise and even depression. That said, winters here can be a thrill, and the following information should help to smooth your way.

APPAREL

Layering is the secret to staying comfortable. Make the layer closest to your skin something that wicks, or draws moisture away from your body. Patagonia long underwear is a favorite here, but there are other high-tech fibers and brands. And though turtlenecks are "out" in most parts of the country, they're always "in," in Minnesota. So are flannel-lined jeans. You'll need a heavy coat. Down-filled is usually considered warmest. Buy it here or from a catalogue company such as L.L. Bean, which rates its clothing for comfort at sub-zero temperatures. Bean's –50° Fahrenheit down hip-length or longer coats and parkas are popular here. For the proper clothing for more strenuous activities, consult the ski and sports stores. There are new fabric systems every year, many of which react with the body's temperature to store or release heat as needed to buffer the body against overheating as well as getting chilled. Finally—feet. Warm feet are key. Snow boots will reduce your chances of suffering a major wipeout on the sidewalk, not to mention frozen toes. Insulated Sorel boots are rated for very cold temperatures and are especially good for those who have to stand around outside. Sorel also makes children's boots and winter booties for infants and toddlers. Other brands to look for include Bugabootoos by Columbia, Kamik's, and Baffin. You can compare many brands of cold-rated apparel at stores here or online at dealers such as Northland Marine (www.northlandmarine.com). Because falling on ice causes many injuries, stores also sell metal-studded detachable soles that fit on the bottoms of your boots. L.L. Bean calls theirs "Stabil-icers." Yaktrax and Yakwalkers are also popular traction devices (sold by L.L. Bean, Northland Marine, and other vendors).

One final category: dressing up. Minnesota couture usually includes long sleeves and boots—and people carry their good shoes. So if you're throwing a winter housewarming, be sure to save room by the front door for the pile of boots.

By the way, your teenager will not dress sensibly, so give it up. Generations of Minnesota teens have proven that you can stand at a bus stop dressed in jeans and a light jacket wearing neither hat nor gloves, with temperatures at 20 below, and survive.

DRIVING

If you have four-wheel drive you may think winter driving will be a cinch, but the truth is although four-wheel drive is better in snow, it is no better on ice. Front-wheel drive cars provide better control in icy conditions than rear-wheel drive, but none of it's any good if you're driving too fast, so slow down.

If the forecast includes bad road conditions, give yourself extra time to get to your destination, including a few minutes to warm up your car. If the weatherman happens to mention "black ice," be especially careful. Black ice is particularly prevalent at intersections, where car exhaust freezes, and causes many accidents on bridges, freeway ramps, and at exposed locations where the wind whips across the pavement. Before winter really kicks in (sometime in October), take the following steps to winterize your vehicle. Change the radiator fluid and add anti-freeze. Some people switch to a lighter oil (more viscous at low temperatures) for winter. If you park outside overnight, 5W-30 or a synthetic oil will help your car start in the morning; if you park in a garage, 10W-30 is sufficient. Do consider buying snow tires and an engine block heater (the origin of the electrical cords you see hanging out of the grilles of some cars). These devices run a low electrical current through your engine to keep it warm overnight. They're particularly helpful if you don't have a garage, although you may find it impractical to run an extension cord out to your car. Finally, think about your battery. Be sure to clean the connections in the fall; and if it is four years old, replace the battery before winter. On those January mornings when it's −20° and you stick your key in the ignition, begging and swearing may not turn your engine over, but that new battery will.

Next, stash the following useful items somewhere inside your car:

- An ice scraper
- A cell phone
- A set of jumper cables, for yourself or for a coworker stranded in the parking lot;
- A bag of kitty litter (for traction) and a small snow shovel, to help dig your way out of a wipeout (car mats work for tire traction, too)
- A "stranded" emergency kit consisting of blankets, a bright-colored piece of cloth to use as a flag, Hot Hands heat packs, a candle in a coffee can (a makeshift heater), matches, a flashlight (with batteries that work), water and a couple of energy bars

Once the Arctic weather has arrived, keep your gas tank from getting near empty—the water content of the fuel will actually freeze in the gas lines, preventing any fuel from getting to the engine. If you've never driven in snowy conditions before, a good place to practice is on a frozen lake. The trick to maintaining control when you start to "fishtail" (when the back wheels slide out to the left or right as you hit the brakes) is to steer, not too fast, into the direction that your back wheels are sliding. Try it; it works. Above all, drive as slowly as conditions demand.

As mentioned, you will have to leave a little extra time to drive anywhere. Many drivers make an extra key for their car, so they can go out, start up their vehicle, lock it, and return to get ready while the inside of the car gets nice and warm. The police however, counsel against doing this, because of the easy (and warm!) target you leave for a car thief. An alternative: On particularly cold nights, start your car up for ten minutes or so before going to bed; it gives your engine and battery an extra charge for the morning. One safety tip: don't run your car while it's parked inside a garage—people here die every year that way.

For specific rules on winter parking, see **Parking** in the **Getting Settled** chapter and check your city's web page. Did we remember to tell you to slow down?

HEATING

TOP TEN WAYS TO SAVE ON YOUR HEATING BILL

Following are the top ten recommendations from the state's Energy Information Center on how to reduce heating costs throughout the winter.

1. Turn your thermostat down 5 to 10 degrees while you are away or asleep. Every degree above 68° adds about 3% to your heating bill.

2. Turn your water heater temperature down to 120° or 125°.
3. Cover the interior of leaky or drafty windows with window film (sold at all hardware stores).
4. Have your furnace and water heater professionally cleaned and inspected annually to make sure they work efficiently and safely. Change your furnace filters monthly.
5. Replace your old furnace with a new, energy-efficient model. Look for the Energy Star label on all new home appliances.
6. Caulk and weatherstrip around doors and windows.
7. Vacuum your heat registers and return air vents regularly. If you have hot water heat, vacuum radiators or baseboard heaters. Make sure furniture and draperies do not block the heat flow.
8. Keep your curtains open when the sun is shining, in order to gain solar heat.
9. Bring your attic insulation up to an R-value of 38, but only after sealing all your attic bypasses. Bypasses leak warm, moist air into the attic, reducing the value of insulation.
10. Call your local utility and schedule a home energy audit, which will pin-point other ways to weatherize your home to make it more energy-efficient.

HOME INSULATION

Insulation is taken seriously in this climate. As of 1999, state building codes began to require a minimum of R-38 in ceilings with attics. To learn more about the state energy code, check with the **Minnesota Department of Commerce Energy Information Center** (651-296-5175, 800-657-3710, www.state.mn.us/portal/mn/jsp/home.do?agency=Commerce). The **Center for Energy and Environment in Minneapolis** (612-335-5858, www.mncee.org) and the **St. Paul Neighborhood Energy Consortium** (651-221-4462, www.spnec.org) are even better resources for information about keeping your house cozy on those below-zero days.

You can actually save a considerable amount of money on heating and cooling by making some relatively modest improvements to your home. Caulking or weather-stripping doors and windows can save as much as 10% on your annual energy bill. Storm doors and windows prevent drafts and can save as much as 15% in cold months. Insulating your attic floor or top floor ceiling reduces energy costs by about 5%, and insulating exterior walls can save on both heating and cooling by 20%.

PETS

The two most important things you can do for your pet in the winter are to provide adequate shelter and plenty of water—animals cannot survive on the moisture in snow. You will also need to protect your pet's feet. Pet stores and catalogues sell dog booties, which protect tender paws from being cut or frozen while walking on the crusty snow. Look for booties that are tall enough to stay on. PetEdge.com sells waterproof tall booties with non-slip soles. You can also pick up booties from local pet stores and vendors at dog shows.

Many people appreciate the convenience of indoor-outdoor runs. It's an easy do-it-yourself project to install a dog door between the studs in a garage wall to create an out-of-the-elements place for your pet to sleep and be fed.

For those who dream of racing through the woods behind a team of huskies, you've come to the right state. See the **Dogsledding** section of the **Sports and Recreation** chapter. Locally, sled dog races are held during St. Paul's Winter Carnival and sometimes on Lake Minnetonka.

WEATHER-RELATED RESOURCES

For current weather conditions as well as a lot of weather-related links, check any of the local radio or TV stations, or call 763-512-1111 for Time and Temperature. If you want to check out the snow cover across the U.S., access www.rap.ucar.edu/weather. Lest you think the only interesting weather comes in winter, check out the Minnesota tornado page (www.tornadoproject.com). Lastly, Minnesota's popular Weatherguide Environment Calendars are sold for $15.95 in most book and grocery stores, or order one from the Freshwater Society (952-471-9773, www.freshwater.org).

TORNADOES

The worst tornadoes in Twin Cities history occurred on May 6, 1965, when six tornadoes swept across the western and northern portions of the metro, killing 13 people and injuring 683.

This was the first night that Twin Cities' sirens were ever used to warn about approaching tornadoes, and they are credited with saving many lives. We still depend on this warning system to let us know when to take cover. Take it seriously when you hear the sirens go off, because tornadoes are the deadliest weather we have. Cities test their civil defense sirens at 1 p.m. on the first Wednesday of the month.

Tornadoes have the power to lift cars and hurl them through the air. Their winds make deadly missiles of ordinary household objects, debris, and broken glass, and they sometimes stay on the ground for many miles. They are among the most violent natural forces on the planet—and by mid-April, we have a reasonable expectation of severe thunderstorms and tornadoes in the metro area.

So if you see strange clouds moving in, or hail, or if the sky starts to turn a sickly green, what should you do? Turn on the radio or television (preferably battery-powered) to any local station to get the weather forecast. They all have Doppler radar and can tell you minute-by-minute where the storm is and where it's going. An "NOAA weather radio" is a special comfort at night. New models can be set so that they are activated when a severe weather warning is issued—and you'll be awakened.

Severe weather warnings fall into two categories: watches and warnings. If a tornado "watch" is issued, it means that a tornado is "possible." If a tornado "warning" is issued and/or you hear a siren, it means that a tornado has actually been spotted, or is strongly indicated on radar, and it is time to go to a safe shelter immediately. What constitutes safe shelter? A basement is best, away from the west and south walls, preferably under a heavy piece of furniture. If you don't have a basement, go to an inside bathroom and get in the tub, or take shelter in a closet, hallway, or stairwell, and put something over you. Even .if it's only a blanket, it might still protect you from flying glass. Outside, if you see a tornado and it isn't moving to your right or left relative to trees and power poles in the distance, it may be heading straight for you, so get down as low as you possibly can. If you're in a car, get out of the car and lie down on the ground or in a ditch, if it isn't raining. If it's raining, the ditch might flood. Do not—DO NOT—take shelter under a highway overpass; you might as well run into a wind tunnel. And do not stay in your car—most tornado deaths occur in mobile homes or cars. If you're out shopping, don't worry; just follow the manager's instructions—all public buildings here have shelters.

Finally, know where you are. Warnings and watches are normally given by county. If the weather service says a warning has been issued for Wright County, you need to know that that's west of Minneapolis and, since storms here usually travel from west to east, if you are in western Hennepin County, you should be thinking about taking precautions. All the warnings in the world won't help if you don't know which city and county you are in. More than likely, you'll never really need to use this advice, but be prepared: Minneapolis does rank number eight on *USA Today*'s list of Top Twenty Tornado-Prone Cities.

BY CAR

FOR BETTER OR WORSE, MOST PEOPLE IN THE TWIN CITIES GET AROUND by car. With increased growth and development, particularly in the outer suburbs, traffic congestion has intensified to the point that Minnesota now ranks fifth worst among 26 metropolitan areas of similar size, according to the **Texas Transportation Institute**'s 2005 Urban Mobility Report. That translates into an average of 43 hours per year that a Twin Cities commuter spends stuck in rush-hour traffic. Another study, by the **Surface Transportation Policy Project**, concluded that a typical Twin Cities family spent nearly $2500 more on transportation in 2003 than a similar family in Portland, Oregon, a more compact city with an extensive public transit system. Be sure to keep these figures in mind when choosing a place to live relative to where you work—unfortunately, it doesn't look like the situation is going to improve anytime soon. In fact, traffic congestion ranks as the No. 1 concern of Twin Cities area residents, according to a survey conducted by the Metropolitan Council.

The state's attempts at addressing the metro's transportation problems start and stop as much as rush hour traffic. The publicly owned **Hiawatha Light Rail Transit** (LRT) line, which began operating between downtown Minneapolis and the Mall of America in 2004, has been carrying double its projected ridership, and is widely hailed as a success. However, its connecting arm, the **Northstar Commuter Rail** (www.mn-GetOnBoard.com), which will run west/northwest from downtown Minneapolis through Coon Rapids, Anoka, Ramsey, and Elk River to Big Lake, is stuck in the "proposal" stage. (For more information about Light Rail, see below.) For the present, most of the state's efforts are focused on roads. The **Minnesota Department of Transportation**, otherwise known as MnDOT (www.dot.state.mn.us) is busily adding lanes to every major road that passes through or around the Twin Cities, and has addressed the problem of congestion on I-394 (the freeway between downtown Minneapolis and the western suburbs) by turning the

High Occupancy Vehicle lane into a **toll lane** during rush hours (see **MN-Pass** below). Other roads in even more serious need of de-congestion (such as the 62 Crosstown) have fallen victim to MnDOT's policy of asking contractors to pay for the construction projects, and then be repaid later by the state.

At the same time, **MetroTransit**, the publicly owned bus company, has been caught in a budget squeeze (ironically caused in part by declining state automobile tax revenues), and has reacted by increasing fares and cutting routes, thus putting many former bus riders back into their cars.

Finally, the state's only other congestion-management tool, **freeway on-ramp metering**, has long been a bugaboo, even to drivers who are used to them. These on-ramp signal lights generally run during morning and evening peak periods, and are meant to keep cars flowing smoothly onto the highway. And yes, they are bona fide traffic lights, so you are required to stop until the light turns green; and yes, again—it is a moving violation to run a red meter.

To find out how the traffic is actually moving each day, keep your radio tuned to **KBEM**, 88.5 FM, www.jazz88fm.com, for real-time accident and gridlock reports.

MN-PASS

For solo commuters caught in the **I-394** bottleneck, there is a way to end-run some of the congestion, albeit an expensive one: I-394's High Occupancy Vehicle (HOV) carpool lanes between Minneapolis and the western suburbs have been converted to rush hour toll lanes. While these express lanes are still free for motorcycles and cars carrying at least one passenger, now solo drivers can use the lanes, too. The catch is the cost of the trips. Using the lanes can be as inexpensive as twenty-five cents one way if there isn't a lot of traffic, but— and this is a big but—as congestion starts to get worse, the tolls go up. Tolls are posted on overhead signs that change every three minutes, and can and do rise to a cost of as much as $8 for a one-way trip at the height of rush hour. You can open a **toll-lane account** in person at 2055 Lilac Drive, Golden Valley; by phone at 866-397-4334; or on the Internet at www.mnpass.net. One last point of information, because the question keeps coming up: According to the people at MN-Pass, an infant does count as a passenger, so if you're driving with an infant in your car, you may use the toll lane without charge.

MAJOR HIGHWAYS

As you get to know the area, you'll find alternatives to the big roads, but until then, here are some of the major arteries:

- **Interstate Hwys 35 and 94** are the main arteries through the cities. I-35 runs north and south and I-94 runs east and west. Both highways connect with the 494/694 ring around the metro area. I-35 splits in Burnsville into **35W**, which heads into Minneapolis, and **35E**, which goes through St. Paul. The two roads run through the northern suburbs before joining again in Lino Lakes and continuing as plain old I-35 up to Duluth.

- Lesser north-south routes serving St. Paul are **State Hwy 3** (**South Robert St**), which connects southeastern suburbs to downtown St. Paul; **State Hwy 61**, which winds along the Mississippi and cuts northwest into St. Paul (a beautiful drive near the river); and **State Hwy 5**, which goes directly east from the airport to West 7th St in St. Paul, or west along I-494 to Eden Prairie, where it becomes plain 5 again and continues through the southwest suburbs. **State Hwy 280** joins I-94 to **State Hwy 36**, an east-west route running north of St. Paul to Stillwater.

- Lesser north-south routes on the Minneapolis side are **State Hwy 77** (**Cedar Ave**), which is a link from Apple Valley to the Mall of America and the airport; **State Hwy 65,** which is a link from Blaine and the other northern suburbs; **State Hwy 100**, which runs from Bloomington through first-ring suburbs to Brooklyn Center; **US 169**, which runs slightly to the west of Hwy 100, from Savage to Maple Grove, and then becomes a state highway heading north.

- **Interstate-94** is the main east-west thoroughfare. It does not split in two the way I-35 does, but instead comes into the Twin Cities at Hudson, Wisconsin, passes directly through downtown St. Paul, then cuts past downtown Minneapolis, turning due north before heading out of town to the northwest. If you are on 94 heading west from St. Paul, to continue westward, get onto **I-394**.

- Minor east-west arteries are **State Hwy 62** (the Crosstown), which runs from I-35W near the airport to Minnetonka, and **I-394**, which heads west out of downtown Minneapolis; I-394 ends at **US 12**, east of Long Lake. US 12 continues due west out of the metro area. **Hwy 55** is a curious road that runs from near the airport, through North Minneapolis, and west to Wright County. The other major east-west route is **State Highway 36**, which runs through suburbs north of St. Paul to Stillwater.

- The main encircling arteries are **I-694** to the north and **I-494** to the south and west. **Minneapolis—St. Paul International Airport** is off I-494/State Highway 5 in Bloomington; see below for best routes by which to approach it. The **Mall of America** is also off I-494 in Bloomington.

COMMUTING OPTIONS

After you've sat on an on-ramp and read an entire newspaper a few afternoons in a row, you might start to consider carpooling or vanpooling. Not only will you save time, but you'll also save money and the environment. The Metropolitan Council estimates that the annual cost of driving a round trip of just 17 miles a day to work can be over $4000 a year. Plug your own numbers into the interactive formula on the Met Council's web site, www.metro commuterservices.org, and find out what commuting by yourself will cost you. Then, if you decide you'd like to travel as part of a group, contact **Metro Commuter Services** (MCS) at 612-373-3333 Option 4, TTY 612-349-7369, or email them at commuter.services@metc.state.mn.us. They will link you with others who work in the same area. In case you're worried about getting trapped downtown in an emergency, with no way home, you can also register for the free **Guaranteed Ride Home Program**. Registered commuters receive two coupons every six months that are good for bus or cab rides in the event of an emergency or schedule conflict.

PARKING

Downtown Minneapolis has 20 parking ramps and 9 lots. A map of the facilities is available on the city's web site at http://parking.ci.minneapolis.mn.us/parking_facilities.htm. Printable maps and parking information can be found on the web site of the Minneapolis Downtown Council, www. downtownmpls.com. Monthly parking rates can be found at http://parking.ci.minneapolis.mn.us/parking_rates.php. Ramps tend to be clustered around Target Center and the Warehouse District, the courthouse, and Orchestra Hall. Monthly parking varies from $127.50 (Hawthorne Transportation Center, 31 North 9th Street) to $250 (Lasalle and 10th). Daily rates range from $7 to $12, and the first hour generally costs at least $3 in the heart of downtown. However, the parking ramps are conveniently located and connected to the skyway system; I-394 from the western suburbs even empties directly into three parking ramps in the Warehouse District, immediately behind Target Center.

Minneapolis also has about 7000 parking meters. They accept only quarters and U.S. dollar coins, but you can purchase a parking card that works in meters the same as money. Cards are sold from dispenser machines located in parking ramps and at City Hall. For further information call 612-673-AUTO (2886) or look online at http://parking.ci.minneapolis.mn.us/parking_card.htm.

These parking cards also work in St. Paul, where much of the parking is on-street and metered, though popular St. Paul venues such as the Xcel Energy Center and the Science Museum do have their own attached ramp parking. For information about these and other ramps, check out the clickable map posted on **St. Paul's Transportation Management Organization's** (TMO's) web site, www.saintpaulparking.com. Click on any facility and see its monthly and hourly rates. TMO also offers commuters other services including interactive ride-matching, information about park & ride lots, and St. Paul's Guaranteed Ride Home plan.

CAR SHARING

Don't want the trouble and expense of keeping a car, but need one some of the time? Consider **Hourcar** car sharing, www.hourcar,org. Managed by the non-profit **Neighborhood Energy Consortium** (NEC), 651-221-4462, Hourcar has car hubs in Uptown, the Wedge, the Minneapolis Riverfront district, Loring/Stevens Square, Minneapolis Depot, University of Minnesota, and Lowertown St. Paul. They offer pay-as-you-go and flat rate plans.

BY BIKE

Surprisingly large numbers of Twin Citians bike to work, and Minneapolis and St. Paul do their best to make their cities bicycle friendly. There are designated bike lanes throughout downtown Minneapolis and 24 bike/pedestrian paths in St. Paul. Download a Minneapolis bike map off the city's web site, www.ci.minneapolis.mn.us/citywork/public-works/transportation/bicycles/maps/downtown.pdf). Download a St. Paul Bike-Hike map at www.stpaul.gov/depts/parks.

For a small fee, Minneapolis Municipal Parking rents weather-sheltered, secure bicycle lockers at several locations in downtown Minneapolis and at the University of Minnesota, as well as at some park & ride lots. Call 612-339-2560 for more information. And don't forget the Guaranteed Ride Home (see above), so you don't have to worry about getting stuck after dark or in bad weather. Register online at www.metrocommuterservices.org or call them at 612-373-3333. They will send you a packet of materials that includes maps, bike locker locations and prices, and can even pair you up with a "bike buddy." For commuter seminars and the latest local developments, check the web site of the Minnesota Bicycle and Pedestrian Alliance, www.bikeped.org.

PUBLIC TRANSPORTATION

BY BUS

Download bus schedules and a transit system map for the entire metro area, create a "Personal Bus Schedule" using the online "Trip Planner," or order transit information and printed schedules to be sent to you by mail by calling Metropolitan Transit Information, 612-373-3333, TTY 612-341-0140, www.metrotransit.org. If you prefer, you can visit one of the following **Metro Transit Stores** to pick up a map, talk to someone in person, or buy a pass:

- **Minneapolis Transit Store**, 719 Marquette Ave, open 7:30 a.m.–5:30 p.m., weekdays.
- **St. Paul Skyway Store**, 101 E Fifth St, US Bank Center, open 7:30 a.m.–5 p.m., weekdays.
- **Mall of America Transit Store**, 60 E Broadway (in the transit station), open 11:30 a.m.–7 p.m. Tuesday–Saturday.
- 150 retail outlets sell **SuperSaver** passes: Cub Foods; Rainbow stores; grocery co-ops; check-cashing stores; city halls; Unbanks; colleges; and some SuperAmericas.

The entire Twin Cities area is included in an integrated public transportation (bus/van/light rail) system known as **MetroTransit**. At the time of the writing of this book, however, with a $60-million shortfall bumping up against the current governor's vow not to raise taxes, MetroTransit is proposing to reduce or eliminate service on over 70% of its 153 bus routes.

It's interesting that the decline in bus service is coming at a time when there is a greater appetite for public transit than there has ever been before.

Consequently, many of the suburbs have stepped up to the plate and are providing their own commuter and local neighborhood service. These include Apple Valley, Elk River, Plymouth, Maple Grove, Eden Prairie, and Woodbury. So if you wish to live in any of those suburbs, you may even be able to get around—or to work, at least—without a car. (See list of suburban bus lines below.) Simply park at a designated **Park & Ride** lot and take the bus into town. Park & Rides and bus stops are both marked with the "**T**" logo. Some Park & Rides and bus stops do not contain posted schedules, so it's a good idea to get a printed map and take it with you until you get comfortable using the system.

An adult non–rush hour base fare ($1.50) gets you one ride plus two transfers to complete a one-way trip. Express routes, which travel between the downtowns and to the suburbs, cost 50 cents extra. Rush hour fares cost an additional 50–75 cents. Seniors and children age 6–12 can ride for 50 cents during non–rush hours, but this fare rises to $2 and $2.75 during rush hours. People with disabilities always ride for 50 cents, but must show some form of proof of disability. (For information on disabled certification, call Customer Relations at 612-373-3333; also see the **Helpful Services** chapter.) Children 5 and under ride free. The fare within either the Minneapolis or St. Paul **Downtown Zones** is 50 cents, anytime. You can pay as you go (drivers take cash, but don't make change), or buy special passes. If you're going to have to take more than one bus, pay the driver when you get on and ask for a transfer. **Transfers** are free and good for up to 2 1/2 hours. If your trip begins on a bus but you need to transfer to light rail, you must ask the bus driver for a **rail-only transfer**. **Light rail fares** are the same as bus fares. You can buy a ticket with cash or a credit card from **vending machines** on the station platforms. A **monthly pass** gives you unlimited rides for a whole calendar month.

Even though all buses are equipped with wheelchair lifts, there is also a special transportation service available for people with disabilities. **Metro Mobility** is the **door-through-door** transportation system available to people in the Minneapolis/St. Paul area and certain adjoining suburbs. Customers who are certified can call transportation providers to schedule their trips. For more information, call 651-602-1111 (TTY 651-291-0904).

If MetroTransit routes aren't convenient for you, there are other options. Check the routes and schedules of the **University of Minnesota Transit Service** (www1.umn.edu/pts/metrobuses.htm or www.metrotransit.org), which runs buses from many locations throughout the city to the University, though usually only on weekdays. Anyone can ride them, and they cost the same as a city bus. **Dial-A-Ride**, a neighborhood-based shared **curb-to-curb** van and minibus service, is another option. Rides must be scheduled in advance, but they do accept standing orders. Your Dial-A-Ride driver can also give you a transfer ticket good for a bus ride. Fares are low, generally under $3. For a list of providers and the numbers to call to schedule a ride, look online at www.metrotransit.org/otherTransOpts/dialARide.asp. Of course, for any service within the metro area, you can always call MetroTransit's main number, 612-373-3333. Here is a small sampling of the areas served and numbers to call to make Dial-A-Ride reservations:

- **Anoka County Traveler**, 763-323-5222
- **Hopkins Hop-A-Ride**, 952-935-8003
- **Maple Grove**, 763-493-2200
- **Northeast Suburban Transit**, 651-227-6378
- **Lake Area Transit**, 651-644-8876
- **Plymouth Dial-A-Ride**, 763-559-5057
- **South (Washington) County Circulator**, 651-275-4315
- **South Shore Lake Minnetonka**, 952-474-7441
- **Woodbury**, 651-735-7433

BUS SAFETY

While generally safe, problems can occur both on buses and at bus stops. **Route 5** between downtown Minneapolis and North Minneapolis has a history of having more problems than most. For your own safety, you may not want to ride this or certain other routes alone.

SUBURBAN BUS LINES

Call Metro Transit, 612-373-3333, www.metrotransit.com, for schedules and connection information for any of these suburban bus lines:

- **Maple Grove Transit**, 763-494-6005, 763-494-5994 (Hotline), http://www.ci.maple-grove.mn.us/content/145/243/802/default.aspx
- **Minnesota Valley Transit Authority**, 952-882-7500, www.mvta.com, serves Apple Valley, Burnsville, Eagan, Rosemount, and Savage
- **Northstar Commuter Coach**, www.commutercoach.org, provides commuter service between Elk River and Minneapolis
- **Plymouth MetroLink**, 3400 Plymouth Blvd, Plymouth, 763-509-5535, www2.ci.plymouth.mn.us
- **SouthWest Metro Transit**, 952-949-2BUS (2287), www.swtransit.org, provides service from the southwest suburbs to downtown Minneapolis, Uptown, Southdale Mall, Normandale Community College, and the University of Minnesota. In summer, it offers special trips to the Como Park Zoo, as well as to Twins games, and many museums.

TROLLEYS AND FUN BUSES

There are also a few fun buses around. Customers with game-day tickets can ride the bus/train for free to Minnesota Wild Hockey games at Xcel Energy Center. Free rides are valid from two hours before face-off until two hours after the game ends. The **RiverCity Trolley** (www.rivercitytrolley.com) offers narrated tours in turn-of-the-century reproduction trolley cars, May through October. The route runs from the Minneapolis Convention Center through downtown Minneapolis to the Mississippi Mile riverfront and back through the Warehouse District. There are stations at St. Anthony Main, Walker Art Center and Sculpture Garden, and the Convention Center. A trolley will also stop every 20 minutes at trolley signs along the route. An all-day pass is $17 for adults and $12 for seniors and children. Call 612-378-7833 for availability, rates, and information. **St. Paul's Capital City Trolley** (www.stpaul.gov/leisure/transportation/trolley or www.capitalcitytrolleys. com) operates between hotels, restaurants, and entertainment. Call 651-223-5600 for trolley routes or check any St. Paul map. **Wayzata** has a free trolley that operates from May through October in downtown Wayzata and up to the Colonial Square shopping center on Wayzata Boulevard. Trolleys can be chartered for parties and to take you to special events like football games or the Symphony Ball.

NATIONAL BUS SERVICE
The **Greyhound Bus Lines** (800-231-2222, www.greyhound.com) has terminals in the following Twin Cities locations:
- **Minneapolis**, 950 Hawthorne, 612-371-3325
- **Minneapolis, University of Minnesota**, 300 Washington Ave SE (Coffman Union), 612-624-4636
- **Minneapolis–St. Paul International Airport**
- **St. Louis Park, Oasis Market**, 530 Blake Rd, 952-935-5409 (Tickets are not sold at this location.)
- **St. Paul, Amtrak Station**, 730 Transfer Rd (Tickets are not sold at this location.)
- **St. Paul**, 166 W University Ave, 651-222-0508

REGIONAL BUSES
There are also a number of **regional** and specialty bus lines you can use:
- **Jefferson Bus Lines**, 2100 26th St, Minneapolis, 888-864-2832, www. jeffersonlines.com, primarily serves the southern part of the state. It also offers service to Brainerd, Duluth, Crookston, Grand Forks, and Winnipeg. Buses leave from the Greyhound depots in St. Paul and Hawthorne Ave in Minneapolis (see addresses above), from Coffman Union at the University, and from the Minneapolis–St. Paul Airport, 612-726-5501.
- **Northfield Lines**, 888-670-8068, www.northfieldlines.com; offers daily shuttles to Northfield.
- **Rochester Direct**, 612-725-0303, www.rochesterdirect.com; offers daily shuttles between Minneapolis–St. Paul International Airport and Rochester

LIGHT RAIL TRANSIT (LRT)

The **Hiawatha Line** provides light-rail service every 7–15 minutes, between 5 a.m. and 1 a.m., to 17 stations along Hiawatha Avenue between the Minneapolis Downtown Warehouse District, airport, and Mall of America in Bloomington. Bus routes are timed to connect with trains.

Park & Ride lots are located at Lake Street/Midtown Station, Fort Snelling Station, and 28th Avenue Station (three blocks east of the Mall of America). For connecting bus schedules, time between stations, and a route map, look online at www.metrotransit.org/rail/station_detail.asp.

Because there are no fare boxes on trains, you must pay before boarding. Rail fares are the same as local bus fares. For a single ride, use cash or a credit card to buy a ticket at the vending machine on the station platform. If your trip begins on a bus, you must ask the bus driver for a rail-only transfer. Those going downtown for a game or movie can buy a **6-Hour Pass** at the rail station. The Hiawatha line's great popularity is giving momentum to the next project on the Twin Cities' LRT wishlist, the **Northstar Commuter Train Route**, which will run 40 miles from downtown Minneapolis through Fridley, Coon Rapids/Riverdale, Anoka, and Elk River to Big Lake. This project was partially funded by the Minnesota legislature in 2005 and (though not yet started) has a projected completion date of 2008. Also under discussion is a light rail line that would run along **University Avenue** and connect Minneapolis and St. Paul.

BY AIR

Minneapolis–St. Paul International Airport, (www.mspairport.com) is the eighth busiest airport in the world, serving 36 million passengers a year. Located on State Highway 5 between Bloomington and St. Paul, it is the commercial aviation center for the entire upper Midwest, and provides connecting service to regional airports including Rochester, Duluth, Fargo, Grand Rapids, and Hibbing. A new north-south runway that opened in October 2005 serves about 37% of the airport's arrivals and 17% of departures, and has increased both air traffic and noise over parts of Bloomington east of the Mall of America, Burnsville, Eagan, Apple Valley, Rosemount, and Inver Grove Heights.

The airport has two terminals. The **Lindbergh (Main) Terminal** serves regularly scheduled flights, while the **Humphrey Terminal** primarily serves charter airlines. A single airline, Northwest, dominates this market.

To reach the airport by car, use the following routes:
- From Minneapolis and points north, take I-35W south to State Hwy 62 east to Hwy 5 west or take Hiawatha Ave all the way south from Minneapolis.
- From St. Paul and points northeast, take I-35E south, then State Hwy 5 west.
- From western, southern and eastern suburbs, take I-494 to State Hwy 5.

The Humphrey Terminal can be reached by going north from I-494 on 34th Avenue. It is well-signed, as are its long-term and off-site parking lots. The airport can also be reached by taking the **Hiawatha Light Rail Transit** train from either downtown Minneapolis or the Mall of America. Trains stop at both the Lindbergh and Humphrey terminals and run between the terminals every few minutes, 24 hours a day. There is no charge for travel between the two terminals. Fares for travel to other locations (such as the Mall of America or downtown Minneapolis) are $2.00 during rush hours (Monday–Friday, 6–9 a.m. and 3–6:30 p.m.) and $1.50 at other times. Tickets are sold at vending kiosks at the rail stations. For more information, visit MetroTransit's web site, www.metrotransit.org/rail. The **Lindbergh Terminal light rail station** entrance is located near the Transit Center, between the Blue and Red Parking ramps. The **Humphrey Terminal Light Rail station** is located outside of the terminal building. A covered walkway connects the station to the Humphrey parking facility and the terminal building. Maps to both the Lindbergh and Humphrey LRT stations are posted on the airport's web site.

If you have a layover and decide you want to go into Minneapolis or the Mall of America, allow about half an hour for the LRT to travel between the airport and warehouse district downtown, and 11 minutes to go to the Mall.

AIRLINES

Service to Minneapolis is dominated by **Northwest Airlines** (www.nwa. com), but a number of other airlines have a smaller presence here.

Airlines serving the **Lindbergh Terminal**:

- **Air Canada Reservations**: 888-247-2262 or 1-316-686-3636, www.aircanada.com
- **Air Tran Airways Reservations**: 800-247-8726, www.airtran.com
- **America West Reservations**: 800-235-9292, TTY 800-526-8077, www. americawest.com
- **American Airlines Reservations**: 800-433-7300, TTY 800-543-1586, www.aa.com
- **ATA Airlines, Inc. Reservations**: 800-435-9282, www.ata.com (Ending Dec. 1, 2006)
- **Continental Airlines Reservations**: 800-525-0280, www. continental.com
- **Delta Air Lines Reservations**: 800-221-1212, TTY 800-831-4488, www. delta.com
- **Frontier Airlines Reservations**: 800-432-1359, www.frontier airlines.com
- **Icelandair Reservations**: 800-223-5500, www.icelandair.com (a local favorite!)
- **KLM Royal Dutch Airlines Reservations**: 800-374-7747, www. klm.com
- **Mesaba (Northwest) Airlines Reservations**: 800-225-2525, TTY 800-328-2298, www.mesaba.com
- **Midwest Connect (Midwest Airlines) Reservations**: 800-452-2022, TTY Phone: 800-872-3608, www.midwestairlines.com; named Best Domestic Airline repeatedly over its 20-plus-year history, its "Signature Service" includes wide, two-across seats and chocolate chip cookies baked onboard.
- **Northwest/KLM Airlines Reservations and Flight Status**: 800-225-2525 or 800-447-4747, TTY 800-328-2298, www.nwa.com
- **SkyWest/Delta Reservations**: 1-435-624-3400, TTY 800-831-4488, www.skywest.com
- **United Airlines Reservations**: 800-241-6522, www.ual.com
- **US Airways/America West Reservations**: 800-428-4322, www. usair.com

Airlines serving the **Humphrey Terminal**:

- **Casino Express Reservations**: 800-258-8800, www.redlioncasino.com
- **Champion Air Reservations**: 800-922-2606, TTY 800-831-4488, www.championair.com
- **Miami Air International Reservations**: 1-305-876-3600, www.miamiair.com
- **Omni Air International Reservations**: 1-877-718-8901, www.omniairintl.com
- **Ryan International Reservations**: 888-443-7926, www.flyryan.com
- **Sun Country Airlines Reservations**: 800-359-6786, www.suncountry.com

PARKING

New **parking ramps at both Lindbergh and Humphrey** terminals have done a lot to ease the parking situation, but you might still want to check availability during busy travel times by calling the **Parking Information Hotline**, 888-868-7001. Off-site parking—and taking a shuttle to the terminal—is cheapest and quite convenient. Terminal parking rates are:

- **Short-term** at the terminal: $5 for the first hour; $8 for the first 2; maximum $36 in a 24-hour period. You can save $2 if you pay with your credit or debit card in the airport's e-Park self-pay system.
- **General Parking**: $8 for the first hour, $2 each additional hour, $18 daily maximum, $98 per week
- Heated under-terminal **valet parking** (use the left inbound lane on the lower level roadway and follow the directional signs to the valet service entrance): $10 first hour, $3 each additional hour; $28 daily, May–October; $40 daily, November–April.

The airport is also served by **off-airport lots**. Find the best price and make reservations for off-airport parking at www.airportparkingreservations.com/airports/minneapolis/index. At the time of the writing of this book, **Park 'N Fly**, www.pnf.com, about 5 minutes away from the airport at 3700 American Boulevard East (south of 494 off 34th Street), offers outdoor parking for $9 a day ($57 per week), indoor ramp parking for $14 ($2 discount for AAA members), and free shuttles from your car to the terminals every 3 to 5 minutes. **Park 'N Go**, 7901 International Drive, Bloomington, is another lot off 34th Street, 952-854-3386. **Team Parking**, three and a half miles from the airport at 1435 Davern Street, St. Paul (off Highway 5/West 7th), also offers outdoor/uncovered parking for $9 a day, and indoor parking for $10. Their free shuttles run around the clock and they tell you to allow 15 minutes to get to the airport.

For jump starts and towing: If you come back from a trip and your car won't start, the airport web page says to call **Mark's Towing** at 651-454-1533.

AIRPORT BUS, SHUTTLE, AND TAXI SERVICE

Taxis are available at both the Lindbergh and Humphrey Terminals. Follow the signs to the cab starter booth, where airport staff will call a taxi up from the queue for you. Downtown Minneapolis is approximately 16 miles (25 minutes) from the airport. Expect to pay around $30. The distance to downtown St. Paul is approximately 12 miles and the fare is around $25.

City **bus** service is provided by MetroTransit. The airport's bus stop is located at the Lindbergh Terminal **Transit Center** on **Level 1** of the **Blue and Red parking ramps**. Passengers who arrive at the Humphrey Terminal will need to take the LRT to the Lindbergh Terminal and catch a city bus there.

Shared ride service between the airport and cities within a 25-mile radius is available from **SuperShuttle**. Shuttles pick up and drop travelers off near the **Green** and **Gold parking ramps** across from the Lindbergh Terminal. To make a reservation, call 612-827-7777 (ext. 1) or 800-BLUEVAN, www.super shuttle.com. **Airport Taxi and Delivery**, 5010 Hillsboro Ave, Minneapolis, 952-928-0000, serves the entire Twin Cities metro area. Vans and smoke-free cabs are available; they take reservations up to 24 hours in advance.

SCHEDULED TRANSPORTATION

Scheduled bus, van, and limousine service is provided by several companies that have **ticket counters** in the **Ground Transportation Center** in the **Lindbergh Terminal**. Advance reservations are highly recommended. Contact the individual companies directly for rates, routes, and other information:

- **Airport Passenger Service** (Service to Wisconsin), 800-869-5796 or 715-835-0399, www.airportpassenger.com
- **Executive Express** (Service to St. Cloud, Brainerd, Camp Ripley, and other cities in central Minnesota), 888-522- 9899, www.executiveexpress.biz
- **Jefferson/Greyhound Bus Lines** (Service to Minnesota, Iowa, Wisconsin, North and South Dakota); buy tickets at the Rochester Direct counter.
- **Land to Air Express** (Service to Mankato and St. Peter), 507-625-3977 or 888-736-9190, www.landtoairexpress.com
- **Premier Transportation** (Hotel shuttle service to St. Paul suburbs), 612-331-7433 or 800-899-7433, www.premierTrans.com
- **Rochester Direct** (Service to Rochester/Mayo Clinic), 507-280-9270 or 800-280-9270, www.rochesterdirect.com
- **Twin City Passenger Service** (Service to Ridgedale Center, Alexandria, Sauk Center, and other points west), 320-762-1544 or 800-950-2930

CAR RENTAL

Rental car companies have phones and touch screen information kiosks at the **Lindbergh Terminal** on the **Baggage Claim Level** opposite baggage carousels 2, 5, and 10. The rental car counters are located in the **Hub** building located between the Blue and Red parking ramps, on Levels 1–3. Passengers can take the underground tram to go between the Lindbergh Terminal and the Hub building.

AT-THE-AIRPORT CAR RENTAL
- **Alamo**, www.alamo.com, 800-327-9633
- **Dollar Rent A Car**, www.dollar.com, 800-800-4000
- **Hertz**, www.hertz.com, 800-654-3131
- **National Car Rental**, Minneapolis, www.nationalcar.com, 800-227-7368
- **Thrifty Car Rental**, 952-854-8080, 800-847-4389, 800-367-2277; Thrifty Car Rental has a branch office at the Millennium Hotel, 1313 Nicollet Ave

OFF-AIRPORT CAR RENTAL
Shuttle buses to the off-airport car rental companies are accessible from the **Transit Center**, between the Blue and Red Parking ramps at the Lindbergh Terminal.
- **Avis Rent-A-Car**, www.avis.com, 800-831-2847
- **Budget**, www.budgetrentacar.com, 800-527-0700
- **Classic Car Rentals and Tours**, 612-529-1337, has a double-decker London bus, vintage sports cars, and chauffeur-driven Rolls Royces
- **Enterprise Rent-A-Car**, www.enterprise.com, 800-325-8007
- **Midwest Motorcycle Rental and Tours**, 612-338-5345, rents Harleys and luxury automobiles, such as Porsches and BMWs
- **Payless Car Rental**, 612-866-4918, 800-729-5377

LIMOS

If you want to arrive in style, all the limousine services make runs to the airport. Check the "Limousine Service" listings in the Yellow Pages or call:
- **Archer Limo**, 763-503-9482, 877-503-9482, http://archerlimo.com
- **Davis Limousine Service**, 952-882-1400, 612-290-2100, 651-231-3338, www.davislimousine.com
- **Star Limousine**, 651-291-8008, 866-440-2907, www.limostar.com

TAXIS

Unless you are in one of the two downtowns or at the airport, you must telephone for a taxi rather than hailing one on the street. Some only work in specific areas, so call the cab that covers your location. (See Taxis and Shuttles in **Useful Numbers and Web Sites**.)

AMTRAK

There are not a lot of passenger trains, but the **Empire Builder** stops in the Twin Cities on its route from **Chicago** (about 8 hours) to **Seattle** (48 hours plus).

- **Amtrak National Route Information**, 800-872-7245, www. amtrak.com
- **Amtrak Twin Cities Passenger Station**, 730 Transfer Rd, St. Paul, 651-644-1127, 800-USA-Rail, www.amtrak.com; the number 16 bus route runs along University Ave, a block south of the station, and you can take that to downtown Minneapolis or St. Paul, but catching a taxi at the train station is probably the easiest way to get to your destination.

WHILE YOU SEARCH FOR A PERMANENT LIVING SITUATION, THE APART-
ment search services listed in the **Finding a Place to Live** chapter
can assist you with a short-term lease. Also consider the following
options, which vary in expense and accommodation.

RESERVATION SERVICES

- **AAA**, www.aaa.com
- **BizTravel**, www.biztravel.com
- **Cheap Tickets**, www.cheaptickets.com
- **Expedia**, 800-EXPEDIA, www.expedia.com
- **Orbitz**, www.orbitz.com
- **Travelocity**, www.travelocity.com
- **Trip Advisor**, www.tripadvisor.com
- **www.hotels.com**

LODGINGS

If you don't want to have to rent a car, stay in downtown Minneapolis or St.
Paul, or along the Hiawatha LRT route.

MINNEAPOLIS DOWNTOWN

- **Courtyard by Marriot—Milwaukee Road Depot**, 225 Third Ave S
  (Washington Ave), 612-375-1700, 800-321-2211, www.marriott.com; features an indoor ice rink and weekend water park.
- **Crowne Plaza–Northstar**, 618 Second Ave S, 612-338-2288, 888-303-
  1746, www.msp-northstar.crowneplaza.com, is located downtown on the
  skyway system.
- **Doubletree Guest Suites**, 1101 La Salle Ave, 612-332-6800, 800-245-
  8011, www.minneapolisdoubletree.com; shuttle service is available within
  five miles of the hotel.

- **Embassy Suites Downtown Minneapolis**, 425 S 7th St, 612-333-3111, 800-EMBASSY, www.embassysuites.com, is located two blocks from the Humphrey Metrodome and Hiawatha LRT.
- **Holiday Inn Metrodome**, 1500 Washington Ave, 612-333-4646, 888-HOLIDAY, 800-448-3663, www.metrodome.com, is located four blocks from the Hiawatha LRT line on the edge of the business district. It offers complimentary shuttle service within a three-mile radius, as well as oversized vehicle parking.
- **The Marquette**, 710 Marquette Ave, 612-333-4545, www.marquette hotel.com, is an older hotel in the IDS Center, an office complex situated on the Nicollet Mall in the middle of downtown Minneapolis.
- **Millennium Hotel Minneapolis**, 1313 Nicollet Mall, 612-332-6000, 866-866-8086, www2.millenniumhotels.com, is connected to the Convention Center through the skyway system.
- **Minneapolis Hilton and Towers**, 1001 Marquette Ave S, 612-376-1000, 800-HILTONS, www.Hilton.com; connected by skyway to the Convention Center.
- **Radisson Plaza Hotel Minneapolis**, 35 S 7th St, 800-333-3333, www.Radisson.com; connected to the city's skyway system.

ST. PAUL

- **Days Inn Midway Minneapolis/St. Paul**, 1964 University Ave W, 651-645-8681, 800-329-7466, www.daysinn.com; other locations throughout the metro; discounts for AAA members; free shuttle to the University of Minnesota hospital; three blocks from the Twin Cities Amtrak station.
- **Embassy Suites Hotel Downtown St. Paul**, 175 E 10th St, 651-224-5400, 800-EMBASSY, http://embassysuites.hilton.com, is near I-94 and I-35E in downtown St. Paul; other locations throughout the metro.
- **Holiday Inn Express–Bandana Square**, 1010 Bandana Blvd W, 651-647-1637, 888-HOLIDAY, www.hibandanasquare.com, is located in an historic setting; offers complimentary shuttle service within a five-mile radius; other locations throughout the metro.
- **Holiday Inn RiverCentre**, 175 W 7th St, 651-225-1515, 888-HOLIDAY, www.holiday-inn.com/stpaulmn, is across the street from Xcel Energy Center/RiverCentre and is also the closest hotel to the Science Museum.
- **Radisson Riverfront**, 11 E Kellogg Blvd, 651-292-1900, 800-333-3333, www.radisson.com/stpaulmn

SUBURBS

- **AmericInn Motel and Suites**, 2200 Hwy 10, Mounds View, 763-786-2000, 800-634-3444, http://americinn.com, operates Splash Adventures water park primarily on weekends; other locations throughout the metro.
- **Baymont Inn and Suites**, 6415 James Circle, Brooklyn Center, 763-561-8400, 877-229-6668, www.baymontinns.com; near Medtronic and 3M; accepts pets.

- **Best Western Kelly Inn–Plymouth**, 2705 N Annapolis Ln, Plymouth, 763-553-1600, 800-528-1234, www.bestwesternplymouth.com
- **Comfort Inn**, 800-424-6423, www.comfortinn.com, has many locations throughout the metro, including St. Cloud.
- **Country Inn & Suites**, 888-201-1746, www.countryinns.com, has many locations throughout the metro.
- **Crowne Plaza North**, 2200 Freeway Blvd, Brooklyn Center, 763-566-8000, 888-303-1746, www.ichotelsgroup.com, is located along highways I-694 and I-94.
- **Days Inn West**, www.daysinn.com, has many locations throughout the metro.
- **Embassy Suites Airport**, 7901 34th Ave S, Bloomington, 952-854-1000, 800-EMBASSY, http://embassysuites.hilton.com, is located one mile from the airport and from the Mall of America; other locations throughout the metro.
- **Four Points by Sheraton**, 1330 Industrial Blvd, Minneapolis, 612-331-1900, 888-625-5144, www.starwoodhotels.com, offers complimentary transportation to downtown Minneapolis, including the Metrodome; other locations.
- **Hampton Inn Minneapolis/St. Paul North**, 800-HAMPTON, www.hamptoninn.com; several locations throughout the metro.
- **Hilton Garden Inns**, 877-STAY HGI (877-782-9444), www.hiltongardeninn.com; numerous locations throughout the metro.
- **Holiday Inn–Burnsville**, 14201 Nicollet Ave S, Burnsville, 888-463-7200 or 952-435-2100, www.hiburnsville.com; located at I-35W/I-35E and County 42.
- **Holiday Inn Select–Minneapolis–St. Paul International Airport**, Three Appletree Sq, Bloomington, 800-465-4329 or 952-854-9000, www.hiselect.com/msp-stpaulapt.
- **Super 8 Hotel–Roseville**, 2401 Prior Ave (I-35 W and Hwy 36), Roseville, 651-636-8888 or 800-800-8000, www.rosevillesuper8.com.

UNIVERSITY AREA

- **Days Inn University**, 2407 University Ave, Minneapolis, 612-623-3999, 800-329-7466; many rooms have microwaves, refrigerators, coffee makers, and full-size irons and ironing boards; a deluxe Continental breakfast is also included.
- **Radisson University Hotel**, 615 Washington Ave Southeast, Minneapolis, 612-379-8888, 800-333-3333, www.radisson.com.

HOSTELS

- **The City of Lakes International House**, 2400 Stevens Ave S, Minneapolis, 612-522-5000, www.minneapolishostel.com, is located among the Victorian homes near the Minneapolis Institute of Arts. Convenient to downtown, it offers private rooms and dormitories, and a group kitchen. This hostel is only open to out-of-the-metropolitan-area and international visitors. Telephone is free for local calls; fax is available. Off street parking is $10 US per night. Contact the management for rates.

SHORT-TERM RENTALS AND EXTENDED-STAY HOTELS

For a comfortable transition, the following hotels offer furnished rooms in convenient locations, such as downtown Minneapolis. Most apartments are equipped with linens, cooking utensils, etc.

- **Baymont Inns**, www.baymontinns.com; AAA Reservation Line, 800-789-4103
- **Bridgestreet Corporate Housing** operates two high-rise apartment hotels, both in downtown Minneapolis, 763-557-5771.
- **Country Inns and Suites**, many locations, 800-456-4000 or www.countryinns.com
- **Extended Stay America,** www.extendedstayamerica.com; efficiency studios; several locations.
- **Holiday Inn Express Hotel & Suites**, 800-HOLIDAY, www.ichotels group.com
- **Northland Inn Luxury Suite Hotel**, 7025 Northland Dr, Brooklyn Park, 763-536-8300, 800-441-6422, www.northlandinn.com; features two- and three-room suites.
- **Oakwood Corporate Housing**, locations throughout the Twin Cities, 800-897-4610; equipped and furnished suites, monthly rates.
- **Park Plaza**, 4460 W 78th St Circle, Bloomington, 952-831-3131, www.parkplaza.com; this hotel has two-room suites.
- **Park Vista**, 387 E Arlington Ave, St. Paul, 651-771-2084; one- and two-bedroom apartments, kitchen and linen packages. Located along Gateway biking and hiking trail.
- **Residence Inn Minneapolis Downtown at the Depot**, 612-340-1300, 800-331-3131, www.marriott.com; ice skating; indoor water park open on weekends.
- **Residence Inn Minneapolis Downtown**, 45 8th St, Minneapolis, 612-677-1000, 800-331-3131, www.marriott.com
- **The Residence Inn**, 3400 Edinborough Way (France Ave and I-494), Edina, 952-893-9300, 800-410-9649, www.marriott.com; guests may use the pool, track, and playground in attached indoor Edinborough Park. Accepts pets. Two-room suites have kitchens. Rates vary with availability; lower rates for longer stays; corporate discounts available.
- **The Residence Inn by Marriott**, 7780 Flying Cloud Dr, Eden Prairie, 952-829-0033, 800-410-9649, www.marriott.com; has one-and two-bedroom units with patios or balconies and fireplaces. Pets are accepted.
- **Richfield Inn Apartments**, 7700 Bloomington Ave S, Richfield, 612-869-3050, 800-245-3050; one- and two-bedroom apartments.
- **Staybridge Suites by Holiday Inn**, 800-238-8000, www.staybridge. com; several locations; feature one bedroom, and two bedroom/two bath suites.

- **TownePlace Suites Minneapolis Downtown**, 525 N 2nd St, Minneapolis, 612-340-1000, www.marriott.com; boast comfy rooms and well-equipped kitchenettes; allow pets.

BED & BREAKFASTS

If you really want to learn about your new hometown, try a bed & breakfast for your initial stay. Innkeepers always know their way around.
- **Chatsworth Bed & Breakfast**, 984 Ashland Ave, St. Paul, 651-227-4288, www.chatsworth-bb.com; Ashland Ave runs parallel to Summit Ave, two blocks north, making this a great location to stay in if you're dropping kids off at one of the local colleges.
- **Evelo's Bed and Breakfast**, 2301 Bryant Ave, Minneapolis, 612-374-9656, www.bedandbreakfast.com
- **Inn on the Farm**, 6150 Summit Dr, Brooklyn Center, in the Earle Brown Heritage Center, 763-569-6330, 800-524-0239, www.earlebrown.com; housed in a cluster of historic farm buildings, this restored Victorian estate has ten rooms including one that is handicapped accessible.
- **Le Blanc House**, 302 University Ave Northeast, Minneapolis, 612-379-2570, 877-379-2570, www.leblanchouse.com, is located within walking distance of a variety of restaurants in downtown Minneapolis.
- **Nan's Bed and Breakfast**, 2304 Fremont Ave, Minneapolis, 612-377-5118, is located only a short walk from Uptown and shopping, restaurants, and the Lake of the Isles walking paths.
- **Ticknor Hill Bed and Breakfast**, 1625 3rd Ave, Anoka, 763-421-9687, 800-484-3954 ext. 6391, www.ticknorhill.com

LUXURY LODGINGS

- **The Grand Hotel Minneapolis**, 615 Second Ave S, Minneapolis, 612-288-8888, 866-THE GRAND, www.grandhotelminneapolis.com, is clubby and quiet; a little out of the action, but only a few blocks.
- **Graves 601**, 601 First Ave N, Minneapolis (formerly Le Meridian), 612-677-1100, 866-523-1100, www.graves601hotel.com; opposite Target Center and First Ave, and connected by skyway to downtown shopping.
- **Nicollet Island Inn**, 95 Merriam St on Nicollet Island, Minneapolis, 612-331-1800, www.nicolletislandinn.com; located in a restored factory on an island in the middle of the Mississippi River.
- **The Saint Paul Hotel**, 350 Market St, St. Paul, 651-292-9292, 800-292-9292, www.stpaulhotel.com, is one of Condé Nast Traveler's "Top 75 Hotels in the U.S." Located across the square from the Ordway and Landmark Center, this historic hotel has always been the place to stay in St. Paul.

ACCESSIBLE ACCOMMODATIONS

A word of warning: if you travel in a large van, the downtown parking ramps will probably not be able to accommodate your vehicle, even though the hotels and skyway system may be able to accommodate you. Some of the hotels do address this issue by offering valet parking, but you may have the best luck finding fully accessible accommodations outside the downtowns. Also note: federal law requires that if a hotel guarantees reservations for its regular rooms, it must also guarantee reservations for handicapped-accessible rooms. Here's a list of some hotels with accessible accommodations:

- **Crowne Plaza Northstar Hotel**, 618 S Second Ave, Minneapolis, 612-338-2288, 800-556-7827, 888-303-1746, www.msp-northstar.crowne plaza.com, is on the skyway system. Call the attached Northstar parking ramp to check on accessibility for your vehicle, 612-333-6127.
- **Days Inn West/Plymouth**, 2955 Empire Ln (Hwys 55 and I-494), Plymouth, 763-559-2400, 800-329-7366, www.daysinn.com
- **Hilton Minneapolis**, 1001 Marquette Ave, 612-376-1000, 800-HILTONS, www.Hilton.com; located on the skyway system, it offers valet parking and can accommodate large vans in an adjacent city-owned parking ramp; pets allowed.
- **Holiday Inn/Bandana Square**, 1010 Bandana Sq W, St. Paul, 651-647-1637, 800-HOLIDAY, www.hibandanasquare.com
- **Holiday Inn Metrodome**, 1500 Washington Ave S, 612-333-4646, 800-448-3663; www.metrodome.com, is near the University of Minnesota campus and the HHH Metrodome.
- **Minneapolis Hyatt Regency**, 1300 Nicollet Mall, 612-370-1234, 800-233-1234, www.Minneapolis.hyatt.com; on the skyway system and connected to the Convention Center. There is no parking for oversize vans.
- **Minneapolis Marriott City Center**, 30 S 7th St in the City Center shopping complex, 612-349-4000, 800-228-9290; www.Marriott.com, is connected to the skyway. The hotel offers valet parking, and can accommodate oversize vans in an open lot a few blocks away.
- **Northland Inn and Executive Conference Center**, 7025 Northland Dr, Brooklyn Park, 763-536-8300, 800-441-6422, www.northlandinn.com, is a suite hotel with fully accessible rooms.

ONCE YOU'VE SETTLED IN, YOU'LL EVENTUALLY WANT TO GET AWAY, IF only for a day or two. Twin Citians tend to frequent the places described below. In addition to these, you may want to join the time-honored tradition of heading **"Up North."** It doesn't matter where you go—there are ten thousand lakes to choose from! Read about them on the Minnesota Tourism web site (www.exploreminnesota.com). One popular destination is **Brainerd**, about two hours' drive north—except on Friday afternoons, when it can take forever. With 465 lakes, 520 holes of golf, two huge waterparks, the 70-mile Paul Bunyan Trail, and International Speedway, Brainerd has plenty of things to do, even on rainy days. Call 800-450-2838 or check www.explorebrainerd lakes.com for specifics. And as long as you're headed that way, don't miss the 26-foot-tall statue of Paul Bunyan at Paul Bunyan Land's This Old Farm and Pioneer Village, seven miles east of Brainerd on Highway 18 (www.thisold farm.net). Don't ask why you should be interested in a giant statue, it's a Minnesota thing, as is breaking the short trip to Duluth at Toby's Restaurant in Hinckley—everybody does it, so you should, too!

HISTORIC VILLAGES AND THEIR VICINITIES

Stillwater, 20 miles east of St. Paul on the St. Croix River, and Excelsior and Wayzata, 20 miles west of Minneapolis on Lake Minnetonka, can only be reached by car. All three of these historic villages offer cute shopping, eating and drinking, and general poking around. Excelsior and Stillwater offer other recreation opportunities as well.

WAYZATA

Wayzata (www.wayzata.org), out I-394, has nothing to offer children, apart from Ben and Jerry's ice cream. Antiquing, however, is world class. Post-shopping, hang with the locals at Sunsets, under the clock tower (www.sunsetsrestaurant.com). For the best lunch around, drive a few minutes west on

Highway 15 to the Minnetonka Art Center (www.minnetonkaarts.org). The café there is open from 9 'til 2, Monday through Friday, as are the galleries, which are filled with local artists' work.

EXCELSIOR

Excelsior (www.ci.excelsior.mn.us), on Highway 7, has a much more family-friendly vibe. Founded in 1853, it has a distinct New England village feel, with a waterfront common area and a variety of colorful houses with cute gardens. Visit during Art on the Lake in June or Apple Days in September, and take a walking tour led by local author Bob Williams, who uses Excelsior as the setting for his books. Browse in the shops on Water Street, swim at the Commons, ride the old-fashioned trolley, or take a day or evening cruise. Excelsior is home port to about a dozen charter cruise lines, among them the Queen of Excelsior (www.qecruise.com). The Minnehaha, a 1906 streetcar boat that was raised and restored by community volunteers after being scuttled in Lake Minnetonka back in the 1920s, runs a scheduled route on weekends and holidays and will drop you off at the Wayzata dock so you can explore that village too (www. steamboatminnehaha.org).

Looking for more action? Rent a jet ski from Bay Rentals (952-474-0366) or a boat or kayak from Excel Boat Club (www.excelboatclub.com). You can even hire a guide to take you fishing. HookMasters (www.HookMasters.net) is based in Excelsior. Other guides can be found in the Yellow Pages under "Fishing Trips."

Don't miss: Excelsior Bay Books (36 Water Street, www.excelsior baybooks.com), an independent bookstore well-known for its children's and fiction sections, and Leipold's Antiques and Gifts (239 Water Street, 952-474-5880). Adele's Frozen Custard & Old Fashioned Ice Cream, on Excelsior Boulevard at the east end of town, is a good place to end your walking tour with a dish of the ultimate in ice cream. Be sure to catch a performance at the world-famous Old Log Theater (5175 Meadville Street, 952-474-5951, www.oldlog.com). The Old Log serves excellent dinners and is renowned for its British farces and for the famous actors who have starred in them. If you decide to stay the night, the Bird House Bed and Breakfast is on Water Street, right in the heart of town (www.birdhouseinn.com). The next closest place to stay is Chanhassen, which has a Country Suites by Carlson (952-937-2424, 800-456-4000, www.countryinns.com/chanhassenmn).

STILLWATER

Stillwater (www.ilovestillwater.com) is another lively town with a history that pre-dates statehood. Nestled into the bluffs of the St. Croix River, this Birthplace of Minnesota was a thriving logging town into the late 1800s and is listed on the National Registry of Historic Places. Visitors can enjoy the antiquing, canoeing and boating on the beautiful St. Croix, one of America's protected Wild and Scenic Waterways—or tour the river valley from a hot air balloon (St. Croix Hot Air Balloons, 651-436-2771, st.croixhotairballoons.com; Stillwater Balloon, Hot

Air Balloon Flights, 651-439-1800, www.stillwaterballoons.com). This is one town that did not tear down its past in order to build its present; consequently many of its elegant old mansions survive and have been turned into bed and breakfasts. Elephant Walk (www.elephantwalkbb.com) and Rivertown Inn Bed & Breakfast (www.rivertowninn.com) are often recommended. The Lowell Inn (www.lowellinn.com) is well known for its Swiss fondue and beautifully restored rooms.

For dining the locals suggest The Dock Café (425 Nelson Street East, 651-430-3770), a great place to sit and watch the river traffic and eat burgers. Or take a trip on the Minnesota Zephyr dinner train (www.minnesota zephyr.com).

Visit Stillwater during Lumberjack Days in July to watch professional and amateur loggers demonstrate logrolling, ax throwing, and other lumberjack skills.

If you love pottery, time your visit to coincide with the **St. Croix Valley Pottery Tour and Sale**. Similar to drive-around weekends in other artsy rural areas of the country, the St. Croix Valley Tour is held every spring—come snow or mosquitoes—on a 75-mile route along Highway 95, between Stillwater and Cambridge. For details and a map to the studios check the potters' web site (www.minnesotapotters.com). Check Minnesota Beds and Breakfasts Online (www.bbonline.com/mn/) for places to stay along the way.

The St. Croix National Scenic Riverway from Stillwater upstream to Taylor's Falls is easy to navigate by canoe or powerboat and also attracts hikers, rock climbers, cross-country skiers, mountain bikers, and fishermen. There are three parks in this area: St. Croix Islands Scenic Reserve, William O'Brien State Park, and Interstate Park at Taylor's Falls. Information is available online from the National Park Service (www.nps.gov/sacn) or from the Minnesota Department of Natural Resources (DNR) (www.dnr.state.mn.us). The St. Croix Boat and Packet Company offers St. Croix River charter cruises departing from the Port of Stillwater, located downtown on the south end of Main Street (651-430-1234, www.andiamo-ent.com).

POINTS NORTH

DULUTH

Duluth (www.visitduluth.com), about two hours' drive north of the Twin Cities up I-35, is an easy weekend destination. There are a lot of things to do, in every season: watch giant cargo ships from around the world enter Duluth's harbor under the Aerial Lift Bridge; downhill ski at city-owned Spirit Mountain (www.spiritmt.com); bike, hike or in-line skate the Willard Munger Trail (www.dnr.state.mn.us/state_trails/willard_munger). At Canal Park, you can stroll the boardwalk and visit the police horse stable, or hop on a tour boat for a narrated harbor cruise. Those looking for real adventure can find it ice climbing on the lake's steep cliffs. The Casket Quarry within the city of Duluth has several "social" climbs. Information about Lake Superior ice climbs, guides, and gear can be found on the Climbing Central web site (www.climbingcentral.com) or call the Ski Hut in Duluth (5607 Grand Avenue, 218-624-5889, and 1032 East 4th Street, 218-724-8525). An equally good source of information is Vertical Endeavors in St. Paul (651-776-1430, www.verticalendeavors.com), or Carnival Thrillz in Duluth (218-279-9980). If you're adventurous, and love the water, try kayaking in Lake Superior. The University of Minnesota–Duluth offers both sea kayaking and rock climbing tours (www.umdrsop.org/kayaking/sea_kayak/index.html).

For those who are looking for something a little less strenuous, walking the quiet residential streets of the historic East End is always a pleasure. The massive mansions and ornate Victorian houses here were built by wealthy turn-of-the century businessmen who could afford to bring master craftsmen over from Europe to build their regal homes. Glensheen at 3300 London Road is a Jacobean mansion on the lake where two infamous murders took place. It is open to the public June–October. Call 218-724-8863 for information, 888-454-4536 for tour reservations, or visit www.d.umn.edu/glen. (Check the **Twin Cities Reading List** chapter for a book about Glensheen that will tell you the things they won't talk about on the tour.)

There are plenty of great places to stay in Duluth. If you're looking for a room with a lake view, try one of these: Fitger's Inn, a renovated brewery at 600 East Superior Street, (888-FITGERS or www.fitgers.com); The Mansion, 3600 London Road, (218-724-0739), an especially elegant bed and breakfast right next door to Glensheen; or the interesting Mountain Villas on top of Spirit Mountain (866-688-4552, www.mtvillas.com). The Canal Park area is another fun place to stay. Accommodations there range from a private "beach cottage" on Park Point (800-774-3004, www.lakesuperiorgetaway.com) to Comfort Suites (800-517-4000, www.stayinduluth.com). For many other options, check out www.visitduluth.com/lodging.

For those who prefer to camp, the Superior National Forest or one of the several state forests along the North Shore are favorite destinations. For Superior National Forest information call 218-626-4300 or 877-550-6777 (reservations), or check out www.fs.fed.us/r9/superior. You can make reservations online. For state forest information and reservations, contact the DNR (651-296-6157, www.dnr.state.mn.us).

Popular events in and near Duluth include Grandma's Marathon, from Two Harbors to Duluth in June, and the North Shore Inline Marathon over the same route in September; The Two Harbors Folk Festival is held in July, with the Bayfront Blues Festival in August. The 400-mile John Beargrease sled dog marathon (www.beargrease.com) starts and ends in Duluth. It is held in late January or early February.

NORTH SHORE OF LAKE SUPERIOR

If you have the time, continue up the **North Shore** of Lake Superior, the largest freshwater lake on earth. Its mild appearance on a calm day belies the fact that these are some of the most dangerous waters anywhere in the world. Highway 61 along the shore is lined with markers memorializing the ships that have wrecked on Superior's iron-red rocks.

The views as you drive along the lake through Superior National Forest are stunning and minimalist, often reduced to a slab of rock against sky and water. Park and hike to Gooseberry Falls and Split Rock Lighthouse—the routes are well-marked from the highway. **Split Rock Lighthouse State Park**, an hour's drive from Duluth, past Two Harbors, boasts a restored lighthouse that is probably Minnesota's most photographed historic attraction (www.mnhs. org/places/sites/srl). You can stay in a working lighthouse at the **Lighthouse Bed and Breakfast at Two Harbors** (218-834-4814 or 888-832-5606, email: lakehist@lakenet.com). (This B&B is said to be haunted, which many visitors consider a plus.) For a North Shore visitors' guide, look online at www. northshoreinfo.com.

A little farther up the coast, **Lutsen** (www.61north.com) is a famous resort area that offers downhill and cross-country skiing and snowmobiling in winter, and hiking, sea kayaking, canoeing, fly fishing, and mountain biking in summer. There are numerous motels and resorts here, but the granddaddy of them all is **Lutsen Resort** (www.lutsenresort.com). Nearby **Bluefin Bay** at Tofte (800-BLUEFIN, www.bluefinbay.com) has been named "Resort Property of the year" by the Minnesota Innkeepers Association.

Grand Marais (www.grandmaraismn.com), just up the road, is an artful little village, home to the **Grand Marais Art Colony** (www.grandmarais artcolony.org), which offers workshops for visual artists and writers throughout the summer. Also here: the **North House Folk School** (www.north house.org), which offers courses in traditional northern crafts, from baking and boatbuilding to weaving and woodworking. **Naniboujou Lodge and Restaurant** (www.naniboujou.com), located 14 miles east of Grand Marais, is the kind of place where high tea is served in the solarium. It was built in the 1920s as an ultra-exclusive private club, with Babe Ruth as one of its charter members. When the stock market crashed in 1929, however, it took Naniboujou down with it. Since then it has been open to the public, and regular people have been able to eat in its colorful Native American–style painted dining room. This room, with its 20-foot-high domed ceiling, has been described as the "North Woods' answer to the Sistine Chapel." Lodging is available in rooms that are substantially more rustic, and don't have telephones or TVs. For lodging at other resorts, call 888-922-2225 or check online at www. grandmaraismn.com.

Seventeen miles north of Grand Marais, the **Gunflint Trail** (www.gun flint-trail.com) takes off into the Boundary Waters Canoe Area Wilderness (BWCAW). The BWCAW, which extends for 150 miles along the Canadian border, is a million-acre labyrinth of portage-linked lakes. Here you can canoe and camp just as primitively as the French-Canadian voyageur fur-traders did back in the 1700s. Cross-country skiing, snowshoeing, dog sled trips, and wolf-calling are popular activities in the wilderness in winter. Whatever the season, you are in close contact with nature including bears, moose, and mosquitoes—so be careful. Guides are available and permits are required for all visitors entering the BWCAW or neighboring Quetico Provincial Park, another million acres of wilderness on the Canadian side of the border. Visit in the middle of the week, or before Memorial Day or after Labor Day, and you will encounter fewer people. The main entry points to the BWCAW are through Crane Lake, Ely, Tofte, and Grand Marais, so that's where the outfitters are located. If you use an outfitter, as most people do, the outfitter will be able to arrange for your permit. For help finding outfitters, look online at the state's tourism web site (www.exploreminnesota.com) or contact the Grand Marais Chamber of Commerce (800-622-4014, www.grandmaraismn.com); the Ely Chamber of Commerce (800-777-7281, www.ely.org); or the Crane Lake Visitor and Tourism Bureau (800-362-7405, www.cranelake.org). For Gunflint Trail lodgings and outfitters call 800-338-6932, www.gunflint-trail.com. Do-it-yourselfers will find Boundary Waters permits available online at www. bwcaw.org.

Seven miles south of the Canadian border, **Grand Portage National Monument** was once a large fur-trading post. Tour the reconstructed fort and hike or cross-country ski the 8.5-mile portage footpath to the awe-inspiring 200-foot-high Pigeon River waterfall. For camping information look online at www.nps.gov/grpo.

Grand Portage is also the place to catch the ferry to **Isle Royale**, a wilderness park of rugged forests and unspoiled lakes located 22 miles out in Lake Superior. Home to wolves and moose, it is accessible only by boat or floatplane, April to October. Eighty percent of Isle Royale National Park is underwater and includes shallow warm-water ponds and fast streams as well as the cold, deep waters of Lake Superior. Sport fishing is popular here and trout, northern pike, walleye, and perch are abundant, especially in spring and fall. Travel in the park is by foot or boat—no pets, no bikes. Campers, including boaters, need a permit (available at any ranger station) and should write for information before traveling to the park: Superintendent, Isle Royale National Park, 800 East Lakeshore Drive, Houghton, Michigan 49931, or call 906-482-0984. For more information, look online at www.nps.gov/isro. Reservations for Rock Harbor Lodge or housekeeping cabins may be made by calling the Lodge at 906-337-4993 or National Park Concessions, Inc., Mammoth Cave, Kentucky 42259, 502-773-2191. Floatplane service is available from Houghton, Michigan (see Superintendent above).

VOYAGEURS NATIONAL PARK

The quiet splash of the voyageurs' paddles dipping into sparkling water is long gone, and has been replaced by crowds of house-boating wilderness-seekers and fishermen, who throng to Voyageurs National Park, on the Canadian border, all summer long. Moose, bears, eagles, loons, and wolves seem to have gotten used to the crowds and are regularly spotted here, as well. Recreation is not limited to the water—the Park Service maintains a number of trails for hiking and cross-country skiing. Snowmobiling and ice fishing are allowed on the frozen lakes in winter. There are primitive boat-in campsites scattered throughout the park, but public and private campsites, accessible by car, are also available. Three park visitor centers offer information, guidebooks, maps, navigational charts, naturalist-guided trips and campfire talks: Rainy Lake Visitor Center is open year round; Kabetogama Lake Visitor Center and Ash

River Visitor Center are open seasonally. There are also narrated boat tours, which depart from Rainy Lake Visitor Center and visit an old lumber camp, gold and mica mines, and the nesting habitats of gulls and cormorants. Reservations are suggested: 218-286-5470.

You can enter Voyageurs Park (www.nps.gov/voya) from four points along US 53 between Duluth and International Falls: Crane Lake, Ash River, Kabetogama, and Rainy Lake. Year-round food, fuel, lodging, and boat rentals are available outside the park at the four access points. Because this park spans the international border, you must report to customs before and after crossing the Canadian border. All passport and identification rules apply. Contact Superintendent, Voyageurs National Park, 3131 US 53, International Falls, MN 56649-8904, 218-283-9821 or www.nps.gov. For lodging and boat rental around Rainy Lake call 800-FALLS-MN or go online (www.international fallsmn.us/index.shtml); for Ash River, call 800-950-2061; for Crane Lake, see BWCAW above.

HEADING SOUTH

SOUTHEAST MINNESOTA BLUFF COUNTRY

In sharp contrast to the rocky wildness of Highway 61 along Lake Superior (the North Shore drive), Highway 61 heading south from the Twin Cities is a pastoral route across rolling farmland and the tall wooded bluffs of the Mississippi River. (See **Scenic Byways** in the **Lakes and Parkways** chapter.) About an hour out of the Twin Cities, **Red Wing** (www.redwing.org) is a popular day or weekend destination. A big rock called Barn Bluff towers over downtown like a nose too big for its face. It's a hard climb, but worth it—the view of Red Wing and the surrounding river valley is breathtaking. People go to Red Wing for many reasons: the scenic drive; Antique Alley; factory outlets; proximity to Welch Village ski area and the Cannon Valley Trail; or to play golf at scenic **Mississippi National Golf Links** (www.wpgolf.com/Mississippi). Many go just to stay at the wonderful **St. James Hotel** (www.st-james-hotel.com). If the St. James is full, there are many other delightful options, including a former dairy farm, **Round Barn Farm Bed and Breakfast and Bread** (www.roundbarnfarm.com).

Lake Pepin at **Lake City** (www.lakecity.org), 60 miles from Minneapolis, is another half-hour south of Red Wing. A natural wide spot in the Mississippi River, this is the place where water skiing was invented. The sailing is wonderful, as well, though it's shared with a lot of big boat recreational and commercial traffic. The lush broad flood plain and majestic river bluffs of Lake Pepin's shoreline make it prime territory for bird watching. The large **Lake City Marina** (651-345-4211, www.lakecitygov.com/Marina/Marinaindex.html) rents boats and has excellent shower and bathroom facilities as well as electric hook-ups, so you can sleep on board your boat if you choose.

A favorite fall color/apple-picking trip is to drive down the Minnesota side of the river on Highway 61, cross at Wabasha or Winona and come back up Wisconsin Route 35, stopping to eat at one of the fun restaurants in **Pepin,**

Wisconsin (www.pepinwisconsin.com). The **Harbor View Café** (www. harborviewpepin.com) is a perennial favorite, but it's first-come-first-served, and the line starts forming an hour before it opens. Laura Ingalls Wilder fans will enjoy seeing the Little House in the Big Woods, which is replicated just north of the town. Laura Ingalls Wilder Days are held annually in September. Along the way, visit **Frontenac** (www.mississippi-river.org/frontenac.html), on the Minnesota side, a village where little has changed since the 1880s. **Frontenac State Park** (www.dnr.state.mn.us/state_parks/frontenac) completely encircles the village and is a sanctuary for migratory warblers and bald and golden eagles. Hiking trails here overlook the valley and lead you to In-Yan-Teopa, a giant boulder that was sacred to the Dakota and Fox Indians. Look for more bald eagles at Read's Landing near **Wabasha** (www.wabashamn.org). Wabasha is home to the **National Eagle Center** (www.nationaleagle center.org), as well as the place where they filmed *Grumpy Old Men*.

At **Winona** (www.visitwinona.com), two hours south of the cities, still on Highway 61, you hit serious apple country. Winona County Road 1 is known as Apple Blossom Drive, but it is **LaCrescent** (www.lacrescent.com) that bills itself as the Apple Capital of Minnesota. Time your trip to catch the Apple Festival held here during the third week in September, or to catch the state's best display of fall color, a little later.

Lanesboro (www.lanesboro.com), a short distance away, was named one of the 50 Best Outdoor Sports Towns in America by *Sports Afield* magazine. Nestled in the Root River Valley, it lives up to its award-winning designation by offering a wide variety of invigorating outdoor activities, including biking, hiking, or cross-country skiing the picturesque 60-mile Root River Trail, paddling the river, hunting, fishing, and golf. Outfitter rentals and shuttle services are available through clickable links from the web site. For those looking for less strenuous activities, a drive along Highway 16, a National Scenic Byway, or a sidetrip down nearly any country road will provide you with a nostalgic glimpse into rural life in Amish country. Back in town, there is professional theater, homemade sauerkraut and root beer at **Das Wurst Haus German Village and Deli** (www.686.us/daswursthaus), and that inimitable local greasy spoon, the **Chat 'n Chew** (www.chatandchew.com). Lodging choices range from camping to B&Bs and full-bore resorts.

GO EAST

WISCONSIN

Two hundred miles northeast of St. Paul, **Bayfield** (www.bayfield.org) and **The Apostle Islands National Lakeshore** (www.nps.gov/apis) are both romantic and sporty. There you can cruise one of the great sailing grounds of the world, fish one of the great fishing holes, bike, hike, golf, or learn about nature from rangers on the islands—or just stroll around and enjoy the ambience.

Start your vacation on the mainland in Bayfield, a gem of a town on the shore of Lake Superior that mixes art, antiques, and Victorian bed and breakfasts with hunting, fishing, camping, and sailing. Take a sailboat cruise on the three-masted schooner, the Zeeto (www.schoonerman.com/zeeto.htm), or charter a boat yourself. **Sailboats, Inc.** at Bayfield and Superior, operates a charter service/sailing school (800-826-7010, www.sailboats-inc.com). If you're adventurous, try sea kayaking. **Midwest Mountaineering** in Minneapolis (www.midwestmtn.com) presents kayaking clinics that cover trip planning details and route information for planning your own paddle through the Apostle Islands. **Living Adventure** (www.livingadventure.com), based in Ashland, Wisconsin, near Bayfield, offers kayak rental as well as guided tours— some strictly for women.

Bayfield is home to several active yacht clubs that conduct a full schedule of regattas. Try to catch the **Blessing of the Fleet** in June when fishing boats, sailboats, kayaks, rowboats, and even ferry boats decorated with flags weave their way through the Bayfield harbor in a colorful parade to welcome the summer season and receive an ecumenical blessing.

When you're ready to head to the islands, you'll find that getting there is half the fun. In the summer take the ferry; in winter, when the lake is frozen, you can drive. In between, and most fun of all, is the windsled, which is used when the ice road is deemed unsafe to travel. The windsled runs on an uncertain schedule, but the ferry travels from Bayfield Dock to Madeline Island every half-hour (www.madferry.com). Sightseeing boats and island shuttles also depart from the Bayfield Dock. The Grand Tour half-day sightseeing trip will take you past all 22 of the Apostle Islands. For campers, there is a shuttle to Stockton Island from the mainland. Stockton is the largest island and has the most extensive trail system, as well as civilized camping facilities and an awesome swimming beach. Devil's Island is famous for its sea caves.

Madeline Island (www.madelineisland.com), the largest of the Apostle Islands, is not part of the park, but is developed with summer and year-round residences, hotels, and bed and breakfasts. Besides water sports, you can play golf and tennis, explore the island on a rented moped or bike, or bird watch in the Madeline Island Wilderness Preserve.

Among the interesting lodging choices on Madeline Island are **The Inn** (800-822-6315), which offers townhouse accommodations and beach cottages, and **Brittany Bed & Breakfast** (www.brittanycabins.com), which is listed on the National Register of Historic Places. This peaceful waterfront complex was built in the style of an Adirondack camp, with a main house and several cottages. Its manicured croquet lawn begs for ladies in long white dresses and gentlemen in boaters. And after you peg out (finish the game, in croquet talk), be sure to stop for a glass of wine in the formal garden's tea house. **The Island Inn** (www.ontheisland.com) takes vacationing in an entirely different direction. It features rooms with a rustic décor and includes winter dogsledding among its entertainments. Two nights lodging and a day on the trail mushing your own dogsled team costs $318 for one person, $518 for two. Other cold weather activities include the Run on Water five-mile race to Madeline Island over the Madeline Island Ice Road, and snowshoe racing.

Wisconsin Dells (www.wisdells.com) is where your kids will want to go—over and over and over. This self-proclaimed "Waterpark Capital of the

World" is located off I-90 and I-94, about 200 miles from St. Paul. It has indoor and outdoor waterparks, adrenaline-pumping roller coasters, jet boats, horses to ride, trains, mini-golf, cabarets, hypnosis shows . . . the list of attractions goes on forever. Be sure to take an amphibious vehicle tour (www.wisconsinduck tours.com and www.dellsducks.com). Two tips from families who go there often: avoid the crowds by staying in a resort that has its own guests-only waterpark; and download all the coupons you can find from the various Dells web sites—it does get expensive.

For more Wisconsin travel information look online at www.travelwiscon-sin.com. The Wisconsin Department of Natural Resources is online at www.dnr.state.wi.us.

A LITTLE FARTHER AFIELD

CHICAGO

This just squeaks in as a "quick" getaway—it's an eight-hour drive, one way—but if you give yourself four days, you won't feel rushed. Or fly—there are often special fares between the Twin Cities and Chicago. Amtrak will get you there as well (800-USA-RAIL, www.amtrak.com). "The Windy City" needs no introduction, but as a reminder, you can visit the Art Institute, the Field Museum of Natural History, the Magnificent Mile of shopping on Michigan Avenue, Millennium Park, the Cloud Gate sculpture, eclectic shops and pubs on Clark Street, Old Town, blues and jazz festivals, and more. Yes, the Cubs still play at Wrigley Field. For a packet of information, call the Chicago Office of Tourism at 877-CHICAGO or www.877chicago.com.

BLACK HILLS, SOUTH DAKOTA

Minnesota was the jumping off point for pioneers headed west in the late 1800s, and to get a taste of those good old days, plan a trip to **Deadwood, South Dakota**, in the heart of the Black Hills.

At 650 miles, this is not a "Quick Getaway" in the strict sense of the word, and the 9- to 10-hour family drive out I-90 all the way across South Dakota to Deadwood (www.deadwood.org) is a whole lot more pleasant if your car has a DVD player. When you finally get there, though, you'll find there's plenty of action—real cowboys and Indians, gunslingers, rodeos and rock-and-roll. In early August, the region roars with motorcyclists who've come to the Black Hills for the **Sturgis Motorcycle Rally**, an event packed with concerts, racing, and general testosterone-testing. Should you miss that event, you can still match wits with one-armed-bandits (slot machines) in gaming halls that date back to the Gold Rush days of the 1870s. Surprisingly, all of Deadwood is actually a national historic landmark, a fact to ponder while standing at the foot of Wild Bill Hickok's grave on the original Boot Hill, or while panning for gold at the Broken Boot Mine. Deadwood is also the gateway to over 300 miles of groomed snow-mobile and bike trails. Lodging is available in cabins, condos, campgrounds, bed and breakfasts, and chain motels. Book reservations online at www.dead wood.net or by calling 866-601-5103. For more South Dakota travel information, look online at the state's tourism web site, www.travelsd.com.

FALL COLOR

Fall color in Minnesota tends to be yellow and short-lived, with leaves falling with the first hard rain. Check the U.S. Forest Service's hotline for weekly updates on peak fall color (800-354-4595, www.fs.fed.us/news/fallcolors). Here are a few places the locals like to go to catch the Fall Color at its height:

- **Chippewa National Forest**, just west of Grand Rapids on Highway 38 (edge of the Wilderness Scenic Byway) or Highway 46 (the Avenue of the Pines), is located at the intersection of Minnesota's three major ecosystems: the aspen, birch, spruce, fir, and pines of the northern boreal forest; the maple-basswood hardwood forests typical in the southern part of the state; and the prairie west of the forest. The combination produces a range of fall colors not found anywhere else in the state.
- **North Shore of Lake Superior**, Highway 61 North (see above)
- **Southeastern Minnesota/Western Wisconsin Bluff Country**, Highway 61 South (see above)
- The **University of Minnesota Landscape Arboretum**, Highway 5 just west of Highway 41 in Chaska, www.arboretum.umn.edu

ADULTS ONLY GETAWAYS

Midwest resorts tend to run to families, fishermen, golfers, and, in winter, snowmobilers. That's fine, if you fit into that mold. But if what you're looking for is something more on the order of a romantic hideaway, there is a **Relais & Chateaux** hotel (www.relaischateaux.com) in Chetek, Wisconsin (www.chetek.com). Rustic and elegant at the same time, **Canoe Bay** (715-924-4594, www.canoebay.com) has been named the top hotel in the Midwest, and one of the Top 10 Most Romantic. It's indulgent, quiet, and expensive—and only a two-hour drive east of the Twin Cities. Be sure to stop in Chippewa Falls for a tour of the Leinenkugel Brewery (www.leinie.com). Reservations are required.

GOLF GETAWAYS

Giants Ridge (www.giantsridge.com) at Biwabik, on the Iron Range in Northern Minnesota, has been named one of *GolfWorld* magazine's "Top Six Golf Destinations in the World." A three-and-a-half hour drive from the Northern Metro, its **Quarry** course, which opened in 2003, was recently cited as "The Best Golf of the 21st Century," by *Golf Digest* and debuted at Number 16 on *Golf Digest*'s 2005-06 rankings of America's 100 Greatest Public Courses. The resort's older course, **The Legend** (No. 88 on the 100 Greatest list), garnered a prestigious 4.5 star rating from *Golf Digest,* and has been named Minnesota's #1 Public Golf Course. Nearby **Fortune Bay Resort Casino** on Lake Vermillion (www.fortunebay.com) is home to **The Wilderness at**

Fortune Bay (www.thewildernessgolf.com), *Golf Digest's* choice for "America's Best New Upscale Public Golf Course for 2005." For the newest, most comfortable lodgings, stay at the resorts.

ADDITIONAL RESOURCES

- For **general travel information** and an excellent comprehensive travel guide for the entire state, look online at the **Minnesota Office of Tourism**'s web site, www.exploreminnesota.com.
- For **trip planning or park maps** call the **Minnesota Department of Natural Resources** at 651-296-6157 or visit www.dnr.state.mn.us. To reserve a campsite at one of the many state parks, call the DNR's reservation line at 866-85PARKS, www.stayatmnparks.com.
- For a free **Wisconsin vacation guide** look online at www.travel wisconsin.com.
- **North Dakota Tourism** information is available at www.ndtourism.com.
- **South Dakota information** is available at www.travelsd.com.
- **Travel Michigan** is online at www.michigan.org/travel.
- The **National Park Service** web site is www.nps.gov.
- For help finding **bed and breakfasts** try Bed and Breakfast Online, www.bbonline.com/mn.
- For **road condition and detour information** call 511 or look online at www.511mn.org.

MOSQUITOES EAT YOU IN SUMMER AND THE COLD FLASH-FREEZES you in winter, but if you're a Minnesotan, you'll be out and about anyway, dismissing such life-threatening conditions as mild annoyances. All four seasons in the Twin Cities offer exciting annual celebrations, festivals, and shows. Here are just a few you may want to experience yourself.

JANUARY

- **Land O'Lakes Kennel Club Dog Show**, River Centre, St. Paul; all breeds. This is the largest indoor show in the region, www.infodog.com.
- **St. Paul Winter Carnival**; this spectacular annual event includes parades, dog sled races, ice carving, a treasure hunt, and fervent attempts by the Vulcans to warm up the winter. It runs into early February, www.winter-carnival.com.

FEBRUARY

- **Chilly Open**; play golf on frozen Lake Minnetonka in Wayzata! There are three courses and lots of hot food and drink, www.wayzatachamber.com.
- **John Beargrease Dogsled Race**, Duluth, www.beargrease.com

MARCH

- **Builders Association Spring Preview of Homes**, offers tours of newly built homes to acquaint you with builders, and the latest trends and developments, www.paradeofhomes.org.
- **Minnesota State High School Basketball Tournaments**, www.mshsl.org
- **Minnesota State High School Hockey Tournaments**, www.mshsl.org
- **St. Patrick's Day Celebration**, March 17, St. Paul, www.stpatsassoc.org

APRIL

- **Annual Smelt Run,** in rivers near Duluth.

MAY

- **Festival of Nations,** RiverCentre, is Minnesota's largest multicultural extravaganza. It features ethnic cafés, folk dancing, and an international bazaar, www.festivalofnations.com.
- **Heart of the Beast May Day Parade**; giant puppets parade through the streets to Powderhorn Park on the first Sunday in May, www.heartofthe beasttheatre.org/mayday.
- **Minnesota Fishing Opener,** this huge event in the land of 10,000 lakes is the weekend we are all reminded that Minnesota has too many fishermen and too few roads heading "Up North."

JUNE

- **Edina Art Fair,** W 50th St and France Ave; outdoor art and craft bazaar featuring artists, food, and entertainment, www.50thandfrance.com/ artfair.html.
- **Gay/Lesbian/Bisexual/Transgender Pride Festival,** Loring Park, Grant and Willow Sts, Minneapolis; includes music, dancing, and drag queens.
- **Grand Old Day,** Grand Ave, St. Paul; this three-mile-long, family-friendly bash in the street includes a parade, food and drink, specials in Grand Ave stores, arts and crafts, and great music on stages in every block, www.GrandAve.com.
- **Grandma's Marathon,** Duluth; the route parallels the shore of Lake Superior from Two Harbors to Duluth and draws competitors from all over the world. Pick up information at local sports stores, www.grandmas marathon.com.
- **Juneteenth,** held in mid-June in Theodore Wirth Park, Glenwood Ave North, Minneapolis, is a family festival celebrating black American culture with food, music, athletic events, and a film festival, www.juneteenth.com.
- **Svenskarnasdag, Swedish Heritage Day,** on the last Sunday in June at Minnehaha Park, Minneapolis, www.svenskarnasdag.com, is a traditional celebration featuring a Swedish/English church service, ethnic food, and the crowning of Miss Svenskarnasdag.

JULY

- **Basilica Block Party,** Basilica of St. Mary, Hennepin Ave and 17th St, Minneapolis; the church trades its choir for funky rock bands, two nights of music, food, drink, and a raffle. Buy tickets by phone, 612-317-3511, or online at www.ticketworks.com.

- **Lumberjack Days**, Stillwater's festival, commemorates its lumber mill days with ax throwing, logrolling, chainsaw carving, pole climbing, free concerts, and a Bunyanesque fireworks display, www.lumberjack days.com.

- **Minneapolis Aquatennial** pays homage to all things water with ten days of free events that appeal to all age groups and interests: Torchlight Parade, Milk Carton Boat Race, the world's highest-purse triathlon, water ski show, sailing regatta, logrolling competition, art fair, concerts, and Fireworks over the Mississippi. This is the biggest event of the summer, with many streets temporarily closed to traffic. This event is always looking for volunteers—it's a great way to feel like you're part of the community. To volunteer, check online at www.aquatennial.org.

- **Minnesota Orchestra's Viennese Sommerfest**, Orchestra Hall, Nicollet Mall; the setting for nearly a month of concerts with famous guest soloists inside Orchestra Hall, and free entertainment, food, and dancing outside in the Peavey Plaza Marketplace. For $50 you can sit on stage with the orchestra. For concert tickets call 612-371-5656 or 800-292-4141, or order online at www.mnorch.org.

- **Rondo Days Festival and Parade**, Martin Luther King Recreation Center Park, St. Paul, is host to the biggest African-American celebration in Minnesota. It includes a parade, arts and crafts, and a drill team competition, http://rondodays.org/history.htm.

- **Taste of Minnesota**, Harriet Island, St. Paul; Fourth of July weekend— three days of music, entertainment, food (some from local restaurants), and capital fireworks, www.tasteofmn.org.

AUGUST

- **Minnesota Renaissance Festival** is a loose recreation of a renaissance town fair. Located off Hwy 169, four miles south of Shakopee, it lasts seven weekends, mid-August to nearly the end of September. Make merry with jousting tournaments, finger food, entertainers, and unique arts and crafts. For directions and ticket information, call 800-966-8215, www.renaissance fest.com.

- **Minnesota State Fair**, State Fairgrounds, Snelling Ave, St. Paul, marks the end of summer with farm animals, art, fried food on a stick, and Princess Kay of the Milky Way carved in butter—what more could you want? Runs through Labor Day, 651-288-4400, TTY 651-642-2372, www.mnstate fair.org. For information about accessibility, wheelchair rental, and other services, contact guestservices@mnstatefair.org or call 651-288-4448. State Fair Express buses operate from the major malls. For automated express bus information, call 612-341-4287.

- **Uptown Art Fair**, Hennepin and Lake in Minneapolis; a street fair crowded with artists' booths, food, and entertainment. This is one of the largest outdoor art fairs in the Midwest, www.uptownminneapolis.com.

- **Wacipi** (Pow Wow), west of Little Six Casino off County Rd 42 in the Shakopee/Prior Lake area, www.ccsmdc.org; live three-day event featuring over 1000 dancers, performed by the Shakopee Mdewakanton (Dakota) Sioux Community.

SEPTEMBER

- **Fall Festival at the Minnesota Landscape Arboretum**, Hwy 5, Chanhassen, invites the public in for live music, children's activities, and apple and plant sales, www.arboretum.umn.edu/.
- **North Shore In-Line Skating Marathon**, Two Harbors to Duluth, www.northshoreinline.com
- **Parade of Homes** is a tour of selected new homes in the Twin Cities, sponsored by the Builders Association of the Twin Cities, www.paradeofhomes.org.

OCTOBER

- **MEA Week**; the Minnesota Education Association holds its annual convention; area schools schedule parent conferences.
- **Twin Cities Marathon**, www.twincitiesmarathon.org

NOVEMBER

- **Holidazzle Parade** down Nicollet Mall in Minneapolis, nightly, Thanksgiving through December.
- **Macy's Holiday Auditorium Show**, 8th Flr, Nicollet Mall, Minneapolis
- **Walk the Wild Side** at the Minnesota Zoo light display, Thanksgiving through December, www.mnzoo.com.

DECEMBER

- **A Capital New Year**, Rice Park and other downtown St. Paul locations, rings in the New Year with ice skating, live music, and midnight fireworks.
- **Holiday Flower Show**, Como Park Conservatory, www.comozoo conservatory.org
- **Holiday Traditions in the Period Rooms**; Minneapolis Institute of Arts, 3rd St, Minneapolis, is decorated for the holidays, www.artsmia.org.

FROM **SINCLAIR LEWIS** AND **F. SCOTT FITZGERALD** TO **CAROL BLY, Garrison Keillor, Jon Hassler,** and **Sandra Benitez**, many fine writers hail from or have written about Minnesota. Is it the weather? Below is a list of a few good reads with a Minnesota connection to get you started. For those who enjoy hearing authors talk about their work, the **Hennepin County Library Foundation** sponsors a series of authors' lectures every year called **"Pen Pals."** Order tickets online at www.hclib.org/foundation or www.uptowntix.com, 651-209-6799; you can also call the **Pen Pals Hotline**, 952-847-8874. For younger readers, the **Children's Literature Network** (www.childrensliteraturenetwork.org) presents an annual fall festival that includes writing workshops for teens, puppet shows, art labs, author presentations, and loads of other book-related fun. Look online for place and date.

FICTION

- *A Superior Death* by Nevada Barr
- *A Thin Town of the Heart* by Patricia Eilola
- *Excelsior* by Bob Williams
- *In the Lake of the Woods* by Tim O'Brien
- *Killing Time in St. Cloud* by Judith Guest
- *Main Street* by Sinclair Lewis is set in Sauk Center.
- *Red Earth, White Earth* by Will Weaver
- *Until They Bring the Streetcars Back* by Stanley Gordon West
- *Welcome to the Great Mysterious* and *Angry Housewives Eating Bon Bons* by Lorna Landvik
- *The Windchill Factor* by Tom Gifford is a mystery set in Stillwater.

REGIONAL HISTORY

- *55000 Sunsets: 150 Years at Linwood Beach, Lake Minnetonka,* by Robert Gerlicher and Michael Peterson

- *All Hell Broke Loose* by William H. Hull is the story of the November 11, 1940 Armistice Day storm—the worst blizzard that ever hit Minnesota.
- *Boundary Waters: The Grace of the Wild* by Paul Gruchow is a mixture of natural history and stories about pioneers on Isle Royale and the Gunflint Trail.
- *Bring Warm Clothes* by Peg Meier
- *Class Action* by Clara Bingham and Laura Leedy Gansler
- *Fitzgerald's Storm: The Wreck of the Edmund Fitzgerald* by Joseph MacInnis
- *Gunflint: Reflections on the Trail* and *Woman of the Boundary Waters* by Justine Kerfoot are by and about an elderly woman who lived alone in the Boundary Waters area.
- *How To Talk Minnesotan* by Howard Mohr (Get the audio version.)
- *Kensington Rune Stone: New Light on an Old Riddle* by Theodore C. Blegen
- *Last Standing Woman* and *All Our Relations: Native Struggles for Land and Life* by Winona LaDuke
- *Me: a Memoir* by Brenda Ueland
- *Minnesota Treasures: Stories Behind the State's Historic Places,* by Denis Gardner
- *Packinghouse Daughter: A Memoir* by Cheri Register
- *Root Beer Lady* by Bob Cary is about Dorothy Molter, a woman who lived alone in her cabin in the Boundary Waters until her death in 1986.
- *Rudy! The People's Governor* by Betty Wilson is about the state's last Democratic governor, Rudy Perpich.
- *Secrets of the Congdon Mansion* by Joe Kimball, tells you everything they won't tell you on the tour of Glensheen in Duluth.
- *The Conscience of a Liberal: Reclaiming the Compassionate Agenda* is by Paul Wellstone, U.S. Senator from Minnesota, 1990–2002.
- *The Days of Rondo* by Evelyn Fairbanks
- *The Street Where You Live: A Guide to Street Names of St. Paul* by Don Emerson
- *Trial at Grand Marais* by Jean Andereck
- *Twin Cities Album: A Visual History* by Dave Kenney
- *Walking the Rez Road* by Jim Northrup

ARCHITECTURE

- *A Guide to the Architecture of Minnesota* by Tom Martinson and David Gebhard, was published by the University of Minnesota Press in 1977, and is still considered the local architectural bible.
- *Cape Cods and Ramblers: A Remodeling Planbook for Post-WWII Houses* will help you time-tune houses from the 1940s, '50s and '60s. Residents of Blaine, Brooklyn Park, Columbia Heights, Coon Rapids, Crystal, Fridley, Golden Valley, Hopkins, Mounds View, New Brighton, New Hope, Robbinsdale, Richfield, Roseville and St. Louis Park can purchase the book for $10 from their city halls. Those who live outside those communities can get a copy for $15 from the City of Brooklyn Park, 763-424-8000.
- *Longfellow Planbook: Remodeling Plans for Bungalows and Other Small Urban Homes* can be purchased from the Longfellow Community Council, 4151

Minnehaha Avenue South, Minneapolis 55406, 612-722-4529; $18.50, $10 for Longfellow residents.

CHILDREN

- *Betsy-Tacy* books by Maud Hart Lovelace
- *Little House in the Big Woods* and *Little House on the Prairie* by Laura Ingalls Wilder are set in this region. The Wilder Pageant, presented every July in an outdoor amphitheater on the banks of Plum Creek, is complete with grasshoppers and the prairie fire. For information and to order tickets look online at www.walnutgrove.org or call 888-859-3102.

GARDENING

- *Growing Perennials in Cold Climates* by Mike Heger and John Whitman
- *Landscaping with Native Plants of Minnesota* by Lynn Steiner
- *Northland Wildflowers: The Comprehensive Guide to the Minnesota Region* by John and Evelyn Moyle
- *Wetlands in Your Pocket, A Guide to Common Plants and Animals of Midwestern Wetlands* by Mark Muller

MINNESOTA IN PHOTOS

- *Barns of Minnesota* by Doug Olman and Will Weaver
- *Chased by the Light: A 90-day Journey* by Jim Brandenburg
- *Minnesota: A State of Beauty* by James LaVigne
- *Minnesota on My Mind* by Paul Gruchow
- *Minnesota Wild* by Les Blacklock

QUICK GETAWAYS

- *Bicycle Vacation Guide, Minnesota and Wisconsin* by Doug Shidell and Vicky Vogels
- *Biking with the Wind: Bicycling Day Trips in Minnesota and Wisconsin* by David Bixen
- *Camper's Guide to Minnesota: Parks, Lakes, Forests, and Trails: Where to Go and How to Get There* by Mickey Little
- *Natural Wonders of Minnesota: Parks, Preserves and Wild Places* by Martin Hintz
- *Romancing Minnesota* by Kate Crowley and Michael Link
- *Scenic Driving: Minnesota* by Phil Davies

SPORTS

- *The Boys of Winter: The Untold Story of a Coach, a Dream, and the 1980 U.S. Olympic Hockey Team* by Wayne Coffey

211, First Call for Help (social services)
311, City of Minneapolis
411, Telephone Directory Assistance
511, Road Conditions
711, Minnesota Relay Assistance
911, Police, Fire, or Medical Emergencies

ALCOHOL AND DRUG DEPENDENCY

- **Alcoholics Anonymous**, Greater Minneapolis, 952-922-0880, www.aaminneapolis.org; St. Paul, 651-227-5502, www. aastpaul.org
- **Crisis Connection** (24-hour), 612-379-6363

ANIMALS (see also "Veterinarians, Emergency Clinics" below)

- **Animal Humane Society of Hennepin County**, www.ahshc.org: 845 N Meadow Ln, Golden Valley, 763-522-4325; 1411 NW Main St, Coon Rapids, 763-862-4030; also boards dogs, cats, and other small animals, and provides pet grief support.
- **Animal Inn Boarding Kennel, Training School, and Pet Cemetery**, 651-777-0255, 888-777-0255, www.animalinnboardingkennel.com
- **Humane Society of Ramsey County**, 651-645-7387, www.visi. com/hsrc
- **Minnesota Online Pet Resources**, www.creatures.com/mn
- **Minnesota Zoo**, www.mnzoo.com
- **St. Paul Animal Control (impound and adoption) Center**, www.stpaul.gov/depts/liep/Animals/ACC.html
- **Wildlife Rehabilitation Center**, 2530 Dale St, Roseville, 651-486-WILD (9453), www.wrcmn.org

APPLIANCE AND ELECTRONICS RECYCLING

- **Carver County Environmental Center**, 116 Peavey Circle, Chaska, 952-361-1835 or 952-361-1800, www.co.carver.mn.us/Divisions/LandWater Services/EnviroServices
- **Eureka Recycling**, 651-633-EASY, www.eurekarecycling.org
- **North Hennepin County Recycling Center and Transfer Station**, 8100, Jefferson Hwy, Brooklyn Park, 612-348-3777, www.hennepin.us
- **South Hennepin County Recycling and Problem Waste Drop-off Center**, 1400 W 96th St, Bloomington, 612-348-3777, www.hennepin.us
- **Twin Cities FreeNet**, www.tcfreenet.or

AUTOMOBILES

- **511**, road conditions
- **AAA**, 952-927-2600, 24-hour line 952-927-2727, www.aaaminneapolis.com
- **Minneapolis Impound Lot**, 612-673-5777
- **Minnesota Department of Public Safety—Motor Vehicle Division**, 651-296-6911, www.dps.state.mn.us
- **St. Paul Impound Lot**, 651-266-5630
- **www.autotrader.com**; useful web site for researching, buying, or selling cars

AUTOMOBILE SERVICE CENTERS—VEHICLE REGISTRATION, DRIVER'S LICENSES AND IDENTIFICATION CARDS

MINNESOTA
For a complete list of service centers, hours of operation, and addresses, check www.dps.state.mn.us/dvs.
- **Anoka County**, www.co.anoka.mn.us: State Exam Station, 530 W Main St, Anoka, 763-422-3401; North Metro Exam Station, Arden Hills, 651-639-4057
- **Carver County**, www.co.carver.mn.us: Chaska Exam Station, 418 Pine St, Chaska, 952-448-3740
- **Dakota County**, www.co.dakota.mn.us: 14955 Galaxie Ave
- **Apple Valley**, 952-891-7570; 1 Mendota Road W, West St. Paul, 651-554-6600; Burnsville Transit Station Hub, 100 E Hwy 13, Burnsville, 952-707-6436; 20085 Heritage Dr
- **Lakeville**, 952-891-7878
- **Hennepin County**, 612-348-8240, www.co.hennepin.mn.us: Hennepin County Government Center, 300 S 6th St—Public Service Level, Minneapolis; Brookdale Service Center, 6125 Shingle Creek Pkwy, Brooklyn Center; Ridgedale Service Center, 12601 Ridgedale Dr, Minnetonka; Southdale Service Center, 7009 York Ave S, Edina; Maple Grove Service Center, 9325 Upland Ln N, Maple Grove; Eden Prairie Service Center, 479 Prairie Center Dr, Eden Prairie

- Minneapolis Driver and Vehicle Licenses, 612-348-8240
- Minnesota Driver's License Exam Station, Chaska, 952-448-3740
- Minnesota Driver's License Exam Station, Plymouth, 952-476-3042
- **Ramsey County**, www.co.ramsey.mn.us: 445 Minnesota St, St. Paul, 651-296-6911; St. Paul/Midway Written Exam Station, 651-642-0808
- **Scott County**, www.co.scott.mn.us: Customer Service Center, Government Services Bldg, 200 W Fourth Ave, Shakopee, 952- 496-8150
- **Sherburne County**, www.co.sherburne.mn.us: Department of Motor Vehicles, 600 Railroad Dr, Elk River; call 763-422-3401 to schedule a road test appointment.
- **Washington County**, www.co.washington.mn.us: Forest Lake License Center, Northland Mall, 1432 S Lake St:
  - Forest Lake, 651-430-8280
  - Stillwater License Center, Valley Ridge, 1520 W Frontage Rd, Stillwater, 651-430-6176
  - Woodbury Service Center, 2150 Radio Dr, Woodbury, 651-275-8600
- **Wright County**, 763-682-3900, 800-362-3667, 10 Second St NW, Buffalo, www.co.wright.mn.us

WISCONSIN
- **Drivers' License Information**, 608-266-2353, www.dot.wisconsin. gov/drivers/drivers/apply/drivrlic.htm
- **Vehicle Registration**, www.dot.wisconsin.gov/drivers/vehicles/ veh-forms.htm
- **Hudson**, Wisconsin, DMV, 2100 O'Neil Rd (near Carmichael Rd); open Wednesdays, 7:45 a.m. to 5:45 p.m.; Thursdays, 8:15 a.m. to 6:15 p.m.; and Fridays, 7:45 a.m. to 5:00 p.m. There is no direct phone number to that location, but the automated phone system number is 800-924-3570. Register vehicles at the St. Croix County Government Center, 1101 Carmichael Rd, Hudson, in the Clerk's Office, 715-386-4609, www.ci.Hudson.wi.us.

BIRTH/ DEATH CERTIFICATES

- **Minnesota Department of Health,** Attention: Office of the State Registrar, P.O. Box 64882, St. Paul, Minnesota 55164-0882, fax 651-291-0101 , www.health.state.mn.us/divs/chs/osr/
- **Wisconsin Vital Records Office**:
  - **Birth**, www.dhfs.state.wi.us/VitalRecords/birth.htm
  - **Death**, www.dhfs.state.wi.us/VitalRecords/death.htm#D1

CHILD ABUSE/PROTECTION

United Way First Call for Help, 211, 651-291-0211 or 800-543-7709, www.211unitedway.org, www.firstcallnet.org

CITIZEN PARTICIPATION

- **Citizens' League**, 651-293-0575, www.citizensleague.net
- **E-Women Win**, www.ewomenwin.org, is an Internet community of multi-partisan women and men dedicated to making women's voices a force on public policy issues in Minnesota. It is a project of the **Minnesota Women's Political Caucus Education Council**, www.mnwpc.org.
- **League of Women Voters of Minnesota**, 800-663-9328, www.lwvmn.org
- **Minnesota Public Interest Research Group**, www.mpirg.org

CONSUMER AGENCIES

- **Better Business Bureau of Minnesota**, 651-699-1111, 800-646-6222, www.mnd.bbb.org
- **Consumer Checkbook**, 651-646-2057, www.checkbook.org; download reports
- **Minnesota Attorney General**, Hotline 651-296-3353, 800-657-3787, TTY 651-297-7206, TTY toll-free 800-366-4812, www.ag.state.mn.us
- **Minnesota Department of Commerce**, 651-296-2488, 651-296-5175, www.commerce.state.mn.us
- **Minnesota Public Utilities Commission**, 651-296-0406, 800-657-3782
- **Telecommunications and Research Action Center**, www.trac.org
- **University of Minnesota Extension Service**, www.extension.umn.edu

CRISIS LINES

- **211, United Way First Call for Help**, is a statewide number that will direct you to the help you need; searchable database online at www.firstcallnet.org.
- **911**, Emergency
- **Drug Abuse Hotline**, 800-662-4357
- **Emergency Contraception**, 888-NOT-2-LATE
- **Jacob Wetterling Foundation** for missing and exploited children, 24-hour helpline, 800-325-HOPE (toll-free), www.jwf.org
- **Minneapolis Sexual Violence Center** (24-hour crisis line), 612-871-5111
- **Minnesota Domestic Abuse Hotline**, 866-223-1111, automatically connects you with resources nearest you.
- **National Runaway Switchboard**, 800-621-4000
- **Suicide Prevention**, 612-347-2222
- **Teens Alone**, 952-988-TEEN, www.teensalone.org, helps homeless teenagers in the west metro.

DISABLED, SERVICES FOR

- **ARC Minnesota** (advocacy and support for those who are developmentally disabled), 651-523-0823, www.arcminnesota.com

- **Courage Center**, 3915 Golden Valley Rd, Golden Valley, 763-588-0811, 888-846-8253, www.courage.org
- **Disabled Certificate/License Plates**, 651-297-3377, www.dps.state.mn.us/dvs/Disability
- **Metropolitan Center for Independent Living**, 651-646-8342, TTY 651-603-2001, www.macil.org
- **Minnesota Deaf and Hard of Hearing Services**, 130 E Seventh St, St. Paul, 651-297-1316, TTY 651-297-1313, fax 651-215-6388, email: dhhs.metro@state.mn.us, www.dhs.state.mn.us
- **Minnesota Library for the Blind**, 800-722-0550, www.loc.gov/nls
- **Minnesota Relay Service**, 800-627-3529 or 800-223-3131
- **Minnesota State Council on Disability** (comprehensive disability resource), 651-296-6785, www.disability.state.mn.us
- **Minnesota State Services for the Blind**, 651-642-0500, TTY 651-642-0506, 800-652-9000, www.mnssb.org
- **National Handicapped Housing Institute** (NHHI), 4556 Lake Dr, Robbinsdale, 651-639-9799; information on barrier-free housing.
- **PACER (Parent Advocacy Coalition for Educational Rights) Center**, 8161 Normandale Blvd, Minneapolis, 952-838-9000, TTY 952-838-0190, toll-free in Greater Minnesota 800-537-2237, fax 952-838-0199, email: pacer@pacer.org, www.pacer.org.

EMERGENCY

- **Fire, Police, Medical**, 911
- **Minnesota Poison Control Center**, 800-222-1222

FOOD

- **Emergency Food Shelf Network**, 763-450-3860 or First Call for Help, 211, www.emergencyfoodshelf.org
- **University of Minnesota Extension Service** (cooking tips), www.extension.umn.edu

GAMBLING

- **Minnesota Compulsive Gambling Hotline**, 800-437-3641

GARDENING

- **University of Minnesota Extension Service and Landscape Arboretum**, 612-624-4771, www.extension.umn.edu, www.gardenminnesota.com, www.arboretum.umn.edu

GOVERNMENT

MINNEAPOLIS
- **City Hall,** general information: 311, www.ci.minneapolis.mn.us

ST. PAUL
- **City Hall,** general information: 651-266-8500, www.stpaul.gov

COUNTY AND REGIONAL
MINNESOTA
- **Anoka County,** www.co.anoka.mn.us, 763-421-4760
- **Carver County,** www.co.carver.mn.us, 952-361-1500
- **Dakota County,** www.co.dakota.mn.us, 651-438-4418
- **Hennepin County,** www.co.hennepin.mn.us, 612-348-3000
- **Isanti County,** www.co.isanti.mn.us, 763-689-3859
- **Metropolitan Council,** www.metrocouncil.org
- **Ramsey County,** www.co.ramsey.mn.us, 651-266-2000
- **Scott County,** www.co.scott.mn.us, 952-445-7750
- **Sherburne County,** www.co.sherburne.mn.us, 763-241-2700
- **Washington County,** www.co.washington.mn.us, 651-439-3220
- **Wright County,** www.co.wright.mn.us, 763-682-3900

WISCONSIN
- **Pierce County,** Courthouse: 414 W Main St, Ellsworth, WI 54011, 715-273-3531, www.co.pierce.wi.us
- **Polk County,** Government Center: 100 Polk County Plaza, Suite 110, Balsam Lake, WI 54810, 715-485-9226, www.co.polk.wi.us
- **St. Croix County,** Government Center: 1101 Carmichael Rd, Hudson, WI 54016, 715-386-4600, www.co.saint-croix.wi.us

STATE
MINNESOTA
- **Attorney General,** www.ag.state.mn.us, 651-296-3353
- **Governor's Office,** 651-296-3391
- **Minnesota State Legislature,** information and bill tracking, www.leg.state.mn.us
- **Secretary of State,** 651-296-2803; Elections: 651-215-1440; www.sos.state.mn.us

WISCONSIN
- **State of Wisconsin,** www.wisconsin.gov
- **Department of Justice,** www.doj.state.wi.us
- **Governor's Office,** 115 E State Capitol, Madison, WI 53702, 608-266-1212, TTY 608-267-6790, www.wisgov.state.wi.us

HEALTH

- **Mayo Clinic Health Oasis**, www.mayohealth.org
- **Minnesota Council of Health Plans**, www.mnhealthplans.org, provides Minnesota health care industry statistics and consumer information, addresses, and links to the ten health care plans.
- **Minnesota Department of Health**, www.health.state.mn.us
- **Minnesota STD/Family Planning Hotline** 800-783-2287, www.std hotline.state.mn.us
- **MnTeenHealth**, 411, www.teenhealth411.org, provides answers to personal health questions.
- **Neighborhood Health Care Network**, 651-489-CARE, www.nhcn.org; medical and dental referrals.
- **Travel Health Resource Line**, 612-676-5588, www2.ncid.cdc.gov/travel

HOMEBUYING AND MAINTENANCE

- **National Association of Home Inspectors**, www.nahi.org; for a list of accredited home inspectors.
- **Twin Cities Bungalow Club**, www.bungalowclub.org, is a great source of advice about old houses of all styles.
- **TwinCitiesMLSDirect.com**, a multiple listing service.

HOSPITALS

(See **Health Care** chapter.)

HOUSING

MINNEAPOLIS (311, www.ci.minneapolis.mn.us)

ST. PAUL (www.ci.stpaul.mn.us)
- **St. Paul Heritage Preservation Commission**, 651-266-9078, www.ci.stpaul.mn.us/depts/liep/HPC
- **St. Paul Housing Information Office**, 651-266-6000

STATE/FEDERAL
- **Minnesota Building Codes**, 651-296-4639
- **Minnesota Department of Human Rights**, 651-296-5663, TDD, 651-296-1283, 800-657-3704
- **Minnesota Department of Public Service Energy Information Center**, www.dpsv.state.mn.us
- **Minnesota Tenant's Union**, 612-871-7485
- **US Department of Housing and Urban Development**, 612-370-3000, www.hud.gov; Discrimination Hotline, 800-669-9777

LIBRARIES

- **Anoka County Library System**, www.anoka.lib.mn.us
- **Carver County Library System**, 952-448-9395, www.carverlib.org
- **Dakota County Library System**, 651-688-1547, www.co.Dakota.mn.us/library
- **Hennepin County**, 952-847-5900, www.hclib.org
- **Hudson, Wisconsin**, www.more.lib.wi.us
- **Minneapolis**, 612-630-6000, www.mplib.org
- **Minnesota Historical Society**, 651-296-2143, www.mnhs.org
- **Ramsey County**, 651-486-2200, www.ramsey.lib.mn.us
- **St. Paul**, 651-266-7073, www.sppl.org
- **Scott County**, 952-707-1760, www.scott.lib.mn.us
- **The State of Minnesota web site**, www.state.mn.us/libraries, provides links to regional and college libraries.
- **Washington County**, 651-275-8500, www.co.washington.mn.us/library

MINNESOTA ONLINE

City/neighborhood specific web sites can be found at the end of each neighborhood profile, or check the **Surrounding Communities** section.
- **About.com**, www.Minneapolis.about.com
- **Minnesota Grown**, www.minnesotagrown.com
- **Newcomers Club**, www.newcomersclub.com/mn.html
- **Photo Tour of Twin Cities**, www.phototour.minneapolis.mn.us
- **Registered Offender List**, www.criminalcheck.com; type in your zip code and find registered offenders living in that neighborhood
- **Twin Cities Online Guide**, http://twincities.citysearch.com
- **Twin Cities Transplants**, www.imnotfromhere.com, is a support group for transplanted professionals.
- **Whatever;** television show by teens for teens on Kare11 TV, www.whatevershow.com

MAPS
- **DNR Fishing Maps**, www.dnr.state.mn.us/lakefind/index.html
- **Metropolitan Council maps** of 46 regional parks and park reserves, 22 trails, and six special recreation areas, www.metrocouncil.org/parks/r-pk-map.htm
- **Minnesota County maps**, www.minnesotabound.com/maps

NEWSPAPERS AND MAGAZINES

For clickable links to newspapers by county, look online at www.mnnews.com/countylist.html.

POLICE

- **Emergency**, 911
- **Hennepin County Sheriff**, Non-Emergency, 763-525-6210
- **Minnesota State Patrol**, Non-Emergency, 651-582-1511

RADIO/TV STATIONS

See **Getting Settled** chapter.

RELOCATION

- **First Books Newcomer's Handbooks**, www.firstbooks.com; relocation resources and information on moving to the USA as a whole, as well as Atlanta, Boston, Chicago, Los Angeles, Minneapolis–St. Paul, New York, Philadelphia, San Francisco Bay Area, Seattle, and Washington, DC, and London, England; also resources for moving pets and children.
- **HousingLink**, 612-522-2500, www.housinglink.org, is a free nonprofit service that provides information about affordable rental housing throughout the metro area.
- **Mothers and More**, www.orgsites.com/mn/mothersandmore-stpaul, is a nonprofit dedicated to improving the lives of "sequencing women."
- **www.moving.com** is the world's largest moving and relocation web site with over 3000 companies in its network of movers, real estate professionals, lenders, and insurance providers.
- **www.moving.org** is the web site of the 3200-member American Moving and Storage Association
- **Newcomers Clubs**, www.newcomersclub.com/mn.html#Minneapolis
- **www.rentnet.com**, apartment rentals, movers, relocation advice, help finding pet-friendly rentals, and more.
- **www.usps.com**; relocation information from the U.S. Postal Service.

ROAD CONDITION INFORMATION (511)

- **Snow Emergency Information, Minneapolis**, 612-348-SNOW, www. ci.minneapolis.mn.us
- **Snow Emergency Information, St. Paul**, 651-266-PLOW, www. stpaul.gov
- **Wisconsin Traveler Information**, 800-ROADWIS (800-762-3947), www.dot.wisconsin.gov/travel/road

SANITATION—GARBAGE & RECYCLING

(see **Getting Settled** chapter)
- **BFI solid waste and recycling**, 763-784-2104 (North Metro), 952-941-5174 (Southwest metro), 651-455-8634 (East metro), www.bfitwincities.com

- **Eureka Recycling**, 651-222-7678, www.eurekarecycling.org
- **Twin Cities Free Market** (web-based, reusable goods exchange), www.twincitiesfreemarket.org
- **Waste Management**, 952-890-1100, www.wm.com; serves most of metro

SENIORS

- **Senior Linkage Line**, 800-333-2433

SOCIAL AGENCIES

- **United Way First Call for Help**, 211, www.firstcallnet.org, acts like directory assistance for those seeking help from social service organizations in Minnesota. This is NOT an emergency number, but it is answered 24 hours a day, and will refer you to the help you need.

SPORTS & RECREATION

COLLEGE/PROFESSIONAL SPORTS
- **Canterbury Park**, www.canterburypark.com; horse racing.
- **Golf Tee Times**, www.teemaster.com
- **Minnesota Lynx**, www.wnba.com/lynx; women's professional basketball.
- **Minnesota Thunder**, www.mnthunder.com; professional soccer.
- **Minnesota Timberwolves**, 612-673-0900, www.nba.com/timberwolves; men's professional basketball.
- **Minnesota Twins**, 612-33-TWINS, http://minnesota.twins.mlb.com
- **Minnesota Vikings**, 612-338-4537, www.vikings.com; professional football.
- **Minnesota Wild**, www.wild.com; NHL hockey.
- **St. Paul Saints**, www.spsaints.com; professional baseball.
- **University of Minnesota** (all teams), 612-624-8080, www.gophersports.com

PARTICIPANT SPORTS & RECREATION
- **Minnesota Ski Areas**, www.twin-cities.com/ski
- **Boundary Waters**, www.canoecountry.com
- **Fishing Network**, www.the-fishing-network.com
- **Ski Conditions and Snow Depths**, www.onthesnow.com/MN/skireport.html
- **Snow Conditions**, 651-296-6157, www.dnr.state.mn.us/current_conditions
- **Snowmobiling**, www.sledcity.com

TAXES

FEDERAL
- **Internal Revenue Service**, 800-829-4477, www.irs.gov
- **Bloomington, Minneapolis, and St. Paul IRS Offices**, 651-312-8082
- **IRS Taxpayer Advocate Service**, 651-312-7999, 877-777-4778

PROPERTY TAXES (CALL YOUR CITY)

STATE

- **Minnesota Department of Revenue**, 600 N Robert St, St. Paul, MN 55101, www.taxes.state.mn.us
- **Income Tax Information and Forms**, 651-296-3781; budget cuts resulted in the shutting down of the state's toll-free number, but you can still access information and file electronically at www.taxes.state.mn.us. People with impairments should call 711 for Minnesota Relay Service.
- **Refund Status**, 651-296-4444
- **Taxpayers Rights Advocate**, 651-556-6013

TAXIS AND SHUTTLES

AIRPORT

- **Airport Taxi and Delivery**, www.airporttaxicabs.com; serves the entire Twin Cities metro area with vans and smoke-free cabs; accepts reservations up to 24 hours in advance; make reservations online.
  - **West Metro**, 952-928-0000
  - **East Metro**, 651-222-0000
  - **Toll free**, 800-464-0555
- **Airport Southwest Taxi**, 952-937-0600; provides service to and from the airport; make reservations 24 hours in advance.
- **SuperShuttle**, 612-827-7777 (ext 1), www.supershuttle.com

MINNEAPOLIS

- **ABC Taxi**, 612-788-1111
- **Blue & White Taxi**, 612-333-3331
- **Red and White Taxi**, 612-871-1600
- **Sky Bird Taxi**, 612-340-0124
- **Suburban and Green & White Taxi**, 612-522-2222
- **Yellow Cab**, 612-824-4000

ST. PAUL

- **Citywide Cab**, 651-489-1111
- **St. Paul All City Cab**, 651-222-8294

SUBURBAN

- **Suburban Taxi**, 763-545-1234, 952-884-8888, www.suburbantaxi.com

TELEPHONE

- **Directory Assistance**, 411
- **Do Not Call List**, 800-921-4110
- **Online Directory**, www.dexonline.com
- **Qwest**, 800-244-1111, www.qwest.com

TOURISM

- **MetroConnections**, 612-333-8687, www.metroconnections.com, offers three-hour tours to various sites in Minneapolis and St. Paul.
- **Minneapolis Heritage Preservation Commission**, 350 5th St S, Minneapolis, 612-673-2597, www.ci.minneapolis.mn.us/hpc, leads free summer walking tours in historic areas of Minneapolis.
- **Minnesota Historical Society**, 345 Kellogg Blvd W, St. Paul, 651-296-6126, www.mnhs.org
- **Minnesota Office of Tourism**, www.exploreminnesota.com
- **Minnesota State Capitol**, 75 Reverend Dr. Martin Luther King Blvd, St. Paul, 651-296-2881, www.mnhs.org; free guided tours on the hour, also self-guided tours.
- **Minnesota Zephyr**, 601 N Main, (Stillwater Depot), Stillwater, 651-430-3000, www.minnesotazephyr.com; 3-hour train trips.
- **Mobile Entertainment's Magical History Tours**, 952-888-9200, www.magicalhistorytour.com; 3 hour tours by Segway of the Minneapolis Riverfront.
- **Padelford Packet Boat Co.**, Harriet Island, St. Paul; 651-227-1100, www.riverrides.com, offers narrated public excursions and private charters on the Mississippi River, May through October, from Boom island, Minneapolis, and Harriet Island, St. Paul.
- **Wabasha Street Caves Tours**, 215 S Wabasha St, St. Paul; 651-224-1191, www.wabashastreetcaves.com
- **Wisconsin Tourism**, www.wisconline.com

TRANSPORTATION

- **Department of Public Safety Driver and Vehicle Services**, www.dps.state.mn.us/dvs
- **Minneapolis–St. Paul International Airport**, www.mspairport.com:
  - **Lindbergh (Main) Terminal**, 4300 Glumack Dr, St. Paul, 612-726-5555
  - **Humphrey Terminal** (charter and other flights), 7150 Humphrey Dr, Minneapolis, 612-726-5800
  - **Airport Police Department** parking ramp escort service, 612-726-5577
- **Mn-PASS toll-lane signup**, 866-397-4334, www.mnpass.org
- **State Department of Transportation**, www.dot.state.mn.us

LOCAL TRANSIT AND COMMUTER SERVICES
- **Metro Transit**, 612-373-3333, TTY 612-349-7369, www.metrotransit.com; find out everything you need to know about local transit by calling this number or looking on this web site—fares, routes, schedules, and commuter information, as well.

NATIONAL TRAIN & BUS SERVICE

- **Amtrak**, Reservations: please call a service representative at 800-USA-RAIL (800-872-7245), TDD/TTY 800-523-6590, www.amtrak.com
- **St. Paul/Minneapolis Midway Amtrak Passenger Station**, 730 Transfer Rd, St. Paul, 651-644-6012
- **Greyhound Bus Lines**, 950 Hawthorne Ave Station, Minneapolis, 612-371-3325, 612-371-3334 (baggage); University of Minnesota, Coffman Union, 300 Washington Ave SE, 612-624-4636; 166 W University Ave, St Paul, 651-222-0507; St. Paul Amtrak Station, 730 Transfer Rd; tickets are not sold at the Amtrak station but may be purchased by mail at least 10 days in advance through the Ticket Center on Greyhound.com or by calling the Telephone Information Center at 800-231-2222, www.greyhound.com.
- **Rochester Direct, Minneapolis International Airport**, 612-726-5501, www.rochesterdirect.com
- **SchoolRider**, 651-227-1905, toll-free 866-55RIDER, www.school rider.com, provides weekend transport for students between the University of Minnesota campuses and Wisconsin destinations, as well as end-of-the-year moving services for Wisconsin students who attend the U of M. They also run bus trips to out-of-town Gopher games.

U.S. POSTAL SERVICE

U.S. Postal Service, 800-275-8777, www.usps.com

UTILITIES

- **Diggers' Hotline** (buried cable locations in Wisconsin), 800-242-8511
- **Gopher State One Call** (buried cable locations in Minnesota) 651-454-0002; call before you dig.

ELECTRICITY
- **Dakota Electric**, 651-463-6212, 800-874-3409, www.dakotaelectric.com
- **Minnesota Valley Electric Co-op**, 952-492-2313 www.mvec.net
- **Xcel Energy**, Billing and New Accounts: 800-895-4999; Street Lights Burned Out/Electrical Outage 800-895-1999; www.xcelenergy.com

NATURAL GAS
- **CenterPoint Energy**, 612-372-4727 or 800-245-2377 for Billing and New Accounts; Emergency Gas Leaks and Repairs, 612-372-5050, www.center pointenergy.com

TELEPHONE
- **Do Not Call**, 888-382-1222, TTY 866-290-4236, www.ftc.gov/donotcall
- **Qwest**, 800-244-1111 Billing and New Accounts (serves almost all of the metro), www.qwest.com

SATELLITE AND CABLE
- **AOL-Time Warner**, 612-522-2000, www.timewarnercable.com (Minneapolis)
- **Charter Communications**, 800-581-0081, www.chartercom.com (Northwest Metro)
- **Comcast**, 800-COMCAST, www.Comcast.com (east side of the cities)
- **Direct TV** satellite service, 800-216-9570, www.directtv.com
- **Dish Network** satellite service, 888-DISHTV1, www.dishtv.com/
- **Mediacom**, 800-332-0245 for Billing and New Accounts; 800-422-1473 Repair, www.mediacomcc.com (west side of the cities)

UTILITY EMERGENCIES
- **Electrical Outage**, 800-895-1999
- **Emergency Furnace Repair**, 612-333-6466 or 800-722-6821
- **Emergency/Gas Odor**, 800-895-2999
- **Gas Leak, Center Point Energy**, 612-372-5050, TTY/Voice 612-342-5471
- **Telephone Outage, Qwest**, 800-573-1311

VETERINARIANS, EMERGENCY CLINICS

- **Affiliated Emergency Veterinary Service** (Minneapolis side of the Twin Cities), www.aevs.com:
  - **Golden Valley**, 4708 Hwy 55, Golden Valley, 763-529-6560
  - **Coon Rapids**, 1615 Coon Rapids Blvd, Coon Rapids, 763-754-9434
  - **Eden Prairie**, 7717 Flying Cloud Dr, Eden Prairie, 952-942-8272
- **Animal Emergency Care** (South Metro)
  - **Apple Valley**, 14690 Pennock Ave, 952-953-3737
- **Animal Emergency Clinic** (St. Paul side of the Twin Cities)
  - **West St. Paul**, 301 University Ave, 651-293-1800;
  - **Oakdale**, Interstate 694 & 10th St, 651-501-3766
- **University of Minnesota Veterinary Hospitals**, 1365 Gartner Ave, St. Paul, 612-625-9711 (24-hour emergency hotline)

VOTING

- **Minnesota Secretary of State Pollfinder**, http://pollfinder.sos.state.mn.us

WORSHIP

- **Minnesota Council of Churches**, www.mnchurches.org
- **Jewish Minnesota**, www.jewishminnesota.org
- **Lutheran Brotherhood**, www.luthbro.com

ZIP CODE INFORMATION

- **USPS**, 800-275-8777, www.usps.com

ELIZABETH CAPERTON-HALVORSON has lived in the Minneapolis area for 30 years. Raised in Virginia, her experience as a newcomer began with her marriage to a Minnesotan—and nearly ended when she realized she had worn her winter coat through the entire summer the first year she lived in the Twin Cities. She and her family soon discovered the exhilaration of Minnesota skiing and the joy of sailing Lake Minnetonka by moonlight, and she now looks forward to the cycle of the seasons. She has worked as an elementary school teacher and newspaper reporter, and is currently a writer and editor of corporate communications. Her family's hobbies revolve around art, bridge, gardening, and sports.

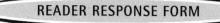

READER RESPONSE FORM

We would appreciate your comments regarding this third edition of the *Newcomer's Handbook® for Moving to and Living in Minneapolis–St. Paul.* If you've found any mistakes or omissions or if you would just like to express your opinion about the guide, please let us know. We will consider any suggestions for possible inclusion in our next edition, and if we use your comments, we'll send you a *free* copy of our next edition. Please send this response form to:

Reader Response Department
First Books
6750 SW Franklin, Suite A
Portland, OR 97223-2542
USA

Comments:

_____

_____

_____

_____

_____

_____

Name: _____

Address _____

_____

_____

Telephone (   ) _____

E-mail

6750 SW Franklin, Suite A
Portland, OR 97223-2542
USA
503-968-6777
www.firstbooks.com

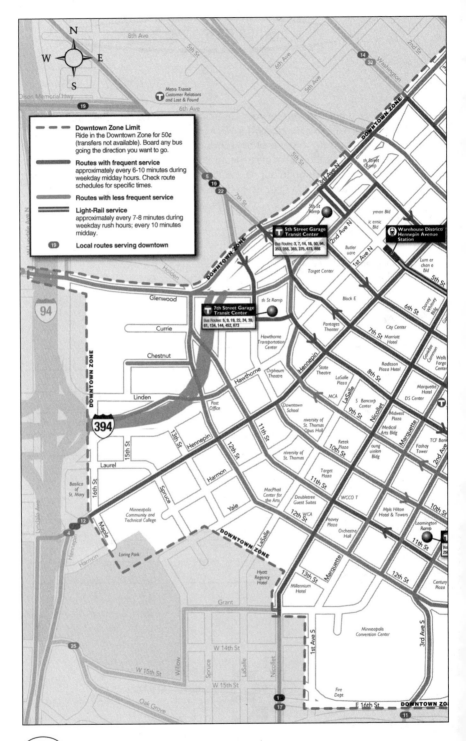

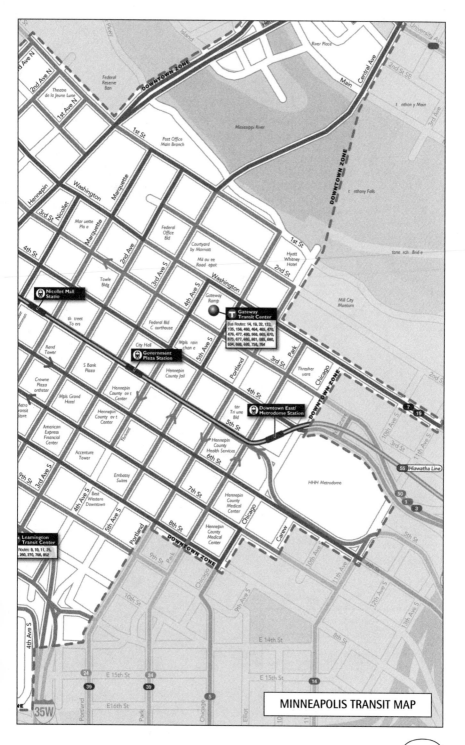

MINNEAPOLIS TRANSIT MAP

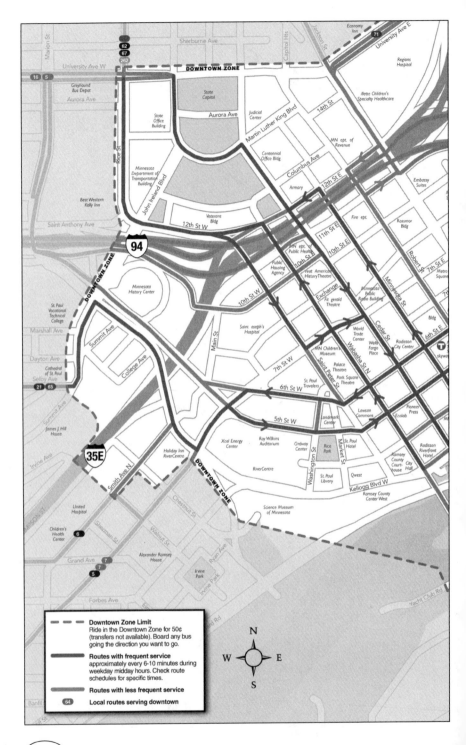

Downtown Zone Limit
Ride in the Downtown Zone for 50¢
(transfers not available). Board any bus
going the direction you want to go.

Routes with frequent service
approximately every 6-10 minutes during
weekday midday hours. Check route
schedules for specific times.

Routes with less frequent service

64   Local routes serving downtown

N
W — E
S

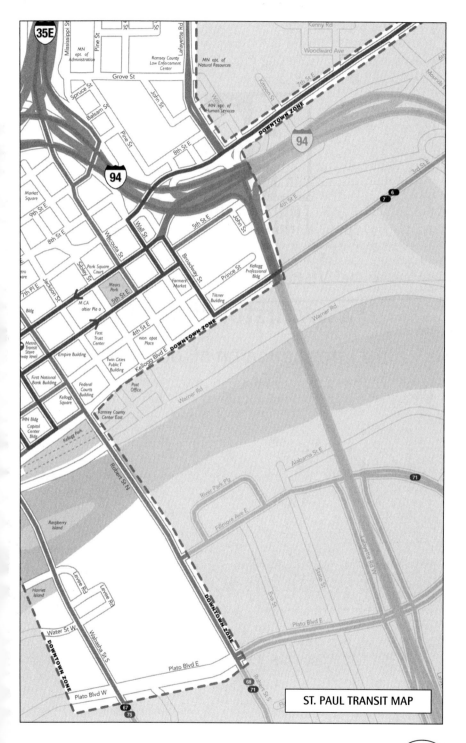

ST. PAUL TRANSIT MAP

FIRST BOOKS®

Visit our web site at

www.firstbooks.com

for information on all our books.